NEW YORK EDITION

3 tres

HOLT McDOUGAL

¡Avancemos!

HOLT McDOUGAL
a division of Houghton Mifflin Harcourt

Cover Photography

Front cover

Plaza de la Constitución at night, Santiago, Chile, © David Noton Photography

Inset: Winter sports in Chile, © Scott Markewitz/Taxi/Getty Images

Back cover

Level 1a: View toward La Fortaleza, San Juan, Puerto Rico, © Steve Dunwell/The Image Bank/Getty Images
Level 1b: View of Buenos Aires through the Puente de la Mujer, © Joseph Rodriguez/Gallery Stock Limited
Level 1: Monumento a la Independencia on the Paseo de la Reforma at night, Mexico City, Mexico, © Panoramic Images/Getty Images
Level 2: Cibeles Fountain and Palacio de Comunicaciones at night, Madrid, Spain, © Doug Armand/Getty Images
Level 3: Plaza de la Constitución at night, Santiago, Chile, © David Noton Photography
Level 4: Santa Catarina Arch, Antigua, Guatemala, © Jeremy Woodhouse/Masterfile

New York Edition Photography and Illustration Acknowledgments

The following acknowledgments supersede those found on Roman numeral pages up through **xxvi** in the Créditos on page R104.

viii *top right* Allan Penn/ Holt McDougal/Houghton Mifflin Harcourt; *bottom left* © 2007 David H. Wells/Odyssey/Chicago; *bottom right* Albert Gea/Reuters/Landov; **ix** Stewart Cohen/Getty Images; **x** Pete Olsen/Holt McDougal/Houghton Mifflin Harcourt; **xi** *top left* Pixel Images, Inc./Holt McDougal/Houghton Mifflin Harcourt; *top right* Greg Johnson/Danita Delimont; **xii** Pete Olsen/Holt McDougal/Houghton Mifflin Harcourt; **xiii** *top left* Jeff Greenberg/Alamy; *top right* Ken Karp/Holt McDougal/Houghton Mifflin Harcourt; **xvi** Pete Olsen/Holt McDougal/Houghton Mifflin Harcourt; **xvii** *top left* Clive Brunskill/Getty Images; *top right* Paulo Cunha/Agencia EFE; **xviii** Pete Olsen/Holt McDougal/Houghton Mifflin Harcourt; **xix** *top left* Patricio Realpe, Stringer/AP Images; *top right* © 2007 Robert Frerck/Odyssey/Chicago; **xx** Pete Olsen/Holt McDougal/Houghton Mifflin Harcourt; **xxi** *top left* Tips Images; *top right* © 2007 Robert Frerck/Odyssey/Chicago; **xxii** Pete Olsen/Holt McDougal/Houghton Mifflin Harcourt; **xxiii** *top left* Timothy Ross/The Image Works, Inc.; *top right* Photograph by Félix Velásquez; **xxiv** Pete Olsen/Holt McDougal/Houghton Mifflin Harcourt; **xxv** *top left* Cy Hire/Tom Stack & Associates; *top right* Allan Penn/Holt McDougal/Houghton Mifflin Harcourt; **xiv** Pete Olsen/Holt McDougal/Houghton Mifflin Harcourt; **xv** *top left* Sonda Dawes/The Image Works, Inc.; *top right* Basco/gtphoto; **NYS2** *background* © PhotoDisc; *all others* © Corbis; **NYS3** *background* © PhotoSpin; *center* © Rubberball; **NYS5** *top right* Jorge Albán/Holt McDougal/Houghton Mifflin Harcourt; **NYS6** *both* © Comstock; **NYS7** © Comstock; **NYS8** *top* © Comstock; *center* © Royalty-Free/Corbis; *bottom* Allan Penn/Holt McDougal/Houghton Mifflin Harcourt.

Printed in the United States of America

ISBN-10: 0-547-25860-7
ISBN-13: 978-0-547-25860-7

2 3 4 5 6 0914 13 12 11 4500286917

Internet: www.holtmcdougal.com

About the Authors

Estella Gahala Estella Gahala received degrees in Spanish from Wichita State University, French from Middlebury College, and a Ph.D. in Educational Administration and Curriculum from Northwestern University. A career teacher of Spanish and French, she has worked with a wide variety of students at the secondary level. Her workshops and publications focus on research and practice in a wide range of topics, including culture and language learning, learning strategies, assessment, and the impact of current brain research on curriculum and instruction. She has coauthored twelve basal textbooks. Honors include the Chevalier dans l'Ordre des Palmes Académiques and listings in *Who's Who of American Women, Who's Who in America,* and *Who's Who in the World.*

Patricia Hamilton Carlin Patricia Hamilton Carlin completed her M.A. in Spanish at the University of California, Davis, where she also taught as a lecturer. Previously she earned a Master of Secondary Education with specialization in foreign languages from the University of Arkansas and taught Spanish and French at the K–12 level. Patricia currently teaches Spanish and foreign language/ESL methodology at the University of Central Arkansas, where she coordinates the second language teacher education program. In 2005, she was awarded the Southern Conference on Language Teaching's Outstanding Teaching Award: Post-Secondary. Her professional service has included the presidency of the Arkansas Foreign Language Teachers Association and the presidency of Arkansas's DeSoto Chapter of the AATSP.

Audrey L. Heining-Boynton Audrey L. Heining-Boynton received her Ph.D. in Curriculum and Instruction from Michigan State University. She is a professor of Education and Romance Languages at The University of North Carolina at Chapel Hill, where she teaches educational methodology classes and Spanish. She has also taught Spanish, French, and ESL at the K–12 level. Dr. Heining-Boynton served as the president of ACTFL and the National Network for Early Language Learning. She has been involved with AATSP, Phi Delta Kappa, and state foreign language associations. In addition, she has published over forty books, articles, and curricula.

Ricardo Otheguy Ricardo Otheguy received his Ph.D. in Linguistics from the City University of New York, where he is currently professor of Linguistics at the Graduate Center. He is also director of the Research Institute for the Study of Language in Urban Society (RISLUS) and coeditor of the research journal *Spanish in Context.* He has extensive experience with school-based research and has written on topics related to Spanish grammar, bilingual education, and Spanish in the United States. He is coauthor of *Tu mundo: Curso para hispanohablantes* and *Prueba de ubicación para hispanohablantes.*

Barbara J. Rupert Barbara Rupert completed her M.A. at Pacific Lutheran University. She has taught Level 1 through A.P. Spanish and has implemented a FLES program in her district. Barbara is the author of CD-ROM activities for the *¡Bravo!* series. She has served as president of both the Pacific Northwest Council for Languages (PNCFL) and the Washington Association for Language Teaching. In 1996, Barbara received the Christa McAuliffe Award for Excellence in Education, and in 1999, she was selected Washington's "Spanish Teacher of the Year" by the Juan de Fuca Chapter of the AATSP.

John DeMado, Creative Consultant John DeMado has been a vocal advocate for second-language acquisition in the United States for many years. He started his career as a middle/high school French and Spanish teacher, before entering the educational publishing profession. Since 1993, Mr. DeMado has directed his own business, John DeMado Language Seminars. Inc., a company devoted exclusively to language acquisition issues. He has authored numerous books in both French and Spanish that span the K--12 curriculum. Mr. DeMado wrote and performed the *¡AvanzaRap!* songs for Levels 1 and 2.

Carl Johnson, Senior Program Advisor Carl Johnson received degrees from Marietta College (OH), the University of Illinois, Université Laval, and a Ph.D. in Foreign Language Education from The Ohio State University. He has been a lifelong foreign language educator, retiring in 2003 after 27 years as a language teacher (secondary and university level), consultant, and Director of Languages Other Than English for the Texas Department of Education. He has completed many publications relating to student and teacher language proficiency development, language textbooks, and nationwide textbook adoption practices. He also served as president of the Texas Foreign Language Association, Chair of the Board of the Southwest Conference on Language Teaching, and president of the National Council of State Supervisors of Foreign Languages. In addition, he was named Chevalier dans l'Ordre des Palmes Académiques by the French government.

Rebecca L. Oxford, Learning Strategy Specialist Rebecca L. Oxford received her Ph.D. in educational psychology from The University of North Carolina. She also holds two degrees in foreign language from Vanderbilt University and Yale University, and a degree in educational psychology from Boston University. She leads the Second Language Education and Culture Program and is a professor at the University of Maryland. She has directed programs at Teachers College, Columbia University; the University of Alabama; and the Pennsylvania State University. In addition, she initiated and edited *Tapestry,* a series of student textbooks used around the world. Dr. Oxford specializes in language learning strategies and styles.

Contributing Writers

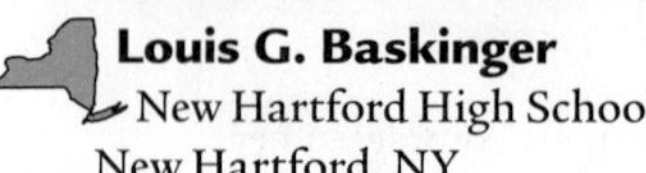

Louis G. Baskinger
New Hartford High School
New Hartford, NY

Jacquelyn Cinotti-Dirmann
Duval County Public Schools
Jacksonville, FL

Consulting Authors

Dan Battisti

Dr. Teresa Carrera-Hanley

Bill Lionetti

Patty Murguía Bohannan

Lorena Richins Layser

Teacher Reviewers

Sue Arandjelovic
Dobson High School
Mesa, AZ

Susan K. Arbuckle
Mahomet-Seymour High School
Mahomet, IL

Kristi Ashe
Amador Valley High School
Pleasanton, CA

Shaun A. Bauer
Olympia High School, *retired*
Orlando, FL

Sheila Bayles
Rogers High School
Rogers, AR

Robert L. Bowbeer
Detroit Country Day Upper School
Beverly Hills, MI

Hercilia Bretón
Highlands High School
San Antonio, TX

Adrienne Chamberlain-Parris
Mariner High School
Everett, WA

Mike Cooperider
Truman High School
Independence, MO

Susan B. Cress
Sheridan High School
Sheridan, IN

Michèle S. de Cruz-Sáenz, Ph.D.
Strath Haven High School
Wallingford, PA

Lizveth Dague
Park Vista Community High School
Lake Worth, FL

Parthena Draggett
Jackson High School
Massillon, OH

Rubén D. Elías
Roosevelt High School
Fresno, CA

Phillip Elkins
Lane Tech College Prep High School
Chicago, IL

Maria Fleming Álvarez
The Park School
Brookline, MA

Michael Garber
Boston Latin Academy
Boston, MA

Marco García
Derry University Advantage Academy
Chicago, IL

David González
Hollywood Hills High School
Hollywood, FL

Raquel R. González
Odessa Senior High School
Odessa, TX

Neyda González-Droz
Ridge Community High School
Davenport, FL

Becky Hay de García
James Madison Memorial High School
Madison, WI

Fatima Hicks
Suncoast High School, *retired*
Riviera Beach, FL

Gladys V. Horford
William T. Dwyer High School
Palm Beach Gardens, FL

Pam Johnson
Stevensville High School
Stevensville, MT

Richard Ladd
Ipswich High School
Ipswich, MA

Patsy Lanigan
Hume Fogg Academic Magnet High School
Nashville, TN

Kris Laws
Palm Bay High School
Melbourne, FL

Elizabeth Lupafya
North High School
Worcester, MA

David Malatesta
Niles West High School
Skokie, IL

Patrick Malloy
James B. Conant High School
Hoffman Estates, IL

Brandi Meeks
Starr's Mill High School
Fayetteville, GA

Kathleen L. Michaels
Palm Harbor University High School
Palm Harbor, FL

Linda Nanos
Brook Farm Business Academy
West Roxbury, MA

Nadine F. Olson
School of Teaching and Curriculum Leadership
Stillwater, OK

Pam Osthoff
Lakeland Senior High School
Lakeland, FL

Nicholas Patterson
Davenport Central High School
Davenport, IA

Daniel N. Richardson
Concord High School, *retired*
Concord, NH

Rita E. Risco
Palm Harbor University High School
Palm Harbor, FL

Miguel Roma
Boston Latin Academy
West Roxbury, MA

Lauren Schultz
Dover High School
Dover, NH

Nona M. Seaver
New Berlin West Middle/High School
New Berlin, WI

Susan Seraphine-Kimel
Astronaut High School
Titusville, FL

Mary Severo
Thomas Hart Middle School
Pleasanton, CA

Clarette Shelton
WT Woodson High School, *retired*
Fairfax, VA

Irma Sprague
Countryside High School
Clearwater, FL

Mary A. Stimmel
Lincoln High School
Des Moines, IA

Karen Tharrington
Wakefield High School
Raleigh, NC

Alicia Turnier
Countryside High School
Clearwater, FL

Roberto E. del Valle
The Overlake School
Redmond, WA

Todd Wagner
Upper Darby High School, *retired*
Drexel Hill, PA

Ronie R. Webster
Monson Junior/Senior High School
Monson, MA

Cheryl Wellman
Bloomingdale High School
Valrico, FL

Thomasina White
School District of Philadelphia
Philadelphia, PA

Jena Williams
Jonesboro High School
Jonesboro, AR

Program Advisory Council

Louis G. Baskinger
New Hartford High School
New Hartford, NY

Linda M. Bigler
James Madison University
Harrisonburg, VA

Flora María Ciccone-Quintanilla
Holly Senior High School
Holly, MI

Jacquelyn Cinotti-Dirmann
Duval County Public Schools
Jacksonville, FL

Desa Dawson
Del City High School
Del City, OK

Robin C. Hill
Warrensville Heights High School
Warrensville Heights, OH

Barbara M. Johnson
Gordon Tech High School, *retired*
Chicago, IL

Ray Maldonado
Houston Independent School District
Houston, TX

Karen S. Miller
Friends School of Baltimore
Baltimore, MD

Dr. Robert A. Miller
Woodcreek High School
Roseville Joint Union High School District
Roseville, CA

Debra M. Morris
Wellington Landings Middle School
Wellington, FL

María Nieto Zezas
West Morris Central High School
Chester, NJ

Rita Oleksak
Glastonbury Public Schools
Glastonbury, CT

Sandra Rosenstiel
University of Dallas, *retired*
Grapevine, TX

Emily Serafa Manschot
Northville High School
Northville, MI

NEW YORK REVIEWERS

New York Program Advisors

Louis G. Baskinger
New Hartford High School
New Hartford, NY

Cherie Bluth
Farmingdale High School
Farmingdale, NY

Elizabeth Bossong
Vestal Senior High School
Vestal, NY

Robert Hughes
Martha Brown Middle School, *retired*
Fairport, NY

New York Reviewers

Joseph T. Baker
LaGuardia Arts High School
New York, NY

Deborah A. Carlson
Sweet Home Middle School
Amherst, NY

Annamaria Falzarano
Greece Central School District
Rochester, NY

Joyce Jackson-Kalinoski, PhD
Jamesville-DeWitt Middle School
Jamesville, NY

Dr. Elaine Margarita
Jericho Schools
Jericho, NY

Frank D. Marino, Jr.
Great Hollow Middle School
Nesconset, NY

Paula Nurse
North Tonawanda High School
North Tonawanda, NY

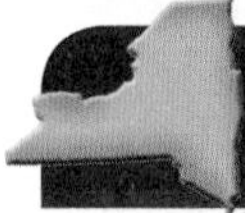

NEW YORK STANDARDS—Checkpoint B

Standard 1: Communication Skills

NY1.1 Listening and speaking are primary communicative goals in modern language learning. These skills are used for the purposes of socializing, providing and acquiring information, expressing personal feelings and opinions, and getting others to adopt a course of action.

Students can:

- Comprehend messages and short conversations when listening to peers, familiar adults, and providers of public services either in face-to-face interactions or on the telephone.
- Understand the main idea and some discrete information in television, radio, or live presentations.
- Initiate and sustain conversations, face to face or on the phone, with native-speaking or more fluent individuals.
- Select vocabulary appropriate to a range of topics, employ simple and complex sentences in present, past, and future time frames, and express details and nuances by using appropriate modifiers.
- Exhibit spontaneity in their interactions, particularly when the topic is familiar, but often rely on familiar utterances.
- Use repetition and circumlocution as well as gestures and other nonverbal cues to sustain conversation.

NY 1.2 Reading and writing are used in languages other than English for the purposes of socializing, providing and acquiring information, expressing personal feelings and opinions, and getting others to adopt a course of action.

Students can:

- Read and comprehend materials written for native speakers when the topic and language are familiar.
- Use cognates and contextual and visual cues to derive meaning from texts that contain unfamiliar words, expressions, and structures.
- Read simple materials independently, but may have to guess at meanings of longer or more complex material.
- Write short notes, uncomplicated personal and business letters, brief journals, and short reports.
- Write brief analyses of more complex content when given the opportunity for organization and advance preparation, though errors may occur more frequently.
- Produce written narratives and expressions of opinion about radio and television programs, newspaper and magazine articles, and selected stories, songs, and literature of the target language.

Standard 2: Cultural Understanding

NY 2.1 Effective communication involves meanings that go beyond words and require an understanding of perceptions, gestures, folklore, and family and community dynamics. All of these elements can affect whether and how well a message is received.

Students can:

- Exhibit more comprehensive knowledge of cultural traits and patterns.
- Draw comparisons between societies.
- Recognize that there are important linguistic and cultural variations among groups that speak the same target language.
- Understand how words, body language, rituals, and social interactions influence communication.

NEW YORK

CONTENTS

New York Student Edition

Liberty Island, New York © Christopher Hill/Alamy

Tradiciones

NEW YORK EDITION

Explora las tradiciones del mundo hispano

NY2 Cultural Understanding

Una tejedora guatemalteca

La fiesta de la Mercé, Barcelona, España

Online at CLASSZONE.COM

Cultura INTERACTIVA *pp. C2–C3, C4–C5, C6–C7, C8–C9, C10–C11, C12–C13, C14–C15, C16–C17, C18–C19, C20–C21, C22–C23, C24–C25*

LECCIÓN PRELIMINAR Estados Unidos

Una vida ocupada

NEW YORK EDITION

New York Standards

NY1.1
- Listening
- Speaking

NY1.2
- Reading
- Writing

NY2 Cultural Understanding
- Gala: un tema importante para Dalí *p. 15*

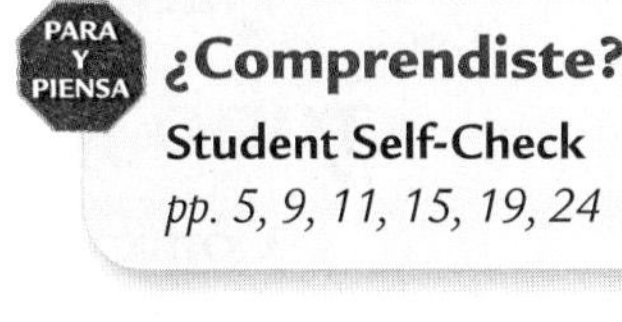

PARA Y PIENSA **¿Comprendiste?**
Student Self-Check
pp. 5, 9, 11, 15, 19, 24

Estudiantes preuniversitarias conversando

UNIDAD 1

México

Nos divertimos al aire libre

NEW YORK EDITION

New York Standards

NY1.1

- Listening 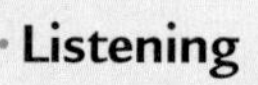
- Speaking 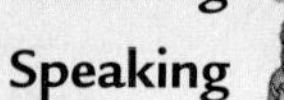

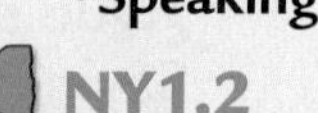

NY1.2

- Reading 
- Writing 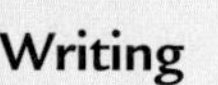

NY2 Cultural Understanding

- Explora México *p. 28*
- La naturaleza y el arte *p. 38*
- Monterrey y sus parques *p. 44*
- «Hermandad», «Viento, agua, piedra» *p. 48*

¿Recuerdas?

- irregular present tense *p. 36*

¿Comprendiste?

Student Self-Check

pp. 34, 36, 39, 41, 44, 47, 51

Online at CLASSZONE.COM

Cultura INTERACTIVA	Animated Grammar	@HomeTutor VideoPlus
pp. 28–29 82–83	*pp. 37, 42, 53 63, 68, 79*	*pp. 84–85*

Video/DVD

El gran desafío

pp. 84–85

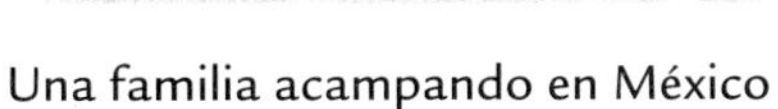

Una familia acampando en México

Playa en la Península de Yucatán, ruinas de Tulum

Lección 2

New York Standards

NY1.1

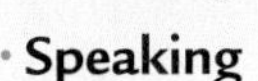

- Listening 
- Speaking 

NY1.2

- Reading
- Writing

NY2 Cultural Understanding

¿Recuerdas?

¿Comprendiste?

Student Self-Check *pp. 60, 62, 65, 67, 70, 73, 77*

UNIT 1 WRAP-UP

UNIDAD 2 Estados Unidos

¡Es hora de ayudar!

NEW YORK EDITION

New York Standards

NY1.1
- Listening 
- Speaking

NY1.2
- Reading 
- Writing

NY2 Cultural Understanding
- Explora Estados Unidos *p. 88*
- El Museo del Barrio *p. 98*
- Pablo O'Higgins *p. 104*
- «En la Ocho y la Doce» *p. 108*

¿Recuerdas?
- irregular preterite *p. 94*
- family relationships *p. 98*
- describing a camping trip *p. 99*
- beach activities *p. 103*
- **ir a** + infinitive *p. 103*

¿Comprendiste?
Student Self-Check
pp. 94, 96, 99, 101, 104, 107, 111

Online at CLASSZONE.COM

Cultura INTERACTIVA *pp. 88–89 142–143*

Animated Grammar *pp. 97, 102, 113 123, 128, 139*

@HomeTutor VideoPlus *pp. 144–145*

Video/DVD
El gran desafío
pp. 144–145

Jóvenes durante el *Hands On Miami Day*, Miami, Florida

Jóvenes haciendo trabajos voluntarios, ciudad de Nueva York

Lección 2

New York Standards

NY1.1
- Listening 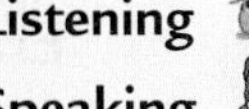
- Speaking 

NY1.2
- Reading 
- Writing 

NY2 Cultural Understanding

- Concierto para todos *p. 124*
- Periódicos estadounidenses en español *p. 130*
- «Las mañanitas» *p. 134*
- Culturas musicales *p. 142*

¿Recuerdas?

- preterite vs. imperfect *p. 120*
- beach activities *p. 125*
- volunteer activities *p. 129*

PARA Y PIENSA **¿Comprendiste?**

Student Self-Check

pp. 120, 122, 125, 127, 130, 133, 137

UNIDAD 3 Centroamérica

¡El futuro de nuestro planeta!

NEW YORK EDITION

New York Standards

NY1.1
- Listening 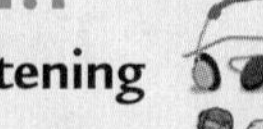
- Speaking 

NY1.2
- Reading 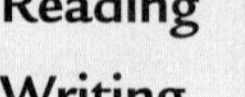
- Writing 

NY2 Cultural Understanding
- Explora Centroamérica *p. 148*
- El lago de Nicaragua *p. 156*
- Especies en peligro *p. 164*
- «La mejor edad» *p. 168*

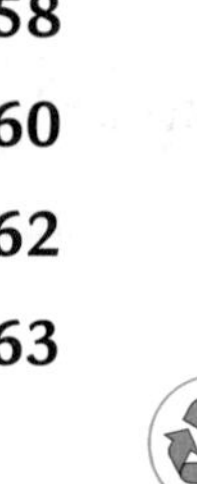

¿Recuerdas?
- **ustedes** commands *p. 154*
- **ir a** + infinitive *p. 156*
- media vocabulary *p. 158*

PARA Y PIENSA **¿Comprendiste?**

Student Self-Check
pp. 154, 156, 159, 161, 164, 167, 171

Online at CLASSZONE.COM

pp. 148–149 202–203

Animated Grammar *pp. 157, 162, 173 183, 188, 199*

@HomeTutor VideoPlus *pp. 204–205*

Video/DVD
El gran desafío
pp. 204–205

El auto del futuro protegerá el medio ambiente

Molinos de viento, Tilarán, Costa Rica

Lección 2

Tema: *Por un futuro mejor* 176

New York Standards

NY1.1
- Listening
- Speaking

NY1.2
- Reading
- Writing

NY2 Cultural Understanding
- **El canal y Panamá** *p. 184*
- **El arte ingenuo** *p. 190*
- **«La tristeza del maya»** *p. 194*
- **Protejamos la naturaleza** *p. 202*

¿Recuerdas?
- **ustedes** commands *p. 180*
- impersonal expressions *p. 184*
- future tense *p. 189*

PARA Y PIENSA **¿Comprendiste?**
Student Self-Check
pp. NYS5, 180, 182, 185, 187, 190, 193, 197

UNIDAD 4

El Caribe

Así quiero ser

NEW YORK EDITION

NY1.1
- Listening 
- Speaking  

NY1.2
- Reading
- Writing

NY2 Cultural Understanding
- Explora El Caribe *p. 208*
- Roberto Clemente *p. 219*
- Juan Luis Guerra *p. 224*
- «El sueño de América» *p. 228*

¿Recuerdas?
- **ser** vs. **estar** *p. 214*
- future tense *p. 219*

¿Comprendiste?
Student Self-Check
pp. 214, 216, 219, 221, 224, 227, 231

Online at CLASSZONE.COM

Cultura INTERACTIVA	Animated Grammar	@HomeTutor VideoPlus
pp. 208–209 262–263	*pp. 217, 222, 233 243, 248, 259*	*pp. 264–265*

Video/DVD
El gran desafío
pp. 264–265

Félix Sánchez, atleta de la República Dominicana

Un bombero en acción

Lección 2

Tema: ¿Quiénes son los héroes? . . 236

New York Standards

NY1.1
- Listening
- Speaking

NY1.2
- Reading
- Writing

NY2 Cultural Understanding
- Un estilo propio *p. 245*
- La pintura y los héroes *p. 250*
- «La ñapa» *p. 254*
- Héroes del Caribe *p. 262*

¿Recuerdas?
- describing people *p. 240*
- superlatives *p. 242*
- family relationships *p. 244*
- **-ísimo** *p. 250*

PARA Y PIENSA **¿Comprendiste?**
Student Self-Check
pp. 240, 242, 245, 247, 250, 253, 257

UNIDAD 5 Los países andinos

Bolivia

Ecuador

Perú

¿Cómo te entretienes?

NEW YORK EDITION

New York Standards

NY1.1
- Listening 
- Speaking 

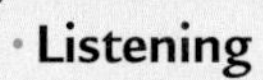
NY1.2
- Reading 
- Writing 

NY2 Cultural Understanding
- Explora los países andinos *p. 268*
- El Museo de Metales Preciosos *p. 278*
- El arte de Tigua, Ecuador *p. 284*
- «La ciudad de los mapas» *p. 288*

¿Recuerdas?
- commands with **tú** *p. 274*
- professions vocabulary *p. 278*

¿Comprendiste?
Student Self-Check
pp. 274, 276, 279, 281, 284, 287, 291

Online at CLASSZONE.COM

Cultura INTERACTIVA *pp. 268–269 322–323*

Animated Grammar *pp. 277, 282, 293 303, 308, 319*

@HomeTutor VideoPlus *pp. 324–325*

Video/DVD
El gran desafío
pp. 324–325

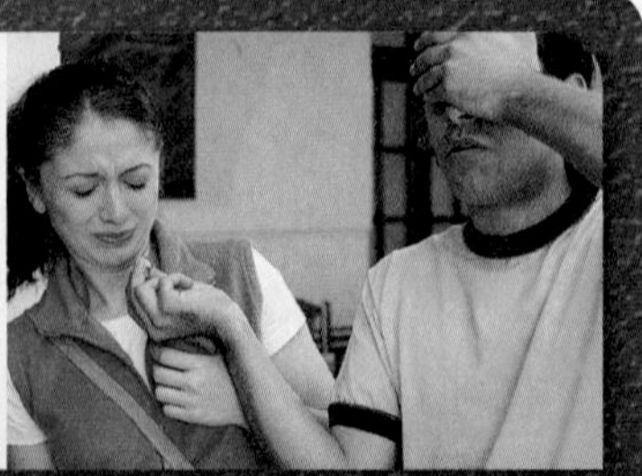

Asamblea de la Organización de Estados Americanos (OEA), Quito, Ecuador

Estudiantes en la Plaza de Armas, Trujillo, Perú

Lección 2

Tema: *Nuevos amigos, nuevas oportunidades* 296

¿Recuerdas?
- preterite *p. 300*
- computer vocabulary *p. 304*

¿Comprendiste?
Student Self-Check
pp. 300, 302, 305, 307, 310, 313, 317

UNIDAD 6

España

¿Dónde vivimos?

NEW YORK EDITION

New York Standards

NY1.1
- Listening 
- Speaking 

NY1.2
- Reading
- Writing

NY2 Cultural Understanding
- Explora España *p. 328*
- Un banco sin fin *p. 336*
- El flamenco: clásico y moderno *p. 344*
- «Manolito Gafotas» *p. 348*

¿Recuerdas?
- preterite *p. 334*
- direct object pronouns *p. 341*

¿Comprendiste?
Student Self-Check
pp. 334, 336, 339, 341, 344, 347, 351

Online at CLASSZONE.COM

Cultura INTERACTIVA *pp. 328–329 382–383*

Animated Grammar *pp. 337, 342, 353 363, 368, 379*

@HomeTutor VideoPlus *pp. 384–385*

Video/DVD
El gran desafío
pp. 384–385

Plaza Real, Barcelona

Vista de Granada

Lección 2

Tema: *Fuera de la ciudad* . . . 356

New York Standards

NY1.1
- **Listening**

- **Speaking**

NY1.2
- **Reading**
- **Writing**

NY2 Cultural Understanding
- **Las autonomías españolas** *p. 362*
- **El Greco y Toledo** *p. 370*
- **«Romance sonámbulo»** *p. 374*
- **Lo moderno y lo tradicional** *p. 382*

¿Recuerdas?
- present perfect *p. 360*
- **tú** commands *p. 360*
- places in the neighborhood *p. 364*
- past participles as adjectives *p. 365*

¿Comprendiste?
Student Self-Check
pp. 360, 362, 365, 367, 370, 373, 377

UNIDAD 7

Colombia y Venezuela

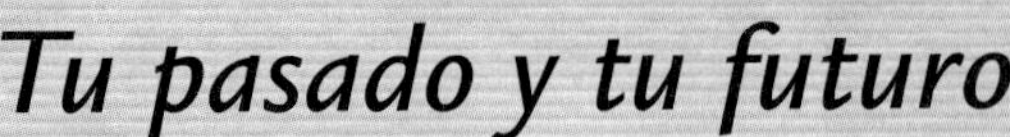

NEW YORK EDITION

NY1.1

- **Listening** 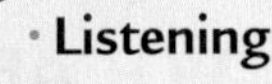
- **Speaking** 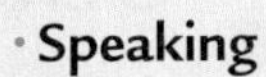

NY1.2

- **Reading** 
- **Writing** 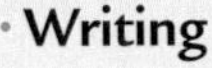

NY2 Cultural Understanding

¿Recuerdas?

¿Comprendiste?

Student Self-Check

pp. NYS9, 394, 396, 399, 401, 404, 407, 411

Online at CLASSZONE.COM

Cultura INTERACTIVA *pp. 388–389 442–443*

Animated Grammar *pp. 397, 402, 413 423, 428, 439*

@HomeTutor VideoPlus *pp. 444–445*

Video/DVD

El gran desafío
pp. 444–445

Estudiantes colombianas vistiendo uniformes, Bogotá, Colombia

Día de graduación en una escuela colombiana

Lección 2

New York Standards

NY1.1
- **Listening** 
- **Speaking** 

NY1.2
- **Reading**
- **Writing**

NY2 Cultural Understanding
- **Los retratos de Fernando Botero** *p. 425*
- **Universidades** *p. 430*
- **«El esqueleto de visita»** *p. 434*
- **Educación especializada** *p. 442*

¿Recuerdas?
- subjunctive with impersonal expressions *p. 420*
- conditional *p. 420*
- future p. 422
- architectural structures p. 424

¿Comprendiste?
Student Self-Check
pp. 420, 422, 425, 427, 430, 433, 437

UNIDAD 8

El Cono Sur

Hablemos de literatura

NEW YORK EDITION

NY1.1
- Listening 
- Speaking 

NY1.2
- Reading
- Writing

NY2 Cultural Understanding
- Explora el Cono Sur *p. 448*
- La literatura y el cine *p. 456*
- Los sueños de Roberto Matta *p. 464*
- «Ardiente paciencia (El cartero de Neruda)» *p. 468*

¿Recuerdas?
- preterite vs. imperfect *p. 459*
- professions *p. 463*

¿Comprendiste?
Student Self-Check
pp. 454, 456, 459, 461, 464, 467, 471

Online at CLASSZONE.COM

Cultura INTERACTIVA *pp. 448–449 502–503*

Animated Grammar *pp. 457, 462, 473 483, 488, 499*

@HomeTutor VideoPlus *pp. 504–505*

Video/DVD
El gran desafío
pp. 504–505

Jóvenes en una feria de libros, Buenos Aires, Argentina

Estudiantes argentinos preparando una obra de teatro

Lección 2

New York Standards

NY1.1
- Listening
- Speaking

NY1.2
- Reading
- Writing

NY2 Cultural Understanding
- **El carnaval gigante** *p. 482*
- **Los teatros: monumentales obras de arte** *p. 490*
- **«Colón agarra viaje a toda costa (parte 4)»** *p. 494*
- **Cuna de autores famosos** *p. 502*

¿Recuerdas?
- **si** clauses *p. 487*
- literary vocabulary *p. 489*

PARA Y PIENSA **¿Comprendiste?**
Student Self-Check
pp. 480, 482, 485, 487, 490, 493, 497

Recursos

NEW YORK EDITION

NEW YORK

TOPIC SUPPORT

TOPIC SUPPORT

Liberty Island, New York © Christopher Hill/Alamy

Presentación de VOCABULARIO

¡AVANZA! **Goal:** Learn about political parties and government. Then practice what you learned by talking about elections and political candidates.

Expand the vocabulary in Unit 3 Lesson 2

A En **una elección,** la gente elige a las personas importantes del gobierno. Las personas que quieren ganar una elección se llaman **candidatos.** Todas las ciudades tienen un jefe de gobierno que se llama **alcalde.** Hoy hay elecciones para alcalde en una ciudad de Centroamérica y éstos son los candidatos.

PARTIDO ECOLÓGICO

CARTA DE RAMÓN SOLÁ, SU CANDIDATO A ALCALDE

Estimados amigos:

¿Quieren tener una ciudad limpia? ¿Quieren proteger los parques? Entonces, yo soy la persona ideal para alcalde.

- Fui **concejal** de esta ciudad por cuatro años. Los concejales representan a cada barrio de la ciudad y la gente les puede contar sus problemas. Yo ya conozco a todos y sé cuáles son los problemas serios.
- Mi **partido** es un grupo de personas que se preocupa por el medio ambiente. Si gano las elecciones para alcalde, todos vamos a respirar mejor.

¡NO TIRE SU **VOTO**!
VOTE PARA RAMÓN SOLÁ.

Ramón Solá

B Los candidatos pertenecen a un partido, que es un grupo político que tiene ideas en común. La lista de esas ideas forman **la plataforma** del partido. Veamos qué ofrece la otra candidata a alcalde.

Más vocabulario

la alcaldía *City Hall*
la dictadura *dictatorship*

¡A responder!

Vas a escuchar unas oraciones. Si la oración tiene lógica, levanta la mano y muestra tu voto (una hoja de papel).

Práctica de VOCABULARIO

1 Las elecciones

Leer

Empareja las columnas para identificar varios aspectos de las elecciones.

1. un grupo de candidatos con ideas similares
2. la persona que tiene su oficina en la alcaldía
3. cuando la gente vota por su candidato(a) favorito(a)
4. un sistema político donde no hay elecciones
5. un sistema político donde hay elecciones frecuentes
6. las opiniones oficiales de un partido político

a. la democracia
b. el partido
c. la dictadura
d. la plataforma
e. el (la) alcalde(sa)
f. la elección

2 ¡A votar!

Leer
Escribir

Lee el siguiente artículo del periódico sobre las próximas elecciones. Complétalo con la palabra correcta de la lista.

el candidato	democracia	el voto
elecciones	la alcaldía	partido

PRÓXIMAMENTE, NUEVO ALCALDE

En el mes de octubre habrá __1.__ para alcalde. El ganador empezará a trabajar en __2.__ en enero. __3.__ del __4.__ ecológico es el favorito. Todos los ciudadanos deben dar su __5.__ para mantener la __6.__.

3 El Partido Azul

Leer
Hablar
Escribir

Lee el volante sobre una elección local y luego contesta las preguntas.

¡VOTE POR EL PARTIDO AZUL!

Los candidatos

Para alcalde: Martín Macías Jaramillo

Para concejales: Lorenzo Robles Olivares
Adriana Laredo Darín

- **Limpiar los parques**
- **Eliminar la pobreza**
- **Mejorar el transporte público**
- **Cuidar a la gente sin hogar**
- **Recaudar fondos para el reciclaje**

¡SU VOTO ES IMPORTANTE! ¡NUESTRO PARTIDO LO NECESITA!

1. ¿Cómo se llama este partido político?
2. ¿Quién es Lorenzo Robles Olivares?
3. ¿Para qué se votará en esta elección?
4. ¿A qué pertenece el punto "Eliminar la pobreza"?
5. Según el volante, ¿cómo es el voto de la gente?
6. Según el volante, ¿qué necesita el Partido Azul?

Expansión
Escoge tres ideas del volante y da tu opinión sobre ellas. ¿En cuál te gustaría participar para ayudar a tu ciudad o pueblo? ¿Por qué?

4 Un debate

Hablar

Las elecciones son muy importantes para el progreso de un país o de una ciudad. Con un(a) compañero(a), formen un partido y hablen de sus ideas usando palabras del vocabulario.

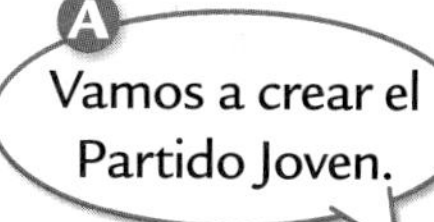

B: ¡Hagamos volantes con nuestra propuesta!

¿Comprendiste? Contesta las siguientes preguntas.

1. ¿Quién gobierna una ciudad?
2. ¿Cómo se llama el sistema político donde la gente vota?
3. ¿Cómo se llama el proceso para elegir a una persona para un puesto político?
4. ¿Qué usa la gente para elegir a sus candidatos en una elección?

Presentación de VOCABULARIO

¡AVANZA! **Goal:** Learn about examination and grading as well as discipline at school. Then practice what you learned by talking about what to do in order to graduate from school.

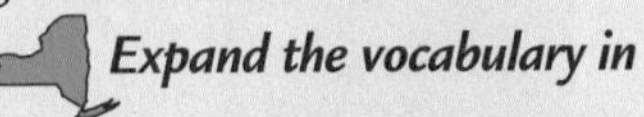

Expand the vocabulary in Unit 7 Lesson 1

A En las escuelas de Latinoamérica, los estudiantes tienen que sacar buenas notas en los exámenes. En algunos países, las notas son en letras. En otros son en números.

B Alicia es de México. ¡En el examen de historia se sacó un 10! Alicia **aprobó** el examen con una nota excelente.

10

¡Excelente!

Nombre: Alicia Pasos

Fecha: 2 de febrero

EXAMEN DE HISTORIA

① Completa las oraciones con la palab...
(10 puntos)

a) Colón llegó a América en 1492 ✓

b) Llegó a una ...

10 de febrero

Rafael Lemos

PARTE I: ÁLGEBRA

1. Escribe el resultado exacto de cada operació...

a. 5 x 5 x 5 = 15 ✗ 125

b. 2^4 = 8 ✗ 16

c. 7 + 3 x 4 = 40 ✗ 19

d. 150 ...

C Rafael es de Puerto Rico. No estudió mucho y en el examen de matemáticas se sacó una F. Rafael **reprobó** el examen.

D Las escuelas tienen requisitos para que los estudiantes se gradúen. Éstos son los requisitos de la Escuela Banderas Unidas.

Más vocabulario

el aplazo *failing grade*
quedarse después de hora *to stay for detention*

REQUISITOS DE GRADUACIÓN

Para graduarse de esta escuela, los estudiantes deben cumplir con lo siguiente:

NOTAS

- Aprobar todas las materias.
- A mitad de año tienen **parciales**. Estos exámenes tienen preguntas generales sobre todo lo que estudiaron hasta ese momento. El estudiante debe aprobar el parcial.
- Si el estudiante reprueba el parcial, tiene la oportunidad de tomar **un recuperatorio** e intentar nuevamente.
- Al terminar el año tienen **finales.** Estos exámenes tienen preguntas generales sobre todo lo que estudiaron en el año. Los finales no tienen recuperatorio.

CONDUCTA

- Los estudiantes deben **portarse bien.** Si no lo hacen tienen que **ir a la Dirección** a hablar con el director de la escuela.
- Los estudiantes que se **portan mal** reciben **una amonestación.**
- Los estudiantes que se portan muy mal reciben **una suspensión** y no pueden ir a la escuela por varios días.
- Los estudiantes que tienen dos suspensiones no se pueden graduar en esta escuela.

¡A responder!

Vas a escuchar unas oraciones. Si la acción representa algo bueno, pon el dedo pulgar hacia arriba. Si representa algo malo, ponlo hacia abajo.

Práctica de VOCABULARIO

1 Un gran cambio

Hablar
Escribir

El año pasado Malena tuvo muchos problemas con la escuela. Elige la palabra correcta entre paréntesis para decir qué hizo cada mes.

1. En enero se portó mal y fue a la ____ (amonestación / Dirección) doce veces.
2. En febrero reprobó cuatro ____ (parciales / suspensiones).
3. En marzo recibió veintidós ____ (amonestaciones / finales).
4. En junio, antes de terminar el año escolar, reprobó dos ____ (parciales / finales).
5. Al empezar el año siguiente, en octubre aprobó un ____ (recuperatorio / aplazo).
6. En noviembre recibió una A y ____ (reprobó / aprobó) todos los parciales.

Expansión
Imagina por qué ha cambiado tanto Malena y escribe una historia que explique qué pasó. Usa todas las palabras del vocabulario que puedas.

2 Tres historias de estudiantes

Hablar
Escribir

Utiliza palabras de la lista para completar las siguientes historias. Usa la forma apropiada de los verbos.

reprobar	portarse bien	aplazo
aprobar	portarse mal	quedarse después de hora

José Antonio
A José Antonio le gustan mucho las ciencias. Es un buen estudiante y __1.__ en todas las clases. Siempre aprueba sus exámenes y nunca ha recibido un __2.__ .

Belkis
A Belkis le encanta dibujar. __3.__ los exámenes de arte es algo fácil para ella. Desgraciadamente, no le gustan las otras materias. El semestre pasado no estudió matemáticas, ciencias ni español y __4.__ tres parciales.

Eduardo
A Eduardo le gusta hablar y reírse mucho. Siempre __5.__ en las clases y los maestros se enojan. La semana pasada, tuvo que __6.__ cuatro veces.

3 ¿Qué hicieron?

Hablar
Escribir

Lee cada descripción. Utiliza las palabras de la lista para decir qué hizo cada persona.

reprobar	portarse bien	tomar un recuperatorio	ir a la Dirección
aprobar	portarse mal	quedarse despúes de hora	

modelo: Susana habló, comió e hizo llamadas telefónicas durante la clase de inglés. Susana se portó mal.

1. Ana recibió buenas notas en sus exámenes. ______
2. José no fue a un examen pero su maestra le dio otra oportunidad. ______
3. Cristina no estudió y recibió una F. ______
4. Esteban escuchó con atención al maestro. ______
5. Eva tuvo que ir a hablar con el director. ______
6. Enrique se portó mal en la clase de álgebra y al final del día no pudo salir de la escuela a las 2 p.m. ______

4 ¿Y tú?

Hablar

Pregúntale a un(a) compañero(a) de clase si ha hecho lo siguiente.

modelo: recibir una amonestación (¿por qué?)

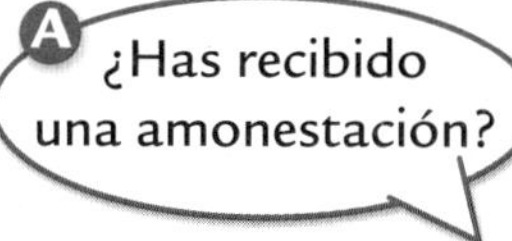

1. reprobar un examen (¿cuál?)
2. ir a la dirección (¿por qué?)
3. quedarse después de hora (¿por qué?)
4. portarse mal en una clase (¿qué hiciste?)
5. tomar un recuperatorio (¿por qué?)

¿Comprendiste? ¿Qué debes hacer si quieres ser un(a) buen(a) estudiante?

1. portarte bien / portarte mal
2. aprobar exámenes / reprobar exámenes
3. quedarte después de hora / salir a la hora normal
4. tomar recuperatorios / recibir suspensiones

En resumen

Vocabulario

Expanded vocabulary for Unit 3 Lesson 2

Talk About Government

el (la) alcalde(sa)	*mayor*
la alcaldía	*city hall*
el (la) candidato(a)	*candidate*
el (la) concejal(a)	*councilor*
la democracia	*democracy*
la dictadura	*dictatorship*
la elección	*election*
el partido	*political party*
la plataforma	*platform*
la propuesta	*proposal*
el voto	*vote*

Expanded vocabulary for Unit 7 Lesson 1

Talk About Examinations and Discipline

la amonestación	*demerit*
el aplazo	*failing grade*
aprobar	*to pass*
el final	*final exam*
ir a la Dirección	*to go to the Principal's office*
el parcial	*mid-term exam*
portarse bien	*to behave well*
portarse mal	*to behave poorly/ misbehave*
quedarse después de hora	*to stay for detention*
el recuperatorio	*make-up exam*
reprobar	*to fail*
la suspension	*suspension*

PARA Y PIENSA **Self-Check Answers**

p. NYS5 1. el alcalde/la alcaldesa 2. democracia 3. elección 4. el voto

p. NYS9 1. portarse bien 2. aprobar exámenes 3. salir a la hora normal 4. tomar recuperatorios

Repaso inclusivo

1 Representa un debate

Hablar
Escribir

Aprendiste varias palabras y expresiones para hablar de los sistemas políticos y las elecciones. Con la clase entera, identifiquen un problema importante que exista en su comunidad. Luego, trabajen en grupos pequeños e imaginen que son políticos del mismo partido. Describan su plataforma por escrito, hablen del problema que identificaron y piensen en una solución. Hagan una investigación en la comunidad o por Internet para buscar información. Luego, escojan a un(a) estudiante del grupo para presentar su partido político y su solución en un debate con los políticos de los otros partidos.

2 Escribe un folleto

Escribir

Aprendiste varias palabras y expresiones para hablar de los exámenes, las notas y la disciplina. Junto(a) con un(a) compañero(a), compara la lista de requisitos para la graduación de la Escuela Banderas Unidas de la página NYS7 con los requisitos para la graduación de tu escuela. Preparen un folleto (*brochure*) sobre los requisitos de tu escuela. Describan los requisitos sobre las notas y la conducta de los estudiantes y expliquen por qué son necesarios estos requisitos.

NEW YORK

SKILL SUPPORT

Liberty Island, New York © Christopher Hill/Alamy

SKILL SUPPORT

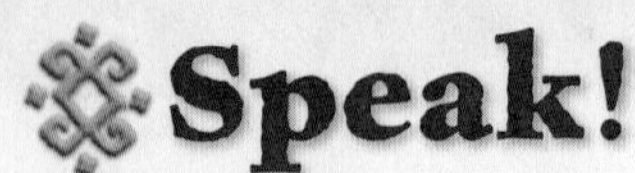

Speak!

Why?

Speaking may be the most important foreign language skill you develop. It allows you to express your needs, feelings, ideas, and opinions. You need speaking skills to ask for information, negotiate, persuade, report, explain, and interact with other people in a meaningful way.

What?

Throughout your year with *¡Avancemos!* you will be speaking about a variety of topics in classroom and simulated real-life situations. You will not only be answering questions in class, but you will also be giving short presentations, conversing with classmates, and engaging in role-plays and skits. By the end of the year, you will be able to describe people and events, obtain information, persuade and advise others, apologize, present and argue your point of view, and express your hopes, plans, and wishes.

How?

Every activity in *¡Avancemos!* marked **Hablar** will help you practice speaking skills. You will find opportunities for speaking interspersed throughout each lesson. Additonally, in the **Todo junto** section of each lesson there is an **Integración** activity that involves giving a short presentation, and after each unit the **Repaso inclusivo** section offers several role-play activities that provide realistic and fun situations for speaking. Whether you're giving a presentation or participating in a conversation, here are some simple strategies that can help you speak with confidence.

- **Relax** Don't be afraid to make mistakes. A native speaker can usually understand what you're trying to communicate even if your verb conjugation or pronunciation isn't perfect. It's better to strive for fluency by just speaking than to keep quiet because you're afraid of how you'll sound.

- **Monitor yourself** It's okay to make mistakes, but it's also okay to stop and correct yourself when you know you've made one.
- **Pay attention to tone, intonation, and appropriate language** Consider the situation and the person you are talking to. Think about what kinds of words and expressions you should use. Make sure your intonation reflects your mood or urgency and whether you are making a statement or asking a question.
- **Prepare** Think about what you're going to say before you say it. Jot down relevant vocabulary and practice common phrases you might need in your situation. Recall a similar real-life situation you may have experienced in your own language.
- **Don't get stuck** If you don't know a particular word, get around it by using words you do know. This is called circumlocution. For example, if you want to say that someone is a carpenter, but you don't know the word **carpintera**, you could say **"Ella construye casas nuevas,"** or **"Ella hace muebles, como mesas, sillas y estantes."**
- **Communicate with gestures** Effective communication relies not only on speaking, but also facial expressions and gestures. This can also help when you are missing certain essential vocabulary words.
- **Ask for clarification** If you don't understand something, don't be afraid to say **Repite, por favor** or **Perdón, no comprendo.**

The Bottom Line

You need to practice to be able to speak Spanish well, so don't be afraid to open up and speak out, even if it means making some mistakes. The more you speak, the more fluent you will become and the fewer mistakes you will make.

Speaking Assessments

Informal speaking is what you do in daily classroom activities. *¡Avancemos!* provides you with many opportunities for creative oral expression. These activities are labeled **Hablar** and take place with a partner or in a small group.

You will also be preparing for **formal speaking assessments,** which consist of specific communication tasks in which you and your partner assume a role. Each task achieves a communication function, such as socializing, providing and obtaining information, expressing personal feelings, or persuading. *¡Avancemos!* prepares you for speaking assessments by having you participate in role-plays, skits, and presentations throughout the lessons, especially in **Todo junto** and **Repaso inclusivo.**

At the end of this course you may take a formal speaking exam in which you will engage in a series of role plays with your teacher. You will be scored according to how well you are able to keep up the conversation and to the level of language that you use. See the chart below for the scoring guidelines.

Each utterance receives		
2 Points *(Checkpoint B)* if it is...	**1 Point *(Checkpoint A)* if it is...**	**0 Points if it is...**
Comprehensible ***AND*** **Appropriate** ***AND*** Contains a preponderance of the following Checkpoint B attributes: Initiates and/or sustains and/or advances the conversation • Uses common verb tense forms (including, past, present, future) • Uses accurate structure • Is articulated comprehensibly • Uses a variety of vocabulary that may expand or clarify meaning • Is extended (may contain more that one short, discrete utterance) • Uses culturally correct gestures, social conventions, and/or idiomatic expressions.	**Comprehensible** ***AND*** **Appropriate** ***BUT*** Is a single, short, discrete utterance consisting exclusively of Checkpoint A vocabulary/structures ***OR*** Contains little or no evidence of Checkpoint B attributes (see Checkpoint B)	**Incomprehensible** ***AND/OR*** **Inappropriate** **Disregard if it is a...** Yes/No response Socializing device Restatement of all or essential parts of what the teacher said Proper nouns(s) in isolation

Here is a sample of how you will be assessed in a formal speaking task (T=teacher; S=student):

TASK	I am your friend. We have just heard the weather report and we are going to make plans for the weekend. I will start the conversation.

2-Point Utterances ***(Checkpoint B)***	**1-Point Utterances** ***(Checkpoint A)***
1. T. Va a llover. ¿Qué vamos a hacer? S. **Tal vez podemos mirar la televisión.** ***Commentary:*** Comprehensible and appropriate; advances the conversation, and demonstrates a preponderance of the attributes of Checkpoint B, including a variety of vocabulary (tal vez).	**1.** T. Va a llover. ¿Qué vamos a hacer? S. **Uhm... mirar el televisión.** ***Commentary:*** Comprehensible and appropriate; uses basic Checkpoint A vocabulary and structure; is a single, short, discrete utterance and includes an error.
2. T. No es una buena idea. S. **¿Por qué no te gusta la idea?** ***Commentary:*** Comprehensible and appropriate; advances the conversation, and demonstrates a preponderance of the attributes of Checkpoint B, including accurate question formation.	**2.** T. No es una buena idea. S. **¿Por qué?** ***Commentary:*** Comprehensible and appropriate; although the response advances the conversation, it is a single, short, discrete utterance.
3. T. Porque siempre miramos la televisión. S. **Vamos al cine y después comemos.** ***Commentary:*** Comprehensible and appropriate; advances the conversation, and demonstrates a preponderance of the attributes of Checkpoint B, including extended response.	**3.** T. Porque siempre miramos la televisión. S. **Vamos al cine.** ***Commentary:*** Comprehensible and appropriate; advances the conversation, uses basic Checkpoint A vocabulary and structure exclusively, and is a single, short, discrete utterance.
4. T. ¿Hay algo interesante en el cine? S. **Sí, una película de horror. Escucho es muy bueno.** ***Commentary.*** Comprehensible and appropriate; advances the conversation, and demonstrates a preponderance of the attributes of Checkpoint B. Utterance contains minor errors in formation.	**4.** T. ¿Hay algo interesante en el cine? S. **Sí, una película de horror.** ***Commentary:*** Comprehensible and appropriate; advances the conversation, uses basic Checkpoint A vocabulary and structure exclusively, and is a single, short, discrete utterance.
5. T. No me gustan las películas de horror. S. **¿Prefieres ver una de ciencia-ficción?** ***Commentary:*** Comprehensible and appropriate; advances the conversation, and demonstrates a preponderance of the attributes of Checkpoint B, including accurate structure.	**5.** T. No me gustan las películas de horror. S. **¿Una de ciencia-ficción?** ***Commentary:*** Comprehensible and appropriate; advances the conversation, uses basic Checkpoint A vocabulary and structure exclusively, and is a single, short, discrete utterance.
6. T. Bueno. ¿Cuándo y dónde? S. **El sábado, a las dos, en el centro comercial.** ***Commentary:*** Comprehensible and appropriate: advances the conversation, and demonstrates a preponderance of the attributes of Checkpoint B, including extended response.	**6.** T. Bueno. ¿Cuándo y dónde? S. **Sábado.** ***Commentary:*** Comprehensible and appropriate; advances the conversation, uses basic Checkpoint A vocabulary and structure exclusively, and is a single, short, discrete utterance.

Try It!

Choose a role-play task from each category and sustain a meaningful conversation with your teacher using the guidelines on the previous two pages.

Socializing

- *(Student initiates)* I am a Mexican teenager. We meet at the beach. We want to get acquainted. You start the conversation.
- *(Teacher initiates)* I am a student. We meet outside the office of the guidance counselor. We talk about our ideas for professions and what we would like to do. I will start the conversation.
- *(Teacher initiates)* I am a classmate. We are in the hall at school. I am going to greet you, and then we will talk about school. I will start the conversation.
- *(Student initiates)* I am a student in a Buenos Aires bookstore. I introduce myself to you and we discuss which books and authors interest us. You start the conversation.

Providing/Obtaining Information

- *(Teacher initiates)* I am a classmate. I am interested in finding out about volunteer opportunities for students in the local community. I will start the conversation.
- *(Student initiates)* I am a volunteer at an environmental information center. You ask me questions about environmental problems and endangered species. You start the conversation.
- *(Teacher initiates)* I am a Peruvian student who is new to your school. We would like to get to know each other better and we talk about our hobbies and interests. I will start the conversation.
- *(Student initiates)* I am the ticket agent at a train station in Spain. You come to me for information about a trip by train. You start the conversation.

Expressing Personal Feelings

- *(Teacher initiates)* I am your classmate. The Spanish teacher is organizing a trip to Cancún this summer. Tell me how you feel about the trip. I will start the conversation.
- *(Student initiates)* I am your Ecuadorian friend. You have been given permission to go on a school trip to Ecuador. Tell me how you feel about it. You start the conversation.
- *(Teacher initiates)* I am your friend. I am running for president of our class. We will discuss how you feel about this. I will start the conversation.
- *(Student initiates)* I am a student. Today the Spanish Club decided it will put on a play in Spanish. You are a teacher. You ask me how I feel about this. You start the conversation.

Persuasion

- *(Student initiates)* I am your Puerto Rican neighbor. You are trying to raise money for your Spanish club. Try to convince me to buy whatever you are selling. You start the conversation.
- *(Teacher initiates)* I am a Latino businessperson. You are a volunteer for a local social service agency. You want to persuade me to get involved in your group's efforts to improve our community. I will start the conversation.
- *(Student initiates)* I am a student. You are the editor of the school yearbook. You ask me who is the school's most inspirational student. I tell you and try to persuade you to name him or her "Student of the Year." You start the conversation.
- *(Teacher initiates)* I am your host parent in Spain. I have planned an all-day trip for the family. You have made other plans. Try to get my permission to do what you want. I will start the conversation.

Listen!

Why?

You receive a lot of information by listening: instructions from your teacher, news from your friends, announcements over the loudspeakers, and information from the radio and television. Listening is an important skill that allows you to understand what others are saying and to stay connected to the community and world around you.

What?

This year you'll listen to statements and questions in face-to-face conversations with peers and familiar adults. You'll also learn to understand the main idea of longer messages and conversations that contain some unfamiliar words.

How?

¡Avancemos! will help you develop listening skills by providing many opportunities to hear a variety of speakers in real-life situations. Every time you see this icon you will engage in active listening. You will learn different listening strategies with each dialogue in the **Todo junto** section of your textbook. Here are some examples of effective listening strategies:

Before you listen:

- Try to anticipate the content of a listening passage by reading the introductory material first and then thinking about what you already know about the topic. (See pages 105 and 431 for examples of this technique.)
- Read the introductory material before you listen and then make predictions about what you will hear. (See page 131 for an example of this technique.)
- Familiarize yourself with the task you will complete after listening. Then, while you listen to the passage, focus your attention on the key words and other information you will need to complete this task. (See pages 71, 191, 251, and 465 for examples of this technique.)

While you listen:

- When you encounter words you don't know, use what you already know about the subject to help you guess their meanings. (See page 105 for an example of this technique.)
- Listen for cognates, words that sound like English words and share the same meaning. (See page 285 for an example of this technique.)
- Use visual cues, such as pictures and facial expressions, to help you determine meaning. (See page 105 for an example of this technique.)
- Pay attention to the different voices you hear to determine who is speaking. Listen to the speaker's intonation to find out how he or she feels. (See pages 105, 371, and 405 for examples of this technique.)
- Take notes and use graphic organizers to analyze the information as you listen. (See pages 45, 165, 225, 311, 345, 371, 405, and 491 for examples of this technique.)

After you listen:

- Listen as many times as necessary to get all the information you need. (See pages 105 and 405 for examples of this technique.)
- Take time after you listen to summarize the information you heard. (See page 371 for an example of this technique.)

The Bottom Line

Like all skills, listening takes practice and time to acquire. The important thing to remember is that it's okay not to understand every word you hear.

Try It!

Try these listening activities.

In Part 1 you will answer multiple choice questions in English. In Part 2 you will answer multiple choice questions in Spanish.

Part 1 Directions

For each question, you will hear some background information in English once. Then you will hear a passage in Spanish twice and a question in English once. After you have heard the question, the teacher will pause while you read the question and the four suggested answers. Choose the best suggested answer. Base your answer on the content of the passage only.

1. Who is invited to this event?
(1) only grandparents and children
(2) you and your entire family
(3) only members of the club
(4) university students and their friends

2. What does the club need student volunteers to do?
(1) plant a vegetable garden in a local park
(2) organize a car and truck wash at the community center
(3) recycle bottles and cans from the school's cafeteria
(4) clean a park and recycle the garbage

3. What product is being advertised?
(1) a new car
(2) an air-conditioning unit
(3) a compact disc cleaner
(4) an instruction manual

4. What did these students receive?
(1) prizes of one-hundred dollars
(2) a trip to the Dominican Republic
(3) a medal for academic achievement
(4) scholarships to City College of New York

5. What is being advertised?
(1) a mini-laptop computer
(2) an antivirus program
(3) a memory card
(4) a Web site for pen pals

Part 2 Directions
For each question, you will hear some background information in English once. Then you will hear a passage in Spanish twice and a question in Spanish once. After you have heard the question, the teacher will pause while you read the question and the four suggested answers. Choose the best suggested answer. Base your answer on the content of the passage only.

1. ¿Qué se puede ver en una excursión por la "Ruta Puuc"?
(1) monumentos modernos
(2) restaurantes elegantes
(3) civilizaciones antiguas
(4) edificios futuristas

2. ¿De qué habla el editor de *La Onda Latina*?
(1) de los fotógrafos que trabajan para su periódico
(2) de una obra caritativa en la comunidad
(3) de un artículo de opinión que escribió
(4) de la primera edición del periódico

3. ¿De qué se trata este comentario?
(1) las plantas indígenas de Centroamérica
(2) los esfuerzos para proteger una especie de pájaro
(3) la posibilidad de reemplazar los bosques de Guatemala
(4) los problemas de contaminación en Guatemala

4. ¿Qué hizo la persona de quien habla tu amiga?
(1) establecer una agencia social
(2) comprar una casa nueva
(3) trabajar de voluntaria
(4) ayudar a un grupo de estudiantes

5. ¿Qué clase de consejos da esta página?
(1) una recomendación de hoteles para el turista
(2) información sobre las cosas necesarias para el viaje
(3) anuncios del horario de los vuelos
(4) ideas para viajar en ciertas líneas aéreas

Read!

Why?

Reading is an essential skill that can help you get important, interesting information from a variety of sources. It can give you access to Spanish-speaking cultures in the print media and in real-world situations. Reading can also provide hours of entertainment and enjoyment! You need reading skills to understand everything from food labels and street signs to newspapers and novels.

What?

This year, you'll read a wide variety of printed materials, such as advertisements, e-mails, newspaper columns, brochures, and literary excerpts. As you progress through the units, you will learn different ways to approach readings and develop your ability to comprehend increasingly difficult texts in Spanish.

How?

There are many ways to approach a complex reading, especially one that includes grammar and vocabulary you haven't learned yet. Throughout *¡Avancemos!* you will use different strategies to analyze readings in the **Contexto** vocabulary and **Lectura literaria** sections. You'll also practice your reading skills as you read the **Conexiones** and **Comparación cultural** sections and the **Todo junto** dialogues. Activities marked **Leer** will also help you practice and develop your reading skills. Here are some of the helpful strategies you can use to improve your reading in Spanish:

- **Look for cognates.** A cognate is a word that is spelled in a similar way and has a similar meaning in two different languages. You may have never seen the words **enorme, murmura,** or **dispersa** in Spanish before, but you can guess their meanings because they resemble English words you already know. See p. 48 for a way to recognize cognates and organize them using a spider map diagram.
- **Skim, scan, and reread.** To get the main idea of a passage, you can first skim it quickly. If you are looking for a specific piece of information, you can scan the passage to locate the fact you need. Rereading allows you to go through a text more slowly in order to absorb secondary ideas and to focus on supporting detail. (See p. 220 for a technique that combines skimming and rereading.)

- **Use visual cues and context.** Photos, illustrations, and symbols can help you guess the general idea of a passage. Also, the context in which they are used can help you guess content. For example, a literary reading may be illustrated with a green-tinted photo of water at night. That, together with the title of the poem *(Romance sonámbulo)* and its first line ("Verde que te quiero verde"), tells you that green will be an important symbol in the poem and that the poem will have a dreamlike quality. (See pp. 375–377 for the poem and illustration.)
- **Use format and organizational cues.** The title, subheads, lists, and other elements of a reading will give you clues to its meaning. Sometimes the author embeds organizational cues, such as repeated words or ideas, that guide you through the passage. (See p. 168 for one way to identify these cues.)
- **Look for and analyze stylistic and grammatical cues.** Punctuation and capitalization are stylistic cues that can help you determine shifts in meaning, such as when someone is speaking directly rather than indirectly. (See p. 194 for an example.) Focusing on the tenses of verbs will help you keep track of the actions and time periods in a passage. Looking at the use of the subjunctive vs. the indicative, for example, will help you understand emotional nuances when characters speak. (See pp. 40, 66, 100, 126, 186, 280, and 306 for examples of how different grammatical structures reinforce meaning.)
- **Use charts and diagrams.** As you read, recording and analyzing information in a graphic organizer can help your comprehension. For example, a cause and effect diagram (see p. 314) is helpful when you are trying to find relationships between different actions. A Venn diagram (see pp. 395, 426) is helpful for comparing and contrasting. A mind map (see pp. 35, 361), a honeycomb story map (pp. 74 and 228), or a chart with multiple rows and columns (see p. 40) can help you organize and keep track of specific details. (See pp. 95, 108, 121, 126, 155, 181, 186, 215, 254, 275, 340, 374, 400, 421, 434, 460, 481, 486, and 494 for a wide variety of charts and graphic organizers you can use to record and analyze information you read.)

The Bottom Line

Whether in English or in Spanish, reading is an important tool for simple day-to-day tasks as well as more complex activities like reading a magazine or a novel. Developing your reading skills can be fun and rewarding.

Try It!

Try the following reading activities.

The readings will be difficult, but you'll find that you can get the main idea if you apply some of the basic skills and strategies you've learned. Use what you know to guess unfamiliar words and phrases.

Part 1 Directions

After the following passage, there are five questions or incomplete statements in Spanish. For each, choose the word or expression that best answers the question or completes the statement according to the meaning of the passage.

El Artista, Fernando Botero

Se le considera a Fernando Botero uno de los pintores y escultores contemporáneos más importantes. Nació y creció en Medellín, ciudad colombiana que en los años 50 no era centro artístico ni cultural. En Medellín se hablaba mucho de arte pero se veía poco, porque no había museos. Las primeras obras que Fernando Botero vio eran cuadros de iglesias y artefactos precolombinos. Un día, por casualidad, encontró un librito de la historia del arte moderno en el que había reproducciones de dibujos de Picasso, Matisse y Cezanne. Así Botero descubrió el arte y este pequeño libro lo inspiró a ser pintor aunque no había visto nunca una pintura original en persona.

Fernando Botero empezó a trabajar cuando tenía 16 años. Siempre había tenido el mismo placer, la misma pasión y la misma necesidad de crear. Era un pintor conocido en su país cuando tenía 21 años. Disfrutaba de una reputación pequeña. Vendió varios cuadros con escenas de la vida cotidiana, muy coloridos y un poco primitivos. Su primer viaje fue a Madrid. Decidió ir allí porque se hablaba español y no tendría dificultad en comunicarse. Más importante era poder visitar el famoso Museo del Prado. Allí Botero vio las obras de los grandes maestros de la pintura que él copió para aprender la técnica.

Viajó por otros países de Europa también. Pasó mucho tiempo en el gran museo de París, el Louvre, fascinado con las esculturas antiguas. Después fue a Italia para estudiar los frescos de los artistas italianos. Entonces regresó a Colombia, donde hizo una exposición de pinturas que no tuvo éxito. Allá le tocó sobrevivir. Fue vendedor y artista gráfico para diarios a los que les vendió algunas ilustraciones. En 1961 el Museo de Arte

Moderno de Nueva York le compró a Botero el *Retrato de Mona Lisa a los 12 años*. El periódico *New York Times* reprodujo el cuadro en una de sus páginas. Botero entonces fue descubierto por el público y comenzó a vender sus pinturas.

La crítica de aquella época, sobre todo en Nueva York, sólo se interesaba en el arte abstracto, y el arte de Botero era figurativo. Desde entonces, Fernando Botero se sentía único porque su arte era difícil de clasificar.

Botero nunca usa modelos. Trabaja sólo con el lienzo frente a él. Para inspirarse usa su memoria e imaginación y esto le ayuda a crear sus formidables pinturas y esculturas. Con esta inspiración Botero intenta sugerir el placer, la plenitud, la abundancia y la expansión.

Hace a sus figuras artísticas con dimensiones enormes. Engorda a sus personajes no para reírse de ellos sino para exaltar su belleza. La gordura no le interesa por sí misma, sino por su cualidad original y personal. Ésta es su "manera" y lo que hace que su estilo sea reconocido de inmediato; estilo que lo ha hecho célebre en todo el mundo. Según Botero, a las personas gruesas se les percibe como amantes de la vida, simpáticas y amables. Para él la gente delgada no provoca la misma reacción. Botero piensa que lo gordo da tranquilidad.

A partir del año 1973 Botero pasó de la pintura a la escultura porque quería crear los volúmenes y las formas de sus cuadros en lo concreto, en el espacio real. La ironía en sus esculturas y sus pinturas está en lo que observa el espectador. A menudo se puede apreciar el buen humor, pero sus personajes no son víctimas de ese humor: son inmóviles, pero nunca ridículos. Según Botero, el artista en nuestra sociedad hace el papel de contribuir a la belleza, a la cultura y al placer. El arte no tiene que ver con la realidad.

Ahora Fernando Botero vive parte del tiempo en Italia pero también en Nueva York, París y Mónaco. No regresa a menudo a Medellín pero sí ama a Colombia con pasión y quiso darle un regalo a su país natal. Por eso, Botero decidió dar a Medellín su colección de obras de arte que adquirió durante 25 años. Su deseo sería morir allí con el pincel en la mano, trabajando en su último cuadro, en la casa que conoció cuando era niño: una casa fresca, rodeada de corredores, con el olor de los naranjos en flor viniendo del patio.

1. ¿Por qué decidió ser artista Fernando Botero?
   (1) Estudió historia del arte en la escuela secundaria.
   (2) Quería ser pintor como su padre.
   (3) Vio reproducciones de obras de arte en un libro.
   (4) Conoció a Pablo Picasso en 1950.

2. Botero fue a Madrid principalmente para
   (1) estar con su familia
   (2) visitar el gran museo de arte
   (3) vender sus cuadros en las calles
   (4) trabajar para el gobierno

3. ¿Cuándo empezó la gente a conocer el arte de Botero?
   (1) cuando una foto de su cuadro apareció en el periódico
   (2) cuando comenzó a regalar sus cuadros
   (3) cuando tuvo una exhibición en una iglesia
   (4) cuando recibió un premio internacional

4. Según la selección, ¿qué usa Botero como inspiración?
   (1) las montañas de Medellín
   (2) los edificios religiosos
   (3) los recuerdos y la imaginación
   (4) las fotos de familiares y amigos

5. ¿Cómo demuestra Botero su amor por Colombia?
   (1) Regaló muchas pinturas a su país.
   (2) Pintó cuadros de todos los presidentes colombianos.
   (3) Contribuyó mucho dinero a causas humanitarias.
   (4) Vivió allí toda su vida.

Part 2 Directions

(Selections 1–6): Below each of the following selections, there is either a question or an incomplete statement in English. For each, choose the word or expression that best answers the question or completes the statement according to the meaning of the selection.

Alquilar casa familiar, *PLAYA DEL CARMEN*

Buscamos personas para alquilar nuestra casa en la playa durante los meses de julio y agosto. Si tiene una familia grande, éste es el sitio perfecto: la casa dispone de cuatro dormitorios, un comedor informal, una cocina, una sala y dos baños. Hay dos motos acuáticas y un velero para el uso de los inquilinos. Aire acondicionado, conexión a Internet, teléfono, lavadora. No se aceptan animales. **2.500 pesos la semana, llame al 55555.**

1. What is being offered in this advertisement?
(1) a package tour to Playa del Carmen
(2) a rental house on the beach
(3) a luxury hotel on the beach
(4) a gated community in Playa del Carmen

A los 25 años decidió que quería ser astronauta y pasaron once años antes de que Miguel López-Alegría viera su sueño cumplido. Hoy tiene 36 años de edad y ha tenido éxito. Algunos lo desean desde los 5, dice. Despegó rumbo al espacio a bordo de un transbordador espacial donde permaneció por 16 días y dio 256 vueltas a la Tierra junto a otros seis tripulantes, dos de ellos mujeres. Ésta fue la primera misión de este madrileño criado en América. Hijo de un militar español y una italiana-americana funcionaria de las Fuerzas Aéreas estadounidenses, sus padres se fueron a vivir a Boston, en Estados Unidos, cuando él sólo tenía dos años. En ese país ha pasado la mayor parte de su vida, allí se casó y luego se divorció; allí se hizo piloto de pruebas. Un día leyó en una revista un artículo sobre la posibilidad de que un piloto de pruebas se hiciera astronauta. No lo dudó. Consiguió entrar en la NASA.

2. What information does this article provide about Miguel López-Alegría?
(1) He completed a mission in space.
(2) He always wanted to be a newspaper reporter.
(3) He worked for the government of Italy.
(4) He became famous when he was 11 years old.

③

Imagínese tener un mundo de conocimientos... ...en su mano

Lleve consigo una referencia electrónica y tendrá información instantánea con sólo pulsar una tecla. Cuando usted lo desee, donde usted lo desee.

Los maestros la recomiendan. Los estudiantes y los profesionales por igual la consideran indispensable. Y los padres de familia saben que puede ayudar a sus hijos a presentar mejores tareas escolares.

No tiene nada de extraño. Con una referencia electrónica usted puede expandir su vocabulario, redactar cartas y reportes de fin de trimestre sin errores gramaticales, hablar en un idioma extranjero, incluso adquirir conocimientos acerca de historia, nutrición o medicina para mencionar algunas de las opciones disponibles.

Y al introducir cualquiera de una selección de "Bookcards" en la ranura posterior de la unidad, literalmente usted duplica la cantidad de información al alcance de su mano.

El conocimiento portátil le abrirá un mundo de posibilidades.

3. What does this product offer?

(1) a fun game for families to play together

(2) a summary of current novels

(3) information at your fingertips

(4) an explanation of medicines and nutrition

④

Mujeres alteradas

En noviembre de 2006 se publicaron por primera vez los cinco libros de la serie Mujeres alteradas en un solo volumen titulado *Todas las mujeres alteradas*. El libro es una recopilación de las historietas y tiras cómicas de la humorista argentina Maitena, quien ha tenido un éxito fenomenal durante los últimos ocho años.

Aunque sus tiras cómicas han sido populares en Argentina por varios años, la humorista logró el éxito internacional en 1999 cuando sus viñetas empezaron a publicarse en *El País Semanal*, la revista dominical del periódico madrileño *El País*. Desde entonces, las viñetas de Maitena han logrado una popularidad enorme dentro y fuera de su país natal. Sus obras se han traducido a diez idiomas y se han publicado en más de veinte países. Por si eso no fuera bastante, ella también goza de la aprobación de la crítica. El periódico *El Mundo* dijo de la serie Mujeres alteradas: "Las Mujeres Alteradas de Maitena son más corrosivas y sarcásticas que Bridget Jones y revelan la compleja condición femenina con ironía y perspicacia."

4. What does Maitena do?

(1) She is a newspaper reporter.

(2) She translates articles for *El País Semanal*.

(3) She writes literary criticism for *El Mundo*.

(4) She writes a popular comic strip.

Part 3 Directions

After the following passage, there are four questions or incomplete statements in English. For each, choose the word or expression that best answers the question or completes the statement according to the meaning of the passage.

Una semana inolvidable en el Transcantábrico

Compartimientos suite, gastronomía regional cuidadosamente elaborada y cuatro coches salones de lujo forman sólo una pequeña parte de esta experiencia inigualable. Pasar una semana viajando en el Transcantábrico es como instalarse en un hotel elegante exclusivo que anda por vías ferroviarias.

El Transcantábrico es un tren de lujo que viaja entre Santiago de Compostela y León, un recorrido pintoresco que pasa por algunas de las escenas y paisajes más impresionantes de España. El itinerario para una excursión de ocho días incluye veinte pueblos y ciudades del norte de España, lugares llenos de historia, tradición y encanto. Situados entre el mar Cantábrico y las montañas empinadas de la Sierra de Cantabria, estos sitios le ofrecen al visitante una variedad de atracciones culturales y regionales, algunas de las mejores de toda España.

Durante cada día del viaje, los pasajeros saldrán del tren para hacer una excursión a uno de los pueblos o ciudades de la ruta. Por ejemplo, un día el grupo puede hacer un paseo en barco por una de las rías entre Galicia y Asturias. Otro día puede aprovechar la oportunidad de comer en un restaurante selecto de Oviedo o visitar la famosa cueva de Altamira. Cada uno de los ocho días del viaje está organizado para incluir una combinación variada de excursiones, visitas, paseos y comidas. Por la noche, los pasajeros duermen en el tren, que permanece en la estación toda la noche. Eso les permite a los viajeros experimentar la vida nocturna de cada lugar sin preocuparse por regresar al tren a una hora determinada.

Por dentro, los compartimientos suite le brindan al viajero la oportunidad de descansar y relajarse dentro de un espacio elegante y de gran confort. Cada compartimiento dispone de artículos para el viajero, como un albornoz de baño, zapatillas, una esponja natural, agua de colonia, un cepillo y un peine. Los compartimientos están completamente amueblados con una cama de matrimonio, un armario ropero, un escritorio y servicio de teléfono con línea exterior. Los baños privados tienen hidrosauna, turbo masaje, baño de vapor y secador de pelo. Todos los compartimientos vienen con climatizador con regulación individual.

Fuera de los compartimientos, el Transcantábrico cuenta con cuatro coches salones de diseño único. Su acabado y decoración interior son distintos, pero cada uno es un ejemplo perfecto de los estilos elegantes de los trenes del pasado. Los coches salones son las zonas comunes del tren y son sitios agradables para tomar algo, charlar, leer o contemplar el paisaje. Uno dispone de juegos de mesa, periódicos, revistas, televisión y una videoteca con una variedad de películas. Otro contiene una pista de baile y está decorado como una alegre sala de fiestas. Un tercer coche está equipado con una biblioteca amplia que ofrece una variedad de libros en español, inglés, francés y alemán. Un cuarto coche sirve como coche-club informal con servicio de mesa.

En cuanto a la gastronomía, los cocineros del Transcantábrico se han inspirado en las comidas típicas del norte de España, en particular de las regiones de Galicia, Asturias, Cantabria, el País Vasco y Castilla y León. Los cocineros aprovechan las mejores materias primas para la elaboración de sus platos gourmet, ofreciendo cada día una combinación deliciosa para la degustación de sus clientes. Un típico menú puede incluir lechazo un día y pescados del Cantábrico, pulpo y bacalao el día siguiente. El desayuno, que se sirve en los coches salones, consiste en un buffet amplio que ofrece desde bollería hasta jamón ibérico.

El precio, que incluye el desayuno y la cena, es 4.600 euros por una suite doble o 3.300 por una suite individual. No es nada barato, pero para los viajeros que buscan una experiencia inolvidable en un ambiente de puro lujo es una oportunidad que no se debe perder.

1. What is unusual about the means of transportation described in the article?
   (1) It is very old.
   (2) It is very inexpensive.
   (3) It is very fast.
   (4) It is very luxurious.

2. Where do the passengers sleep?
   (1) in a hotel
   (2) in individual suites
   (3) in the houses of host families
   (4) in inns and small hostels

3. What kind of food is served?
   (1) gourmet cuisine from around the world
   (2) sandwiches and boxed lunches
   (3) regional specialities from northern Spain
   (4) vegetarian cuisine prepared by famous chefs

4. What comes with the room?
   (1) a variety of items for personal care
   (2) a video player and movies
   (3) a library of books in different languages
   (4) a laptop computer with an Internet connection

Write!

Why?

Writing is a good way to organize your thoughts and ideas about a subject. When you write, you can take the time to present your message in a polished form. Writing develops your analytical and organizational abilities and increases your options for communicating with others.

What?

This year you'll write about a wide variety of topics in realistic informal and formal situations. You'll be writing various kinds of finished pieces: e-mails, brochures, descriptions, short narratives, persuasive essays, journal entries, and much more.

Who?

One of the most important parts of the writing process actually happens before you write. That's when you determine who your audience is. In informal writing, such as e-mails, lists, and journal entries, the intended audience is usually yourself or someone you know well. With more formal writing, such as brochures, essays, and reports, the audience is usually someone you do not know or do not know well.

How?

The writing process in any language is similar: brainstorm and organize, create a rough draft, and revise. *¡Avancemos!* provides you with specific strategies for writing in the **Escritura** sections. Writing tasks throughout the lesson are labeled **Escribir** . The **Todo junto** open ended writing activity gives you a task and a list of criteria so you know exactly what you need to do in order to succeed.

Before you write:

- Brainstorm ideas and jot them all down.
- Narrow your ideas down to one topic you can cover comfortably in your composition. (See page 318 for an example of this technique.)
- Organize and refine your thoughts and ideas using charts, idea maps, and other kinds of graphic organizers. (See pages 78, 82, 138, 142, 202, 262, 323, 378, 438, 442, 498, and 502 for examples.)

While you write:

- Begin with an opening or topic sentence.
- Try to write as freely and quickly as you can. Don't worry about editing yet.
- Support your statements with facts and examples. (See page 198.)
- Remember who your audience is and why you are writing to them. Use formal or informal language that is appropriate to that audience.
- Remember to make a concluding sentence.

After you write:

- Go back and reread your work several times. The first time through, focus on making sure your audience, purpose, and message are clear.
- Read again to check the content of your piece. Can you make it clear?
- Ask a peer to check your writing and offer suggestions.
- Incorporate your revisions and your peer's comments into a final draft. Reread it to correct errors of spelling, capitalization, and grammar. (See the revision checklists in each of the **Escritura** sections.)

Writing Criteria

The following chart shows the criteria used to evaluate and grade written pieces. It tells you what you need to do to write a piece that is coherent, well organized, and accurate. Keep these criteria in mind as you try some of the writing tasks below.

Dimension	A response receiving maximum credit:
Purpose/Task	Accomplishes the task, includes many details that are clearly connected to the development of the task, but there may be minor irrelevancies.
Organization The extent to which the response exhibits direction, shape, and coherence.	Exhibits a logical and coherent sequence throughout, provides a clear sense of a beginning, middle, and end. Makes smooth transitions between ideas.
Vocabulary	Includes a wide variety of vocabulary that expands the topic, but there may be minor inaccuracies.
Structure/Conventions • Subject-verb agreement • Tense • Noun-adjective agreement • Correct word order • Spelling/diacritical marks	Demonstrates a high degree of control of Checkpoint B (Regents level) structure/conventions: • Subject-verb agreements • Present, past, future ideas expressed as appropriate • Noun-adjective agreement • Correct word order • Spelling/diacritical marks (e.g., accents) Errors *do not* hinder overall comprehensibility of the passage.
Word Count	Contains 100 words or more.

The Bottom Line

Writing is a process. When you focus on using strategies and improving your skills in each step, the more confident and accomplished you'll become.

Try It!

Writing Tasks

Write your answer to the writing task. It should be written entirely in Spanish and should contain a minimum of 100 words. Place names and brand names written in Spanish count as one word. Contractions are also counted as one word. Salutations and closings, as well as commonly used abbreviations in Spanish, are not included in the word count. Numbers, unless written as words, and names of people are not counted as words. You must satisfy the purpose of the task. Be sure to organize your response and to include a beginning, middle, and ending. The sentence structure and/or expressions used should be connected logically and should demonstrate a wide range of vocabulary with minimal repetition.

Task 1

You recently visited a relative who lives in a distant city. Write a letter to your pen pal in Spanish telling him or her about the visit. You may wish to include:

- who the relative is
- where the relative lives
- when you visited the relative
- how you traveled
- the purpose of the visit
- gifts that you bought
- activities during your visit
- how you felt about seeing your relative

Task 2

In Spanish, write a journal entry about what you will be doing in ten years. You may wish to include:

- where you will be living
- why you chose to live there
- what your residence will be like
- what job you will have or what work you will be doing
- why you will enjoy that job or work
- what you will do in your leisure time
- if or where you will travel
- information about your friends
- information about your family
- how you will use your foreign language ability

Task 3

In Spanish, write a story about the situation shown in the picture. It must be a story relating to the picture, not a description of the picture. Do **not** write a dialogue.

SKILL SUPPORT

EL GRAN DESAFÍO

VIDEO DVD

Welcome to the Gran Desafío Internacional! In this video you will meet six teenagers from Argentina, Chile, Mexico, and the Dominican Republic who are going to take part in the second phase of a competition. Each contestant has already participated in and won the first phase of the competition and is now here to win the grand prize. Teams of two will participate in eight different challenges and each challenge is worth one point. The team with the most points wins. The grand prize is a year of studies at the UNAM, an apartment in Mexico City, and 100,000.00 pesos living expenses for one year.

El director: Profesor Miguel Dávila

Meet the participants!

José de la Argentina y Carmen de la República Dominicana

Marco de Chile y Ana de México

Luis de México y María de Chile

1

El desafío Each team has to pitch a tent in the least amount of time.

2

El desafío One person from each team takes a turn as the guest vocalist of a local mariachi band.

3

El desafío The teams partake in specific activities to help protect the environment.

4

El desafío The teams must guess how each contestant describes him or herself.

5

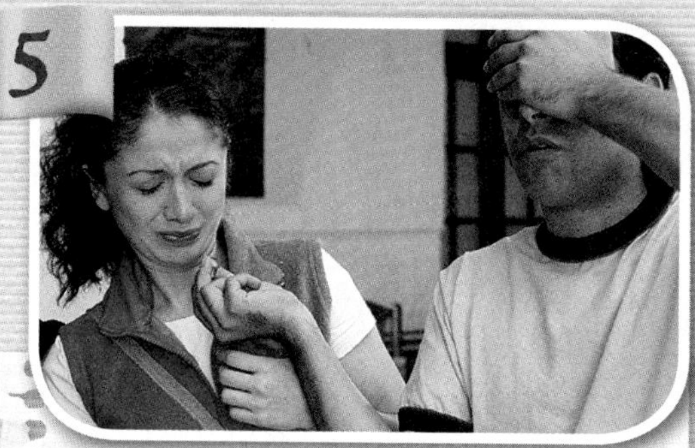

El desafío Each team has to research and make guacamole from scratch for a famous restaurant in Cuernavaca.

6

El desafío The teams are given clues to search for specific objects in different locations in a neighborhood.

7

El desafío Each team must come up with a way to earn the most amount of money by the end of the day.

8

El desafío The teams write and perform a play.

Why Study Spanish?

Discover the world

Deciding to learn Spanish is one of the best decisions you can make if you want to travel and see the world.

More than 400 million people around the globe speak Spanish. After Chinese, English and Spanish are tied as the two most frequently spoken languages worldwide. Spanish is now the third most-used language on the Internet. In Europe, Spanish is the most popular foreign language after English. People who speak both Spanish and English can communicate with people from all around the globe, no matter where they find themselves.

Explore your community

Inside the United States, Spanish is by far the most widely spoken language after English.

There are currently about 30 million Spanish speakers in the U.S. When you start to look and listen for it, you will quickly realize that Spanish is all around you—on the television, on the radio, and in magazines and newspapers. You may even hear your neighbors speaking it. Learning Spanish will help you communicate and interact with the rapidly growing communities of Spanish speakers around you.

Experience a new perspective

Learning a language is more than just memorizing words and structures.

When you study Spanish, you learn how the people who speak it think, feel, work, and live. Learning a language can open your eyes to a whole new world of ideas and insights. And as you learn about other cultures, you gain a better perspective on your own.

Create career possibilities

Knowing Spanish opens many doors.

If you speak Spanish fluently, you can work for international and multinational companies anywhere in the Spanish-speaking world. You can create a career working as a translator, an interpreter, or a teacher of Spanish. And because the number of Spanish speakers in the U.S. is growing so rapidly, being able to communicate in Spanish is becoming important in almost every career.

What Is Vocabulary?

Building Your Spanish Vocabulary

Vocabulary is a basic building block for learning a foreign language. By learning just a few words, you can start to communicate in Spanish right away! You will probably find that it is easier to understand words you hear or read than it is to use them yourself. But with a little practice, you will start to produce the right words in the right context. Soon you will be able to carry on conversations with other Spanish speakers.

 How Do I Study Vocabulary?

First Steps

- Read all of the new words in **blue** on the Vocabulary presentation page in your textbook.
- Point to each word as you say it out loud.

Be Creative

- Make flashcards with your new vocabulary words. You could also draw pictures of the words on the back of the flashcards.
- Group vocabulary words by theme. Add other words that fit the categories you've learned.
- Imagine a picture of the word.
- Create a rhyme or song to help you remember the words.

Make It Personal

- Use vocabulary words to write original sentences. Make them funny so you'll be sure to remember!
- Label everyday items in Spanish.
- Create reminders for difficult words. Put note cards inside your locker door, or on your mirror at home.
- See it, and say it to yourself! For example, if you are learning colors and clothing words, think of the Spanish word to describe what your friends are wearing.

el cuaderno

Practice Makes Perfect

- Say your vocabulary words out loud and repeat each word several times.
- Write each word five times, keeping its meaning in mind.
- Use Spanish words with your classmates outside of class—if you're having lunch in the cafeteria, use the words you know for food. Greet your classmates in the hallway in Spanish!

Create Your Own System

- Practice a little bit every day. Many short sessions are better than one long one.
- Focus on the words that are the hardest for you.
- Find a buddy. Quiz one another on the vocabulary words.
- Keep a vocabulary notebook and update it regularly.
- Use the study sheets in the back of your workbook to review vocabulary.

What Is Grammar?

Some people think of grammar as the rules of a language, rules that tell you the "correct" way to speak a language. For instance, why do you say *big red house,* not *red big house*? Why do you say *how much money do you have* instead of *how many money*? If English is your first language, you probably don't think about the rule. You make the correct choice instinctively because it *sounds right.* Non-native speakers of English have to learn the rules. As you begin your study of Spanish, you will need to learn the grammar rules of Spanish.

Why Should I Study Grammar?

Grammar helps you to communicate.

For instance, using the past tense or future tense makes it clear when something happens. (*I did my homework* versus *I will do my homework.*) Using subject pronouns lets you know who is performing the action. (*I gave the book to her* versus *She gave the book to me.*) Using correct grammar when speaking Spanish will help you communicate successfully with native speakers of Spanish.

How Do I Study Grammar?

Read the English Grammar Connection before each grammar explanation.

Think about how you use the same type of grammar in English. Understanding your own language will help you to better understand Spanish.

> **English Grammar Connection:** Some impersonal expressions show uncertainty that something will happen. In both English and Spanish, such expressions are followed by verbs in the **subjunctive.**
>
> It's important that he **leave.** Es importante que él **salga.**

Practice the new forms that you are learning.

Completing the practice activities in your student book and workbook will help you to learn the correct way to say things.

Use the Spanish you know as often as you can.

After all, that's how you learned to speak English, by hearing and speaking it every day.

What Is Culture?

To communicate with people from Spanish-speaking countries in a meaningful way, you need to know something about their culture. Vocabulary and grammar will help you learn what words to say and how to put them together, but culture will give you a better understanding of "how, when, and why to say what to whom."

What exactly is culture?

Culture includes . . .

Art
History
Traditions
Relationships
Music
Holidays
Food
Architecture
Pastimes

and more!

How can I learn about another culture?

- Read the **Comparación cultural** information to find out more about the cultures that you are studying.
- Think about the answers to the questions in the **Comparación cultural.**
- Think about the perspectives and practices that shape and influence the culture.
- Compare your own culture with the cultures you are studying.

El mundo

OCÉANO ÁRTICO
Mar de Siberia Oriental
RUSIA
Mar de Bering
Alaska (EE.UU.)
Mar de Beaufort
Bahía de Baffin
GROENLANDIA (DINAMARCA)
Bahía de Hudson
Mar del Labrador
CANADÁ
ESTADOS UNIDOS
OCÉANO ATLÁNTICO
Golfo de México
REP. DOMINICANA
ISLAS BAHAMAS
PUERTO RICO (EE.UU.)
SAN CRISTÓBAL Y NEVIS
HAITÍ
CUBA
ANTIGUA Y BARBUDA
GUADALUPE (FRANCIA)
DOMINICA
MARTINICA (FRANCIA)
SAN VICENTE Y GRANADINAS
BARBADOS
TRINIDAD Y TOBAGO
SANTA LUCÍA
GRANADA
JAMAICA
BELICE
Mar Caribe
MÉXICO
Islas Hawai (EE.UU.)
ISLAS MARSHALL
OCÉANO PACÍFICO
GUATEMALA
EL SALVADOR
HONDURAS
NICARAGUA
COSTA RICA
PANAMÁ
VENEZUELA
COLOMBIA
GUAYANA FRANCESA (FRANCIA)
GUYANA
SURINAM
Islas Galápagos (Ecuador)
ECUADOR
NAURU
KIRIBATI
ISLAS TUVALU
ISLAS SALOMÓN
SAMOA
Samoa Americana (EE.UU.)
VANUATÚ
FIDJI
TONGA
NUEVA CALEDONIA (FRANCIA)
PERÚ
BRASIL
BOLIVIA
PARAGUAY
CHILE
URUGUAY
ARGENTINA
NUEVA ZELANDA
Islas Malvinas (R.U.)

OCÉANO ÁRTICO
Mar de Kara
Mar de Laptev
Mar de Barents
Mar de Noruega
ISLANDIA
SUECIA
FINLANDIA
NORUEGA
1 DINAMARCA
2 HOLANDA
3 BÉLGICA
4 LUXEMBURGO
5 SUIZA
6 REPÚBLICA CHECA
7 ESLOVAQUIA
8 HUNGRÍA
9 ESLOVENIA
10 CROACIA
11 BOSNIA Y HERZEGOVINA
12 SERBIA Y MONTENEGRO
13 ALBANIA
14 MACEDONIA
15 BULGARIA
RUSIA
ESTONIA
LETONIA
LITUANIA
REINO UNIDO
Mar del Norte
Mar Báltico
IRLANDA
BIELORRUSIA
ALEMANIA
POLONIA
UCRANIA
Lago Baikal
Mar de Ojotsk
60°N
KAZAKSTÁN
MONGOLIA
FRANCIA
AUSTRIA
MOLDAVIA
RUMANIA
Mar de Aral
ANDORRA
ESPAÑA
PORTUGAL
ITALIA
Mar Negro
GEORGIA
Mar Caspio
UZBEKISTÁN
KIRGUISTÁN
TURQUÍA
TURKMENISTÁN
COREA DEL NORTE
Mar de Japón
GRECIA
ARMENIA
TADJIKISTÁN
GIBRALTAR (R.U.)
MALTA
SIRIA
AZERBAIYÁN
COREA DEL SUR
JAPÓN
TÚNEZ
Mar Mediterráneo
CHIPRE
LÍBANO
IRAQ
IRÁN
AFGANISTÁN
CHINA
MARRUECOS
Islas Canarias (Esp.)
ISRAEL
JORDANIA
KUWAIT
QATAR
BHUTÁN
ARGELIA
LIBIA
EGIPTO
BAHREIN
PAQUISTÁN
NEPAL
30°N
SAHARA OCCIDENTAL
E.Á.U
BANGLADESH
Trópico de Cáncer
ARABIA SAUDITA
OMÁN
INDIA
MYANMAR
TAIWÁN
CABO VERDE
MAURITANIA
Mar Rojo
LAOS
OCÉANO PACÍFICO
MALÍ
NÍGER
CHAD
ERITREA
YEMEN
TAILANDIA
VIETNAM
FILIPINAS
GUAM (EE.UU.)
SENEGAL
BURKINA FASO
SUDÁN
JIBUTI
Mar Arábigo
Golfo de Bengala
CAMBOYA
Mar de China
GAMBIA
GUINEA
BENIN
NIGERIA
COSTA DE MARFIL
TOGO
REP. CENTRO-AFRICANA
ETIOPÍA
MICRONESIA
GUINEA BISSAU
GHANA
CAMERÚN
BRUNEI
PALAU
LIBERIA
SOMALIA
ISLAS MALDIVAS
SRI LANKA
MALAYSIA
SIERRA LEONA
GUINEA ECUATORIAL
CONGO
UGANDA
KENIA
GABÓN
REP. DEM. DEL CONGO
Ecuador 0°
RUANDA
SANTO TOMÉ Y PRÍNCIPE
BURUNDI
TANZANÍA
SEYCHELLES
SINGAPUR
INDONESIA
PAPUASIA NUEVA GUINEA
CABINDA (ANGOLA)
COMORES
ANGOLA
TIMOR ORIENTAL
ZAMBIA
MALAWI
MOZAMBIQUE
NAMIBIA
ZIMBABWE
MADAGASCAR
MAURICIO
OCÉANO ÍNDICO
BOTSWANA
Trópico de Capricornio
AUSTRALIA
SUAZILANDIA
SUDÁFRICA
LESOTHO
30°S
N
O
E
S
0
1,000
2,000 millas
0
1,000
2,000 kilómetros
60°S
ANTÁRTIDA

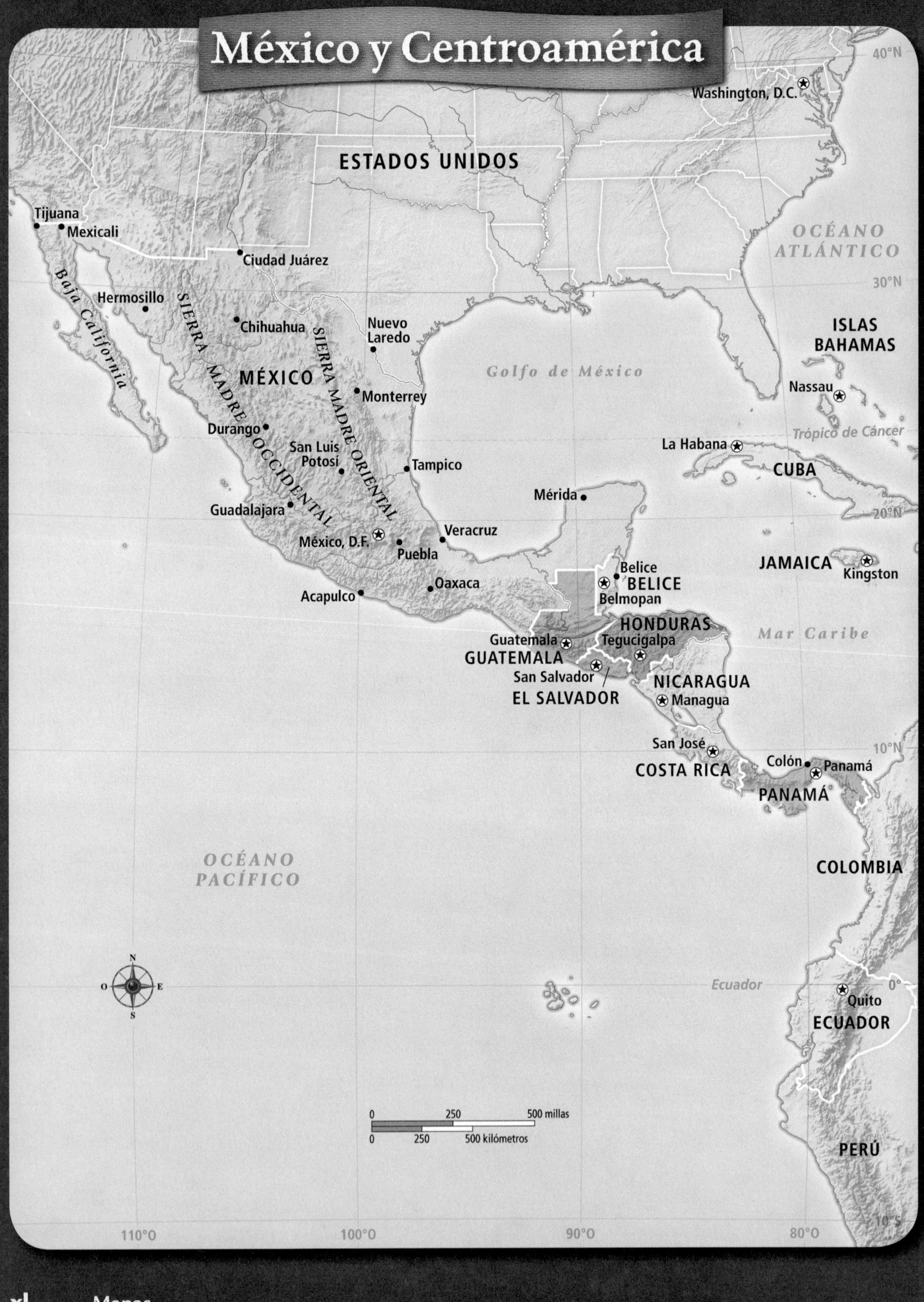
México y Centroamérica
ESTADOS UNIDOS
Washington, D.C.
OCÉANO ATLÁNTICO
Tijuana
Mexicali
Ciudad Juárez
Baja California
Hermosillo
SIERRA MADRE OCCIDENTAL
Chihuahua
SIERRA MADRE ORIENTAL
Nuevo Laredo
MÉXICO
Golfo de México
ISLAS BAHAMAS
Nassau
Monterrey
Durango
San Luis Potosí
Tampico
Trópico de Cáncer
La Habana
CUBA
Mérida
Guadalajara
Veracruz
México, D.F.
Puebla
Oaxaca
Acapulco
Belice
BELICE
Belmopan
JAMAICA
Kingston
HONDURAS
Tegucigalpa
Guatemala
GUATEMALA
San Salvador
EL SALVADOR
NICARAGUA
Managua
Mar Caribe
San José
COSTA RICA
Colón
Panamá
PANAMÁ
COLOMBIA
OCÉANO PACÍFICO
Ecuador
Quito
ECUADOR
PERÚ
N
O
E
S
0
250
500 millas
0
250
500 kilómetros
40°N
30°N
20°N
10°N
0°
10°S
110°O
100°O
90°O
80°O

El Caribe

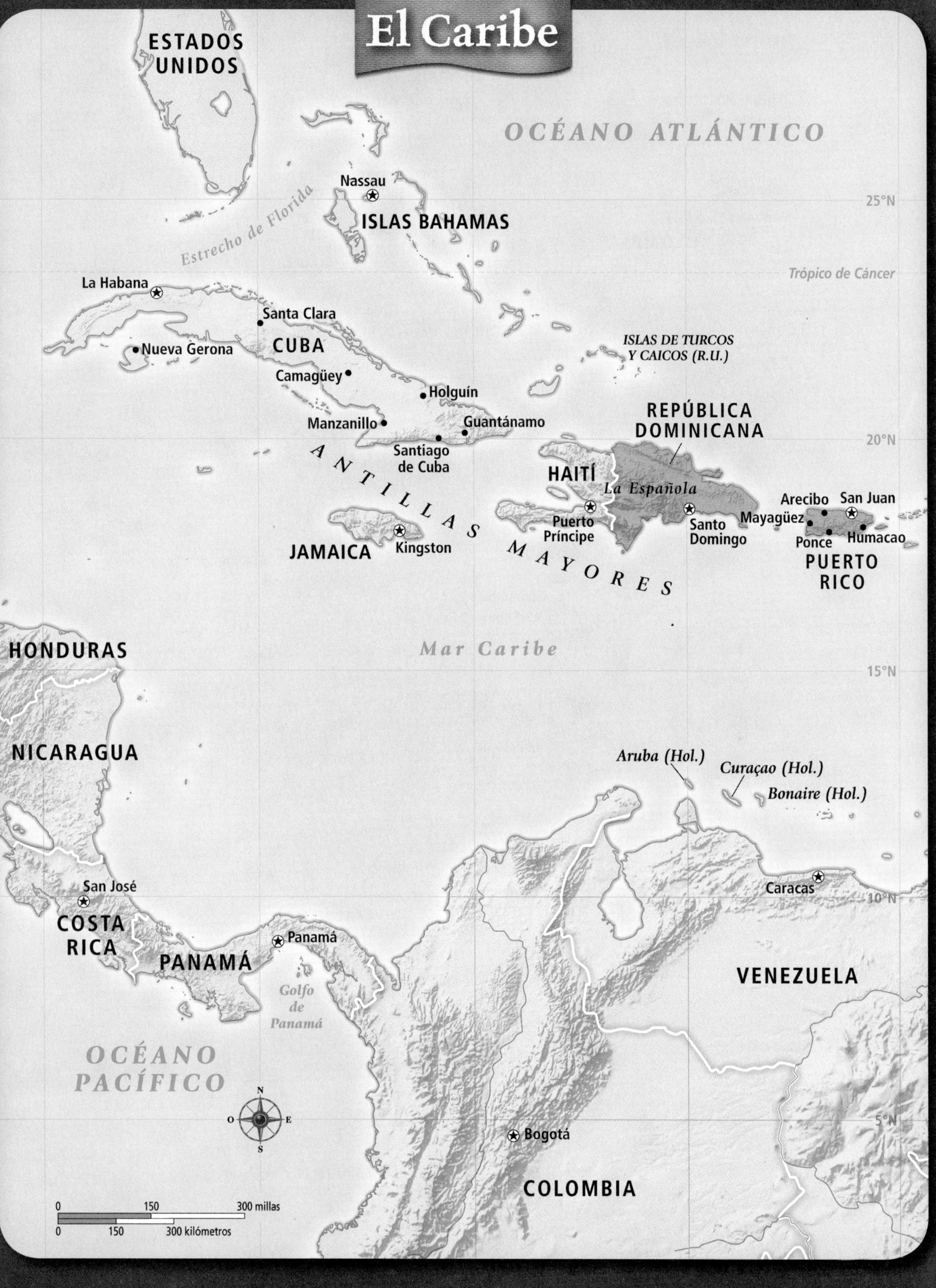

ESTADOS UNIDOS
OCÉANO ATLÁNTICO
Nassau
ISLAS BAHAMAS
Estrecho de Florida
25°N
Trópico de Cáncer
La Habana
Santa Clara
CUBA
Nueva Gerona
Camagüey
Holguín
ISLAS DE TURCOS Y CAICOS (R.U.)
Manzanillo
Guantánamo
Santiago de Cuba
REPÚBLICA DOMINICANA
20°N
ANTILLAS MAYORES
HAITÍ
La Española
Puerto Príncipe
Santo Domingo
Arecibo
San Juan
Mayagüez
Ponce
Humacao
PUERTO RICO
JAMAICA
Kingston
HONDURAS
Mar Caribe
15°N
NICARAGUA
Aruba (Hol.)
Curaçao (Hol.)
Bonaire (Hol.)
San José
Caracas
10°N
COSTA RICA
Panamá
PANAMÁ
VENEZUELA
Golfo de Panamá
OCÉANO PACÍFICO
N
O
E
S
Bogotá
5°N
COLOMBIA
0
150
300 millas
0
150
300 kilómetros

Sudamérica

Mar Caribe
Barranquilla
Cartagena
Maracaibo
Lago Maracaibo
Caracas
TRINIDAD Y TOBAGO
Puerto España
Río Orinoco
VENEZUELA
Georgetown
GUYANA
Paramaribo
SURINAM
Cayena
GUAYANA FRANCESA (FRANCIA)
OCÉANO ATLÁNTICO
Medellín
Manizales
Bogotá
Cali
COLOMBIA
Otavalo
Quito
ECUADOR
Guayaquil
Cuenca
Río Negro
Río Amazonas
Ecuador 0°
PERÚ
Río Madeira
Río Tapajóz
Río Xingú
Río Tocantins
Río São Francisco
Trujillo
BRASIL
CORDILLERA DE LOS ANDES
Callao
Lima
Lago Titicaca
BOLIVIA
La Paz
Cochabamba
Santa Cruz
Sucre
Brasilia
OCÉANO PACÍFICO
Islas Galápagos (Ecuador)
PERÚ
0 200 400 millas
0 200 400 kilómetros
GRAN CHACO
PARAGUAY
Asunción
Trópico de Capricornio
CHILE
Salta
San Miguel de Tucumán
Resistencia
Córdoba
Valparaíso
Mendoza
Rosario
URUGUAY
Santiago
Buenos Aires
Montevideo
ARGENTINA
La Plata
OCÉANO PACÍFICO
Concepción
PAMPAS
Mar del Plata
Temuco
Bahía Blanca
PATAGONIA
N
O
E
S
0 250 500 millas
0 250 500 kilómetros
Estrecho de Magallanes
Islas Malvinas (R.U.)
Tierra del Fuego
Cabo de Hornos
10°N
10°S
20°S
30°S
40°S
50°S
100°O
90°O
80°O
70°O
50°O
40°O
30°O
20°O

España

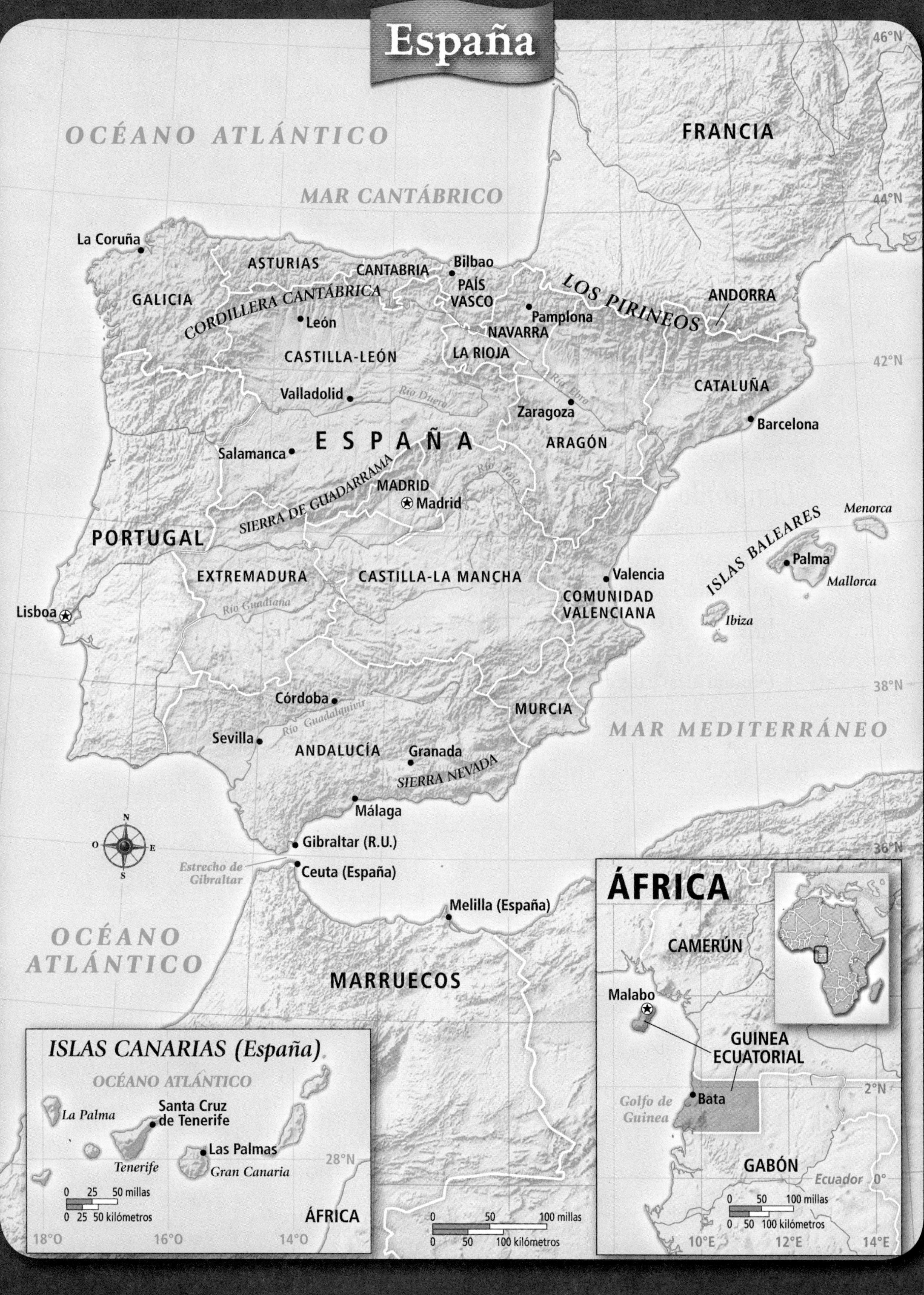

OCÉANO ATLÁNTICO
MAR CANTÁBRICO
FRANCIA
La Coruña
ASTURIAS
CANTABRIA
Bilbao
PAÍS VASCO
GALICIA
CORDILLERA CANTÁBRICA
León
LOS PIRINEOS
ANDORRA
Pamplona
NAVARRA
LA RIOJA
CASTILLA-LEÓN
Valladolid
Río Duero
Río Ebro
Zaragoza
CATALUÑA
Barcelona
ESPAÑA
Salamanca
ARAGÓN
SIERRA DE GUADARRAMA
MADRID
Madrid
Río Tajo
PORTUGAL
ISLAS BALEARES
Menorca
Palma
Mallorca
Ibiza
EXTREMADURA
CASTILLA-LA MANCHA
Valencia
COMUNIDAD VALENCIANA
Lisboa
Río Guadiana
Córdoba
Río Guadalquivir
MURCIA
MAR MEDITERRÁNEO
Sevilla
ANDALUCÍA
Granada
SIERRA NEVADA
Málaga
Gibraltar (R.U.)
Estrecho de Gibraltar
Ceuta (España)
Melilla (España)
OCÉANO ATLÁNTICO
MARRUECOS
N
O
E
S
46°N
44°N
42°N
38°N
36°N
0
50
100 millas
0
50
100 kilómetros
ISLAS CANARIAS (España)
OCÉANO ATLÁNTICO
La Palma
Santa Cruz de Tenerife
Tenerife
Las Palmas
Gran Canaria
ÁFRICA
28°N
18°O
16°O
14°O
0 25 50 millas
0 25 50 kilómetros
ÁFRICA
CAMERÚN
Malabo
GUINEA ECUATORIAL
Golfo de Guinea
Bata
GABÓN
Ecuador
2°N
0°
10°E
12°E
14°E
0 50 100 millas
0 50 100 kilómetros

Las tradiciones

Las siguientes lecciones sobre tradiciones te enseñarán más sobre la cultura del mundo hispanohablante. Son lecciones adicionales que puedes leer en tus ratos libres o cuando tu maestro o maestra las presente en una clase especial.

El *mundo hispano es grande y variado* y sus tradiciones son múltiples. Los países hispanos comparten (share) algunas tradiciones, pero cada país hispano, y a veces cada región de un país, también tiene tradiciones únicas. La diversidad de estas tradiciones refleja la diversidad de las personas hispanas. En las siguientes páginas verás algunas de estas tradiciones, las semejanzas (similarities) y las diferencias.

Contenido

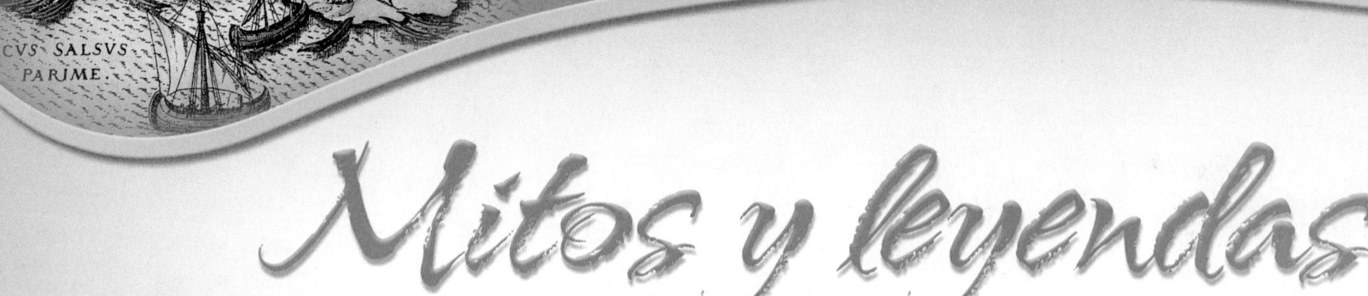

Mitos y leyendas

Vocabulario para los mitos y las leyendas

la fuerza natural *natural force*
el relato *tale*
el ser sobrenatural *supernatural being*
el símbolo *symbol*

Los pueblos indígenas de Latinoamérica tienen una rica tradición de mitos y leyendas. Los mitos y las leyendas son relatos orales o escritos que explican el origen de las cosas, las relaciones sociopolíticas y los fenómenos naturales. Los mitos generalmente incluyen a dioses o a otros seres sobrenaturales que representan las fuerzas naturales. La leyenda es un relato aparentemente histórico, pero con muchos elementos imaginarios o distorsionados *(distorted)*.

Guatemala

El quetzal Según la leyenda maya, durante la invasión de los conquistadores, el quetzal se paró *(landed)* encima del rey maya Tecún Umán mientras *(while)* moría. La sangre *(blood)* del rey manchó *(stained)* el quetzal y desde entonces el pájaro tiene el pecho *(chest)* de color rojo brillante.

Florida

La fuente de la juventud Cuando Juan Ponce de León era gobernador de Puerto Rico, él oyó una leyenda sobre una fuente *(fountain)* en la isla de Bimini donde uno podía recuperar la juventud *(youth)* si bebía de o se bañaba en las aguas. Entonces formó una expedición para encontrarla. Nunca encontró ni la isla ni la fuente, pero sí encontró Florida en el año 1513.

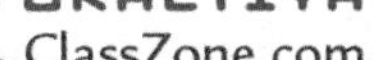

Cultura INTERACTIVA ClassZone.com *See these pages come alive!*

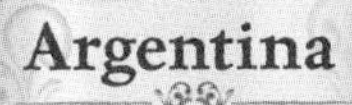

Las cataratas del Iguazú Según un mito guaraní, el dios del río *(river)* Iguazú se enamoró de la muchacha Naipú. Pero Naipú estaba enamorada de un guerrero guaraní y trató de *(tried to)* escaparse con él en una canoa. El dios, furioso, formó las cataratas *(waterfalls)* para atraparlos. Transformó al guerrero en un árbol al lado del río y atrapó a su querida Naipú en las cataratas para siempre.

México

El dios Yum K'aax En la mitología de los mayas hay unos 190 dioses. Yum K'aax era el dios del maíz, una comida básica de la dieta maya. Para tener una buena cosecha *(harvest)*, en sus ritos y mitos los mayas honraban a Yum K'aax y a Chac, el dios de la lluvia.

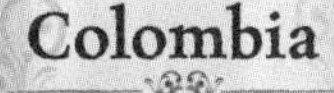

El Dorado Según una leyenda muisca, El Dorado era el rey de una tribu andina que llegaba todos los años a un lago *(lake)* para hacer un rito religioso. El rey, cubierto *(covered)* en polvo *(dust)* de oro, subía a una balsa *(raft)* y tiraba objetos de oro al lago. Luego, se bañaba en el agua. Los españoles buscaron a El Dorado y su lago por años, pero nunca lo encontraron.

Comparación cultural

1. ¿Conoces alguna leyenda sobre un animal, un fenómeno geográfico o un lugar mítico? Descríbela y compárala con una de las leyendas que leíste aquí.
2. ¿Qué otras culturas explican el mundo humano y las fuerzas naturales con leyendas sobre dioses y diosas ? Compara lo que hacen los dioses en esas leyendas con lo que hacen los dioses en las leyendas de aquí.

Comida de las Américas

Vocabulario para la comida de las Américas

el aguacate *avocado*
el alimento *food*
el cacao *cacao tree*
la cocina *cuisine*
ser originario(a) de *to come from*

Muchos alimentos que hoy asociamos con la comida de los países europeos son productos que ningún europeo conocía antes de 1492. La introducción en Europa de alimentos del Nuevo Mundo tuvo un gran impacto en la cocina y en la economía de los países europeos. Hoy en día muchos platos populares de Estados Unidos usan alimentos que son originarios de las culturas indígenas de Latinoamérica.

El aguacate Hace más de 7000 años que se cultiva el aguacate en el sur de México y en Centroamérica. Los aztecas comían esta fruta en un puré con tomates que hoy conocemos como el guacamole.

El tomate Los tomates probablemente son originarios de la costa de Perú. Los italianos fueron los primeros europeos en adoptarlos en su cocina. Hoy el tomate es esencial en muchos platos españoles, como el gazpacho.

La papa La papa, o patata, tiene una historia de cultivo de más de 7000 años en los valles *(valleys)* andinos de Sudamérica. Los incas cultivaban más de 200 variedades, y hoy en día hay más de 1000. Los españoles fueron los primeros europeos en comer la papa, pero se popularizó rápidamente en toda Europa.

El chocolate El cacao era un árbol sagrado *(sacred)* para los mayas. Los mayas y los aztecas usaban las bayas *(beans)* de cacao para preparar una bebida de chocolate con pimienta (¡y sin azúcar!) para las ceremonias religiosas. Cuando los conquistadores introdujeron el chocolate en Europa, lo preparaban con azúcar y vainilla.

Comparación cultural

1. Piensa en dos o tres platos típicos de tu región e identifica los ingredientes del Nuevo Mundo en cada uno.
2. ¿Qué frutas y verduras se producen en tu región? ¿Son «nativos» de esa región o son productos originarios de otro continente?

Ferias de España

Vocabulario para las ferias de España

la batalla *battle; fight*
la carroza *float*
el desfile *parade*
los fuegos artificiales *fireworks*
el santo patrón / la santa patrona *patron saint*

Todas las comunidades de España, desde las ciudades grandes hasta los pueblos *(towns)* más pequeños, celebran sus ferias. Muchas ferias tienen orígenes religiosos, por ejemplo, para honrar al santo patrón o a la santa patrona de la ciudad o del pueblo, o conmemorar fechas religiosas importantes. Otras ferias son cívicas o estacionales. Algunas ferias son modernas o recientes; otras tienen más de mil años. Típicamente las ferias pueden incluir música, desfiles, bailes tradicionales, fuegos artificiales y comida especial, pero las ferias de muchas regiones también tienen tradiciones únicas.

Laredo, Cantabria

La Batalla de Flores (agosto) Esta joven participa en el desfile de la Batalla de Flores. Las carrozas están decoradas con miles de flores y tienen diferentes temas. Compiten en la «batalla» para ganar el gran premio de la feria.

Pamplona, Navarra

La feria de San Fermín (del 7 al 14 de julio) Esta feria tiene fama por el recorrido del encierro *(running of the bulls)*. El recorrido empieza a las ocho de la mañana todos los días de la fiesta. Los participantes vienen de todas partes del mundo.

Buñol, Valencia

La Tomatina (agosto) Según el *Libro Guinness de los Récords,* es la batalla de comida más grande del mundo. Dicen que empezó en 1944 ó 1945 como una broma *(joke)* entre amigos, pero hoy hay más de 30.000 participantes y unas 90.000 libras *(pounds)* de tomates.

Barcelona, Cataluña

La fiesta de la Señora de Mercé (24 de septiembre) La atracción más fascinante de la fiesta es la competencia de los *castellers* en la Plaça Sant Jaume. Estas torres *(towers)* humanas pueden llegar a ser de ocho, nueve y diez niveles.

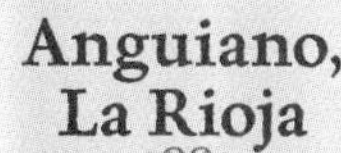

Anguiano, La Rioja

Las Fiestas de María Magdalena (julio) La danza de los zancos *(stilts)* es la gran tradición de los padres e hijos durante esta feria. Los bailadores bajan las escaleras de la iglesia y giran *(spin)* por las calles estrechas *(narrow)* y empinadas *(steep)*.

Comparación cultural

1. Haz una lista de todas las ferias o festivales de tu región. ¿Cuántas incluyen desfiles? ¿Música? ¿Bailes típicos? ¿Carrozas? ¿En qué se parecen a las ferias de España?
2. ¿Conoces ferias o festivales que incluyan una «batalla»? ¿Cómo es? ¿Es más parecida a la batalla de flores de Laredo o a la batalla de tomates de Buñol?

Bailes típicos

Vocabulario para los bailes típicos

el bailarín / la bailarina *dancer*
el (la) cantante *singer*
el conjunto *(dance) group*
interpretar *to perform (a dance)*
el paso *(dance) step*

El baile expresa las tradiciones y costumbres de una cultura. En el mundo hispano, los bailes típicos son una fusión de culturas. En el flamenco de España vemos tradiciones de los españoles, los moros y los gitanos. Los bailes del Caribe son una mezcla de las culturas indígenas, africanas y europeas. Aunque *(Although)* puedes ver algunos de los bailes típicos principalmente durante celebraciones culturales, otros bailes, como el merengue de la República Dominicana y la cumbia de Colombia, son populares durante cualquier ocasión. Los elementos más importantes del baile típico son los pasos y la música, y en los festivales, la ropa tradicional también es importante.

España

Una danza tradicional de Navarra Las presentaciones de bailes folklóricos son parte de la fiesta de San Fermín en Pamplona.

Bolivia

La Morenada La Festividad del Señor del Gran Poder es conocida por las presentaciones de bailes folklóricos. Este conjunto presenta La Morenada, un baile que se originó en la comunidad afroboliviana.

Puerto Rico

La bomba y la plena Estos dos bailes son los más típicos de Puerto Rico. En la bomba, el bailarín «dialoga» con los tambores.

México

La danza de la Flor de Piña Esta danza es una de las atracciones de la Guelaguetza, una celebración de Oaxaca para dar gracias por la cosecha *(harvest)*. Miles de turistas asisten a este festival.

Perú

Bailes peruanos tradicionales Durante la Copa América en Lima, varios conjuntos interpretan bailes típicos de Perú en ropa tradicional. Algunos de los bailes de Perú son la marinera, el huayno, el festejo y el vals criollo.

Comparación cultural

1. ¿Cuáles son algunos de los bailes típicos de este país? Describe la música, la ropa y los pasos de un baile típico que conoces.
2. En el mundo hispano, los bailes típicos se interpretan durante las fiestas nacionales y regionales, en los desfiles y eventos deportivos y cívicos. ¿Durante qué celebraciones y eventos podemos ver bailes típicos en este país?

¡FÚTBOL!

El fútbol es el deporte más popular del mundo. Los hispanos aprenden a jugar al fútbol desde muy jóvenes, practicando con amigos en los parques durante el tiempo libre. Generalmente, no hay equipos de fútbol en las escuelas. Para competir, un joven hispano tiene que afiliarse a *(join)* un club de fútbol. Hay competencias de la comunidad y de nivel *(level)* nacional. Casi todos los países hispanos tienen ligas profesionales de fútbol y equipos nacionales. Aunque *(Although)* el fútbol era un deporte principalmente masculino en los países hispanos, hoy en día también hay clubes para chicas y mujeres.

Colombia

La Copa América Este aficionado colombiano tiene un modelo del trofeo de la Copa América, una competencia que se estableció en 1916 para los países americanos.

Ecuador

Parque Carolina Estos muchachos practican el fútbol en el Parque Carolina de Quito, Ecuador.

Cultura INTERACTIVA ClassZone.com *See these pages come alive!*

Vocabulario para el fútbol

el Campeonato Mundial Juvenil *World Youth Championship*
la Copa Mundial *World Cup*
el (la) aficionado(a) *fan*
la liga *league*
el torneo *tournament*
el trofeo *trophy*

Perú

La Copa Mundial Estos aficionados peruanos animan a *(cheer for)* su equipo durante un partido contra *(against)* el equipo ecuatoriano en la Copa Mundial de la FIFA (Federación Internacional de Fútbol Asociado).

Argentina

El Campeonato Mundial Juvenil El equipo de Argentina celebra el triunfo después de ganar el torneo del Campeonato Mundial Juvenil de la FIFA en Holanda.

Comparación cultural

1. ¿Qué tipo de equipos de fútbol hay en tu comunidad? ¿Sólo hay clubes privados de fútbol o también hay equipos escolares o de la comunidad?
2. La Copa Mundial tiene más televidentes *(viewers)* que ningún otro evento del mundo. En algunos países hispanos, los partidos se emiten *(are broadcast)* en televisores gigantes en las calles, en las oficinas y por Internet. ¿Qué eventos atraen a muchos televidentes en este país?

Telas y tejidos

Vocabulario para las telas y los tejidos

el algodón *cotton*
el encaje *lace*
la lana *wool*
el lino *linen*
la seda *silk*
los tejidos *woven materials*
la tela *cloth, fabric*

Las telas y los tejidos del mundo hispano reflejan su diversidad y tienen una larga historia. Las culturas prehispánicas usaban el algodón, fibras de otras plantas y la lana de la llama para hacer los tejidos. Para dar color, usaban tintes *(dyes)* que derivaban de *(came from)* insectos, mariscos *(shellfish)* y plantas. Hacían los tejidos para los ritos culturales, el comercio *(trading)* y también para identificar la posición social, la edad o la región de donde era la persona. Un tejido importante, el encaje, se originó en Europa. En los siglos *(centuries)* XVII y XVIII, el encaje era un lujo *(luxury)* de la clase alta española. Las técnicas del encaje se exportaron a partes de Latinoamérica como Puerto Rico y Argentina. La seda y el lino son los hilos *(threads)* principales para el encaje.

México

De moda Las telas y los tejidos tradicionales están de moda. Esta joven lleva un chal colorido, un tejido tradicional de México.

Guatemala

Ropa tradicional Los tejedores *(weavers)* de Guatemala diseñan tejidos y ropa de colores brillantes y diseños intrincados *(intricate)*. Los colores y diseños identifican orígenes culturales y a veces cuentan una historia. Muchos guatemaltecos, como estas mujeres, todavía usan la ropa tradicional.

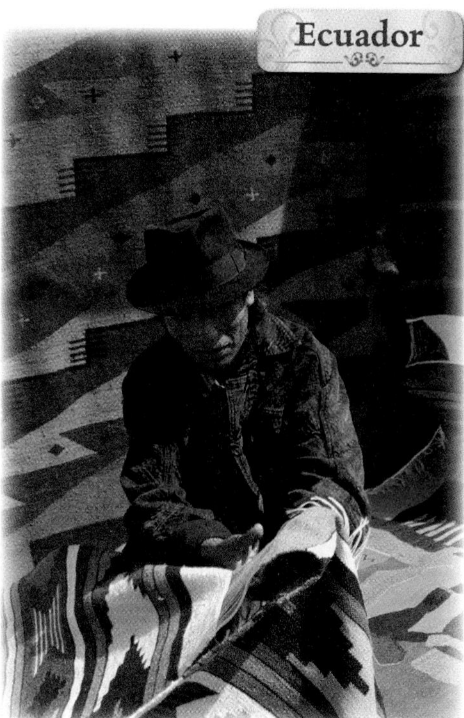

Ecuador

Una tradición prehispánica En los Andes han encontrado evidencia de todas las técnicas conocidas del tejido entre grupos indígenas prehispánicos. Este hombre vende tejidos de lana típicos de los indígenas de Otavalo, Ecuador.

España

El encaje Estas jóvenes españolas llevan encajes tradicionales para una exhibición en Sevilla. Antes los hombres y las mujeres de clase social alta usaban la ropa de encaje, pero ahora lo usan las mujeres o en decoraciones de la casa.

Panamá

La mola La mola, un tejido de los kunas de Panamá, es una serie de sobrepuestos *(overlays)* de cinco o seis capas *(layers)* de tela. Ellos cortan y bordan *(embroider)* los diseños con hilos de colores brillantes.

Comparación cultural

1. ¿Cuáles son algunos de los tejidos o ropa tradicionales de Estados Unidos? ¿Hay grupos que todavía llevan ropa tradicional?
2. Frecuentemente la moda moderna incorpora telas y tejidos tradicionales o «étnicos». Describe artículos de ropa que tienes o que has visto *(you have seen)*, que tienen elementos de telas y tejidos tradicionales.

¡Buena suerte!

Vocabulario para la buena suerte

el amuleto *good-luck charm*
atraer *to attract*
la costumbre *custom*
evitar *to avoid*
el gesto *gesture*

En todas las culturas, hay amuletos, gestos y otras tradiciones para atraer la buena suerte y evitar la mala suerte. Algunas de las tradiciones, como echar *(throwing)* sal detrás del hombro o tocar *(touching)* la madera, son internacionales. Otras tradiciones son regionales. En los Andes, por ejemplo, se dice que los huayruros, un tipo de frijol, traen la buena suerte, y los artesanos crean y venden collares, pulseras y aretes de huayruros. Aunque podemos trazar *(trace)* el origen y la historia de algunas de estas tradiciones, el origen de otras es un misterio.

Guatemala

Muñecas de las preocupaciones Antes de dormirse, algunos niños de Guatemala les cuentan todos sus problemas a sus muñecas de las preocupaciones *(worry dolls)* y las ponen debajo de la almohada *(pillow)*. En la mañana, las muñecas les han quitado *(have taken away)* todas las preocupaciones.

Perú

Los toritos de Pucará Los artesanos y alfareros *(potters)* de Pucará son famosos por sus toritos *(little bulls)*. Para atraer la buena suerte, la gente pone los toritos en el techo *(roof)* de la casa.

Bolivia

El Ekeko En la tradición aymara, Ekeko es el dios de la abundancia. Es costumbre darle alasitas, o representaciones en miniatura de un objeto que deseas. Si quieres un coche nuevo, le das al Ekeko una alasita que representa un coche. Cada enero, es costumbre darle alasitas al Ekeko. Lo que le das en miniatura, recibirás de verdad durante el año, según la tradición.

Chile

Los chanchitos En el pueblo de Pomaire, la gente cree que los cerdos traen la buena suerte, especialmente los chanchitos, figuras de cerdos de tres patas *(legs)*. Es una tradición darles chanchitos de cerámica a los amigos para desearles la buena fortuna.

España

Las arras Las arras son trece monedas *(coins)* de oro o plata que, durante una boda *(wedding)* española, el novio *(groom)* le da a su novia *(bride)*. Las arras representan la fortuna futura de la pareja que se casa.

Comparación cultural

1. ¿Qué tradiciones practicas para atraer la buena suerte o evitar la mala suerte? ¿Practicas alguna que se parece a estas tradiciones?
2. Haz una lista de amuletos, gestos y otros actos que son populares en tu comunidad para atraer la buena suerte o evitar la mala suerte. Compara estas costumbres con las del mundo hispano.

VAQUEROS

Muchos países comparten la figura folklórica del vaquero. Los vaqueros llevan una vida solitaria y representan la independencia y la libertad. La geografía, la ropa, la música y la comida de los vaqueros varían de país en país. El vaquero tradicional todavía existe en muchos países, y el folklore del vaquero se celebra en las fiestas y los rodeos. Estas celebraciones incluyen exhibiciones y competencias, y aunque algunos de los competidores son vaqueros de verdad, también hay muchos vaqueros que lo hacen como pasatiempo *(hobby)*.

México

Los charros Los charros, símbolos de lo ideal del carácter nacional, participaron en la lucha por la libertad e independencia mexicana. Este charro muestra su talento con el lazo durante un rodeo, una tradición mexicana.

Los huasos Los huasos de Chile se identifican por los colores de su poncho. En la única competencia del rodeo chileno, dos huasos trabajan juntos para atrapar, sin soga, a un toro contra la pared.

Chile

Vocabulario para los vaqueros

el (la) competidor(a) *competitor*
el ganado *cattle*
el lazo *lasso*
la soga *rope*
los zahones *chaps*

Perú

El pastor Este pastor peruano vive en los altiplanos *(high plains)* andinos y cuida llamas y alpacas. Su vida solitaria se parece a la de los vaqueros de otros países.

Estados Unidos

El cowboy y el español La Fiesta de los Vaqueros se celebra en febrero en Tucson, Arizona. Muchas palabras del vocabulario del *cowboy,* como *rodeo, lasso* y *bronco,* vienen del español.

Argentina

El gaucho El gaucho es un símbolo folklórico nacional y las fiestas y celebraciones argentinas siempre incluyen desfiles *(parades)* o competencias de gauchos. Estos gauchos de la provincia de Tucumán llevan zahones tradicionales para trabajar.

Comparación cultural

1. Haz una lista de la ropa típica de un *cowboy* de Estados Unidos. Compara esa ropa con la ropa de los diferentes vaqueros de estas fotos.
2. Piensa en las características y la vida del *cowboy* norteamericano, por ejemplo, su independencia, su vida solitaria y la geografía donde vive. ¿Crees que los gauchos, los huasos y los otros vaqueros tienen las mismas características y estilo de vida? ¿Por qué?

Quinceañeras

Vocabulario para las quinceañeras

el chambelán *male atttendant*
la corona *tiara*
la corte *entourage, attendants*
la dama *female attendant*
hacerse mujer *to become a woman*

La quinceañera celebra la transición de niña a mujer. Estas celebraciones, típicas en los países de habla hispana americanos, ahora se realizan con exuberancia en Estados Unidos. Para la celebración, la muchacha escoge una corte de honor, típicamente de siete damas y siete chambelanes que son parientes y amigos. La celebración puede tener todo el esplendor de una gran boda. Empieza con un servicio religioso. Luego, todos van a la casa de la muchacha o a una sala de baile para la recepción. El primer baile es entre la muchacha y su padre o padrino. Antes de bailar, el padre de la quinceañera la ayuda a quitarse los zapatos de muchacha y ponerse tacones *(high heels)*. Ella también recibe regalos tradicionales de sus padres, como la última muñeca o un anillo o una pulsera.

Kansas

Un día emocionante La madre y la tía de esta joven la ayudan a prepararse para su fiesta de quinceañera. La celebración es un evento familiar y un día emocionante para todos.

Pennsylvania

Las damas y las fotos Esta joven de Pennsylvania y sus damas de honor se preparan para una foto antes de la fiesta de quinceañera.

México

Los mariachis Los mariachis dan una serenata a la quinceañera mexicana la noche antes de su cumpleaños. También cantan en la ceremonia y durante el baile.

Cuba

El vestido El vestido de gala, un elemento importante y personal de esta tradición, generalmente es blanco o de color pastel. Esta joven lleva un vestido azul claro y la corona.

Texas

El vals Estas quinceañeras gemelas bailan el vals tradicional con sus damas y chambelanes para iniciar el baile de la fiesta.

Comparación cultural

1. ¿Cuáles son algunos cumpleaños especiales en las tradiciones de este país? Describe cómo se celebran. ¿Cuál se parece a la tradición de la quinceañera? Descríbela.
2. Compara la fiesta de quinceañera con otras fiestas tradicionales de este país, por ejemplo una boda o un baile de gala *(prom)*.

Actuaciones callejeras

Vocabulario para las actuaciones callejeras

la actuación callejera *street performance*
la comparsa *dance troupe*
el desfile *parade*
entretener *to entertain*
la farsa *farce; comical play*
el (la) intérprete *performer*

La tradición de la farsa es una forma de arte dramático que data desde *(dates from)* antes de la Edad Media *(Middle Ages)* en Europa. La farsa generalmente contaba situaciones absurdas, cómicas o crudas. Muchas veces eran actuaciones informales, que se presentaban en las calles para llamar la atención de los peatones *(pedestrians)*. En Latinoamérica, la influencia de la farsa se ve en las actuaciones durante celebraciones oficiales, en las actuaciones de intérpretes que trabajan en la calle para entretener y ganar dinero, y en los personajes y la coreografía de los bailes folklóricos. Es natural que las actuaciones callejeras en los países hispanos sean populares porque los hispanos pasan parte de su tiempo libre en las plazas y otras zonas públicas de la ciudad.

Nicaragua

El güegüense El baile del güegüense, una farsa típica de Nicaragua, tiene orígenes precolombinos. Representa la resistencia indígena a los españoles.

Chile

Estatuas vivas Esta estatua humana posa delante de la Catedral de Santiago en la capital de Chile. Las estatuas vivas son comunes en muchas ciudades grandes.

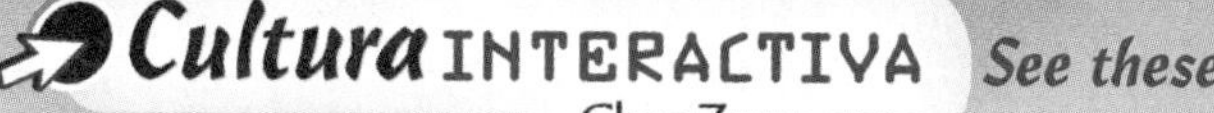

See these pages come alive!

Uruguay

El Desfile de Llamadas Estos músicos tocan con su comparsa. Están en el Desfile de Llamadas, una atracción tradicional del carnaval de Montevideo.

México

Los voladores de Papantla Para los totonacas, esta tradición era un rito religioso, pero hoy los voladores entretienen a turistas por todo el mundo. Un hombre se balancea encima de un poste de 30 metros, y toca música y canta mientras los cuatro voladores, atados a cuerdas *(tied to ropes)*, vuelan *(fly)* hacia la tierra *(ground)*.

Guatemala

El Baile de la Conquista Estos jóvenes llevan trajes para el Baile de la Conquista, una danza satírica sobre la invasión española en las tierras mayas. Es parte del festival de San Tomás en Chichicastenango.

Comparación cultural

1. ¿Qué tipos de actuaciones callejeras son comunes en Estados Unidos? ¿Dónde son comunes las estatuas vivas?
2. ¿Durante qué festivales norteamericanos es posible ver comparsas como la Serenata Africana?

Los mercados

Vocabulario para los mercados

el pueblo *town*
el (la) vendedor(a) *vendor*
el puesto *stand*

Hoy hay más y más supermercados y grandes almacenes en los países hispanos, pero todavía son comunes y populares los mercados al aire libre. En los pueblos y en las ciudades pequeñas, generalmente el mercado está cerca del centro. En las ciudades grandes, hay un mercado en casi todas las zonas principales, y a veces hay un mercado muy grande e histórico en el centro. Aunque *(Although)* muchos turistas visitan los mercados, especialmente los de artesanías, muchos residentes los visitan diariamente para comprar productos frescos para la preparación de sus comidas.

Bolivia

Pan de los muertos En este mercado de Bolivia, venden pan de los muertos para las celebraciones de Todos los Santos y del Día de los Muertos en noviembre.

México

Mercado de Ocotlán Esta vendedora prepara frutas para los clientes que visitan su puesto. Los mercados, como las plazas, son un lugar para socializar y a veces para comer.

España

Mercat de Sant Josep Estas mujeres están en el Mercado de la Boquería, o el Mercat de Sant Josep, el mercado más famoso de Barcelona. En esta sección venden frutas y verduras. En otras secciones venden carnes, pescado y flores.

Ecuador

Mercado de flores Este mercado en Cuenca está en el centro, cerca del Parque de Calderón y la catedral. Aquí venden flores, plantas de jardín y árboles ornamentales los siete días de la semana.

Perú

Flores y artesanías en Lima En este puesto de un mercado de flores en Lima se venden flores secas y artesanías hechas de las flores. Algunos puestos están decorados de una manera muy artística.

Comparación cultural

1. ¿Dónde hay mercados al aire libre en este país? Compara los mercados o los lugares que venden frutas y verduras en tu ciudad con los mercados de Ocotlán y Barcelona.
2. En muchos de los mercados, los precios no son fijos *(fixed)* y los clientes regatean con los vendedores. ¿Dónde puedes regatear en este país?

Banderas nacionales

Vocabulario para las banderas nacionales

la bandera *flag*
el desfile *parade*
el escudo *coat of arms*
la estrella *star*
el significado *meaning*

Las banderas son símbolos importantes de la identidad nacional. A veces los colores tienen significados especiales, por ejemplo, el color verde representa la fertilidad de la tierra *(land)* en las banderas de México y Bolivia. El rojo significa la valentía *(bravery)* en las banderas de Venezuela y Bolivia, pero en las banderas de Puerto Rico y México simboliza la sangre *(blood)* de la gente. El blanco significa la paz *(peace)* en la bandera de Panamá, la libertad en la de Puerto Rico y la pureza *(purity)* en la de México. Algunas banderas incluyen estrellas, escudos y otras imágenes simbólicas.

Nueva York

La hispanidad Estos espectadores del Desfile de la Hispanidad llevan banderas de varios países hispanos: Bolivia (rojo, amarillo y verde), España (rojo y amarillo), Puerto Rico (rojo, blanco y azul) y Ecuador (amarillo, azul y rojo). Se pueden ver los escudos en las banderas españolas y ecuatorianas.

Panamá

Dos estrellas La atleta panameña Eileen Coparropa lleva los colores de su bandera durante los Juegos Panamericanos. El blanco representa la paz, el azul es la pureza y el rojo, la autoridad.

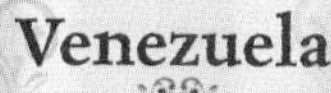

Venezuela

La valentía venezolana Durante la Copa Davis en Caracas este aficionado tiene la cara pintada de los colores de la bandera venezolana. El rojo es la valentía y el azul, la independencia de España. Las ocho estrellas representan las siete provincias del país, más Guyana, que originalmente formaba parte de la República de Venezuela. El escudo *(seal)* tiene símbolos que representan las ideas de unión, victoria y libertad.

Puerto Rico

Una bandera caribeña Aníbal Acevedo Vilá lleva la bandera puertorriqueña durante la campaña para gobernador de la isla. El triángulo azul de la bandera representa el cielo, el Caribe y las tres ramas *(branches)* del gobierno.

México

La historia El mexicano Antonio Pérez celebra con sus compañeros después de ganar el campeonato Renault Fórmula 2000. En la bandera de México, la rama de encina *(oak)* representa la fuerza y la rama de laurel, la victoria. El águila *(eagle)* y la serpiente son de la mitología azteca.

Comparación cultural

1. Compara los eventos en que estas personas llevan la bandera de su país. ¿Cuándo llevas la bandera de tu país? ¿En qué eventos públicos usamos las banderas?
2. Compara el significado de los colores y las estrellas de la bandera de Estados Unidos con el significado de los elementos de las banderas de los países hispanos.

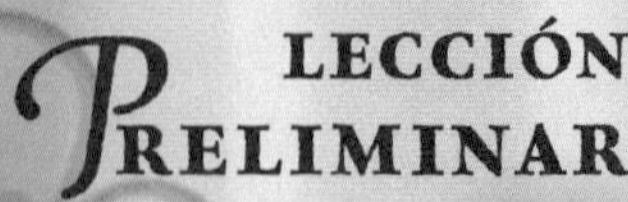

Lección Preliminar
Estados Unidos

Tema:
Una vida ocupada

¡AVANZA! 

¿Recuerdas?

- talk about yourself and your friends
- say what you know how to do
- talk about people and places you know
- describe your daily routine
- make comparisons

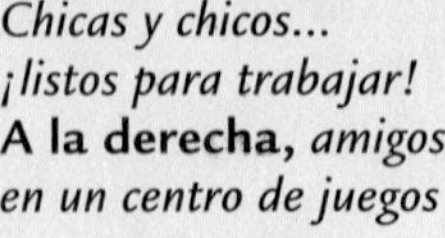

Chicas y chicos... ¡listos para trabajar! **A la derecha,** *amigos en un centro de juegos*

Estudiantes preuniversitarias conversando

Mis amigos y yo

¡AVANZA! **Goal:** Read about Lucía and her friends in her personal web blog. Then practice the review vocabulary by talking about yourself and your friends. ***Actividades 1–3***

A Lucía es una chica que tiene un blog. Éste se llama *El mundo de Lucía.*

@ El mundo de Lucía

Atrás Adelante Detener Actualizar Inicio | Imprimir Correo

Dirección: http://www.blog.net/lucia/98542

El mundo de Lucía

07 septiembre
Estoy en una clase **avanzada** de ciencias y me gusta mucho. Pero mañana vamos a **hacer una excursión** de dos días al campo y ¡no quiero ir!

10 septiembre
¡Tengo una nueva **cámara digital**! Me gusta mucho **tomar fotos.** Aquí hay algunas fotos de la excursión.

Aquí ***acampamos.***

Yo
¿Quién soy? Mi nombre es Lucía. Tengo diecisiete años y soy estudiante. No tengo muchos amigos pero sí tengo dos o tres muy buenos.
Me gusta la música tecno y me encantan los libros de **ciencia ficción.** Mi **actor** favorito es Orlando Bloom.
No me gusta hacer la tarea. Tampoco me gusta hacer cola, ni en la cafetería, ni en el cine, ni en ninguna parte. Prefiero estar en casa, navegar por Internet, **estar en línea,** escribir...

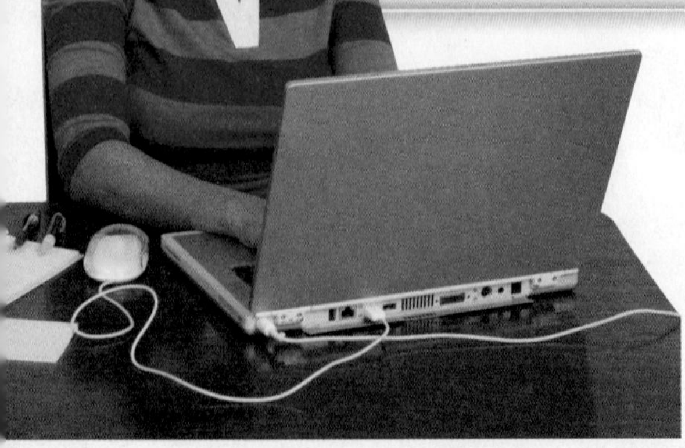

B Y aquí continúa el blog de Lucía.

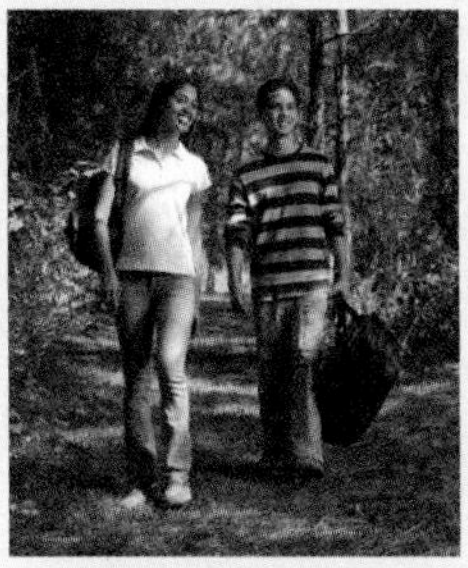

Damos una caminata.

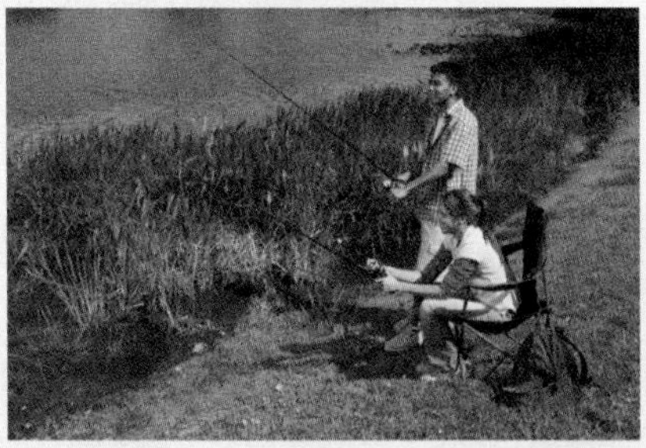

Vamos a pescar.

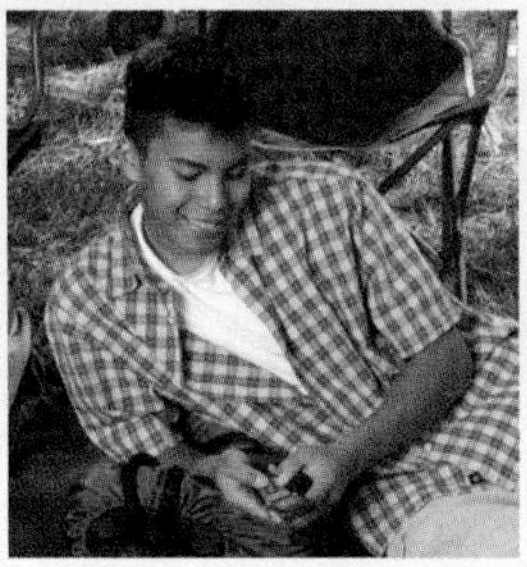

José Antonio y su teléfono. ¡Le encanta el mensajero instantáneo!

Mis amigos

José Antonio, conocido como «Gato». A él también le gusta crear páginas web. ¿Qué más? Le gusta **dibujar**, ir al cine, escuchar música, salir con amigos y hablar por teléfono. Su **actriz** favorita es Michelle Rodríguez. Ella tiene ojos negros y bonitos como Orlando Bloom.

Alma, inteligente y guapa. Le encanta el arte. Le gusta **visitar los museos** de arte y leer libros de arte. También le encanta ir de compras. ¡**Regatea** muy bien! Su actor favorito: Gael García Bernal.

Enviar comentarios

¡A responder! Escuchar

Vas a escuchar una serie de oraciones. Para cada una, indica la persona a quien se refiere. Si se refiere a Lucía, levanta la mano derecha. Si se refiere a José Antonio, levanta la mano izquierda. Si se refiere a Alma, levanta las dos manos.

REPASO Verbs Like gustar

Gustar, encantar and **interesar** are used to talk about what people like, love or are interested in. An **indirect object pronoun (me, te, le, nos, os, les)** always precedes the verb, and the verb endings always agree with the thing that is liked or disliked.

Me gustan las verduras.
I like vegetables.

¿**Te gusta** el arte?
Do you like art?

Nos encanta acampar.
We love to camp.

A Victoria no **le interesan** los museos.
Victoria is not interested in museums.

1 ¿Te gusta?

Hablar

Pregúntale a tu compañero(a) si le gusta hacer las siguientes actividades.

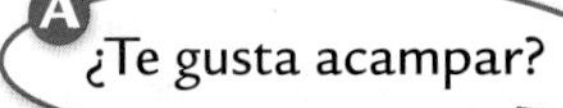

B No, no me gusta acampar.

1. 
2. 
3. 
4. 
5. 
6. 

2 ¿Qué les gusta?

Escribir

Combina las palabras de cada columna para escribir seis oraciones.

modelo: A mí me encanta regatear.

a mí	encantar	visitar museos
a ti	(no) gustar	regatear
a los maestros	(no) interesar	los libros de arte
a los estudiantes		la música tecno

REPASO Present Tense of Regular Verbs

To form the present tense of a regular verb, drop the **-ar, -er,** or **-ir** ending and add these endings:

	-ar **hablar**	**-er** **vender**	**-ir** **compartir**
yo	**hablo**	**vendo**	**comparto**
tú	**hablas**	**vendes**	**compartes**
usted, él, ella	**habla**	**vende**	**comparte**
nosotros(as)	**hablamos**	**vendemos**	**compartimos**
vosotros(as)	**habláis**	**vendéis**	**compartís**
ustedes, ellos(as)	**hablan**	**venden**	**comparten**

3 Las vacaciones de José Antonio

Leer
Escribir

¿Qué hace José Antonio todos los veranos? Completa el párrafo con el tiempo presente de los verbos que están entre paréntesis.

Todos los veranos, mi familia y yo **1.** ____ (viajar) a México. Muchas veces nosotros **2.** ____ (acampar) en la playa. Mi padre **3.** ____ (correr) por la playa y yo **4.** ____ (montar) en bicicleta. Mi madre **5.** ____ (visitar) los mercados y **6.** ____ (regatear). Ella **7.** ____ (comprar) collares de plata y luego los **8.** ____ (vender) en su tienda. Mis hermanas **9.** ____ (tomar) muchas fotos. A mí me gusta ir a los cibercafés. Allí **10.** ____ (navegar) por Internet y les **11.** ____ (escribir) correos electrónicos a mis amigos.

Pronunciación Las letras b y v

Las letras **b** y **v** generalmente tienen la misma pronunciación. Como letra inicial o antes o después de una consonante, se pronuncian las dos como el sonido *b* de la palabra *boy* en inglés. Entre vocales, la **b** y la **v** tienen un sonido más suave como la *b* de la palabra *able* en inglés.

barrio **sabroso** **visitar** **avanza**

Trabalenguas

Pablito clavó un clavito. ¿Qué clavito clavó Pablito?

¿Comprendiste? Nombra dos cosas que a Lucía le gusta hacer y dos actividades que no le gusta hacer.

¿Qué saben hacer?

¡AVANZA! **Goal:** Read about what four famous Spanish speakers know how to do well. Then practice the review vocabulary by naming three things you know how to do. ***Actividades 4–10***

Ⓐ Juanes

Este joven delgado, con pelo largo, toca la guitarra muy bien. Se llama Juanes y es de Colombia. Juanes también canta y escribe canciones. Con muchos **premios** y éxitos *(hits)*, este carismático artista tiene un futuro musical brillante.

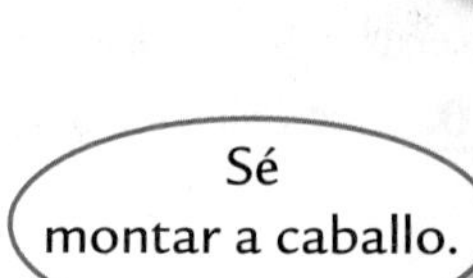

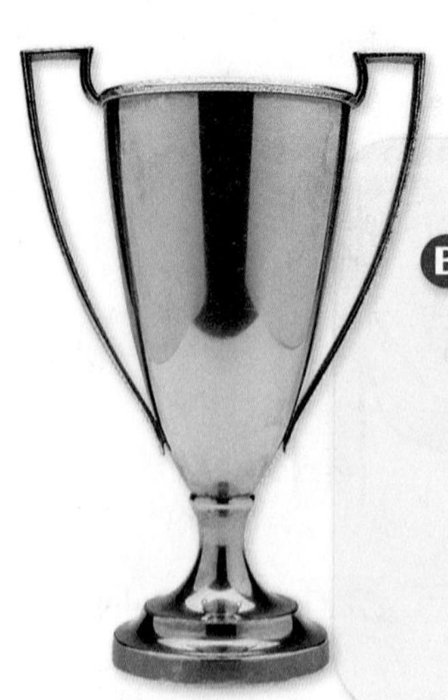

Ⓑ Beatriz Ferrer-Salat

Beatriz Ferrer-Salat es la mejor amazona *(horsewoman)* de España. **Compite** internacionalmente y gana premios. Tiene doce caballos pero compite normalmente con Beauvalais, un caballo rápido y **musculoso.** Beatriz **monta a caballo** y también va al gimnasio para **hacer ejercicio** todos los días.

C Alberto Medina

Alberto Medina es un jugador de fútbol de México. Es joven pero ya **juega** profesionalmente para el **equipo** Guadalajara y la selección nacional. Medina es muy **rápido,** sabe correr y **¡mete muchos goles!**

Sé escribir.

D María Amparo Escandón

María Amparo Escandón es una escritora y profesora de California. Ella sabe **contar** muy bien las experiencias de los mexicoamericanos. Es bilingüe: escribe novelas y guiones de películas en inglés y en español.

¡A responder! Escuchar

Escucha cada oración. Si es cierta, indícalo con el pulgar hacia arriba *(thumbs up)*. Si es falsa, indícalo con el pulgar hacia abajo *(thumbs down)*.

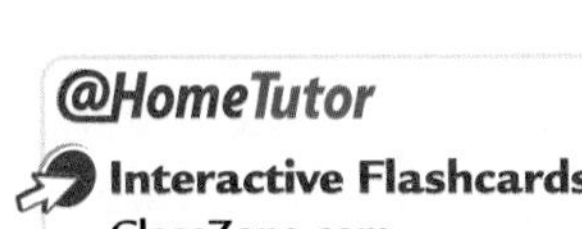

REPASO Present Tense of Irregular Verbs

Ser, estar and **ir** are irregular verbs because they do not follow the pattern of regular verbs.

ser		estar		ir	
soy	somos	estoy	estamos	voy	vamos
eres	sois	estás	estáis	vas	vais
es	son	está	están	va	van

4 ¿De dónde soy?

Hablar
Escribir

Mira los dibujos y di de dónde son las siguientes personas.

modelo: ustedes
Ustedes son de Estados Unidos.

1. yo

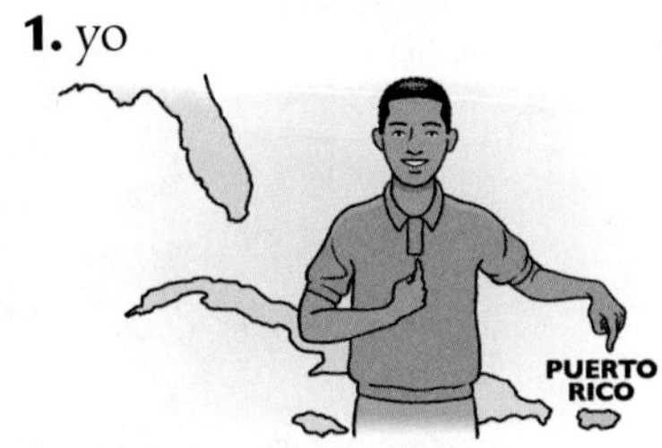

2. tú

3. ellas

4. nosotros

5 La familia Núñez

Leer
Escribir

Completa el párrafo sobre la familia Núñez utilizando **ser, estar** o **ir,** según corresponda. Conjuga correctamente cada verbo.

La Sra. Núñez __1.__ de Venezuela; el Sr. Núñez __2.__ de California. Ella __3.__ vendedora y __4.__ a Venezuela con frecuencia. El Sr. Núñez también __5.__ vendedor. Trabaja para una compañía que __6.__ en Madison, Wisconsin. Pablo y María Núñez __7.__ ahora en la escuela secundaria. El mes que viene todos __8.__ a ir a California para visitar al padre del Sr. Núñez, que vive en Los Ángeles.

REPASO Present Tense of Irregular yo Verbs

Some verbs are irregular only in the **yo** form.

	conocer *to know; to meet*	**dar** *to give*	**saber** *to know*	**ver** *to see*
yo	**conozco**	**doy**	**sé**	**veo**
tú	**conoces**	**das**	**sabes**	**ves**

	hacer *to make; to do*	**poner** *to put*	**salir** *to go out; to leave*	**traer** *to bring*
yo	**hago**	**pongo**	**salgo**	**traigo**
tú	**haces**	**pones**	**sales**	**traes**

6 Yo también

Escribir Hablar

Di si tú también haces las siguientes actividades.

modelo: Hernán da caminatas.
Yo también doy caminatas. / Yo no doy caminatas.

1. Leonor va al gimnasio.
2. Mónica sabe montar a caballo.
3. Fernando ve mucha televisión.
4. Carlos sale con amigos.
5. Ada trae un diccionario a clase.
6. Jaime siempre está en línea.
7. David hace cola en la cafetería.
8. Patricia pone música para estudiar.
9. Eva conoce a Juanes.

7 ¿Qué sabes hacer?

Hablar

Pregúntale a tu compañero(a) si sabe hacer las siguientes cosas.

modelo:

A: ¿Sabes montar a caballo?

B: Sí, sé montar a caballo. / No, no sé montar a caballo.

1. pescar
2. meter goles
3. tocar la guitarra
4. regatear
5. tomar fotos
6. jugar al béisbol
7. dibujar
8. tocar el piano

PARA Y PIENSA

¿Comprendiste? Empareja cada sujeto con la terminación correcta.

Get Help Online ClassZone.com

1. Nosotros
2. Yo
3. Ella
4. Ellos

a. está emocionada.
b. somos estudiantes.
c. van a pescar.
d. salgo para México.

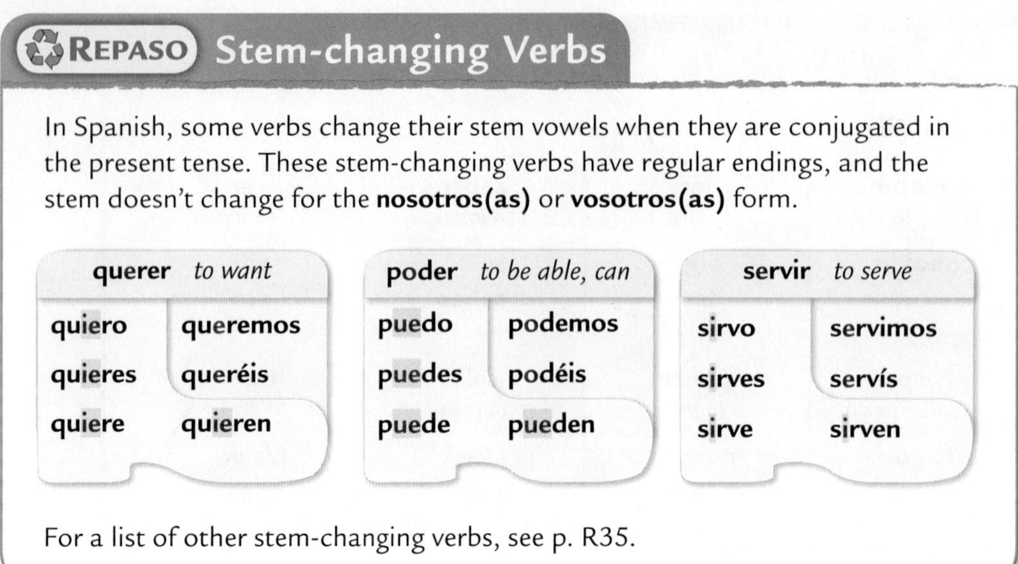

REPASO Stem-changing Verbs

In Spanish, some verbs change their stem vowels when they are conjugated in the present tense. These stem-changing verbs have regular endings, and the stem doesn't change for the **nosotros(as)** or **vosotros(as)** form.

querer *to want*	
quiero	**queremos**
quieres	**queréis**
quiere	**quieren**

poder *to be able, can*	
puedo	**podemos**
puedes	**podéis**
puede	**pueden**

servir *to serve*	
sirvo	**servimos**
sirves	**servís**
sirve	**sirven**

For a list of other stem-changing verbs, see p. R35.

8 ¡Otra vez a la escuela!

Escribir
Leer

Marta le escribe a su amiga Lucía un correo electrónico sobre los primeros días de clase en su escuela. Completa el texto con el tiempo presente de los verbos que están entre paréntesis.

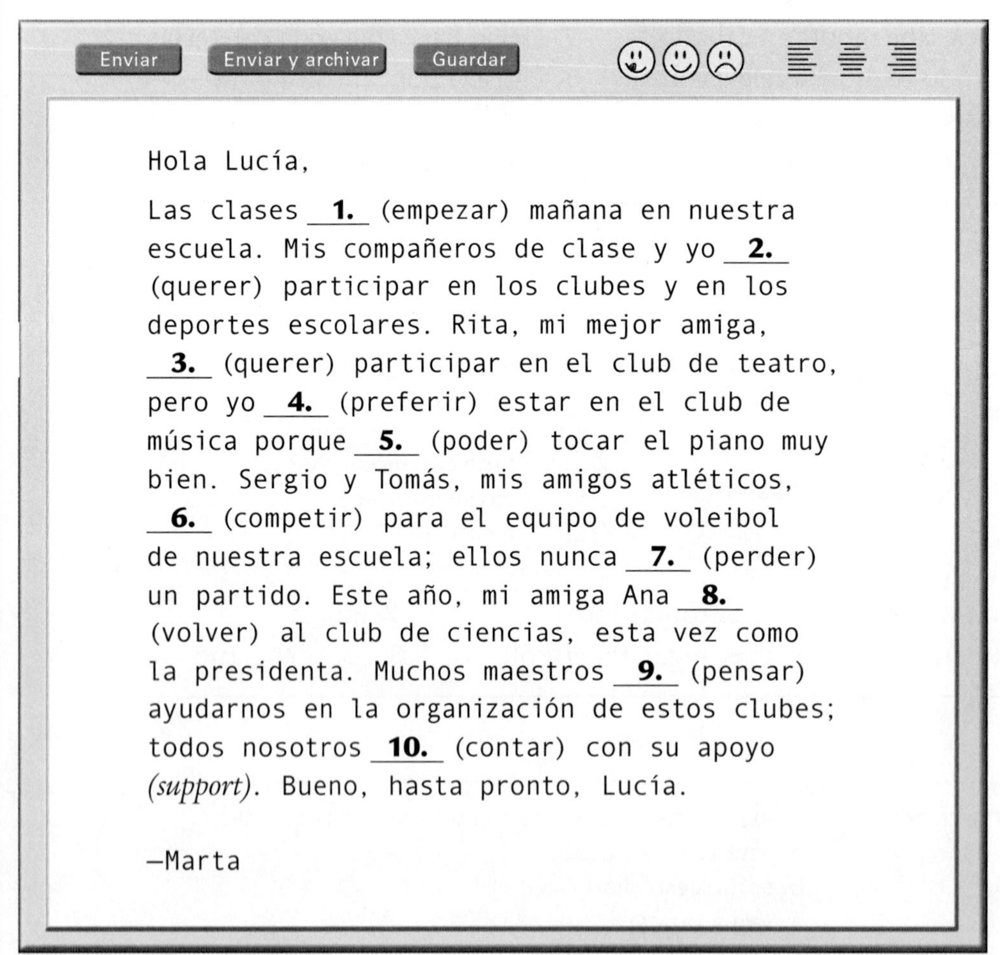

Hola Lucía,

Las clases __**1.**__ (empezar) mañana en nuestra escuela. Mis compañeros de clase y yo __**2.**__ (querer) participar en los clubes y en los deportes escolares. Rita, mi mejor amiga, __**3.**__ (querer) participar en el club de teatro, pero yo __**4.**__ (preferir) estar en el club de música porque __**5.**__ (poder) tocar el piano muy bien. Sergio y Tomás, mis amigos atléticos, __**6.**__ (competir) para el equipo de voleibol de nuestra escuela; ellos nunca __**7.**__ (perder) un partido. Este año, mi amiga Ana __**8.**__ (volver) al club de ciencias, esta vez como la presidenta. Muchos maestros __**9.**__ (pensar) ayudarnos en la organización de estos clubes; todos nosotros __**10.**__ (contar) con su apoyo *(support)*. Bueno, hasta pronto, Lucía.

—Marta

REPASO The Verbs decir, tener, and venir

Three stem-changing verbs with irregular **yo** forms are **decir, tener,** and **venir.**

	decir (e → i) *to say, to tell*	**tener (e → ie)** *to have*	**venir (e → ie)** *to come*
yo	**digo**	**tengo**	**vengo**
tú	**dices**	**tienes**	**vienes**

9 ¿A qué hora?

Hablar

Pregúntale a tu compañero(a) a qué hora hace las siguientes actividades.

modelo: competir

A ¿A qué hora compites?

B Mañana compito a las cuatro de la tarde.

1. almorzar
2. dormir
3. tener que ir a trabajar
4. preferir desayunar
5. venir a la escuela
6. empezar a hacer la tarea
7. volver a casa
8. tener clase de español
9. poder salir de noche
10. servir el almuerzo

10 Pequeño cuestionario

Leer
Escribir

Una universidad desea conocerte y saber algo más sobre tu vida escolar. Recibes el siguiente cuestionario. Contéstalo.

Estimado estudiante:

Contesta las siguientes preguntas sobre tu vida escolar.
Tu información nos ayuda a conocerte mejor.

1. ¿Cuándo empiezan las clases en tu escuela?
2. Generalmente, ¿cuántas horas duermes?
3. ¿Qué clases tienes este año?
4. ¿Qué cosas (actividades) prefieres hacer?
5. ¿Qué piensas estudiar en el futuro?
6. ¿Quieres visitar nuestra universidad? ¿Cuándo puedes visitarnos?

¿Comprendiste? Conjuga los verbos.

1. Yo (venir).
2. Juan (entender).
3. Ustedes (competir).
4. Tú (contar).
5. Yo (tener).
6. Ellas (decir).

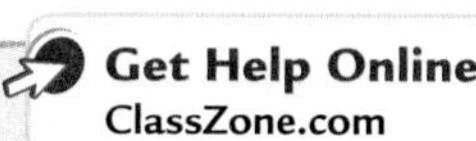

¿Lo conoces?

¡AVANZA! **Goal:** Read these conversations in which friends talk about famous people and places they know. Then practice the review vocabulary by talking about the people and places you know in your neighborhood. ***Actividades 11–14***

AUDIO

A Cecilia y Julia son dos amigas que viven en Tampa, Florida. En estos momentos están conversando en un café.

B **Cecilia:** Julia, **estoy muy emocionada.** Mi familia y yo vamos a México. ¿Conoces México?

Julia: Sí. Allí viven mis tíos. Me encanta esa ciudad: los museos, **teatros,** restaurantes, **tiendas, joyerías...**

Cecilia: Es grande y moderno, ¿verdad?

Julia: Sí, es muy grande. Y también muy moderno. Aquí traigo algunas fotos de mi querido México. Deseo enseñártelas. Mira: hay muchos **rascacielos.** La Torre Mayor es **el edificio** más alto de Latinoamérica.

C **Cecilia:** Tengo que verlo.

Julia: También tienes que ir a Sanborns.

Cecilia: No lo conozco. ¿Qué es?

Julia: Son **almacenes** que tienen **librería, farmacia** y restaurante. El más famoso está en la Casa de los Azulejos, en la calle de Madero.

Cecilia: Está bien. También quiero visitar **el barrio** de Coyoacán. Sabes, allí está la Casa Azul, de Frida Kahlo. Sabes quién es, ¿verdad?

Julia: Sí, conozco muy bien algunas de sus pinturas. Frida Kahlo es mi artista favorita. ¡Qué vida! Tengo un libro sobre su vida que **me hace llorar.**

D Cecilia y Julia salen del café y caminan porque van a tomar el autobús para ir al cine.

Cecilia: Mira, Julia. Ahí está Nicolás en **la parada de autobús.** Hola, Nico. ¿Qué tal? ¿Conoces a Julia?

Nicolás: No. Mucho gusto, Julia. ¿Adónde van?

Julia: Vamos al cine a ver **una película** de Robert Rodríguez. ¿Sabes quién es?

Nicolás: Sí. Es el joven director mexicoamericano. Conozco sus películas muy bien; algunas **me hacen reír** mucho.

E **Cecilia:** Pues, nosotras vamos a ver su última película; varias personas me dijeron que **les dio miedo.** ¿Quieres venir con nosotras?

Nicolás: **Me encantaría,** pero no puedo. Busco un libro que es un poco difícil de conseguir.

Cecilia: **¡Qué lástima!**

Nicolás: ¿Conocen una buena librería?

Julia: Sí, hay una en la calle North Tampa, cerca de **la zapatería.** Se llama Old Tampa Book Company.

¡A responder! Escuchar 

Vas a escuchar una serie de oraciones. Para cada una, indica la persona a quien se refiere. Si se refiere a Cecilia, levanta la mano derecha. Si se refiere a Julia, levanta la mano izquierda. Si se refiere a Nicolás, levanta las dos manos.

@HomeTutor
Interactive Flashcards
ClassZone.com

REPASO Saber or conocer

Saber and **conocer** both mean *to know.* Use **saber** to talk about factual information you know and to say you know how to do something.

No **sé** cómo se llama la nueva estudiante.
I don't know what the new student's name is.

Ella **sabe** tocar la guitarra.
She knows how to play the guitar.

Use **conocer** when you want to say that you are familiar with a person, place, or thing and to talk about meeting someone for the first time.

¿**Conoces** Nueva York?
Do you know (are familiar with) New York?

Quiero **conocer** a tu hermano.
I want to meet your brother.

11 Mi amigo Marcos

Leer Escribir

Completa las oraciones con la forma correcta de **saber** o **conocer.**

1. ¿_____ ustedes a mi amigo Marcos?
2. Marcos _____ jugar al fútbol muy bien.
3. Yo no _____ a qué hora es el partido.
4. Marcos y yo queremos _____ a los jugadores del equipo Chivas.
5. ¿_____ tú de dónde son los Chivas?
6. Son de Guadalajara, pero yo no _____ esa ciudad.

12 Personas famosas

Hablar

Piensa en personas famosas. Pregúntales a tus compañeros(as) si las conocen y si saben de dónde son.

modelo:

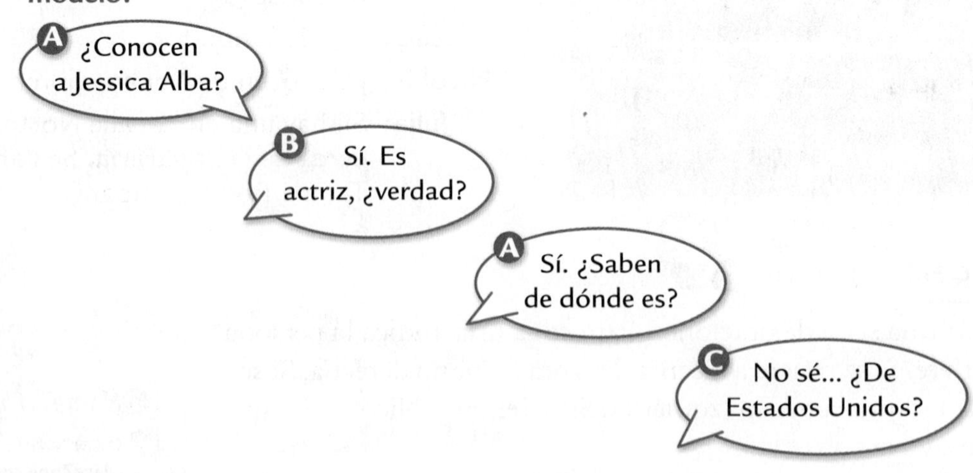

REPASO Ser or estar

Ser and **estar** both mean *to be.* **Ser** is used to indicate origin, to describe personal traits and physical characteristics, and to indicate professions.

Rafael **es** de Panamá. **Es** alto y simpático. Su padre **es** maestro.
Rafael is from Panama. He is tall and nice. His father is a teacher.

Estar is used to indicate location and to describe conditions, such as how someone feels.

Carmen **está** en casa; **está** enferma.
Carmen is at home; she is sick.

13 Un político estadounidense

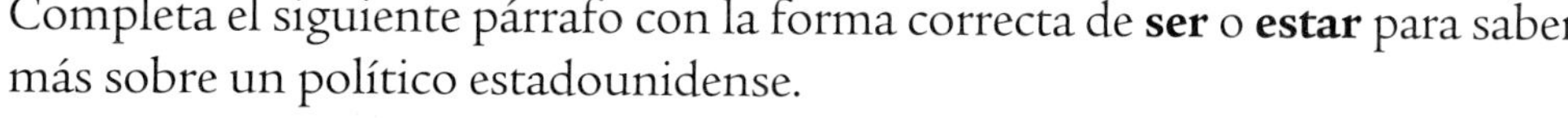

Leer
Escribir

Completa el siguiente párrafo con la forma correcta de **ser** o **estar** para saber más sobre un político estadounidense.

¿Sabes quién __**1.**__ Mel Martínez? Mel Martínez __**2.**__ un político del estado de la Florida. Mel __**3.**__ originalmente de Cuba. Todos los políticos __**4.**__ personas muy ocupadas. Y Mel no __**5.**__ excepción: un día él __**6.**__ en Washington y otro día __**7.**__ en Miami. Probablemente, él __**8.**__ emocionado porque su papel en la política __**9.**__ muy importante.

14 Describe la pintura

Leer
Hablar
Escribir

Comparación cultural

Dalí de espaldas pintando a Gala de espaldas *(1972–73), Salvador Dalí*

Gala: un tema importante para Dalí

¿Por qué los artistas repiten ciertos temas? Salvador Dalí (1904–1989) era un pintor *(painter)* de **España.** Su esposa Gala es un tema frecuente en la obra de Dalí. En esta pintura *(painting)* Dalí y Gala están de espaldas, pero el reflejo *(reflection)* de sus caras se ve en el espejo.

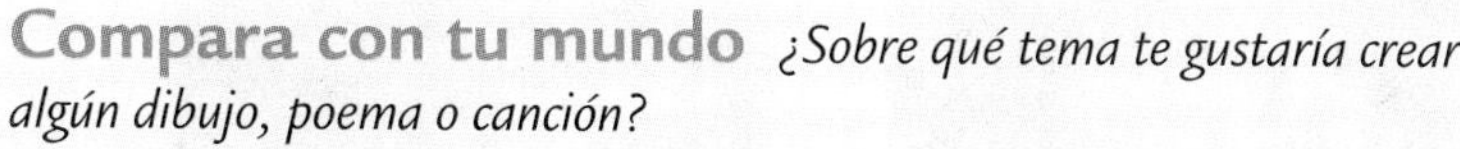

Compara con tu mundo *¿Sobre qué tema te gustaría crear algún dibujo, poema o canción?*

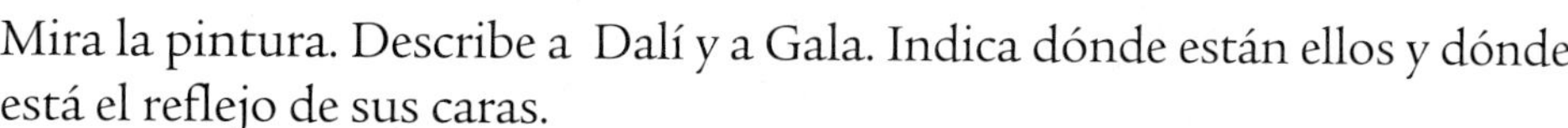

Mira la pintura. Describe a Dalí y a Gala. Indica dónde están ellos y dónde está el reflejo de sus caras.

PARA Y PIENSA

¿Comprendiste? Empareja cada oración con la terminación correcta.

1. No conozco... **2.** Soy... **3.** Beto está...
a. enojado. **b.** Miami. **c.** estudiante.

Get Help Online
ClassZone.com

Mi rutina diaria

¡AVANZA! **Goal:** Read about a typical day in the life of Jimena, a sixteen-year old student from Florida. Then practice the review vocabulary by saying what you do to get ready in the morning. ***Actividades 15–18***

AUDIO

Jimena

A Mi vida es ocupada, trabajo mucho, no tengo mucho tiempo libre, pero... ¡me encanta mi vida! Me llamo Jimena y soy una persona muy **activa.** La escuela y los deportes son muy importantes para mí. Saco buenas notas. Corro, hago ejercicio y juego al tenis. También toco el piano y me gusta ayudar en el club de teatro.

B Mi día empieza temprano. **Me despierto** a las seis de la mañana. Escucho la radio por quince minutos y luego **me levanto.**

Me despierto.

C Me **lavo la cara y las manos, me cepillo los dientes, me visto** y voy a la escuela. Después de la escuela, comparto con mis compañeros y hago la tarea.

Me lavo la cara.

Voy a la escuela.

Hago la tarea.

D Luego practico el piano, juego al tenis o voy al club de teatro. ¡A veces hago las tres cosas!

Toco el piano.

Juego al tenis.

Voy al club de teatro.

E Ceno en casa y hago más tarea. Cuando termino, escucho música. Luego **me ducho** (o **me baño**), **me seco, me pongo la ropa** de dormir y **me acuesto** alrededor de las diez y media.

Me seco.

Me acuesto.

F Muchas veces no tengo tiempo para pasar un rato con mis amigos. Y muchas veces estoy muy cansada. Pero me gusta mi vida ocupada.

¡A responder! Escuchar

Escucha cada oración. Si es cierta, indícalo con el pulgar hacia arriba. Si es falsa, indícalo con el pulgar hacia abajo.

REPASO Reflexive Verbs

Reflexive verbs describe people doing things to or for themselves. In Spanish, all reflexive verbs are expressed with a **reflexive pronoun.**

bañarse *to take a bath*			
yo	**me baño**	nosotros(as)	**nos bañamos**
tú	**te bañas**	vosotros(as)	**os bañáis**
usted, él, ella	**se baña**	ustedes, ellos(as)	**se bañan**

The **reflexive pronoun** always appears before the conjugated **reflexive verb.**

Me lavo las manos antes de comer.
I wash my hands before eating.

When the **reflexive verb** follows a **conjugated verb,** the **reflexive pronoun** can be attached to the infinitive or be placed before the **conjugated verb.**

Los niños no quieren **acostarse.** / Los niños no **se quieren** acostar.
The children don't want to go to bed.

15 ¿Qué van a hacer?

Escribir

¿Qué van a hacer todos antes de salir de la casa? Usa las palabras para escribir oraciones completas.

modelo: Francisco / bañarse
Francisco va a bañarse. (Francisco se va a bañar.)

1. Daniela / secarse el pelo
2. tú / cepillarse los dientes
3. los niños / ponerse los zapatos
4. nosotros / lavarse las manos
5. Rodrigo / ponerse la camisa
6. yo / vestirse
7. tú / lavarse la cara
8. Eduardo / ducharse

16 Hábitos

Escuchar
Hablar

Escucha la narración de Ramón sobre los hábitos diarios de él y de sus dos hermanos, Laura y Carlos. Luego contesta las preguntas sobre esta narración de Ramón.

1. ¿A qué hora se levanta Laura? ¿Se baña o se ducha?
2. ¿Quién se levanta más temprano: Ramón o Carlos?
3. ¿Cuándo se ducha Ramón?
4. ¿A qué hora se acuesta Carlos?

17 Un día típico

Hablar

¿Cómo es el día típico de Sergio? Con un(a) compañero(a), mira los dibujos y describe lo que hace Sergio. Usa palabras como **primero, entonces, luego, más tarde, por fin.**

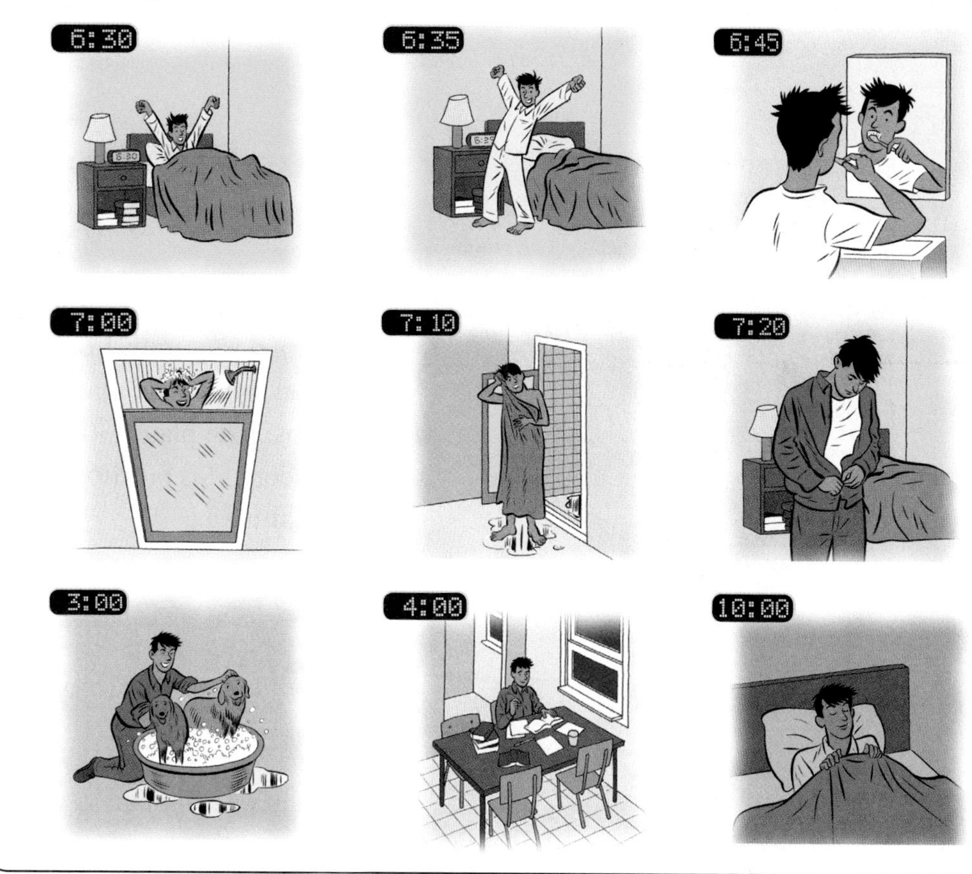

18 ¿Y tú?

Hablar
Escribir

Contesta las siguientes preguntas.

1. ¿A qué hora te despiertas los lunes? ¿Y los sábados?
2. ¿Prefieres levantarte tarde o temprano?
3. ¿Te duchas por la mañana o por la noche?
4. ¿Te cepillas los dientes antes o después de bañarte?
5. ¿Te vistes antes o después de desayunar?
6. ¿Te lavas las manos antes de comer?
7. ¿Cuándo te pones sandalias?
8. ¿A qué hora te acuestas los fines de semana?

¿Comprendiste? Conjuga los verbos.

1. Yo (ducharse) _____ .
2. Paco (levantarse) _____ .
3. Nosotros (acostarse) _____ .
4. Tú (vestirse) _____ .

Get Help Online
ClassZone.com

Guía de restaurantes

¡AVANZA! **Goal:** Read the following restaurant guide. Then practice the review vocabulary by comparing the food from two of your favorite eating spots. ***Actividades 19–25***

Señor Burrito

Comida rápida y barata. Un buen lugar para **desayunar.** Los huevos **fritos** con tortillas de maíz son deliciosos. Este plato no es tan **picante** como los burritos pero es más **sabroso**.

El Chalet

Un restaurante romántico y elegante. Tiene su propia **panadería**. Los camareros son **lentos** pero **amables**. Es imposible **cenar** aquí y no probar los ricos **postres** del chef Hildebrand.

El Jardín

Restaurante con una decoración de buen gusto y un menú excelente. **La sopa** de **verduras**, el pollo al **ajo** y el **pescado** en salsa **agria** son algunas de **las especialidades**.

Café Tropical

Excelente café para comer **la merienda**. El ceviche —pescado que es **cocido** solamente con limón— compite con los mejores ceviches de Perú. También hay que probar los famosos tostones —(plátanos hervidos y luego fritos), que ya salen con **sal** de la cocina.

La Casa de Leyla

Este restaurante popular tiene un nuevo chef. ¡Qué lástima! Las sopas ahora son más **saladas** y los jugos más **dulces** que antes. Las **papas** a veces salen un poco **crudas**. Pero los precios son tan buenos como antes.

Pollos Campo

Hay pocos restaurantes que preparan un **pollo asado** más sabroso que aquí. Este pollo tiene más **pimienta** que otros y la carne está cocida perfectamente. A los adultos les encanta tanto como a los niños.

¡A responder! Escuchar 

Escucha cada oración. Si es cierta, indícalo con el pulgar hacia arriba. Si es falsa, indícalo con el pulgar hacia abajo.

@HomeTutor
Interactive Flashcards
ClassZone.com

REPASO Unequal Comparisons

To compare differences between people and things, Spanish uses these comparatives:

más + **adjective, adverb,** or **noun** + **que**

Estos camareros son **más amables que** aquéllos.
*These waiters are **nicer than** those.*

menos + **adjective, adverb,** or **noun** + **que**

El supermercado tiene **menos verduras que** el mercado.
*The supermarket has **fewer vegetables than** the market.*

To compare differences between actions, use these adverbial phrases:

más que... *more than . . .*	Me gusta la comida salada **más que** la comida dulce. *I like salty foods **more than** sweet foods.*
menos que... *less than . . .*	Yo como **menos que** tú. *I eat **less than** you.*

The following comparative words are irregular.

mayor	**menor**	**mejor**	**peor**
older	*younger*	*better*	*worse*

19 Arturo y Mariana

Escuchar

Escucha unas comparaciones entre Arturo y Mariana. Para cada una, di si es cierta o falsa, según los dibujos.

Arturo

Mariana

20 Haz comparaciones

Leer
Escribir

Escribe comparaciones con la siguiente información.

modelo: La salsa roja es picante, pero la salsa verde es muy picante.
La salsa roja es menos picante que la salsa verde.

1. La maestra tiene 40 años y el estudiante tiene 17 años.
2. Hay 19 chicos y 12 chicas en la clase.
3. El té negro es agrio. El té verde es más agrio.
4. A Eva le gusta la cena pero le encanta la merienda.
5. El caldo cuesta $5 y el gazpacho cuesta $8.

REPASO Equal Comparisons

To compare similarities between people and things, use these phrases:

tan + **adjective** or **adverb** + **como** *as . . . as*	La tarta es **tan sabrosa como** el flan. *The cake is **as tasty as** the custard.*
tanto (a, os, as) + **noun** + **como** *as many/much . . . as*	La sopa tiene **tanta pimienta como** sal. *The soup has **as much pepper as** salt.*
tanto como... *as much . . . as*	Cocino **tanto como** tú. *I cook **as much as** you do.*

21 Mi amigo y yo

Leer Escribir

Completa el párrafo con las palabras apropiadas.

Mi amigo Guillermo y yo somos muy parecidos *(alike)*. Guillermo es __1.__ alto __2.__ yo, __3.__ pelirrojo __4.__ yo y __5.__ cómico __6.__ yo. Guillermo tiene __7.__ camisetas rojas __8.__ yo, lee __9.__ libros __10.__ yo, y le gusta la comida picante __11.__ __12.__ a mí.

22 No eres mejor

Escribir

Rebeca y Sofía tienen, cada una, un restaurante. Rebeca piensa que el suyo *(hers)* es mejor. Vuelve a escribir las oraciones según Sofía, usando comparativos de igualdad.

modelo: Rebeca: Mi restaurante es más elegante que tu restaurante.
Sofía: Mi restaurante es tan elegante como tu restaurante.

1. Mi restaurante tiene más mesas que tu restaurante.
2. Mi menú tiene más postres que tu menú.
3. Mi comida es más sabrosa que tu comida.
4. Mis camareros son más amables que tus camareros.
5. Cocinamos más rápido que ustedes.
6. Somos mejores que ustedes.

23 Compárate con tu amigo(a)

Escribir

¿Cómo te comparas con tu mejor amigo(a)? Escribe ocho comparaciones.

alto(a)	estudioso(a)	vida ocupada	atlético(a)
mayor	dibujar	dormir	gustar las verduras

modelo: Mi mejor amigo es más alto que yo...

24 En tu opinión

Hablar Combina las palabras para hacer comparaciones. Luego comparte tus opiniones con un(a) compañero(a).

modelo: hay / cafés / panaderías

B No. Hay más cafés que panaderías.

1. comida mexicana / picante / comida italiana
2. comida de la cafetería / buena / comida rápida
3. en el desayuno / comer / en la cena
4. las manzanas / dulce / los plátanos
5. hay / restaurantes / almacenes

25 ¿Qué piensas?

Hablar Pregúntale a tu compañero(a) qué opina entre las dos cosas. Usa **más... que, menos... que** y **tan... como.**

modelo: interesante

A ¿Es más interesante ir a pescar o tomar fotos?

B Para mí, tomar fotos es más interesante que ir a pescar.

1. divertido  / 
2. aburrido 
3. sabroso 
4. bueno 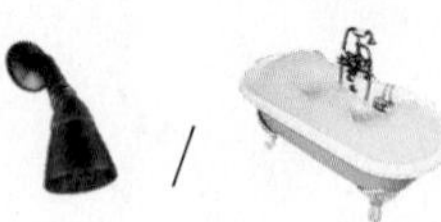
5. delicioso 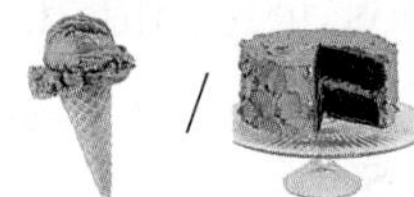
6. saludable 
7. fácil 
8. caro 

PARA Y PIENSA

¿Comprendiste? Completa las comparaciones según la información.

Get Help Online ClassZone.com

1. Rosa tiene 60 años. — Soy _____ Rosa.
2. Rosa mide 4´10˝. — Soy _____ alta _____ Rosa.
3. Rosa y tú tienen los mismos amigos. — Tengo _____ amigos _____ Rosa.

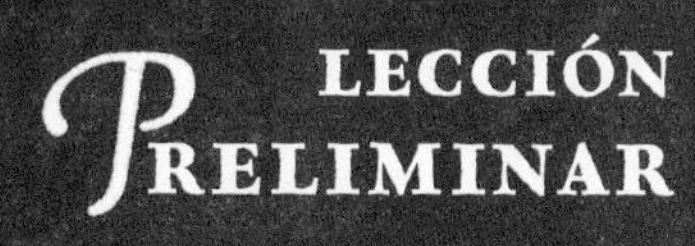

En resumen

Vocabulario

Vocabulario

Talk About Yourself and Your Friends

People and Activities

el actor	*actor*
la actriz	*actress*
la cámara digital	*digital camera*
la ciencia ficción	*science fiction*
el mensajero instantáneo	*instant messaging*

More Activities

acampar	*to camp*
dar una caminata	*to hike*
dibujar	*to draw*
estar en línea	*to be online*
hacer una excursión	*to go on a day trip*
pescar	*to fish*
regatear	*to bargain*
tomar fotos	*to take photos*
visitar un museo	*to visit a museum*

What You Know How To Do

competir (i, i)	*to compete*
contar (ue)	*to tell (a story)*
hacer ejercicio	*to exercise*
jugar en equipo	*to play on a team*
meter un gol	*to score a goal*
montar a caballo	*to ride a horse*
el premio	*prize, award*

Talk About Places and People You Know

Places

el almacén	*department store*
el barrio	*neighborhood*
el edificio	*building*
la farmacia	*pharmacy*
la joyería	*jewelry store*
la librería	*bookstore*
la panadería	*bakery*
la parada de autobús	*bus stop*
la película	*film*
el rascacielos	*skyscraper*
el teatro	*theater*
la tienda	*store*
la zapatería	*shoe store*

Emotions

Estoy muy emocionado(a).	*I am overcome with emotion.*
Me encantaría.	*I would love to.*
Me hace llorar.	*It makes me cry.*
Me hace reír.	*It makes me laugh.*
Me / te / le da miedo.	*It scares (me, you, him / her).*
¡Qué lástima!	*What a shame!*

Describe Your Daily Routine

acostarse (ue)	*to go to bed*
bañarse	*to take a bath*
cepillarse los dientes	*to brush one's teeth*
despertarse (ie)	*to wake up*
ducharse	*to take a shower*
lavarse (la cara, las manos)	*to wash oneself (one's face, one's hands)*
levantarse	*to get up*
ponerse la ropa	*to put on clothes*
secarse	*to dry oneself*
vestirse (i, i)	*to get dressed*

Make Comparisons

Food

el ajo	*garlic*
cenar	*to have dinner*
desayunar	*to have breakfast*
la especialidad	*specialty*
la merienda	*afternoon snack*
la papa	*potato*
el pescado	*fish*
la pimienta	*pepper*
el pollo asado	*roasted chicken*
el postre	*dessert*
la sal	*salt*
la sopa	*soup*
las verduras	*vegetables*

Adjectives

activo(a)	*active*
agrio(a)	*sour*
amable	*kind*
avanzado(a)	*advanced*
cocido(a)	*cooked*
crudo(a)	*raw*
dulce	*sweet*
frito(a)	*fried*
hervido(a)	*boiled*
lento(a)	*slow*
musculoso(a)	*muscular*
picante	*spicy, hot*
rápido(a)	*fast*
sabroso(a)	*tasty*
salado(a)	*salty*

Repaso de la lección

¡LLEGADA!

@HomeTutor
ClassZone.com

Now you can
- talk about yourself and your friends
- say what you know how to do
- talk about people and places you know
- describe your daily routine
- make comparisons

Using
- verbs like **gustar**
- present tense
- reflexive verbs
- comparisons

To review
- activities pp. 2–3, 6–7
- **gustar** p. 4

1 Listen and match descriptions

AUDIO

Escucha las siguientes descripciones. Escribe el número de la descripción al lado de la foto que corresponde.

a.

b.

c.

d.

To review
- regular present-tense verbs p. 5
- irregular present-tense verbs p. 8
- irregular **yo** present-tense verbs p. 9
- stem-changing verbs p. 10
- **decir, tener,** and **venir** p. 11

2 Say what you know how to do

Primero di si sabes hacer la actividad. Luego di con qué frecuencia la haces: **(casi) nunca, a veces, muchas veces, (casi) siempre.**

modelo: tocar el piano
No sé tocar el piano. Nunca toco el piano.

1. jugar en equipo
2. contar historias
3. regatear en español
4. montar en bicicleta
5. poner la mesa
6. hacer blogs
7. pescar
8. usar el mensajero instantáneo

To review
- **saber** or **conocer** p. 14
- **ser** or **estar** p. 15

3 Talk about people and places you know

Lee el siguiente párrafo sobre El Corte Inglés. Completa las oraciones con el presente del verbo correcto.

¿ __1.__ (Saber / Conocer) tú El Corte Inglés? Todas las personas en España lo __2.__ (saber / conocer) porque __3.__ (ser / estar) un almacén famoso. El Corte Inglés __4.__ (ser / estar) en muchas ciudades de España. Allí la calidad __5.__ (ser / estar) buena y cuando un cliente no __6.__ (ser / estar) contento con el producto, lo puede devolver.

To review
- reflexive verbs p. 18

4 Describe your daily routine

Combina palabras de cada columna para escribir seis oraciones sobre lo que las personas hacen generalmente.

modelo: Mi hermano se acuesta temprano.

yo	levantarse	tarde
tú	acostarse	temprano
mi hermano(a)	ducharse	por la noche
nosotros	vestirse	por la mañana

To review
- unequal comparisons p. 22
- equal comparisons p. 23

5 Make comparisons

Vas a leer las descripciones de dos chicas: Ana y Raquel. Utiliza las palabras de la lista para hacer cuatro comparaciones.

modelo: Ana dibuja mucho. A Raquel no le gusta dibujar.
Raquel dibuja menos que Ana.

tarde	más (...) que	tanto tiempo como
temprano	menos (...) que	tantas veces como

Ana	Raquel
Dibuja mucho.	No le gusta dibujar.
Se levanta a las 7:30 de la mañana.	Se levanta a las 5:30 de la mañana.
Se ducha por la noche.	Se ducha por la mañana.
Le gusta mucho correr.	Le gusta poco correr.
Se cepilla los dientes cuatro veces al día.	Se cepilla los dientes cuatro veces al día.

Get Help Online
ClassZone.com

UNIDAD 1

México

Nos divertimos al aire libre

Lección 1

Tema: ***Vamos a acampar***

Lección 2

Tema: ***Vamos a la playa***

«*¡Bienvenidos a México!*
Me llamo Javier y soy del D.F. Mi amiga se llama Sandra; es de Veracruz.»

Almanaque cultural

Población: 109.955.400 habitantes

Área: 761.606 millas cuadradas

Capital: México D.F.

Nombre oficial: Estados Unidos Mexicanos

Estados: 31

Moneda: peso mexicano

Comida típica: tamales, ceviche, tacos, enchiladas

Gente famosa: Octavio Paz (escritor), Paulina Rubio (cantante), Gael García Bernal (actor)

Enchiladas

Pirámide de Chichén-Itzá

◀ **Ruinas arqueológicas** La Península de Yucatán es una zona muy rica en sitios arqueológicos. Las ruinas más famosas son Chichén-Itzá y Uxmal, que conservan las maravillas de la civilización maya. *¿Conoces sitios arqueológicos en Estados Unidos?*

Diversión en el agua En las costas de México puedes practicar surf y otros deportes acuáticos, como en Cabo San Lucas y Puerto Escondido, en el Pacífico. En la costa de la Bahía de Campeche hay playas muy famosas, como Cancún. *¿Qué deportes acuáticos se practican en Estados Unidos? ¿En qué ciudad?* ▶

Joven haciendo surfing en Cabo San Lucas

La gran capital El Distrito Federal, o México D.F., tiene más de ocho millones de habitantes, es una zona cosmopolita, donde se concentra la actividad financiera y las principales universidades del país. *¿Cuáles son las ciudades de Estados Unidos con más habitantes?* ▼

Monumento a la Independencia (El Ángel), Paseo de la Reforma, México D.F.

UNIDAD 1

México

Lección 1

Tema:

Vamos a acampar

¡AVANZA! **In this lesson you will learn to**

- describe a camping trip
- talk about what you did with friends
- talk about nature

using

- preterite tense of regular verbs
- irregular preterites

¿Recuerdas?

- irregular present tense
- stem-changing verbs in the preterite

Comparación cultural

In this lesson you will learn about

- nature in Mexico
- geography of Mexico

Compara con tu mundo

Esta familia está acampando. Acaba de preparar su tienda de campaña *(tent)*. *¿Hay lugares para acampar en tu región? ¿Cómo son?*

¿Qué ves?

Mira la foto

¿Cómo está la familia? ¿Contenta? ¿Seria?

¿Qué ropa llevan todos?

¿Cómo son los hijos? ¿Y los padres?

¿Cuántos años crees que tienen?

Online SPANISH CLASSZONE.COM

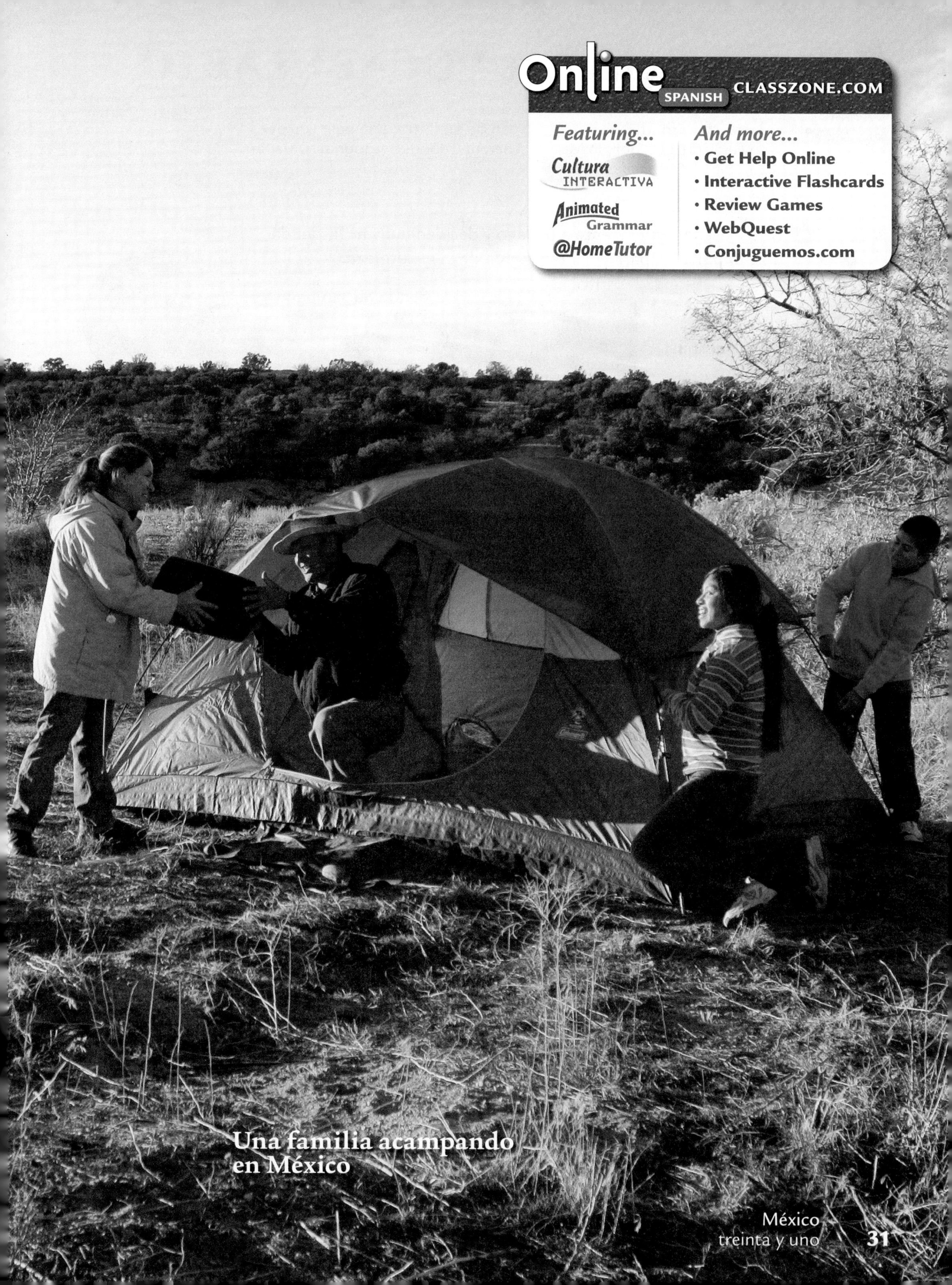

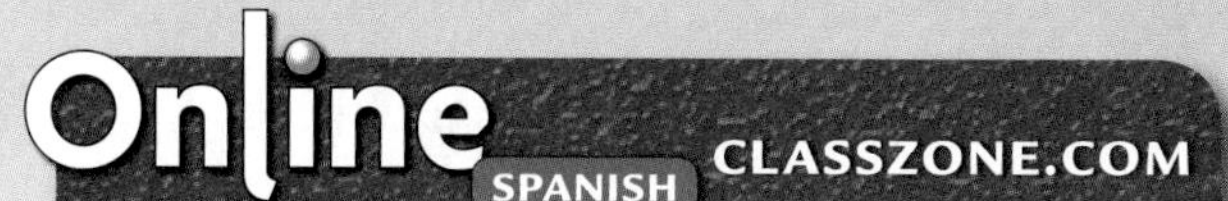

Featuring...
- Cultura INTERACTIVA
- Animated Grammar
- @HomeTutor

And more...
- Get Help Online
- Interactive Flashcards
- Review Games
- WebQuest
- Conjuguemos.com

Una familia acampando en México

Presentación de VOCABULARIO

¡AVANZA! **Goal:** Learn what activities you can do and the equipment you need to enjoy the outdoors in Mexico. Then talk about outdoor activities and camping. ***Actividades 1–3***

AUDIO

A Estos jóvenes están **frente a** un lago y deciden **montar la tienda de campaña** allí para estar más cerca de **la naturaleza.**

B La tienda debe quedar cerrada para **las arañas, serpientes** u otros animales. Deben estar **sin** zapatos **dentro** de la tienda; por eso, antes de **meterse,** deben dejar los zapatos **fuera.**

C Es necesario tener **fósforos** para **encender la fogata** y una **cantimplora,** que siempre deben **llenar** con agua.

D Hay muchas actividades que pueden hacer **al aire libre.** Por ejemplo, pueden **hacer caminatas** por los **senderos del bosque** y mirar **los árboles** y **las flores,** o **hacer una excursión junto al río.**

la estufa de gas

las ollas

el saco de dormir

hacer una caminata

escalar montañas

Más vocabulario

agotador *exhausting*
el albergue juvenil *youth hostel*
la camioneta *SUV, truck*
el equipo *equipment*
al extranjero *abroad*
observar *to observe*
la selva *jungle*
Expansión de vocabulario p. R2
Ya sabes p. R2

E Antes de encontrar un lugar para acampar deben **conseguir** información sobre **las tarifas.** Muchos lugares **ofrecen descuentos** a los estudiantes y pueden **ahorrar** dinero.

¡Inolvidable!

El Sol Mexicano es el lugar perfecto para **divertirse,** acampar y tener una experiencia **inolvidable.**

Pueden ver muchos **pájaros** y **mariposas.** Les damos **una guía** con fotos del lugar y con las direcciones que deben **seguir** para llegar.

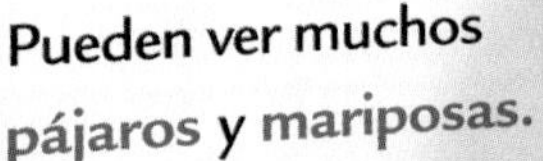

Pueden **utilizar el transporte público;** la parada del autobús está a cinco minutos de aquí.

¡Tarifas especiales para estudiantes!

¡Actividades y deportes!

A muchas personas les gusta **remar** en **el río** y pasar horas en **kayac.**

¡Los más valientes deciden **navegar por rápidos!**

En los lugares de **agua dulce** hay una variedad de **peces** para las personas que desean pescar.

¡Llamen **con anticipación** para hacer reservaciones!

Nuestro teléfono: (888)111-1111

¡A responder! Escuchar

Escucha la lista de actividades. Para cada actividad, haz la mímica que corresponde. *(Mimic the activities as you hear them.)*

@HomeTutor
Interactive Flashcards
ClassZone.com

Práctica de VOCABULARIO

1 ¿Para qué es?

Hablar
Escribir

Escoge uno de los verbos para explicar el uso de los siguientes artículos.

cocinar	poner líquido
dormir	conseguir información
encender	acampar

modelo: la tienda de campaña: acampar

1. el saco de dormir
2. las ollas
3. la cantimplora
4. la estufa de gas
5. la guía sobre la región
6. los fósforos

2 ¿Por qué prefieres eso?

Hablar

Entrevista a un(a) compañero(a) para saber sus preferencias.

modelo: transporte público / automóvil

A: ¿Prefieres utilizar el transporte público o un automóvil? ¿Por qué?

B: Prefiero el transporte público para ahorrar dinero.

1. albergue juvenil / tienda de campaña
2. fogata / estufa de gas
3. frente al río / junto a un árbol
4. remar / pescar
5. usar una guía / perderse en el bosque
6. las arañas / las serpientes
7. escalar montañas / remar en kayac
8. los pájaros / los peces

Expansión
Compara tus preferencias con las de tu compañero(a). ¿Ustedes son compatibles para viajar? Escribe un resumen.

3 ¡Preguntas, preguntas!

Hablar
Escribir

Contesta las siguientes preguntas. Recuerda las palabras que aprendiste.

1. ¿Qué tipos de transporte público hay donde tú vives?
2. ¿Qué haces para ahorrar antes de un viaje?
3. ¿Cómo te diviertes al aire libre?
4. ¿Qué te gusta de la naturaleza?
5. ¿Qué miras cuando caminas por un sendero del bosque?
6. ¿Te parecen interesantes los albergues juveniles? ¿Por qué?

Más práctica Cuaderno *pp. 1–3* Cuaderno para hispanohablantes *pp. 1–4*

¿Comprendiste?
1. ¿Qué equipo necesitas para acampar?
2. Menciona tres actividades para hacer al aire libre.

VOCABULARIO en contexto

¡AVANZA! **Goal:** Learn about the outdoor activities Javier is planning for his trip. Then talk about these activities and who will be doing them. ***Actividades 4–5***

 *¿Recuerdas?* Irregular present tense p. 8

Contexto 1 *Póster*

ESTRATEGIA **Leer**

Make a mind-map In the center, write **el viaje.** In attached circles, write key phrases from the reading **(las fechas, el equipo, los compañeros de viaje)**. Attach more circles to show as many details as you can.

AUDIO

Javier Medina preparó un póster para la sección de anuncios del Club Deportivo de su escuela. Busca dos compañeros para hacer una excursión con él y con su padre desde México D.F. hasta la Península de Yucatán este verano.

Club Deportivo
ANUNCIOS

¡Viaje de aventura inolvidable!
¡Tengo camioneta, necesito compañeros (y equipos)!

Excursión por México, este verano

Vamos a visitar:
- la selva de la Península de Yucatán para observar su naturaleza: pájaros y peces exóticos, mariposas raras y flores bonitas
- las ruinas de Chichén Itzá y Uxmal
- un albergue juvenil frente a un parque ecológico con todo tipo de flora y fauna
- el río Pahuatlán para navegar por rápidos en kayac
- los volcanes al sur de la ciudad de México para escalar montañas

Todavía tenemos que decidir:
- las fechas exactas del viaje
- el equipo que tenemos que utilizar durante el viaje y una lista de las cosas que tenemos que conseguir
- el itinerario y los sitios donde podemos acampar en la ruta

Para formar parte del grupo tienes que escribir a 2medina05@mexnex.net con anticipación.
¡Sólo tengo espacio para cuatro personas en total, además del equipo!

¿Te animas?

4 Comprensión del póster

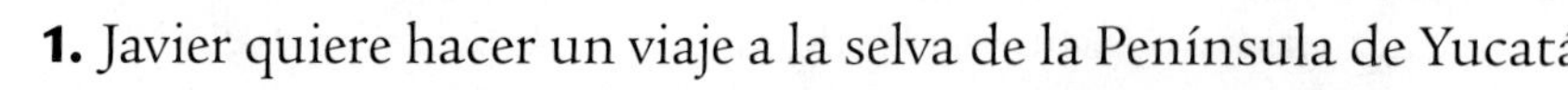

Hablar
Escribir

Di si las siguientes oraciones sobre la lectura son ciertas o falsas. Si son falsas, corrígelas.

1. Javier quiere hacer un viaje a la selva de la Península de Yucatán.
2. En la camioneta hay espacio para cuatro personas.
3. Javier ya tiene todo el equipo que necesita para hacer un viaje inolvidable.
4. Las personas interesadas deben escribir con anticipación.
5. Los planes incluyen escalar montañas, navegar por rápidos y acampar.
6. Javier debe hacer un itinerario con sitios para montar la tienda de campaña en la ruta.

5 ¿Qué tienen que hacer? *¿Recuerdas?* Irregular present tense p. 8

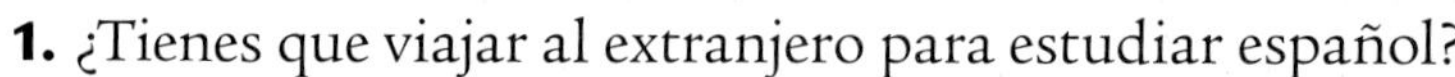

Hablar
Escribir

Contesta las siguientes preguntas con oraciones completas.

modelo: ¿Tienes que ahorrar dinero?
Sí, tengo que ahorrar dinero.

1. ¿Tienes que viajar al extranjero para estudiar español?
2. ¿A cuántas personas tiene que observar el (la) maestro(a) en la clase de español?
3. ¿Qué tienen que llevar las personas cuando van a acampar al bosque?
4. ¿Qué tiene que hacer Lorena cuando está en un kayac?
5. ¿Tienes que hacer reservaciones para ir a un albergue juvenil?
6. ¿Qué tienes que leer para no perderte en un área para acampar?

Expansión
Con un(a) compañero(a), escribe una lista de cinco cosas que tienen que hacer antes de salir de vacaciones.

AUDIO

Pronunciación La letra c con a, o, u

La combinación de la **c** con las vocales **a, o, u,** o con una consonante produce el sonido /k/. Su posición en la palabra no afecta nunca la pronunciación.

cargar	**conseguir**	**cuatro**	**crudo**
escalar	**saco de dormir**	**descuento**	**activo**

Trabalenguas

¿Cómo come usted en Como?
Como en Como como en Como come usted.

PARA Y PIENSA

¿Comprendiste? ¿Cuáles de las siguientes actividades menciona Javier en su póster?

1. navegar por rápidos
2. tomar el transporte público
3. escalar montañas
4. meterse en la tienda de campaña

Presentación de GRAMÁTICA

¡AVANZA! **Goal:** Review the conjugations of regular verbs in the preterite. Then practice by talking about what happened during a trip or vacation. ***Actividades 6–9***

English Grammar Connection: In English, the past tense of a regular verb is formed by simply adding *-ed* to the end of the infinitive form.

to climb *becomes* **I climbed** **escalar** *becomes* **Yo escalé**

REPASO Preterite Tense of Regular Verbs

Animated Grammar ClassZone.com

Use the **preterite** to talk about actions that you or others completed in the past.

Here's how:

Note that **-er** *and* **-ir** *verbs have the same endings.*

Preterite of Regular Verbs

	escalar	correr	salir
yo	**escalé**	**corrí**	**salí**
tú	**escalaste**	**corriste**	**saliste**
usted, él, ella	**escaló**	**corrió**	**salió**
nosotros(as)	**escalamos**	**corrimos**	**salimos**
vosotros(as)	**escalasteis**	**corristeis**	**salisteis**
ustedes, ellos(as)	**escalaron**	**corrieron**	**salieron**

Escalé una montaña hoy.
I climbed *a mountain today.*

Salimos de la casa a las cinco de la mañana.
We left *the house at five o'clock in the morning.*

Verbs ending in **-car, -gar,** and **-zar** have a spelling change in the **yo** form to preserve pronunciation. All other forms are regular.

Verbs with Spelling Changes in the Preterite yo Form

	(c → qu)	(g → gu)	(z → c)
	practicar	**navegar**	**organizar**
yo	**practiqué**	**navegué**	**organicé**
tú	**praticaste**	**navegaste**	**organizaste**

¿Quién **organizó** la excursión?
Who ***organized*** *the trip?*

Yo **organicé** la excursión.
I organized *the trip.*

Más práctica
Cuaderno *pp. 4–6*
Cuaderno para hispanohablantes *pp. 5–7*

Conjuguemos.com

@HomeTutor
Leveled Practice
ClassZone.com

Práctica de GRAMÁTICA

6 ¿Qué pasó el fin de semana?

Escuchar
Escribir

Escucha el diálogo y escribe oraciones para decir cómo pasaron el fin de semana. Usa las actividades del banco de frases.

modelo: Marta
Marta navegó por rápidos.

1. Alberto
2. Ernesto
3. Marta y Alberto
4. Silvia

navegar por rápidos
divertirse
escalar una montaña
limpiar la olla
llenar las cantimploras

Expansión
Escoge tres verbos regulares más y escribe lo que tú y tus amigos hicieron durante una aventura al aire libre.

7 ¡Qué divertido!

Escribir

Sara le escribió un correo electrónico a su amigo Víctor para contarle lo que pasó durante su aventura en el campo. Completa su mensaje con la forma correcta de los siguientes verbos.

pasarlo bien	asustarse
quedarse	aprender
descubrir	cocinar
observar	remar

Hola Víctor,

Mi hermana y yo viajamos al campo la semana pasada. ¡Pensamos **1.** y fue genial! Yo **2.** mucho sobre la naturaleza de la zona y **3.** muchos árboles y mariposas. Silvia **4.** por horas en su kayac. En la noche, nosotras **5.** cerca del río. ¡Qué ricos son los peces de agua dulce! Luego **6.** en los sacos de dormir, al aire libre, fuera de la tienda. Una noche Silvia **7.** una araña en su saco de dormir y **8.** un poco. Fue una semana agotadora pero inolvidable.

Comparación cultural

La naturaleza y el arte

¿En qué se inspiran los artistas? El muralista Gerardo Murillo nació en **México** en 1875. Cambió su nombre a «Dr. Atl», que quiere decir «Doctor Agua» en náhuatl. Dr. Atl se inspiró en la naturaleza de su país para pintar paisajes.

Compara con tu mundo *¿Qué tipo de geografía ves en esta pintura? Menciona lugares así en Estados Unidos.*

Volcán Iztlaccíhuatl *(1934), Gerardo Murillo*

8 Las vacaciones pasadas

Hablar

Pregúntale a tu compañero(a) si hizo las actividades que se muestran en las fotos.

modelo: abrazar

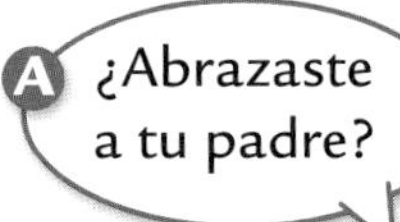

B Sí, (No, no) abracé a mi padre.

1. buscar

2. sacar

3. llegar

4. navegar

5. utilizar

6. almorzar

7. organizar

8. tocar

9. jugar

9 Cosas en común

Escribir
Hablar

Escribe una lista con las diez actividades más interesantes de tus últimas vacaciones. Luego, di qué actividades hicieron tus amigos.

modelo: Yo visité el parque nacional de Yellowstone y mi amigo Joaquín visitó el parque nacional Glacier.

Más práctica Cuaderno *pp. 4–6* Cuaderno para hispanohablantes *pp. 5–7*

¿Comprendiste? Usa el pretérito para explicar estas actividades:

Get Help Online
ClassZone.com

1. yo / utilizar la estufa de gas
2. los vendedores / ofrecer un descuento
3. nosotros / seguir el sendero
4. yo / pagar la tarifa más barata

GRAMÁTICA en contexto

¡AVANZA! **Goal:** ***Show what you know*** Notice how Luis, Roberto, and Tomás use the preterite in their emails to Javier. Then practice using the preterite to talk about the outdoor activities they discussed. ***Actividades 10–12***

Contexto 2 *Correos electrónicos*

ESTRATEGIA Leer
Use a table to review verb tenses in context Copy and complete this table with verbs from the reading.

Verbo	Tiempo		Frase
	presente	pretérito	
quiero	√		*quiero formar parte del grupo*

AUDIO

Javier Medina busca dos compañeros con equipo de acampar para hacer un viaje a la Península de Yucatán este verano. Tres estudiantes contestaron el anuncio de Javier y escribieron para reservar un sitio en su camioneta.

Enviar | Enviar y archivar | Guardar

¡Hola, Javier!
¡Leí tu anuncio y quiero formar parte del grupo! No puedo viajar durante el mes de junio, pero sí en julio o agosto. Mi familia y yo viajamos a EE.UU. el verano pasado y acampamos en varios parques. Tengo una tienda de campaña para cuatro personas y cuatro sacos de dormir.
Espero tu respuesta con más información sobre el viaje. ¡Hasta pronto!

Luis Mendoza :-)

Hola,

Quiero participar en el viaje que describiste en tu anuncio. El problema es que sólo puedo ir durante los meses de junio y julio. Mis amigos y yo acampamos mucho, pero no tengo mucho equipo. Tengo una estufa de gas y unas ollas que usé en el último viaje. También tengo una cantimplora y un kayac. ¿Tenemos espacio para el kayac?

¡Gracias!

Roberto Durín

Hola,

Leí tu anuncio sobre el viaje. ¡Qué padre! El año pasado conseguí una tienda de campaña para dos personas y tres sacos de dormir. También compré una estufa de gas. Pero sólo puedo ir durante el mes de julio.

¿Piensas ir a Cancún? Mis amigos y yo organizamos una excursión allí hace dos años y nos divertimos mucho. ¡Es genial! ¡Espero más información!

Tomás Gutiérrez

También se dice

En el correo electrónico, Tomás usa la palabra **padre** para decir que la idea del viaje le gusta mucho y le parece genial.

- **Argentina** **bárbaro**
- **España** **guay**
- **Cuba** **volao**
- **Venezuela** **chévere**

10 Comprensión de los correos electrónicos

Hablar
Escribir

Contesta las siguientes preguntas según la información de los correos electrónicos.

1. ¿Qué tipo de tienda de campaña tiene Tomás?
2. ¿Adónde viajó Tomás con sus amigos hace dos años?
3. ¿Adónde viajó la familia de Luis?
4. ¿Qué quiere llevar Roberto para usar en el agua?
5. ¿En qué mes puede viajar Tomás?
6. ¿Roberto tiene experiencia para acampar?

11 ¡A escribir!

Escribir

Responde a uno de los correos electrónicos de la página 40. Usa las pistas para organizar tu respuesta:

Pistas: ¿Qué escribió esa persona y qué información adicional quieres? ¿Qué quieres preguntarle a esa persona sobre alguna experiencia que mencionó en su correo electrónico? ¿Tienes alguna pregunta más sobre equipo o fechas? ¿Tienes alguna pregunta sobre personalidad, gustos o preferencias de esa persona?

Expansión
Escribe un correo electrónico a un(a) amigo(a) para invitarlo(la) a un viaje.

12 ¿Cómo te divertiste?

Hablar

Habla con un(a) compañero(a) sobre sus últimas vacaciones. Usa las siguientes pistas:

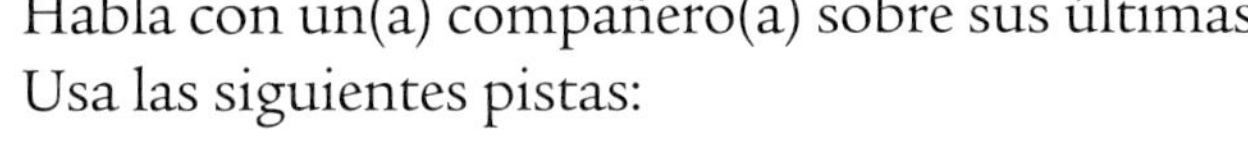

Pistas: ¿viajar?, ¿conocer lugares?, ¿ practicar deportes?, ¿disfrutar de actividades al aire libre?, ¿usar equipo para acampar?, ¿actividades más y menos preferidas?, ¿tarifas caras?

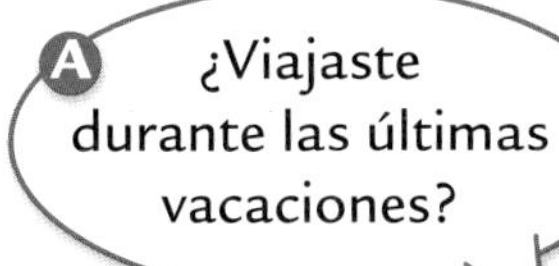

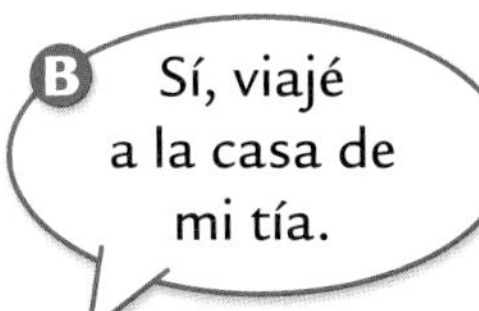

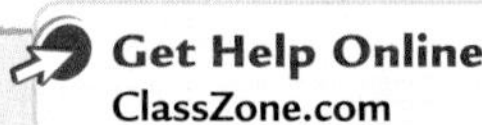

¿Comprendiste? Escoge el verbo correcto, según la lectura, e indica la conjugación apropiada para cada oración.

1. Tomás _____ una excursión a Cancún hace dos años.
2. Luis y su familia _____ a Estados Unidos el verano pasado.
3. Yo _____ una estufa de gas cuando viajé.

Presentación de GRAMÁTICA

¡AVANZA! **Goal:** Review the forms of irregular verbs in the preterite. Then practice by talking about outdoor activities in the past. ***Actividades 13–16***

English Grammar Connection: Many verbs in English and in Spanish have irregular forms in the past tense.

you **bring** *becomes* you **brought** tú **traes** *becomes* tú **trajiste**

REPASO Irregular Preterites

Animated Grammar ClassZone.com

The following verbs have **irregular stems** and **irregular endings** in the **preterite.**

Here's how:

i-Stem Verbs		u-Stem Verbs		uv-Stem Verbs		Preterite Endings	
hacer	**hic-/hiz-***	**haber**	**hub-**	**andar**	**anduv-**	**-e**	**-imos**
querer	**quis-**	**poder**	**pud-**	**estar**	**estuv-**	**-iste**	**-isteis**
venir	**vin-**	**poner**	**pus-**	**tener**	**tuv-**	**-o**	**-ieron**
		saber	**sup-**				

*The stem of **hacer** is **hiz-** for the **usted/él/ella** form only. *(Ella **hizo** la tarea.)*

j-Stem Verbs		Preterite Endings	
decir	**dij-**	**-e**	**-imos**
traer	**traj-**	**-iste**	**-isteis**
conducir	**conduj-**	**-o**	**-eron**

Other Irregular Verbs in the Preterite

ser *and* ir	dar	ver
fui	di	vi
fuiste	diste	viste
fue	dio	vio
fuimos	dimos	vimos
fuisteis	disteis	visteis
fueron	dieron	vieron

*The verbs **dar** and **ver** have regular **-er/-ir** preterite endings but with no written accent marks.*

Más práctica

Cuaderno *pp. 7–9*

Cuaderno para hispanohablantes *pp. 8–11*

Conjuguemos.com

@HomeTutor Leveled Practice ClassZone.com

Práctica de GRAMÁTICA

13 ¿Qué hicieron?

Escribir

Completa las oraciones según el modelo. Usa cada verbo en la forma apropiada del pretérito.

modelo: Irma / andar / por el sendero con tres amigos
Irma anduvo por el sendero con tres amigos.

1. Javier / ir / a la tienda de deportes
2. Lupita y Marín / hacer / una excursión inolvidable
3. todos / decir / que era hora de comer
4. yo / caminar / al centro comercial
5. tú / traer / la tarjeta de crédito
6. nosotros / tener que / sacar dinero del banco

REPASO gramatical Stem-changing verbs in the preterite p. R32

Verbs ending in **-ar** and **-er** that have a stem change in the present tense do not have a stem change in the preterite. Verbs ending in **-ir** that have a stem change in the present tense change from **o** → **u** or **e** → **i** in the forms of **usted/él/ella** and **ustedes/ellos/ellas** in the preterite.

dormir (**ue**, **u**)	**divertir** (**ie**, **i**)
Nosotros **dormimos** en casa.	Yo **me divertí** mucho.
Ellas **durmieron** al aire libre.	Usted **se divirtió** también.

14 Una excursión al campo

Hablar
Escribir

Describe qué hicieron estas personas durante su excursión al campo.

modelo: Ana y Marta se despidieron antes de ir a casa.

Ana y Marta	divertirse	agua para todos
Jorge	dormir	navegar por rápidos
Mis amigos y yo	seguir	con botas
ustedes	despedirse	en el kayac
Tú	conseguir	en el saco de dormir
Silvia	preferir	el sendero
Jaime	vestirse	antes de ir a casa

15 ¡Qué aventura!

Hablar

Uno(a) de los (las) estudiantes se perdió durante la excursión. Entrevista a ese(a) estudiante para saber algo de sus experiencias.

modelo: ¿cuántos días / estar perdido?

A ¿Cuántos días estuviste perdido(a)?

B Estuve perdido(a) cuatro días.

1. ¿cómo / conseguir comida y agua?
2. ¿qué / utilizar para hacer una fogata?
3. ¿dónde / tener que dormir?
4. ¿tener problemas con algún animal?
5. ¿tener mucho o poco miedo?
6. ¿cómo / sentirse cuando te encontraron?
7. ¿qué / decirte tus amigos(as) cuando te vieron?

Expansión
Escribe un artículo con las respuestas de la entrevista.

16 A acampar en Chipinque

Leer
Escribir

Comparación cultural

Monterrey y sus parques

¿Cómo influye la geografía de un país en las formas de diversión? Cerca de la ciudad de Monterrey, en el norte de **México,** hay varios parques ecológicos famosos: El parque Cola de Caballo con su hermosa cascada *(waterfall)*, La Mesa Chipinque y el Parque Ecológico de Chipinque, que está en las montañas de La Sierra Madre. La gente siempre utilizó este lugar al aire libre, hizo excursiones y se divirtió sin dañar la naturaleza. Allí se puede montar tiendas de campaña y ayudar a conservar el lugar.

Cascada Cola de Caballo

Compara con tu mundo *¿Qué parques ecológicos hay en tu estado? ¿Qué actividades ofrecen? ¿Cómo es el paisaje?*

Contesta las preguntas con oraciones completas.

1. ¿Qué actividades hizo la gente en el Parque de Chipinque?
2. ¿Qué pudieron montar los que quisieron dormir en el parque?
3. ¿Desde cuándo la gente utilizó este lugar?

Más práctica Cuaderno *pp. 7–9* Cuaderno para hispanohablantes *pp. 8–11*

Get Help Online
ClassZone.com

¿Comprendiste? Pregúntales a tus amigos(as) si hicieron lo siguiente. ¡Cuidado con los cambios verbales!

1. tener descuentos en las tarifas
2. poner el equipo en la camioneta
3. dormir bien en el saco de dormir

Todo junto

¡AVANZA! **Goal:** ***Show what you know*** Notice the preterite verb forms that Javier and his family use to talk about the emails he received. Then talk about outdoor activities using verbs in the preterite. ***Actividades 17–20***

Resumen contextos 1 y 2 Javier Medina recibió tres correos electrónicos como resultado de un póster que puso en su escuela. Cada persona escribió con información sobre el equipo para acampar y la experiencia que tienen para hacer un viaje desde el D.F. hasta la Península de Yucatán este verano.

Contexto 3 *Diálogo*

ESTRATEGIA **Escuchar**
Analyze the situation with a flow chart List the concerns raised by Javier's mother and father. What do they do to help? What happens as a result?

AUDIO

Ahora, Javier habla con sus padres para escoger a las dos personas ideales para hacer el viaje a Yucatán.

Javier: Mamá, es difícil escoger a las dos personas ideales.

Madre: Claro, pero tienes que enfocarte en el equipo necesario para el viaje. Van a ser cuatro personas, incluido tu papá, y como tú no tienes nada más que la camioneta...

Javier: Papá me puede dar más dinero.

Padre: ¡Ya te di mucho, Javier! ¡Te presté la camioneta y me escogiste como la persona adulta para ir con ustedes!

Javier: ¡Sí, sí, papi, ya lo sé! A ver... Luis dijo que tiene una tienda de campaña para cuatro personas y cuatro sacos de dormir. Tomás dijo que tiene una tienda para dos personas y tres sacos de dormir. Y Roberto... no tiene tienda, pero tiene una estufa de gas, unas ollas, una cantimplora y un kayac.

Madre: Tenemos que considerar las fechas posibles para el viaje. Luis dijo que no puede viajar en junio, y Tomás dijo que sólo puede viajar en julio.

Javier: Y Roberto dijo que sólo puede viajar en junio o julio.

Padre: Ay, ¡basta! Es como un problema de lógica... ¡demasiado agotador para mí!

Madre: Mira, Javier, busqué papel y lápiz, y preparé una tabla comparando todos los datos.

Javier: ¡Mucho mejor! Hiciste la tabla y ahora puedo ver la situación con más detalle.

Padre: Bueno, es demasiado para mí. Nunca me gustó este tipo de problemas. ¡Me voy a ver la tele!

Madre: Bueno, Javier, ¿empezamos a decidir quién viaja?

Javier: ¡Manos a la obra!

17 Comprensión del diálogo

Escuchar
Hablar

Di a quién describen las siguientes oraciones.

1. Dijo que no le gustan los problemas de lógica.
2. Hizo una tabla para analizar la información.
3. Dijo que lo más importante es pensar en el equipo necesario.
4. Dijo que es difícil escoger a las dos personas ideales.
5. Salió y no participó en la solución del problema.
6. Dijo que alguien puede darle más dinero.

18 ¡A decidir quién viaja!

Escribir

Según el diálogo, haz una tabla como la que hizo la mamá de Javier. Compara el equipo de Luis, Roberto y Tomás, y las fechas en que pueden viajar. Luego, decide quiénes son los candidatos apropiados para el viaje y escribe por qué.

	Luis	Roberto	Tomás
Equipo			
Fechas			

19 Integración

Leer
Escuchar
Hablar

Lee este artículo de una revista sobre un campamento en México. Luego, escucha el mensaje sobre el problema con tu reservación. Decide qué quieres hacer y llama al campamento para explicar tu decisión.

Fuente 1 Artículo de opinión

Aire y Sol
Correo de lectores

Un campamento inolvidable
por Leandro Mir

El mes pasado fui al campamento Sol Maya, cerca de la reserva natural Agua Azul. Tuvimos que hacer reservaciones con anticipación para conseguir el mejor lugar: un sitio frente al río. Cuando llegamos, montamos la tienda de campaña y encendimos una fogata. Esa noche dormimos muy bien. Al día siguiente hicimos caminatas por el bosque. Un día navegamos por los rápidos en un kayac y el último día utilizamos el transporte público para visitar las ruinas de Uxmal. Son increíbles.

Fuente 2 Un mensaje por teléfono

Escucha y apunta

- ¿Qué problema hay con tu reservación?
- ¿Qué tienes que hacer?

modelo: Hola, llamo porque quise hacer una reservación en su campamento pero me dijeron que no hay lugar. No puedo ir en otra fecha pero ustedes me dijeron que me pueden recomendar otro campamento.

20 Una tarjeta postal

Escribir

Escríbele una tarjeta postal a un(a) amigo(a) o pariente y explica qué hiciste en ese lugar durante tus vacaciones. Usa verbos regulares e irregulares.

Pistas: ¿Adónde fuiste? ¿Con quién(es)? ¿Qué hiciste? ¿Qué sorpresa tuviste?

Writing Criteria	Excellent	Good	Needs Work
Content	Your postcard addresses all of the questions.	Your postcard addresses some of the questions.	Your postcard addresses few of the questions.
Communication	Your postcard is organized and easy to follow.	Parts of your postcard are organized and easy to follow.	Your postcard is disorganized and hard to follow.
Accuracy	You make few mistakes in grammar and vocabulary.	You make some mistakes in grammar and vocabulary.	You make many mistakes in grammar and vocabulary.

Más práctica Cuaderno *pp. 10–11* Cuaderno para hispanohablantes *pp. 12–13*

PARA Y PIENSA

¿Comprendiste? Escribe las siguientes oraciones en el pretérito.

1. Tienes que enfocarte en el equipo necesario.
2. ¡Es como un problema de lógica!
3. El padre le presta la camioneta.

Get Help Online
ClassZone.com

Lectura literaria

¡AVANZA! **Goal:** Read and listen to the poetry of a Mexican author and analyze the references to nature.

Para leer 

ESTRATEGIA Leer

Look for cognates Draw a spider map like the one below, and write down at least four cognates that you find in the poems "Hermandad" or "Viento, agua, piedra."

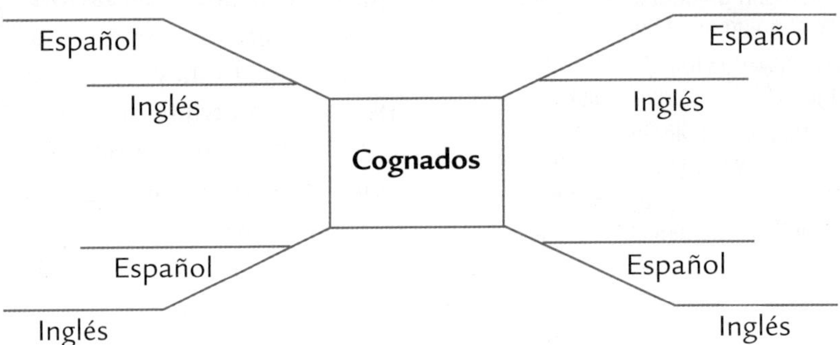

Vocabulario para leer

Hermandad

durar *mantenerse en un lugar, permanecer*
hacia *preposición que indica a dónde nos dirigimos*
deletrear *nombrar las letras que forman una palabra*

Viento, agua, piedra

horadar *hacer una perforación en un objeto*
la copa *vaso con pie, que sirve para beber*
giros *cambios de dirección, cambios de movimiento*
vacío *que no contiene nada*
desvanecerse *no existir más, desaparecer, deshacerse*

Nota cultural

Sobre el autor ***Octavio Paz (1914–1998)***
Obtuvo gran fama con su libro *El laberinto de la soledad,* donde describe la psicología de los mexicanos. En 1990 recibió el premio Nobel de literatura. Al aceptar el premio comentó: «Los españoles encontraron en México no sólo una geografía sino una historia».

Sobre la naturaleza Muchos poetas se inspiran en la naturaleza. México presenta una geografía muy variada: sierras, desierto, costas y bosques. Frecuentemente, los poetas y escritores mexicanos reflejan esta riqueza natural en sus obras, como hizo Octavio Paz en «Viento, agua, piedra».

Big Dipper, *El Hortelano*

Hermandad

AUDIO

Soy hombre: duro poco
y es enorme la noche.
Pero miro hacia arriba:
las estrellas escriben.
Sin entender comprendo:
también soy escritura
y en este mismo instante
alguien me deletrea.

A pensar
¿Con qué se compara el narrador del poema?

Reflexiona

¿Qué características tienen el narrador, la noche y las estrellas en el poema? ¿Cómo crees que se siente el narrador?

Tornado *(1941), Mario Carreño*

VIENTO, AGUA, PIEDRA

AUDIO

El agua horada la piedra,
el viento dispersa el agua,
la piedra detiene al viento.
Agua, viento, piedra.

El viento esculpe[1] la piedra,
la piedra es copa del agua,
el agua escapa y es viento.
Piedra, viento, agua.

El viento en sus giros canta,
el agua al andar murmura,
la piedra inmóvil se calla[2].
Viento, agua, piedra.

Uno es otro y es ninguno:
entre sus nombres vacíos
pasan y se desvanecen
agua, piedra, viento. ❖

---

[1] carves [2] **se...** stops talking

❖ A pensar
¿Qué acciones se asocian con el agua, el viento y la piedra? ¿Con qué puedes comparar el agua, el viento y la piedra?

Reflexiona

¿Qué relación hay entre los tres elementos descritos en el poema?

¿Comprendiste?

1. ¿Por qué el autor usa el título «Hermandad»?
2. En el poema «Hermandad», ¿cómo cambia la actitud del narrador desde el principio hasta el final?
3. ¿Por qué cambia el autor el orden de los elementos en el título y en la última línea de cada estrofa de «Viento, agua, piedra»?
4. ¿Qué describe la conclusión del poema «Viento, agua, piedra»?

¿Y tú?

¿Cómo presentan los dos poemas la naturaleza? ¿Estás de acuerdo con el autor?

Conexiones *Las ciencias naturales*

Mariposas migratorias

¿Sabes que la mariposa monarca es el insecto nacional de Estados Unidos? Esta hermosa mariposa anaranjada y negra alegra la naturaleza del país durante el verano. En el otoño, comienza su viaje al sur, para pasar el invierno en los bosques de las montañas de México central. En marzo, los insectos abandonan México y comienzan su viaje de regreso a Estados Unidos.

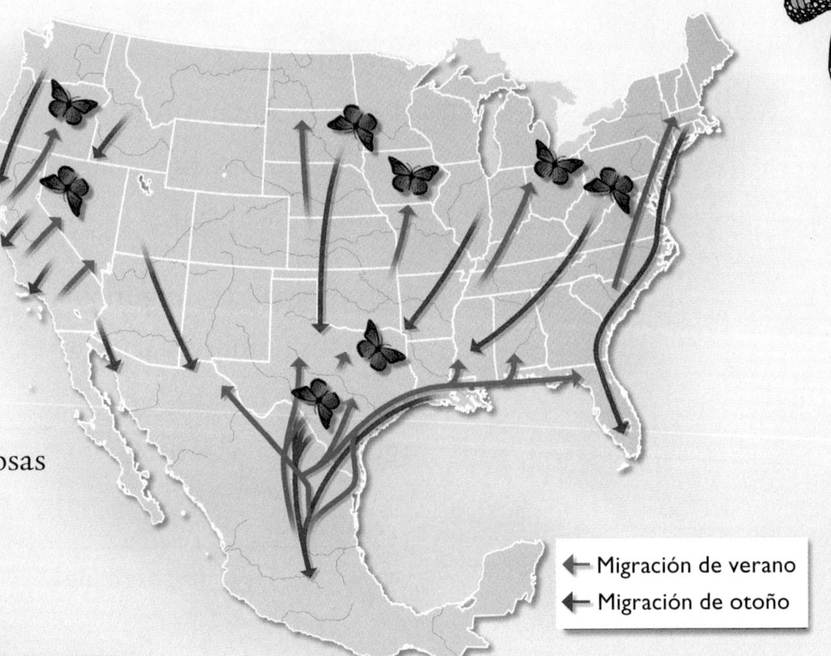

Después de una larga migración, más de 250 millones de mariposas monarcas descansan en grandes colonias de más de 10 mil, que cubren los troncos[1] y las ramas[2] de los árboles. Hay reservas importantes de mariposas monarcas cerca del D.F., en Valle de Bravo y en el estado de Michoacán.

El ciclo de vida de una mariposa monarca es bastante[3] corto. Muchos de los insectos que completan la migración a México nacieron[4] durante el viaje y pueden ser los nietos[5] o biznietos[6] de las mariposas que empezaron el viaje en Estados Unidos.

[1] trunks [2] branches [3] quite
[4] were born [5] grandchildren [6] great-grandchildren

Proyecto Investiga el ciclo de vida de las mariposas monarcas en una página web en español. ¿Cuántas etapas *(stages)* tiene? ¿Qué formas toma el insecto durante su ciclo de vida? ¿Cuánto tiempo toma cada etapa, desde el huevo hasta la muerte?

En tu comunidad

¿Hay mariposas monarcas en tu comunidad? ¿Hay muchas o pocas? ¿Qué plantas y flores prefieren?

Haz un análisis del ecosistema donde tú vives y determina hasta qué punto tu comunidad les ofrece a las mariposas monarcas el hábitat que necesitan.

Lección 1

En resumen

Vocabulario y gramática

Vocabulario

Describe a Camping Trip

al aire libre	*outdoors*	la fogata	*campfire*	la tienda de campaña	*tent*
el albergue juvenil	*youth hostel*	el fósforo	*match*	el transporte público	*public transportation*
la camioneta	*SUV, truck*	la guía	*guide*	hacer una caminata	*to take a walk*
la cantimplora	*water bottle, canteen*	el kayac	*kayak*		
el descuento	*discount*	la olla	*pot*		
el equipo	*equipment*	el saco de dormir	*sleeping bag*		
la estufa (de gas)	*(gas) stove*	la tarifa	*fare*		

Talk About What You Did with Friends

ahorrar	*to save (money, time)*	hacer una excursión	*to go on an excursion, guided tour*	navegar	*to navigate, to sail*
conseguir	*to get, to find*	llenar	*to fill up*	observar	*to observe*
divertirse (ie, i)	*to enjoy, to have fun*	meterse en	*to go into*	ofrecer	*to offer*
encender (ie)	*to light (a match), to make a fire, to turn on*	montar	*to put up*	remar	*to row*
escalar montañas	*to climb mountains*	navegar por rápidos	*to go whitewater rafting*	seguir (i, i)	*to follow*
				utilizar	*to use*

Talk About Nature

el agua dulce	*fresh water*	la naturaleza	*nature*
la araña	*spider*	el pájaro	*bird*
el árbol	*tree*	el pez	*fish*
el bosque	*forest, woods*	el río	*river*
la flor	*flower*	la selva	*jungle*
la mariposa	*butterfly*	el sendero	*path*
		la serpiente	*snake*

Other Words and Phrases

agotador(a)	*exhausting*
al extranjero	*abroad*
con anticipación	*in advance*
dentro	*inside*
frente a	*facing*
fuera (de)	*outside (of)*
inolvidable	*unforgettable*
junto a	*next to*
sin	*without*

Gramática

Nota gramatical: Stem-changing verbs in the preterite *p. 43*

REPASO Preterite Tense of Regular Verbs

Add the following endings to the stems of regular verbs.

-ar verbs		-er/-ir verbs	
-é	-amos	-í	-imos
-aste	-asteis	-iste	-isteis
-ó	-aron	-ió	-ieron

Verbs ending in **-car, -gar,** and **-zar** have a spelling change in the **yo** form.

practicar → **yo practiqué**
navegar → **yo navegué**
organizar → **yo organicé**

REPASO Irregular Preterites

These verbs have **irregular stems** in the **preterite**.

i-Stem	u-Stem	uv-Stem	j-Stem
hacer hic-/hiz-	**haber** hub-	**andar** anduv-	**decir** dij-
querer quis-	**poder** pud-	**estar** estuv-	**traer** traj-
venir vin-	**poner** pus-	**tener** tuv-	**conducir** conduj-
	saber sup-		

- **Ser** and **ir** have the same irregular conjugations.

fui	fuimos
fuiste	fuisteis
fue	fueron

- **Dar** and **ver** have regular **-aer/-ir** endings but with no written accent marks.

Lección 1

Repaso de la lección

¡LLEGADA!

@HomeTutor ClassZone.com

Now you can
- describe a camping trip
- talk about what you did with friends
- talk about nature

Using
- preterite tense of regular verbs
- irregular preterite
- stem-changing verbs in the preterite

To review
- vocabulary pp. 32–33

1 Listen and understand

AUDIO

Escucha a estas personas hablar de sus planes para el fin de semana. Luego, contesta las preguntas que siguen.

1. ¿Por qué quiere Susana salir de la ciudad este fin de semana?
2. ¿Qué sitio le recomienda Margarita a Susana?
3. ¿Qué planes tiene Margarita?
4. ¿Qué llevan Margarita y sus amigas?
5. ¿Qué piensan hacer Margarita y sus amigas para preparar la comida?
6. ¿Qué cosa necesita Susana para poder hacer la excursión?

To review
- preterite of regular verbs p. 37

2 Talk about nature

Usa los verbos entre paréntesis para completar la siguiente conversación sobre una excursión al campo que organizaron Marcos y sus hermanos.

Leo: Oye, Marcos, ¿(pasar) __1.__ unas vacaciones buenas?

Marcos: Sí, ¡estupendas! Mis hermanos y yo (organizar) __2.__ una excursión a las montañas para acampar.

Leo: ¡Qué suerte! ¿(Observar) __3.__ animales interesantes?

Marcos: Sí, yo (ver) __4.__ muchos pájaros exóticos y unas mariposas raras. Mis hermanos y yo (caminar) __5.__ por un sendero donde (descubrir) __6.__ unas flores increíbles.

Leo: ¿Y te (gustar) __7.__ dormir en la tienda de campaña?

Marcos: Sí, más o menos... Un hombre __8.__ (encontrar) una serpiente en el campamento, pero por suerte no (entrar) __9.__ en nuestra tienda.

Leo: ¡Qué susto!

Marcos: ¡Sí! Pero también (aprender) __10.__ mucho sobre la naturaleza.

To review
- preterite of irregular verbs p. 42
- preterite of stem-changing verbs p. 43

3 Describe a camping trip

Di qué hicieron las siguientes personas durante su excursión al aire libre.

modelo: yo / hacer una excursión al aire libre
Yo hice una excursión al aire libre

1. tú y yo / ir al Campamento Juventud
2. Elena / divertirse al aire libre
3. Javier / leer una guía sobre la Península de Yucatán
4. Marcela y Paula / dormir en una tienda de campaña
5. yo / llegar al albergue juvenil
6. Andrés / traer su perro al campo

To review
- regular and irregular verbs in the preterite pp. 37, 42

4 Talk about what you did with friends

Mira la siguiente lista de quehaceres y escribe oraciones para indicar qué tuvieron que hacer las personas indicadas durante su excursión al aire libre. Sigue el modelo.

modelo: Ricardo
Ricardo hizo la reservación.

yo: pagar al guía, organizar el equipaje
Esteban: conseguir tres sacos de dormir, ir al río por agua
Alicia: organizar el equipaje, llevar a todos en su auto
Ricardo: hacer la reservación, ir al río por agua
todos: montar las dos tiendas de campaña

1. Alicia y yo
2. Esteban y Ricardo
3. Alicia
4. Esteban
5. yo
6. todos

To review
- **Comparación cultural** pp. 38, 44

5 Nature and geography in Mexico

Comparación cultural

1. ¿Qué temas representó el Dr. Atl en sus pinturas?
2. ¿Por qué Gerardo Murillo se cambió el nombre?
3. ¿Qué hay cerca de la ciudad de Monterrey?
4. ¿Qué puedes hacer en el parque Chipinque?

Más práctica Cuaderno *pp. 12–23* Cuaderno para hispanohablantes *pp. 14–23*

Get Help Online
ClassZone.com

UNIDAD 1

México

Lección 2

Tema: Vamos a la playa

¡AVANZA! **In this lesson you will learn to**

- talk about family vacations
- discuss activities, skills, and abilities
- describe a place and its climate

using

- imperfect tense
- preterite vs. imperfect

¿Recuerdas?

- **saber** and **conocer**
- expressions of emotion

Comparación cultural

In this lesson you will learn about

- sports in Mexico
- Mexican fine art and family relationships
- cultural contrasts between two Mexican regions

Compara con tu mundo

Este sitio arqueológico de los mayas está en la costa del mar Caribe. Sus ruinas incluyen un castillo *(castle)* y un templo con pinturas en las paredes. *¿Hay un sitio arqueológico o un museo con objetos antiguos en tu región?*

¿Qué ves?

Mira la foto

¿Qué hay en la playa?

¿Qué hacen las personas?

¿Cómo son las ruinas?

Online SPANISH CLASSZONE.COM

Featuring...

Cultura INTERACTIVA

Animated Grammar

@HomeTutor

And more...

- Get Help Online
- Interactive Flashcards
- Review Games
- WebQuest
- Conjuguemos.com

Playa en la Península de Yucatán, ruinas de Tulum

Presentación de VOCABULARIO

¡AVANZA! **Goal:** Learn about the activities of various family members during a reunion in Mexico. Then talk about what you can do at the beach. ***Actividades 1–3***

AUDIO

A Hola, me llamo Sandra Zapata y soy de México. Mi familia siempre **se reúne** una vez al año. La reunión de **los parientes** puede durar varios días o puede ser una **escapada** de fin de semana.

La reunión de la familia Zapata

En esta foto que tomé hace dos años, vemos a mi familia en la playa. Algunas de estas personas **se parecen** muchísimo y otras no se parecen **en absoluto.** Claro, también hay personas con otro **apellido.** Por ejemplo, la hija del Sr. Patricio Zapata, Beba, es **la esposa** de Ricardo Ríos, que es **el yerno** del Sr. Zapata. Y el padre de Ricardo también es Ríos, se llama Miguel y es **el suegro** de Beba.

Más vocabulario

el (la) bebé *baby*
el (la) bisabuelo(a) *great-grandfather / great-grandmother*
el (la) biznieto(a) *great-grandson / great-granddaughter*
el (la) cuñado(a) *brother-in-law / sister-in-law*
la madrina *godmother*
el matrimonio *marriage; married couple*
el (la) novio(a) *fiancé / fiancée*
la nuera *daughter-in-law*
el padrino *godfather*
el (la) sobrino(a) *nephew / niece*
ver el amanecer *to watch the sunrise*
Expansión de vocabulario p. R3
Ya sabes p. R3

B Muchos viajamos desde distintas partes de México para **juntarnos** en la costa del Pacífico. Algunos llegaron **conduciendo el carro.** Algunos parientes que viven en Estados Unidos llegaron en **casas rodantes.**

C Para **refrescarnos** y **refugiarnos** del calor, todos vamos al agua. Los más jóvenes conducimos **motos acuáticas.** Otros van a remar aunque, a veces, es difícil **mantener** el equilibrio en un bote.

el velero

el surfista

el chaleco salvavidas

la canoa

el voleibol playero

D Los abuelitos generalmente **se paran** en **la orilla** para ver a sus **nietos** jugar al voleibol playero en **la arena.** Los niños también se divierten y **recogen caracoles** en una bolsa. Para descansar, es ideal **recostarse** debajo de **una sombrilla.**

E Cuando en la playa hace un **calor agobiante,** podemos **hacer un crucero** para sentir **la brisa** del mar. También es divertido **merendar** en **la cubierta** del barco, pero allí es muy común **marearse.** A la hora de cenar **hace fresco** y todos vamos a un restaurante del **puerto** a comer y ver **la puesta del sol.**

la puesta del sol

¡A responder! Escuchar

Escucha las siguientes actividades y representa cada una con movimientos.

Práctica de VOCABULARIO

1 Asociaciones

Hablar
Escribir

¿Dónde ocurre lo siguiente *(the following)*? Las respuestas están en el banco de palabras.

en la arena
bajo la sombrilla
en la orilla
en la canoa
en el velero

modelo: jugar al voleibol playero
en la arena

1. marearse
2. recoger caracoles
3. recostarse
4. merendar
5. ponerse el chaleco salvavidas

2 Actividades playeras

Hablar

Usa las fotos del folleto *(brochure)* para hacerle preguntas a un(a) compañero(a) sobre sus actividades en la playa.

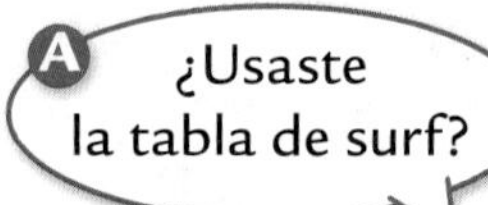

B Sí, usé muchas veces la tabla de surf.

3 ¡De vacaciones!

Hablar

Entrevista a tres compañeros(as) para saber qué les gustaría hacer en sus próximas vacaciones. Hablen sobre el equipo necesario para cada actividad y el lugar ideal.

Expansión
Escribe un resumen de las actividades más populares entre tus compañeros(as).

Más práctica Cuaderno *pp. 24–26* Cuaderno para hispanohablantes *pp. 24–27*

Get Help Online
ClassZone.com

¿Comprendiste? ¿Cuál de estas actividades haces para tener momentos emocionantes en la playa?
1. hacer surf **2.** pararse en la orilla **3.** merendar **4.** ver el amanecer

VOCABULARIO en contexto

¡AVANZA! **Goal:** Read what Sandra wrote on her web page about her family vacation last year. Then discuss what her family members did on the trip. ***Actividades 4–5***

Contexto 1 *Blog*

ESTRATEGIA Leer

Make a family tree Draw Sandra's family tree, including all the family members that appear in the reading. In addition, indicate each person's relationship to one other relative of Sandra's.

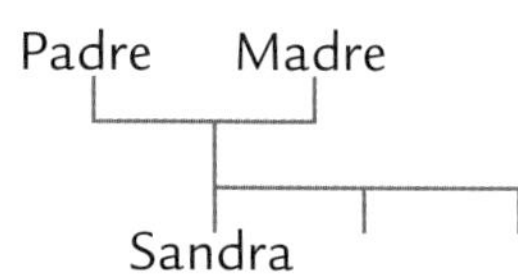

Sandra Zapata es una joven mexicana de Veracruz. Ella tiene un blog donde describe sus experiencias. Aquí habla de sus últimas vacaciones con su familia.

¡Bienvenidos al blog de Sandra!

SÚPER SANDRA

LIBROS QUE ME GUSTAN | MIS AMIGOS | MIS VACACIONES | MIS POEMAS | MI NOVELA GRÁFICA

Jueves 24 de abril

Hoy supe que vamos a pasar dos semanas de vacaciones en la playa con la familia entera. :(

La última vez hicimos un crucero por el Caribe y fuimos todos: Sergio, mi hermano mayor, con su esposa Olga y su bebé Rosita; mis padres y yo. Lo peor fue que nos acompañaron los suegros de Sergio (el Sr. y la Sra. Oliveros), los cuñados de Sergio (Daniel, Lorenzo y Luisa), y los sobrinos de Olga (Rafael y Renata).

Yo traté de refugiarme en mi cabina, pero no pude. Sergio, Olga y Rosita se marearon y yo pasé la semana cuidándolos. Los suegros de Olga se asustaron y pasaron el viaje entero con los chalecos salvavidas sin parar de llorar. Por suerte mis padres se recostaron todo el día en las hamacas.

El último día conocí a Santiago, un surfista. Vive en Cabo San Lucas, tiene un velero y me dijo que le gusta la playa. Fue la única persona interesante entre todos, pero me quedó poco tiempo para hablar con él.

¡No me parezco en absoluto a mi familia! Así que, queridos lectores, ya saben por qué no quiero pasar las próximas vacaciones con la familia.

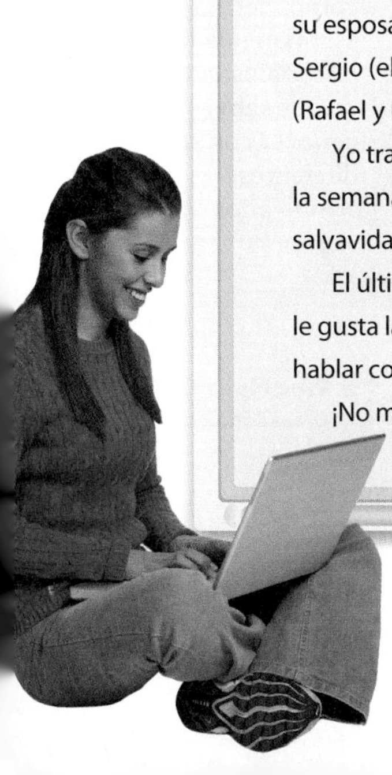

4 Comprensión del blog

Hablar

Empareja las personas de las ilustraciones con la relación familiar que aparece abajo.

Sergio **Rafael** **Luisa** **Renata** **Rosita** **Olga**

1. el nieto de la Sra. Oliveros
2. la sobrina de Sandra
3. la sobrina de Olga
4. la cuñada de Sandra
5. el hermano de Sandra
6. la cuñada de Sergio

REPASO gramatical

The verbs **saber** and **conocer** p. 14

The verbs **saber** *(to know a fact, to know something)* and **conocer** *(to know a person, to be familiar with)* take on a different meaning when used in the preterite. **Saber** in the preterite means *found out* and **conocer** in the preterite means *met*.

Hoy **supe** que vamos a pasar dos semanas de vacaciones en la playa.
*Today **I found out** that we're going to spend two weeks of vacation at the beach.*

El último día del viaje, **conocí** a un surfista que se llama Santiago.
*The last day of the trip, **I met** a surfer named Santiago.*

5 ¿Qué pasó en la fiesta?

Hablar
Escribir

Después de una fiesta, la mamá de Sandra le hizo muchas preguntas. Completa su diálogo con la forma correcta de **saber** o **conocer** en el pretérito.

Mamá: Sandra, ¿qué tal estuvo la fiesta anoche? ¿Quiénes fueron? ¿ __**1.**__ a alguien interesante?

Sandra: No, fueron los amigos de siempre. No __**2.**__ a nadie nuevo.

Mamá: Pues, ¿ __**3.**__ algo de las vacaciones que pasaron Elena y su familia?

Sandra: Bueno, __**4.**__ que Elena __**5.**__ a un chico muy simpático.

Mamá: ¿Ah, sí? ¿Un novio? ¿Qué les pareció a los papás de Elena?

Sandra: Ellos lo __**6.**__ y están contentos. ¡Pero es sólo un amigo!

Expansión
Con un(a) compañero(a), escriban una breve historia usando los verbos **saber** y **conocer** con sus diferentes significados.

¿Comprendiste?

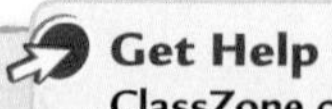

1. ¿Qué les pasó a Sergio, Olga y Rosita durante las vacaciones?
2. ¿Qué llevaron los suegros de Olga durante el viaje entero?
3. ¿Qué le pasó a Sandra el último día del viaje?

Presentación de GRAMÁTICA

¡AVANZA! **Goal:** Review the regular and irregular conjugations of verbs in the imperfect tense. Then practice using the imperfect to describe events that occurred in the past. ***Actividades 6–9***

English Grammar Connection: In English, you use the simple past tense *(I wanted to surf)* or expressions like *used to* or *always* to describe actions that were ongoing or recurring.

I used to go to the beach in the afternoon. **Iba** a la playa por la tarde.

REPASO Imperfect Tense

In Spanish, use the **imperfect tense** for actions that were ongoing, recurring, or incomplete in the past. How do you conjugate verbs in the **imperfect**?

Here's how:

Regular Verbs in the Imperfect

	parar	mantener	reunir
yo	**paraba**	**mantenía**	**reunía**
tú	**parabas**	**mantenías**	**reunías**
usted, él, ella	**paraba**	**mantenía**	**reunía**
nosotros(as)	**parábamos**	**manteníamos**	**reuníamos**
vosotros(as)	**parabais**	**manteníais**	**reuníais**
ustedes, ellos(as)	**paraban**	**mantenían**	**reunían**

Siempre **manteníamos** el carro limpio. ***We*** *always* ***kept*** *the car clean.*

Irregular Verbs in the Imperfect

ir	ser	ver
iba	era	veía
ibas	eras	veías
iba	era	veía
íbamos	éramos	veíamos
ibais	erais	veíais
iban	eran	veían

Eran las ocho y **veíamos** la puesta del sol.
It was *eight o'clock and* ***we were watching*** *the sunset.*

Más práctica
Cuaderno *pp. 27–29*
Cuaderno para hispanohablantes *pp. 28–30*

Conjuguemos.com

@HomeTutor
Leveled Practice
ClassZone.com

Práctica de GRAMÁTICA

6 ¿Cómo pasaban las vacaciones?

Escuchar
Escribir

Escucha la narración en que Roberto describe las vacaciones de su familia. Presta atención a las actividades. Escribe oraciones completas.

modelo: sus abuelos
Sus abuelos hacían un crucero.

1. su hermano	**4.** su cuñada	**7.** sus padrinos
2. Roberto	**5.** sus sobrinos	**8.** todos
3. sus bisabuelos	**6.** otros parientes	**9.** sus papás

Expansión
Escribe un resumen de lo que hacías en las vacaciones cuando eras niño(a).

7 Un diario

Escribir

Encontraste el diario de tu abuelita, en el que contaba sus experiencias sobre un viaje a Puerto Escondido con tu abuelito. Complétalo con los verbos indicados.

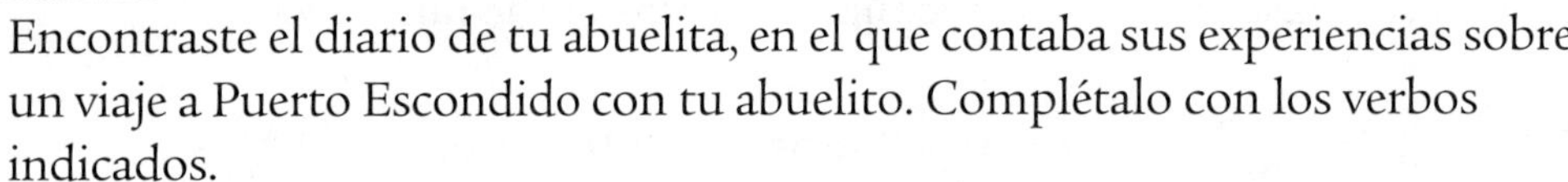

Querido diario,

Hoy fue un día muy interesante. Pedro y yo alquilamos un velero para explorar la costa un poco. __1.__ (ser) una mañana hermosa con mucho sol y una brisa muy agradable. Yo, por supuesto, __2.__ (llevar) mi chaleco salvavidas, pero no (tener) __3.__ miedo. ¡Pedro __4.__ (navegar) como un capitán profesional! Siempre __5.__ (ir) despacio. Yo no me mareé en absoluto. En la orilla, nuestros amigos __6.__ (refrescarse) en la olas y se divertían mucho. Después de varias horas, decidimos reunirnos con ellos y volvimos al puerto. Allí __7.__ (haber) mucha gente que __8.__ (pescar) tranquilamente.

Comparación cultural

Los clavadistas de Acapulco

¿Por qué participa la gente en deportes extremos? Acapulco es una de las ciudades turísticas más importantes de la costa del Océano Pacífico de **México.** Entre sus espectáculos más interesantes está el de los famosos clavadistas de La Quebrada. Estos hombres se zambullen *(dive)* desde un acantilado *(cliff)* de más de cien pies de altura. Este deporte extremo es una tradición que empezó en 1934.

Compara con tu mundo *¿Te interesa algún deporte extremo? ¿Por qué?*

Clavadista en La Quebrada

8 Mucha gente en la playa

Hablar
Escribir

Mira las fotos de un día típico en la playa y describe qué hacía cada persona.

modelo: mi papá y yo
Mi papá y yo navegábamos en un velero estupendo.

1. mis hermanos

2. mi mamá

3. mis amigos

4. mi abuelito

5. Silvia y Roberto

6. mis tíos

7. mi hermano y yo

8. Mauricio

9. los niños

9 Tú y yo

Hablar
Escribir

Compara las actividades que tú hacías cuando estabas de vacaciones el año pasado con las actividades que hacía tu compañero(a).

Más práctica Cuaderno *pp. 27–29* Cuaderno para hispanohablantes *pp. 28–30*

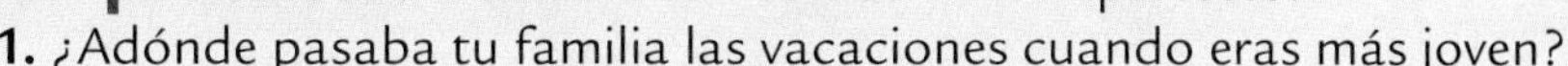

¿Comprendiste? Contesta con verbos en el imperfecto.

1. ¿Adónde pasaba tu familia las vacaciones cuando eras más joven?
2. ¿Qué hacían? ¿Dónde se quedaban?

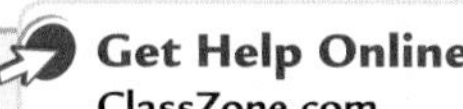

GRAMÁTICA en contexto

¡AVANZA! **Goal:** Notice how Sandra uses forms of the preterite and imperfect tenses to talk about a day at the beach in her graphic novel. Then use these tenses to write your own description of activities that occurred in the past. ***Actividades 10–11***

Contexto 2 *Novela gráfica*

ESTRATEGIA **Leer**

Transform verbs in context Count the phrases containing the imperfect tense in the graphic novel and list these in box A. If the imperfect-tense verb in box A is singular, change the phrase to the corresponding plural form in box B and vice versa.

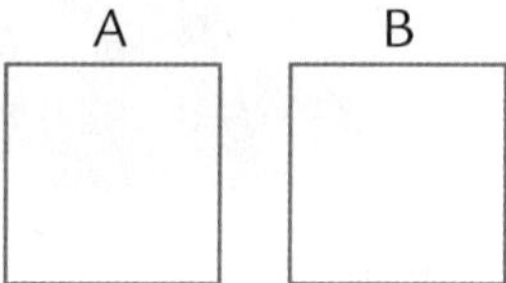

Sandra no se divierte cuando va de vacaciones con su familia. Hace un mes, tuvo que pasar otra vez dos semanas de vacaciones con ellos. Como no quería hacer actividades con sus parientes, se divertía dibujando una novela gráfica para su blog.

Las aventuras de Súper Sandra en la playa...

SÚPER SANDRA

LIBROS QUE ME GUSTAN | MIS AMIGOS | MIS VACACIONES | MIS POEMAS | MI NOVELA GRÁFICA

ERA UN DÍA TÍPICO EN UNA PLAYA TÍPICA DE BAJA CALIFORNIA... SÚPER SANDRA ANDABA POR LA PLAYA SOLA, TRATANDO DE ESCAPARSE DE SU FAMILIA Y SUS ACTIVIDADES ABURRIDAS.

LA FAMILIA DE SÚPER SANDRA SE DIVERTÍA EN LA PLAYA... SU MADRE SE RECOSTABA, SU PADRE RECOGÍA CARACOLES... SU HERMANO SERGIO Y SU ESPOSA OLGA SE REFRESCABAN EN EL AGUA CON SU HIJA ROSITA...

Y LOS SUEGROS, CUÑADOS Y SOBRINOS DE SERGIO CONDUCÍAN MOTOS ACUÁTICAS. NO ERA NADA NUEVO PARA SÚPER SANDRA.

SÚPER SANDRA SE REFUGIABA EN UN LUGAR TRANQUILO PARA PENSAR.

¡QUÉ ABURRIDA ESTOY!

LUEGO SÚPER SANDRA OBSERVABA LA PUESTA DEL SOL Y PENSABA EN SU VIDA PATÉTICA CUANDO... DE REPENTE...

¡¿SANTIAGO?!

¡UNA SORPRESA INCREÍBLE! ¡NO LO PODÍA CREER! ¡ERA EL SURFISTA QUE CONOCIÓ EN EL CRUCERO HACE UN AÑO!

10 Comprensión de la novela gráfica

Hablar
Escribir

Según la novela gráfica de Sandra, ¿quién o quiénes hacían lo siguiente?

1. conducían motos acuáticas
2. recogía caracoles
3. se refrescaban en el agua
4. se recostaba debajo de una sombrilla
5. surfeaba
6. estaba muy aburrida

11 Y entonces...

Hablar
Escribir

Con tus compañero(as), describe las siguientes escenas de la novela gráfica sobre la reunión de Sandra y Santiago en la playa. Luego, completa las oraciones con el imperfecto de los verbos indicados.

¡ __1.__ (ser) tan extraño! Súper Sandra __2.__ (encontrarse) en una escena completamente romántica y no __3.__ (saber) qué decir.

Sandra __4.__ (hacer) todo lo que Santiago __5.__ (sugerir). La familia de Sandra ya no la __6.__ (conocer); ¡ __7.__ (estar) transformada!

Durante la cena, Santiago __8.__ (hablar) de reunirse el próximo verano, pero Sandra sólo __9.__ (escuchar) su voz y no __10.__ (oír) sus palabras.

Expansión
Escribe la escena de una novela gráfica con una experiencia de tu vida. Debes tener tres o cuatro cajas con dibujos y usar el imperfecto.

PARA Y PIENSA

¿Comprendiste? Usa la forma correcta del verbo en el imperfecto para describir la escena en la playa:
Sergio y Olga (refrescarse) __1.__ con Rosita. La madre de Sandra (recostarse) __2.__ . Sandra (observar) __3.__ la puesta del sol y (pensar) __4.__ en su vida.

Get Help Online
ClassZone.com

Presentación de GRAMÁTICA

¡AVANZA! **Goal:** Review the differences between the preterite and the imperfect and how each tense is used in Spanish. Then practice by narrating a situation in the past. ***Actividades 12–16***

 *¿Recuerdas?* Expressions of emotion p. 12

English Grammar Connection: In English, you can use the simple past tense for actions in the past, whether they were completed or not. To emphasize that an action was in progress, you use the past progressive tense *(Pedro was swimming)*.

REPASO Preterite vs. Imperfect

Animated Grammar ClassZone.com

You already know two tenses that refer to the past, the **preterite** and the **imperfect.** How is each tense used?

Here's how:

- Use the **preterite tense** to describe an action or series of actions completed in the past.

Aquel día, Pedro **fue** a la playa y **jugó** al voleibol playero.	*That day, Pedro **went** to the beach and **played** beach volleyball.*

- Use the **imperfect tense** for ongoing actions or states of being in the past without focusing on their beginning or end. Always use the imperfect to say what time it was or what the weather was like in the past.

Elena siempre **iba** a la playa cuando **hacía** buen tiempo.	*Elena always **used to go** to the beach when the weather **was** nice.*

- Sometimes you need the **imperfect** and the **preterite** in the same sentence.

  Use the **imperfect** to tell what was going on in the background.
  Use the **preterite** for the interrupting action or main event.

Yo **nadaba** cuando Pedro **llegó** a la playa.	*I **was swimming** when Pedro **arrived** at the beach.*

Más práctica

Cuaderno *pp. 30–32*
Cuaderno para hispanohablantes *pp. 31–34*

Conjuguemos.com

@HomeTutor Leveled Practice ClassZone.com

Práctica de GRAMÁTICA

12 ¿Qué pasó?

Hablar
Escribir

Usa el pretérito y el imperfecto del verbo apropiado para explicar qué pasó durante otra actividad en proceso.

1. Mientras Alberto y Susana ____ su moto acuática, Susana ____ . (conducir, caerse)
2. Karina ____ a buscar la merienda mientras Gustavo ____ la puesta del sol. (ir, observar)
3. Yo todavía ____ la canoa cuando mi sobrino ____ el chaleco salvavidas. (preparar, ponerse)
4. Tú ____ un pájaro cuando nosotros ____ por el sendero. (ver, caminar)
5. Nosotros ____ cinco debajo de la sombrilla cuando tú nos ____ para jugar al voleibol playero. (ser, llamar)
6. José ____ al aire libre pero ____ a llover. (leer, empezar)
7. Felipe ____ en el crucero pero ____ la calma. (marearse, mantener)
8. Carla ____ en la casa rodante cuando ____ con sus padrinos para comer. (estar, juntarse)

13 ¿Qué verbo?

Hablar
Escribir

Completa las oraciones con el verbo apropiado del banco de palabras. Ten cuidado con el pretérito y el imperfecto.

viajar
merendar
cortar
ir
cenar

1. El esposo de Noemí ____ al cine cuando se cayó.
2. María Inés y su madrina ____ con pan y leche.
3. Los señores Quijano ____ con sus hijos, su nuera y su yerno en el restaurante.
4. De repente, ____ la luz.
5. De niño, Matías ____ todos los años a Acapulco.

AUDIO

Pronunciación La letra c con e, i y la letra z

En Latinoamérica la combinación de la **c** con las vocales **e, i** produce el sonido /s/, al igual que la **z**. En cambio, en España **ce, ci** y la **z** se pronuncian como la *th* de la palabra *thin* en inglés. Su posición en la palabra no afecta nunca la pronunciación.

cenar	**cinturón**	**Zapata**
amanecer	**conducir**	**biznieta**

Refrán

Come poco y cena temprano si quieres llegar a ser anciano.

14 ¿Qué hacían en la playa?

Hablar

Pregúntale a tu compañero(a) qué hacían sus parientes cuando él o ella llegó a la playa. Escoge una actividad del banco de palabras para las respuestas.

surfear
navegar en velero
remar en la canoa
leer debajo de una sombrilla
jugar al voleibol playero
recoger caracoles en la orilla

A ¿Qué hacía tu abuela cuando llegaste a la playa?

B Mi abuela leía cuando llegué a la playa.

1. tu abuela **2.** los novios **3.** tu bisabuela **4.** tu cuñada

Expansión
Describe qué hacían los estudiantes y la maestra cuando llegaste a la clase.

15 ¡Pasó esto!

¿Recuerdas? Expressions of emotion p. 12

Escribir

Escríbele un correo electrónico a un(a) compañero(a) para contarle algo de una excursión con tu familia. Incluye elementos de descripción (imperfecto), algunas actividades que hicieron tú y tu familia (pretérito) y expresiones de emoción con el tiempo verbal apropiado.

modelo: Estaba muy contento. Hacía calor... comimos en la playa...

16 ¿Qué crees?

Leer
Escribir

Comparación cultural

De español y mestiza, castiza
Miguel Cabrera (1695–1768)

En familia

¿Cómo representan los artistas los temas que les interesan? Durante el siglo dieciocho, los pintores de Nueva España se dedicaron a representar la diversidad social de aquel entonces. Esta preocupación con el mestizaje entre europeos, indígenas y africanos dio luz a un género artístico: el retrato de castas. Los retratos representaban a un hombre, a su mujer y a los hijos de ellos, todos de diversos grupos étnicos.

Compara con tu mundo *¿A quién elegirías* (would you choose) *para representar en un retrato? ¿Por qué?*

Mira la pintura. ¿Cómo crees que eran estas personas? ¿Qué pensaban? ¿Qué crees que hicieron antes y después de hacerse el retrato?

Más práctica Cuaderno *pp. 30–32* Cuaderno para hispanohablantes *pp. 31–34*

¿Comprendiste? Contesta las siguientes preguntas sobre tus últimas vacaciones con las formas correctas del imperfecto o pretérito.
1. ¿Adónde fuiste? **2.** ¿Qué tiempo hacía cuando llegaste? **3.** ¿Qué hiciste?

Get Help Online
ClassZone.com

Todo junto

¡AVANZA! **Goal:** ***Show what you know*** Notice how Sandra and her best friend Carmen use the preterite and the imperfect tenses in the following conversation. Then talk about what happened on the vacation Sandra took with her family. ***Actividades 17–19***

Resumen contextos 1 y 2 Sandra Zapata escribió acerca de las vacaciones con su familia. Ella hizo una novela gráfica en su blog con sus experiencias.

Contexto 3 *Diálogo*

ESTRATEGIA **Escuchar**
Cause and effect As you listen, pay attention to the descriptions of Santiago and Jorge to find out what causes Sandra's confusion. In the chart, include Santiago and Jorge's description and what Sandra could share with each of them.

AUDIO

Sandra regresó de sus vacaciones en la playa con su familia. Ahora le cuenta a Carmen lo que pasó durante las vacaciones.

Carmen: Sandra, ¿qué onda? ¿Cómo pasaste las vacaciones?

Sandra: Bueno, las vacaciones empezaron como siempre: todo el mundo estaba en la playa haciendo lo que le gustaba, y yo estaba sola y aburrida.

Carmen: ¡Claro! ¡Como siempre!

Sandra: Era como una película de terror. Estaba muy deprimida y hacía un calor agobiante cuando, sin esperarlo, vi otra vez al chico del crucero.

Carmen: ¿Santiago? ¿El surfista? ¡Qué padre!

Sandra: Sí... qué casualidad, ¿no? Lo interesante es que somos muy diferentes, pero nos gustaba hacer cosas juntos. Hicimos un crucero, caminamos por la arena todos los días, ¡hasta condujimos motos acuáticas!

Carmen: ¿Tú? ¡Imposible! ¡No lo creo!

Sandra: ¡Ni yo! Pero nos divertimos mucho. Yo era una persona completamente diferente. Y mientras hacíamos todas estas cosas, también hablábamos mucho... Creo que lo conozco bien, aunque sólo estuve dos semanas en Baja California.

Carmen: ¿Y qué dijeron tus padres?

También se dice

La expresión **¿qué onda?** es muy común en México para saludar a un amigo.
- **Colombia** **¿quiubo?** (viene de **qué hubo**)
- **España** **¿qué pasa?**
- **Argentina** **¿qué tal?**
- **República Dominicana** **¿y qué?**

Sandra: Pues, tuve que presentarlo a la familia entera... ¡qué horror! No puedo ni hablar de eso. ¡Eso sí! Santiago se divirtió con todos.

Carmen: ¿Y conociste a su familia?

Sandra: Sí, sí, todos en la familia Aguirre fueron muy amables. Tienen una casa rodante y me invitaron a hacer un viaje con ellos a Los Ángeles durante todo el mes de agosto.

Carmen: ¡No puedes ir en agosto! Ese mes viene mi primo Jorge a Monterrey y ya te dije que tienes que conocerlo. Es el amigo perfecto para ti: el año pasado dirigió su propia película independiente, y a la vez que hacía la película, escribía una novela gráfica sobre sus experiencias... y una casa editorial la publicó hace dos meses.

Sandra: ¡Ay!, no sé qué hacer. En mi vida nunca pasa nada, y cuando pasa, pasa todo junto. ¡Realmente no sé qué hacer!

Carmen: Bueno, Sandra, recuerda que en realidad no te gusta mucho estar al aire libre ni hacer deportes. El surfista fue un buen amigo para pasar las vacaciones, pero... ¿crees que tú y Santiago son compatibles de verdad?

Sandra: Pues, no lo sé. Santiago fue muy bueno conmigo. Por otro lado, tu primo publicó una novela gráfica. ¡Lo mismo que me interesa a mí!

Carmen: Pues, amiga, tienes que decidirte pronto... ¡ya estamos en julio!

17 Comprensión del diálogo

Escuchar
Hablar
Escribir

Escoge la opción correcta para completar las oraciones y di si son ciertas o falsas.

1. Al principio de las vacaciones Sandra (estuvo / estaba) aburrida.
2. El día que Sandra vio a Santiago (hizo / hacía) fresco.
3. A Sandra y a Santiago les (gustó / gustaba) hacer cosas juntos.
4. Sandra (fue / era) una persona diferente con Santiago.
5. Sandra (tuvo / tenía) que presentar a Santiago a su familia entera.
6. Sandra le (dijo / decía) a Carmen que el apellido de Santiago es González.
7. La familia Aguirre (invitó / invitaba) a Sandra a una escapada de fin de semana a Los Ángeles.
8. Santiago (se divirtió / se divertía) con los parientes de Sandra.
9. Mientras (dirigió / dirigía) la película, Jorge también escribía una novela gráfica.
10. Santiago (fue / era) muy bueno con Sandra.

Expansión
Piensa en una persona que sea compatible contigo. Escribe una historia breve con actividades que hicieron juntos, usando el pretérito y el imperfecto.

18 Integración

Leer
Escuchar
Hablar

Te gusta mucho la telenovela «Seres queridos». Lee este artículo sobre uno de los actores. Luego escucha las noticias de la radio sobre su visita a la playa. Cuenta las noticias.

Fuente 1 Artículo periodístico

NOVELAS EN LA PLAYA

El famosísimo actor de la telenovela «Seres queridos», Eduardo Ríos, llegó a Acapulco ayer con su familia para celebrar su cumpleaños.

A Eduardo lo acompañaron Nina, su esposa, y sus dos hijas. Se quedaron en el elegantísimo hotel Miramar, de cinco estrellas, y pasaron el primer día de su escapada de fin de semana en la playa. Eduardo practicó el surf mientras el resto de la familia andaba en velero. Por la tarde se hizo una fiesta de cumpleaños en la terraza del hotel, desde donde vieron una maravillosa puesta del sol – **¡el regalo perfecto!**

Fuente 2 Reporte de radio

Escucha y apunta
- ¿Por qué decidió Eduardo celebrar su cumpleaños en Acapulco?
- ¿Con quién fue y qué hizo allí?

modelo: Mi actor favorito, Eduardo Ríos, fue a Acapulco a celebrar su cumpleaños. Lo acompañó su esposa. Cuando era niño fue a Acapulco y le encantó, por eso quiso volver.

19 Querido diario...

Escribir

Volviste ayer de un viaje maravilloso. En tu diario, escribe algo sobre tus aventuras, actividades y las personas que conociste. Di lo que hiciste y lo que pasaba mientras hacías esas cosas.

Writing Criteria	Excellent	Good	Needs Work
Content	Your diary entry includes many details about your trip.	Your diary entry includes some details about your trip.	Your diary entry includes few details about your trip.
Communication	Your diary entry is organized and easy to follow.	Parts of your diary entry are organized and easy to follow.	Your diary entry is disorganized and hard to follow.
Accuracy	You make few mistakes in grammar and vocabulary.	You make some mistakes in grammar and vocabulary.	You make many mistakes in grammar and vocabulary.

Más práctica Cuaderno *pp. 33–34* Cuaderno para hispanohablantes *pp. 35–36*

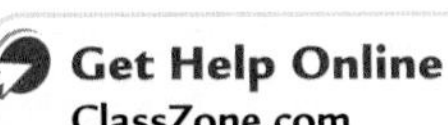

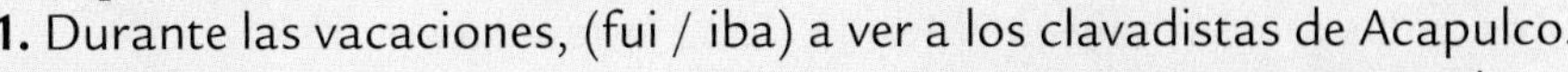

¿Comprendiste? Escoge la opción correcta.

1. Durante las vacaciones, (fui / iba) a ver a los clavadistas de Acapulco.
2. Liliana (fue / era) joven cuando (hizo / hacía) su primera escapada.
3. Mientras (miré / miraba) el retrato (pensé / pensaba) en mi familia.

 Lectura literaria

¡AVANZA! **Goal:** Read and listen to the excerpt of a story by a Mexican author and analyze the roles of women in the early 1900's.

Para leer 

ESTRATEGIA **Leer y escribir**

Read more effectively with a honeycomb story map As you read, complete a honeycomb story map like the one below. Using your honeycomb map for guidance, summarize the story and your reflections in a paragraph.

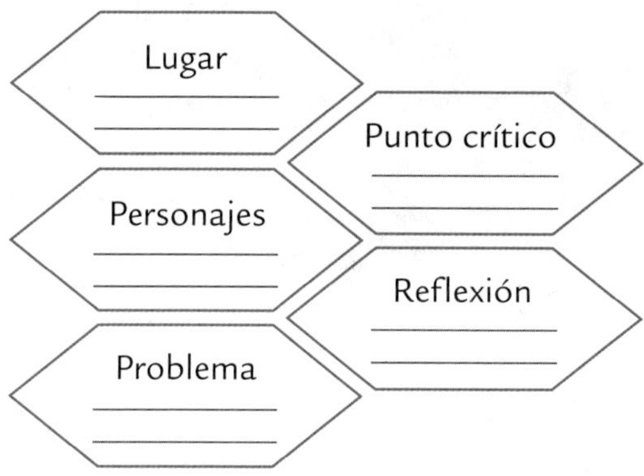

Vocabulario para leer

el chorizo *tipo de salchicha*
moler *deshacer granos u otros elementos sólidos para hacerlos polvo*
planchar *sacar las arrugas de la ropa con una plancha*
bordar *adornar una tela o ropa con dibujos hechos con hilo*
coser *unir dos pedazos de tela con hilo y aguja*

Nota cultural

Sobre la autora ***Laura Esquivel (1951–)***
Nació en México D.F. Empezó su carrera literaria como guionista *(scriptwriter)*. Obtuvo el reconocimiento mundial con su primera novela, *Como agua para chocolate,* que cuenta la historia de una familia mexicana de principios de 1900. También se filmó una película basada en la novela.

Sobre la vida familiar en 1900 En el año 1900 había muchos ranchos pequeños en las áreas rurales de México. Toda la familia compartía los quehaceres; tenían que cuidar los animales y las cosechas *(harvests)*, limpiar la casa y preparar la comida. Los ranchos funcionaban como una comunidad.

COMO AGUA PARA Chocolate

AUDIO

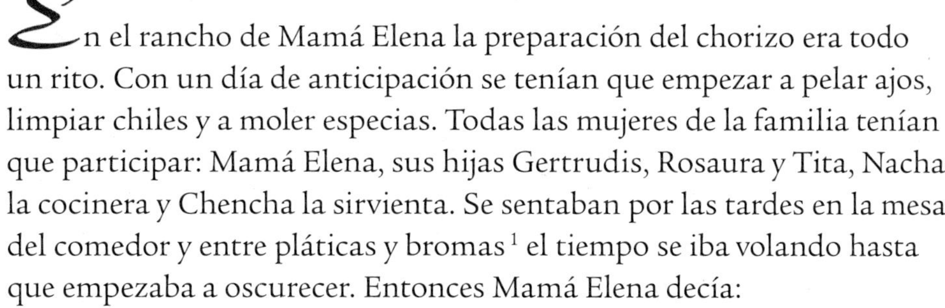

En el rancho de Mamá Elena la preparación del chorizo era todo un rito. Con un día de anticipación se tenían que empezar a pelar ajos, limpiar chiles y a moler especias. Todas las mujeres de la familia tenían que participar: Mamá Elena, sus hijas Gertrudis, Rosaura y Tita, Nacha la cocinera y Chencha la sirvienta. Se sentaban por las tardes en la mesa del comedor y entre pláticas y bromas[1] el tiempo se iba volando hasta que empezaba a oscurecer. Entonces Mamá Elena decía:

—Por hoy ya terminamos con esto.

Dicen que a buen entendedor pocas palabras[2], así que después de escuchar esta frase todas sabían qué era lo que tenían que hacer. Primero recogían la mesa y después se repartían las labores: una metía a las gallinas[3], otra sacaba agua del pozo[4] y la dejaba lista para utilizarla en el desayuno y otra se encargaba de la leña[5] para la estufa. Ese día ni se planchaba ni se bordaba ni se cosía ropa. Después todas se iban a sus recámaras[6] a leer, rezar[7] y dormir. Una de esas tardes, antes de que Mamá Elena dijera que ya se podían levantar de la mesa, Tita, que entonces contaba con[8] quince años, le anunció con voz temblorosa que Pedro Muzquiz quería venir a hablar con ella...

—¿Y de qué me tiene que venir a hablar ese señor?

Dijo Mamá Elena luego de un silencio interminable que encogió el alma de Tita.

Con voz apenas perceptible respondió:

—Yo no sé.

A pensar
¿Puedes decir el significado de las palabras **pelar** y **especias** a partir del contexto, en el momento en que preparan el chorizo?

A pensar
¿Cómo crees que Tita se siente con la reacción de su madre ante el pedido de Pedro? ¿Puedes deducir el significado de **encogió el alma** y **voz apenas perceptible?** Recuerda que aunque tu deducción no sea exacta, aún puedes comprender la idea general a partir del contexto.

[1] **pláticas...** chatting and joking
[2] **a buen...** a popular refrain meaning "one who understands well needs few words"
[3] hens [4] well [5] firewood [6] bedrooms [7] to pray
[8] **contaba...** was

Reflexiona

¿Qué le dice Tita a su madre? ¿Cómo reacciona Mamá Elena?

Escena de la película Como agua para chocolate, *de Alfonso Arau*

Mamá Elena le lanzó[9] una mirada que para Tita encerraba[10] todos los años de represión que habían flotado sobre la familia y dijo:

—Pues más vale[11] que le informes que si es para pedir tu mano, no lo haga. Perdería su tiempo y me haría perder[12] el mío. Sabes muy bien que por ser la más chica de las mujeres a ti te corresponde cuidarme hasta el día de mi muerte.

Dicho esto, Mamá Elena se puso lentamente de pie, guardó sus lentes dentro del delantal[13] y a manera de orden final repitió:

—¡Por hoy, hemos terminado con esto!

---

[9] threw (like a lance) [10] contained [11] **más...** it's better
[12] **me...** would make me [13] apron

Reflexiona

Según la madre, ¿qué tiene que hacer Tita con su vida?

Tita sabía que dentro de las normas de comunicación de la casa no estaba incluido el diálogo, pero aun así, por primera vez en su vida intentó protestar a un mandato[14] de su madre.

—Pero es que yo opino que...

—¡Tú no opinas nada y se acabó! Nunca, por generaciones, nadie en mi familia ha protestado ante esta costumbre y no va a ser una de mis hijas quien lo haga.

Tita bajó la cabeza y con la misma fuerza con que sus lágrimas cayeron sobre la mesa, así cayó sobre ella su destino. Y desde ese momento supieron ella y la mesa que no podían modificar ni tantito la dirección de estas fuerzas desconocidas que las obligaban, a la una, a compartir con Tita su sino[15], recibiendo sus amargas[16] lágrimas desde el momento en que nació, y a la otra a asumir esta absurda determinación. ❖

[14] command [15] fate [16] bitter

❖ A pensar
¿Qué crees que significa la palabra **asumir**? Luego, usa el diccionario para ver cuál es la definición apropiada en este caso.

¿Comprendiste?

1. ¿Dónde vivían Tita y su familia?
2. ¿Quiénes participaban en la preparación del chorizo?
3. ¿Qué otras actividades eran parte de la vida diaria de las mujeres?
4. ¿Quién era Pedro Muzquiz?
5. ¿Cómo era la relación entre Mamá Elena y sus hijas?

¿Y tú?

¿Qué opinas tú de la costumbre familiar que Tita necesita seguir?

Escritura

Una experiencia inolvidable

Escribe sobre una experiencia inolvidable y cómo te afectó personalmente. Para hacerlo, usa la siguiente secuencia de estrategias.

1 Prepárate para escribir

ESTRATEGIA **Haz una lista** Toma algunos minutos para hacer una lista de experiencias inolvidables de tu vida. Escribe todas las ideas que se te ocurran. Haz un círculo alrededor de la experiencia más inolvidable.

2 Escribe

ESTRATEGIA **Usa una tabla como ayuda para escribir un borrador** ***(draft)*** Crea una tabla como la de abajo y contesta las preguntas de cada columna. Usando las respuestas, escribe un primer borrador de tres a cinco párrafos describiendo tu experiencia y cómo te afectó personalmente. Incluye una introducción y una conclusión.

Información descriptiva (usa el imperfecto)	Acciones específicas (usa el pretérito)	Cómo me afectó la experiencia (usa formas apropiadas)
• ¿Cómo era el día? • ¿Qué tiempo hacía? • ¿Cómo eran las personas que estaban presentes?	• ¿Qué hiciste? • ¿Qué hicieron las otras personas? • ¿Qué pasó?	• ¿Cómo me sentía? • ¿Qué aprendí? • ¿Qué descubrí?

3 Revisa tu composición

Lee el borrador de tu compañero(a). Subraya *(underline)* todos los verbos, y para cada verbo conjugado haz lo siguiente:

- Decide si es correcto su uso del imperfecto o del pretérito.
- Decide si es correcta la conjugación del verbo.
- Haz un círculo alrededor de los verbos con errores.
- Escribe las correcciones.

Usando toda la información, revisa tu composición hasta que esté correcta.

"Mi familia y yo navegábamos por rápidos por primera vez. Nos divertíamos mucho cuando, de repente, el guía se caía (cayó) al agua. Mi hermana y yo empezaron (empezamos) a gritar pero mis padres seguían remando sin observar que el guía estaba en el río. Yo me sentí..."

Lección 2

En resumen

Vocabulario y gramática

Vocabulario

Talk About Family Vacations

Family relationships

el apellido	*last name*	el (la) esposo(a)	*husband; wife; spouse*	la nuera	*daughter-in-law*
el (la) bebé	*baby, infant*	la madrina	*godmother*	el padrino	*godfather*
el (la) bisabuelo(a)	*great-grandfather / great-grandmother*	el matrimonio	*marriage; married couple*	el pariente	*relative*
el (la) biznieto(a)	*great-grandson / great-granddaughter*	el (la) nieto(a)	*grandson / granddaughter*	el (la) sobrino(a)	*nephew / niece*
el (la) cuñado(a)	*brother-in-law / sister-in-law*	el (la) novio(a)	*boyfriend / girlfriend fiancé / fiancée*	el (la) suegro(a)	*father-in-law / mother-in-law*
				el yerno	*son-in-law*

Describe a Place and its Climate

la arena	*sand*	la orilla	*shore*
la brisa	*breeze*	el puerto	*port*
el calor agobiante	*stifling heat*	la sombrilla	*parasol*
el caracol	*shell*	ver el amanecer	*to watch the sunrise*
hacer fresco	*to be cool (weather)*	ver la puesta del sol	*to watch the sunset*

Trips and Transportation

el carro	*car*
la casa rodante	*RV*
conducir	*to drive*
la cubierta	*deck (of boat)*
la escapada	*getaway*
hacer un crucero	*to go on a cruise*

Discuss Activities, Skills and Abilities

la canoa	*canoe*	en absoluto	*not at all*	parecerse a (alguien)	*to look like (someone), to be like (someone)*
el chaleco salvavidas	*life jacket*	juntarse	*to get together with*	recoger	*to pick up*
la moto acuática	*personal watercraft*	mantener (el equilibrio)	*to keep (one's balance)*	recostarse	*to lie down*
el (la) surfista	*surfer*	marearse	*to get seasick / to become dizzy*	refrescarse	*to cool down*
la tabla de surf	*surfboard*	merendar	*to have a snack*	refugiarse	*to take refuge from*
el velero	*sailboat*	pararse	*to stand up*	reunirse	*to get together, to meet*
el voleibol playero	*beach volleyball*				

Gramática

Nota gramatical: The verbs **saber** and **conocer** *p. 62*

REPASO Imperfect Tense

Add the following endings to the stems of **regular verbs.**

-ar verbs		-er/-ir verbs	
-aba	-ábamos	-ía	-íamos
-abas	-abais	-ías	-íais
-aba	-aban	-ía	-ían

Irregular Verbs

ir:	iba	ibas	iba	íbamos	ibais	iban
ser:	era	eras	era	éramos	erais	eran
ver:	veía	veías	veía	veíamos	veíais	veían

REPASO Preterite vs. Imperfect

Use the **preterite tense** for:

- actions completed in the past
- actions that interrupt
- the main event

Use the **imperfect tense** to describe:

- the time or weather
- ongoing actions or states of being
- background information

Lección 2

Repaso de la lección

¡LLEGADA!

@HomeTutor ClassZone.com

Now you can
- talk about family vacations
- discuss activities, skills, and abilities
- describe a place and its climate

Using
- imperfect
- preterite vs. imperfect
- **saber** and **conocer**

To review
- vocabulary pp. 58–59

1 Listen and understand

AUDIO

Escucha a una radioyente que habla con un locutor de radio sobre una escapada de fin de semana que ella ganó en un concurso. Luego, completa las oraciones siguientes con las palabras que faltan.

1. La Sra. Ramos ganó una _____ a Acapulco.
2. Los Sres. Ramos viajaron en _____ hasta Acapulco.
3. Todos los días los Sres. Ramos _____ en la playa.
4. Por las tardes, _____ con jugo de coco.
5. Después del desayuno, se _____ en la playa.
6. La Sra. Ramos y su _____ tuvieron una experiencia inolvidable.

To review
- imperfect p. 63

2 Describe a place and its climate

Completa la siguiente descripción de un día en la playa.

Abuelito,

¿Qué le puedo decir de mi día en la playa? (Ser) **1.** un día estupendo. (Hacer) **2.** un calor agobiante y el sol (brillar) **3.** . (Haber) **4.** mucha gente en la playa. Algunas personas (recostarse) **5.** en la arena y otros (caminar) **6.** por la orilla. Mis amigos y yo (conducir) **7.** motos acuáticas mientras tú (pasear) **8.** en velero. Pero, de repente, empezó a llover y todos se fueron. Mis amigos y yo (estar) **9.** muy aburridos porque ya (hacer) **10.** fresco y no (poder) **11.** estar en la playa. (Ser) **12.** las seis y volvimos al hotel. Ya son las once y tengo sueño.

To review
- preterite vs. imperfect p. 68

3 Talk about family vacations

Di qué hacían las personas indicadas cuando algo inesperado ocurrió. Sigue el modelo y usa el banco de palabras.

modelo: Laura y Gerardo / nadar en la piscina / empezar a llover
Laura y Gerardo nadaban en la piscina cuando empezó a llover.

1. yo
2. Marcos y Anita
3. tú
4. Hernando
5. nosotros

refrescarse en el agua	nadar en la piscina
empezar a llover	llegar sus amigos
encontrar unas llaves	pasear en velero
conducir una moto acuática	tener un accidente
marearse	ver la puesta del sol

To review
- **saber** and **conocer** p. 62

4 Discuss activities, skills, and abilities

Completa las siguientes oraciones con la forma correcta de **saber** o **conocer** en el pretérito o el imperfecto.

1. La semana pasada tú y yo ____ que Marcos puede navegar un velero.
2. Ayer Paula ____ al padrino de César.
3. Aunque yo ____ la ciudad bien, no pude encontrar el hotel.
4. Mi bisabuelo ____ manejar la casa rodante.
5. Tú ____ a un surfista profesional en la playa.
6. Mis padres ____ nadar.

To review
- **Comparación cultural** pp. 64, 70

5 Sports, fine art, and family relationships in Mexico

Comparación cultural

1. ¿En qué ciudad mexicana se encuentran los clavadistas de La Quebrada?
2. ¿En qué año empezó este deporte en México?
3. En el retrato de la página 70, ¿quiénes son los miembros de la familia? ¿Qué profesión tiene el hombre? ¿Cómo lo sabes?
4. ¿De qué preocupación social surgió el género artístico de los retratos de castas?

Más práctica Cuaderno *pp. 35–46* Cuaderno para hispanohablantes *pp. 37–46*

Comparación cultural

AUDIO

Tierra de contrastes

Lectura y escritura

WebQuest
ClassZone.com

1. **Leer** Juan y Diana son de zonas muy diferentes de México. Lee la descripción de las dos regiones.

2. **Escribir** Después de leer lo que dicen Juan y Diana, escribe una composición sobre la región donde tú vives.

ESTRATEGIA **Escribir**

Gather and organize cultural information Gather cultural information using the Internet or the library. Organize the information using a chart showing region name, location, and comments/details.

Nombre de la región	Lugar	Comentarios / Detalles

Paso 1 Usa la información de tu tabla para ayudarte a escribir. Escribe tu introducción en el primer párrafo.

Paso 2 Escribe un párrafo sobre cada característica que quieres explicar.

Paso 3 Escribe un párrafo como una conclusión con tus comentarios. Luego revisa la gramática y la ortografía.

Compara con tu mundo

Usa el párrafo que escribiste y compara tu ciudad o región con las regiones donde viven Juan y Diana. ¿Son parecidas? ¿Son diferentes? Explica.

Cuaderno *pp. 47–49* Cuaderno para hispanohablantes *pp. 47–49*

El Noreste y Monterrey

Juan

Me llamo Juan Aguilar y vivo en Monterrey, en el noreste de México. Ésta es una zona agrícola y hay muchos ranchos. A mi ciudad le dicen «la ciudad de las montañas» porque aquí las montañas tienen formas muy interesantes. Algunos ejemplos son el Cerro de la Silla, y la Sierra Madre (donde está el parque ecológico Chipinque). La ciudad también tiene museos y dos universidades muy importantes: la Universidad de Monterrey y el Tecnológico de Monterrey, donde yo estudio. La ciudad es moderna pero también puedes escuchar música ranchera e ir a rodeos con toda la familia.

El Distrito Federal

Diana

Me llamo Diana Figueras y mis iniciales son iguales a las de mi ciudad: el D.F. (Distrito Federal). El D.F. es la capital de México y una de las ciudades más grandes del mundo. Tiene más de ocho millones de habitantes.

Yo vivo cerca de la Plaza Hidalgo, en el barrio de Coyoacán. Es famosa por sus artesanos. Aquí está el museo de Frida Kahlo.

En el valle de México vivieron grupos indígenas importantes. Los aztecas establecieron la primera ciudad, Tenochtitlán, en 1325. Esta ciudad, hoy es el D.F.

Aquí hay muchas pirámides y templos de la época precolombina. Además, es tierra de escritores y artistas muy importantes, como Carlos Fuentes (escritor) y Cantinflas (actor). El centro de la ciudad está lleno de vida.

Plaza de la Conchita, Coyoacán, México, D.F.

EL DESAFÍO

VIDEO DVD

En este primer desafío, después de observar la naturaleza y decir lo que piensan, cada equipo debe conseguir las partes necesarias para montar una tienda de campaña. El equipo más rápido gana el desafío.

Antes del video

1. ¿Dónde está Marco? ¿Qué crees que está haciendo?

2. ¿Qué están haciendo Carmen y José? ¿Crees que encuentran las partes que necesitan?

3. Describe lo que ves en esta foto. ¿Qué crees que va a pasar?

El profesor explica el desafío.

Mira el video: Toma apuntes

- Escribe las diferentes cosas que observó Luis.
- ¿Qué opina Marco sobre el parque? ¿Qué prefiere hacer él?
- ¿Qué le da el profesor a Marco?
- Describe lo que hacen Luis y María.
- ¿Qué equipo monta la tienda de campaña primero?
- ¿Qué equipo se divirtió más en este desafío?

Después del video

1. ¿Qué equipo ganó este primer desafío? Describe a los ganadores.
2. En tu opinión, ¿qué pasó con la tienda de campaña de Luis y María?
3. ¿Crees que el profesor es muy estricto? Explica tu respuesta.
4. ¿Cómo es Marco?

UNIDAD 1

Repaso inclusivo

Options for Review

1 Escucha, comprende y compara

Escuchar
Hablar

Escucha este reportaje sobre un problema medioambiental y contesta las preguntas.

1. ¿Qué lugar visitó Silvia?
2. ¿Con quién habló?
3. ¿Qué pasó con las mariposas monarcas? ¿Por qué?
4. ¿Qué ocurrió en el bosque?
5. ¿Qué pidió el director de la reserva?

2 Da una presentación oral

Hablar

Muchos artistas mexicanos exploran los temas de la naturaleza, la familia y la revolución mexicana. Investiga a un artista en particular y prepara una presentación oral sobre sus obras, temas y técnicas. Otra opción es investigar uno de los temas en la obra de varios artistas mexicanos. Trae ejemplos para ilustrar tu presentación. La presentación debe durar por lo menos cinco minutos.

3 Realiza una dramatización

Hablar

La novela gráfica de Sandra se va a convertir en una telenovela. Con un(a) compañero(a) presenta un episodio de la vida-novela de Súper Sandra. La dramatización debe durar por lo menos cinco minutos.

4 Escribe un folleto

Escribir

Escribe un folleto *(brochure)* promocionando un viaje estudiantil a una reserva ecológica o a una de las playas famosas de México. Incluye información sobre las fechas y la duración del viaje, medio de transporte, alojamiento, actividades, equipo necesario, costos y los contactos para más información. No olvides ilustrar tu folleto con fotos apropiadas.

5 Ve a una entrevista

Hablar

Tienes una entrevista con el (la) director(a) de un albergue estudiantil, cerca de una reserva ecológica, un lugar para acampar o una playa. Tú vas a ser el (la) entrevistado(a) y un(a) compañero(a) va a ser el (la) director(a). El (La) director(a) busca un(a) asistente de actividades y te hace preguntas sobre tus conocimientos y experiencias. Contesta sus preguntas relatando las actividades que te gustan y lo que sabes hacer, además de tu experiencia en el pasado con ese tipo de actividades. La entrevista debe durar por lo menos cuatro minutos. Recuerda usar el pretérito y el imperfecto correctamente.

6 Presenta un informe

Hablar
Escribir

Eres un(a) reportero(a) de la revista popular *Gente de hoy* y acabas de entrevistar a un(a) mexicano(a) famoso(a) durante sus vacaciones en el campo o en la playa. Escribe tu reportaje basado en cómo contestó esa persona seis preguntas que le hiciste. Incluye una foto de la persona en tu informe.

7 Escribe un correo electrónico

Leer
Escribir

Escribiste un correo electrónico a Sandra después de leer la novela gráfica en su blog y recibiste esta respuesta de ella. Cuéntale una experiencia de tu vida que ella pueda convertir en una novela gráfica.

Hola,

Gracias por tu interés en mi novela gráfica. La escribí después de las vacaciones familiares en una playa de México. Yo pasé unos días muy aburridos, pero por suerte conocí a un amigo simpático e interesante. Al final, hice muchas cosas nuevas con él y me divertí muchísimo. Esas fueron las mejores vacaciones de mi vida. Creo que las experiencias de tu vida te pueden dar muchas ideas para escribir. ¿Te ocurrió algo interesante con tu familia o tus amigos? ¡Dime qué pasó! Te puedo ayudar a convertir tus experiencias verdaderas en una novela gráfica.

Tu amiga, Sandra

UNIDAD 2

Estados Unidos

¡Es hora de ayudar!

Lección 1

Tema: ***¡Todos para uno y uno para todos!***

Lección 2

Tema: ***¿Cómo nos organizamos?***

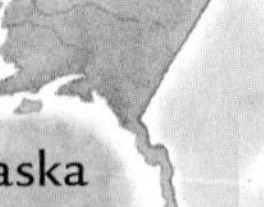

«¿Cómo estás?
Yo soy Irma, de Los Ángeles, y Roberto es de Nueva York.»

Almanaque cultural

Número de hispanos por estado:

CA	11.500.000	IL	1.560.000
TX	7.078.000	AZ	1.412.000
NY	2.890.000	NJ	1.160.000
FL	2.860.000	NM	790.000

Comidas: influencia mexicana (burritos, jaitas), influencia caribeña (puerco, yuca y moros).

Gente famosa: Jennifer López (actriz/cantante), Roberto Fernández (escritor), Sandra Cisneros (escritora), Óscar de la Hoya (boxeador)

Burritos

Festival puertorriqueño en Nueva York

Noreste En los estados de Nueva York y Nueva Jersey se concentran las comunidades puertorriqueña y dominicana más grandes de Estados Unidos. Estas comunidades mantienen sus costumbres y fiestas. *¿Hay alguna celebración latina en tu comunidad?*

Costa Oeste El estado de California tiene una zona agrícola muy importante y es muy famoso por sus viñedos *(vineyards)*. También es conocido por las misiones establecidas por los españoles. Además, en la ciudad de Los Ángeles está la industria del espectáculo más grande del mundo: Hollywood. *¿Qué se cultiva en tu estado? ¿Qué industria hay?*

Misión de Santa Bárbara

Jóvenes hispanas observando murales en Chicago

Estados centrales En la ciudad de Chicago, Illinois, la población mexicana contribuye a la riqueza cultural. La música, pinturas y comida distinguen a Chicago como una ciudad especial. *¿Conoces ejemplos de contribución cultural latina en tu ciudad o estado?*

UNIDAD 2

Estados Unidos

Lección 1

Tema:

¡Todos para uno y uno para todos!

¡AVANZA! **In this lesson you will learn to**

- describe volunteer activities
- organize people to do a project
- persuade or influence others

using

- **tú** commands
- **usted(es), nosotros** commands
- polite requests

¿Recuerdas?

- irregular preterite
- family relationships
- camping and beach activities

Comparación cultural

In this lesson you will learn about

- museums of Latin art
- artists and the community

Compara con tu mundo

Estos jóvenes están en Miami, Florida. Participan en *Hands On Miami Day,* un día en que se hacen trabajos comunitarios. *¿Qué trabajos crees que se pueden hacer en tu comunidad en un día como ése?*

¿Qué ves?

Mira la foto

¿Qué hacen los jóvenes de la foto?

¿Crees que forman un equipo? ¿Por qué?

¿A quién(es) piensas que ayudan?

Online SPANISH CLASSZONE.COM

Featuring...

Cultura INTERACTIVA

Animated Grammar

@HomeTutor

And more...

- Get Help Online
- Interactive Flashcards
- Review Games
- WebQuest
- Conjuguemos.com

Jóvenes durante el *Hands On Miami Day*,
Miami, Florida

Presentación de VOCABULARIO

¡AVANZA! **Goal:** Learn about activities based on volunteer work. Then talk about ways that volunteers can help in their own communities. ***Actividades 1–3***

 *¿Recuerdas?* Irregular preterites p. 42

AUDIO

A Una forma de ayudar es **trabajar de voluntario. Los voluntarios** deben **organizar** actividades en equipo o individualmente para **colaborar** con la comunidad. **La cooperación** es muy importante para **cumplir** con los objetivos.

BUSCAMOS VOLUNTARIOS PARA TRABAJAR EN...

...EL HOGAR DE ANCIANOS

Necesitamos personas para **colaborar** en **proyectos de acción social** para **recaudar fondos**.

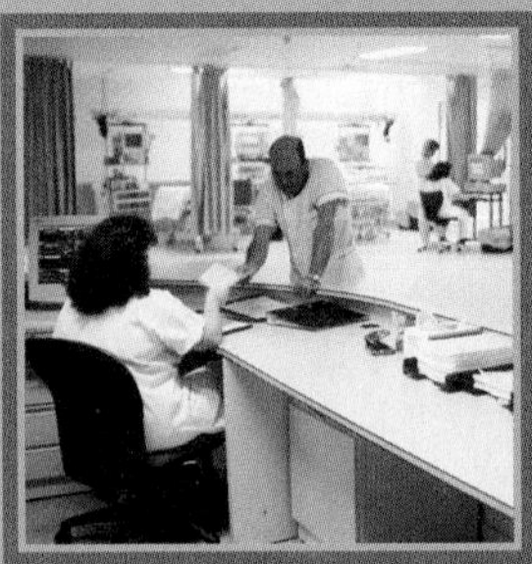

...EL HOSPITAL

Puedes **elegir** una tarea para hacer: puedes leer **los artículos** de **los periódicos** y **revistas** a los pacientes o colaborar en **el diseño** de **los letreros** y pósteres.

...EL COMEDOR DE BENEFICENCIA

Necesitamos hacer un **presupuesto** para la comida y un plan para **gastar** bien el dinero.

NUESTRO TELÉFONO ES: 1-800-VOLUNTA

Más vocabulario

contar con los demás *to count on others*
delegar *to delegate*
el envase *container*
juntar fundos *to fundraise*
el lema *motto*
las noticias *news*
la pobreza *poverty*
prestar *to lend*
la prioridad *priority*
tirar basura *to litter*
Expansión de vocabulario p. R4
Ya sabes p. R4

B Los voluntarios limpian los parques y las calles. También recogen la basura y **reciclan las latas** y otros **artículos** de papel o plástico.

C **La publicidad** es muy importante. Los grupos voluntarios presentan su **campaña** poniendo **anuncios** en **la prensa,** en **las emisoras de radio** o en **los canales de televisión.** **Las agencias de publicidad** trabajan con mucha **creatividad.**

el guante de trabajo

el lema

la lata

la bolsa de plástico

las revistas

los periódicos

D Las campañas son para **solicitar** dinero para comprar comida para **la gente sin hogar,** medicinas o artículos para limpiar la ciudad. Las personas mandan **cheques** para apoyar estas campañas.

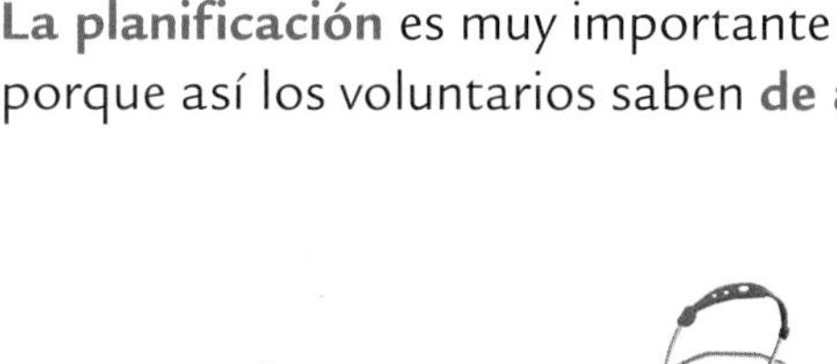

E **La planificación** es muy importante en los trabajos voluntarios, porque así los voluntarios saben **de antemano** qué van a hacer.

¡A responder! Escuchar

Vas a escuchar ocho oraciones. Si la oración describe un ejemplo de ayudar a otros, indícalo con el dedo pulgar hacia arriba. Si la oración no describe un ejemplo de ayudar a otros, indícalo con el dedo pulgar hacia abajo.

Práctica de VOCABULARIO

1 ¡Mucho que hacer!

Escuchar

Escucha este mensaje telefónico que te dejó la coordinadora de una campaña para ayudar a la gente sin hogar. ¿Qué se menciona en la lista de organización?

1. solicitar la cooperación de la prensa
2. depositar los cheques
3. contactar la emisora de radio
4. recoger los letreros
5. hacer un diseño para los letreros
6. solicitar la colaboración del hospital
7. organizar a los voluntarios
8. llamar a la agencia de publicidad

2 Trabajos voluntarios

 ***¿Recuerdas?*** Irregular preterite p. 42

Hablar
Escribir

Usa el pretérito para expresar qué hicieron estas personas como voluntarios.

modelo: **Milton / juntar fondos para el hogar de ancianos**
Milton juntó fondos para el hogar de ancianos.

1. Alicia y Ana / poner un anuncio para reciclar latas y plástico en la comunidad
2. Jorge / hacer un presupuesto para el comedor de beneficencia
3. Elena / conseguir un cheque para pagar el anuncio en el canal de televisión
4. yo / hacer un letrero con mucha creatividad
5. Martín y yo / tener que establecer las prioridades
6. tú / decir que la campaña contra la pobreza era buena

3 ¡A cambiar el mundo!

Hablar

Tus compañeros(as) hicieron trabajos voluntarios. Entrevístalos para saber más. ¿Dónde trabajaron? ¿Qué actividades hicieron en cada lugar? ¿Cuánto tiempo trabajaron? ¿Qué medio de comunicación usaron para anunciar su campaña?

Expansión
Escribe un ensayo breve para resumir los trabajos voluntarios de tus compañeros.

Más práctica Cuaderno *pp. 50–52* Cuaderno para hispanohablantes *pp. 50–53*

¿Comprendiste? Contesta con oraciones completas.

1. ¿Qué eventos especiales organizan los (las) voluntarios(as)?
2. ¿Qué medios de comunicación son útiles para las campañas?
3. ¿Qué puedes recoger y reciclar en tu comunidad?

 VOCABULARIO en contexto

¡AVANZA! **Goal:** Notice how the following letters make suggestions and inspire volunteer participation. Then practice persuading others to do things using language that is courteous. ***Actividades 4–5***

Contexto 1 *Cartas*

ESTRATEGIA **Leer**

Remember phrases by grouping them Following the example, group key phrases from the reading into four categories. Include as many appropriate phrases as possible in each category.

Para empezar la carta	Para terminar la carta	Sobre el concurso	Sobre acción social

AUDIO

Un canal de televisión local de Los Ángeles organizó un concurso para crear un anuncio de publicidad en español para un proyecto de acción social. El gran premio es la oportunidad de filmar el anuncio en cooperación con el canal. Ahora los empleados del canal tienen que elegir al ganador del concurso entre uno de estos tres candidatos.

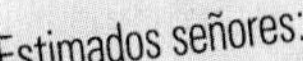

Estimados señores:

Soy una estudiante de Los Ángeles. Mis amigos y yo vimos que hay muchos parques llenos de basura. Queremos limpiar los parques y reciclar el papel, el vidrio, las latas y los envases de plástico que se encuentran allí.

No tenemos un presupuesto para promover y organizar un proyecto como éste, pero podemos contar con otros estudiantes para recoger basura y reciclarla.

Nuestro lema es «Las latas son una lata... nuestros parques no son basureros».

Espero recibir noticias de ustedes,

Irma Rodríguez
Irma Rodríguez

Señores del canal:

Soy voluntaria en un hogar de ancianos y mi obligación es juntar fondos para organizar actividades para los ancianos.

Quiero promover el centro con un anuncio publicitario. Mi lema es «Los ancianos y los jóvenes representan nuestro pasado y futuro».

Mis compañeros y yo pensábamos trabajar con una agencia de publicidad para hacer la campaña, pero si ganamos el concurso vamos a ahorrar mucho dinero. Gracias por su consideración.

Muy atentamente,

Dorotea Cisneros
Dorotea Cisneros

Señores:

Quiero hacer un anuncio publicitario para un comedor de beneficencia.

En el área metropolitana hay mucha pobreza y también mucha gente sin hogar. Quiero promover los proyectos del comedor y también atraer a voluntarios nuevos.

Mi lema para el anuncio es «Cuenta con nosotros para combatir el hambre». ¿Necesito algo más para completar mi propuesta?

En espera de sus noticias,

Ernesto Vargas
Ernesto Vargas

También se dice

Ser una lata es una expresión popular en México y significa «ser muy molesto». Un sinónimo de **molesto** es **latoso.**

- **Argentina** ser un plomo
- **Ecuador** ser molestoso
- **España** ser pesado
- **Cuba** ser una bomba

4 Comprensión de las cartas

Escribir
Hablar

Responde correctamente a las siguientes preguntas.

1. ¿A qué organización quiere apoyar Ernesto?
2. ¿A quiénes quiere atraer Ernesto?
3. ¿Dónde trabaja Dorotea?
4. ¿Cuál es el tema principal del lema de Ernesto?
5. ¿Para qué junta fondos Dorotea?
6. ¿Qué quieren hacer Irma y sus compañeros?
7. ¿Qué problema encontró Irma?
8. ¿Qué observa Ernesto en el área metropolitana?

Repaso gramatical

Polite Requests Many Spanish-speakers avoid direct commands and look for a way of making their suggestions more courteous. Here is one way to make indirect requests.

podrías/podría/podríais/podrían + verb infinitive

¿**Podrías aprobar** el plan? ***Could/Would you approve** the plan?*

5 ¿Podría colaborar?

Hablar

Solicita donaciones de la gente para el hogar de ancianos de tu comunidad. Persuade a tu compañero(a), solicitando sus donaciones con preguntas amables.

modelo: unas latas de comida

A ¿Podrías donar unas latas de comida para el hogar de ancianos?

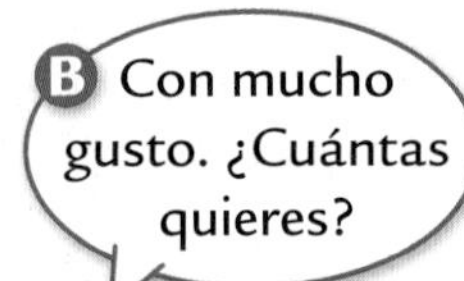

1. recaudar fondos
2. donar una bolsa de ropa
3. comprar unos libros
4. colaborar con nuestra campaña
5. contribuir con un cheque
6. unir los esfuerzos de todos
7. saber el presupuesto para la campaña
8. recoger los envases de plástico

Expansión
Escoge un lugar de tu comunidad (una oficina, un centro comercial, etc.) y escribe cinco preguntas para persuadirlos de que ayuden en tu campaña.

¿Comprendiste? ¿Qué puedes decir para...

1. convencer a tu profesor(a) de que no debe dar tarea?
2. convencer a tus padres de que deben comprarte un carro?
3. solicitar la ayuda de un amigo en la planificación de un proyecto?

Presentación de GRAMÁTICA

¡AVANZA! **Goal:** Review affirmative and negative commands used with **tú.** Then practice by telling others what to do or not to do. ***Actividades 6–9***

¿Recuerdas? Family relationships pp. 58–59, Camping trip pp. 32–33

English Grammar Connection: In English, command forms are the same as the infinitive, but without *to*. Simply add *don't* to make them negative. In Spanish, the **tú command** has an affirmative form and a negative form.

Be good. **Sé** bueno. Don't **be** rude. No **seas** mal educado.

Tú Commands

To tell someone to do or not to do something, use command forms. How do you form the **affirmative tú command?**

Here's how: Regular **affirmative tú commands** are the same as the **usted/él/ella** form in the present tense.

Present Tense: Juan **recoge** y **recicla** las latas.
*Juan **collects** and **recycles** the cans.*

Affirmative tú Command: Juan, ¡**recoge** y **recicla** las latas, por favor!
*Juan, **collect** and **recycle** the cans, please!*

The following verbs are **irregular** in the **affirmative tú command** form.

decir	hacer	ir	poner	salir	ser	tener	venir
di	haz	ve	pon	sal	sé	ten	ven

¡**Ve** a la tienda! ***Go** to the store!* ¡**Di** la verdad! ***Tell** the truth!*

You form **negative tú commands** by changing the **yo** form of the present tense.

-ar verbs **-o** *changes to* **-es**
-er, -ir verbs **-o** *changes to* **-as**

Yo **gasto** mucho dinero. ¡No **gastes** demasiado dinero!

The following verbs are **irregular.**

dar	estar	ir	ser
no des	no estés	no vayas	no seas

No **estés** triste. ***Don't be** sad.*

Más práctica
Cuaderno *pp. 53–55*
Cuaderno para hispanohablantes *pp. 54–56*

Conjuguemos.com

@HomeTutor
Leveled Practice
ClassZone.com

Práctica de GRAMÁTICA

6 ¡Los deberes!

 *¿Recuerdas?* Family relationships pp. 58–59

Escuchar
Escribir

Tus papás están de vacaciones en la playa pero tu mamá te llamó por teléfono con algunas instrucciones. Escucha su mensaje telefónico y apunta los mandatos que usa tu mamá para decirte qué tienes que hacer y no hacer.

modelo: ¡No gastes todo el dinero!

7 ¡Quiero ayudar!

Hablar
Escribir

Un(a) amigo(a) te pidió sugerencias para ayudar en la comunidad. Haz mandatos con los siguientes verbos para recomendar actividades.

modelo: ____ (trabajar) de voluntario(a) en el hospital
Trabaja de voluntario(a) en el hospital.

1. ____ (prestar) tus guantes de trabajo para limpiar el parque.
2. ____ (leer) el periódico en el hogar de ancianos.
3. ____ (apoyar) la campaña de reciclaje.
4. ____ (conseguir) la cooperación de una revista.
5. ____ (colaborar) en la planificación de la campaña.
6. ¡No ____ (esperar) cambiar el mundo en un solo día!
7. No ____ (olvidar) a la gente sin hogar.

Expansión
Tu amigo(a) quiere instrucciones para usar los medios de comunicación. Dale cuatro recomendaciones más relacionadas con ese tema.

Comparación cultural

El Museo del Barrio

Museo del Barrio

¿Por qué es importante conservar las diferentes culturas que tiene un país? El Museo del Barrio está en la ciudad de Nueva York. Los artistas y activistas de **Puerto Rico** lo fundaron en 1969. Ahora, muchos años más tarde, es el museo de Nueva York que mejor conserva, refleja y apoya las culturas y las tradiciones de las comunidades caribeñas y latinas en esta ciudad.

El museo organiza exposiciones y programas muy interesantes. Su prioridad es mostrar la creatividad de los latinoamericanos. Por eso, podemos decir que es un ejemplo importante del intercambio cultural entre las comunidades de **Estados Unidos.**

Compara con tu mundo *¿Hay influencias de la cultura latina en tu ciudad? Descríbelas. ¿Hay un museo en tu ciudad? ¿Qué muestra?*

8 Organiza el campamento

 *¿Recuerdas?* Camping trip pp. 32–33

Hablar

Con un(a) compañero(a), túrnense *(take turns)* para decirles a las personas siguientes qué deben hacer para organizar el campamento. Usen mandatos afirmativos y negativos.

modelo: Jaime, no busques las partes de la tienda ahora. Saca el equipo del carro.

Ana	buscar	estufa de gas
Jaime	recoger	partes de la tienda
Ramón	cerrar	sacos de dormir
Ernesto	sacar	a nosotros
Carmen y Ramón	traer	cantimplora
Ernesto y Carmen	ayudar	latas de refresco
Carmen y Jaime	contar	equipo
Ana, Ramón y Jaime	guardar	tienda de campaña
Todos	organizar	puerta del carro
	montar	mochilas
	descansar	

9 ¡Gracias por tu ayuda!

Escribir

Organizaste una campaña en un comedor de beneficencia. Escríbele una nota a un(a) compañero(a) que te quiere ayudar la semana que tú no puedes ir. Dile qué tiene que hacer y qué no debe hacer. Usa por lo menos cuatro mandatos afirmativos y cuatro negativos en tu nota.

Julián:
¡Gracias por tu ayuda!
La semana...

Expansión
Escribe la nota que te dejó tu compañero(a) después de su semana de voluntario. ¿Qué hizo? ¿Qué mandatos incluye en su nota para tu regreso al trabajo de voluntario(a)?

Más práctica Cuaderno *pp. 53–55* Cuaderno para hispanohablantes *pp. 54–56*

PARA Y PIENSA

¿Comprendiste? ¿Qué debe hacer y qué no debe hacer un(a) nuevo(a) estudiante en tu escuela? Escribe tres mandatos afirmativos y tres mandatos negativos para darle consejos.

GRAMÁTICA en contexto

¡AVANZA! **Goal:** Notice how commands are used in the following proposal for a public service announcement to be aired on television. Then practice using commands to give suggestions to peers. ***Actividades 10–12***

Contexto 2 *Bosquejo*

ESTRATEGIA **Leer**

Use a chart to compare commands
As you read, make a list of the commands you find, placing them into two columns. Notice the forms used for each.

Afirmativos	Negativos

AUDIO

Un canal local de Los Ángeles organizó un concurso para apoyar un proyecto de acción social en la comunidad. El gran premio es la oportunidad de filmar un anuncio de publicidad. Irma Rodríguez ganó el concurso e hizo un bosquejo *(story board)* del anuncio.

Nuestros parques no son basureros...

Tenemos que organizarnos para mantenerlos limpios. ¡Usa un poco de tu tiempo para ayudarnos! ¡Haz un esfuerzo y mejora tu comunidad!

Recuerda esta fecha: sábado 7 de abril. Ven al parque que está frente al canal. ¡No lo olvides! Prepárate para limpiar el parque y reciclar.

¡Lleva tus guantes de trabajo y colabora con la limpieza! Invita a tus amigos a recoger latas y envases de plástico.

¡Ven a ayudarnos! ¡Recoge y recicla para limpiar nuestros espacios públicos!

Recuerda: ¡Las latas son una lata... nuestros parques no son basureros!

10 Comprensión del bosquejo

Hablar
Escribir

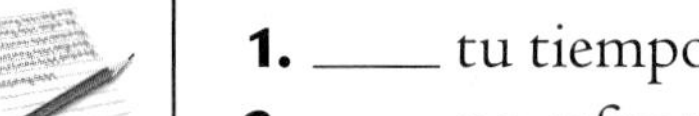

Completa los siguientes mandatos al telespectador *(TV viewer)*, según la información del anuncio.

1. _____ tu tiempo.	**6.** _____ con la limpieza.
2. _____ un esfuerzo.	**7.** _____ a tus amigos.
3. _____ la fecha.	**8.** _____ latas y envases de plástico.
4. No _____ la fecha.	**9.** No te _____ .
5. _____ los guantes.	**10.** _____ : «Las latas son una lata.»

11 ¡Colabora!

Escribir

Con un(a) compañero(a) ayuda a Irma a diseñar un póster para promocionar su evento. Usa ideas de su anuncio como inspiración, ¡pero no las copies directamente! Debes incluir al menos cuatro mandatos. Explica por qué la gente tiene que participar en el evento.

Expansión
Prepara otro póster para Irma. Esta vez, usa algunas ideas propias.

12 Una campaña

Hablar

Tú y tus compañeros(as) deben crear su propio anuncio promocionando un proyecto de acción social en su comunidad. Primero, hablen de los programas que consideran importantes. Luego preparen una campaña para presentar en la clase. Usen vocabulario y verbos apropiados en forma de mandato.

AUDIO

Pronunciación El sonido ch

La combinación **ch** se pronuncia exactamente como la **ch** de la palabra *choose* en inglés. Su posición en una palabra no afecta nunca la pronunciación de la **ch.**

chapotear	**cheque**
chaleco	**ducharse**

Trabalenguas

Pancha plancha con cuatro planchas.
¿Con cuántas planchas Pancha plancha?

¿Comprendiste? Utiliza tres mandatos afirmativos y tres mandatos negativos para dar sugerencias a un(a) compañero(a) que quiere ayudar en la comunidad escolar.

Get Help Online
ClassZone.com

Presentación de GRAMÁTICA

¡AVANZA! **Goal:** Review **usted, ustedes,** and **nosotros** command forms. Then practice by persuading or influencing others. ***Actividades 13–16***

¿Recuerdas? Beach activities pp. 58–59, **ir a** + infinitive p. R33

English Grammar Connection: In English, **commands** almost always stay the same, whether they are given to one or more people. When you include yourself in a group, you simply add the word *let's* in front of the verb.

	¡Para! *(tú)*		
Stop!	**¡Pare!** *(usted)*	**Let's stop** here!	¡**Paremos** aquí!
	¡Paren! *(ustedes)*		

REPASO Other Command Forms

Animated Grammar ClassZone.com

To use affirmative and negative **commands** for **usted, ustedes,** and **nosotros,** start with the **yo** form of the present tense.

Here's how: For regular verbs, drop the **-o,** and add the command ending.

		Command Forms		
Infinitive	**Present Indicative**	**Usted**	**Ustedes**	**Nosotros**
tirar	**yo tiro**	¡(No) **tire**!	¡(No) **tiren**!	¡(No) **tiremos**!
hacer	**yo hago**	¡(No) **haga**!	¡(No) **hagan**!	¡(No) **hagamos**!
elegir	**yo elijo**	¡(No) **elija**!	¡(No) **elijan**!	¡(No) **elijamos**!

Profesora, ¡**elija** a un representante!
*Professor, **choose** a representative!*

¡No **tiremos** basura en el parque!
***Let's not litter** in the park!*

- To say *let's go,* use **vamos.**
- To say *let's not go,* use **no vayamos.**

Verbs ending in **-car, -gar,** and **-zar** require a spelling change (**c→qu, g→gu, z→c**) in **usted, ustedes,** and **nosotros** command forms.

organizar Representantes, ¡**organicen** sus papeles antes de salir!
*Representatives, **organize** your papers before leaving!*

Más práctica
Cuaderno *pp. 56–58*
Cuaderno para hispanohablantes *pp. 57–60*

Conjuguemos.com

@HomeTutor Leveled Practice ClassZone.com

Práctica de GRAMÁTICA

13 En la playa

 ***¿Recuerdas?*** Beach activities pp. 58–59

Hablar
Escribir

Un grupo de niños está en la playa para hacer actividades. Tú les das mandatos para decirles qué tienen que hacer.

modelo: ¡Levanten las manos!

1. recoger

2. mantener

3. refrescarse

4. jugar

5. recostarse

6. pararse

14 ¡Vamos a comenzar!

 ***¿Recuerdas?*** **ir a** + infinitive p. R33

Hablar

Tú y un(a) compañero(a) quieren colaborar en un proyecto para su comunidad. Usen los mandatos **nosotros** o la expresión **vamos a** para expresar sus sugerencias.

modelo: trabajar de voluntarios en el hospital / trabajar de voluntarios en el hogar de ancianos

A ¡Trabajemos de voluntarios en el hospital!

B No, ¡vamos a trabajar de voluntarios en el hogar de ancianos!

1. escribir el lema / elegir más voluntarios
2. comprar bolsas de plástico / escribir el artículo para el periódico
3. dar la noticia en todo el barrio / hacer publicidad en la radio
4. llamar al coordinador / delegar la tarea
5. contar con los demás / buscar soluciones de antemano
6. trabajar de voluntario en dos proyectos / cumplir con un proyecto primero

Expansión

Prepara un cartel invitando al público a participar en un proyecto. Usa cinco ejemplos de mandatos en la forma de **nosotros** y **vamos a.**

15 ¡Organicémonos!

Escribir

Organizas una campaña para ayudar a la gente sin hogar. Tienes que decirle al (a la) director(a) de la escuela lo que tiene que hacer. Escribe un correo electrónico con las instrucciones. Usa mandatos en la forma de **usted.**

```
Sr./Sra. Director(a),
Tenemos mucho que hacer para organizar nuestra campaña.
1) Por favor, prepare el anuncio para la prensa.
2) ...
```

16 Los artistas y la comunidad

Leer
Escribir

Comparación cultural

Pablo O'Higgins

The Market
(c. 1940), Pablo O'Higgins

¿Qué papel juegan los artistas dentro de la comunidad? Antes del comienzo del siglo XX la mayoría de los artistas pintaban solamente la vida de los ricos. Pero, entre los años 1910 y 1950 esto se hizo más democrático, cuando muchos artistas se dedicaron a la representación de la vida y las ocupaciones de la gente común. Entre ellos está Pablo O'Higgins. O'Higgins nació en Salt Lake City, **Estados Unidos,** en 1904 y su nombre original era Paul Higgins. Fue a **México** a estudiar con los muralistas mexicanos y trabajó con Diego Rivera por cuatro años. El movimiento del muralismo mexicano pintó a la clase obrera *(working class)*.

Compara con tu mundo *¿Hay artistas en tu comunidad? ¿Qué temas usan? ¿Crees que los artistas tienen la obligación de tratar de mejorar la vida en su comunidad? ¿Por qué?*

Piensa en un tema para pintar un mural. Puede ser un tema sobre tu comunidad. Luego, escribe un párrafo corto para dar instrucciones a los artistas. Usa por lo menos cinco mandatos formales en tu párrafo.

Más práctica Cuaderno *pp. 56–58* Cuaderno para hispanohablantes *pp. 57–60*

PARA Y PIENSA

¿Comprendiste? Tus compañeros(as) voluntarios(as) necesitan tu ayuda para organizar sus tareas en el comedor de beneficencia. Diles qué tienen que hacer. Usa la forma apropiada del mandato.

1. Jorge y Luis: poner los platos en las mesas
2. Sr. Ramos: encender la estufa
3. Martín y Rosa: preparar la comida

Get Help Online
ClassZone.com

Todo junto

¡AVANZA! **Goal:** ***Show what you know*** Notice how Irma uses command forms to give instructions in the following dialogue. Then practice by explaining how to do something. ***Actividades 17–19***

Resumen contextos 1 y 2 Irma ganó un concurso con una propuesta publicitaria para televisión. El objetivo de su anuncio es invitar a voluntarios a limpiar un parque de Los Ángeles.

Contexto 3 *Diálogo*

ESTRATEGIA **Escuchar**

Use what you know to sharpen the focus
Before listening, examine the photo and consider what you already know about environmental clean-up and recycling. While listening several times, use these clues, plus the speakers' voice intonation, to bring the meaning into focus.

AUDIO

Muchos voluntarios vinieron para ayudar con la limpieza de un parque de Los Ángeles. Irma tiene que decirles qué deben hacer. Irma habla con el grupo y también con su amigo Darío, que está ayudando con la organización del evento.

Irma: Tenemos mucho que hacer, pero no se preocupen, podemos completar todo si nos organizamos bien.

Darío: Mira, Irma, los Sres. Ramírez trajeron estas bolsas de plástico.

Irma: ¡Qué bien! Sr. y Sra. Ramírez, si no les molesta, repartan las bolsas entre los voluntarios.

Sra. Ramírez: Claro, Irma. No dudes en decirnos si hay otra cosa que podemos hacer.

Irma: Gracias, Sra. Ramírez. Si no tenemos suficientes bolsas, vaya a comprar más a la tienda, por favor. Sr. Ramírez, tome el dinero de la campaña, está allí. A ver... Darío, ¿podrías formar un grupo de personas para recoger artículos de vidrio y papel, cerca del lago? Pónganlos aquí en estas bolsas. ¡No olviden usar los guantes de trabajo!

Darío: No hay problema. ¡Vamos!

Irma: Esteban, ¿nos puedes ayudar a reciclar los envases de plástico y las latas? Escoge a cinco voluntarios para recoger esos materiales y luego pónganlos aquí. Pero, no los mezclen con el vidrio.

Esteban: ¡Enseguida, Irma! A ver... ustedes, por favor, ¿por qué no vienen conmigo? Vamos a empezar aquí, junto a estos árboles.

Darío: ¡Irma, Irma, no te imaginas qué pasó!

Irma: ¿Qué pasó? ¡Dime!

Darío: ¡Adivina quiénes acaban de llegar!

Irma: ¿Quién? ¿Quiénes? ¡Cuéntame! ¡Me muero de curiosidad!

Darío: Oye, ya sabes que están filmando una película muy cerca de aquí...

Irma: Sí, sí..., ¡no me hagas esperar ni un segundo más! Dime qué pasa.

Darío: Bueno, las estrellas de la película vinieron para ayudar con el proyecto de limpieza... ¡Salma Hayek, Antonio Banderas, Benicio del Toro, Gael García Bernal y Penélope Cruz!

Irma: ¡No me digas! Darío, llama al canal de televisión. ¡Y a los periódicos! ¡Y a la radio! ¡Tenemos una oportunidad increíble para hacer la publicidad de nuestra campaña!

Darío: ¡De acuerdo! Préstame tu celular. ¡Ya llamo a todos!

17 Comprensión del diálogo

Escuchar
Hablar
Escribir

Según el diálogo, di qué actividad(es) asocias con quién(es).

Irma | Los señores Ramírez | Darío | Esteban

1. dijo a todos lo que tenían que hacer
2. formó un grupo para reciclar cosas
3. pidió el teléfono celular
4. recogió artículos de papel y vidrio
5. repartió las bolsas de plástico
6. trabajó cerca del lago
7. trajeron bolsas de plástico
8. vio a unas estrellas de cine

18 Integración

Leer
Escuchar
Hablar

Lee el folleto solicitando voluntarios para la comunidad. Luego escucha el discurso de Jaime en el parque. Después di cuáles son las oportunidades para voluntarios que hay en la comunidad. Usa palabras para persuadir a la gente a trabajar como voluntario(a).

Fuente 1 Folleto

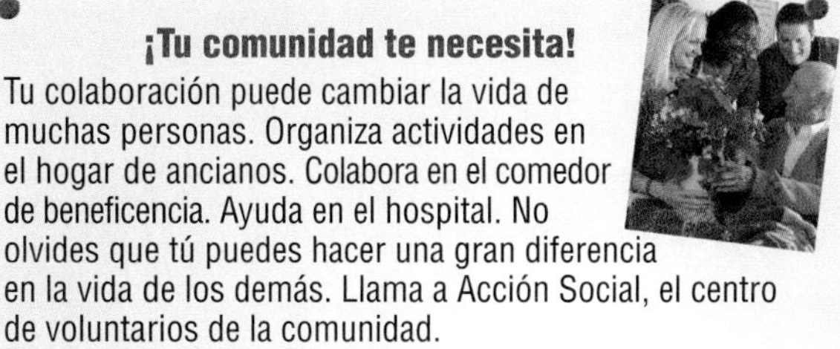

¡Tu comunidad te necesita!

Tu colaboración puede cambiar la vida de muchas personas. Organiza actividades en el hogar de ancianos. Colabora en el comedor de beneficencia. Ayuda en el hospital. No olvides que tú puedes hacer una gran diferencia en la vida de los demás. Llama a Acción Social, el centro de voluntarios de la comunidad.

1-800-CCENTRO
www.accionsocial.org

¡La comunidad cuenta contigo!

Fuente 2 Discurso

Escucha y apunta

- ¿Qué pide Jaime Lagos en su discurso?
- ¿Qué oportunidades para voluntarios hay en esa comunidad?

modelo: Jaime Lagos busca gente para trabajar en la comunidad. Se puede trabajar en hogares de ancianos y juntar fondos.

19 ¡Un evento memorable!

Escribir

Escribe un artículo sobre una campaña para limpiar un parque. Utiliza expresiones para dar órdenes y las siguientes pistas *(hints)* para escribirlo.

Pistas: lugar, día, describir el lugar antes y después de limpiarlo, da nombres de los que participaron, las tareas de cada cual y los materiales que utilizaron.

Writing Criteria	Excellent	Good	Needs Work
Content	You include all of the important information and quote several commands.	You include some of the important information and quote some commands.	You include little information and quote few commands.
Communication	Your article is organized and easy to follow.	Parts of your article are organized and easy to follow.	Your article is disorganized and hard to follow.
Accuracy	You make few mistakes in grammar and vocabulary.	You make some mistakes in grammar and vocabulary.	You make many mistakes in grammar and vocabulary.

Más práctica Cuaderno *pp. 59–60* Cuaderno para hispanohablantes *pp. 61–62*

¿Comprendiste? Da instrucciones a un(a) compañero(a) para explicar cómo hacer algo, por ejemplo: llegar a tu casa, estudiar para un examen, preparar una comida o jugar a algún deporte. Usa la forma **tú** de los mandatos e incluye dos mandatos negativos.

Lectura literaria

¡AVANZA! **Goal:** Read the following story and notice how two different cultures have become intertwined in the characters' lives.

Para leer 

ESTRATEGIA **Leer**

Play the Circle Game to enhance understanding Copy the diagram below, taking notes about the main theme and the interrelated story parts: (a) people; (b) setting; (c) events, actions, or changes; and (d) reasons for events, actions, or changes.

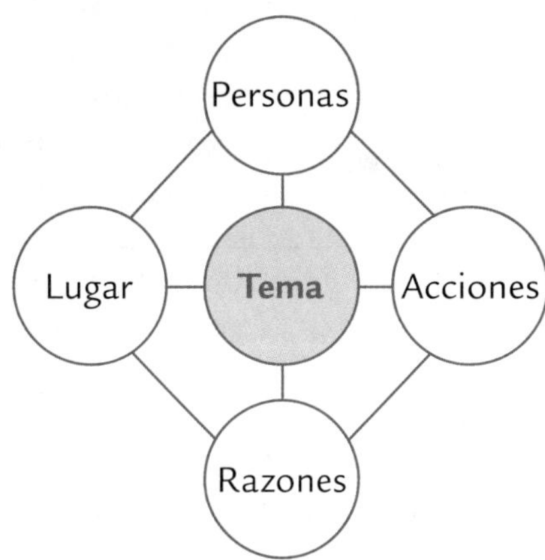

Vocabulario para leer

el tilo	*té que se prepara con las hojas aromáticas de un árbol*
la nevera	*aparato electrodoméstico que sirve para refrigerar alimentos*
el pavo	*animal que se come tradicionalmente el Día de Acción de Gracias*
el chisme	*noticia que se dice de boca en boca; puede ser verdadera o falsa*
la ciudadanía	*derechos que adquieren las personas al ser ciudadanos de un país*

Nota cultural

Sobre el autor **Roberto G. Fernández (1955–)**
Nació en Cuba y a la edad de ocho años se trasladó *(he moved)* a Miami. Entre sus libros figuran *Holy Radishes* y *En la Ocho y la Doce,* donde presenta los conflictos culturales de los cubanoamericanos.

Sobre la migración Entre los años 1959 y 1963, muchos cubanos emigraron a Estados Unidos. Hoy hay más de un millón de cubanoamericanos en Estados Unidos. Miami todavía tiene la mayor población, pero también hay grupos grandes en las ciudades de Nueva York, Los Ángeles y Chicago.

En la Ocho y la Doce

—¡Oye, ábreme, es Barbarita!

—¿Qué está pasando?

—Perdone, Ramiro, ¿Tita se encuentra?

—Pase, pase, que sale en seguida. Está en el baño. No tenga pena. Siéntese que se ve agitada.

—Pero mujer, ¿qué te ocurre que oía la gritería[1] desde el traspatio[2]?

—Ay, Tita, he pasado el susto más grande de toda mi vida, ni siquiera cuando a Many le explotó la cocinita de kerosén en los cayos[3] pasé más susto.

—Te voy a hacer una taza de tilo para que te calmes un poco. Estás muy pálida.

—No te molestes.

—Tú estate tranquila aquí sentada que yo vengo en menos de tres minutos. ¡El micronda nuevo que me compré es una maravilla! Ponte a hojear una revista mientras regreso que eso calma mucho los nervios. ❋

....

—Ay, Tita, estaba yo repasando el comienzo de la constitución, ¿te dije que me voy a hacer *American citizen*?, y en ese momento cuando estaba diciendo en voz alta *We the people*...

❋ A pensar
¿Cuál crees que es el escenario de esta historia? ¿Una tienda? ¿Una casa? ¿Una oficina? ¿Qué pistas del contexto usaste para determinar el lugar?

---

[1] shouting [2] backyard [3] The Florida Keys

—Güi di pipol, ¿qué es eso?

—¡Por eso te vuelvo a decir que tienes que volverte normal igual que yo! Tita, así empieza la constitución, en inglés se dice constituchon. Oye, Tita, es que no me dejas acabarte el cuento[4] y me va a dar más estrés.

—Sigue, sigue, que no te interrumpo más.

—Y estaba repasando el preámbulo a la constituchon y...

... Y de pronto veo algo sobre la nevera y como soy miope[5] pues na' ma' veía un bulto[6] y me figuré que era un melón que Many había comprado del frutero que pasa por aquí a las tres, el marido de la lavandera, y seguí practicando el *We the People,* pero me entró sed y cuando voy a abrir la puerta de la nevera para sacar el litro de Diet Coke pasé el susto de la vida. Había un hombre transparente sentado arriba de la nevera con un pavo bajo el brazo. Me asusté mucho, me sentí como cucaracha en fiesta de gallinas[7], y con el susto le dije en inglés, «¿Gua du yu guan?» El hombre me respondió: «Soy San Guiven».

Entonces yo le dije: «¿San Guiven, el de la novela?»[...] Y él me respondió: «Tranquilícese que eso es sólo en la novela. Yo soy San Guiven de verdad. Vengo pa' que me empieces una colecta[8] y me

A pensar
Tita dice algunas frases en inglés con un acento muy fuerte. ¿Qué frase en inglés suena como «Güi di pipol»? ¿Y «constituchon»?

[4] **acabarte...** to finish the story for you
[5] nearsighted [6] **na'...** I only saw a thing
[7] **como...** *fig.* afraid (*lit.* feeling like a roach in a party of chickens)
[8] fundraiser, collection

hagas un santuario[9]». Entonces sí que me turbé[10], tú sabes bien Tita que no es todos los días que a uno se le aparece un santo. Y ya algo más tranquila le dije: «¿Tú sabes cómo termina la novela?» Él me dijo con la cabeza que sí, y siguió hablándome: ❖

A pensar
«San Guiven» es la pronunciación incorrecta de *Thanksgiving.* «La novela» *(soap opera)* se refiere a un programa de televisión que menciona esta celebración y que las dos mujeres ven todos los días. ¿Cuál crees que es la confusión de Barbarita y Tita?

Reflexiona

¿Por qué Barbarita se asustó tanto?

«Ve al pantry y saca una lata de arándanos». «¿Arándanos?» le pregunté yo y él tan atento me contestó: «Así se les dice a los *cranberries* en *Spanish*». Imagínate la pena que pasé con el santo, yo casi una maestra y no sabía decir *cranberries* en español. Y continuó: «Sácale los arándanos y limpia bien la lata. Ésta será la primera lata para la colecta. Quiero que esta lata esté en el punto más alto del santuario una vez se construya». Y en seguida dijo «Mi fiesta debe ser celebrada siempre el último jueves de noviembre, *the last Thursday in November*».

—¿Di las serdei in nobemver?

—¡Ay Tita! ¿Cuándo vas a aprender inglés? Eso es el último jueves de noviembre. Él lo repitió en inglés pa' asegurarse que su fiesta fuera bilingüe.[...] Entonces como mismito[11] vino se desapareció, tú sabes, Tita, se esfumó[12], pero dejó el pavo que tenía bajo el brazo.

Esto te lo digo a ti porque sé que no vas a ir a nadie con el chisme y pa' que me ayudes a hacer más latas pa' la colecta. Yo sé que el santo dijo una lata, pero con una lata no se puede. Toma más tiempo y con lo de la ciudadanía y el trabajo de tícher assistan no tengo el tiempo ni pa' arrascarme el ombligo. ❖

A pensar
Busca todos los mandatos que aparecen en esta página.

[9] sanctuary [10] **me...** I got nervous [11] **como...** just like
[12] he vanished

¿Comprendiste?

1. ¿Por qué fue Barbarita a ver a Tita?
2. ¿Qué le dio Tita a Barbarita para calmarla?
3. ¿Qué estaba haciendo Barbarita cuando San Guiven apareció?
4. ¿Qué traía San Guiven y qué le mandó hacer a Barbarita?
5. ¿Aceptó Barbarita la misión? ¿Qué piensa hacer?

¿Y tú?

¿Conoces a alguien que hable como los personajes de este relato? ¿Puedes dar ejemplos de algunas frases o palabras?

Conexiones *La historia*

Un líder latino

Uno de los líderes latinos más influyentes del siglo XX es César Chávez. Nació en 1927 cerca de Yuma, Arizona. Hijo de padres mexicanos, desde niño experimentó la dificultad de seguir una vida migratoria, pasando de una ciudad a otra en busca de trabajo.

Desde muy joven trabajó en las cosechas de uvas *(grapes)*, damascos *(apricots)* y aceitunas *(olives)*. Chávez decía que la cosecha más difícil era la de aceitunas: «Son tan pequeñas que nunca llenas los cubos *(buckets)*».

Chávez simpatizaba con los trabajadores migratorios y decidió ayudarlos. En 1962 creó la National Farm Workers Association, que luego se transformó en la United Farm Workers Union. Usó tácticas no violentas como manifestaciones, huelgas *(strikes)* y ayunos *(fasts)* para conseguir leyes a favor de los trabajadores del campo.

Después de una vida de sacrificios y esfuerzos en nombre de los trabajadores migratorios, Chávez murió en su casa, cerca de Yuma. Ahora, para conmemorar sus esfuerzos, se celebra el *César Chávez Day of Service and Learning* en siete estados (Arizona, California, Colorado, Missouri, Nuevo México, Texas, Utah) y muchas ciudades de Estados Unidos.

Proyecto En la biblioteca o en Internet, investiga las celebraciones del *César Chávez Day of Service and Learning.* ¿Qué actividades se organizan? ¿Hay diferencias entre las celebraciones de un estado y otro?

Investiga sobre otro(a) líder latino(a) en Estados Unidos. ¿Qué causa social apoya? ¿Qué quiere hacer para mejorar su comunidad?

En tu comunidad

¿Se celebra el *César Chávez Day of Service and Learning* en tu estado o ciudad? ¿Hay comunidades de latinos en tu estado o ciudad? ¿Hay líderes latinos importantes en tu comunidad? ¿Hay otras celebraciones que se asocian con líderes de tu comunidad?

Lección 1

En resumen

Vocabulario y gramática

Vocabulario

Describe Volunteer Activities

los ancianos	*the elderly*	el hogar de ancianos	*nursing home*
la bolsa de plástico	*plastic bag*	el hospital	*hospital*
el comedor de beneficencia	*soup kitchen*	la lata	*metal can*
el envase	*container*	la pobreza	*poverty*
la gente sin hogar	*the homeless*	el proyecto de acción social	*social action project*
los guantes de trabajo	*work gloves*	el (la) voluntario(a)	*volunteer*

Organize People to do a Project

apoyar	*to support*	juntar fondos	*to fundraise*
el cheque	*check*	organizar	*to organize*
colaborar	*to collaborate*	la planificación	*planning*
contar con los demás	*to count on others*	prestar	*to lend*
la cooperación	*cooperation*	el presupuesto	*budget*
cumplir	*to fulfill, to carry out*	la prioridad	*priority*
de antemano	*beforehand*	recaudar fondos	*to raise funds*
delegar	*to delegate*	reciclar	*to recycle*
elegir (i)	*to choose*	solicitar	*to ask for, to request*
gastar	*to spend*	tirar basura	*to litter*
		trabajar de voluntario	*to volunteer*

Persuade or Influence Others

la agencia de publicidad	*ad agency*
el anuncio	*announcement, ad*
el artículo	*article*
la campaña	*campaign*
el canal de televisión	*T.V. channel*
la creatividad	*creativity*
el diseño	*design*
la emisora (de radio)	*radio station*
el lema	*motto*
el letrero	*sign, poster*
las noticias	*news*
el periódico	*newspaper*
la prensa	*press*
la publicidad	*publicity*
la revista	*magazine*

Gramática

Nota gramatical: Polite requests *p. 96*

REPASO Tú Commands

Regular **affirmative tú commands** are the same as the **usted/él/ella** form in the present tense.

The following verbs are **irregular:**

decir: di	**hacer:** haz	**ir:** ve	**poner:** pon
salir: sal	**ser:** sé	**tener:** ten	**venir:** ven

You form negative **tú commands** by changing the **yo** form of the present tense.

For **-ar** verbs: **-o** *changes to* **-es**.
For **-er/-ir** verbs: **-o** *changes to* **-as**.

The following verbs are **irregular:**

dar: no des	**estar:** no estés
ir: no vayas	**ser:** no seas

REPASO Other Command Forms

Command Forms

Usted	Ustedes	Nosotros
¡(No) **tire**!	¡(No) **tiren**!	¡(No) **tiremos**!
¡(No) **haga**!	¡(No) **hagan**!	¡(No) **hagamos**!
¡(No) **elija**!	¡(No) **elijan**!	¡(No) **elijamos**!

To say *let's go,* use **vamos.**
To say *let's not go,* use **no vayamos.**

Verbs ending in **-car, -gar,** and **-zar** require a spelling change (c→qu, g→gu, z→c) in **usted, ustedes,** and **nosotros** command forms.

Lección 1

Repaso de la lección

¡LLEGADA!

@HomeTutor ClassZone.com

Now you can
- describe volunteer activities
- organize people to do a project
- persuade or influence others

Using
- **tú** commands
- other command forms
- polite requests

To review
- **tú** commands p. 97
- vocabulary pp. 92–93

1 Listen and understand

AUDIO

Una estudiante de una escuela secundaria escribió un artículo para el periódico estudiantil sobre las leyes de oro *(golden rules)* para los voluntarios. Escucha mientras ella las lee e indica si dice lo siguiente o no.

1. Gastar dinero sin pedir permiso. ____
2. Reciclar todos los materiales que ya no usas. ____
3. Participar en proyectos de acción social en tu comunidad. ____
4. Delegar lo que tú mismo puedes hacer. ____
5. Cumplir con tus obligaciones. ____
6. Solicitar fondos por teléfono después de las nueve de la noche. ____

To review
- **tú** commands p. 97
- **usted, ustedes,** and **nosotros** commands p. 102

2 Organize people to do a project

Oscar organiza un proyecto para apoyar un comedor de beneficencia de su comunidad. Completa los mandatos que Oscar les da a varios voluntarios.

1. Susana, ____ (elegir / nosotros) a dos voluntarios más para calcular el presupuesto.
2. Sra. Ramos, ____ (leer) el anuncio para ver si hay errores.
3. Miguel y Manuel, ____ (llevar) estos letreros a la escuela, por favor.
4. Luis, ____ (organizar) un grupo para juntar fondos. No (olvidar) ____ pedir donaciones en la emisora de radio.
5. Sr. Menéndez, ¡no ____ (olvidarse)! Necesitamos un lema para la campaña de publicidad. ____ (consultar) con los otros voluntarios para pedir sus opiniones. Luego, entre todos, ____ (inventar) un lema.
6. Marilú, no ____ (gastar) más dinero por el momento. Primero ____ (depositar) este cheque en el banco, por favor.

To review
- commands with the form **vamos a** + infinitive p. 103

3 Describe volunteer activities and opportunities

Mira las siguientes escenas y di qué mandato usa cada persona para decir a todos lo que tienen que hacer. Usa la forma **vamos a** y el vocabulario apropiado.

1. Olivia

2. Elena y Enrique

3. Guillermo

4. Alberto y Ana

To review
- polite requests p. 96

4 Persuade or influence others

Irma escribió un correo electrónico para enviárselo a un grupo de voluntarios. Ahora quiere hacerlo un poco más cortés *(polite)*. Escribe de nuevo las siguientes oraciones según el modelo.

modelo: ¡Ayuda con el proyecto!
¿Podrías ayudar con el proyecto?

1. ¡Da tu ropa vieja a la gente sin hogar!
2. ¡Colaboren con la campaña!
3. ¡Junten fondos para el comedor de beneficencia!
4. ¡Solicita donaciones de dinero!
5. ¡Elige más voluntarios!
6. ¡Recicle artículos de vidrio, plástico y papel!

To review
- **Comparación cultural** pp. 98, 104

5 Museums of Latin art, artists, and the community

Comparación cultural

Contesta las siguientes preguntas sobre la cultura en el mundo hispano de Estados Unidos.

1. ¿Qué actividades organiza el Museo del Barrio?
2. ¿Cuándo y quiénes lo fundaron?
3. ¿Dónde nació Pablo O'Higgins?
4. ¿Por qué el muralismo mexicano fue un estilo de pintura más democrático?

Más práctica Cuaderno *pp. 61–72* Cuaderno para hispanohablantes *pp. 63–72*

Get Help Online
ClassZone.com

UNIDAD 2

Estados Unidos

Lección 2

Tema:

¿Cómo nos organizamos?

¡AVANZA! **In this lesson you will learn to**

- make requests and recommendations
- express opinions
- talk about media and the community

using

- pronouns with commands
- impersonal expressions + infinitive
- impersonal constructions with **se**

¿Recuerdas?

- preterite vs. imperfect
- beach activities
- volunteer activities

Comparación cultural

In this lesson you will learn about

- celebrities who raise money
- Spanish newspapers in the United States
- different types of music in the United States

Compara con tu mundo

Estos estudiantes de Nueva York están organizando un grupo de voluntarios para colaborar en proyectos de acción social. Preparan letreros mientras un adulto da información sobre los proyectos. *¿Trabajaste de voluntario alguna vez? ¿Qué hiciste?*

¿Qué ves?

Mira la foto

¿Qué hacen los estudiantes?

¿Qué ropa llevan?

¿Qué tipos de edificios ves?

¿Qué tiempo hace?

Online SPANISH CLASSZONE.COM

Featuring...

- Cultura INTERACTIVA
- Animated Grammar
- @HomeTutor

And more...

- Get Help Online
- Interactive Flashcards
- Review Games
- WebQuest
- Conjuguemos.com

Jóvenes haciendo trabajos voluntarios,
ciudad de Nueva York

Presentación de VOCABULARIO

¡AVANZA! **Goal:** Learn about the different media that are used to communicate information. Then practice the vocabulary you learned to talk about various aspects of newspapers and television. ***Actividades 1–3***

¿Recuerdas? Preterite vs. imperfect p. 68

AUDIO

A Hola, me llamo Roberto y trabajo en el periódico de mi escuela. Aquí ves mi escritorio. Quiero **explicarles** mi trabajo. Junto con un **fotógrafo, entrevisto** a la gente, **investigo cuestiones** importantes y **presento** las noticias en mis **artículos de opinión** con fotos excelentes. También escribo **reseñas** de libros y **describo** exposiciones de pintura. Pero lo que más me gusta es tener **un debate** con otra persona sobre un tema en que **no estamos de acuerdo.**

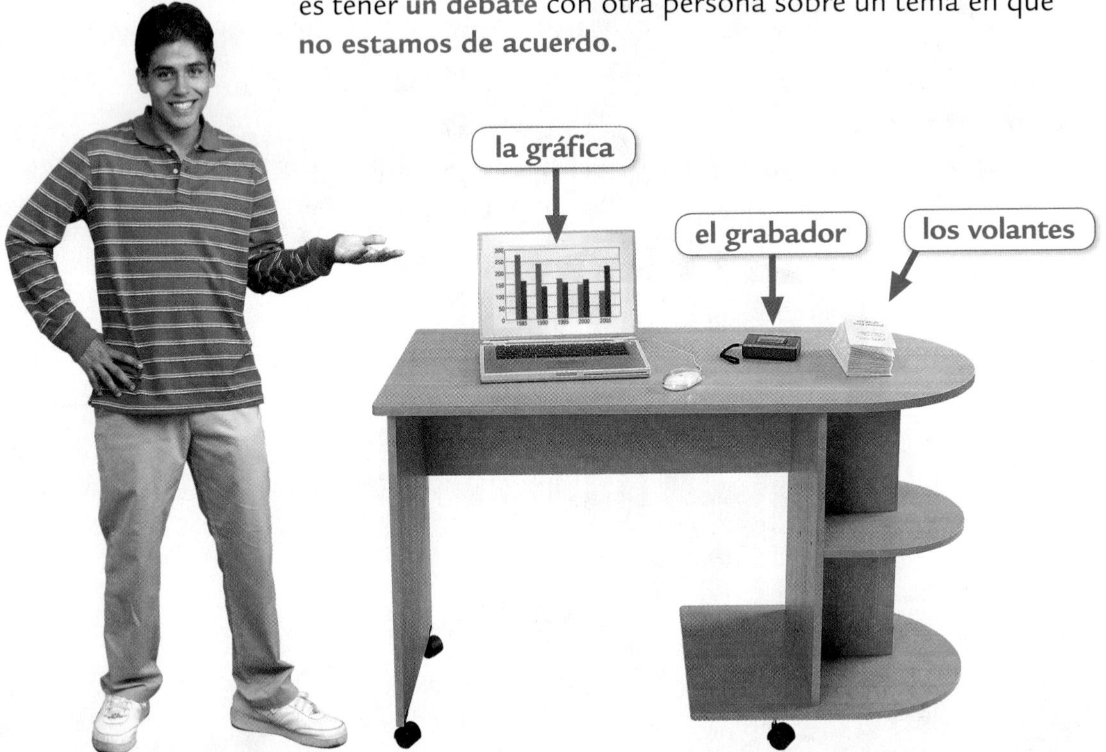

B El periódico se **publica** y se **distribuye** cada día. Por eso tengo **una fecha límite** para terminar los textos. Luego, **el editor** escribe **los titulares** y **un artículo de opinión** que se llama «**La columna** del editor», que es uno de los favoritos del **público.**

Más vocabulario

- **el acceso** *access*
- **el anuncio clasificado** *classified ad*
- **el anuncio personal** *personal ad*
- **la cita** *quote*
- **el cortometraje** *short documentary*
- **los dibujos animados** *cartoons*
- **la entrevista** *interview*
- **el largometraje** *feature, full-length movie*
- **el noticiero** *news broadcast*
- **otorgar** *to grant*
- **la publicidad por correo** *mailing*

Expansión de vocabulario p. R5
Ya sabes p. R5

 Ayer escribí este **anuncio** para el periódico.

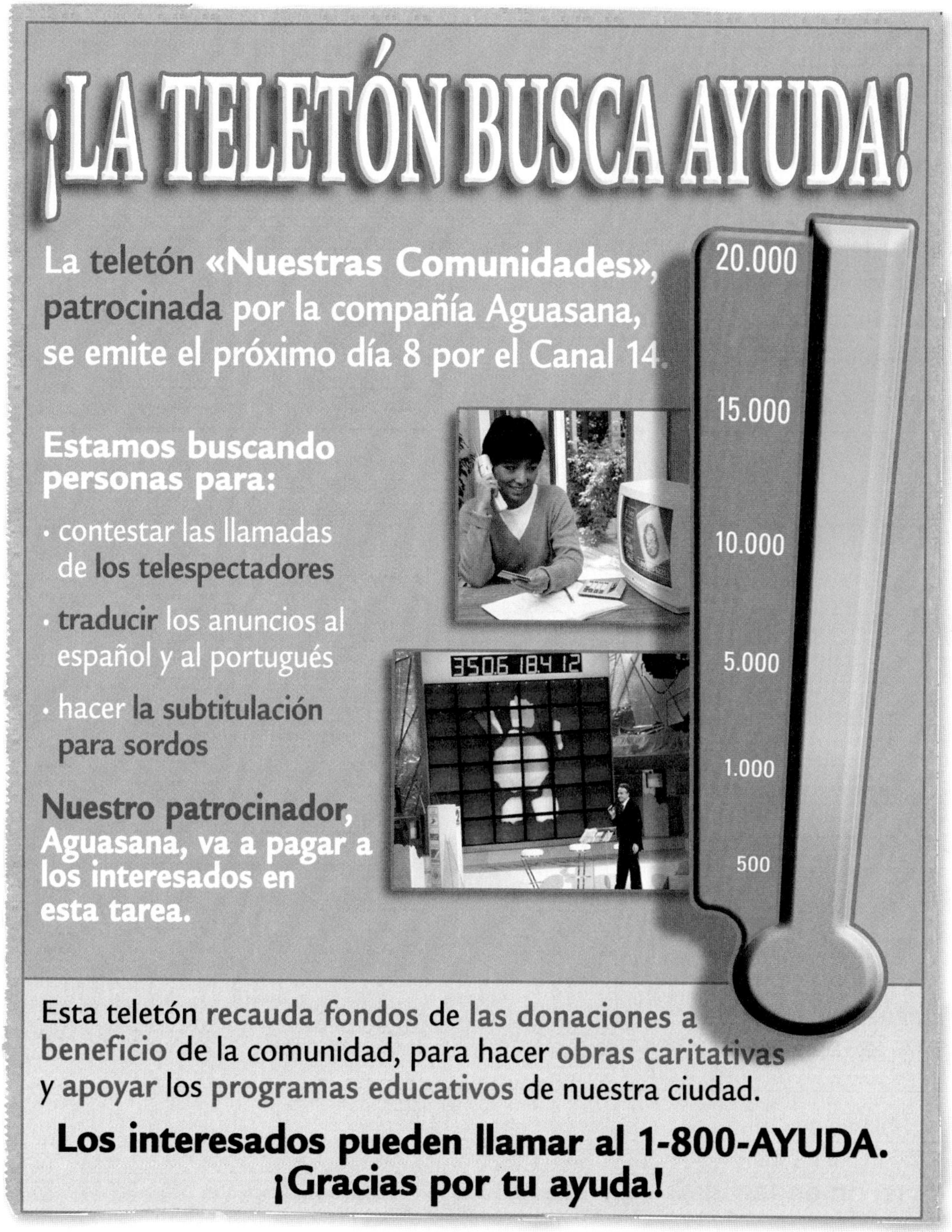

¡LA TELETÓN BUSCA AYUDA!

La teletón **«Nuestras Comunidades»**, **patrocinada** por la compañía Aguasana, **se emite** el próximo día 8 por el Canal 14.

Estamos buscando personas para:

- contestar las llamadas de **los telespectadores**
- **traducir** los anuncios al español y al portugués
- hacer **la subtitulación para sordos**

Nuestro patrocinador, Aguasana, va a pagar a los interesados en esta tarea.

20.000
15.000
10.000
5.000
1.000
500

Esta teletón **recauda fondos** de las **donaciones a beneficio** de la comunidad, para hacer **obras caritativas** y **apoyar** los **programas educativos** de nuestra ciudad.

Los interesados pueden llamar al 1-800-AYUDA.
¡Gracias por tu ayuda!

¡A responder! Escuchar 

Vas a escuchar ocho oraciones. Si estás de acuerdo con la opinión expresada en la oración indícalo con el dedo pulgar hacia arriba. Si no estás de acuerdo, indícalo con el dedo pulgar hacia abajo.

Práctica de VOCABULARIO

1 Las partes del periódico

Escribir

Empareja las columnas para identificar las partes de un periódico.

modelo: el título de un artículo: el titular

1. las palabras exactas que dijo alguien
2. el artículo que expresa un punto de vista
3. el anuncio para vender o anunciar algo
4. el comentario sobre algún artículo
5. las recomendaciones
6. el resumen

a. el anuncio clasificado
b. el artículo de opinión
c. la carta al editor
d. la cita
e. la columna de consejos
f. la reseña

2 ¿Qué hay en la tele?

Leer Hablar Escribir

Lee la guía de programas para hoy y luego contesta las preguntas.

Miércoles	8:00 p.m.	9:00 p.m.	10:00 p.m.
Canal de Acceso Público	*Zorro,* película con Antonio Banderas y Catherine Zeta Jones (con subtitulación). Teletón a beneficio del comedor de beneficencia.		*Su mundo mejor,* programa que solicita donaciones y otorga dinero a obras caritativas (con subtitulación)
Canal 13	*Cara a cara,* con los actores Miguel Ramírez y Sonia Palacios comentando su nueva película.	*¿Vamos a bailar?,* película con Jennifer López y Richard Gere (con subtitulación).	
Canal 15	*El perro Fermín,* dibujos animados (con subtitulación)	*La historia del español,* nacimiento y expansión del idioma (con subtitulación).	*Hoy a las diez,* noticiero (con subtitulación).

1. ¿Qué tipo de programa es *La historia del español*?
2. ¿Cómo se titula el programa de entrevistas?
3. ¿Cuáles son los largometrajes de esta noche?
4. ¿Quiénes son los telespectadores de *El perro Fermín*?
5. ¿Qué programas son accesibles a las personas sordas *(deaf)*?

Expansión
Escoge dos programas de la guía que tú quieres ver. Explica por qué.

3 ¿Qué vieron en la tele?

¿Recuerdas? Preterite vs. imperfect p. 68

Escribir

Con tu compañero(a) escribe qué programas vieron en la tele el fin de semana. ¿Qué tipo de programas eran? ¿A qué hora los vieron? ¿Que hacían sus familiares mientras veían la tele? Usen el pretérito y el imperfecto.

Más práctica Cuaderno *pp. 73–75* Cuaderno para hispanohablantes *pp. 73–76*

¿Comprendiste? Para ti, ¿cuáles son las partes más importantes de un periódico?

Get Help Online
ClassZone.com

VOCABULARIO en contexto

¡AVANZA! **Goal:** Notice the vocabulary that is used to discuss a telethon in the following selections from a school newspaper. Then discuss the event and identify different parts of the newspaper. ***Actividades 4–5***

Contexto 1 *Periódico escolar*

ESTRATEGIA **Leer**

Find numerical expressions As you read the newspaper clippings below, pay attention to different kinds of numerical expressions. In a diagram like the one to the right, group them all into three categories: a) *para las fechas,* b) *para las personas,* and c) *para el dinero.*

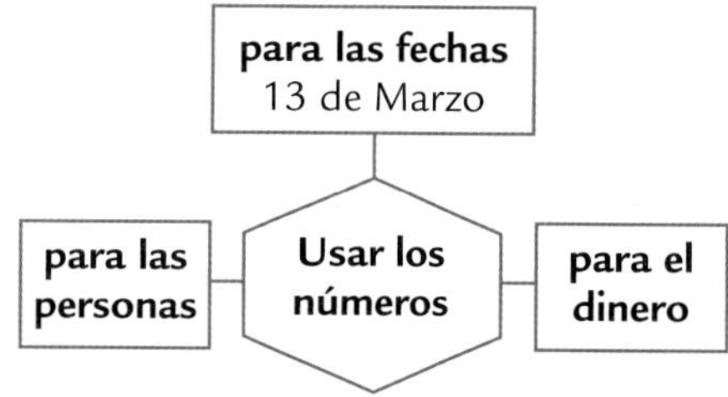

Roberto vive en la ciudad de Nueva York y es un reportero nuevo del periódico de su escuela, *El Nuevo Vocero.* Su primer artículo es sobre la teletón anual a beneficio de la agencia social Nuestras Comunidades. Para escribir sobre el evento, Roberto mira los archivos de la teletón del año pasado.

= El Nuevo Vocero =

13 de Marzo

¡Este año la teletón junta más de $13.000 para Nuestras Comunidades!

«Sin los fondos que este evento nos otorga, es imposible proveer nuestros proyectos sociales. Es muy grande el entusiasmo de los estudiantes y de la comunidad.»

Mercedes Huerta, presidenta de Nuestras Comunidades, le agradece a Pablo Morales los Fondos recaudados por el teletón, que contó con más de 15.000 telespectadores. Más de 600 personas contribuyeron a esta campana para solicitar fondos.

12 de Febrero

Teletón anual

La fecha es el 10 de marzo a las siete de la tarde. Nuestras Comunidades es una agencia social local que organiza proyectos a beneficio de nuestra comunidad, como jardines comunales, la limpieza de los parques y donaciones de dinero.

El año pasado juntamos más de $10.000. Este año, la meta es $12.000. Invitamos a todos los comerciantes a patrocinar este evento. Ya conseguimos setenta y tres patrocinadores con donaciones de $100 cada uno. Recuerden que la fecha límite para donar es el 9 de marzo.

Contamos con la colaboración de todos. ¡Siempre se puede más!

Pablo Morales
Presidente, Comité Teletón

4 Comprensión del periódico escolar

Hablar
Escribir

Empareja los números de la izquierda y los datos a la derecha, según la información de la lectura.

1. $13.142	**a.** número de telespectadores este año
2. más de 15.000	**b.** número de patrocinadores que ya donaron este año
3. más de 600	**c.** meta para las donaciones este año
4. más de $10.000	**d.** fecha límite para las donaciones de los patrocinadores
5. $12.000	**e.** total del dinero donado este año
6. 9 de marzo	**f.** total del dinero donado el año pasado

REPASO gramatical

Impersonal Constructions with se You can use the pronoun **se** in order to avoid specifying the person who is doing the action of the verb. If an infinitive or a singular noun follows the verb, you use the **usted/él/ella** form. If a plural noun follows the verb, you use the **ustedes/ellos/ellas** form.

Se **habla** español aquí.
*Spanish **is spoken** here.*

Se **publican** todas las entrevistas.
*All the interviews **are published.***

5 ¿Qué se hace en la teletón?

Hablar
Escribir

Con un(a) compañero(a), túrnense *(take turns)* para contestar las siguientes preguntas sobre una teletón. Usen la construcción impersonal con **se.**

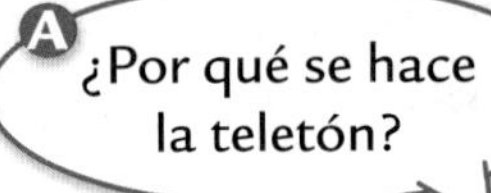

1. ¿Cuándo se hace la teletón este año?
2. ¿Para qué se dan volantes?
3. ¿Cómo se distribuyeron los fondos el año pasado?
4. ¿Qué programas se apoyan con las donaciones?
5. ¿Cuánto dinero se espera recaudar este año?
6. ¿Qué se hace con el dinero que otorgan los patrocinadores?
7. ¿Para qué se hacen los debates?
8. ¿Para qué se hace publicidad por correo?

PARA Y PIENSA

¿Comprendiste? Di cuáles de las siguientes partes de un periódico se ven en la lectura.

1. _____ titular
2. _____ cita
3. _____ gráfica
4. _____ columna de consejos
5. _____ carta al editor
6. _____ foto

Get Help Online
ClassZone.com

Presentación de GRAMÁTICA

¡AVANZA! **Goal:** Review the use of pronouns with command forms. Then practice by giving commands that include pronouns. ***Actividades 6–9***

¿Recuerdas? Beach activities pp. 58–59

English Grammar Connection: You often use **object pronouns** with commands to direct the action of the **verb** at someone or something. In English, you always place pronouns *after* the command.

after — **Give me** that! *attaches* — ¡**Dame** eso!

after — **Don't read it!** *before* — ¡**No lo leas!**

REPASO Pronouns with Commands

Animated Grammar ClassZone.com

In Spanish, the placement of **object pronouns** depends on whether a command is affirmative or negative.

Here's how: In **affirmative commands** you *attach* **object pronouns** to the end of the **verb.** In **negative commands,** they go *before* the **verb** and after **no.**

affirmative: Julia, **describe** tu comunidad. → **Descríbela.**

negative: **No me digas** la respuesta. → **No me la digas.** (*before*)

Remember: If both **object pronouns** begin with the letter **L,** change the **indirect object pronoun** to **se.**

Enrique, **explícale** tu punto de vista a Raquel. → **Explícaselo.**

When using the command form of a **reflexive verb** with an object pronoun, the **reflexive pronoun** comes before the **object pronoun.**

¡**Ponte** las botas! → ¡**Póntelas!** (*before*)

¡**No te pongas** las botas! → ¡**No te las pongas!** (*before*)

With the **nosotros** command, drop the **-s** of the ending before adding the **reflexive pronoun nos.**

¡**Organicemos** una reunión! (*drop*)
***Let's organize** a meeting!*

¡**Organicémonos!** (*attaches*)
Let's get organized!

Más práctica

Cuaderno *pp. 76–78*

Cuaderno para hispanohablantes *pp. 77–79*

@HomeTutor Leveled Practice ClassZone.com

Práctica de GRAMÁTICA

6 Instrucciones editoriales

Leer
Escribir

Lee la siguiente nota que escribió el editor del periódico escolar. Escribe los mandatos con pronombre. Indica a qué o a quiénes se refiere el pronombre.

> Chicos y chicas,
> Tengo trabajo esta tarde y no puedo ayudarlos con la próxima edición. Hagan lo siguiente. En primer lugar, tenemos que presentar la información correcta; léanla dos veces. Contesten las cartas al editor y pónganlas en un documento electrónico. Finalmente, lean el artículo de Sharon sobre el acceso a la educación y tradúzcanlo al español. Si tienen preguntas, escríbanme un mensaje. ¡Gracias!

Expansión
Descubriste que hay que hacer otros trabajos antes de la próxima edición. Diles a tus compañeros lo que tienen que hacer. Usa al menos cinco mandatos.

7 Preparemos el programa

Hablar

Tu compañero(a) y tú están preparando un programa nuevo para el canal de televisión que tiene su comunidad. Contesta las preguntas de tu compañero(a) usando mandatos para decirle qué debe hacer.

A ¿Debo darle la carta al director?

B Sí, dásela. (No, no se la des.)

modelo: dar la carta al director

1. llamar al fotógrafo
2. pedir la gráfica a Margarita
3. poner el anuncio personal
4. incluir una cita
5. prestar el grabador a los reporteros
6. explicarte la cuestión

Comparación cultural

Concierto para todos

Carlos Santana

¿Por qué son importantes las donaciones de los artistas famosos? Carlos Santana es uno de los más grandes guitarristas del rock. Carlos Santana toca la guitarra con el corazón, y sus raíces latinas se sienten en canciones como «Oye como va» y «Smooth». Carlos Santana nació en **México** y conoció la música a los siete años, por su padre José, que era un mariachi violinista. Él combina la técnica que aprendió de su padre con el sonido de los grandes músicos de **Estados Unidos** que oía desde niño en la radio. En 1998, Carlos Santana creó la Fundación Milagro. Su prioridad es organizar, apoyar y patrocinar campañas para donar dinero y otorgar fondos a beneficio de los niños y jóvenes pobres.

Compara con tu mundo *Menciona otros artistas que donan fondos para ayudar a los demás. Explica tu respuesta con ejemplos concretos.*

8 ¡A la playa!

¿Recuerdas? Beach activities pp. 58–59

Leer Escribir

Julia piensa pasar una semana en la playa. Como sabe que el año pasado tú fuiste a Cancún, te mandó un correo electrónico para pedirte sugerencias. Léelo y contéstalo usando al menos ocho mandatos con pronombres. Puedes agregar más sugerencias.

> ¡Hola! ¡Salimos para Cancún en dos semanas y no sé qué llevar ni qué hacer allí! Tú fuiste el año pasado con tu familia, ¿verdad? ¿Podrías darme algunas sugerencias? ¿Debo llevar una sombrilla? ¿Es muy agobiante el calor? ¿Debo usar bloqueador de sol? ¿Qué actividades recomiendas? ¿Crees que debo practicar voleibol playero? ¿Me recomiendas comer en el puerto? ¿Te compro un regalo? ¿Te escribo una postal?
>
> Gracias. ¡Contéstame pronto!
>
> Julia

modelo: Querida Julia:
¡No te preocupes! Vas a pasarlo muy bien en Cancún.
La sombrilla, sí, llévala.

Expansión
Julia te pide más sugerencias sobre la moto acuática y el amanecer en la playa. Escribe sus preguntas y contéstalas con mandatos con pronombres.

9 ¡Nuestra teletón!

Hablar Escribir

Tus compañeros(as) y tú están organizando una teletón para juntar fondos para una obra caritativa. Primero, escojan una obra caritativa e inventen un lema. Después, elaboren sus ideas para anunciar la campaña y la teletón. Finalmente, creen un anuncio para la teletón y escríbanlo. Incluyan la siguiente información en su anuncio:

Pistas: el lema, fecha límite de la teletón, a beneficio de... fondos para... , donar, patrocinadores, el público, entrevistar, punto de vista, (no) estar de acuerdo

Más práctica Cuaderno *pp. 76–78* Cuaderno para hispanohablantes *pp. 77–79*

PARA Y PIENSA

¿Comprendiste? Contesta las siguientes preguntas de tu(s) compañeros(as) con mandatos afirmativos y negativos con pronombres.

Get Help Online ClassZone.com

1. ¿Tengo que describir la obra caritativa en mi artículo?
2. ¿Necesitamos publicar las cartas al editor?
3. ¿Cuándo debo organizar los anuncios clasificados?
4. ¿Te envío las cartas?

GRAMÁTICA en contexto

¡AVANZA! **Goal:** Notice how pronouns are used with commands in the following selection from the annual report of a social services agency. Then practice using object pronouns with commands to make suggestions to others. ***Actividades 10–12***

Contexto 2 *Informe*

ESTRATEGIA **Leer**

Use a diagram for commands While reading the annual report, find each verb that is in the command (imperative) form and copy it in the top box. Then write the entire sentence that contains the verb in the lower box. Review your work and reflect: Are these commands formal or informal? Are any commands from irregular verbs? If so, which ones?

Oración completa
Por favor, díganos cuáles de los programas les gustan más y por qué.

AUDIO

La agencia social Nuestras Comunidades recibió las donaciones de una teletón anual organizada por los estudiantes de la escuela local.

Carmen Delgado
«Nos encanta cultivar vegetales para preparar platos sanos y deliciosos. Los vegetales son importantes, ¡no los olvides! ¡Cómelos todos los días!»

Benito Candelaria
«Nuestro proyecto es pintar un mural. No tenemos suficiente dinero. Por favor, ¡dénnoslo!»

Lorenzo Rivas
«Acompáñenos para limpiar los parques. Y recuerde: la basura es una lata. No la tire en los parques.»

INFORME ANUAL

Distribución de donaciones para nuestros programas

Estimados patrocinadores:

En la última teletón recibimos un número récord de donaciones. En este informe presentamos cómo distribuimos el dinero entre nuestros programas. Estúdienlos con atención.

Por favor, díganos cuáles de los programas les gustan más. Siempre tenemos en cuenta los comentarios de nuestros patrocinadores.

Atentamente,

Mercedes Huerta

Mercedes Huerta
Presidenta, Nuestras Comunidades

Donaciones recibidas 2005:
$23.492,00

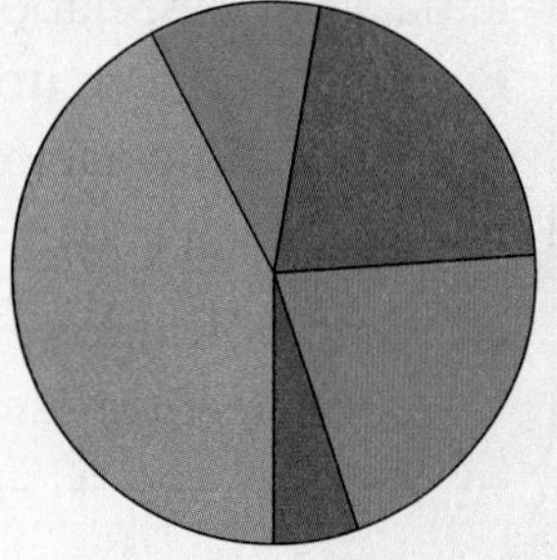

25% proyecto jardín comunal
5% proyecto mural escolar
40% centro recreativo
10% limpieza de parques
20% programa de lectura

10 Comprensión del informe

Hablar
Escribir

Di a quién o a qué cosa se refieren los siguientes pronombres. Busca las respuestas en el informe. Sigue el modelo.

modelo: díga**nnos**
las personas que trabajan para Nuestras Comunidades

1. estúdien**los**
2. no **los** olvides
3. dén**nos**lo
4. acompáñe**nos**
5. no **la** tire
6. cóme**los**

11 ¡Elige uno!

Escribir

Con tu compañero(a) considera los cinco programas que apoya Nuestras Comunidades. Decidan cuál quieren apoyar y por qué. Luego, preparen un anuncio breve para emitir por radio o publicar en el periódico solicitando la colaboración de más voluntarios. Usen al menos cinco mandatos con pronombres.

modelo: La lectura
Imagina un mundo sin la lectura! No hay periódicos, no hay revistas, no hay letreros, no hay libros, no hay Internet... Ayúdanos en la organización Pro-lectura. Llámanos al 800-PRO-LEER.

Expansión
Piensa en una actividad que quieres hacer con tu compañero(a). Prepara las instrucciones con mandatos con pronombres para explicar a tu compañero(a) cómo hacer esa actividad.

12 ¡A pintar!

Hablar

Tus compañeros(as) y tú están colaborando en un mural para embellecer *(beautify)* su comunidad. Usen mandatos con o sin pronombres.

pintar	borrar	darse prisa	investigar
dibujar	cambiar	dar	elegir
poner	quitar	describir	organizar

modelo: Arturo, pinta un árbol cerca de las flores pero no le pongas hojas verdes. Dale hojas de muchos colores.

PARA Y PIENSA

¿Comprendiste? Escribe la forma correcta del mandato y agrégale el pronombre correspondiente.

1. (ustedes) decir / a nosotros
2. (ustedes) dar / dinero / a nosotros
3. (tú) no olvidar / los vegetales
4. (usted) no traducir / el anuncio

Presentación de GRAMÁTICA

¡AVANZA! **Goal:** Review the use of impersonal expressions with infinitives. Then practice making suggestions or requests. ***Actividades 13–16***

¿Recuerdas? Volunteer activities pp. 92–93

English Grammar Connection: In English, as in Spanish, you can use **impersonal expressions** with **infinitives** to state an opinion or to make indirect or subtle suggestions.

It's important to tell the truth. **Es importante decir** la verdad.

REPASO Impersonal Expressions + Infinitive

To state an opinion, or to suggest that something should be done without indicating who should do it, use an **impersonal expression** plus an **infinitive.**

Here's how: **Impersonal expressions** combine the **usted/él/ella** form of the verb ser and an **adjective.** The verb ser can be in any tense.

Form of ser		Adjective
Es Fue Era Va a ser	+	**bueno** **difícil** **fácil** **importante** **imposible** **interesante** **malo** **mejor** **necesario** **posible**

Add the **infinitive** to state your opinion.

Es malo presentar información falsa. *It's bad to present false information.*

Fue bueno entrevistar al director. *It was good to interview the director.*

Era interesante escuchar las entrevistas. *It was interesting to listen to the interviews.*

Va a ser difícil cancelar la teletón. *It's going to be difficult to cancel the telethon.*

Más práctica

Cuaderno *pp. 79–81*

Cuaderno para hispanohablantes *pp. 80–83*

@HomeTutor Leveled Practice ClassZone.com

Práctica de GRAMÁTICA

13 ¡Es importante!

Escuchar
Hablar

Escucha este anuncio sobre una reunión para donar tiempo a las obras caritativas. Luego, decide si las siguientes frases son ciertas o falsas.

1. Es bueno colaborar.
2. Es importante ver el noticiero.
3. Es malo patrocinar una teletón.
4. No es posible hacer cambios.
5. No es necesario trabajar juntos.
6. Es útil ver los cortometrajes de la campaña.
7. No es importante ser creativos.
8. Es imposible leer los volantes.

14 ¿Qué dices?

¿Recuerdas? Volunteer activities pp. 92–93

Hablar

Tu compañero(a) y tú ven las siguientes escenas y quieren hacer comentarios usando expresiones impersonales. ¿Qué pueden decir en cada situación?

modelo: Es importante ayudar a los demás.

1. 

2. 

3. 

4. 

5. 

6. 

AUDIO

Pronunciación La letra d

La letra **d** tiene dos sonidos en español. Al principio de una palabra o después de una consonante, es como la *tt* de la palabra *better* en inglés. Al fin de una palabra o entre dos vocales, es como la *th* en la palabra *father.*

describir **editor** **donar** **comunidad**

Trabalenguas

Dos alcaldes, David Machado y Daniela Amador, danzan el fandango el sábado.

15 Unos letreros

Hablar
Escribir

Tu compañero(a) y tú quieren promocionar la acción social en su comunidad. Hablen de varias obras caritativas y proyectos sociales que creen importantes. Luego, escriban un bosquejo de tres letreros para promocionar sus proyectos. Usen expresiones impersonales.

modelo: ¡Es importante reciclar todo lo posible!

Expansión
Preparen uno de los letreros con todos los detalles posibles para presentar en clase y poner en la escuela.

16 Es interesante leer...

Leer
Hablar
Escribir

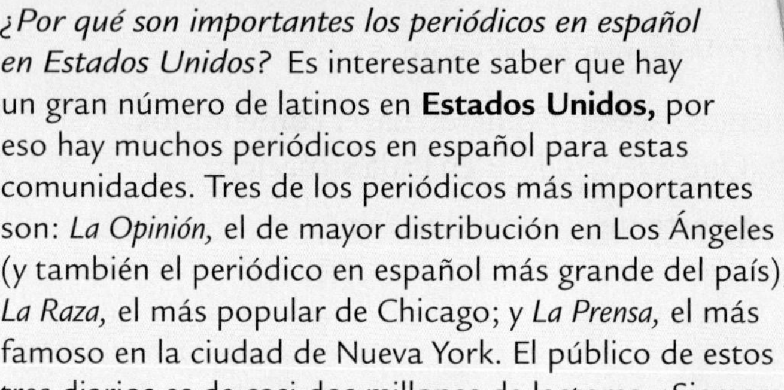

Comparación cultural

Periódicos estadounidenses en español

¿Por qué son importantes los periódicos en español en Estados Unidos? Es interesante saber que hay un gran número de latinos en **Estados Unidos,** por eso hay muchos periódicos en español para estas comunidades. Tres de los periódicos más importantes son: *La Opinión,* el de mayor distribución en Los Ángeles (y también el periódico en español más grande del país); *La Raza,* el más popular de Chicago; y *La Prensa,* el más famoso en la ciudad de Nueva York. El público de estos tres diarios es de casi dos millones de lectores. ¡Siempre se necesita la información cultural!

Periódicos estadounidenses en español

Compara con tu mundo *¿Qué periódicos en español hay en tu comunidad, ciudad o estado? ¿Salen cada día o cada semana? ¿Se publica(n) en inglés también? ¿Qué tipo de artículos tienen?*

Escribe un párrafo para dar tu opinión de qué temas debe presentar un periódico de tu comunidad. Utiliza expresiones impersonales con el verbo en infinitivo: **(No) Es importante... , (No) Es interesante... , (No) Es buena idea... , (No) Es necesario...**

Más práctica Cuaderno *pp. 79–81* Cuaderno para hispanohablantes *pp. 80–83*

PARA Y PIENSA

¿Comprendiste? Cambia los mandatos a una expresión impersonal. Utiliza expresiones como: *Es una buena idea...*

1. Apoya la teletón.
2. Escribe una carta al editor.
3. Incluyan subtitulación para sordos en los programas.

Get Help Online
ClassZone.com

Todo junto

¡AVANZA! **Goal:** ***Show what you know*** Listen to the following interview with Roberto and others who are participating in this year's telethon to benefit a social services agency. Focus on the commands and impersonal expressions that are used in the conversation. ***Actividades 17–19***

Resumen contextos 1 y 2 Roberto trabaja para el periódico escolar. Tiene que escribir un artículo sobre una teletón anual y revisó los archivos de la teletón del año pasado para estar bien informado.

Contexto 3 *Diálogo*

ESTRATEGIA **Escuchar**

Predict, listen, and compare What topics do you think Sra. Huerta and Sr. Sandoval will mention during the interview? Write down your predictions and then list the topics *actually* discussed. Compare the two lists. Which predictions were correct? Were there any surprises?

AUDIO

Ahora Roberto va a hacerle una entrevista a la Sra. Huerta, presidenta de la agencia social Nuestras Comunidades, y al Sr. Sandoval, un patrocinador importante que va a organizar un concurso *(contest)*.

Roberto: Sra. Huerta, pienso que usted está muy contenta con las donaciones que estamos recibiendo esta noche, ¿no?

Sra. Huerta: ¡Sí, Roberto! Como sabes, este año nuestra meta es juntar $15.000. Nuestros patrocinadores y el público ya donaron $11.400. ¡Es emocionante ver la generosidad de todos!

Roberto: ¡De acuerdo! ¿Y cómo se llama el señor que la acompaña esta noche?

Sra. Huerta: Permíteme presentarte al Sr. Sandoval, el presidente de la corporación Imagen. Sr. Sandoval, él es Roberto Torres, el reportero del periódico escolar.

Roberto: Un placer, Sr. Sandoval.

Sr. Sandoval: El gusto es mío, Roberto... Tengo un anuncio para el público y los telespectadores. Eh... ¿hay un fotógrafo aquí? ¿Sí? Llámalo, por favor... Y es importante tener presentes a todos los reporteros. Y trae también unas cámaras de video... y...

Un momento después...

Sr. Sandoval: Señores y señoras, creo que es necesario hacer algo por nuestra comunidad. Por eso voy a patrocinar un nuevo programa educativo.

Sra. Huerta: ¡Qué sorpresa! ¡Muchísimas gracias, Sr. Sandoval!

Sr. Sandoval: Creemos que es una buena idea crear un programa a beneficio de nuestros vecinos. Por eso hoy donamos $10.000.

Sra. Huerta: ¿Y cómo se va a decidir el enfoque del programa?

Sr. Sandoval: Con un concurso. El público envía sus propuestas para el enfoque del programa; luego, un comité especial elige la mejor. El 1° de julio es la fecha límite para recibir las propuestas.

Sra. Huerta: ¡Fabuloso, Sr. Sandoval!

Sr. Sandoval: ¡Y eso no es todo! Nuestra empresa tiene dinero para producir un cortometraje para el público adulto y una tira de dibujos animados para los niños. ¡Y todo se traduce! El inglés y el español sirven para unir a nuestras comunidades.

Sra. Huerta: Estoy muy emocionada. Muchas gracias de nuevo.

Sr. Sandoval: ¡Un placer, señora! A ver, Roberto, ¿tienes todos los datos necesarios para escribir el artículo? Y no te olvides de mi foto.

Roberto: ¡Sí, sí, Sr. Sandoval! Pero, discúlpenme, por favor... ¡tengo mucho que escribir!

También se dice

Los niños llaman a los dibujos animados de maneras diferentes y divertidas:
- **México** caricaturas
- **Argentina** dibujitos
- **Colombia** monitos
- **Cuba y República Dominicana** muñequitos

17 Comprensión del diálogo

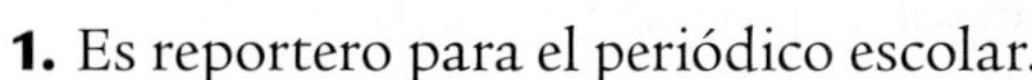

Escuchar
Hablar
Escribir

¿Con quién(es) asocias las siguientes frases? ¿Roberto, la señora Huerta o el señor Sandoval?

modelo: Está muy satisfecha con las donaciones: Sra. Huerta

1. Es reportero para el periódico escolar.
2. Trabaja en la organización Nuestras Comunidades.
3. Quiere patrocinar un nuevo programa educativo.
4. Va a organizar un concurso para decidir el enfoque del nuevo programa.
5. Se preocupa por la publicidad.
6. Está muy emocionada por la donación.
7. Colaboran para anunciar el concurso.
8. Quieren hacer cosas a beneficio de la comunidad.

18 Integración

Leer
Escuchar
Hablar

Lee el anuncio para limpiar tu comunidad que hay en el tablero del parque. Escucha la llamada telefónica que te hace la organización para informarte de algunos cambios. Explica cuáles son los cambios para participar en el evento.

Fuente 1 Tablero de anuncios

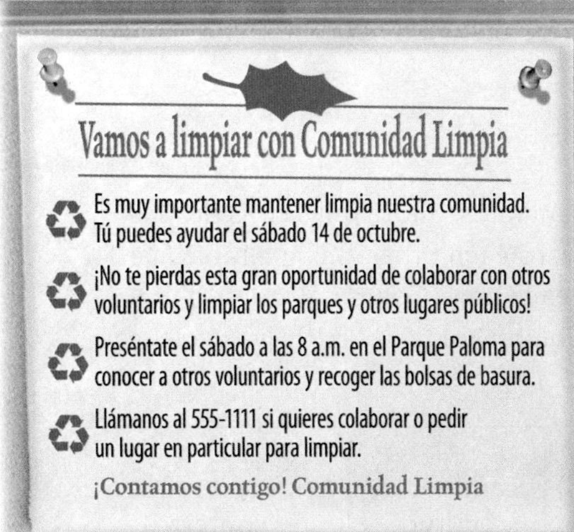

Fuente 2 Llamada telefónica

Escucha y apunta

- ¿Dónde va a trabajar el grupo ahora? ¿Dónde pensaba trabajar antes?
- ¿Qué deben llevar y qué van a hacer los miembros del grupo? ¿Qué otros cambios hay?

modelo: El grupo va a trabajar en el parque San Francisco. Tienen que llevar guantes de trabajo al parque.

19 Un artículo de opinión

Escribir

Elige una organización real o imaginaria que apoyas. Escribe un artículo de opinión para el periódico. Di por qué crees que es una buena organización y por qué crees que otras personas deben apoyarla con dinero y actividades. Usa por lo menos tres mandatos con pronombres y tres expresiones impersonales.

Writing Criteria	Excellent	Good	Needs Work
Content	Your argument includes several persuasive reasons for supporting the organization.	Your argument includes some persuasive reasons for supporting the organization.	Your argument includes few persuasive reasons for supporting the organization.
Communication	Your argument is organized and easy to follow.	Parts of your argument are organized and easy to follow.	Your argument is disorganized and hard to follow.
Accuracy	You make few mistakes in grammar and vocabulary.	You make some mistakes in grammar and vocabulary.	You make many mistakes in grammar and vocabulary.

Más práctica Cuaderno *pp. 82–83* Cuaderno para hispanohablantes *pp. 84–85*

PARA Y PIENSA

Get Help Online
ClassZone.com

¿Comprendiste? Convierte los mandatos en expresiones impersonales y las expresiones impersonales en mandatos con **ustedes.**

1. Trae unas cámaras de video.

2. Es emocionante ver la generosidad de todos.

Lectura literaria

¡AVANZA! **Goal:** Read and understand the following passage about the Mexican tradition of singing *Las mañanitas* to celebrate someone's birthday. Then discuss this tradition and compare it to the traditions of your family.

Para leer 

ESTRATEGIA Leer

Track the relationships To understand "Las mañanitas" more fully, consider the feelings and attitudes that the characters hold toward each other. Using a table like the one shown, describe the relationship between each pair (Column B), describe any changes in the relationship during the story (Column C), and briefly list evidence supporting your descriptions in B and C (Column D).

A Relación familiar	B Descripción	C Cambios de actitud	D Evidencias [frases o contexto]
Narradora ←→ Abuela			
Madre ←→ Abuela			
Padre ←→ Abuela			

Vocabulario para leer

enojona *que se enoja fácilmente*
desfilar *pasar un grupo de gente delante de alguien*
la recámara *lugar de la casa donde se duerme*
regañar *retar a alguien y decirle lo que no debe hacer*
dar vergüenza *sentirse incómodo ante una situación*
felicitar *saludar a alguien por un motivo especial, como un cumpleaños*

Nota cultural

Sobre la autora ***Sandra Cisneros (1954–)***
Nació en Chicago y ahora vive en San Antonio, Texas. Su familia es de origen mexicano. Ella escribe poesía y ficción, y recibió muchos premios literarios. Entre sus libros más famosos están *La casa en Mango Street* y *Caramelo.* Algunas de sus obras se tradujeron a más de doce idiomas.

Sobre las canciones populares «Las mañanitas» es una canción tradicional que se canta para celebrar los cumpleaños. Es una costumbre mexicana muy típica pero también es popular en otros países de habla hispana. En algunos casos, la letra *(lyrics)* varía y se pueden agregar *(add)* algunos versos.

Las mañanitas

AUDIO

Como lo obligaron a despertarse temprano todos los días de su infancia, papá tiene un sueño atroz[1]. No hay cosa que le guste más que despertarse tarde. Especialmente en su cumpleaños.

Y así, todos los demás ya están vestidos y listos para saludar la mañana de su nacimiento con una canción. *—Despierta, mi bien, despierta...* Pero esto quiere decir todos. La abuela enojona, el abuelito, la tía Güera y la prima Antonieta Araceli, la niña Oralia, exhausta por tener que cocinar y limpiar para dieciocho personas más de lo normal, y hasta Amparo la lavandera y su hermosa hija, Candelaria.

Además de cualquier otro a quien puedan forzar a presentar sus respetos —los primos, las tías y tíos, mis seis hermanos— todos desfilan por nuestra recámara mientras todavía estamos dormidos bajo las sábanas, parpadeando[2] con los ojos legañosos[3], el aliento agrio[4], el pelo chueco[5] como escobas: mi mamá, mi papá y yo, porque, olvidé contarte, yo también duermo en su cuarto cuando estamos en México, a veces en el catre con ruedas[6] enfrente de ellos y a veces en la misma cama.

---

[1] **tiene...** He is terribly tired [2] blinking [3] **con...** with sleep in our eyes
[4] **aliento...** sour breath [5] crooked [6] **catre...** cot on wheels

Reflexiona

¿Qué día ocurre esta historia?

—Parecen rancheros —nos regaña la abuela después de que se acaba la canción del cumpleaños—. Sinvergüenza[7] —me dice—. ¿No crees que ya estás grandecita como para dormir sola?

Pero ¿a quién le gusta dormir solo? ¿A quién se le ocurriría[8] dormir solo a menos que tuviera que hacerlo[9], chico o grande?

Da vergüenza que te canten y te griten antes del desayuno cuando todavía estás en tu camiseta con olanes[10] y tus calzones[11] floreados. ¿A mamá también le da pena? Estamos clavados[12] a la cama, sin poder levantarnos hasta que todos hayan felicitado a papá por su cumpleaños.

A pensar
Aquí aparecen las palabras **vergüenza** y **pena.** ¿Por qué siente vergüenza la narradora? ¿Por qué la mamá puede sentir pena?

¡Felicidades! ¡*Happinesses!*

—Sí, gracias—dice papá pestañeando[13]. *Trae la barba gris sin rasurar*[14]*, su camiseta ya no es tan blanca,* piensa mamá, *y ¿por qué tuvo que ponerse ésa con el hoyo*[15]*?*

—¿Adivina qué te guardé nada más para ti, m'ijo? ¡La nata[16] de hoy! ¿Prefieres vestirte y bajar a desayunar, o te traigo una charola[17]?

—Gracias, mamá. Me voy a vestir. Gracias a todos. Gracias, muchas gracias.

Luego, después de lo que parece un largo rato mientras la abuela asiente[18] y supervisa los buenos deseos de todo el mundo, todos salen en fila.

Mamá se levanta de un brinco[19] y se ve en el espejo del tocador.

—Me veo horrible, dice, cepillándose el pelo con furia.

Sí se ve horrible, el pelo parado como si se estuviera incendiando[20], pero nadie le dice, —Ay, no, no te ves horrible para nada, y esto sólo hace que se sienta peor.

---

[7] shameless [8] **A...** Who would think about
[9] **a menos...** unless he(she) had to [10] frilly [11] underwear
[12] nailed [13] blinking [14] **sin...** unshaven
[15] hole [16] cream [17] bowl [18] agrees
[19] **de...** she jumps [20] burning

Reflexiona

En general, ¿cómo se siente la gente que vive en la casa después de recibir la visita?

Apúrate y vístete —me dice de esa manera que me hace obedecerla sin preguntar por qué.

—¡Tu mamá! Te apuesto a que se cree muy chistosa cuando entra todos los años sin tocar siquiera. Despierta a todo el barrio más y más temprano. ¿Qué cree? ¿Que me ve la cara de taruga[21] o qué? ❖

Papá no hace caso de las quejas de mamá. Papá ríe esa risa que siempre ríe cuando el mundo le parece divertido. Esa risa como las chicharras[22], una risa como la letra «k».

❖ A pensar
¿Es la primera vez que esta visita ocurre? ¿A quién definen las palabras **chistosa** y **taruga** en este párrafo? ¿Por qué?

---

[21] **Que...** Does she think I'm a blockhead? [22] cicadas

¿Comprendiste?

1. ¿Son muchas o pocas las personas que felicitan al papá?
2. ¿Qué diferencia hay entre el aspecto de las personas que llegan a la casa y el aspecto de la narradora y sus padres?
3. ¿Cómo reaccionan la narradora y sus padres ante la visita?
4. ¿Cuál es el papel *(role)* de la abuela en la celebración?
5. ¿Qué relación crees que hay entre la narradora y la abuela, la mamá y la abuela y el papá y la abuela?

¿Y tú?

¿Cómo se celebran los cumpleaños en tu familia? ¿Tienen alguna tradición especial? ¿Cómo preferirías *(would you prefer)* celebrar tu cumpleaños?

Escritura

La importancia del trabajo voluntario

Escribe un discurso para promover el trabajo voluntario entre los estudiantes de tu escuela. Usa la siguiente secuencia de estrategias para organizar tus ideas.

1 Prepárate para escribir

ESTRATEGIA Selecciona trabajos voluntarios Haz una lista de trabajos voluntarios en los que quieres participar. Luego haz otra lista con trabajos voluntarios que no te gustan.

2 Escribe

ESTRATEGIA Establece un punto de vista Para establecer un punto de vista es bueno estudiar los aspectos del tema y ver si son positivos o negativos. Luego, se escogen las mejores razones para convencer al público. De la lista que hiciste, escoge un trabajo que te gusta y uno que no te gusta. Completa una tabla como la siguiente con los aspectos positivos y negativos de cada trabajo. Luego escribe un ensayo para persuadir a la gente de que participe en los dos trabajos. Plantea la importancia del trabajo voluntario. Incluye los elementos positivos y convence a la gente para superar los aspectos negativos.

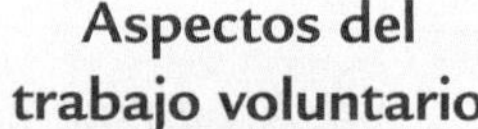

Aspectos del trabajo voluntario	Positivo	Negativo

Se trabaja gratis.	**Se contribuye con trabajo y tiempo.**	**A veces la gente no toma sus obligaciones en serio porque no recibe dinero.**

3 Revisa tu composición

Lee el borrador de tu compañero(a).

- Comprueba que use suficientes mandatos en la forma correcta de **ustedes** y expresiones impersonales con infinitivo para pedir, recomendar o sugerir. Subraya lo correcto y corrige si es necesario.
- ¿Están claros la opinión y los lados positivos que presenta?
- ¿Hay una introducción y una conclusión interesantes?

Después de las correcciones, revisa tu ensayo.

> ¡Trabajen de voluntarios en el hospital! Miren ~~Mira~~ el lado positivo: podemos ayudar a mucha gente que está enferma. ¿El lado negativo? Sí, es triste estar enfermo y muchos días en el hospital, pero es importante ayudar a la gente que está sola.

En resumen

Vocabulario y gramática

Vocabulario

Talk About the Media

el acceso	*access*
el anuncio clasificado	*classified ad*
el anuncio personal	*personal ad*
el artículo de opinión	*editorial*
la cita	*quote*
la columna	*column*
el cortometraje	*short documentary*
la cuestión	*issue, question*
los dibujos animados	*cartoons*
el (la) editor(a)	*editor*
la entrevista	*interview*
la fecha límite	*deadline*
el (la) fotógrafo(a)	*photographer*
el grabador	*tape recorder*
la gráfica	*graphic*
el largometraje	*feature, full-length movie*
el noticiero	*news broadcast*
la publicidad por correo	*mailing*
el público	*audience*
la reseña	*review*
la subtitulación para sordos	*closed captioning for the hearing-impaired*
el (la) telespectador(a)	*TV viewer*
la teletón	*telethon*
el titular	*headline*

Actions

distribuir	*to distribute*
emitir	*to broadcast*
entrevistar	*to interview*
investigar	*to investigate*
presentar	*to present*
publicar	*to publish*
traducir	*to translate*

Express Opinions

el debate	*debate*
describir	*to describe*
estar / no estar de acuerdo con	*to agree / disagree with*
explicar	*to explain*

Talk About the Community

a beneficio de	*to the benefit of*
donar	*to donate*
la obra caritativa	*charitable work*
otorgar	*to grant*
el (la) patrocinador(a)	*sponsor*
patrocinar	*to sponsor*
el programa educativo	*educational program*
los volantes	*flyers*

Gramática

Nota gramatical: Impersonal constructions with **se** *p. 122*

Repaso: Pronouns with Commands

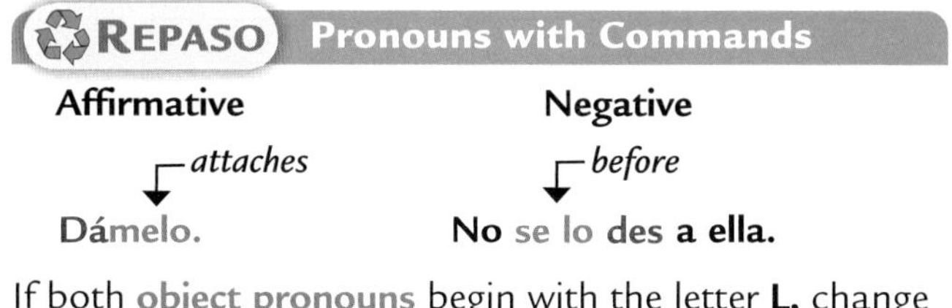

If both object pronouns begin with the letter **L**, change the le or les to se.

The reflexive pronoun always comes before the object pronoun.

before — ¡Póntelas!

before — ¡No te las pongas!

With the **nosotros** command, drop the -s of the ending before adding the **reflexive pronoun** nos.

¡Organicemos una reunión! ¡Organicémonos!

Repaso: Impersonal Expressions + Infinitive

To state an opinion, or to suggest that something should be done, use an **impersonal expression** plus an **infinitive.**

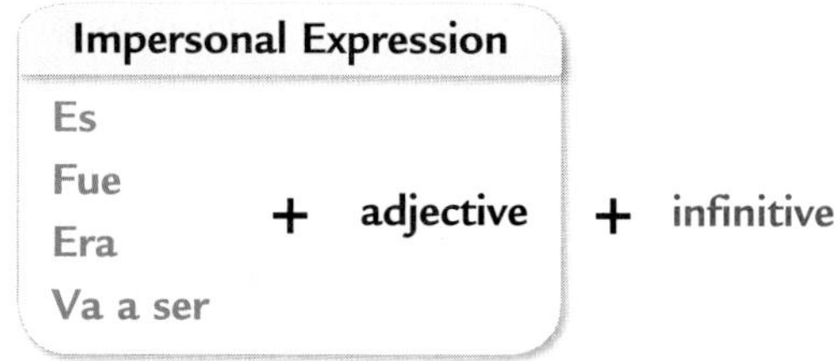

Es malo presentar información falsa.
It's bad to present *false information.*

Lección 2

Repaso de la lección

¡LLEGADA!

@HomeTutor
ClassZone.com

Now you can
- make requests and recommendations
- express opinions
- talk about media and the community

Using
- pronouns with commands
- impersonal expressions + infinitive
- impersonal constructions with **se**

To review
- vocabulary pp. 118–119

1 Listen and understand

AUDIO

Dos estudiantes son candidatos para el puesto de editor del periódico escolar. Hoy dan discursos para presentar sus ideas para atraer a más lectores al periódico. Escucha los dos discursos y luego indica a quién se refiere cada una de las siguientes oraciones, ¿a Natalia o a Francisco?

1. Dijo que es necesario usar titulares grandes.
2. Dijo que quiere tener un traductor.
3. Dijo que quiere publicar el periódico dos veces por semana.
4. Dijo que es necesario incluir citas de personas importantes.
5. Dijo que es importante tener más gráficas.
6. Dijo que es una buena idea dedicar una página entera a las cartas al editor.
7. Dijo que quiere añadir una sección de anuncios clasificados.
8. Dijo que quiere añadir una columna de consejos.

To review
- impersonal constructions with **se** p. 122

2 Talk about media and the community

Escribe las preguntas según el modelo.

modelo: revista / publicar / español
¿Se publica la revista en español?

1. anuncios escritos en inglés / traducir / al español
2. anuncios clasificados / vender / a un precio muy bajo
3. columnas de consejos / considerar necesarias / para la comunidad
4. las noticias / explicar / al detalle
5. historias / investigar / interesantes
6. escritores y fotógrafos / emplear / hispanohablantes

To review
- pronouns with commands p. 123

3 Make requests and recommendations

Varias personas opinan sobre la tele-educación. Completa sus comentarios con el mandato correcto y sustituye las palabras subrayadas *(underlined)* con pronombres. Sigue el modelo.

modelo: «Me gusta este proyecto.» (apoyar / Ud.)
Apóyelo.

1. «Necesitamos investigar las finanzas antes de apoyar el proyecto.» (analizar / ustedes)
2. «Es importante tener una fecha límite.» (fijar / usted)
3. «Queremos hacer entrevistas a los empleados.» (hacer / ustedes a ellos)
4. «Es mucho dinero para un solo proyecto.» (no gastar / ustedes)
5. «Necesito saber más sobre el proyecto.» (describir / usted a mí)
6. «No me gustó el programa piloto.» (no emitir / ustedes)

To review
- impersonal expressions with infinitives p. 128

4 Express opinions

Responde a las siguientes opiniones. Usa las expresiones impersonales que aparecen entre paréntesis.

modelo: No presentan programas educativos en este canal. ((No) Es importante)
Es importante presentar programas educativos en este canal.

1. No hay anuncios traducidos al español. ((No) Es mala idea)
2. Queremos publicar muchas cartas al editor. ((No) Es interesante)
3. El artículo no incluye varios puntos de vista. ((No) Es buena idea)
4. En general, la tele-educación no cuenta con muchos patrocinadores. ((No) Es necesario)

To review
- **Comparación cultural** pp. 124, 130

5 Celebrities who raise money; Spanish newspapers

Comparación cultural

Escribe un párrafo sobre cada uno de los temas que aparecen a continuación. Sigue las pistas en cada caso.

1. ¿Quién es Carlos Santana?
2. ¿Qué hace la Fundación Milagro?
3. ¿Cuáles son los tres periódicos en español más grandes de Estados Unidos?
4. ¿Cuánto público tienen estos periódicos?

Más práctica Cuaderno *pp. 84–95* Cuaderno para hispanohablantes *pp. 86–95*

Get Help Online ClassZone.com

Comparación cultural

AUDIO

Culturas musicales

Lectura y escritura

1. **Leer** Lee sobre la música que se escucha en los estados donde viven Rolando y Mariana.

2. **Escribir** Escribe una composición sobre la música que se escucha en la región donde tú vives.

ESTRATEGIA **Escribir**

Use shapes as a reminder Use different shapes to remind yourself of what to include in your composition: circle = introduction, squares = type of music, and triangle = conclusion.

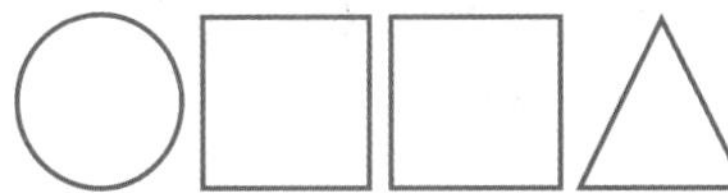

Paso 1 Escoge los tipos de música que se escucha en tu región.

Paso 2 Haz un diagrama como el que se muestra. En el círculo escribe una oración como introducción. En cada cuadrado escribe un tipo de música. En el triángulo escribe una conclusión breve.

Paso 3 Usa lo que escribiste en el diagrama para escribir un ensayo completo con más detalles sobre la música de tu región. Luego revisa la gramática y la ortografía.

Compara con tu mundo

Usa el ensayo que escribiste y compara la música de tu ciudad o región con la que escuchan Rolando y Mariana. ¿Escuchan la misma música? ¿Hay elementos comunes? ¿Tienen influencias diferentes?

Cuaderno *pp. 96–98* Cuaderno para hispanohablantes *pp. 96–98*

California

Mariana

Me llamo Mariana Villegas, vivo en Los Ángeles. Esta zona tiene una tradición musical muy grande. Aquí se escucha mucha música ranchera porque hay muchos mexicanos. Pero aquí también se crea una música menos tradicional, el hip-hop latino con raíces mexicanas. A mí me gusta el grupo Akwid, formado por los hermanos Sergio y Francisco Gómez, que emigraron desde México y crecieron en Los Ángeles. Son unos raperos que cantan en español, con trompetas y otros instrumentos de banda mexicana. Su disco *Proyecto Akwid* ganó un disco de platino.

Rolando

Hola. Me llamo Rolando Bravo y vivo en Miami, la capital de la música latina.

Aquí se oye todo tipo de música: salsa (con origen en Cuba y Nueva York), el merengue (de la República Dominicana y Cuba), el dance remix (como la nueva música de Thalía y Shakira) y el reggaeton, una nueva forma caribeña que combina el reggae, el rap y el hip-hop. Tenemos muchas canciones en español y muchas otras en español e inglés al mismo tiempo. En Miami hay muchos productores de música latina y muchos jóvenes que llegan allí para hacerse famosos.

Florida

EL DESAFÍO

VIDEO
DVD

En el desafío de hoy cada equipo debe prepararse para cantar, pero primero tienen que hacer unos anuncios de publicidad para presentar a sus equipos a los invitados. Sólo una persona de cada equipo tiene que cantar.

Antes del video

1. Describe el letrero de Luis y María. ¿Qué colores ves?

2. ¿Qué está haciendo Marco? ¿Crees que su actuación es buena o mala? ¿Por qué?

3. ¿Quiénes son estas personas? ¿Qué equipo crees que va a ganar este desafío?

Practicando la canción

Mira el video: Toma apuntes

- ¿Qué dibuja Marco?
- ¿Qué piensa Luis sobre los colores que está usando María?
- ¿Con quién habla Ana por teléfono?
- Describe el letrero de Carmen y José.
- ¿A quién le va a donar el premio el equipo ganador?
- Describe cómo canta Carmen.
- ¿A quién se le olvida parte de la canción?

Después del video

1. Lee tus predicciones. ¿Sabías quién iba a ganar el desafío?
2. En tu opinión, ¿cuál fue el mejor anuncio? ¿Por qué?
3. Compara la actuación de Luis y Marco.
4. Piensa cómo es Marco. En tu opinión, ¿fue buena idea elegirlo para cantar?

@HomeTutor VideoPlus
ClassZone.com

UNIDADES 1-2

Repaso inclusivo

Options for Review

1 Escucha, comprende y decide

Escuchar
Hablar

Escucha el anuncio sobre una organización que necesita apoyo. Después, habla con tu compañero(a) para decidir si quieren colaborar o no. Tengan en cuenta cómo pueden mejorar los programas. Expliquen sus razones a la clase.

2 Pregunta, contesta y escribe

Hablar

Hazle diez preguntas a un(a) compañero(a) sobre las cosas interesantes que pasaron la semana pasada. Luego, cambien de papel: tu compañero(a) te hace diez preguntas y tú contestas. Usen las formas apropiadas del pretérito y el imperfecto en las preguntas y las respuestas.

modelo:

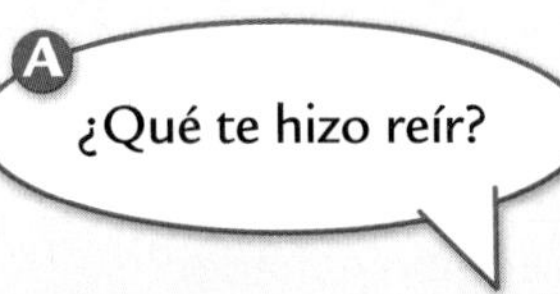

B El programa de TV me hizo reír.

3 ¡Un programa nuevo!

Hablar

Tus compañeros(as) y tú son parte de un comité que recomienda nueva programación para el canal de televisión de su comunidad. En particular, ustedes van a considerar la programación para los jóvenes entre quince y diecisiete años. Juntos, analicen los programas que hay en la tele y decidan qué falta. Diseñen un programa nuevo para llenar ese vacío *(gap)* y presenten sus ideas al comité (la clase).

Pistas: Consideren lo siguiente:
tipo de programa
tipo de público
por qué creen que es necesario
por qué creen que va a ser exitoso
a qué hora y por qué
cuántas veces por semana
patrocinadores posibles
otras recomendaciones específicas

4 ¡Qué hacer y dónde!

Escribir

Tú escribes una columna de consejos para el periódico estudiantil y recibes varias cartas de estudiantes que preguntan qué hacer y qué no hacer en un viaje para acampar. Escribe una columna dándoles consejos específicos. Incluye información sobre adónde ir (o no ir), qué llevar (y no llevar), qué hacer (y no hacer). Usa mandatos y expresiones impersonales para dar tus consejos.

5 Haz una entrevista

Hablar
Escribir

La televisión o radio de tu escuela o comunidad va a ofrecer una serie de programas sobre la inmigración y tú vas a hacer una de las entrevistas con un(a) inmigrante. Primero, prepara una lista de preguntas para aprender cuándo, de dónde, cómo, con quién(es) y por qué esa persona decidió venir a tu comunidad. Haz la entrevista y toma apuntes para recordar lo que contesta tu compañero(a). No te olvides de preguntar sobre sus experiencias e impresiones en los primeros meses y cómo cambió su vida.

6 Escribe un artículo

Escribir

Escribe un artículo para el periódico estudiantil sobre la llegada de un inmigrante a tu comunidad. Puedes usar los apuntes de la actividad anterior (5.) o puedes entrevistar a otra persona sobre sus experiencias antes de escribir tu artículo. ¡Si hay estudiantes inmigrantes en tu escuela puedes entrevistar a uno(a) de ellos(as)!

7 Informa sobre la ciudadanía

Escribir

Investiga los requisitos que tienen que cumplir los inmigrantes que quieren hacerse ciudadanos de Estados Unidos. Luego, escribe un artículo informativo sobre lo que aprendiste. Ten en cuenta algunos detalles de la lectura *En la Ocho y la Doce.*

Inmigrantes celebrando la ceremonia de ciudadanía estadounidense

UNIDAD 3

Centroamérica

El futuro de nuestro planeta

Lección 1

Tema: ***¿Cómo será el futuro?***

Lección 2

Tema: ***Por un futuro mejor***

México

Honduras

Guatemala

Sololá

Tegucigalpa

San Salvador

Guatemala

El Salvador

Nicaragua

Managua

Mar Caribe

Costa Rica

Panamá

Tilarán

Limón

Puntarenas

San José

Panamá

Océano Pacífico

«¡Saludos!
Soy Mario, de Panamá.
Ella es Liliana, de Honduras.»

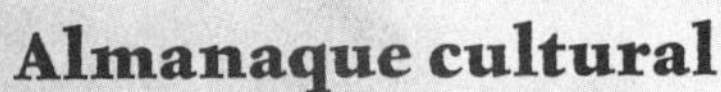

Almanaque cultural

Clima: Frío en las tierras altas. Cálido y húmedo en las tierras bajas

Geografía: Volcán Tajumulco (Guatemala, pico más alto de Centroamérica, 4.220 m); bosques tropicales y playas

Idiomas indígenas (mayas): garífuna, xinca, mam, kaqchiquel, akateco, quiché

Comidas: pupusas, tamales, gallo pinto, tortillas, ceviche

Gente famosa: Rubén Darío (poeta; Nicaragua); Claribel Alegría (escritora; El Salvador); Ricardo Arjona (cantante; Guatemala), Gabriela Núñez (política; Honduras)

Pupusas

◀ **Artesanías indígenas** Las artesanías indígenas de Centroamérica tienen una combinación de hermosos colores. En los mercados al aire libre puedes encontrar ropa hecha por los mayas, los indígenas de la región. *¿Qué tipo de artesanías hay en tu ciudad o estado?*

Joven vendiendo ropa maya en el mercado de Sololá, Guatemala

Arqueología Centroamérica es uno de los lugares preferidos por los arqueólogos de todo el mundo. Aquí descubrieron ruinas, sitios y artefactos de la civilización maya. En el año 2000 descubrieron un palacio maya. *¿Qué ruinas hay cerca de tu ciudad?* ▶

Arqueólogos estudiando imágenes de ceremonias de los reyes mayas

Ciudades llenas de vida Las estructuras modernas también forman parte de Centroamérica. Sus ciudades capitales tienen edificios grandes y son centros de actividad industrial y cultural. La ciudad de Panamá tiene uno de los puertos más importantes de Latinoamérica. *¿Qué estructuras modernas hay en tu ciudad?* ▼

Avenidas Balboa y Paitilla, ciudad de Panamá

UNIDAD 3

Centroamérica

Lección 1

Tema:

¿Cómo será el futuro?

¡AVANZA! **In this lesson you will learn to**

- discuss the impact of technology
- express environmental concerns and possibilities
- make predictions and discuss causes and effects

using

- future tense
- the prepositions **por** and **para**

¿Recuerdas?

- **ustedes** commands
- **ir a** + infinitive
- media vocabulary

Comparación cultural

In this lesson you will learn about:

- lakes in Nicaragua
- endangered species in Central America

Compara con tu mundo

Estos estudiantes hacen una excursión en un bosque tropical *(rain forest)* de Costa Rica. Su guía les habla sobre la naturaleza. *¿Hiciste alguna vez una excursión con tu clase? ¿Adónde fuiste? ¿Qué viste y qué aprendiste?*

¿Qué ves?

Mira la foto

¿Cuántas personas ves?

¿Qué ropa llevan?

¿Qué llevan para su excursión?

¿Piensas que la excursión les interesa? ¿Por qué?

Featuring...

Cultura INTERACTIVA

Animated Grammar

@HomeTutor

And more...

- Get Help Online
- Interactive Flashcards
- Review Games
- WebQuest
- Conjuguemos.com

Excursión en un bosque tropical
Costa Rica

Presentación de VOCABULARIO

¡AVANZA! **Goal:** Learn about issues that affect the environment. Then practice the vocabulary that you have learned to discuss these issues and possible solutions. ***Actividades 1–3***

 *¿Recuerdas?* **Ustedes** commands p. 102

REPORTE ANUAL

AUDIO

Porque un nuevo **porvenir** es posible... ¡para todos!

Nuestra empresa ve el futuro con optimismo. Por eso, trabajamos en **el desarrollo** de **inventos** nuevos y soluciones para los problemas más urgentes del **medio ambiente:**

el aire puro

- Conservar **el aire puro.**
- **Fomentar** el uso de **los recursos naturales** para **reemplazar los recursos no renovables,** como **el petróleo.**

Hacemos **investigaciones** para **proteger** a **las especies en peligro de extinción** y **mejorar la biodiversidad** en general.

los recursos naturales

las especies en peligro de extinción

¡Trabajamos en **la transformación** de este **planeta** en un lugar limpio y bello! ¡Queremos **respirar** y vivir mejor! Por eso pensamos que nuestra **responsabilidad** es **desarrollar innovaciones** para **proteger la capa de ozono** y **disminuir los riesgos** de **la contaminación.**

En Soluciones Nuevas **valoramos** mucho todas nuestras investigaciones. En esta página, puedes **informarte** de cómo usamos nuestros fondos.

Trabajamos para eliminar...

Más vocabulario

el basurero *garbage container*
el clima *climate*
el derrumbe *landslide*
el temblor *earthquake*
amenazar *to threaten*
apreciar *to appreciate*
dañar *to harm*
destruir *to destroy*
extinguirse *to become extinct*
reutilizar *to reuse*
volar *to fly*
votar *to vote*
complejos *complex*
responsable *responsible*

Expansión de vocabulario p. R6
Ya sabes p. R6

¡A responder! Escuchar 

Escucha la lista de palabras y frases. Si es algo que quieres tener en el futuro indícalo con el dedo pulgar hacia arriba. Si es algo que no quieres tener en el futuro indícalo con el dedo pulgar hacia abajo.

@HomeTutor
Interactive Flashcards
ClassZone.com

Práctica de VOCABULARIO

1 ¿Qué es?

Hablar
Escribir

Haz las preguntas usando las palabras de la lista.

la biodiversidad
la sequía
el petróleo
la erosión
la inundación
el aire puro

modelo: todas las especies diferentes de un lugar
¿Qué es la biodiversidad?

1. un recurso natural
2. ocurre cuando el suelo no está protegido por plantas
3. cuando no llueve
4. lo que todos queremos respirar
5. cuando llueve demasiado

2 Una campaña ecológica

¿Recuerdas? **Ustedes** commands p. 102

Hablar
Escribir

Usa mandatos en la forma de **ustedes** para una campaña sobre el medio ambiente. Utiliza verbos de la lista.

dañar
votar
informarse
usar
desarrollar
proteger
disminuir

modelo: ¡No dañen el medio ambiente!

1. ¡ _____ las especies en peligro de extinción!
2. ¡ _____ nuevas técnicas para un porvenir seguro!
3. ¡ _____ sobre los riesgos de la deforestación!
4. ¡No _____ la biodiversidad!
5. ¡ _____ por los candidatos que valoran el medio ambiente!
6. ¡ _____ los basureros!

3 Me preocupa...

Hablar

Pregúntale a un(a) compañero(a) si los siguientes problemas le preocupan y qué recomienda para mejorarlos.

modelo: deforestación

A ¿Te preocupa la deforestación?

B Sí, es muy importante proteger nuestros bosques y...

1. el smog
2. la erosión
3. la contaminación
4. las inundaciones
5. los derrumbes
6. el efecto invernadero

Expansión
Escribe un correo electrónico donde expresas tus ideas sobre un problema del medio ambiente en tu comunidad.

Más práctica Cuaderno *pp. 99–101* Cuaderno para hispanohablantes *pp. 99–102*

¿Comprendiste? Contesta con oraciones completas.
1. ¿Qué causa el smog y la contaminación?
2. ¿Qué podemos hacer para resolver los problemas?

Get Help Online
ClassZone.com

VOCABULARIO en contexto

¡AVANZA! **Goal:** Review the words that Nicolás uses in his science project. Then identify and discuss the environmental problems that he mentions. ***Actividades 4–5***

¿Recuerdas? **ir a** + infinitive p. R33

Contexto 1 *Informe escolar*

ESTRATEGIA **Leer**

Use a problem chart On a chart, summarize the three environmental problems that Nicolás mentions. Explain why these problems are important.

Problema 1	Problema 2	Problema 3

Nicolás, un estudiante panameño, hizo una investigación sobre los problemas del medio ambiente. El profesor escribió sus comentarios en rojo.

Nicolás García - Grado 11
Ciencias Naturales
Profesor Ludueña
4 de Abril

B

¡Buen trabajo, Nicolás!

EL PORVENIR DEPENDE DEL PRESENTE

El uso de cuatro litros de gasolina produce nueve kilogramos de dióxido de carbono (CO_2). Durante los últimos diez años la cantidad de emisiones de CO_2 en Panamá aumentó en más del 86 por ciento. Si vamos a conservar el petróleo, es necesario comprar coches pequeños que no usan tanta gasolina.

No te olvides de los recursos renovables.

A consecuencia de la deforestación y la destrucción de los hábitats naturales, hay muchas especies en peligro de extinción. En Panamá hay más de veinte especies de pájaros en peligro de extinción. Estas prácticas también contribuyen a la erosión del suelo y a los derrumbes.

También tenemos 192 especies de plantas en peligro de extinción.

Algunos científicos creen que la destrucción de la capa de ozono crea el efecto invernadero, y, como resultado, vamos a tener más sequías e inundaciones. La Organización de las Naciones Unidas estima que, en el futuro, el 50 por ciento de la población mundial va a correr el riesgo de sufrir condiciones climáticas extremas.

Las estadísticas de la ONU se refieren al año 2025.

4 Comprensión del informe escolar

Leer Hablar Escribir

Contesta las preguntas según el informe de Nicolás.

1. ¿Cuántos kilogramos de dióxido de carbono (CO_2) producen cuatro litros de gasolina?
2. ¿Cómo cambiaron las emisiones de CO_2 durante los últimos diez años?
3. Menciona tres consecuencias de la deforestación.
4. ¿Qué porcentaje de la población del mundo va a estar en riesgo de sufrir condiciones climáticas extremas en el año 2025?
5. ¿Cuál puede ser la causa de los problemas con el clima?

5 ¿Cómo ves el futuro?

¿Recuerdas? **ir a** + infinitive p. R33

Hablar Escribir

Haz predicciones sobre el futuro usando la construcción **ir** + **a** + **infinitivo.**

modelo: La contaminación va a destruir la capa de ozono.

destruir	los recursos naturales
desarrollar	las especies en peligro de extinción
respirar	la contaminación
disminuir	la capa de ozono
mejorar	el aire puro

Expansión
Escribe un párrafo sobre la contaminación y sus efectos en el futuro.

Comparación cultural

El Lago de Nicaragua

¿Cómo cambian las formas geográficas con los años?
El Lago de **Nicaragua** es el lago más grande de Centroamérica, con un área de 4.791 millas cuadradas. Antes era parte del Mar Caribe, pero cuando subió el nivel *(level)* de la tierra, se formó el lago. Con los años, el agua salada del lago se transformó y ahora es agua dulce. Las especies de peces que viven allí se adaptaron, para poder vivir en el nuevo ambiente. Por eso, en el Lago de Nicaragua es posible encontrar tiburones *(sharks)*.

El Lago de Nicaragua

Compara con tu mundo *¿Sabes cuáles son los lagos más grandes de Estados Unidos? ¿Dónde están? ¿Sabes cuál es el lago más grande? ¿Hay un lago en tu región?*

¿Comprendiste? Di cuál de los siguientes problemas del medio ambiente se menciona en el trabajo de Nicolás.

los temblores   el smog   las inundaciones   los derrumbes

Get Help Online
ClassZone.com

Presentación de GRAMÁTICA

¡AVANZA! **Goal:** Learn about the formation of the future tense. Then practice using these forms to talk about what will happen in the future. ***Actividades 6–9***

¿Recuerdas? Media vocabulary pp. 92–93

English Grammar Connection: The **future tense** indicates that something will happen in the future. You form the **future tense** in English with the word *will* before an infinitive, minus the word *to*: *We **will** play.*

Future Tense

You have already learned how to refer to future events by using **ir** + **a** + infinitive. Spanish verbs can also be conjugated in the **future tense.**

Here's how: You add endings directly to the infinitive to form the **future tense** of regular verbs.

Infinitive		Future Endings	
jugar		**-é**	**-emos**
proteger	+	**-ás**	**-éis**
traducir		**-á**	**-án**

All verbs have the same endings in the future tense.

Él **traducirá** el informe para mañana.
*He **will translate** the report for tomorrow.*

Protegeremos a nuestros niños.
***We will protect** our children.*

Some verbs are irregular in the **future tense.** You change their stems before adding the regular future tense endings.

Irregular Future Stems

Infinitive	Stem	Infinitive	Stem	Infinitive	Stem
haber	**habr-**	**poner**	**pondr-**	**decir**	**dir-**
poder	**podr-**	**salir**	**saldr-**	**hacer**	**har-**
querer	**querr-**	**tener**	**tendr-**		
saber	**sabr-**	**venir**	**vendr-**		

You can also use the **future tense** to wonder or make a guess about something.

¿Qué **hará** Carlos hoy?
***I wonder** what Carlos **is doing** today.*

Jugará al tenis con Emiliano.
***He's probably playing** tennis with Emiliano.*

Más práctica

Cuaderno *pp. 102–104*

Cuaderno para hispanohablantes *pp. 103–105*

Conjuguemos.com

@HomeTutor Leveled Practice ClassZone.com

Práctica de GRAMÁTICA

6 ¡A organizarnos!

 **¿Recuerdas?** Media vocabulary pp. 92–93

Escuchar
Escribir

Escucha al editor de un periódico semanal de Costa Rica explicar qué tendrán que hacer los empleados para la próxima edición. Luego, completa una tabla, como la siguiente, con el plan de trabajo.

¿Quién?	¿Qué?	¿Para cuándo?
Jorge	sacará fotos	para esta tarde
<1>	<2>	para mañana
Silvia y Martín	<3>	<4>
<5>	completará la columna de consejos	<6>

7 El anuario

Escribir

Escribe una predicción para acompañar cada foto del anuario *(yearbook)*.

modelo: Raúl y Carolina
Raúl y Carolina inventarán una solución para eliminar la contaminación.

1. Elena

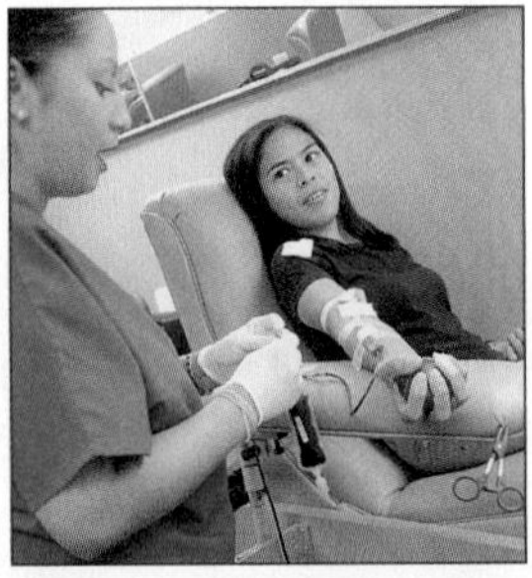

2. Alfredo y Rosa

3. Raquel

4. todos nosotros

5. yo

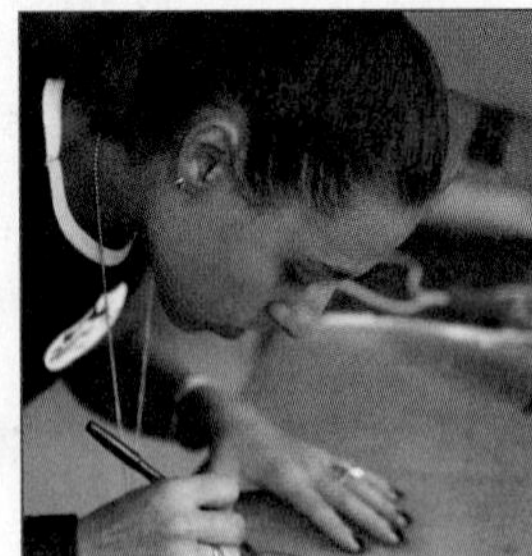

6. tú

8 No sé exactamente

Hablar

Tu compañero te hace muchas preguntas el día de una excursión escolar. Tú no estás seguro(a). Contéstale con el futuro de probabilidad *(for making guesses)*.

modelo: dónde / estar / Ricardo (en casa)

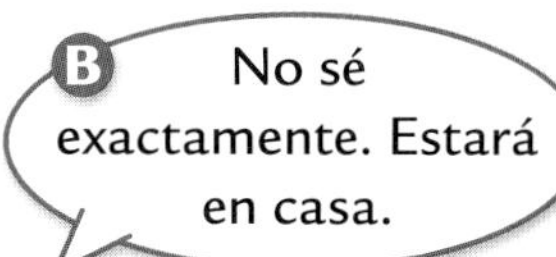

1. adónde / ir / nosotros / de excursión (algún museo)
2. cómo / llegar / allí (en autobús o en tren)
3. cuándo / venir / el autobús (en unos cinco minutos)
4. qué hora / ser (las ocho o las ocho y media)
5. cuántos años / tener / esa señora (unos sesenta años)
6. quién / ser / ella (nuestra guía)
7. dónde / comer / todos (en la cafetería)
8. dónde / estar / mi boleto (en tu bolsillo)
9. qué / tener que hacer / nosotros / para mañana (escribir algo)
10. cuándo / salir / nosotros (el jueves o el viernes)

9 ¿Cómo será tu futuro?

Hablar

Pregúntale a un(a) compañero(a) cómo será su futuro. Haz diez preguntas con los verbos de la lista.

inventar	amenazar	saber	poder
tener	investigar	hacer	reutilizar
fomentar	ser	vivir	apreciar
reciclar	querer	ir	haber

A: ¿Inventarán coches grandes, pero más eficientes?

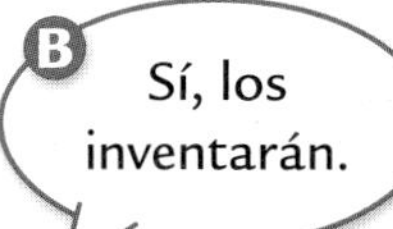

Expansión
Escribe cinco predicciones sobre los cambios en el mundo dentro de veinte años.

Más práctica Cuaderno *pp. 102–104* Cuaderno para hispanohablantes *pp. 103–105*

¿Comprendiste? Cambia las siguientes oraciones del presente al futuro para decir qué hará tu familia en un día libre.

1. Mis abuelos descansan en la playa.
2. Yo voy al museo con mi hermana.
3. Nosotros volvemos a las seis.
4. Mi madre quiere cenar a las siete.

Get Help Online
ClassZone.com

GRAMÁTICA en contexto

¡AVANZA! **Goal:** Note how Nicolás uses the future tense in his journal entry. Then use what you have learned to talk about the future. ***Actividades 10–12***

Contexto 2 *Cuaderno personal*

ESTRATEGIA Leer

Analyze the dream Nicolás is having a nightmare! Analyze what Nicolás sees in the dream and what "Nicolás 2050" tells him. Then write down Nicolás' response (feelings, words).

Analizar el sueño	
Lo que Nicolás ve	
Lo que «Nicolás 2050» dice	
Cómo responde Nicolás	

AUDIO

Nicolás escribió un trabajo para la clase sobre los problemas del medio ambiente en Panamá y en el mundo. Al día siguiente describió en su cuaderno personal un sueño extraño que tuvo.

¡LO QUE VENDRÁ!

Soñé que conocí a un chico del futuro que se llamaba Nicolás 2050. Era exactamente igual que yo, pero vivía en el año 2050. Inmediatamente le pregunté, "¿Cómo será el futuro? ¿Estaré contento? ¿Qué pasará?"

Nicolás 2050 me dijo: "En el futuro vivirás en una ciudad protegida del medio ambiente. La ciudad será muy compleja y estará dentro de un globo de vidrio. La contaminación será tan fuerte que no podrás salir al aire libre y la capa de ozono no te protegerá del sol. Las innovaciones tecnológicas solucionarán algunos de los problemas, pero no habrá árboles, ni flores, ni plantas. Los recursos no renovables no existirán."

"¡No puede ser!" le dije con horror. "¿No tendremos nada bueno en el futuro?" "Claro, hombre," me dijo. "Tendrás un auto especial. ¡Los autos volarán! Usarán la energía solar y no necesitarán gasolina. Y, para divertirte, podrás ir al cine y ver cualquier película que quieras..." "¡Ay, pero todo será aún peor...!" le dije. Y de repente, me desperté.

Ahora sé que tengo que hacer algo para cambiar el futuro... No viviré en un mundo sin aire puro, sin árboles... ¡Qué horror! Los autos que usan energía solar son interesantes... Mañana empezaré a investigar más sobre las energías alternativas.

También se dice

Nicolás utiliza la expresión **¡Qué horror!** para expresar sorpresa y emoción intensa.

- **Centroamérica y el Caribe** **¡Alabao!** (forma informal de «alabado»)
- **España** **¡Qué barbaridad!**
- **Colombia** **¡Caramba!**

10 Comprensión del cuaderno personal

Leer Hablar

Completa las siguientes oraciones con el futuro de los verbos de la lista.

1. Nicolás ____ en una ciudad compleja.
2. Los autos que vuelan ____ a los autos comunes.
3. Las innovaciones ____ algunos problemas.
4. La capa de ozono ____ muy pequeña.
5. Los recursos no renovables no ____ .

ser
existir
solucionar
reemplazar
vivir

11 Consecuencias

Hablar Escribir

Ayuda a Nicolás a analizar las consecuencias de los problemas del futuro.

modelo: nosotros / luchar / contra la destrucción
Nosotros lucharemos contra la destrucción.

1. la gente / buscar / transformación

2. todos /apreciar / inventos

3. tú / aceptar / responsabilidad
4. nosotros / valorar / aire puro
5. yo / no dañar / suelo

6. gobiernos / proteger / especies

Expansión
Escribe una carta al editor de tu periódico local y expresa las posibles consecuencias de algunos problemas del medio ambiente en tu comunidad.

12 Inventos ecológicos

Hablar Escribir

Con tus compañeros(as), identifiquen un problema ecológico e inventen algo para mejorar el problema. Preparen un anuncio de prensa *(press release)* para presentar su invento. Usen el futuro. Presenten su invento en clase.

PARA Y PIENSA

¿Comprendiste? Según «Nicolás 2050», ¿qué será diferente en el futuro? Contesta con tres oraciones completas usando verbos en el futuro.

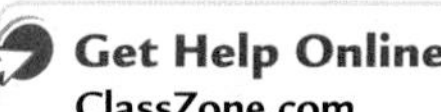

Presentación de GRAMÁTICA

¡AVANZA! **Goal:** Learn about the proper uses of the prepositions **por** and **para.** Then practice using them in a variety of contexts. ***Actividades 13–16***

English Grammar Connection: In English, the preposition *for* can indicate exchange *(We already paid **for** our food)* or destination *(I'm leaving **for** school)*. Spanish has two prepositions to express these ideas: **por** and **para.**

Por and Para

The prepositions **por** and **para** have distinct uses in Spanish. How do you know which one to use?

Here's how:

Use **por** to indicate. . .

• the idea of **passing through**	El tren pasa **por** Panamá.
• **general** rather than specific **location**	¿Hay un basurero **por** aquí?
• **how long** something lasts	Vivimos en San Salvador **por** muchos años.
• the **cause** of something	No tenemos agua **por** la sequía.
• an **exchange**	Cada día pagamos más **por** el petróleo.
• doing something **in place of** or instead of someone else	Estoy muy enfermo hoy. ¿Puedes trabajar **por** mí?
• a **means** of completing an action	Hablamos **por** teléfono.

Use **para** to indicate. . .

• **for whom** something is done	Damos una fiesta **para** mamá.
• **destination**	María sale **para** Panamá mañana.
• the **recipient** of an item	Este regalo es **para** la abuelita.
• the **purpose** of an action	Leemos el periódico **para** informarnos.
• an **opinion**	**Para** mí, la innovación es importante.
• a **comparison** or contrast	Miguel es alto **para** tener dos años.
• a **deadline**	Hay que terminar la tarea **para** mañana.

Más práctica

Cuaderno *pp. 105–107*
Cuaderno para hispanohablantes *pp. 106–109*

@HomeTutor
Leveled Practice
ClassZone.com

Práctica de GRAMÁTICA

13 Un viaje ecológico

Leer
Escribir

Usa **por** o **para** y completa la carta que Anita le escribió a su amiga describiendo el viaje que va a hacer con su clase de ecología.

Querida Julia,

Mi clase de ecología hará un viaje __**1.**__ varias regiones de Costa Rica. Saldremos __**2.**__ San José el viernes y nos quedaremos __**3.**__ dos semanas. Visitaremos seis parques nacionales y reservas ecológicas. __**4.**__ ser un país pequeño, Costa Rica tiene muchísima variedad natural y el gobierno se preocupa mucho __**5.**__ el medio ambiente. Pasaremos __**6.**__ los parques a pie, __**7.**__ ver más. Llevaré una cámara digital __**8.**__ sacar fotos. Después del viaje, te las mandaré __**9.**__ correo electrónico. Tendré que pagar mucho __**10.**__ el viaje, pero será inolvidable. Bueno, Julia, te escribiré más la semana que viene.

—Anita

14 Lo haremos

Escribir

Escribe oraciones completas en el futuro. Usa **por** o **para.**

modelo: nosotros / lavar coches / juntar fondos
Nosotros lavaremos coches para juntar fondos.

1. Marcela / desarrollar un invento / disminuir la erosión
2. nosotros / leer el periódico / informarse
3. yo / hacer las investigaciones / Internet
4. tú / no poder acercarse a las tortugas / tocarlas
5. Edelmiro y Rinaldo / regresar mañana / la noche
6. Muchos animales / extinguirse / la contaminación

Expansión
Escribe cinco actividades que hiciste la semana pasada. Usa **por** o **para.**

AUDIO

Pronunciación La letra g con a, o, u, L, o r

Delante de las vocales **a, o, u,** y las consonantes **L** y **r,** la letra **g** tiene un sonido duro como la *g* de la palabra *go* en inglés. Su posición en una palabra no afecta la pronunciación.

tortuga **riesgo** **gustar** **peligro** **globo**

Trabalenguas

Si su gusto no gusta del gusto que gusta mi gusto,
qué disgusto se lleva mi gusto al saber que su gusto
no gusta del gusto que gusta mi gusto.

15 Una campaña para todos

Hablar

Con un(a) compañero(a), habla de ideas para mejorar la cafetería de tu escuela. Discutan estas preguntas y luego presenten sus ideas a la clase.

A ¿Por qué mejoraremos la cafetería?

B La mejoraremos porque queremos comer mejor.

1. Para la gente de la escuela, ¿cómo es la comida de nuestra cafetería ahora?
2. ¿Qué comidas reemplazaremos por otras? ¿Por qué?
3. Para nosotros, ¿por qué es importante comer mejor?
4. ¿Por cuántas horas podremos usar la cafetería durante el día?
5. ¿Para quiénes serán los cambios que sugerimos?
6. ¿Para cuándo haremos los cambios?

Expansión
Escribe un breve anuncio con tus ideas para mejorar la cafetería. Usa verbos en el futuro y las preposiciones **por** y **para.**

16 ¿Qué pasará?

Escribir

Comparación cultural

Especies en peligro

¿Por qué es importante proteger las especies en peligro de extinción? Las selvas de **Centroamérica,** con su gran variedad de flora y fauna, son un ecosistema maravilloso. Pero, si no paramos la deforestación y la contaminación, estos problemas van a terminar con su existencia. Cuando una especie se extingue, esto daña el equilibrio biológico. Por ejemplo, si desaparecen las tortugas, las algas *(algae)* que ellas comen van a aumentar *(increase)* y pueden contaminar el agua. También los jaguares (que comen tortugas) comerán más venados *(deer)* u otros animales de la zona.

Una tortuga en peligro de extinción

Compara con tu mundo *Menciona dos animales típicos de Estados Unidos. ¿Qué crees que puede pasar si se extinguen?*

Menciona una especie en peligro de extinción de Estados Unidos. Escribe un párrafo para decir qué crees que pasará con esa especie y qué va a pasar si se extingue. Utiliza las preposiciones **por** y **para** en expresiones como: **para mí..., por muchos años..., por eso...**

Más práctica Cuaderno *pp. 105–107* Cuaderno para hispanohablantes *pp. 106–109*

¿Comprendiste? Completa las siguientes frases con **por** o **para.**

1. El desarrollo excesivo no es bueno _____ el medio ambiente.
2. En nuestro viaje, pasamos _____ zonas de mucha erosión.
3. Quiero ir a Honduras _____ el buen tiempo y _____ ver Copán.

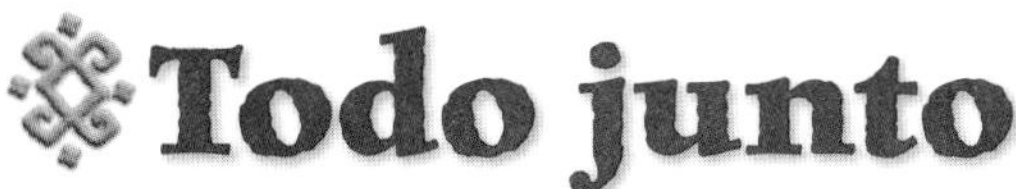

Todo junto

¡AVANZA! **Goal:** ***Show what you know*** Listen to the conversation that Nicolás has with the school guidance counselor. Notice how he expresses concern about the future and how he uses the prepositions **por** and **para.** ***Actividades 17–19***

Resumen contextos 1 y 2 Nicolás es un estudiante panameño que escribió un informe sobre los problemas del medio ambiente. Esa misma noche, tuvo un sueño sobre los efectos de esos problemas.

Contexto 3 *Diálogo*

ESTRATEGIA **Escuchar**
Create a dialogue map Make a "dialogue map" of the conversation between Nicolás and Sr. Zamora. Try not to write down every word. Instead, write the main things they say to each other.

AUDIO

Nicolás decide hablar con el consejero de su escuela sobre proyectos sociales en Centroamérica, donde él puede trabajar de voluntario.

Nicolás: Hola, Sr. Zamora. ¿Será posible hablar con usted sobre mis planes para el verano? Puedo regresar más tarde si está ocupado.

Sr. Zamora: No, no. Está bien, Nicolás. Siéntate. Dime, ¿en qué estás pensando?

Nicolás: Quiero saber más sobre los programas de acción social en Centroamérica… Tuve un sueño horrible sobre el futuro y decidí que quiero hacer todo lo que pueda para mejorar la situación mundial. Quiero hacerlo por las generaciones del porvenir.

Sr. Zamora: Buena idea, Nicolás. ¿En qué tipo de proyecto quieres trabajar?

Nicolás: Tal vez algo relacionado con la energía solar. Sé que no tendremos suficiente petróleo para los vehículos en el futuro. Necesitaremos más innovaciones tecnológicas para solucionar el problema.

Sr. Zamora: Bueno, ése es un buen objetivo. A ver, aquí tengo información sobre un programa en Nicaragua que apoya la energía renovable y mejora las prácticas agrícolas en el país... También hay otro programa que tiene proyectos por toda Centroamérica, trabajando en los pueblos para implementar el uso de cocinas solares.

Nicolás: Los dos programas parecen muy buenos. Tendré que hablar con mis padres y pensar más en las posibilidades, pero en unos días podré decidir.

Sr. Zamora: Otro programa, en Costa Rica, construyó un sitio en Tilarán, donde los productores de café pueden usar la energía solar para ayudar con la producción. Aquí, en Panamá, hay un grupo que trabaja para eliminar la deforestación, que causa problemas con los niveles del agua en el Canal de Panamá.

Nicolás: ¡Cuántos programas interesantes! ¿Cómo escogeré el mejor?

Sr. Zamora: Bueno, Nicolás, tendrás que pensarlo bien y decidir si viajarás por varios lugares o si te quedarás aquí, en Panamá, este verano. ¿Qué te parece?

Nicolás: ¡Me parece que tengo cuatro opciones muy interesantes! Voy a pensarlo bien y haré otra cita con usted para hablar más.

Sr. Zamora: Bien, Nicolás. Toma estos papeles con información. Tenlos por cinco días. Muéstraselos a tus padres, habla con ellos durante el fin de semana y regresa a verme la semana que viene. Esperaré tu visita y ¡buena suerte con tu decisión!

17 Comprensión del diálogo

Escuchar
Escribir

Completa una tabla como la que sigue con la información sobre los programas que mencionó el Sr. Zamora.

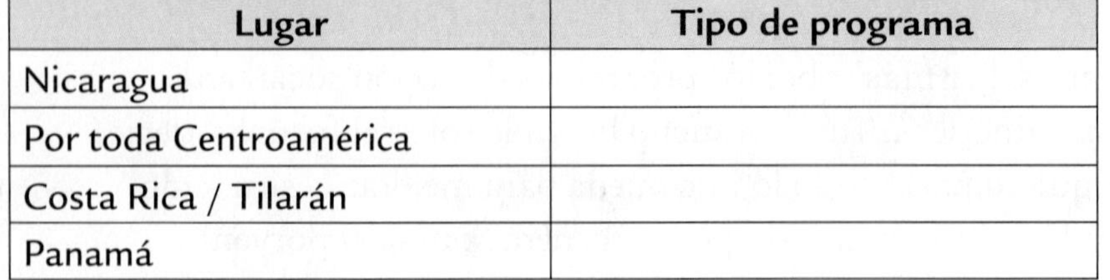

Lugar	Tipo de programa
Nicaragua	
Por toda Centroamérica	
Costa Rica / Tilarán	
Panamá	

Expansión
¿Qué programa quieres elegir tú? Escribe un informe breve explicando por qué.

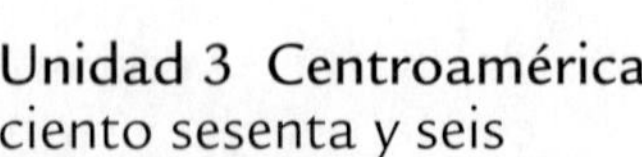

18 Integración

Leer
Escuchar
Hablar

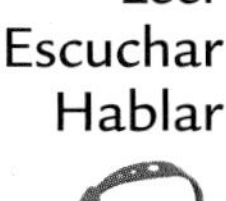

Lee el artículo sobre cambios medioambientales. Luego escucha el anuncio de un nuevo vehículo ecológico, que pasan por la radio. Después, explica cómo será nuestro planeta en el año 2025 si todos usamos el nuevo vehículo.

Fuente 1 Revista científica

AMBIENTE EN PELIGRO

Nuestro planeta tendrá muchos problemas medioambientales en el futuro. Para el año 2025 la

destrucción de la capa de ozono será un problema enorme. La contaminación del aire y la deforestación causarán daños irreparables en el medio ambiente. Habrá más especies de plantas y animales en peligro de extinción. Tenemos que actuar ahora para disminuir el efecto invernadero e implementar cambios para asegurar el porvenir del planeta. Debemos hacerlo para nosotros y para las generaciones del futuro.

Fuente 2 Anuncio por la radio

Escucha y apunta

- ¿Cuándo se puede comprar el nuevo carro?
- ¿Qué efectos se verán en el futuro?

modelo: El nuevo carro Verde se puede comprar hoy mismo. Si todos usamos ese carro, en el año 2015 no habrá contaminación y los animales y plantas no estarán en peligro...

19 Un programa interesante

Escribir

Escribe un ensayo corto con las soluciones ideales para evitar un riesgo para el medio ambiente. Debes incluir una introducción para describir el problema y sus posibles efectos en el futuro, un párrafo con posibles soluciones y una conclusión para describir los beneficios de esas soluciones.

Writing Criteria	Excellent	Good	Needs Work
Content	Your essay proposes several solutions and clearly explains their benefits.	Your essay proposes some solutions and somewhat clearly explains their benefits.	Your essay proposes few solutions and does not clearly explain their benefits.
Communication	Your argument is organized and easy to follow.	Parts of your argument are organized and easy to follow.	Your argument is disorganized and hard to follow.
Accuracy	You make few mistakes in grammar and vocabulary.	You make some mistakes in grammar and vocabulary.	You make many mistakes in grammar and vocabulary.

Más práctica Cuaderno *pp. 108–109* Cuaderno para hispanohablantes *pp. 110–111*

PARA Y PIENSA

Get Help Online
ClassZone.com

¿Comprendiste? Según la lectura, contesta cada pregunta.

1. ¿Por qué a Nicolás le interesa un proyecto relacionado con la energía solar?
2. ¿Para qué usan la energía solar en Tilarán, Costa Rica?

Lectura literaria

¡AVANZA! **Goal:** Notice how the author characterizes and describes the stages of life in the following story. Then discuss your interpretations of the text as well as your own opinions about which stage is the best.

Para leer 

ESTRATEGIA **Leer**

Anticipate content through organizational clues The author of the following selection gives wonderful organizational clues to lead us through the essay. These clues relate to age. On a separate sheet of paper, draw pictures of the different ages mentioned in the reading. Next to the corresponding picture, summarize what people of each age think about "the best age."

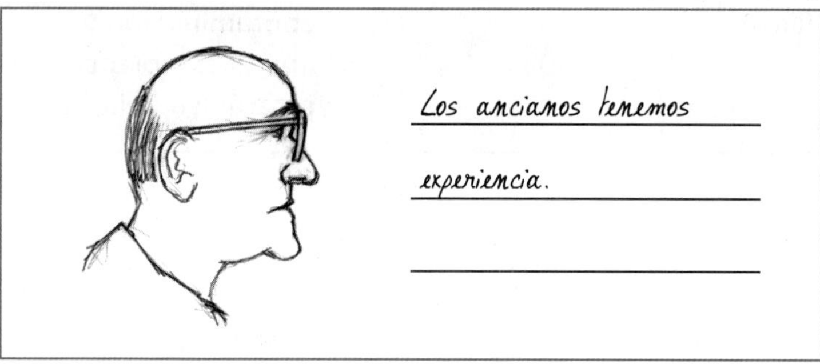

Vocabulario para leer

gozo *sensación de placer y alegría*
desdicha *tristeza, mala suerte*
devenir *lo que ocurre en el futuro*
vejez *edad de los ancianos*
esplendor *momento en que algo llega a la perfección*

Nota cultural

Sobre el autor *Carlos Balaguer (1952–)*

Nació en San Salvador, El Salvador. De joven empezó a escribir poemas y decidió irse a vivir al campo. Allí descubrió su fascinación por la naturaleza, un tema que se manifiesta en muchas de sus obras. Estudió psicología en la Universidad Católica (UCA) y empezó a escribir para el periódico *El Diario de Hoy* de San Salvador. Entre sus obras figuran ensayos, novelas, leyendas y fábulas.

Feria, (2006), Graciela Genovés

La mejor edad

AUDIO

El hombre puede hacer de su vida gozo o desdicha; puede crear su paraíso o, si lo quiere, su infierno. De la elección de su corazón depende su alegría. ❖

Si de pronto, al estar en un lugar rodeado[1] de muchas personas, empezáramos a preguntar a cada quién cuál es la mejor edad[2] de la vida, cada cual diría[3] su propia respuesta.

Para un niño, la mejor edad de la vida será la de ser niño, porque así podría[4] comer caramelos[5], jugar, cazar[6] estrellas y mariposas. En los caballos de nube[7] de su imaginación estará el trote[8] de sus ilusiones por el anchuroso[9] universo de la ilusión.

❖ **A pensar**
¿Quién es el responsable de la alegría o la tristeza de una persona?

---

[1] surrounded [2] age [3] **cada...** everyone would say [4] could
[5] candies [6] to hunt [7] **En...** In the clouds shaped like horses
[8] trot [9] wide

Calle del Cabañal, Valencia *(1902), Joaquín Sorolla Bastida*

Para otros, la mejor edad de la vida será la juventud, pues en ella la naturaleza expresará su fuerza, esperanza y encanto[10]. La belleza de la juventud está en lo que promete[11]. Sus rosas y sus luces; sus encantos y sus ilusiones. En la juventud, es cuando los caminos se abren al hombre, que trata de conquistar su devenir, su ideal.

A pensar
¿Cómo cambia la vida en la juventud?

[10] enchantment [11] **está...** is in what it promises

Reflexiona

¿Cuál crees que es la posición del autor con respecto a las diferentes edades?

Para un anciano, en cambio, la alegría de la vida ya no estará únicamente en sus emociones de lucha, sino en la contemplación de la naturaleza; la paz del guerrero[12] después de la victoria de vivir... La mejor edad de la vida para el viejo, estará en la paz de la naturaleza y en su sensación de eternidad y de grandeza[13]. La sabiduría[14] de la vejez, otro de sus encantos, será un fuerte motivo de hacer de la vejez, si se quiere, la mejor edad de la vida... ❖

En fin, y si continuamos más allá, veríamos[15] que para el derrotista[16] no existen mejores edades de la vida y que, para el árbol, cada edad de su vida tiene su propio esplendor, su verdor[17], su floración[18] y sus frutos... cuando no el oro de su otoño[19].

❖ **A pensar**
¿Qué tienen los ancianos que les permite considerar la vejez como la mejor edad?

---

[12] warrior, soldier [13] greatness
[14] wisdom [15] we would see
[16] defeatist [17] greenness [18] flowering
[19] **cuando...** even the gold of its autumn

¿Comprendiste?

1. ¿Cuáles son las tres edades que menciona el autor?
2. ¿Cuáles son las características de cada edad según el autor?
3. Según el autor, ¿de qué depende la felicidad del ser humano?
4. En tu opinión, ¿qué significa la conclusión del ensayo?

¿Y tú?

En tu opinión, ¿cuál es la mejor edad?

Conexiones *Los estudios sociales*

Los símbolos patrióticos

La importancia del quetzal Los países de Centroamérica comparten un símbolo importante: el pájaro quetzal. El quetzal figura en la mitología indígena como imagen del dios Quetzalcóatl, la serpiente emplumada *(feathered)*. Además, este pájaro representa la libertad, porque según las leyendas, no puede vivir en cautiverio *(captivity)*. En la actualidad el quetzal es el símbolo de un medio ambiente sano y hay reservas para su protección. Guatemala adoptó el quetzal como símbolo nacional y su imagen aparece en la bandera *(flag)*, en el escudo *(seal)* y en la moneda *(currency)*, que también se llama «quetzal».

Un poema a la libertad

El siguiente poema patriótico guatemalteco expresa la importancia del quetzal como símbolo de libertad y de la patria.

Poema a la Bandera
Autor anónimo

Yo tengo una Bandera
Bandera bicolor,
Que indica que sigamos
la senda del honor.
Mi Bandera y mi Escudo
con su bello quetzal
simbolizan la patria,
Guatemala inmortal.

Proyecto Escoge un país o ciudad de Centroamérica y haz una investigación sobre sus símbolos patrióticos. Prepara un informe sobre la importancia actual y el significado histórico de los símbolos. Explica por qué los símbolos representan bien a la gente de esa región.

En tu comunidad

¿Cuáles son los símbolos principales de Estados Unidos?

¿Hay un pájaro nacional? ¿Qué otros símbolos nacionales existen y dónde se ven?

En resumen

Vocabulario y gramática

Vocabulario

Express Environmental Concerns and Possibilities

el aire puro	*clean air*
el basurero	*garbage container*
la biodiversidad	*biodiversity*
la capa de ozono	*ozone layer*
el clima	*climate*
la contaminación	*pollution, contamination*
la deforestación	*deforestation*
el derrumbe	*landslide*
el efecto invernadero	*greenhouse effect*
la erosión	*erosion*
las especies en peligro de extinción	*endangered species*
la inundación	*flood*
el medio ambiente	*environment*
no renovable	*nonrenewable*
el petróleo	*oil*
el planeta	*planet*
el recurso natural	*natural resource*
la responsabilidad	*responsibility*
el riesgo	*risk*
la sequía	*drought*
el smog	*smog*
el suelo	*ground, soil*
el temblor	*earthquake*

Actions

dañar	*to harm*
destruir	*to destroy*
disminuir	*to diminish, to decrease*
fomentar	*to foment, to support*
proteger	*to protect*
respirar	*to breathe*
reutilizar	*to reuse*
valorar	*to value*

Impact of Technology

apreciar	*to appreciate*
complejo(a)	*complex*
desarrollar	*to develop*
el desarrollo	*development*
la innovación	*innovation*
el invento	*invention*
la investigación	*research*
mejorar	*to improve*
reemplazar	*to replace*

Make Predictions

amenazar	*to threaten*
extinguirse	*to become extinct*
informarse	*to keep informed*
el porvenir	*future*
responsable	*responsible*
la transformación	*transformation*
volar	*to fly*
votar	*to vote*

Gramática

Future Tense

Infinitive +

Future Endings	
-é	-emos
-ás	-éis
-á	-án

Irregular Future Stems

Infinitive	Stem	Infinitive	Stem
haber	habr-	**salir**	saldr-
poder	podr-	**tener**	tendr-
querer	querr-	**venir**	vendr-
saber	sabr-	**decir**	dir-
poner	pondr-	**hacer**	har-

You can also use the **future tense** to wonder or make a guess about something.

Por and Para

Use **por** to indicate . . .

- **passing through**
- **general location**
- **how long**
- **cause**
- **exchange**
- **in place of**
- **means**

Use **para** to indicate . . .

- **for whom**
- **destination**
- **recipient**
- **purpose**
- **opinion**
- **comparison**
- **deadline**

Lección 1

Repaso de la lección

¡LLEGADA!

@HomeTutor
ClassZone.com

Now you can
- discuss the impact of technology
- express environmental concerns and possibilities
- make predictions and discuss causes and effects

Using
- future tense
- **por** and **para**

To review
- vocabulary pp. 152–153

1 Listen and understand

AUDIO

Escucha el siguiente anuncio publicitario y di si los siguientes comentarios son ciertos o falsos. Si son falsos, corrígelos según la información del anuncio.

1. En el futuro no será necesario cambiar nuestra forma de vida.
2. AlertAmbiental va a proteger el medio ambiente.
3. Si no protegemos nuestros recursos naturales, no habrá agua limpia.
4. En el futuro tampoco habrá inundaciones ni sequías.
5. AlertAmbiental va a trabajar para aumentar el efecto invernadero.
6. AlertAmbiental cuidará el planeta.

To review
- future tense p. 157

2 Express environmental concerns and possibilities

Mira las fotos y escribe oraciones para indicar qué hará cada persona para mejorar el medio ambiente.

1. Carlos / querer un vehículo económico

2. Mónica y Rafaela / reemplazar los árboles cortados

3. Luisa y Beatriz / informarse sobre el medio ambiente

4. ellos / proteger el agua

5. nosotros / votar por el candidato «verde»

6. yo / fomentar el reciclaje

To review
• **por** and **para** p. 162

3 Discuss the impact of technology

Completa el siguiente párrafo con **por** o **para,** según el contexto.

Mis amigos, Lorenzo y Teresa, siempre tratan de conservar los recursos naturales. El año pasado, hicieron una investigación __**1.**__ buscar información sobre inventos nuevos, desarrollados __**2.**__ proteger el medio ambiente. Estudiaron __**3.**__ un año __**4.**__ saber más sobre la contaminación. __**5.**__ mí, la tecnología y el desarrollo son importantes, pero también tenemos que cuidar los recursos. Debemos viajar __**6.**__ carretera en autos económicos __**7.**__ gastar menos gasolina y __**8.**__ ahorrar dinero.

To review
• future tense p. 157

4 Make predictions and discuss causes and effects

Haz predicciones sobre el futuro, usando los verbos y la información dada.

modelo: **nosotros / tener aire y agua puros / eliminar la contaminación**
En el futuro tendremos aire y agua puros porque eliminaremos la contaminación.

1. las especies en peligro de extinción / no extinguirse / valorar la biodiversidad
2. los vehículos / no usar petróleo / reemplazarlo con recursos renovables
3. yo / informarse / todos tener la responsabilidad de ayudar
4. la capa de ozono / no estar en peligro / haber menos contaminación
5. mis amigos y yo / hacer una campaña / querer disminuir la deforestación
6. En las ciudades / disminuir el smog / desarrollar los recursos renovables

To review
• **Comparación cultural** pp. 156, 164

5 Environmental concerns and official symbols

Comparación cultural

1. ¿Cómo es el agua del Lago de Nicaragua? ¿Por qué?
2. Explica por qué los tiburones pueden vivir en el lago.
3. ¿Qué amenaza a las especies en las selvas centroamericanas?
4. ¿Qué pasará si se extinguen las tortugas?

Más práctica Cuaderno *pp. 110–121* Cuaderno para hispanohablantes *pp. 112–121*

UNIDAD 3

Centroamérica

Lección 2

Tema: *Por un futuro mejor*

¡AVANZA! **In this lesson you will learn to**

- discuss obligations and responsibilities
- present and support an opinion
- express a point of view and make recommendations

using

- present subjunctive of regular verbs
- more subjunctive verb forms

¿Recuerdas?

- **ustedes** commands
- impersonal expressions
- future tense

Comparación cultural

In this lesson you will learn about

- the Panama Canal
- native art in Central America
- ways to protect the environment in Central America

Compara con tu mundo

Estos molinos de viento *(windmills)* son una fuente *(source)* de electricidad para la región. El viento es un ejemplo de energía renovable. *¿Viste molinos de viento en Estados Unidos? ¿Dónde? Si no los viste, ¿dónde crees que hay?*

¿Qué ves?

Mira la foto

¿Cuántos molinos puedes ver?

¿Cómo es el paisaje?

¿Qué hora del día crees que es?

Featuring...

Cultura INTERACTIVA

Animated Grammar

@HomeTutor

And more...

- Get Help Online
- Interactive Flashcards
- Review Games
- WebQuest
- Conjuguemos.com

Molinos de viento
Tilarán, Costa Rica

 Presentación de VOCABULARIO

¡AVANZA! **Goal:** Learn new vocabulary relating to government, society, and business. Then practice the vocabulary to talk about ways of achieving success. ***Actividades 1–3***

¿Recuerdas? **Ustedes** commands p. 102

AUDIO

A Liliana ganó el premio «**Ciudadana** Modelo» de su comunidad por su **conciencia social** y porque **lucha** cada día contra **la irresponsabilidad** y por **la mejora** de **la sociedad.**

B Liliana es un ejemplo para todos. Ella siempre quiere **solucionar** problemas de su ciudad y de los ciudadanos. «Operación Barrio» tiene muchas responsabilidades: desde plantar árboles y limpiar la ciudad, hasta ayudar a las personas pobres con sus **sufrimientos.** La organización ayuda a las personas a **superar obstáculos** y a **seguir adelante** con sus vidas.

C Además, **se encarga de advertir** a los más jóvenes de los **errores** que pueden **cometer** y cómo evitar **fracasos** en el futuro. Liliana siempre dice en las reuniones: «**Es imprescindible persistir, emprender** y **progresar**».

Más vocabulario

la advertencia *warning*
la política *politics*
el principio *principle*
la unidad *unity*
criticar *to criticize*
insistir *to insist*
penalizar *to penalize*
respetar *to respect*
es raro que... *it is strange that . . .*
por el otro lado... *on the other hand . . .*
por un lado... *on one hand . . .*

Expansión de vocabulario p. R7
Ya sabes p. R7

D Ahora, Liliana tiene una idea para un invento que quiere desarrollar para mejorar su comunidad. Ella buscó información sobre cómo se debe introducir un producto nuevo al público.

Un **producto novedoso** es el resultado de una idea nueva.

La Oficina de **Patentes evalúa** el producto y lo registra.

Liliana hace un **compromiso** con una compañía que **invierte** para **comercializar** el producto.

¡El producto **satisface** al público y todos **prosperan**!

¡A responder! Escuchar

Escucha la lista de palabras y frases. Si es algo que puede ayudar a hacer un negocio, indícalo con el dedo pulgar hacia arriba. Si es algo que es un obstáculo para hacer un negocio, indícalo con el dedo pulgar hacia abajo.

@HomeTutor
Interactive Flashcards
ClassZone.com

Práctica de VOCABULARIO

1 Los inventos

Hablar
Escribir

Usa palabras de la lista para completar el párrafo sobre el proceso de inventar.

persistir
fracasos
emprender
comercializar
solucionar
evaluar
una patente
superar

Siempre es una aventura __1.__ la invención de un producto novedoso. Pero no es fácil __2.__ los obstáculos. Si hay __3.__ , no importa, tienes que __4.__ . Es mejor __5.__ los problemas y tratar de __6.__los. Si luego piensas __7.__ tu nuevo producto, es preferible sacar __8.__ para proteger tu idea.

2 Una campaña política

¿*Recuerdas?* **Ustedes** Commands p. 102

Hablar
Escribir

Elige el verbo apropiado y escribe el mandato en la forma de **ustedes** para inventar lemas para una campaña política.

modelo: (solucionar / comercializar)

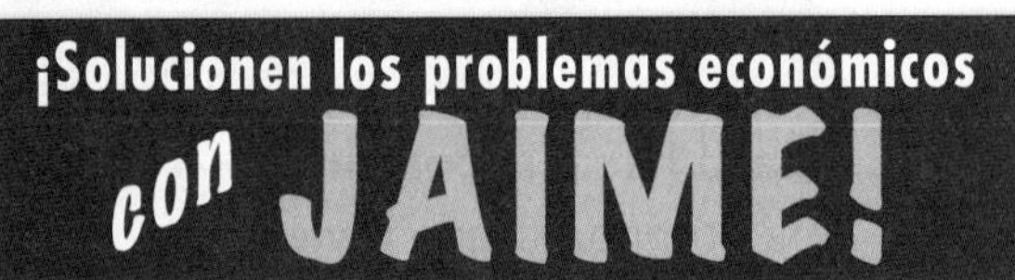

1. (invertir / advertir) ¡ ____ en la sociedad! ¡Voten por Silvia!
2. (seguir adelante / satisfacer) ¡ ____ ! ¡Avancen con Darío!
3. (evaluar / respetar) ¡ ____ los valores de los ciudadanos y ciudadanas!
4. (prosperar / criticar) ¡ ____ con Walter y su plan de negocios!
5. (penalizar / luchar) ¡ ____ contra el sufrimiento con Regina!

3 Un producto nuevo

Hablar

Con tu compañero(a), resuman las características de un producto nuevo para presentar a los directores de su compañía. Consideren lo siguiente: ¿Qué tipo de producto es? ¿Qué necesidad satisface? ¿Qué mejora ofrece? ¿Cómo piensan comercializarlo?

Expansión
Preparen un anuncio de su producto para una campaña de publicidad.

Más práctica Cuaderno *pp. 122–124* Cuaderno para hispanohablantes *pp. 122–125*

¿Comprendiste? ¿Qué debe hacer una persona o un negocio para prosperar? Usa las siguientes palabras en tu respuesta: invertir, respetar, persistir, solucionar.

Get Help Online
ClassZone.com

 VOCABULARIO en contexto

¡AVANZA! **Goal:** In her notes describing a new product, learn the words that Liliana uses to make her ideas convincing. Then identify and talk about the benefits her product offers. ***Actividades 4–5***

Contexto 1 *Folleto técnico*

ESTRATEGIA **Leer**

Analyze benefits with a pyramid chart In the bottom part of the pyramid, write the name of Liliana's invention and a short description of it. In the rest of the pyramid write four benefits in order of importance, with the most important benefit (N°1) at the very top.

Liliana Estrella, una estudiante hondureña, tuvo la idea de inventar un aparato que ayude a los que practican deportes y sufren de asma, como ella. Por eso, escribió unas notas y dibujó un posible invento.

Este aparato novedoso, combina las funciones de un reproductor de MP3 con un monitor del aire. Soluciona los problemas de los atletas con problemas respiratorios (alergias, asma) que quieren practicar deportes al aire libre. Evalúa la calidad del aire a cada momento y le avisa al atleta cuando hay contaminación o un nivel de polen alto. Así, el atleta no cometerá el error de seguir haciendo ejercicio.

MejorAire

El monitor es fácil de leer e interpretar. Indica cuando el atleta debe seguir adelante y le advierte cuando debe volver a casa.

El aparato está disponible en dos versiones: para las altitudes normales y para las altitudes extremas.

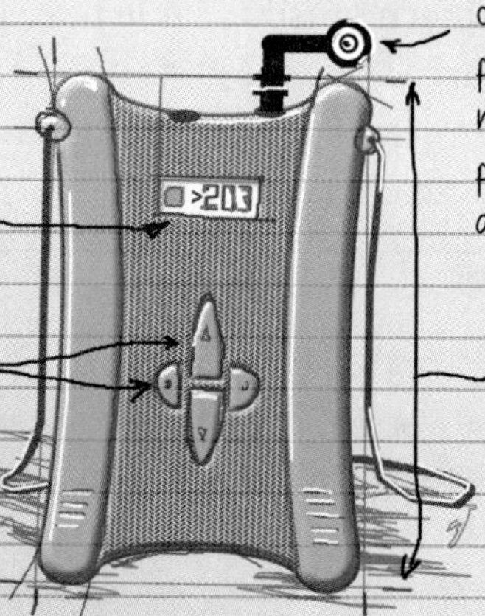

La variedad de funciones elimina la necesidad de llevar dos aparatos cuando se emprende una excursión larga.

Satisface las necesidades de los atletas con una máquina ligera y pequeña.

¿Es posible comercializarlo? ¡Tal vez necesito sacar una patente! Por un lado, es buena idea. Por el otro lado, ¡puede ser caro!

4 Comprensión del folleto técnico

Hablar
Escribir

Usa palabras de la lista para completar las siguientes oraciones.

advertir	novedoso	solucionar
comercializar	satisfacer	cometer un error
evaluar	patente	

1. El MejorAire es un aparato ____ .
2. ____ los problemas de los atletas con asma.
3. El aparato ____ la calidad del aire.
4. Le ____ al atleta cuando el aire está contaminado.
5. Liliana piensa ____ su invento.
6. Liliana se pregunta si debe sacar una ____ para el invento.
7. El atleta no ____ si el aire está contaminado.
8. El MejorAire ____ las necesidades de los atletas.

5 ¿Qué opinas?

Hablar
Escribir

Expresa tus opiniones y contesta las siguientes preguntas usando las expresiones **por un lado** y **por el otro lado.**

modelo: ¿Crees que es una buena idea tener clases en el verano? Por un lado es importante seguir aprendiendo, pero, por el otro lado, es necesario tener tiempo libre.

1. ¿Deben los estudiantes poder evaluar sus escuelas?
2. ¿Deben comercializar productos no saludables en la televisión?
3. ¿Debemos penalizar a las personas que contaminan el medio ambiente?
4. En tu opinión, ¿es el gobierno responsable por el sufrimiento de los ciudadanos sin hogar?
5. Para una compañía, ¿es mejor satisfacer a los inversionistas *(investors)* o tener una conciencia social?

Expansión
Escribe un párrafo sobre la pregunta que te interesa más.

¿Comprendiste? Usa las siguientes palabras para describir las cualidades que un producto nuevo debe tener: **satisfacer, solucionar, novedoso.**

Get Help Online
ClassZone.com

Presentación de GRAMÁTICA

¡AVANZA! **Goal:** Learn about the formation of the present subjunctive for regular verbs. Then use the subjunctive to discuss your opinions. ***Actividades 6–9***

¿Recuerdas? Impersonal expressions p. 128

English Grammar Connection: Some impersonal expressions show uncertainty that something will happen. In both English and Spanish, such expressions are followed by verbs in the **subjunctive.**

It's important that he **leave.** Es importante que él **salga.**

Present Subjunctive of Regular Verbs

The **present subjunctive** is formed in the same way as most command forms.

Here's how: Start with the present tense **yo** form. Drop the **-o** and add **-e** to **-ar** verbs and **-a** to **-er**/**-ir** verbs.

These forms are the same.

	hablar	tener	escribir
yo	**hable**	**tenga**	**escriba**
tú	**hables**	**tengas**	**escribas**
usted, él, ella	**hable**	**tenga**	**escriba**
nosotros(as)	**hablemos**	**tengamos**	**escribamos**
vosotros(as)	**habléis**	**tengáis**	**escribáis**
ustedes, ellos(as)	**hablen**	**tengan**	**escriban**

Es imprescindible que **hables** claramente. *It is imperative that **you speak** clearly.*

You have to change the spelling of some verbs to maintain proper pronunciation.

	becomes
criticar	**critique**
investigar	**investigue**
penalizar	**penalice**
proteger	**proteja**
extinguir	**extinga**

Es raro que un músico **critique** su música.
*It's strange that a musician **criticize** his own music.*

Es necesario que él **proteja** a los ciudadanos.
*It's necessary that he **protect** the citizens.*

Más práctica
Cuaderno *pp. 125–127*
Cuaderno para hispanohablantes *pp. 126–128*

Conjuguemos.com

@HomeTutor
Leveled Practice
ClassZone.com

Práctica de GRAMÁTICA

6 Es importante...

Hablar
Escribir

Completa cada oración con la forma correcta del verbo.

modelo: Es importante que todos nosotros (respetar) las leyes.
Es importante que todos nosotros respetemos las leyes.

1. Es una lástima que ellos no (superar) los obstáculos.
2. Es mejor que tú te (encargar) de tus problemas.
3. Es una buena idea que yo (conseguir) una patente.
4. Es una pena que unos negocios (insistir) en tener precios altos.
5. Es necesario que nosotros (leer) las advertencias públicas.

Expansión
Escribe cinco oraciones más con información original que se relacione con tu escuela o comunidad.

7 La ecóloga

¿Recuerdas? Impersonal expressions p. 128

Escuchar
Escribir

Escucha lo que dice la ecóloga sobre el medio ambiente. Completa las oraciones con las expresiones impersonales y el subjuntivo para dar tu opinión.

modelo: Es triste que...
Es triste que no respiremos aire puro.

1. Es una lástima que...
2. Es raro que...
3. Es lamentable que...
4. Es mejor que...
5. Es importante que...
6. Es imprescindible que...

Comparación cultural

El canal y Panamá

¿Cómo se beneficia un país de su posición geográfica? El Canal de Panamá conecta a los océanos Atlántico y Pacífico. Es importante que todos sepan que es uno de los logros más grandes de la ingeniería mundial. ¡La tierra y las piedras excavadas *(excavated)* en el Canal eran suficientes para construir una réplica de la Gran Muralla China, desde San Francisco hasta Nueva York! Como resultado de la construcción del canal, la historia y las costumbres de **Panamá** cambiaron para siempre. Antes, era un país pequeño y poco conocido, y ahora es uno de los centros de tráfico de mercancías *(merchandise)* más grandes del mundo. Además, los trabajadores chinos que participaron en su construcción formaron una de las minorías más importantes de la población panameña actual.

Un barco de carga en el Canal de Panamá

Compara con tu mundo *¿Conoces alguna construcción importante cerca de tu comunidad que ayuda al comercio? ¿Cómo ayudan estas construcciones a tu comunidad?*

8 ¿Qué opinas?

Hablar
Escribir

Usa expresiones impersonales y el subjuntivo para expresar tu opinión sobre las situaciones en las fotos.

(no) es bueno que...	(no) es peligroso que...
(no) es importante que...	(no) es posible que...
(no) es malo que...	(no) es raro que...

modelo: No es raro que los periódicos digan la verdad.

1. 
2. 
3. 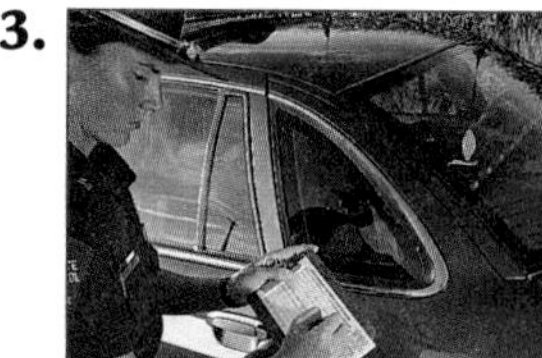
4. 
5. 
6. 

Expansión
Expresa tu opinión sobre las fotos. Usa el subjuntivo y dos expresiones impersonales más.

9 Los expertos

Hablar

Según los expertos, es necesario que hagamos ciertas cosas para proteger el medio ambiente. ¿Por qué es necesario que hagamos estas cosas? Habla con un(a) compañero(a) sobre estos temas. Usen el subjuntivo.

modelo: valorar la innovación

1. disminuir la contaminación
2. hacer investigaciones
3. usar recursos naturales
4. proteger las especies en peligro de extinción

A ¿Por qué es necesario que valoremos la innovación?

B Es necesario que valoremos la innovación para solucionar problemas nuevos.

Más práctica Cuaderno *pp. 125–127* Cuaderno para hispanohablantes *pp. 126–128*

¿Comprendiste? Termina las siguientes frases con el subjuntivo para expresar tus opiniones:

1. Es mejor que... **2.** Es importante que... **3.** Es raro que...

GRAMÁTICA en contexto

¡AVANZA! **Goal:** Notice how the advertisement below uses the subjunctive with impersonal expressions. Then practice by talking about innovative products. ***Actividades 10–11***

Contexto 2 *Anuncio*

ESTRATEGIA **Leer**

Different uses of the subjunctive In a hierarchy chart like the one to the right, write three different uses of the subjunctive and give examples of each. Start with phrases in this reading where the subjunctive is used to express an opinion.

Usos del subjuntivo

AUDIO

Liliana inventó un aparato que evalúa la calidad del aire. Al día siguiente, vio este anuncio en un periódico local.

Se buscan jóvenes inventores

En enero se realiza el Primer Congreso Hondureño de Inventores Jóvenes. Todos los estudiantes de escuela secundaria pueden participar. Deben enviar la información necesaria antes del 10 de diciembre.

Es necesario que los inventos...

- solucionen un problema medioambiental que afecta a la población hondureña.
- despierten la conciencia social sobre el problema y respeten la filosofía de la conservación ecológica.

Además es importante que...

- el invento se base en una idea novedosa y útil.
- cada participante envíe sus datos y una foto o dibujo del invento.

IMPORTANTE: Es preferible que el maestro o la maestra del joven inventor escriba una carta de recomendación.

Los estudiantes que quieran participar deben mandar sus datos y fotos a:
Centro Educativo de la Comunidad
Caja Postal 999
Tegucigalpa, 111

10 Comprensión del anuncio

Leer
Escribir

Completa las oraciones con el verbo en la forma correcta.

1. Es imprescindible que los estudiantes ____ la información necesaria.
2. Es necesario que ____ a la dirección indicada.
3. Es mejor que el invento ____ una filosofía ecológica.
4. Es importante que los maestros ____ a los estudiantes.
5. Es necesario que el invento ____ novedoso y útil.

ser
escribir
respetar
apoyar
enviar

11 Un invento novedoso

Hablar
Escribir

Con tus compañeros(as), identifiquen un problema y piensen en un invento para solucionarlo.

Paso 1 Preparen una explicación usando expresiones impersonales.

modelo:
Problema: el smog
Soluciones posibles: una máscara, filtros nasales
Invento y explicación: Es imprescindible que resolvamos el problema del smog. Es recomendable llevar máscaras...

Paso 2 Preparen un anuncio de televisión para promocionar el invento. Incluyan por lo menos cinco ejemplos de expresiones impersonales con el subjuntivo.

Expansión
Considera con tus compañeros(as), los inventos de los demás grupos. ¿Qué recomendaciones pueden dar a los demás grupos para mejorar su invento?

AUDIO

Pronunciación La letra g con e, i

Delante de las vocales **e, i,** la **g** tiene un sonido suave como la *h* de la palabra *hello* en inglés. Recuerda que la **g** tiene un sonido duro en combinación con **a, o, u** y **r.**

generación **proteger** **gigante** **lógico**

Refrán

Genio y figura hasta la sepultura.

PARA Y PIENSA

¿Comprendiste? Completa las oraciones con verbos en el subjuntivo.

1. Es preferible que los inventos... un problema y... la conciencia social.
2. Es necesario que cada participante... una solicitud y... una foto.

Get Help Online
ClassZone.com

Presentación de GRAMÁTICA

¡AVANZA! **Goal:** Learn about the subjunctive of irregular and stem-changing verbs. Then talk about your hopes and opinions. ***Actividades 12–16***

¿Recuerdas? Future tense p. 157

English Grammar Connection: In English, the subjunctive is the same as the infinitive without *to (It's important that you **be** here)*, or the simple past *(I wish I **were** older)*. In Spanish, verbs are conjugated to form the subjunctive.

More Subjunctive Verb Forms

Some verbs are **irregular** in the **subjunctive.** How are they conjugated?

Here's how:

dar	estar	ir	saber	ser
dé	esté	vaya	sepa	sea
des	estés	vayas	sepas	seas
dé	esté	vaya	sepa	sea
demos	estemos	vayamos	sepamos	seamos
deis	estéis	vayáis	sepáis	seáis
den	estén	vayan	sepan	sean

The subjuntive of **haber** *is* **haya.**

Verbs ending in **-ar** and **-er** have the same stem changes as in the present indicative.

cerrar (e → **ie**)

Es importante que **cierres** la puerta.
It's important that you close the door.

volver (o → **ue**)

Es bueno que yo **vuelva** pronto.
It's good that I am returning soon.

The stem changes for **-ir** verbs follow the same pattern as in the present indicative for all forms except **nosotros** and **vosotros,** where they change **e** → **i** or **o** → **u.**

divertirse (e → **ie, i**)

Es imprescindible que **se diviertan.**
It's important that they have fun.

dormir (o → **ue, u**)

Es necesario que todos **durmamos** aquí.
It's necessary that we all sleep here.

Verbs that change **e** → **i** in the present indicative have the same stem change in all forms of the present subjunctive.

pedir (e → **i**)

Es mejor que tú **pidas** primero y que nosotros **pidamos** después de ti.
It is best that you order first and that we order after you.

Más práctica

Cuaderno *pp. 128–130*
Cuaderno para hispanohablantes *pp. 129–132*

Conjuguemos.com

@HomeTutor
Leveled Practice
ClassZone.com

Práctica de GRAMÁTICA

12 La acción social

Hablar
Escribir

Tu clase va a emprender una serie de eventos para fomentar la acción social en tu comunidad. Completa las ideas con el subjuntivo de los verbos de la lista.

invertir
encargarse
ser
hacer
saber
estar

modelo: Es importante que nosotros <u>invirtamos</u> tiempo suficiente en la planificación.

1. No es bueno que yo ____ todo.
2. Es necesario que la política de un país ____ defender el aire puro.
3. Es mejor que todos nosotros ____ unidos porque la unidad es una fuerza positiva.
4. Es importante que la sociedad ____ de proteger el medio ambiente.
5. Es imprescindible que la sociedad ____ los principios para cuidar el medio ambiente.

Expansión
Piensa en una campaña de acción social para tu comunidad. Usa expresiones impersonales para explicar los cambios que recomiendas.

13 Unos consejos  *¿Recuerdas?* Future tense p. 157

Hablar

Usa una expresión impersonal como «es mejor» o «es raro» para darle consejos a tu compañero(a). Él (Ella) debe responder usando el futuro. Túrnense.

modelo: ir

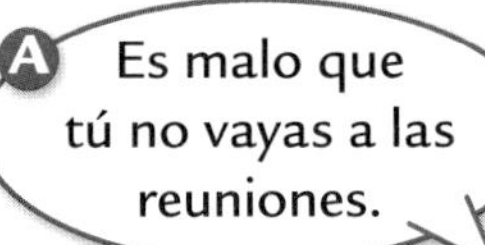

B Es verdad. Iré a la próxima reunión.

1. dormir	**3.** saber	**5.** invertir	**7.** criticar
2. ser	**4.** pedir	**6.** dar	**8.** haber

14 Un viaje a Honduras

Hablar
Escribir

Mónica va a viajar a Tegucigalpa, Honduras, para visitar a sus abuelos. ¿Qué consejos le da su abuelita?

modelo: hacer las reservaciones
Es importante que hagas las reservaciones por teléfono.

1. despertarse temprano
2. cerrar bien las maletas
3. llevar tu pasaporte
4. saber el número del vuelo
5. ser cortés
6. buscarme en el aeropuerto

15 Un futuro próspero

Hablar
Escribir

Prepara un discurso breve para que los inversionistas te den dinero para un invento. Usa un mínimo de cinco expresiones impersonales con el subjuntivo. Presenta tu discurso en clase.

modelo: Señoras y señores, gracias por su apoyo. Ahora es muy importante que sigamos adelante. Es imprescindible que emprendamos proyectos novedosos para progresar. Espero que estén listos para terminar con la irresponsabilidad.

Expansión
Prepara tres preguntas con expresiones impersonales para saber más sobre los proyectos.

16 Es interesante que...

Leer
Escribir

Comparación cultural

El arte ingenuo

¿Cómo representan los artistas el mundo que los rodea? El pintor José Antonio Velásquez (1906–1983) nació en **Honduras.** Él pintó sus cuadros pensando en cómo pintaban los hombres primitivos y en cómo pintan los niños. Este género de pintura se llama arte ingenuo o primitivista.

Velásquez fue minucioso *(detail-oriented)* en sus obras, ¡pintaba las tejas *(tiles)* de las casas una por una! ¡Es increíble que sus cuadros tengan tantos detalles! Un dato interesante es que en sus cuadros las personas siempre están haciendo algo.

Vista de San Antonio de Oriente *(1957), José Antonio Velásquez*

Compara con tu mundo *Describe con detalles la calle donde vives. Utiliza el estilo de José Antonio Velásquez.*

Escribe tres opiniones sobre el cuadro de José Antonio Velásquez. Utiliza algunas de las siguientes expresiones: **es necesario que, es importante que, es interesante que, es increíble que...**

Más práctica Cuaderno *pp. 128–130* Cuaderno para hispanohablantes *pp. 129–132*

PARA Y PIENSA

¿Comprendiste? Escribe oraciones con el subjuntivo utilizando los elementos siguientes:

1. Es increíble / haber
2. Es difícil / ir
3. Es mejor / invertir
4. Es imprescindible / advertir

Get Help Online
ClassZone.com

Todo junto

¡AVANZA! **Goal:** ***Show what you know*** Listen to the following conversation between Liliana and her friend Ernestina. Focus on the language they use to present and support their opinions. ***Actividades 17–19***

Resumen contextos 1 y 2 Liliana Estrella, una estudiante hondureña que sufre de asma, inventó un aparato novedoso que evalúa la calidad del aire. Luego, vio el anuncio para un congreso de inventores jóvenes. ¡Es la oportunidad perfecta para mostrar su invento!

Contexto 3 *Diálogo*

ESTRATEGIA **Escuchar**
Make a cost-benefit comparison
As you listen, make a list of the costs and potential benefits to help you come to a decision. Which seems to "weigh" the most: the costs or the benefits?

AUDIO

Liliana llenó una solicitud y la invitaron a participar en un congreso para inventores jóvenes hondureños. Va a mostrar su invento, el MejorAire, que es un aparato que combina las funciones de un reproductor de MP3 con un monitor del aire y está diseñado para los deportistas que tienen problemas respiratorios. Ahora, Liliana habla con su amiga Ernestina en la sala de exhibiciones del congreso.

Liliana: ¡Es increíble que tantas personas quieran hablar conmigo sobre el MejorAire!

Ernestina: ¡De veras! Ojalá que alguien te ofrezca la oportunidad de comercializarlo.

Liliana: ¿No te lo dije? ¡La directora de una compañía de ropa y equipos atléticos dijo que quiere comprar los derechos del MejorAire!

Ernestina: ¡Es lógico! Tu invento puede ser muy útil. Pero, ¿no es mejor que hables con otras compañías antes de aceptar su oferta? Es importante que busques más información antes de comprometerte.

También se dice

Para afirmar lo que se dice, muchas veces se usa la expresión: **¡Es lógico!**
- **Centroamérica** **¡Pues claro!**
- **El Caribe** **¡Se cae de la mata!**
- **Argentina** **¡Obvio!**

Liliana: Tal vez tienes razón. Pero la señora me dijo que es necesario que yo tome una decisión hoy mismo. No va a esperar hasta la semana que viene.

Ernestina: Liliana, si dijo eso, no sé. No tengo confianza en esa señora. No quiero criticar, pero, ¿no es un poco raro que ella te pida actuar con tanta prisa? Tal vez es preferible que investigues la posibilidad de sacar una patente para proteger tu idea. Es necesario que consultes con un abogado.

Liliana: ¡Pero las patentes salen muy caras! El costo total puede llegar a las 100.000 lempiras. La señora me ofreció 150.000 lempiras en efectivo si firmo un contrato con ella hoy mismo.

Ernestina: No sé, Liliana... Es mucho dinero, pero ojalá que no cometas un error. ¿No es posible que primero saques una patente y luego vendas los derechos por más dinero?

Liliana: Ay, ¿qué hago? Es lógico que un abogado puede ayudarme con la decisión, pero también puede ser caro y yo no conozco a ninguno.

Ernestina: Tienes razón. Creo que es importante que lo pienses bien y que busques la ayuda de otros antes de tomar tu decisión. Tú no debes encargarte de todos los detalles, sola.

Liliana: Gracias, Ernestina. Respeto mucho tu opinión. Consideraré tu advertencia antes de seguir adelante.

17 Comprensión del diálogo

Escuchar
Escribir

Contesta las preguntas.

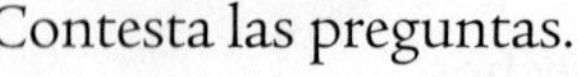

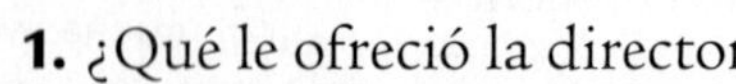

1. ¿Qué le ofreció la directora de una compañía a Liliana?
2. Según Ernestina, ¿qué debe hacer Liliana?
3. ¿Cuándo es necesario que Liliana tome su decisión?
4. ¿Qué tiene que hacer Liliana para sacar una patente?
5. ¿Cómo reaccionó Liliana con el comentario de Ernestina?
6. ¿Por qué debe Liliana pensarlo más antes de tomar su decisión?

Expansión
¿Cual es tu opinión sobre el invento de Liliana? ¿Qué piensas de la señora que le hizo la oferta? ¿Qué debe hacer Liliana?

18 Integración

Leer
Escuchar
Hablar

Lee el anuncio de un horno *(oven)* solar en un periódico. Escucha los comentarios de un inventor durante un congreso para inventores. Explica de qué manera el horno solar que viste cumple con las ideas del inventor.

Fuente 1 Publicidad en el periódico

¿Es necesario que cambiemos la forma de cocinar? *¡Sí!*

¡Presentamos el producto más novedoso del año!

Es económico, portátil y fácil de usar. Sólo necesita la energía del sol.

HornoSol satisface las necesidades de los cocineros de todo el mundo – en la ciudad y en el campo.

HornoSol, la tecnología sigue adelante.

Advertencia: Este producto depende de la energía solar para funcionar. No funciona sin el sol.

Es importante que ahorremos energía... Y **HornoSol** nos ayudará.

Fuente 2 Congreso de inventores

Escucha y apunta

- ¿Cuáles son las responsabilidades de los inventores hoy?
- ¿Qué características deben tener los inventos con conciencia social?

modelo: Es necesario que los inventos sean económicos y prácticos. El **HornoSol** que vi en el anuncio es un buen ejemplo porque...

19 ¡A escribir!

Escribir

Efraín inventó un carro que vuela y tiene que decidir si quiere vender su nuevo invento a unos inversionistas o comercializarlo él mismo. Él te pide consejos. Contéstale utilizando cinco expresiones impersonales con el subjuntivo.

Writing Criteria	Excellent	Good	Needs Work
Content	Your response includes five clear suggestions using impersonal expressions.	Your response includes somewhat clear suggestions using impersonal expressions.	Your response includes few clear suggestions using impersonal expressions.
Communication	Your message is organized and easy to follow.	Parts of your message are organized and easy to follow.	Your message is disorganized and hard to follow.
Accuracy	You make few mistakes in grammar and vocabulary.	You make some mistakes in grammar and vocabulary.	You make many mistakes in grammar and vocabulary.

Más práctica Cuaderno *pp. 131–132* Cuaderno para hispanohablantes *pp. 133–134*

PARA Y PIENSA

¿Comprendiste? Presenta y defiende tu opinión sobre estas ideas.

1. MejorAire es un invento novedoso.
2. Liliana debe aceptar la oferta.
3. Liliana debe sacar una patente.
4. Liliana necesita un abogado.

Get Help Online
ClassZone.com

Lectura literaria

¡AVANZA! **Goal:** Read the following Guatemalan fable about mankind's relationship to the natural world. Then consider why this relationship is important.

Para leer 

ESTRATEGIA Leer

Use dialogue clues from punctuation and wording To understand a written dialogue in Spanish, find clues in the markers before each segment of dialogue. Dialogue in Spanish is either preceded by an extended hyphen (—) or is enclosed in brackets (<<...>>) instead of the English form of quotation marks (" . . . "). You can also find clues in words such as **dijo.** Such words tell you who is saying the first line. You might find it useful to write on a sheet of paper the sequence of speakers as they shift from one to the next and back. See the example below.

Texto original
El maya dijo:
—Quiero ser feliz.
La lechuza respondió:
—¿Quién sabe lo que es la felicidad?...

El maya: Quiero ser feliz.
La lechuza: ¿Quién sabe lo que es la felicidad?...

Vocabulario para leer

la lechuza *owl*	**el zorro** *fox*
el zopilote *vulture*	**la ardilla** *squirrel*
el venado *deer*	**la chachalaca** *chachalaca (a type of guan, a bird with a distinctive call)*
el ruiseñor *nightingale*	

Nota cultural

Sobre la civilización maya La civilización maya existió entre 2600 a.C. y 1511 d.C. en lo que hoy son Guatemala, Honduras, El Salvador, Belice y la parte este de México. Tenían una civilización muy avanzada; entre sus contribuciones culturales podemos contar con un calendario y un sistema de jeroglíficos que los científicos todavía no pueden descifrar *(decipher)* por completo.

Sobre las leyendas Los mayas tenían mucho respeto por el medio ambiente y todo lo que éste incluía: los pájaros, los reptiles, los insectos y las plantas. «La tristeza del maya» es una leyenda que muestra este amor por la naturaleza.

Guerreros con máscaras *(c. 750–900 d.C.), pintura maya*

La tristeza del maya

Un día los animales se acercaron a un maya y le dijeron:

—Es una pena que estés triste. Pídenos lo que quieras y lo tendrás.

El maya dijo:

—Quiero ser feliz.

La lechuza respondió:

—¿Quién sabe lo que es la felicidad? Pídenos cosas más humanas.

—Bueno —añadió el hombre—, es importante que tenga buena vista[1].

El zopilote le dijo:

—Tendrás la mía.

—Es mejor que sea fuerte.

A pensar
¿Por qué no pueden los animales dar la felicidad al maya?

[1] sight

Reflexiona

¿Quién dice «Es mejor que sea fuerte»?

Procesión de animales *(c. 750–900 d.C.), pintura maya*

El jaguar le dijo:
—Serás fuerte como yo.
—Quiero caminar sin cansarme.
El venado le dijo:
—Te daré mis piernas.
—Quiero adivinar[2] la llegada de las lluvias.
El ruiseñor le dijo:
—Te avisaré con mi canto.
—Es preferible que sea astuto[3].

[2] guess
[3] clever

Reflexiona

¿Cómo reaccionan los animales ante los deseos del maya?

Figura haciendo una ofrenda al Dios Itzamná
(c. 750–900 d.C.) Pintura en una vasija maya

El zorro le dijo:

—Te enseñaré a serlo.

—Quiero trepar[4] a los árboles.

La ardilla le dijo:

—Te daré mis uñas[5]. ❖

—Será bueno que conozca las plantas medicinales.

La serpiente le dijo:

—¡Ah, ésa es cosa mía porque yo conozco todas las plantas! Te las marcaré en el campo.

Y al oír esto último, el maya se alejó[6].

Entonces la lechuza les dijo a los animales:

—El hombre ahora sabe más cosas y puede hacer más cosas, pero siempre estará triste. ❖

Y la chachalaca se puso a gritar:

—¡Pobres animales! ¡Pobres animales! Ojalá el hombre aprenda a pedir menos y dar más. Sólo así encontrará su felicidad.

❖ A pensar
¿Crees que la naturaleza puede solucionar los problemas del hombre? Da ejemplos.

❖ A pensar
¿Por qué crees que los animales piensan que el hombre siempre estará triste?

---

[4] climb
[5] nails
[6] **se...** he left

¿Comprendiste?

1. ¿En dónde crees que tiene lugar el diálogo?
2. Explica la relación entre lo que quiere el hombre y el regalo que le da cada animal.
3. ¿Por qué crees que la chachalaca gritó «Pobres animales» al final?
4. ¿Por qué el hombre pide tantas cosas?
5. La chachalaca cree que el hombre sólo encontrará su felicidad si aprende a pedir menos y dar más. ¿Estás de acuerdo o no? Explica tus razones.

¿Y tú?

En tu opinión, ¿qué puede el maya aprender de los animales? ¿Qué cualidad debe pedir el maya para ser feliz?

Escritura

La necesidad de apoyar un invento

Escribe una propuesta para un(a) inversionista local, pidiéndole dinero para apoyar un invento que puede beneficiar a toda la comunidad. Usa la siguiente secuencia de estrategias para organizar tus ideas.

1 Prepárate para escribir

ESTRATEGIA **Selecciona un invento** Piensa en un invento que pueda ser útil para la comunidad. Piensa en algo que pueda ayudar a las personas, al medio ambiente o al tránsito.

2 Escribe

ESTRATEGIA **Apoya tus opiniones con datos y ejemplos** Quieres que tu opinión sea persuasiva para que algunas personas den el dinero para el invento. Dibuja dos flechas como las siguientes. En el medio escribe tu opinión sobre el invento. En las flechas escribe datos, como qué elementos tiene y para qué sirve, y ejemplos de cómo se puede usar.

Luego escribe un breve discurso para persuadir al inversionista de que su dinero servirá para algo importante para la comunidad. Incluye tu opinión y las características de tu invento. Cada párrafo debe tener una oración principal con tu opinión, seguida de oraciones que la apoyen con datos y ejemplos.

3 Revisa tu composición

Lee el borrador de tu compañero(a).

- ¿Están claros la explicación y los beneficios del invento?
- ¿Está clara la opinión del inventor?
- ¿Usó el (la) escritor(a) el subjuntivo y las expresiones impersonales con precisión?
- ¿Hay una oración principal en cada párrafo?
- ¿Son precisas las oraciones que dan información adicional?
- ¿Es realmente persuasivo el discurso para conseguir dinero del inversionista?

Revisa tu composición incorporando las correcciones y sugerencias de tu compañero(a) que te parezcan apropiadas.

El nuevo invento Puro Aire es importante para que nuestra comunidad ~~está~~ esté saludable. Con este pequeño invento el aire estará siempre limpio.

Es importante que ~~sabemos~~ sepamos usar este invento. Es muy fácil, sólo hay que presionar esta tecla.

Su compañía puede donar dinero para producir este invento. Ayudará a la comunidad y será muy famosa entre toda la gente.

Lección 2

En resumen

Vocabulario y gramática

Vocabulario

Discuss Obligations and Responsibilities

Social Awareness

el (la) ciudadano(a)	*citizen*	penalizar	*to penalize*
el compromiso	*commitment*	la política	*politics*
la conciencia social	*social awareness*	el principio	*principle*
encargarse de	*to take charge of, to make oneself responsible for*	respetar	*to respect*
la irresponsabilidad	*irresponsibility*	satisfacer	*to satisfy*
		la sociedad	*society*
		la unidad	*unity*

Inventions

comercializar	*to market*
invertir(ie, i)	*to invest*
novedoso(a)	*novel, original*
la patente	*patent*
el producto	*product*

Mistakes and Persistence

advertir (ie)	*to warn*	progresar	*to progress*
cometer	*to make (a mistake)*	prosperar	*to prosper*
emprender	*to undertake*	seguir adelante	*to continue on, to carry on*
el error	*mistake, error*	solucionar	*to solve*
insistir	*to insist*	superar	*to overcome*
luchar	*to struggle*		
persistir	*to persist*		

Other Words

la advertencia	*warning*
el fracaso	*failure*
la mejora	*improvement*
el obstáculo	*obstacle*
el sufrimiento	*suffering*

Present and Support an Opinion

criticar	*to criticize*	es raro que...	*it is strange that . . .*	por un lado...	*on one hand . . .*
es imprescindible que...	*it is indispensable / imperative that . . .*	evaluar	*to evaluate*	por el otro lado...	*on the other hand . . .*

Gramática

Present Subjunctive of Regular Verbs

hablar	**tener**	**escribir**
hable	**tenga**	**escriba**
hables	**tengas**	**escribas**
hable	**tenga**	**escriba**
hablemos	**tengamos**	**escribamos**
habléis	**tengáis**	**escribáis**
hablen	**tengan**	**escriban**

Spelling Changes

	becomes
criticar	**critique**
investigar	**investigue**
penalizar	**penalice**
proteger	**proteja**
extinguir	**extinga**

More Subjunctive Verb Forms

Irregular Subjunctive Forms

dar	**estar**	**ir**	**saber**	**ser**
dé	**esté**	**vaya**	**sepa**	**sea**
des	**estés**	**vayas**	**sepas**	**seas**
dé	**esté**	**vaya**	**sepa**	**sea**
demos	**estemos**	**vayamos**	**sepamos**	**seamos**
deis	**estéis**	**vayáis**	**sepáis**	**seáis**
den	**estén**	**vayan**	**sepan**	**sean**

The subjuntive of **haber** is **haya.**

- Verbs ending in **-ar** and **-er** change **e** → **ie** or **o** → **ue** in all forms except **nosotros** and **vosotros.**
- Verbs ending in **-ir** that change **e** → **ie** or **o** → **ue** have a different change (**e** → **i** or **o** → **u**) in the **nosotros** and **vosotros** forms.
- Verbs that change **e** → **i** have the same stem change in all forms.

Lección 2

Repaso de la lección

¡LLEGADA!

@HomeTutor
ClassZone.com

Now you can
- discuss obligations and responsibilities
- present and support an opinion
- express a point of view and make recommendations

Using
- present subjunctive of regular verbs
- more subjunctive verb forms
- impersonal expressions

To review
- vocabulary pp. 178–179
- present subjunctive of regular verbs p. 183
- more subjunctive verb forms p. 188

1 Listen and understand

AUDIO

Escucha el siguiente segmento de un programa de radio donde participan el locutor, la Dra. Delgado y dos radioyentes. Luego, completa las siguientes oraciones con las palabras que faltan.

1. La Dra. Delgado dice que el peor problema medioambiental que tenemos es la ____ .
2. Según la doctora, es imprescindible que todos ____ para cambiar la situación.
3. Un oyente le pide que no ____ mucho dinero.
4. La doctora dice que es preferible que nos ____ de dos cosas.
5. La doctora dice que ojalá los proyectos ____ más baratos en el futuro.

To review
- present subjunctive of regular verbs p. 183

2 Discuss obligations and responsibilities

Luis y Virginia sueñan con la idea de crear una compañía perfecta. Completa sus descripciones de esta compañía con las formas correctas de los verbos indicados.

En la compañía ideal, es necesario que cada empleado **1.** (participar) en las decisiones más importantes. Es imprescindible que todos **2.** (compartir) los mismos valores. Es preferible que todos **3.** (respetar) a los demás, sin tener prejuicios. Es lógico que, juntos, nosotros **4.** (resolver) los problemas y que **5.** (superar) los obstáculos que se presenten. No es preferible que un empleado **6.** (emprender) algo sin la ayuda de los demás: es mejor que todos **7.** (solucionar), juntos, los problemas.

To review
- more subjunctive verb forms p. 188

3 Express a point of view and make recommendations

Gonzalo inventó un aparato que recicla el calor *(heat)* del horno y lo usa para calentar *(to heat)* agua. Ahora todo el mundo le da consejos sobre cómo comercializar el aparato.

1. es lógico / tú sacar una patente
2. es imprescindible / el aparato ser barato
3. es preferible / los científicos analizar el invento
4. es importante / nosotros hacer una campaña de publicidad
5. es necesario / el invento satisfacer al público

To review
- expressions for giving opinions p. 178

4 Present and support an opinion

Mirta y Francisco son amigos pero nunca tienen la misma opinión. Completa su conversación con palabras de la lista.

creo que	por un lado
en mi opinión	por el otro lado
estoy de acuerdo con	según

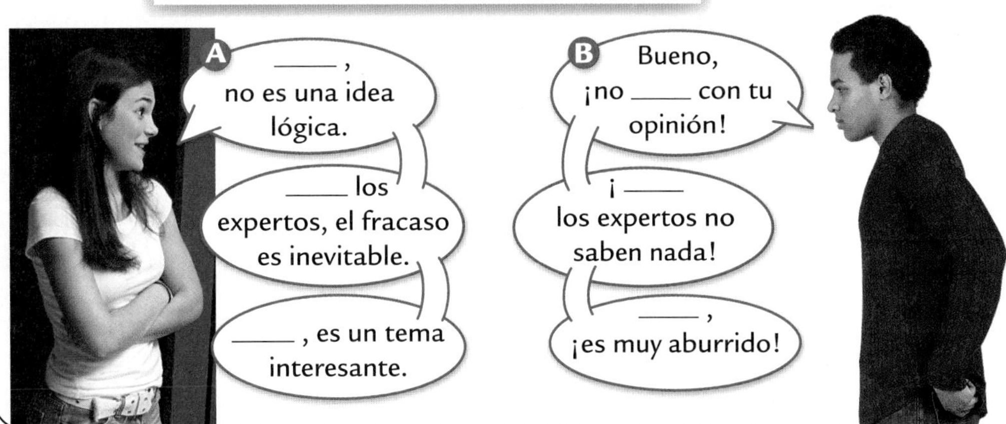

To review
- **Comparación cultural** pp. 184, 190

5 Technology and art

Comparación cultural

Contesta las preguntas según lo que leíste en esta lección.

1. ¿Qué océanos conectan el canal de Panamá?
2. ¿Cómo cambió el país y su población después de la construcción del canal?
3. ¿Quién era José Antonio Velásquez?
4. Menciona dos características del arte ingenuo.

Más práctica Cuaderno *pp. 133–144* Cuaderno para hispanohablantes *pp. 135–144*

Get Help Online
ClassZone.com

Protejamos la naturaleza

Lectura y escritura

1. **Leer** Lee las actividades que hacen Manuela y Ruth para proteger la naturaleza.

2. **Escribir** Usa la información de Manuela y de Ruth como modelo, y escribe una composición sobre la naturaleza de tu zona, cómo la cuidan y quiénes participan.

ESTRATEGIA Escribir

Use "LAP" diagrams for projects
For each environmental preservation project, create a diagram that shows the place (***l**ugar*), the activities (***a**ctividades*), and the people (***p**ersonas*).

Paso 1 En una parte del círculo escribe el nombre del lugar, los animales y el tipo de vegetación que hay allí.

Paso 2 En otra parte del círculo haz una lista de las actividades que se hacen para proteger el lugar.

Paso 3 En la tercera parte escribe qué personas participan para cuidar el lugar. Usa la información de los círculos para escribir tu ensayo. Luego revisa la gramática y la ortografía.

Compara con tu mundo

Usa el ensayo que escribiste y compara la naturaleza de tu ciudad o región con la de los países de Manuela y de Ruth. ¿Hay animales parecidos? ¿Hacen tareas similares para cuidar la naturaleza? ¿Qué diferencias hay entre tu región y las de ellas?

Cuaderno *pp. 145–147* Cuaderno para hispanohablantes *pp. 145–147*

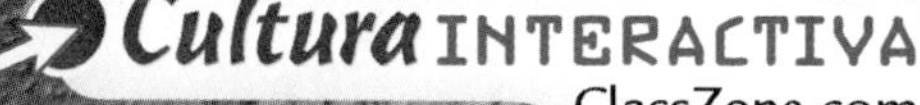

Guatemala

Manuela

Hola, me llamo Manuela Samalea. Soy de Guatemala, y creo que es imprescindible que en nuestros países haya reservas y refugios que conserven la naturaleza. El año pasado participé en un programa del Proyecto Ecológico Quetzal (PEQ). El programa protege los bosques de la región, donde hay muchos pájaros en peligro de extinción. El PEQ también cree que es importante que trabajemos con las comunidades indígenas locales, maya quiché, para conservar los recursos naturales de la zona. En Guatemala y en otros países de Centroamérica, la naturaleza está en peligro. Es necesario que la cuidemos.

Ruth

¡Hola! Soy Ruth Blanes. Soy costarricense y vivo cerca del Parque Nacional Braulio Carrillo. Es lamentable que el desarrollo industrial destruya la vida natural. Por eso es importante que cuidemos a los animales y las plantas de esta región.

Este parque es una de las zonas protegidas más grandes de Costa Rica, con cinco ecosistemas diferentes. Allí se pueden ver más de 600 especies de árboles, 500 especies de pájaros, 135 especies de mamíferos y cien especies de mariposas. ¡Imagínate!

También soy voluntaria en la Fundación Salvemos al Manatí. En esta reserva no hay botes a motor, cacería ilegal ni pesticidas que pongan en peligro la vida de los manatíes.

Costa Rica

EL DESAFÍO

VIDEO DVD

En este desafío, los equipos deben conservar, proteger y valorar el medio ambiente. El profesor les va a dar varios papeles con actividades relacionadas con el medio ambiente. Cada equipo debe elegir una de estas actividades.

Antes del video

1. ¿Qué actividad relacionada con el medio ambiente crees que Luis y María están haciendo? ¿Crees que forman un buen equipo? ¿Se llevan bien o mal?

2. Describe lo que ves en esta foto. ¿Qué crees que está pasando?

3. ¿Qué actividad crees que José y Carmen deben hacer? ¿Dónde puede estar José? ¿Qué crees que está haciendo?

Los grupos eligen sus actividades.

Mira el video: Toma apuntes

- ¿Está escuchando María lo que dice el profesor?
- ¿Qué equipo elige «suelo y erosión»? ¿Qué deben hacer?
- ¿Qué actividad deben hacer José y Carmen?
- Describe cómo piensa José hacer su actividad.
- ¿Por qué se enoja Carmen con José?
- ¿Qué equipo elige el reciclaje?
- ¿Por qué no quiere ir al basurero Ana?
- ¿Dónde está la bolsa con los plásticos?

Después del video

1. ¿Qué equipo ganó este desafío? ¿Por qué crees que ganaron?
2. Lee tus apuntes y di por qué los otros equipos no ganaron.
3. Piensa en la actitud de Ana y Marco. Escribe unos consejos para ellos.

@HomeTutor VideoPlus
ClassZone.com

UNIDADES 1-3

Repaso inclusivo

Options for Review

1 Escucha, comprende y contesta

Escuchar
Hablar

Escucha el informe sobre un desastre natural en Copán, una ciudad importante por sus ruinas mayas. Luego, contesta las preguntas.

1. ¿En qué país está el reportero?
2. ¿Sobre qué desastres informa?
3. Nombra uno de los problemas que causaron los derrumbes.
4. ¿Cuál es el pronóstico para los próximos días?
5. ¿Qué es importante que lleven los visitantes a la zona?

2 Informa sobre los desastres

Hablar
Escribir

Investiga uno de los siguientes temas en Centroamérica y prepara un informe sobre los eventos más recientes, sus efectos y la colaboración de otros países. Presenta tu informe en clase. Debes incluir material visual.

- los temblores
- las erupciones volcánicas
- los incendios
- la desertificación
- los derrumbes
- las inundaciones

3 Haz una propuesta

Hablar
Escribir

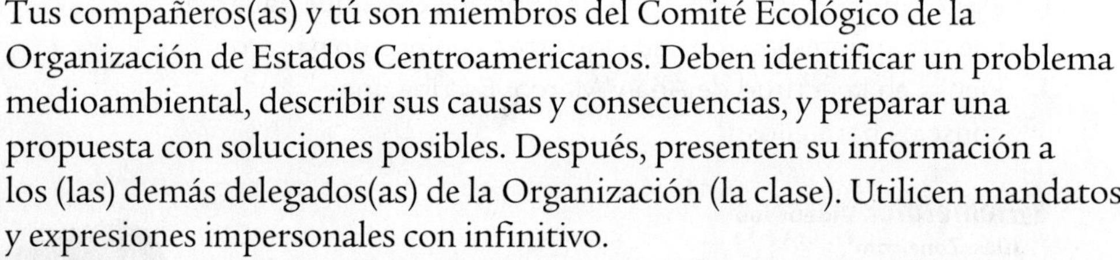

Tus compañeros(as) y tú son miembros del Comité Ecológico de la Organización de Estados Centroamericanos. Deben identificar un problema medioambiental, describir sus causas y consecuencias, y preparar una propuesta con soluciones posibles. Después, presenten su información a los (las) demás delegados(as) de la Organización (la clase). Utilicen mandatos y expresiones impersonales con infinitivo.

4 Planea un programa

Hablar
Escribir

Con unos(as) compañeros(as), diseñen un programa ecológico para atraer a voluntarios a tu comunidad o estado. El programa debe incluir elementos de intercambio cultural como: visitas a lugares de interés y un proyecto ecológico concreto que necesite la colaboración de muchos voluntarios. Incluyan en su presentación una descripción detallada de los dos aspectos del programa y sus ideas para promocionarlo. Utilicen el futuro y las preposiciones **por** y **para.**

5 Compara plantas

Hablar
Escribir

Investiga sobre las plantas medicinales y la ecología de los países centroamericanos. Prepara una presentación sobre tres plantas específicas que puedes cultivar en tu jardín o en el jardín ecológico de tu escuela. Identifica las plantas, muestra fotos y explica para qué y cómo se usa cada una. Utiliza comparaciones y la forma **se** impersonal.

Por ejemplo:

La manzanilla (chamomile) *es una hierba fácil de cultivar. Sirve para calmar los nervios y el dolor de estómago. Además, es relajante y ayuda a las personas a dormir. Se hace un té de las hojas de la planta y se bebe.*

6 Colabora en grupo

Hablar
Escribir

Los países centroamericanos son nuestros vecinos y, como tales, tenemos muchos puntos de contacto. Con unos(as) compañeros(as), piensen en la economía, la ecología, la educación, el desarrollo tecnológico y la cultura, para identificar tres intereses comunes entre Estados Unidos (o tu comunidad) y los países centroamericanos. Luego, hagan una lista de sugerencias para fomentar la colaboración internacional y solucionar problemas en una de las áreas que identificaron. Presenten sus ideas a la clase. Utilicen el subjuntivo con expresiones impersonales.

7 Escribe sobre las edades

Escribir

Escribe un ensayo sobre cuál crees que sea la mejor edad. Describe tu propia niñez (*childhood*), tu vida actual e imagina tu vida como adulto. Usa el pretérito, el presente y el futuro.

Organiza tus ideas según las épocas siguientes:

Mi niñez: ¿Cómo era?
¿Qué hacía?

Mi vida actual: ¿Cómo es?
¿Qué hago?

Mi vida adulta: ¿Cómo será?
¿Qué haré?

UNIDAD 4

El Caribe

Así quiero ser

Lección 1

Tema: ***¿Quién te inspira?***

Lección 2

Tema: ***¿Quiénes son los héroes?***

La Habana

Cuba

Mar Caribe

«¡Oye!
Somos Inés, de Puerto Rico, y Enrique, de la República Dominicana. Somos caribeños. »

Almanaque cultural

Clima: Tropical. Dos estaciones: la seca (poca humedad y mucho calor) y la lluviosa (humedad y temperaturas más frescas)

Geografía: Islas llanas con algunas montañas

Comidas: arroz moro, frijoles negros, masas de puerco, congrí, plátanos maduros fritos

Gente famosa: Ricky Martin (cantante, Puerto Rico), Pedro Martínez (pelotero, República Dominicana), Gloria Estefan (cantante, Cuba), Julia Álvarez (escritora, República Dominicana), Alejo Carpentier (escritor, Cuba), Olga Tañón (cantante, Puerto Rico)

Arroz con mariscos

Máscara del Carnaval de Ponce, Puerto Rico

◀ **Festivales con máscaras** En el Caribe es muy común ver festivales de máscaras gigantes. Esto ocurre especialmente durante el Carnaval. Algunos nombres de estos personajes de cabeza grande son vejigantes, cabezones y cojuelos. *¿Qué tipo de disfraces* (costumes) *se usan en tu comunidad?*

Jóvenes divirtiéndose en Santo Domingo, República Dominicana

Diversión en la calle Los fines de semana, los jóvenes caribeños se juntan y pasean por las calles de sus ciudades. Por las tardes salen a caminar y a tomar un refresco, y más tarde van a bailar. Salir en grupo es parte de la cultura hispana. *¿Adónde vas a pasear los fines de semana?* ▶

Venta de cocos en Santo Domingo

◀ **Frutas tropicales** El Caribe tiene una producción muy importante de frutas. Las frutas tropicales son deliciosas y tienen mucho jugo. En las calles del Caribe puedes comprar fruta fresca o beber jugos de muchos sabores, como piña, mango y guayaba. *¿Qué frutas son las más populares de tu región?*

UNIDAD 4

El Caribe

Lección 1

Tema:

¿Quién te inspira?

¡AVANZA! **In this lesson you will learn to**

- describe people
- tell others what to do
- express wishes and desires

using

- subjunctive with **ojalá** and verbs of hope
- subjunctive with verbs of influence
- suffixes

¿Recuerdas?

- **ser** vs. **estar**
- future

Comparación cultural

In this lesson you will learn about

- how sports celebrities help disaster victims
- how singers help people

Compara con tu mundo

Félix Sánchez es el único atleta dominicano con una medalla de oro de los Juegos Olímpicos. Él ganó la medalla en la carrera de 400 metros con vallas *(hurdles)*. También ganó una medalla de oro en los Juegos Panamericanos. *¿Te gusta mirar los Juegos Olímpicos? ¿Cuál evento te interesa más? ¿Por qué?*

¿Qué ves?

Mira la foto

¿Cómo es Félix Sánchez?

¿Cómo se viste?

¿Qué hay en su uniforme?

¿Cómo está Sánchez en este momento? ¿Serio o contento?

Online SPANISH CLASSZONE.COM

Featuring...

Cultura INTERACTIVA

Animated Grammar

@HomeTutor

And more...

- Get Help Online
- Interactive Flashcards
- Review Games
- WebQuest
- Conjuguemos.com

Félix Sánchez, atleta de la República Dominicana

Presentación de VOCABULARIO

¡AVANZA! **Goal:** Learn about personal characteristics and ways to describe people. Then practice what you learned by talking about the characteristics that are most important for specific professions as well as for life in general. ***Actividades 1–3***

 *¿Recuerdas?* **Ser** vs. **estar** p. 15

A Hola, mi nombre es Inés. Ahora tengo que completar este cuestionario para ver qué vocación me recomiendan los consejeros.

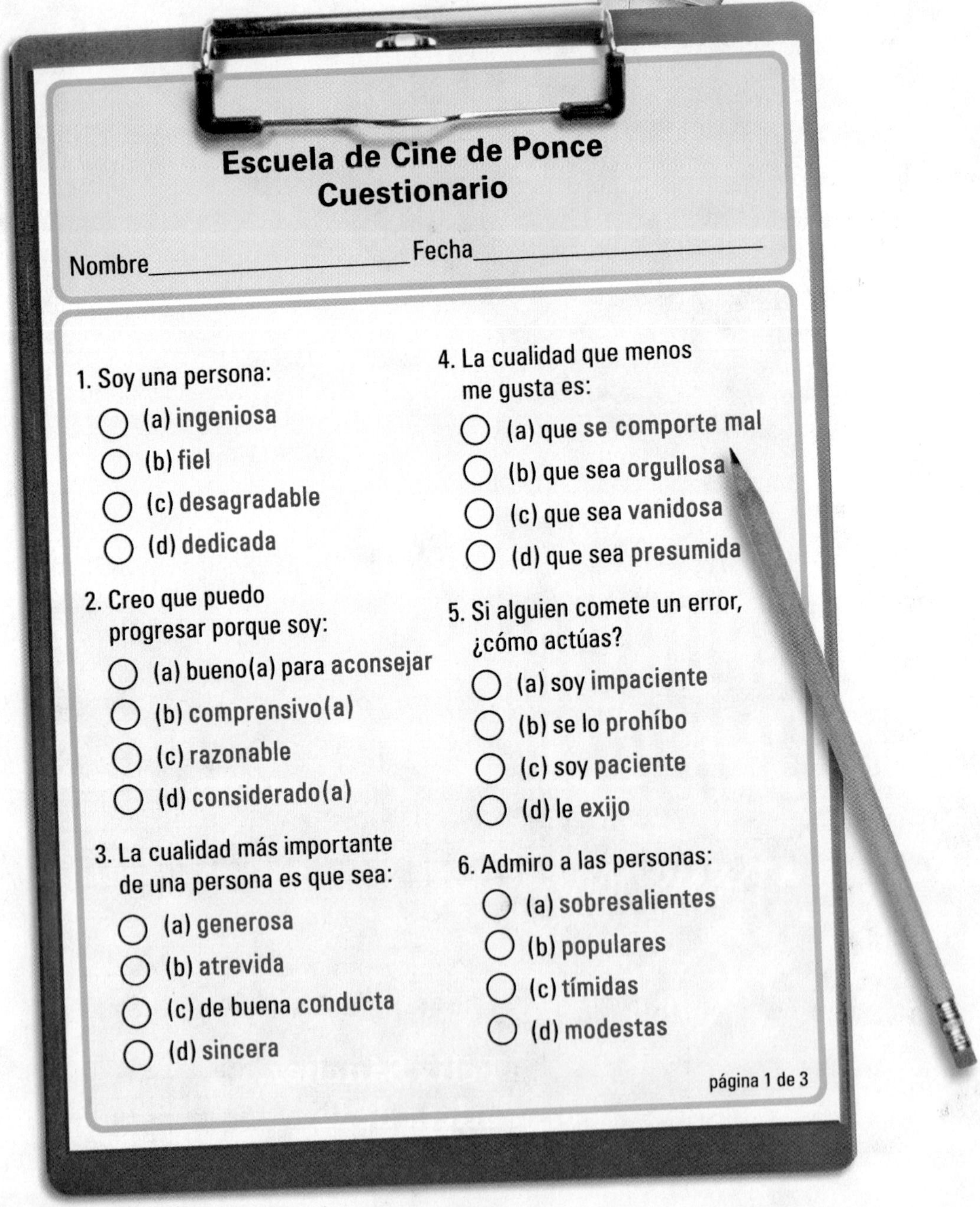

Escuela de Cine de Ponce
Cuestionario

Nombre________________ Fecha________________

1. Soy una persona:
   - (a) ingeniosa
   - (b) fiel
   - (c) desagradable
   - (d) dedicada

2. Creo que puedo progresar porque soy:
   - (a) bueno(a) para aconsejar
   - (b) comprensivo(a)
   - (c) razonable
   - (d) considerado(a)

3. La cualidad más importante de una persona es que sea:
   - (a) generosa
   - (b) atrevida
   - (c) de buena conducta
   - (d) sincera

4. La cualidad que menos me gusta es:
   - (a) que se comporte mal
   - (b) que sea orgullosa
   - (c) que sea vanidosa
   - (d) que sea presumida

5. Si alguien comete un error, ¿cómo actúas?
   - (a) soy impaciente
   - (b) se lo prohíbo
   - (c) soy paciente
   - (d) le exijo

6. Admiro a las personas:
   - (a) sobresalientes
   - (b) populares
   - (c) tímidas
   - (d) modestas

página 1 de 3

B Bueno, ya hice el cuestionario para saber cuál es mi vocación. ¡Yo quiero ser escritora y directora de cine! Son profesiones en que hay que pensar, planear y tomar riesgos.

C Existen muchas profesiones para elegir. Pero cada persona tiene su vocación. ¿Te interesan algunas de las siguientes profesiones?

el detective

la mecánica

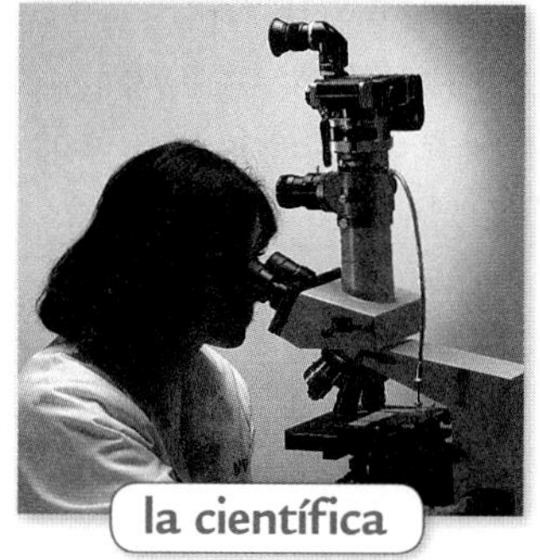
la científica

el piloto

el astronauta

el electricista

Más vocabulario

el (la) empresario(a) *business person*
el (la) entrenador(a) *trainer, coach*
el (la) obrero(a) *laborer*
el (la) programador(a) *programmer*
el (la) trabajador(a) social *social worker*
dejar que *to allow*
destacarse por... *to be remarkable for . . .*
exigir *to demand*
idealizar (a alguien) *to idealize (someone)*
imitar *to imitate*
mandar que *to order, command that*
personificar *to personify*
representar *to represent*
sugerir que *to suggest that*
Expansión de vocabulario p. R8
Ya sabes p. R8

¡A responder! Escuchar

Escucha la lista de características personales. Para cada una, haz la representación de una persona que tenga la característica.

Práctica de VOCABULARIO

1 ¿Cómo es?

 ***¿Recuerdas?*** **Ser** vs. **estar** p. 15

Hablar
Escribir

Completa cada descripción con el verbo apropiado (**ser** o **estar**) y con un adjetivo de la lista.

impaciente
generoso(a)
popular
atrevido(a)

1. Silvia siempre ____ lista para ayudar a otras personas. Es muy ____ con su tiempo.
2. Arturo tiene muchos amigos. ____ muy ____ .
3. A la señora García le gusta su rutina. Prefiere no hacer grandes cambios en su vida porque no ____ muy ____ .
4. Diana ____ ____ porque su hermana no llegó a tiempo.

2 Características deseables e indeseables

Hablar
Escribir

Con tu compañero(a), identifica tres características deseables y tres indeseables para las siguientes profesiones.

profesión	características deseables	características indeseables
un(a) piloto		
un(a) entrenador(a)		
un(a) detective		

Expansión
Escojan tres profesiones más e identifiquen los dos tipos de características.

3 ¿A quién admiras?

Leer
Escribir

Lee el artículo sobre Cristina Saralegui. Haz una lista de seis características de Cristina según lo que leíste.

CRISTINA SARALEGUI,
periodista con más de treinta años de experiencia, es una mujer determinada, práctica y atrevida que conquistó el éxito gracias a la visión que la llevó a personificar sus ideales. Fue directora de la revista *Cosmopolitan en Español* y luego se convirtió en la productora ejecutiva y presentadora de «El Show de Cristina» en Univisión, el programa de discusión con mayor impacto en todo el mundo hispano.

Más práctica Cuaderno *pp. 148–150* Cuaderno para hispanohablantes *pp. 148–151*

¿Comprendiste? Menciona algunas características que deben tener estas personas.

1. un profesor 2. una madre 3. una científica

VOCABULARIO en contexto

¡AVANZA! **Goal:** Notice the language that Inés uses to describe the characters in her description. Then identify and discuss the main characteristics of each person. ***Actividades 4–5***

Contexto 1 *Caracterización de los personajes*

ESTRATEGIA **Leer**

Get to know the characters Using "Capitán" as a model, fill in this chart to help you compare and expand your knowledge of the **solucionistas.**

Los Solucionistas					
	Gonzalo	Ramona	Carmen	Manuel	Capitán
Características					cariñoso con el equipo

AUDIO

Inés Delgado, una estudiante puertorriqueña, está escribiendo un programa de televisión para su clase de escritura. Antes de escribir la primera escena, hizo una lista de los personajes principales y una descripción de cada uno.

«Los Solucionistas» por Inés Delgado

Los Solucionistas son cuatro expertos en diferentes especialidades. Este grupo sobresaliente viaja por todas partes del globo en su superavión privado, solucionando problemas grandes y pequeños.

Gonzalo Domínguez Es guapo, atrevido y orgulloso. Es piloto y tiene su propio avión, el más grande del mundo, diseñado especialmente para enfrentar grandes problemas.

Ramona Salgado Es una mecánica y muy capaz, sabe reparar cualquier aparato o máquina. Aunque es muy inteligente, también es presumida e impaciente. Su conducta puede ser desagradable.

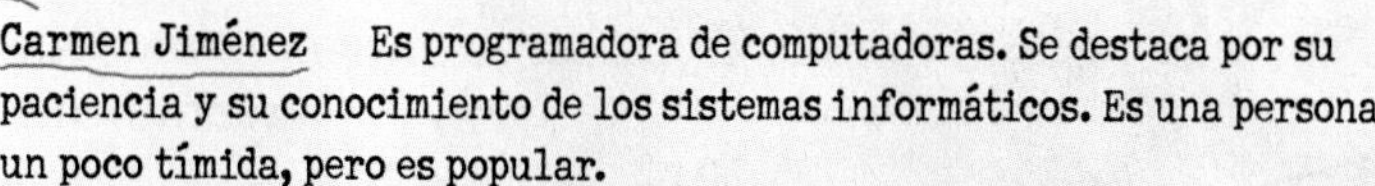

Carmen Jiménez Es programadora de computadoras. Se destaca por su paciencia y su conocimiento de los sistemas informáticos. Es una persona un poco tímida, pero es popular.

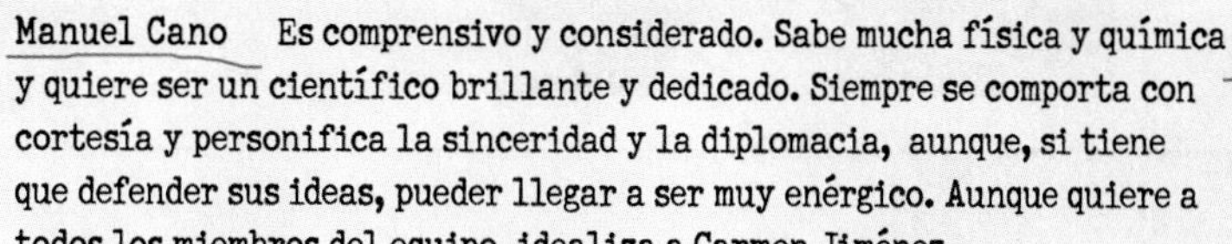

Manuel Cano Es comprensivo y considerado. Sabe mucha física y química y quiere ser un científico brillante y dedicado. Siempre se comporta con cortesía y personifica la sinceridad y la diplomacia, aunque, si tiene que defender sus ideas, pueder llegar a ser muy enérgico. Aunque quiere a todos los miembros del equipo, idealiza a Carmen Jiménez.

Capitán Tiene dos años. Es fiel y cariñoso con todos los miembros del equipo.

1.

4 Comprensión de la caracterización de los personajes

Hablar
Escribir

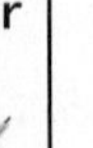

Di si las siguientes oraciones son ciertas o falsas. Si son falsas, corrígelas.

1. Ramona Salgado trabaja con las manos.
2. Carmen Jiménez usa la computadora en su trabajo.
3. A Gonzalo Domínguez no le gusta el avión.
4. Manuel Cano ahora trabaja como trabajador social.
5. Capitán no es fiel, pero es cariñoso.
6. Manuel Cano es una persona muy desagradable.

Nota gramatical

Suffixes Many of the adjectives you have learned can be changed to nouns by adding some common suffixes. These suffixes **(-cia, -ez, -dad, -ción)** create feminine nouns.

Adjective	Noun	Adjective	Noun
paciente *patient*	la pacien**cia** *patience*	tímido *shy*	la timid**ez** *shyness*
sincero *sincere*	la sinceri**dad** *sincerity*	considerado *considerate*	la considera**ción** *consideration*

Norma es **impaciente.** Se destaca por su impacien**cia.**
*Norma is **impatient.** She stands out for her **impatience.***

5 Cualidades admirables

Hablar
Escribir

Tu compañero(a) te pregunta qué tres cualidades de él o ella admiras más y qué tres te gustan menos. Contéstale con las palabras de la lista y explícale por qué.

dedicación	consideración
modestia	timidez
vanidad	(im)paciencia
generosidad	comprensión
sinceridad	popularidad

modelo:

¿Comprendiste? Busca tres adjetivos para describir a cada persona.

1. Gonzalo Domínguez
2. Carmen Jiménez
3. Ramona Salgado
4. Manuel Cano

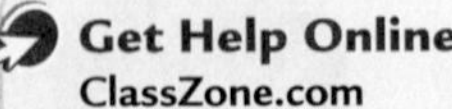

Presentación de GRAMÁTICA

¡AVANZA! **Goal:** Learn to use the subjunctive with verbs that express hopes or wishes. Then talk about what you and others hope will happen. ***Actividades 6–9***

¿Recuerdas? Future tense p. 157

English Grammar Connection: In English, you express what you want someone *to do* with an infinitive, you express what you hope someone *does* with the present tense, and you express what you wish someone *would do* with the conditional. In Spanish, you can express all three with the **subjunctive.**

Infinitive: I want John **to arrive.**
Present: I hope John **arrives.**
Conditional: I wish John **would arrive.**

Subjunctive: Quiero / Espero / Deseo que John **llegue.**

Subjunctive with Ojalá and Verbs of Hope

Animated Grammar ClassZone.com

You have already learned how to form the **subjunctive.** After **verbs of hope,** use the **subjunctive** if there is a change of subject.

Here's how: Use the **indicative** for the verb expressing a hope or wish and the **subjunctive** for the verb with a new subject.

Verbs of Hope						
desear **esperar** **querer**	+	**que**	+	**different subject**	+	**subjunctive**

indicative → *subjunctive* →

Ella **quiere** que **su hijo se comporte** bien.
She wants her son to behave well.

Use the **infinitive** and omit **que** if there is no change of subject.

El niño **quiere comportarse** bien.
The boy wants to behave well.

Ojalá also expresses hope. It has only one form and cannot be conjugated. **Ojalá** can be used with or without **que.** Either way, it is used with the **subjunctive.**

Ojalá no **llueva** mañana.
I hope it doesn't rain tomorrow.

Ojalá que tengamos tiempo.
I hope we'll have time.

Más práctica

Cuaderno *pp. 151–153*

Cuaderno para hispanohablantes *pp. 152–154*

@HomeTutor Leveled Practice ClassZone.com

Práctica de GRAMÁTICA

6 ¿Qué queremos?

Hablar
Escribir

Completa cada oración con el subjuntivo, el indicativo o el infinitivo de los verbos, según corresponda.

modelo: **los ciudadanos / querer / que el presidente / representar / sus intereses**
Los ciudadanos quieren que el presidente represente sus intereses.

1. (yo) esperar / que mi hijo / tener / buena conducta
2. los padres / desear / que sus hijos / comportarse bien
3. mis primos / desear / que yo / venir / a jugar con ellos
4. mi mamá / desear / que yo / sacar / notas sobresalientes
5. tú / esperar / que Anita / idealizar / a las celebridades generosas
6. Octavio / querer / imitar / las buenas acciones de su padre

Expansión
Ahora, di qué esperan las segundas personas de las primeras. Por ejemplo, el presidente de los ciudadanos.

7 Las esperanzas

Hablar
Escribir

Usa el subjuntivo para decir qué esperan las personas de la lista de las otras. Usa **(no) querer, (no) desear** o **(no) esperar.**

modelo: **los maestros**
Los maestros no quieren que los estudiantes copien las respuestas en un examen.

los estudiantes
el (la) entrenador(a)
mi papá
nosotros(as)
el (la) director(a) de la escuela
el (la) empresario(a)

1. los (las) jugadores(as)
2. yo
3. el programador
4. los (las) maestros(as)
5. sus clientes

8 ¿Qué esperas?

Hablar

Usa el subjuntivo para hacerle preguntas a un(a) compañero(a). Luego cambien de papel.

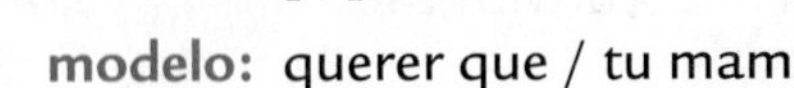

modelo: **querer que / tu mamá**

1. desear que / tus hermanos(as)
2. no querer que / tu amigo(a)
3. esperar que / tu gato(a)
4. desear que / tu abuelo(a)
5. no esperar que / tu maestro(a)

A ¿Tu mamá quiere que vayas al cine los sábados?

B Sí, pero espera que vuelva temprano.

9 ¿Qué deseas? ¿Recuerdas? Future tense p. 157

Escribir

Es el primer día de clases. Escribe ocho cosas que Jorge desea que haga Rafael en su primer día en el bachillerato. Usa verbos de deseo con los adjetivos de la lista.

presumido	vanidoso	orgulloso	tímido
comprensivo	dedicado	modesto	razonable

modelo:

Jorge: Deseo que no seas presumido.

Rafael: Está bien, no seré presumido.

Comparación cultural

Roberto Clemente

¿Deben las personas famosas ayudar a los demás? El sobresaliente beisbolista Roberto Clemente nació en Carolina, **Puerto Rico,** en 1934. Jugó con los Piratas de Pittsburgh durante toda su carrera en las ligas nacionales. Fue nombrado líder de bateo *(batting champion)* de la Liga Nacional cuatro veces y fue el Jugador Más Valioso del año 1966. Clemente era una persona popular y generosa que estaba en la cima *(height)* de su carrera cuando murió trágicamente en un accidente de avión cuando llevaba unas donaciones para las víctimas del terremoto de 1972, en **Nicaragua.**

Roberto Clemente

Compara con tu mundo *¿Qué atletas profesionales admiras y por qué?*

Más práctica Cuaderno *pp. 151–153* Cuaderno para hispanohablantes *pp. 152–154*

PARA Y PIENSA

Get Help Online ClassZone.com

¿Comprendiste? Escribe oraciones completas con el subjuntivo.

1. tú / querer / que yo / conservar / agua
2. mis hermanos / esperar / que su entrenador / darles / una oportunidad
3. nosotros / desear / que ustedes / reciclar los periódicos
4. yo / no querer / que tú / gastar / todo tu dinero

GRAMÁTICA en contexto

¡AVANZA! **Goal:** In the following script of the T.V. show "Los Solucionistas," notice when the characters use the subjunctive and when they use the indicative. Then practice by talking about what the characters hope to do. ***Actividades 10–12***

Contexto 2 *El guión*

ESTRATEGIA **Leer**

Read using different techniques Try reading Inés' script using different reading methods. First skim the entire reading to get a "big picture" view of the text; then read it again more slowly, focusing on all of the individual details. What are the reasons to use the subjunctive? What information did you understand only on your second reading?

AUDIO

Como tarea para su clase de escritura creativa, Inés está escribiendo un guión *(script)* para un programa de televisión. «Los Solucionistas» son un equipo de cuatro héroes que viajan por el mundo solucionando problemas.

Episodio 1:
Huracán en Puerto Rico

Escena 1: En la oficina de Los Solucionistas

Manuel entra, preocupado y con urgencia.

Manuel: Tengo malas noticias. Espero que la situación no sea tan grave como parece. El radar muestra un huracán grande que pasará muy cerca de Puerto Rico, dirigido hacia la ciudad de Ponce.

Carmen: ¡No podemos dejar que llegue a la ciudad! ¿Qué hacemos?

Gonzalo: ¡Vamos al Superavión! ¡Ahora mismo!

Escena 2: En el avión de Los Solucionistas

Manuel, Ramona y Carmen pasan a la parte del avión donde están los equipos científicos de Manuel.

Manuel: Quiero que miren el monitor. ¿Ven? Es un huracán de categoría cinco y es muy peligroso. Ojalá podamos prevenir la destrucción de Ponce...

Ramona: Oye, 'mano, ¡es importante que hagamos algo!

8.

También se dice

Ramona se dirige a Manuel diciéndole **'mano.** Esta expresión informal para hablar con amigos es la abreviatura de **hermano.**

- **Venezuela** pana
- **España** tío
- **Costa Rica** mae
- **Cuba** compadre

10 Comprensión del guión

Hablar
Escribir

Escribe las preguntas correctamente y da respuestas completas.

1. ¿Quién espera que las noticias no (ser) tan graves como parecen?
2. ¿Quién espera que el huracán no (destruir) la ciudad?
3. ¿Quién quiere que todos (ir) al avión?
4. ¿Quién quiere que los otros (mirar) el monitor?
5. ¿Quién espera que todos (hacer) algo?

11 ¡Viene el huracán!

Hablar
Escribir

Una oficial de la Cruz Roja piensa hablar por televisión para aconsejar a los ciudadanos de Ponce ante el peligro del huracán. Usa elementos de las cuatro columnas para escribir cinco consejos posibles de la oficial.

modelo: Yo espero que los ciudadanos no tengan miedo.

yo	querer	los ciudadanos	no hacer daño
los científicos	esperar	todos	comportarse con calma
la policía	desear	el huracán	quedarse en casa
los ciudadanos		los trabajadores sociales	ayudar
todos nosotros			no tener miedo

Expansión
Inventa cinco comentarios más de la oficial de la Cruz Roja. Usa las expresiones impersonales: Ojalá que... ; Es mejor que...

12 Después de la crisis

Hablar
Escribir

En grupo, completen el diálogo entre «Los Solucionistas». Deben escribir su propio final. Comparen sus versiones con otros grupos.

Ramona: Oye, 'mano, ¡Es importante que sigas pensando! Siempre hay una solución. A ver... ¿no me dijiste que cuando los huracanes pasan sobre el agua fría pierden su energía?

Manuel: Quiero que busquemos alguna manera de hacer que el agua o el aire estén más fríos.

Ramona: Es necesario que yo examine nuestro sistema de aire acondicionado para ver cómo funciona. ¡Tal vez podemos echarle aire frío del Superavión!

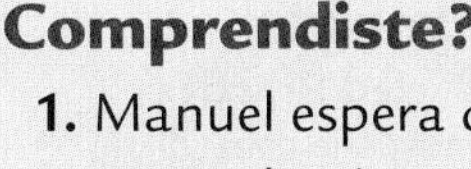

¿Comprendiste? Completa las oraciones con formas del subjuntivo.

1. Manuel espera que la situación no...
2. Manuel quiere que todos...
3. Es importante que Manuel...
4. Es necesario que Ramona...

Get Help Online
ClassZone.com

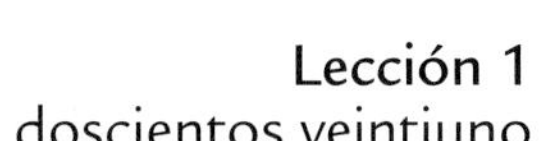

Presentación de GRAMÁTICA

¡AVANZA! **Goal:** Learn to use the subjunctive with verbs of influence. Then practice by discussing actions or behaviors that are suggested, allowed, or prohibited. ***Actividades 13–16***

English Grammar Connection: In English, you can use the **infinitive** or the **subjunctive** after verbs that are used to influence the actions of others. In Spanish, if there is a change of subject, you must use the **subjunctive.**

His parents allow him **to drive.**	Sus padres permiten que **conduzca.**
They demand that we **be** on time.	Ellos exigen que **estemos** a tiempo.

Subjunctive with Verbs of Influence

Animated Grammar
ClassZone.com

You already know how to use the subjunctive after verbs that express hope. You also use the **subjunctive** after verbs used to influence the actions of others by, for example, suggesting or prohibiting an action.

Here's how: Use the indicative for the verb of influence and the **subjunctive** for the second verb.

Verbs of Influence		
aconsejar	**insistir (en)**	**prohibir**
dejar	**mandar**	**recomendar**
exigir	**pedir**	**sugerir**

verb of influence + que + different subject + subjunctive

indicative ↓ *subjunctive* ↓

Sugiero que **llegues** temprano. *I suggest that you arrive early.*

The indicative is used for the first verb because it states a fact. The **subjunctive** is used for the second verb because it expresses a possibility rather than a fact, and because there is a change of subject.

Más práctica

Cuaderno *pp. 154–156*

Cuaderno para hispanohablantes *pp. 155–158*

@HomeTutor
Leveled Practice
ClassZone.com

Práctica de GRAMÁTICA

13 ¿Quién hace qué?

Escribir

Completa la nota que la mamá de Marta le escribió. Usa la forma correcta del subjuntivo.

> Marta, tengo que trabajar hasta tarde; por eso te exijo que hoy (llegar) __**1.**__ temprano a casa. Hay muchas cosas que hacer. Te sugiero que (leer) __**2.**__ la lista de tareas que te dejé sobre la mesa. Te aconsejo que (hacer) __**3.**__ primero las tareas más difíciles. Luego, recomiendo que (descansar) __**4.**__ unos minutos. Hay que ir a buscar pan y leche al supermercado, pero te prohíbo que (ir) __**5.**__ en bicicleta. Hay mucho tráfico a esa hora. ¡Tu ayuda es importante!
>
> Un beso,
> Mamá

Expansión
Dile a un compañero(a) qué aconsejas, sugieres, esperas, quieres, recomiendas y prefieres que él o ella haga. Luego, cambien de papel.

14 ¿A quién eliges?

Hablar

Estás muy ocupado(a) y le recomiendas a un(a) compañero(a) que otras personas hagan las actividades que te pide. Túrnense para hacer las preguntas.

mandar	insistir en
sugerir	recomendar
dejar	preferir

modelo: entrevistar al detective / Álex y Silvia

A ¿Quieres entrevistar al detective?

B No, no puedo. Sugiero que Álex y Silvia lo entrevisten.

1. llamar al mecánico / tú
2. pagar al programador / José
3. hacer una cita con la empresaria / ellos
4. escribir el artículo sobre los obreros / Elena
5. buscar al electricista / tú
6. avisar al astronauta / Ana y Marta

AUDIO

Pronunciación La letra q

La **q** siempre va seguida por **u** y la **u** por las vocales **e** o **i.** La combinación **qu** siempre tiene el sonido /k/, como en la palabra *key* o *cane.*

quitar **búsqueda**
quien **orquesta**

Refrán

Quien anda de prisa es el que tropieza.

15 ¿Qué te piden otros?

Escuchar
Escribir

Escucha los mensajes en tu contestadora y escribe una lista de las cosas que las otras personas quieren que hagas.

modelo: Mi mamá insiste en que yo regrese a casa antes de las diez.

16 Famosos que ayudan a la comunidad

Escribir

Comparación cultural

Juan Luis Guerra

¿De qué manera la educación formal puede afectar el talento de un músico y su forma de pensar? Juan Luis Guerra Seijas, el gran cantante de merengue, nació el 7 de julio de 1956 en Santo Domingo, **República Dominicana.** Guerra estudió Filosofía y Letras en la Universidad de Santo Domingo y después obtuvo una beca para estudiar música en Berklee College of Music en Boston. «Mi casa siempre fue musical, hasta los aguacates cantaban», recuerda el artista a quien muchos consideran un poeta también. Junto con su amigo Herbert Stern creó la Fundación 440 que se encarga de ayudar a los que necesitan recursos médicos en todo el mundo.

Juan Luis Guerra

Compara con tu mundo *¿Conoces a un(a) cantante, un actor o una actriz que contribuya con mucho dinero o tiempo a obras caritativas? ¿Qué tipos de proyectos apoya?*

Escoge a una personalidad que ayude a la comunidad y escribe cinco oraciones para describir a esta persona y sus proyectos, usando las siguientes expresiones: **querer que... ; esperar que... ; dejar que... ; sugerir que... ; permitir que...**

Más práctica Cuaderno *pp. 154–156* Cuaderno para hispanohablantes *pp. 155–158*

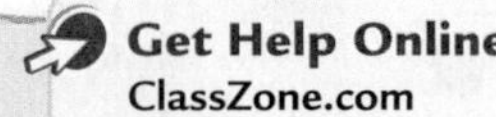

¿Comprendiste? Completa cada oración con el subjuntivo del verbo indicado.

1. Me gustan los aviones, pero mamá me prohíbe que _____ (ser) piloto.
2. Arturo es razonable. Aconsejo que él _____ (estudiar) para ser detective.
3. Tu invento es muy novedoso. Sugiero que _____ (sacar) una patente.

Todo junto

¡AVANZA! **Goal:** ***Show what you know*** Notice how Inés, the actors, and a 7-year-old boy use the subjunctive to talk about their hopes and desires. Then practice by talking about actions that you or others hope will occur.
Actividades 17–19

Resumen contextos 1 y 2 Inés Delgado es una estudiante puertorriqueña. Ella escribió un guión *(script)* para un programa de televisión que se llama «Los Solucionistas». Ellos son cuatro personas que viajan por el mundo solucionando problemas.

Contexto 3 *Diálogo*

ESTRATEGIA **Escuchar**
Use a "story frame" to understand the story While listening, use a story frame to consider how similar or different the "real" people in the story are from the TV characters. The story frame consists of the following questions: Who are the two "real" people? Who are the four TV characters? Do the actors always stay in character?

AUDIO

Inés está filmando el último episodio de su programa «Los Solucionistas» en el gimnasio de la escuela. Luego presentará el video en la escuela.

Inés: Bueno, vamos a filmar la escena final otra vez. Quiero que todos hablen con mucha sinceridad y que sigan el guión sin errores. Tres, dos, uno... ¡empecemos!

Carmen: «Ramona, eres una mecánica increíble. ¡Deja que se lo diga a todos!»

Ramona: «Gracias, Carmen. Pero lo importante es que pudimos salvar a Ponce del huracán... »

Gonzalo: «Ramona, eres demasiado modesta. Tú eres una gran mecánica».

De repente, llega un niño.

Gonzalo: Un momento... A ver... ¿Qué te pasa, niño?

Inés: ¡Corten! ¿Qué pasa?

Ricardo: ¡Por favor! ¡Necesito su ayuda!

Gonzalo: Bueno... cúentanos tu problema... tranquilo. Quiero que empieces desde el principio. ¿Cómo te llamas?

Ricardo: Me llamo Ricardo Alonso. Tengo siete años y estoy en segundo grado. Veo que ustedes son superhéroes o algo así y espero que me puedan ayudar. Pero tiene que ser rápido, mi mamá está en la puerta esperándome y quiere que vuelva pronto.

Carmen: Bueno, cuéntanos... ¿Cuál es el problema?

Ricardo: El problema es que mi carrito eléctrico se dañó. No sé qué hacer.

Manuel: ¡Pobrecito! ¡No te preocupes!

Ricardo: Y como vi que esa mujer es mecánica y sabe reparar las cosas...

Ramona: ¿Yo? Ay, Ricardito, la verdad es que no soy mecánica... ¡Soy actriz! ¿Qué podemos hacer?

Carmen: Seguro son las baterías. Bueno, por suerte yo sé un poco sobre carritos eléctricos. Trataré de repararlo, pero queremos que sepas que no somos superhéroes.

Ricardo: ¡Gracias, amigos! ¡Vengan, vengan conmigo!

17 Comprensión del diálogo

Escuchar
Hablar
Escribir

Contesta las preguntas según el diálogo.

1. ¿Qué les pide Inés a todos en la filmación de la última escena?
2. ¿Qué cualidades tiene Ramona que admiran Carmen y Gonzalo?
3. ¿Qué problema tiene Ricardo?
4. ¿Por qué cree Ricardo que Carmen, Ramona y Gonzalo pueden ayudarlo?
5. ¿Dónde está la mamá de Ricardo?
6. ¿Quién sabe algo de mecánica?

18 Integración

Leer
Escuchar
Hablar

Lee el sitio web de la organización Líderes para el Futuro. Escucha la videoconferencia donde te dan respuestas a un mensaje que pusiste en la sección «Contáctanos». Luego, toma parte en la videoconferencia y da más detalles sobre las cualidades de un líder.

Fuente 1 Sitio web

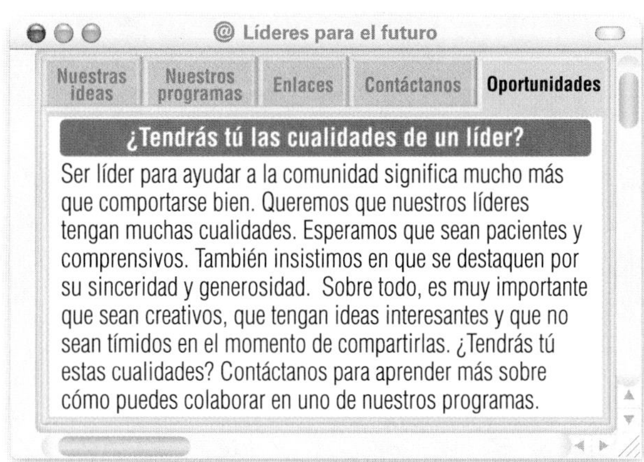

@ Líderes para el futuro

Nuestras ideas | Nuestros programas | Enlaces | Contáctanos | Oportunidades

¿Tendrás tú las cualidades de un líder?

Ser líder para ayudar a la comunidad significa mucho más que comportarse bien. Queremos que nuestros líderes tengan muchas cualidades. Esperamos que sean pacientes y comprensivos. También insistimos en que se destaquen por su sinceridad y generosidad. Sobre todo, es muy importante que sean creativos, que tengan ideas interesantes y que no sean tímidos en el momento de compartirlas. ¿Tendrás tú estas cualidades? Contáctanos para aprender más sobre cómo puedes colaborar en uno de nuestros programas.

Fuente 2 Videoconferencia

Escucha y apunta

- ¿Cómo reaccionó la persona al mensaje que pusiste en el sitio web?
- ¿Qué quieren que hagas ahora?

modelo: La persona dijo que le gustó el mensaje. Quiere que mañana participe en otra videoconferencia. Creo que las cualidades de un líder deben ser la sinceridad...

19 ¡A escribir!

Escribir

Escribe una nueva escena de las aventuras de «Los Solucionistas». Puedes basar tu escena en los cuatro personajes de las lecturas o presentar algún personaje nuevo. Incluye por lo menos cinco ejemplos del subjuntivo y tres ejemplos de adjetivos o sustantivos de carácter y personalidad.

Writing Criteria	Excellent	Good	Needs Work
Content	Your scene includes many interesting details.	Your scene includes some interesting details.	Your scene includes few interesting details.
Communication	Your scene is organized and easy to follow.	Parts of your scene are organized and easy to follow.	Your scene is disorganized and hard to follow.
Accuracy	You make few mistakes in grammar and vocabulary.	You make some mistakes in grammar and vocabulary.	You make many mistakes in grammar and vocabulary.

Expansión
Practica tu escena con algunos compañeros(as) y preséntenla en clase.

Más práctica Cuaderno *pp. 157–158* Cuaderno para hispanohablantes *pp. 159–160*

PARA Y PIENSA

¿Comprendiste? Escribe oraciones con el verbo dado y otro verbo en el subjuntivo para indicar qué quieren las personas siguientes.

1. mis padres / dejar
2. mi profesor(a) / prohibir
3. yo / esperar
4. mi amigo(a) / aconsejar

Get Help Online
ClassZone.com

Lectura literaria

¡AVANZA! **Goal:** Read the following segment from a novel about a mother's concerns about raising her children. Then think about how different friends and family members have served as role models for you.

Para leer 

ESTRATEGIA **Leer**

Use a honeycomb map to summarize the reading While reading the excerpt of a story by Esmeralda Santiago, use the honeycomb map to summarize the story. First draw the honeycomb map on a separate sheet. Next complete all the parts of the map. You might need to make some intelligent guesses (inferences) based on the context. After filling the entire map, you are ready to write full answers to the reflection questions contained in the story.

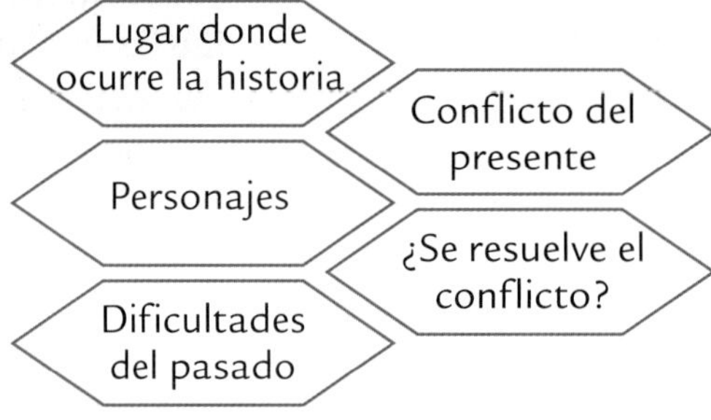

Vocabulario para leer

entrometerse	*meterse sin permiso en una conversación o en la vida de otra persona*
salirle bien	*tener los resultados esperados*
nena	*expresión familiar para dirigirse a una mujer más joven*
encajar	*hacer que una cosa coincida o esté relacionada con otra*
sufrimiento	*preocupación que pasan las personas en algunos momentos de su vida*

Nota cultural

Sobre la autora ***Esmeralda Santiago (1948–)***
Nació en San Juan, Puerto Rico, y su familia vino a Estados Unidos cuando ella tenía trece años. Entre sus obras más famosas están *Cuando era puertorriqueña* y *El sueño de América.* Esta última ya se ha publicado en seis idiomas y fue seleccionada por Literary Guild.

Sobre la inmigración Puerto Rico es un Estado Libre Asociado de Estados Unidos. Los puertorriqueños son ciudadanos estadounidenses que no necesitan pasaporte para entrar a EE.UU. En la novela *El sueño de América,* una puertorriqueña llega a EE.UU. y visita a su tía que vino a este país hace muchos años.

Plazoleta Rodolpho Walsh (2000), *Graciela Genovés*

El sueño de América

—Así son nuestros domingos —Paulina le explica más tarde—. Todas las semanas que pueden, vienen los hijos y la nieta. Y casi siempre Rufo y Lourdes y Darío y, por supuesto, los mellizos[1].

—¿Todas las semanas?

—Sí, m'ija[2], todas las semanas. Y a veces vienen otros parientes o los vecinos. Pero siempre tengo la casa llena los domingos.

....

—Usted parece tener una relación tan linda con sus hijos, Tía. América dice con tanta sinceridad que Paulina se infla de orgullo.

—Sí, es verdad. Leopoldo y yo tratamos de no entrometernos mucho en sus vidas. Les permitimos cometer errores.

—Eso es lo que yo traté de hacer con Rosalinda, pero no me salió bien.

—El darles la libertad de cometer errores no quiere decir que no los cometerán, América.

---

[1] twins [2] my daughter *(mi hija)*

Reflexiona

¿Qué relación tiene Paulina con la gente que la visita los domingos?

Ella considera esto un minuto, y la tensión de siempre vuelve a su pecho, un dolor tan profundo que no puede nombrarlo, no puede separarlo de su ser. Se deslizan[3] lágrimas por sus mejillas.

—Lo has tomado tan personalmente —Paulina dice con verdadera sorpresa, como si nunca se le hubiera ocurrido[4] que los errores de sus hijos se reflejarían[5] en ella.

—¿Usted no lo haría[6], Tía? —América dice resentida[7].

—Nena, tú no tienes ni idea del sufrimiento que me han ocasionado mis hijos —Paulina sube sus manos a su pecho.

América la mira como si la estuviera viendo[8] por primera vez.

—¿Ellos la han hecho[9] sufrir? —no encaja con la imagen de las caras sonrientes[10] en las tarjetas de Navidad en la pared de memorias de Ester.

—Si yo contara[11] las horas que pasé sentada en esta misma silla esperando que Orlando regresara a casa de estas calles peligrosas, o de las batallas que tuve con Carmen sobre sus amigos...

—Ay, no, nena, tú no quieras saber —Paulina mira sus manos fijamente, manos arrugadas[12], manchadas[13] por la edad, con uñas desafiladas[14] y cutículas gruesas[15].

A pensar
¿Por qué reacciona América tan fuertemente al comentario de su tía? ¿Quién es Rosalinda y qué crees que hizo?

---

[3] Roll down [4] **como...** as if it had never occurred to her
[5] **se...** would reflect [6] **no...** wouldn't do it [7] resentfully
[8] **como...** as if she were seeing her [9] **la...** they made you
[10] smiling [11] **Si...** If I were to count [12] wrinkled
[13] speckled [14] rough [15] thick

Reflexiona

¿Qué descubre América de su tía?

—Lo que yo no comprendo —América dice— es qué tiene que hacer una madre para prevenir que sus hijos no repitan sus errores. ¿Cómo se les enseña que nuestra vida no es su modelo?

—No se les puede enseñar[16], nena, ellos tienen que aprender eso por sí mismos. ❖

—Yo no puedo estar de acuerdo con eso, Tía. ¿Para qué somos madres si no es para enseñarles?

—No se les puede enseñar —Paulina insiste—. Sólo puedes escucharles y orientarlos. Y después sólo si te lo piden puedes guiarles.

[16] **No...** they can't be taught

❖ **A pensar**
Paulina usa frecuentemente la expresión **nena** para dirigirse a América. ¿Por qué crees que la usa tanto? Ten en cuenta el tono en que Paulina le habla a su sobrina.

¿Comprendiste?

1. ¿Qué deduce América de los domingos en casa de Paulina?
2. ¿Quién es Leopoldo?
3. ¿Por qué crees que América se pone triste cuando piensa en su hija?
4. ¿Qué tipo de fotos vio América en la casa de Ester?
5. Según Paulina, ¿cuál es la responsabilidad de una madre?

¿Y tú?

¿Crees que los niños aprenden del modelo de sus padres o tienen que aprender de sus propios errores? Explica tus razones.

Conexiones *Las matemáticas*

Promedios en el béisbol

El béisbol es una pasión en muchos países latinoamericanos, particularmente en los países del Caribe. En 1902, Luis Castro fue el primer beisbolista latinoamericano que jugó en las Grandes Ligas de Estados Unidos. Éstas son las estadísticas de cuatro jugadores caribeños que están en el Salón de la Fama.

El promedio *(average)* de bateo de un jugador se obtiene dividiendo su cantidad de hits entre sus veces al bate. Luego, ese resultado lo multiplicas por mil.

$$\underset{\text{hits}}{(3} \div \underset{\text{veces al bate}}{10)} \times 1000 = \underset{\text{promedio de bateo}}{300}$$

Caribeños en el Salón de la Fama

Proyecto

1. Según estas estadísticas, ¿quién bateó más hits en total?
2. ¿Quiénes batearon más jonrones?
3. ¿Quién tuvo el promedio más alto?
4. Usa una calculadora para saber el promedio de bateo de un jugador que bateó 6 hits en 20 veces al bate y de otro jugador que bateó 4 hits en 15 veces al bate. ¿Quién tuvo el promedio más alto?

En tu comunidad

¿Hay jugadores latinos en el equipo de las Grandes Ligas más cercano a tu ciudad? ¿Quiénes son? ¿De qué país son o cuál es su origen? ¿En qué equipo juegan?

- Escoge a un jugador de béisbol del Caribe que juegue en las Grandes Ligas de Estados Unidos. Busca información sobre sus datos biográficos y sus estadísticas en este momento. Aquí hay una lista con algunos beisbolistas del Caribe.
  - Adrián Beltré (República Dominicana)
  - José Contreras (Cuba)
  - David De Jesús (Puerto Rico)
  - David Ortiz (República Dominicana)
  - Rubén Gotay (Puerto Rico)
  - Liván Hernández (Cuba)

Lección 1

En resumen

Vocabulario y gramática

Vocabulario

Describe People

comportarse bien / mal	*to behave well / badly*	destacarse por...	*to be remarkable for, to stand out (from others) for . . .*	imitar	*to imitate*
la conducta	*behavior*	idealizar (a alguien)	*to idealize (someone)*	personificar	*to personify*
				representar	*to represent*

Personal characteristics

atrevido(a)	*daring*	impaciente	*impatient*	razonable	*reasonable*
comprensivo(a)	*understanding*	ingenioso (a)	*clever*	sincero(a)	*sincere*
considerado(a)	*considerate*	modesto(a)	*modest*	sobresaliente	*outstanding*
dedicado(a)	*dedicated*	orgulloso(a)	*proud*	tímido(a)	*shy*
desagradable	*disagreeable*	paciente	*patient*	vanidoso(a)	*vain*
fiel	*faithful*	popular	*popular*		
generoso(a)	*generous*	presumido(a)	*presumptuous*		

Professions

el (la) astronauta	*astronaut*	el (la) mecánico(a)	*mechanic*
el (la) científico(a)	*scientist*	el (la) obrero(a)	*laborer*
el (la) detective	*detective*	el (la) piloto	*pilot*
el (la) electricista	*electrician*	el (la) programador(a)	*programmer*
el (la) empresario(a)	*businessperson*	el (la) trabajador(a) social	*social worker*
el (la) entrenador(a)	*trainer, coach*		

Tell Others What To Do

aconsejar que	*to advise that*
dejar que	*to allow that*
exigir que	*to demand that*
mandar que	*to order, command that*
prohibir que	*to prohibit that*
sugerir (ie, i) que	*to suggest that*

Gramática

Nota gramatical: Suffixes *p. 216*

Subjunctive with Ojalá and Verbs of Hope

Verbs of Hope
desear
esperar
querer

Verbs of Hope + que + different subject + subjunctive

Ella **quiere** que **su hijo se comporte** bien.

Use the **infinitive** and omit **que** if there is no change of subject.

El niño **quiere comportarse** bien.

Ojalá can be used with or without **que.** It is always used with the **subjunctive.**

Ojalá que no **llueva** mañana.

Subjunctive with Verbs of Influence

Verbs of Influence		
aconsejar	**insistir**	**prohibir**
dejar	**mandar**	**recomendar**
exigir	**pedir**	**sugerir**

verb of influence + que + different subject + subjunctive

indicative → *subjunctive* →

Sugiero que **llegues** temprano.

I suggest that you arrive early.

Lección 1

Repaso de la lección

¡LLEGADA!

@HomeTutor ClassZone.com

Now you can
- describe people
- tell others what to do
- express wishes and desires

Using
- suffixes
- subjunctive with **ojalá** and verbs of hope
- subjunctive with verbs of influence

To review
- vocabulary p. 212
- suffixes p. 216
- subjunctive with verbs of influence p. 222

1 Listen and understand

AUDIO

En este episodio de la telenovela «La Familia Suárez», Luisa habla con su hermano, Álvaro. Después de una ausencia misteriosa de veinte años, Álvaro quiere hablar con su madre. Escucha parte de la escena y luego contesta las preguntas.

1. ¿Qué tipo de cualidad tiene Álvaro, según él?
2. ¿Qué quiere Álvaro que su mamá vea?
3. ¿De qué tipo de cosas quiere hablar Álvaro con su mamá?
4. ¿Qué tipo de persona piensa Álvaro que es su mamá?
5. Según Álvaro, ¿qué característica tiene su hermana al final de la conversación?

To review
- subjunctive with verbs of influence p. 222

2 Tell other people to do something

Usa la información de la tabla y escribe oraciones para expresar lo que insisten las personas indicadas. Sigue el modelo.

modelo: mi madre / nosotros
Mi madre insiste en que nosotros nos comportemos bien.

	tú	nosotros	yo
mi madre	ayudar en la cocina	comportarse bien	ser más considerado(a)
la maestra	hacer la tarea	no hablar en clase	estudiar más
los amigos	ser más generoso	ir mañana a la playa	dar una fiesta

1. mi madre / tú
2. mi madre / yo
3. la maestra / tú
4. la maestra / nosotros
5. los amigos / nosotros
6. los amigos / yo

To review
- suffixes p. 216

3 Describe people

Completa las siguientes oraciones con los adjetivos o sustantivos correctos.

1. Andrés se destaca por su dedicación. Es muy ____ .
2. Elisa personifica la sinceridad. Es muy ____ .
3. Sandra, tú representas la ____ . Eres muy considerada.
4. Nosotras nos destacamos por la ____ . Somos muy tímidas.
5. Ellos personifican la vanidad. ¡Son tan ____ !
6. Marisol y Rafael se destacan por su ____ . Son muy populares.

To review
- subjunctive with **ojalá** and verbs of hope p. 217
- subjunctive vs. indicative p. 222

4 Express wishes and desires

Completa la siguiente descripción con las formas correctas de los verbos indicados. Usa el infinitivo, el subjuntivo o el indicativo, según el contexto.

5 de agosto

Ay, ¡qué vida más difícil! Quiero **1.** (describir) todos mis problemas... ¡Los maestros quieren que yo **2.** (leer) cinco libros por semana! Mis padres mandan que mis hermanos y yo **3.** (hacer) todos los quehaceres de la casa. Y mis amigos esperan que yo **4.** (salir) con ellos todos los días. Yo les sugiero a ellos que **5.** (tener) más paciencia conmigo, pero ellos no quieren **6.** (oír).

To review
- **Comparación cultural** pp. 219, 224

5 People and places

Comparación cultural

1. ¿Cuál es el origen nacional de Juan Luis Guerra? ¿Qué proyectos de caridad patrocina?
2. ¿Conoces a una persona famosa que financia proyectos semejantes en tu comunidad o estado?
3. ¿Dónde nació Roberto Clemente? ¿Qué premios ganó durante su carrera con los Piratas de Pittsburgh?
4. ¿Qué proyecto humanitario emprendió?

Más práctica Cuaderno *pp. 153–170* Cuaderno para hispanohablantes *pp. 161–170*

UNIDAD 4

El Caribe

Lección 2

Tema:

¿Quiénes son los héroes?

¡AVANZA! **In this lesson you will learn to**

- describe people and things
- express doubt, denial, and disbelief
- express positive and negative emotions

using

- subjunctive with doubt
- subjunctive with emotion

¿Recuerdas?

- superlatives
- the suffix **-ísimo**
- describe people
- family relationships

Comparación cultural

In this lesson you will learn about

- Caribbean artists and their artwork
- Independence heroes from Puerto Rico and Dominican Republic

Compara con tu mundo

El Morro es una fortaleza *(fortress)* construida por los españoles para proteger San Juan. Ahora es un sitio histórico y turístico muy popular. *¿Hay algún lugar turístico en tu región? ¿Cuál es su importancia histórica o cultural?*

¿Qué ves?

Mira la foto

¿Qué tipo de geografía ves?

¿Cómo son los edificios y estructuras que ves?

¿Qué símbolo ves en el helicóptero? ¿Con qué asocias sus colores?

Featuring...

Cultura INTERACTIVA

Animated Grammar

@HomeTutor

And more...

- Get Help Online
- Interactive Flashcards
- Review Games
- WebQuest
- Conjuguemos.com

Helicóptero guardacostas sobre El Morro
San Juan, Puerto Rico

❖ Presentación de VOCABULARIO

¡AVANZA! **Goal:** Read the following. Then talk about what qualities people need for different professions. ***Actividades 1–2***

 *¿Recuerdas?* Describe people pp. 212–213

AUDIO

A Enrique Rivera escribe en su libreta de notas.

Hoy llegaron los resultados del cuestionario vocacional y ¡**me sorprende que** digan que seré mejor **bombero** que escritor! Imagínense, ¡Enrique el Bombero!

Para ser bombero hay que **actuar** con **valentía** y **arriesgar** la vida con **el propósito** y **la meta** de ayudar a los demás. Creo que es un **honor**, pero **no estoy seguro de que** pueda **convertirme en** bombero. Me gusta más ser escritor o **periodista. Por eso,** estos resultados son **sorprendentes.** Existen otras formas de **lograr** ser un héroe **auténtico** y cumplir con los **deberes** sociales. **Por lo tanto, no creo que** los resultados del cuestionario sean **prácticos** para mí.

Más vocabulario

el logro *achievement*
el sacrificio *sacrifice*
el (la) técnico(a) *technician*
el (la) vecino(a) *neighbor*
alegrarse de que *to be happy that*
es dudoso que *it is doubtful that*
no es cierto que *it is not certain that*
no es verdad que *it is not true that*
sentir que *to be sorry that, to feel*

Expansión de vocabulario p. R15
Ya sabes p. R15

B Yo siempre pienso en escribir libros y artículos en los periódicos. Quiero entrevistar a **músicos** con **fama**, a **carpinteros** o a **políticos**; no tienen que ser famosos. Creo que mi misión en la vida es contar historias sobre **amistades verdaderas** y describir **imágenes** bellas de otros lugares. **Sin embargo, es improbable que** todos mis textos sean **realistas** porque me gustan las historias en que **aparecen** personajes o lugares fantásticos. No **dudo que** seré escritor y podré **figurar en** las librerías algún día, como mi autora favorita, Zoe Valdés.

Zoe Valdés, escritora cubana

C ¿Y tú? ¿Qué trabajo te interesa hacer? Hay muchas profesiones para elegir.

¡A responder! Escuchar

Escucha la lista de profesiones. Para cada una, haz un movimiento que represente las acciones típicas de la profesión.

Práctica de VOCABULARIO

1 Cualidades y profesiones

 *¿Recuerdas?* Describe people pp. 212–213

Hablar
Escribir

Usa elementos de las cuatro columnas para escribir siete oraciones sobre la cualidad apropiada para cada profesión.

modelo: político(a) / tener que ser / honesto / con las personas
El político tiene que ser honesto con las personas.

músico(a)	tener que ser	atrevido(a)	con sus clientes
bombero(a)	deber ser	dedicado(a)	para triunfar
policía		ingenioso(a)	para proteger a los demás
cartero		popular	con sus herramientas
carpintero(a)		paciente	con las entregas del correo
maestro(a)		considerado(a)	con sus alumnos
político(a)		honesto(a)	

2 Una actriz famosa

Leer
Escribir

Utiliza los verbos de la lista para completar el párrafo sobre la famosa actriz Juliana Tejera.

lograr
figurar
creer
actuar
convertirse en
aparecer

Juliana Tejera siempre deseó __1.__ una gran actriz con el propósito de tener fama. Por lo tanto, para poderlo __2.__ , tuvo que __3.__ en muchas películas durante muchos años. También debió __4.__ en programas donde invitan a los famosos y __5.__ en revistas populares, entrevistada por periodistas. Seguramente, tres cosas fueron necesarias: trabajar mucho, __6.__ mucho en sí misma y hacer muchos sacrificios.

Más práctica Cuaderno *pp. 171–173* Cuaderno para hispanohablantes *pp. 171–174*

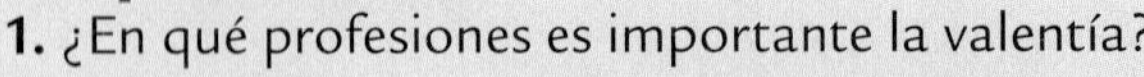

¿Comprendiste?

1. ¿En qué profesiones es importante la valentía?
2. ¿Qué profesiones pueden traer la fama?
3. ¿En qué profesiones no se arriesga la vida?

VOCABULARIO en contexto

¡AVANZA! **Goal:** Notice the words that Enrique uses to describe his father in the following editorial. Then talk about what qualities can make people heroes in their own community. ***Actividades 3–4***

Contexto 1 *Artículo de opinión*

ESTRATEGIA Leer

Infer In Enrique's article, he reveals what he values in other people. Make a list of qualities he admires in his father to help you infer why he says that everyday people can be called true heroes.

El padre de Enrique
1. vive con sinceridad
2.
3.

AUDIO

Enrique Rivera es editor de la revista de su escuela en la República Dominicana. Para la próxima edición, quiere hacer un foto ensayo *(photo essay)* sobre los héroes. Por eso, acaba de escribir un artículo de opinión. En éste, les pide recuerdos personales a sus lectores y habla de la importancia de los héroes en la comunidad.

Nuestros héroes

Mientras muchas películas y novelas gráficas cuentan las historias de los superhéroes, es importante recordar que no todos los héroes son de fantasía. Los héroes verdaderos viven al lado de nosotros: pueden ser nuestros familiares, nuestros vecinos o nuestros maestros. Todos tenemos la capacidad para actuar heroicamente: los bomberos, los artistas, los policías, los periodistas, incluso los estudiantes.

Por ejemplo, mi héroe es mi padre. No logra éxitos sorprendentes, no tiene fama mundial ni una vida extraordinaria, pero todos los días se comporta como un héroe verdadero. Vive con sinceridad, honor y valentía; va al trabajo todos los días, cuida de nosotros y siempre está listo para hacer cualquier sacrificio por su familia.

Mi padre y yo

Para la edición del próximo mes, quiero que me cuenten sobre los héroes que ustedes conocen. Mándenme sus sugerencias y seleccionaremos las tres historias más emocionantes para que figuren en un foto ensayo sobre los héroes de todos los días.

A la espera de sus historias...

Enrique Rivera

3 Comprensión del artículo de opinión

Hablar
Escribir

Contesta las siguientes preguntas sobre la lectura.

1. ¿Qué es importante recordar de los héroes?
2. Según Enrique, ¿quiénes pueden ser héroes?
3. ¿Quién es el héroe de Enrique? ¿Cuáles son sus cualidades?
4. ¿Qué quiere Enrique que los lectores le cuenten?

REPASO gramatical

Superlatives When you want to say that something is "the most," you use superlative forms. Follow this formula to talk about superlatives:

el / la / los / las + **noun** + **más** + **adjective** *(agrees with article and noun)*

Ana María es **la artista más famosa** que conozco.
*Ana María is **the most famous artist** I know.*

Los señores Gómez son **los vecinos más agradables** del barrio.
*Mr. and Mrs. Gómez are **the most pleasant neighbors** in the neighborhood.*

4 El más...

Hablar
Escribir

Tu compañero(a) y tú colaboran en un comité escolar que reconoce a personas y lugares por su excelencia, méritos y servicios. Escriban una lista de posibles candidatos para presentar al comité.

modelo: la calle más interesante

1. el vecino más amable
2. las personas más sorprendentes
3. el trabajador más arriesgado
4. el logro más ingenioso
5. el político más auténtico
6. la mujer (chica) más valiente
7. el hombre (chico) más considerado
8. la tienda más atractiva
9. el restaurante más moderno
10. la maestra más buena
11. el artista más talentoso
12. el parque más limpio

Expansión
Expliquen por qué recomiendan cada lugar o miembro de la comunidad.

PARA Y PIENSA

¿Comprendiste? Busca tres características y dos acciones del padre de Enrique que hacen que su hijo lo considere como un héroe.

Get Help Online
ClassZone.com

Presentación de GRAMÁTICA

¡AVANZA! **Goal:** Learn how to use the subjunctive with expressions of doubt. Then practice by speaking about things you disagree with or doubt. ***Actividades 5–8***

 *¿Recuerdas?* Family relationships pp. 58–59

English Grammar Connection: In English, you use the **indicative** after **expressions of doubt.** In Spanish, you use the **subjunctive.**

I don't believe that fame **is** important. (↑ indicative) **No creo** que la fama **sea** importante. (↑ subjunctive)

Subjunctive with Doubt

You need to use the **subjunctive** after **expressions of doubt** because they suggest that the second verb may be untrue.

Here's how:

Expressions of Doubt			
dudar	**es imposible**	**no es cierto**	**no estar de acuerdo con**
es dudoso	**es improbable**	**no es verdad**	**no estar seguro(a) de**

expression of doubt + **que** + **different subject** + **subjunctive**

Marta **no está segura de** que **tengamos** tiempo para ver la película.
Marta is not sure that we have time to see the movie.

Note that the word **no** can change the meaning of an expression and affect whether you need to use the **subjunctive** or **indicative** form of the second verb.

expresses doubt / *subjunctive*
Dudamos que Jorge **conozca** al músico.
***We doubt** that Jorge knows the musician.*

expresses certainty / *indicative*
No dudamos que él **tiene** talento.
***We do not doubt** that he has talent.*

Más práctica
Cuaderno *pp. 174–176*
Cuaderno para hispanohablantes *pp. 175–177*

@HomeTutor
Leveled Practice
ClassZone.com

Práctica de GRAMÁTICA

5 ¡Qué noticias!

Escuchar Escribir

Escucha este mensaje telefónico de tu amiga Marisa y luego decide si las siguientes frases son ciertas o falsas.

1. Es dudoso que Marisa acepte los boletos.
2. Es improbable que los jugadores permitan la entrevista.
3. No es verdad que Marisa vaya a escribir un artículo.
4. Marisa no cree que los jugadores acepten su invitación a comer.
5. No creo que los jugadores quieran pasar tiempo con una chica que no es famosa.

6 Dudas y certezas

 ***¿Recuerdas?*** Family relationships pp. 58–59

Hablar Escribir

Haz oraciones con las expresiones indicadas, utilizando el subjuntivo o el indicativo, según corresponda.

modelo: dudamos / nuestro tío / poder levantar el carro
Dudamos que nuestro tío pueda levantar el carro.

1. no es cierto / mi padrino / ser atrevido
2. creo / mi papá / conocer a un cantante dominicano
3. Raúl y Martín no creen / su cuñada / saber cocinar
4. no dudo / tu hermanito / comportarse bien
5. estoy seguro / ese matrimonio / figurar en la revista *Gente de hoy*
6. es imposible / mi madre / actuar en la telenovela
7. pienso / mi primo / tener que cambiar su imagen
8. no es cierto / mi sobrino / parecerse a su bisabuelo

7 Exageraciones

Hablar

Tu compañero(a) siempre exagera. Tú no le crees y se lo dices.

modelo: conocer al beisbolista Pedro Martínez

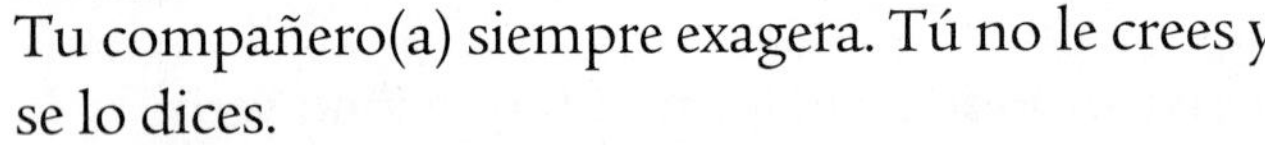

no es cierto que...
no es verdad que...
no estar seguro(a) de que...
es dudoso que...
es improbable que...

1. ser muy famoso
2. viajar cada año a París
3. tener mucha fama en Cuba
4. comerse diez perros calientes
5. tener que leer cien libros hoy
6. convertirse en perro todas las noches

8 ¿Lo lograré?

Escribir Hablar

Escribe una lista de cinco cosas que quieres hacer en tu vida pero que no estás seguro(a) de que puedas lograr. Luego comparte tu lista con un(a) compañero(a). Él o ella va a expresar una opinión más positiva.

A Quiero ser músico(a), sin embargo, no estoy seguro(a) de que pueda ganar suficiente dinero para vivir.

B En mi opinión, es muy importante que sigas tus metas y las logres. Por eso, debes...

Expansión
Escribe un párrafo breve sobre una de las metas de tu compañero(a). ¿Por qué crees que es importante que haga lo que quiere?

Comparación cultural

Un estilo propio

¿Qué importancia tiene crear un estilo propio en el arte? Amelia Peláez fue una pionera entre los pintores modernistas latinoamericanos. La artista de **Cuba** tenía un estilo muy personal y original. Ella logró combinar la arquitectura y las artes decorativas del período colonial con la pintura de su tiempo. Amelia dibujaba con una línea ancha y negra el perímetro de los objetos o las personas de sus cuadros. El resto del cuadro siempre lo pintaba con colores muy brillantes. Esto produce un efecto similar a los vitrales *(stained glasses)* del tiempo colonial.

Marpacífico *(Hibiscus)* *(1943), Amelia Peláez*

Compara con tu mundo *Di alguna actividad en que tú tienes un estilo propio. Describe cuál es la diferencia entre cómo lo haces tú y cómo lo hacen los demás.*

Más práctica Cuaderno *pp. 174–176* Cuaderno para hispanohablantes *pp. 175–177*

PARA Y PIENSA

Get Help Online
ClassZone.com

¿Comprendiste? Repite las oraciones siguientes usando expresiones de duda o negación. Haz los cambios necesarios para usar el subjuntivo.

1. Todos los estudiantes de tu escuela tienen que escribir un artículo para el periódico escolar.
2. Tu maestro(a) de español toca la guitarra con tres músicos caribeños.
3. Tus vecinos son superhéroes que protegen a los ciudadanos.

GRAMÁTICA en contexto

¡AVANZA! **Goal:** In the letters below, notice how Gladys, Pablo, and Grisel use the subjunctive. Then practice using the subjunctive with expressions of doubt. ***Actividades 9–11***

Contexto 2 *Cartas al editor*

ESTRATEGIA Leer

Compare the heroes Three readers of Enrique's school newspaper explain whom they consider the most esteemed person in their lives. Compare the three heroes using the graphic organizer.

Héroe	Cualidades
Dulce	
Abuelo	
Maestra	

AUDIO

Enrique Rivera, el editor de la revista escolar *Nuestro Mundo,* solicitó a sus lectores algunas historias sobre héroes y recibió las siguientes respuestas.

Mi hermana Dulce es la chica más valiente que conozco. Dudo que ella sepa cuánto la admiramos. Hace tres años sufrió un accidente de coche malísimo. Como resultado, tiene que usar silla de ruedas *(wheelchair).* Pero siempre mantiene el buen humor y actúa de una manera muy positiva. Ahora juega al béisbol en silla de ruedas. Ella es mi heroína.

-Gladys Rubio

Admiro mucho a mi abuelo. La hija de su vecina toca el piano y tiene muchísimo talento. Quería asistir a un conservatorio de música, pero no tenía dinero. Mi abuelo le dio el dinero para pagar sus estudios y luego estableció un fondo para los músicos jóvenes sin recursos financieros. ¡No creo que vaya a tener problemas en encontrar candidatos!

Pablo Castaño

Mi maestra es una persona extraordinaria. Su valentía es increíble. Un día hubo un incendio *(fire)* en nuestra escuela. Nuestra maestra se arriesgó para volver al edificio y ayudar a salir a un estudiante que tenía miedo. No es cierto que todos los héroes estén en las películas...

Grisel Bravo

9 Comprensión de las cartas al editor

Hablar Escribir

tocar	tener
saber	existir

Completa las siguientes oraciones con las formas correctas de los verbos de la lista.

1. La hermana de Dulce duda que ella ____ cuánto la admira su familia.
2. El nieto no cree que su abuelo ____ que buscar mucho para encontrar candidatos.
3. No es verdad que el abuelo ____ el violín.
4. La estudiante dice que no es cierto que los héroes ____ solamente en las películas.

10 Héroes y heroínas

Hablar

no es verdad	no estar seguro(a)
no es cierto	dudar
no creer	

Con un(a) compañero(a), haz comentarios sobre los héroes y las heroínas que Enrique considera para el foto ensayo.

modelo: Dulce / pesimista

A: Yo creo que Dulce es una chica pesimista.

B: No es verdad que Dulce sea pesimista. Es una chica optimista.

1. Dulce / saber jugar al básquetbol
2. Dulce / ser voluntaria en el hogar de ancianos
3. el abuelo / tocar el violín
4. el abuelo / no quiere ayudar a su vecina
5. la maestra / ser tímida
6. la maestra / buscar la fama

11 ¿Quién es tu héroe?

Escribir

Escoge a una persona que sea considerada héroe o heroína por la gente. Di quién es y completa las siguientes frases con una opinión personal para decir que tienes algunas dudas sobre esa persona.

1. Dudo que...
2. No creo que...
3. No es verdad que...
4. No estoy seguro(a) de que...

Expansión
Escribe una nominación de un héroe para un reconocimiento. Usa las historias que Enrique recibió.

PARA Y PIENSA

¿Comprendiste? Completa las frases con la forma apropiada del subjuntivo o indicativo, según la lectura.

1. Dudo que Dulce ____ (saber) cuánto la admiramos.
2. No creo que mi abuelo ____ (ir) a tener problemas en encontrar candidatos.
3. No es cierto que todos los héroes ____ (estar) en las películas.

Get Help Online
ClassZone.com

Presentación de GRAMÁTICA

¡AVANZA! **Goal:** Learn how to use the subjunctive with expressions of emotion. Then practice by discussing both positive and negative emotions. ***Actividades 12–16***

 *¿Recuerdas?* The suffix **-ísimo** p. R31

English Grammar Connection: Expressions of emotion are followed by the **indicative** in English, but the **subjunctive** in Spanish.

I am sorry that you **are** sad. (indicative) **Siento** que **estés** triste. (subjunctive)

Subjunctive with Emotion

Animated Grammar ClassZone.com

After **expressions of emotion** in Spanish, you must use the **subjunctive** regardless of whether or not the information is true.

Here's how: Use the **indicative** for the verb that expresses emotion and the **subjunctive** for the verb that follows.

Expressions of Emotion			
alegrarse (de)	**es sorprendente**	**estar triste**	**temer**
encantar	**es triste**	**gustar**	**tener celos de**
enojarse	**estar contento(a)**	**sorprenderse (de)**	**tener miedo de**
es una lástima	**estar emocionado(a)**	**sentir**	**es una pena**

expression of emotion + **que** + **different subject** + **subjunctive**

Nos alegramos de que tú **actúes** con honor.
We're happy that you act honorably.

Me **gusta** que **podamos** elegir.
I like that we can choose.

No **me sorprendo de** que **sea** difícil.
I'm not surprised that it's difficult.

Temo que no me **entiendas.**
I'm afraid you don't understand me.

Más práctica
Cuaderno *pp. 177–179*
Cuaderno para hispanohablantes *pp. 178–181*

@HomeTutor Leveled Practice ClassZone.com

Práctica de GRAMÁTICA

12 ¿Cómo se sienten?

Hablar
Escribir

Elige un verbo de emoción apropiado y haz oraciones completas con el subjuntivo para describir las emociones de cada sujeto.

alegrarse de que
sentir que
es una lástima que
estar contento(a)
sorprenderse de que

modelo: yo / (tú) sacar buenas notas
Yo me alegro de que tú saques buenas notas.

1. tú / (yo) lograr mis metas
2. Daniel / (sus hermanos) no jugar con él
3. nuestros papás / (nosotros) ser famosos
4. Alberto y Rosa / (tú) ser realista
5. Raúl / Luciana no creer en la amistad

13 ¡Qué emoción!

Escribir
Hablar

Completa los mensajes instantáneos con el subjuntivo del verbo apropiado. Después practícalo con tu compañero(a) y preséntalo en clase.

conocer	viajar
poder	saber
tener	ir

boricua43: Me alegro de que __**1.**__ buenas noticias. ¿Qué pasa?
salsa007: ¡Voy a estudiar español en Puerto Rico!
boricua43: ¡Qué bueno que tú __**2.**__ a Puerto Rico!
salsa007: Vamos a estudiar con artistas, músicos, periodistas...
boricua43: Espero que __**3.**__ a mi tío. Es un artista muy famoso en Puerto Rico. Siento que yo no __**4.**__ acompañarte.
salsa007: Bien, pero espero que __**5.**__ conmigo el año que viene.
boricua43: ¿Ya planeas volver el año que viene?
salsa007: ¡Claro! Me sorprende que no __**6.**__ que me encanta Puerto Rico.

Expansión
Expresa cuatro dudas sobre el viaje de «salsa007» y hazle cuatro recomendaciones. Usa el subjuntivo.

AUDIO

Pronunciación La letra j

La **j** se pronuncia como la **g** suave en la palabra **generoso.** Es importante no confundirse entre la **j** y la **g** al escribir una palabra con ese sonido.

jamás **trabajador social**
jefe **mejorar**

Refrán

Jóvenes y viejos, juntos necesitamos consejos.

14 ¡Grandísimo!

 *¿Recuerdas?* The suffix **-ísimo** p. R31

Hablar
Escribir

Contesta las siguientes preguntas usando el subjuntivo y expresiones de emoción con el superlativo del adjetivo terminado en **-ísimo(a).**

modelo: ¿Son inteligentes los estudiantes?
Espero que sean inteligentísimos.

1. ¿Es simpático el cartero?
2. ¿Es cuidadoso el veterinario?
3. ¿Es importante el deber?
4. ¿Son ingeniosos los carpinteros?
5. ¿Es organizada la secretaria?
6. ¿Es inteligente el técnico?

15 ¡Qué sorprendente!

Hablar
Escribir

Haz una lista de cinco cosas interesantes de tu vida o personalidad. Díselas a tu compañero(a). Él o ella responderá con una expresión de emoción y el subjuntivo. Luego, cambien de papel.

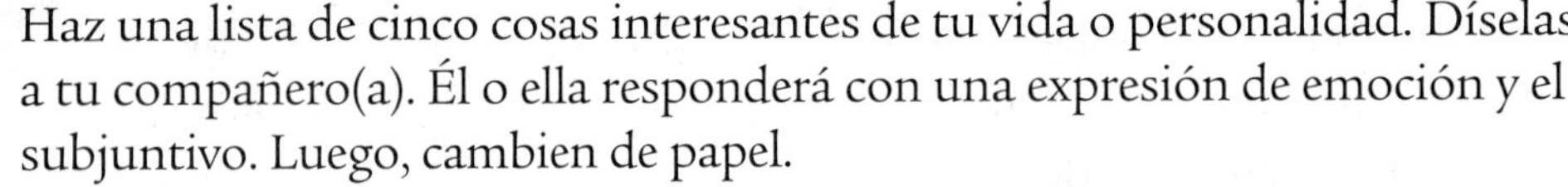

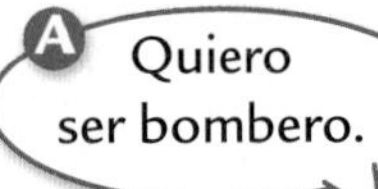

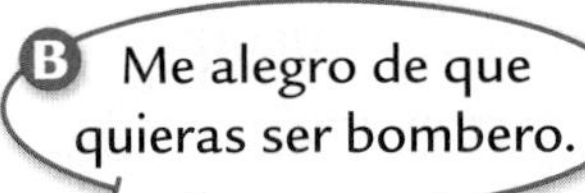

Expansión
Escoge tres de los ejemplos de tu compañero(a) y explica tu reacción.

16 Me gusta, no me gusta

Leer
Escribir

Comparación cultural

La pintura y los héroes

¿Cómo puede representar un artista a sus héroes? Óscar Ortiz nació en Nueva York y pasó su niñez en **Puerto Rico**. De niño, le encantaba hacer dibujos de los super-héroes de las tiras cómicas. En sus pinturas usa líneas sencillas, colores vivos y un estilo alegre. Muchas de sus obras representan al jíbaro, el campesino puertorriqueño. Ortiz considera al jíbaro como un héroe por sus valores tradicionales. En este cuadro, un jíbaro cuida a su hijo y trabaja la tierra.

Mi futuro y mi tierra *(2003)*, Óscar Ortiz

Compara con tu mundo *¿Qué incluirías en una pintura sobre el heroísmo y los héroes de tu sociedad?*

Escribe sobre el cuadro. Usa las siguientes expresiones.

1. El jíbaro está contento de que...
2. Me gusta que...
3. Creo que...

Más práctica Cuaderno *pp. 177–179* Cuaderno para hispanohablantes *pp. 178–181*

Get Help Online
ClassZone.com

¿Comprendiste? Completa las frases con terminaciones diferentes.

1. Me enoja que...
2. Mis tíos sienten que...
3. Yo me alegro de que...

Todo junto

¡AVANZA! **Goal:** ***Show what you know*** Notice the ways that Enrique, Rebeca, and Silvia use the subjunctive in the following dialogue. Then use the subjunctive with expressions of doubt and emotion to talk about people you admire. ***Actividades 17–19***

Resumen contextos 1 y 2 Enrique es el editor de una revista escolar. Él solicitó, de sus lectores, historias sobre héroes de la vida diaria con el propósito de usarlas en un foto ensayo *(photo essay)* para la revista. Recibió tres cartas interesantes.

Contexto 3 *Diálogo*

ESTRATEGIA **Escuchar**
Listen for the plan, the possibility, and the problem As you listen, identify the following three things: Rebeca and Enrique's plan, the new possibility, and the problem that arises. Write your answers on a three-column chart.

Enrique piensa hacer un foto ensayo sobre los héroes. Ahora está preparando su trabajo con la ayuda de su amiga Rebeca.

Enrique: Bueno, Rebeca, ¿qué te parece?

Rebeca: Me gustan todas las historias. Y podemos usar muchas más.

Enrique: ¡Olvídate de eso! Seguramente los lectores enviarán más cartas hoy, pero dudo que podamos usar más. Tenemos que terminar el foto ensayo en una hora. ¡A ver! ¡Rápido! ¿Qué historias tenemos?

Rebeca: Primero, Dulce, la niña que usa silla de ruedas, juega al béisbol y trabaja como voluntaria enseñando ese deporte a otros jóvenes en sillas de ruedas.

Enrique: Segundo, el abuelo que estableció un fondo para ayudar a los músicos jóvenes...

Rebeca: Sí, y la maestra que salvó a un estudiante de un incendio en la escuela.

Enrique: Perfecto. Cuánto me alegra que haya una selección buena.

También se dice

Enrique usa la expresión **¡Olvídate de eso!** para decirle a Rebeca que no insista en la idea de utilizar todas las historias.

- **Puerto Rico y Cuba** **¡Olvídate de los peces de colores!**
- **España** **Dale vuelta a la página.**
- **Perú** **Échale tierra al asunto.**

Suena el teléfono...

Enrique: Un momento, Rebeca... ¿Hola? Sí, Enrique Rivera.

Silvia: Hola, Enrique. No creo que me conozca... Me llamo Silvia Martínez. Ojalá no sea demasiado tarde para contarle la historia de un héroe auténtico.

Enrique: No, no. Estamos trabajando en el foto ensayo ahora mismo.

Silvia

Silvia: Es sólo un minuto; nuestro cartero es un hombre muy dedicado... Pues, ayer se arriesgó a salvar a una niñita de tres años que corrió hacia la calle enfrente de un coche... Es un verdadero héroe, porque sólo pensó en la niña.

Enrique: ¡Qué bueno que la niña esté bien! ¿Tiene una foto del cartero?

Silvia: Sí. ¿Quiere que la lleve a la oficina? Luego puedo contarle los detalles.

Enrique: Gracias, señorita Martínez. Hasta pronto...

Rebeca: ¿Qué pasa?

Enrique: Espera y te lo cuento... ¿Crees que podamos usar una historia más?

17 Comprensión del diálogo

Escuchar
Hablar
Escribir

¿Con quién(es) asocias las siguientes oraciones?

Enrique

Rebeca

Silvia

el cartero

modelo: **Están preparando un foto ensayo sobre los héroes locales.**
Enrique y Rebeca

1. Cree que se puedan usar muchas más historias.
2. Se alegra de que haya una buena selección de historias.
3. Llama para explicar lo que pasó en su calle.
4. Espera que no sea demasiado tarde para nominar a otro héroe.
5. Actuó con mucha valentía.
6. Cambió de opinión y considerará a otro héroe.

Expansión
Escoge tu carta preferida y explica por qué debe ser el héroe N° 1.

18 Integración

Leer
Escuchar
Hablar

Lee la contracubierta *(back cover)* del libro *Un verdadero héroe.* Luego escucha la presentación de la obra en la Feria del Libro de Puerto Rico. Después, escoge dos elementos del artículo y dos del discurso y explica si estás de acuerdo o no con ellos.

Fuente 1 Contracubierta del libro

Muchos dicen que hoy día ya no hay políticos que se dediquen a luchar por la gente común. Pues, Ariel Vasconcelos no es el típico político. Este hombre sorprendente por su visión realista y práctica no busca la fama. Su meta es lograr cambios auténticos que permitan que todos los jóvenes de nuestra comunidad tengan las oportunidades educativas y laborales necesarias para convertirse en adultos capaces de destacarse en cualquier profesión. No hay estudiante que no pueda aprender, dice Vasconcelos, y no hay joven que no sea responsable de sus acciones. Lo importante es ofrecerles verdaderas oportunidades. Este libro, *Un verdadero héroe*, es el más importante de su carrera como político. Aquí, Vasconcelos da consejos importantísimos para todos los jóvenes.

Fuente 2 Presentación

Escucha y apunta

- ¿Qué cualidades tiene Ariel Vasconcelos?
- ¿Por qué es importante su libro?

modelo: Ariel Vasconcelos es un político sincero pero dudo que su libro sea el más importante de su carrera. Sin embargo, me encanta que les dé consejos a los jóvenes...

19 ¡A escribir!

Escribir

Escoge a una persona que admiras y escribe una descripción de tres párrafos. El primer párrafo debe identificar y describir a la persona. El segundo debe explicar por qué admiras a la persona. En tu conclusión, incluye algún comentario sobre lo que esperas de esa persona.

Writing Criteria	Excellent	Good	Needs Work
Content	Your description includes many interesting details.	Your description includes some interesting details.	Your description includes few interesting details.
Communication	Your description is organized and easy to follow.	Parts of your description are organized and easy to follow.	Your description is disorganized and hard to follow.
Accuracy	You make few mistakes in grammar and vocabulary.	You make some mistakes in grammar and vocabulary.	You make many mistakes in grammar and vocabulary.

Más práctica Cuaderno *pp. 180–181* Cuaderno para hispanohablantes *pp. 182–183*

¿Comprendiste? Usa cada expresión para escribir oraciones sobre otras personas. Usa el subjuntivo.

1. dudar / él dormir
2. no estar seguro / ella venir temprano
3. alegrarse / tú tener éxito
4. sorprenderse / ellos volver hoy

Get Help Online
ClassZone.com

Lectura literaria

¡AVANZA! **Goal:** Read the following selection by an author who has lived in the United States and the Dominican Republic. Then talk about customs that vary from one culture to another.

Para leer 

ESTRATEGIA **Leer**

Use categories to compare the two places In the story, Tía Lola makes comparisons between the U.S. and the Dominican Republic. Make a chart in which you list all the comparisons she makes.

Estados Unidos	La República Domincana
1. saludar con la mano 2.	1. saludar con besos 2.

Vocabulario para leer

asentir *decir que sí, estar de acuerdo*

avergonzarse *sentir vergüenza o sentirse incómodo ante una situación*

cabina *oficina pequeña donde trabajan los oficiales de inmigración*

apretón de manos *saludo formal que se dan las personas, extendiendo el brazo y agarrando la mano de la otra persona*

Nota cultural

Sobre la autora ***Julia Álvarez (1950–)***

Aunque Julia Álvarez nació en la ciudad de Nueva York, su familia regresó a la República Dominicana cuando ella todavía era bebé. Entre sus obras están *Cómo las García perdieron su acento, Antes de ser libres* y *Cuando tía Lola vino de visita a quedarse.* La selección que vas a leer pertenece a este último libro, donde la autora habla de unas Navidades en la República Dominicana.

Sobre las costumbres populares La palabra **ñapa** viene de la palabra quechua **yapay,** que significa «dar más». Esta palabra se refiere a la costumbre que existe en los mercados y en las tiendas pequeñas de darle al cliente un poquito más de lo que ha comprado. Esta tradición sirve para agradecerle al cliente y animarlo a que vuelva a comprar allí. Esta costumbre existe en muchos países, como Argentina, donde se llama la **yapa;** en Cuba, donde se llama la **contra,** y aun en Nueva Orleans, donde la palabra mantiene su pronunciación española pero con ortografía francesa: *lagniappe.*

Vista aérea de la República Dominicana

La ñapa

AUDIO

Miguel mira desde su asiento en el avión, junto a la ventanilla[1]. La República Dominicana se extiende bajo sus ojos como una enorme alfombra verde esmeralda, bordeada de playas de arena blanca como la nieve. Hace algunas horas, la tierra era un borrón[2] gris. Cuesta creer[3] que es diciembre, y que en dos días será Navidad.

Junto a él, en el asiento del medio, tía Lola les da unos consejos de última hora sobre las costumbres de la isla.

—Los americanos saludan de mano —dice— pero los dominicanos preferimos saludarnos con besos.

En el asiento del pasillo[4], Juanita escucha la lección atentamente.

—¿Por eso siempre nos das besos, tía Lola?

—¿Es que acaso les doy tantos besos? —les pregunta ella.

Miguel asiente con la cabeza, para que tía Lola no le pregunte si está prestando atención. Observa los exuberantes campos verdes acercarse más y más. Los árboles diminutos se vuelven[5] de tamaño natural y las figuras que parecían hormigas[6] se transforman en gente de verdad.

---

[1] plane window [2] blur [3] **Cuesta...** It is hard to believe
[4] aisle [5] **se...** become [6] ants

Reflexiona

¿Dónde están los personajes? ¿Adónde van? ¿De dónde vienen?

Lectura literaria *continuación*

Arte naif de la República Dominicana

En cuanto a los besos de tía Lola, Juanita tiene razón. Tía Lola les da un beso cuando llegan a casa, así como cuando salen. Les da un beso al acostarse por la noche y cuando se levantan por la mañana. Si quiere darles las gracias o decirles que lo siente o felicitarlos[7] por ayudarle a limpiar la casa, también les da un beso. De pronto, Miguel se pone nervioso. Está a punto de encontrar una isla llena de gente a la que le gusta dar besos tanto como a su tía.

A pensar
Si Miguel está acostumbrado a que tía Lola les dé besos, ¿por qué se pone nervioso ante el comentario de su tía?

—Si van al mercado —dice tía Lola—, y compran una docena de mangos, no olviden pedir su ñapa.

—¿Y eso qué es? —pregunta Juanita.

—Una ñapa es un poquitico más que te dan al final. Si compras una funda[8] de naranjas y pides tu ñapa, te dan una naranja de más o tal vez una guayaba[9] o un cajuil[10] o un caramelo. Si comes flan y pides tu ñapa, te dan un poco más. Digamos que una familia tiene siete hijos y luego nace otro. A ese último lo llaman la ñapa.

....

Es el primer viaje de Miguel a la isla de donde vienen sus padres. ¿Cómo será?

De pronto, piensa que debería haberle puesto[11] más atención a las lecciones de tía Lola durante el recorrido[12] desde Vermont.

Cuando entran a la terminal, un conjunto musical empieza a tocar un merengue. Todo el mundo se pone a bailar[13], entre ellos tía Lola y mami y Juanita. Miguel se alegra de que ninguno de sus amigos viva aquí, así no tiene por qué avergonzarse.

---

[7] congratulate them [8] bag [9] guava [10] cashew
[11] **debería...** he should have paid [12] journey, trip [13] **se...** starts dancing

Se paran en una larga cola a esperar su turno. Algunas de las personas tienen pasaportes rojos. Los suyos son azules.

—¿Por qué? —le pregunta Juanita a mamá.

—Porque somos ciudadanos de Estados Unidos. Los dominicanos tienen pasaportes rojos.

Juanita se siente orgullosa de tener un pasaporte de Estados Unidos, aunque le gustaría que Estados Unidos hubieran escogido [14] el rojo, su color preferido.

El agente de la cabina de vidrio revisa sus pasaportes, y mira a Miguel y luego a Juanita.

—No parecen americanos —le dice a su mamá.

—¡Sí somos americanos! —Miguel suelta de sopetón [15]. Se pregunta qué lo hace ser un verdadero americano. ¿Haber nacido en Nueva York y no en la República Dominicana como sus papás? ¿Hablar en inglés? ¿Que su equipo preferido de béisbol sean los Yanquis? ¿Que todavía le gusten más los *hot dogs* que el arroz con habichuelas [16]?

En realidad, cuando Miguel mira a su alrededor, se parece más a los dominicanos de pasaportes rojos que a sus compañeros de escuela de Vermont.

Miguel recuerda parte de la lección que tía Lola les ha dado en el avión. Quizá la manera de probar que es americano es actuar como tal. Le sonríe al agente, luego se para de puntillas [17] para darle un apretón de manos. ❈

❈ A pensar
¿Cómo se siente Miguel cuando el agente le dice que no parecen americanos? ¿Crees que está orgulloso de serlo o no?

---

[14] **hubieran...** had chosen [15] **suelta...** blurts out unexpectedly
[16] beans [17] **de...** on tip toes

¿Comprendiste?

1. ¿En dónde nacieron Miguel y Juanita? ¿Y sus padres?
2. ¿Qué diferencias culturales se describen en la selección?
3. ¿Qué consejos les da la tía Lola a Miguel y a Juanita?
4. Según Miguel, ¿qué cosas hace ser americano de verdad?
5. ¿Qué quiere demostrar Miguel cuando se para y saluda al agente?

¿Y tú?

1. ¿Fuiste alguna vez a otro país? Explica tus experiencias.
2. En tu opinión, ¿en qué consiste ser un(a) verdadero(a) ciudadano(a) de Estados Unidos?

Escritura

Un bosquejo biográfico

Vas a entrevistar a una persona y luego escribir un bosquejo *(sketch)* biográfico. Usa la siguiente secuencia de estrategias como ayuda.

1 Prepárate para escribir

ESTRATEGIA **Elige a la persona** Piensa en una persona que conozcas. Si esa persona hizo algo que te interesa, tenlo en cuenta para tus preguntas.

2 Escribe

ESTRATEGIA **Haz preguntas** Una buena técnica de preparación para una entrevista es hacer una lista de preguntas. Las respuestas te servirán para preparar el bosquejo. Enfoca tus preguntas en los aspectos de la vida de la persona que quieres examinar. Recuerda que necesitas información sobre la historia de la persona y también sobre su vida actual *(current)*. Usa las siguientes palabras interrogativas de la tabla para escribir tus preguntas.

¿Quién?	¿Cómo?	¿Qué?	¿Cuándo?	¿Dónde?	¿Por qué?

- Si es posible, usa un grabador para grabar la entrevista.
- Escucha la entrevista que grabaste y toma apuntes. Para organizarlos, agrupa la información de la siguiente manera:

Primer párrafo (información del presente): *Mi veterinario se llama Norberto Núñez. Tiene cuarenta y dos años y es de Puerto Rico. Tiene dos hijos... Vive...*

Segundo párrafo (información del pasado): *Nació en Mayagüez y decidió estudiar para ser veterinario cuando tenía doce años... Fue a...*

Tercer párrafo Da tu opinión sobre la vida actual de la persona y sobre su futuro posible. Trata de usar varias expresiones con el subjuntivo: *Me alegro de que el Doctor Núñez sea nuestro veterinario. Deseo que trabaje aquí muchos años.*

3 Revisa tu composición

Después de escribir tu primer borrador *(draft)*, intercámbialo con un(a) compañero(a) de clase. Lee el párrafo de tu compañero(a) y corrígelo.

- ¿Es necesario agregar detalles?
- ¿Usó el (la) escritor(a) las formas del pretérito y del imperfecto con precisión en el segundo párrafo?
- ¿Son correctas las formas del subjuntivo en el tercer párrafo?
- Revisa las correcciones que hizo tu compañero(a) y escribe la versión final.

Mi veterinario es el Dr. Rodríguez.

Viajó a Estados Unidos cuando ~~tuvo~~ tenía dieciocho años...

Ojalá que el Dr. Rodríguez siempre ~~será~~ sea el veterinario de mi perrito.

Lección 2

En resumen

Vocabulario y gramática

Vocabulario

Describe People and Things

Descriptions

auténtico(a)	*authentic*	realista	*realistic*
práctico(a)	*practical, down-to-earth*	sorprendente	*surprising*
		verdadero(a)	*real, true, sincere*

Professions

el (la) artista	*artist*	el (la) político(a)	*politician*
el (la) bombero(a)	*firefighter*	el (la) secretario(a)	*secretary*
el (la) carpintero(a)	*carpenter*	el (la) técnico(a)	*technician, repairperson*
el (la) cartero(a)	*mail carrier*		
el (la) músico(a)	*musician*	el (la) vecino(a)	*neighbor*
el (la) periodista	*journalist*	el (la) veterinario(a)	*veterinarian*
el (la) policía	*police officer*		

Express Positive and Negative Emotions

alegrarse de que	*to be happy that*	no es verdad que	*it is not true that*
dudar que	*to doubt that*	no estar seguro(a) (de) que	*not to be sure that*
es dudoso que	*it is doubtful that*		
es improbable que	*it is improbable / unlikely that*	sentir (siento) que	*to be sorry that, to feel*
no creer que	*not to believe that*	sorprenderse de que	*to be surprised that*
no es cierto que	*it is not certain that*		

Actions

actuar	*to act*
aparecer	*to appear*
arriesgarse	*to risk*
convertirse en	*to turn into*
figurar en	*to appear in*
lograr	*to attain, to achieve*

Other Words

la amistad	*friendship*
el deber	*duty*
la fama	*fame*
el honor	*honor*
la imagen	*image*
el logro	*achievement, success*
la meta	*goal*
por eso	*for that reason, that's why*
por lo tanto	*therefore*
el propósito	*purpose, aim*
el sacrificio	*sacrifice*
sin embargo	*nevertheless, however*
la valentía	*bravery*

Gramática

Repaso gramatical: Superlatives *p. 242*

Subjunctive with Doubt

expression of doubt + **que** + **different subject** + **subjunctive**

Marta **no está segura de** que **tengamos** tiempo para ver la película.

Note that the word **no** can affect whether or not you need to use the **subjunctive.**

expresses certainty → **No dudamos** · *indicative* → **tiene**

No dudamos que él **tiene** talento.
***We do not doubt** that he has talent.*

Subjunctive with Emotion

expression of emotion + **que** + **different subject** + **subjunctive**

Nos alegramos de que tú **actúes** con honor.
We're happy that you act with honor.

No **me sorprendo de** que **sea** difícil.
I'm not surprised that it's difficult.

Lección 2

Repaso de la lección

¡LLEGADA!

@HomeTutor
ClassZone.com

Now you can
- describe people and things
- express doubt, denial, and disbelief
- express positive and negative emotions

Using
- subjunctive with doubt
- subjunctive with emotion
- superlatives

To review
- subjunctive with doubt p. 243
- subjunctive with emotion p. 248

1 Listen and understand

AUDIO

Ramona está escuchando uno de sus programas de radio favoritos. Escucha los comentarios de Diana Diamante y completa las oraciones.

1. No es cierto que Víctor Vargas y su esposa ____ .
2. Le sorprende a Diana que Esmeralda no le ____ Diamante a su perrito.
3. No es verdad que Julia Jiménez ____ cinco casas.
4. Es una lástima que Lorenzo Lima no ____ proyectos mejores.
5. Le emociona a Diana que Paloma Palmares ____ pintar tan bien.

To review
- subjunctive with emotion p. 248

2 Express positive and negative emotions

Marisol habla por teléfono con su abuela. Completa las reacciones de Marisol a los comentarios de la abuela. Usa las formas correctas de los verbos indicados.

— Bueno, Marisol, me siento muy bien hoy.

— Ay, abuelita, ¡me alegro de que __1.__ (estar) mejor hoy!

— Pero tengo mucho que hacer y estoy un poco nerviosa.

— Es una pena que __2.__ (tener) tanto que hacer.

— Sí, tengo que llevar el gato al veterinario. Está enfermo y no quiere comer.

— ¡Es una lástima que el gatito no __3.__ (comer)!

— Y tengo que hablar con la vecina... está escuchando la radio muy alto.

— Me sorprende que ella __4.__ (comportarse) así.

To review
- subjunctive with doubt p. 243

3 Express doubt, denial, and disbelief

Reacciona a los comentarios usando expresiones como: **no es cierto que... , dudar que... , no creer que...**

1. La amistad no existe.
2. Los políticos son todos muy honestos.
3. Todo el mundo busca la fama.
4. La valentía no importa.

To review
- superlatives p. 242

4 Describe people and things

Mira los dibujos de las personas y compáralas. Usa formas del superlativo y adjetivos con **-ísimo,** según el modelo.

modelo: cartero / alto
Élmer es el cartero más alto. Es altísimo.

1. superhéroe / atrevido

2. político / bajo

3. bombero / rápido

4. policía / fuerte

To review
- **Comparación cultural** pp. 245, 250

5 Artists and their work

Comparación cultural

1. ¿En qué se inspiró Amelia Peláez para pintar sus cuadros?
2. Menciona dos características de su pintura.
3. ¿Qué significa el jíbaro en el cuadro *Mi futuro y mi tierra,* de Óscar Ortiz?

Más práctica Cuaderno *pp. 182–193* Cuaderno para hispanohablantes *pp. 184–193*

Get Help Online
ClassZone.com

Comparación cultural

Héroes del Caribe

Lectura y escritura

1. **Leer** Lee los datos históricos que mencionan Inés y Fernando sobre la independencia de sus países.

2. **Escribir** Basándote en la narración de Inés y Fernando, escribe una biografía en forma de ensayo sobre un héroe o una heroína de tu comunidad o estado.

ESTRATEGIA Escribir

Follow a model for your essay Use the model for the four parts of the essay: (a) introduction (person's name and reason for being a hero/heroine), (b) person's main qualities and ideals, (c) key dates and events, and (d) summary or final insight.

- Introducción
- Nombre del héroe
- ¿Qué hizo?

Cualidades e ideales

Fechas y hechos

Conclusión

Paso 1 Dibuja cuatro óvalos como los de arriba. Cada óvalo representa un párrafo de la biografía sobre un héroe o una heroína de tu comunidad o estado.

Paso 2 Usando las narraciones de Inés y de Fernando como guía, escribe tu ensayo de cuatro párrafos.

Paso 3 Revisa la gramática y la ortografía.

Compara con tu mundo

Usa el ensayo que escribiste y compara tu héroe o heroína con las heroínas de Inés y de Fernando. ¿Hicieron cosas parecidas? ¿Tenían ideales similares? ¿Fueron héroes para el país o para una comunidad? Explica.

Cuaderno *pp. 194–196* Cuaderno para hispanohablantes *pp. 194–196*

Puerto Rico

Inés

Hola. Soy Inés Costa y vivo en San Juan, la capital de Puerto Rico. Su parte vieja es muy famosa. Allí se encuentra el Fuerte San Felipe del Morro, una fortaleza española construida entre 1540 y 1783. ¡Es enorme! Tiene 140 pies de altura. Es un sitio del Patrimonio Cultural de la UNESCO. Sugiero que lo visites.

A mí me encanta la historia. Una de nuestras heroínas es Mariana Bracetti. Ella vivió entre 1825 y 1903 y la admiramos por su valor, patriotismo y apoyo a la lucha por la independencia. Hizo la primera bandera de Puerto Rico y participó en el Grito de Lares, el primer movimiento independentista de Puerto Rico. Aunque esa iniciativa fracasó, Puerto Rico por fin ganó su independencia de España en 1897.

Fernando

¿Cómo estás? Me llamo Fernando Burgos y vivo en la ciudad de Santo Domingo. Aquí se estableció la primera colonia española en el Nuevo Mundo. La zona colonial de mi ciudad tiene unos edificios muy antiguos, como la Catedral Santa María la Menor, que es la primera catedral del Nuevo Mundo.

La República Dominicana es una isla que se llamaba Quisqueya. Luego los españoles la llamaron La Española. Nuestro país tuvo muchos conflictos con España y con Haití, que comparte la isla con nosotros. Entre nuestros héroes de la independencia tenemos a Juana Trinidad, conocida como la «coronela inmortal». No creo que haya nadie más valiente que ella. Luchó contra el ejército haitiano en Santiago, donde arriesgó su vida para llegar al río Yaque y llevarles agua a sus compañeros.

República Dominicana

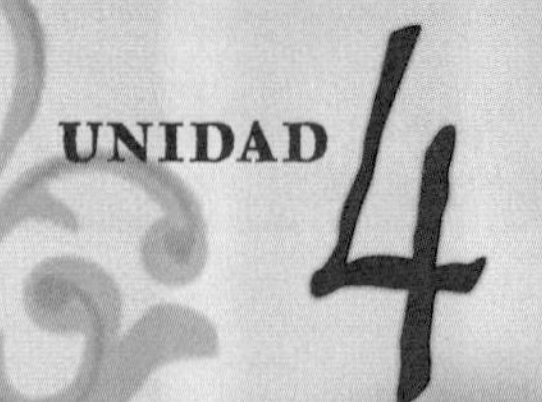

EL DESAFÍO

VIDEO DVD

En este desafío, todos deben descansar un poco y tomarse unos minutos para conocerse un poco mejor. Luego, cada uno debe escribir en una tarjeta el adjetivo que mejor describa su personalidad. Los otros equipos deben adivinar el adjetivo, pero sólo tienen una oportunidad.

Antes del video

1. ¿Cómo es Marco? ¿Qué adjetivo crees que describe mejor la personalidad de Marco?

2. ¿Qué crees que está leyendo Carmen? Escribe un adjetivo que describa la personalidad de Carmen.

3. ¿Qué adjetivos describen mejor a María? ¿Cómo describirán los otros a ella?

Comparando descripciones

Mira el video: Toma apuntes

- ¿Qué le recomienda el profesor a Carmen?
- ¿Qué quiere el profesor que hagan todos antes del próximo desafío?
- ¿A quién le gusta leer sobre la vida de los artistas famosos?
- Según Ana, ¿cómo es José?
- ¿Quién escribe «orgullosa» en la tarjeta?
- ¿Por qué se enoja María con Luis?

Después del video

1. ¿Qué equipo ganó este desafío? ¿Qué pasó?
2. Lee la lista de adjetivos que escribiste sobre los personajes. ¿Cuántos adjetivos adivinaste?
3. En tu opinión, ¿por qué crees que fue difícil adivinar los adjetivos correctos?

@HomeTutor VideoPlus
ClassZone.com

"DEDICADO"

UNIDADES 1-4

Repaso inclusivo

Options for Review

1 Escucha, comprende y compara

Escuchar

Escucha este comentario sobre Celia Cruz. Luego contesta las preguntas.

1. ¿De dónde era Celia Cruz?
2. ¿Cuál era su profesión?
3. ¿A qué país inmigró?
4. ¿Era valiente y atrevida o presumida y vanidosa?
5. ¿Qué personifica?

2 Investiga y describe

Hablar
Escribir

Con un(a) compañero(a), investiga la vida y contribuciones de un(a) caribeño(a) famoso(a). Por ejemplo, Gloria Estefan, Pedro Martínez, Víctor Rasuk, Celia Cruz, Ricky Martin, Juan Luis Guerra, Roberto Clemente o José Martí. Luego, preparen un breve reportaje sobre la vida y las características admirables de esa persona y preséntenlo en clase.

3 Escribe un artículo periodístico

Escribir
Hablar

Prepara un artículo sobre un héroe o heroína de tu comunidad o estado. Incluye una foto de tu héroe e información sobre su vida, su profesión, su personalidad, sus logros y sus esperanzas para el futuro. Luego, un(a) compañero(a) deberá leerlo e indicar cuáles son las características más importantes.

4 Solicita colaboración

Escribir

Escribe una carta en la que pides la colaboración de alguna persona famosa de México, Centroamérica o el Caribe para un proyecto en tu comunidad. Explica el proyecto y por qué puede ser interesante para esa persona. Incluye al menos cinco ejemplos del subjuntivo en tu carta.

5 Presenta un programa de televisión

Hablar

Con tus compañeros(as), preparen un programa de charla *(talk show)* en que un(a) locutor(a) invita a dos personas famosas de México, Centroamérica o el Caribe. Piensen, por ejemplo, en el encuentro de dos políticos, dos artistas o dos escritores. ¿Qué tienen en común esas dos personas? ¿Cuáles son sus diferencias? Preparen una conversación realista. El (La) locutor(a) debe presentar a sus dos invitados y dirigir la conversación con preguntas apropiadas. Usen mandatos.

6 Da tu opinión por la radio

Hablar

Eres locutor(a) de radio. Háblales a tus oyentes, diciendo cómo crees que será el mundo en los próximos años y lo que deseas para el futuro. Utiliza también expresiones impersonales.

7 Organiza un viaje

Hablar
Escribir

Tú y tus compañeros(as) son agentes de viaje y quieren organizar un viaje de una semana a México, algún país de Centroamérica o el Caribe, con un enfoque histórico, ecológico o cultural. Como el viaje es de tiempo limitado, deben considerar con cuidado qué pueden incluir en el itinerario. Preparen un folleto informativo para distribuir durante la presentación promocional que hacen en clase. Incluyan verbos en el futuro.

UNIDAD 5

Los países andinos

¿Cómo te entretienes?

Ecuador
Quito
Tigua
Coca
Guayaquil
Machala
Islas Galápagos
Trujillo
Perú
Lima
Machu Picchu
Cuzco
Bolivia
La Paz
Sucre
Océano Pacífico

Lección 1

Tema: ***Comuniquémonos entre naciones***

Lección 2

Tema: ***Nuevos amigos, nuevas oportunidades***

«¡Hola a todos!
Somos Raúl, de Bolivia, y Gladys, de Perú.»

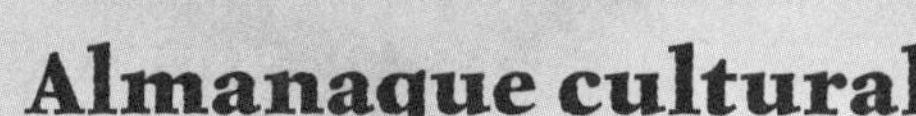

Almanaque cultural

Capitales: Ecuador: Quito; Perú: Lima; Bolivia: La Paz y Sucre

Geografía y clima: Zonas más bajas: (con calor durante el día y fresco por la noche). Zonas altas, como Machu Picchu (temperatura extremadamente fría).

Comidas: llapingachos, ceviche, papas a la huancaína, llunca, picante de pollo, fricasé

Lenguas indígenas: quechua, aymara

Gente famosa: Franklin Briones (director de cine, Ecuador), Tania Libertad (cantante, Perú), Mario Vargas Llosa (escritor, Perú), Claudia Cornejo (atleta, Bolivia)

Sopa de pimientos

Jóvenes viendo un partido de fútbol de la selección de Ecuador

◀ **La amistad** Los jóvenes latinoamericanos comparten sus gustos con sus amigos. Los deportes, la música y el cine sirven para reunirse y divertirse en compañía de los mejores amigos. No importa el lugar ni la hora; lo importante es la amistad. *¿Qué gustos compartes con tu mejor amigo(a)?*

Historia indígena En las ruinas de los países andinos puedes ver la riqueza de la cultura indígena. En lugares como Machu Picchu (Perú), Ingapirca (Ecuador) y Tiwanaku (Bolivia) puedes ver cómo vivían las antiguas civilizaciones. *¿Qué indígenas vivían en tu estado?* ▶

Camino Inca, Perú

El lago Titicaca Está entre Bolivia y Perú, y es el lago más alto del mundo (3800 m). Aquí estuvo el imperio inca, por eso esta zona está llena de misterios y leyendas. Sus montañas eran ricas en oro y plata, y sus tierras apropiadas para cultivar papas. *¿Qué lago hay cerca de tu ciudad?* ▼

Indígena aymara navegando en el lago Titicaca

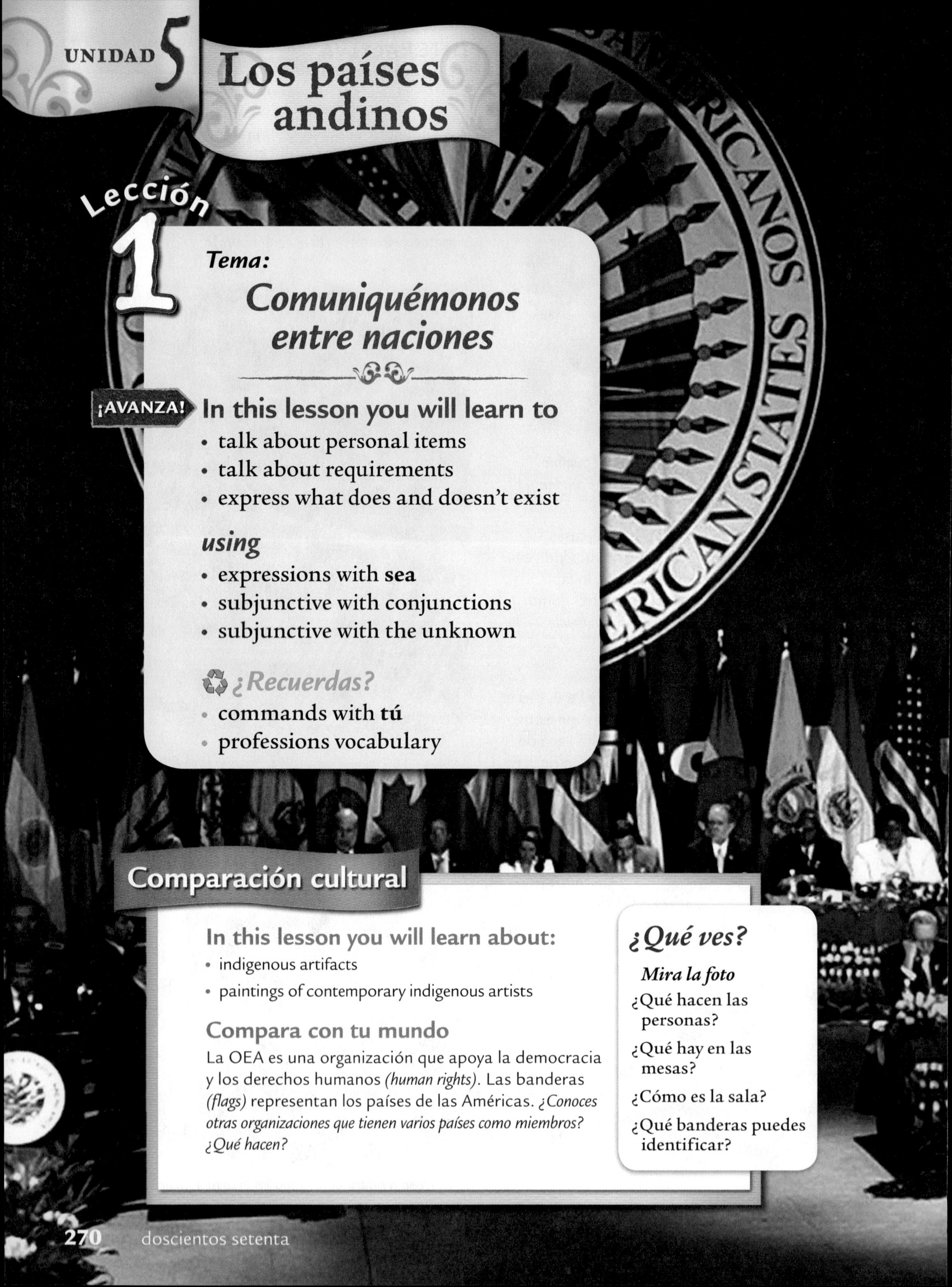

UNIDAD 5

Los países andinos

Lección 1

Tema:

Comuniquémonos entre naciones

¡AVANZA! **In this lesson you will learn to**

- talk about personal items
- talk about requirements
- express what does and doesn't exist

using

- expressions with **sea**
- subjunctive with conjunctions
- subjunctive with the unknown

¿Recuerdas?

- commands with **tú**
- professions vocabulary

Comparación cultural

In this lesson you will learn about:

- indigenous artifacts
- paintings of contemporary indigenous artists

Compara con tu mundo

La OEA es una organización que apoya la democracia y los derechos humanos *(human rights)*. Las banderas *(flags)* representan los países de las Américas. *¿Conoces otras organizaciones que tienen varios países como miembros? ¿Qué hacen?*

¿Qué ves?

Mira la foto

¿Qué hacen las personas?

¿Qué hay en las mesas?

¿Cómo es la sala?

¿Qué banderas puedes identificar?

Online SPANISH CLASSZONE.COM

Featuring...
Cultura INTERACTIVA
Animated Grammar
@HomeTutor

And more...
- Get Help Online
- Interactive Flashcards
- Review Games
- WebQuest
- Conjuguemos.com

Asamblea de la Organización de Estados Americanos (OEA)
Quito, Ecuador

Presentación de VOCABULARIO

¡AVANZA! **Goal:** Learn vocabulary relating to computers and other valuable items. Then talk about personal items and about how to use the Internet. ***Actividades 1–3***

¿Recuerdas? Commands with **tú** p. 97

AUDIO

A Raúl está buscando información en Internet sobre una conferencia, en Lima, en que va a participar. Él ve que su abuela quiere aprender a usar Internet y se ofrece a enseñarle.

B «Bueno, abuela, veo que **estás ilusionada** con aprender a **conectarte a Internet** y **sospecho que** quieres que te enseñe. Por eso te voy a **dar unas sugerencias.**

Antes de que te conectes, debes escribir tu nombre y **la contraseña.** Si quieres, utiliza mi **computadora portátil, a fin de que** puedas conectarte desde **distintos** lugares de la casa.»

C «Saber conectarse a Internet es una información muy **valiosa.** Podrás hacer **búsquedas** sobre tus temas favoritos, **descargar** fotos y participar en **los salones de charlas** que te interesen. ¡Recuerda que nunca debes dar información personal! **Te darás cuenta de** cómo pasar de un **sitio web** a otro; sólo tienes que seguir **los enlaces** que aparecen en ellos. Y otra cosa muy importante, ¡aprenderás a **enviar** correos electrónicos **en caso de que** quieras comunicarte conmigo mientras yo esté en la conferencia!»

D Raúl **teme que** su equipaje para la conferencia no esté completo. Él no sabe qué quiere **guardar** en su maleta.

Más vocabulario

a menos que... *unless*
con tal (de) que... *as long as*
hasta que... *until*
para que... *in order that*
sin que... *without*
los ahorros *savings*
el documento (de identidad) *(identification) document*
el monedero *coin purse*
precioso(a) *precious*
sin valor *worthless*
dar consejos *to give advice*
disfrutar de *to enjoy*
esconder *to hide*
evitar *to avoid*
imprimir *to print*
ponerse de acuerdo *to agree*

Expansión de vocabulario p. R10
Ya sabes p. R10

¡A responder! Escuchar

Escucha la lista de palabras. Si es una cosa física que puedes llevar contigo, levanta la mano derecha. Si es una cosa relacionada con las computadoras y que no puedes llevar contigo, levanta la mano izquierda.

Práctica de VOCABULARIO

1 ¿Qué es?

Hablar
Escribir

Identifica cada artículo.

la cartera	el escáner
la bolsa	la agenda electrónica
el paraguas	el salón de charlas
la contraseña	

modelo: un lugar en el ciberespacio para reunirse con gente: el salón de charlas

1. un aparato portátil para guardar información
2. un objeto para llevar otros artículos
3. un aparato para copiar documentos o imágenes
4. un artículo para protegerse de la lluvia o el sol
5. un objeto para meter dinero y documentos de identidad
6. una palabra que te permite tener acceso a tu computadora

2 La computadora nueva

¿Recuerdas? Commands with **tú** p. 97

Hablar
Escribir

Acabas de comprar una nueva computadora portátil. Tu papá te da instrucciones usando mandatos afirmativos y negativos.

modelo: no conectarse por muchas horas
No te conectes por muchas horas.

1. no olvidarse tu contraseña
2. enviar un correo electrónico a tus abuelos
3. imprimir pocas hojas
4. hacer búsquedas con cuidado
5. no descargar de sitios malos
6. no publicar fotos
7. ponerse de acuerdo para trabajar con tus compañeros
8. leer los enlaces

Expansión
Prepara una lista sobre el uso seguro de las computadoras. Usa mandatos para incluir al menos seis recomendaciones.

3 Mi cartera

Hablar
Escribir

Mira los artículos que tienes en tu cartera o mochila y di cuáles son, para ti, las cosas valiosas y las que no tienen valor.

modelo: La foto de mi perro es muy importante para mí, pero no es valiosa.

Más práctica Cuaderno *pp. 197–199* Cuaderno para hispanohablantes *pp. 197–200*

¿Comprendiste? ¿Qué sitio web visitas para hacer lo siguiente?

1. entrar a un salón de charlas
2. descargar juegos o música
3. hacer una búsqueda
4. comprar juegos o música

Get Help Online
ClassZone.com

VOCABULARIO en contexto

¡AVANZA! **Goal:** Notice how the language used in the following chat room entries reflects each person's personality. Then discuss what you have learned about these characters. ***Actividades 4–5***

Contexto 1 *Salón de charlas*

ESTRATEGIA **Leer**

Summarize the chat room conversation On a separate sheet of paper, sketch three large, connected computers, each identifying a participant in the chat room. Use arrows to show the directions of the conversation (who talks to whom). On each person's screen, write the person's main topic(s).

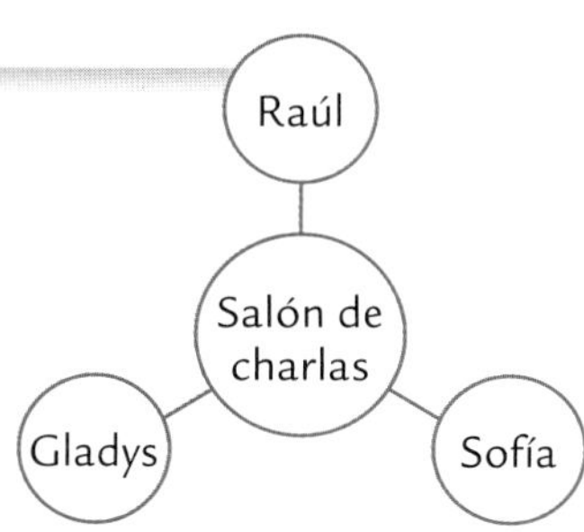

Raúl Méndez es un estudiante boliviano que va a ir a una conferencia estudiantil en Lima, Perú. Como Raúl sale para la conferencia dentro de una semana, participa en un salón de charlas con otros participantes para hablar sobre algunos detalles.

envía | cancela

Raúl — La Paz
Sofía — Guayaquil
Gladys — Lima

09/09 20:23:24 Raúl
<Raúl007@raul4cero.net> escribió:
Hola, estoy muy ilusionado con la idea de participar en la reunión... pero no sé qué debo llevar. ¿Alguien me puede dar sugerencias?

Mensajero instantáneo con Sofía

Sofía <Sofiazul@yahaa.com.ec>
09/09 20:28:42
Hola, Raúl. Soy ecuatoriana y estoy lista para ir a Lima. Pues, yo siempre llevo paraguas ***y*** gafas de sol... nunca se sabe, ¿verdad? También llevo un monedero. Es más seguro que una bolsa grande. Tienes que llevar tus documentos de identidad: el pasaporte y la tarjeta de identidad estudiantil. ¿Recibiste la lista de información del comité de la reunión? Si no, te la puedo enviar o la puedes descargar del sitio web. Tu maestro también te puede dar más sugerencias.
¡Hasta pronto!

Mensajero instantáneo con Gladys

09/09 20:38:17 Gladys
<superestrellaperu@correo.rr.pe> escribió:
¡Bienvenidos, Raúl y Sofía! Soy de Lima, así que les puedo dar algunos consejos. Traigan una cartera y un monedero, pero tengan cuidado de guardarlos en un sitio seguro. Sólo pongan los artículos sin mucho valor. Como vamos a ir a muchas reuniones, mi maestra recomienda que lleve una agenda electrónica para organizar todos los detalles... y también una computadora portátil, si la tienen. Me alegra decirles que hace muy buen tiempo en este momento... ¡Ojalá que siga así para poder disfrutar de un paseo! Bueno, eso es todo. Escríbanme si hay algo más que quieran saber. ¡¡¡Los veo la semana próxima!!!

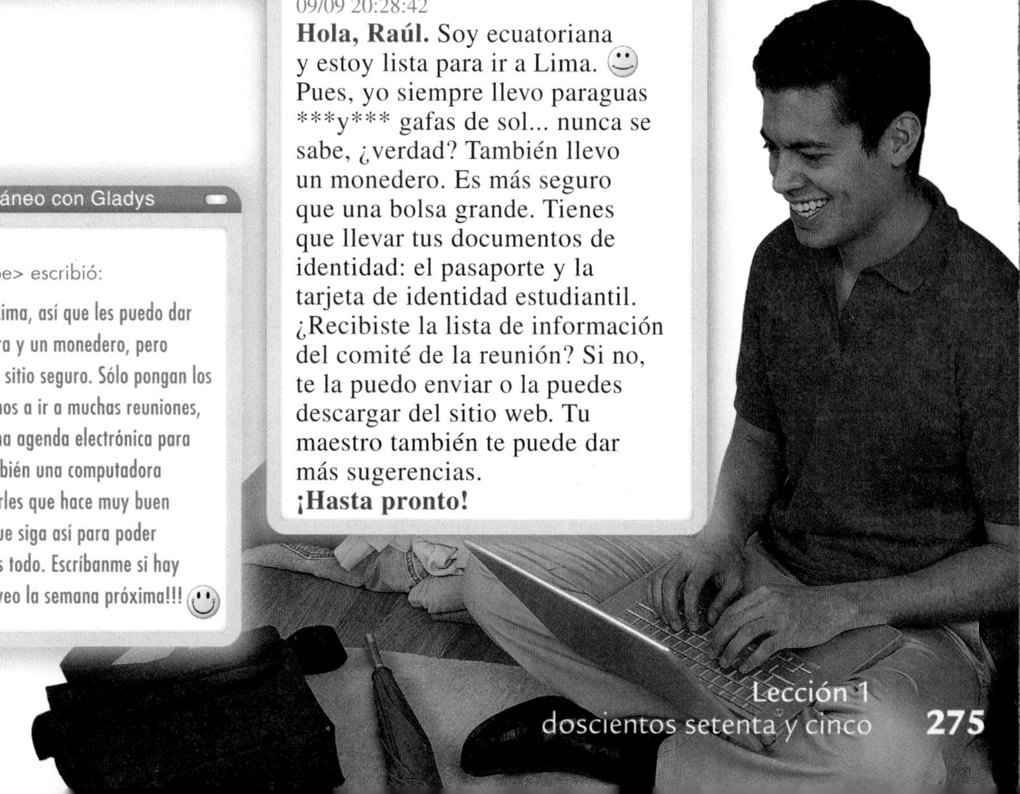

4 Comprensión del salón de charlas

Leer
Hablar

Contesta las siguientes preguntas sobre la lectura.

1. ¿De qué país es Raúl?
2. ¿De qué país es Sofía?
3. ¿De qué país es Gladys?
4. ¿Qué cosas recomienda Sofía que lleve Raúl?
5. ¿Qué cosas recomienda Gladys que Raúl y Sofía traigan?
6. ¿Cuándo va a ser la conferencia?

Expansión
¿Qué recomiendas tú llevar a la conferencia de Lima?

Nota gramatical

Expressions with sea If you are not sure about the details of who, when, what or where, you can use the following expressions with **sea** to indicate your uncertainty.

a la hora que sea *at whatever time that may be*	**donde sea** *wherever that may be*	**lo que sea** *whatever that may be*
cuando sea *whenever that may be*	**quien sea** *whoever that may be*	**como sea** *however that may be*

Por favor, llámame cuando llegues, **a la hora que sea.**
Please, call me when you arrive, ***at whatever time that may be.***

Siempre lo pasamos bien en la playa, en la ciudad, o **donde sea.**
We always have a good time at the beach, in the city or ***wherever (we may be).***

5 Como sea

Hablar
Escribir

Completa cada oración con una de las expresiones de la lista.

donde sea
cuando sea
quien sea
lo que sea
como sea

modelo: No sé cómo, pero tenemos que completar la tarea... **como sea.**

1. No sé a la hora que van a llegar, pero voy a estar allí...
2. Juliana te da consejos aunque no quieras oírlos; los da...
3. Me emociona enviarle correos electrónicos a...
4. Guarda las cosas preciosas que tengas: el monedero, la cartera o...
5. ¿No sabes si perdiste tu agenda electrónica? Pues, búscala...
6. Dime ...pero yo voy a comprar estos juegos de computadora.

PARA Y PIENSA

¿Comprendiste? Indica cuáles de las siguientes cosas no se mencionan en el salón de charlas.

1. paraguas
2. escáner
3. computadora portátil
4. agenda electrónica
5. monedero
6. mochila

Presentación de GRAMÁTICA

¡AVANZA! **Goal:** Learn how to use the subjunctive after certain conjunctions. Then talk about actions that may happen in the future. ***Actividades 6–9***

 *¿Recuerdas?* Professions vocabulary pp. 212–213

English Grammar Connection: Expressions like *unless, so that,* and *in case* are conjunctions that connect two parts of the same sentence. In English, they are followed by the indicative. In Spanish, they are followed by the **subjunctive.**

I'll take my umbrella **in case** it rains. Traeré mi paraguas **en caso de que llueva.**

Subjunctive with Conjunctions

Some conjunctions must be followed by a **subjunctive** verb form. How do you know which ones?

Here's how: Always use the subjunctive after the following conjunctions because they express doubt or uncertainty about whether or not the events in the second part of the sentence will happen.

Conjunctions Used with Subjunctive			
a fin de que	**antes (de) que**	**en caso (de) que**	**sin que**
a menos que	**con tal (de) que**	**para que**	

No gastes tus ahorros **a menos que sea** necesario.
*Don't spend your savings **unless** it's necessary.*

Voy a imprimir las fotos **para que** todos las **miren.**
*I'm going to print the photos **so that** everyone can look at them.*

When the conjunctions above are used without **que,** the verb that follows must be in the **infinitive** form.

Tendrás que comer **antes de que salgas.**
You'll have to eat before you leave.

Tendrás que comer **antes de salir.**
You'll have to eat before leaving.

Más práctica

Cuaderno *pp. 200–202*

Cuaderno para hispanohablantes *pp. 201–203*

@HomeTutor
Leveled Practice
ClassZone.com

Práctica de GRAMÁTICA

6 Todo depende

¿Recuerdas? Professions vocabulary pp. 212–213, 238–239

Hablar
Escribir

Completa cada oración con la conjunción apropiada.

modelo: **Seré policía (sin que / hasta que) consiga otro trabajo.**
Seré policía hasta que consiga otro trabajo.

1. Los carpinteros deben ser dedicados (para que / sin que) no se aburran de su trabajo.
2. El cartero trabaja (en caso de que / a menos que) esté enfermo.
3. No idealizaremos a los artistas (con tal de que / hasta que) sean famosos.
4. Los bomberos siempre están preparados (en caso de que / a fin de que) haya un incendio.

7 En caso de que

Hablar
Escribir

Completa cada oración con una conjunción de la lista y una idea apropiada.

modelo: Yo voy a llevar el monedero...
Yo voy a llevar el monedero en caso de que tú quieras comprar algo.

para (que)
a menos que
antes de (que)
con tal de (que)
en caso de que

1. Tú usarás los ahorros...
2. María entrará en el salón de charlas...
3. Yo compraré la computadora portátil...
4. Ustedes esconderán...
5. Nosotros estudiaremos el sitio web...

Comparación cultural

El Museo de Metales Preciosos

¿Por qué son valiosos los objetos históricos? El Museo de Metales Preciosos de La Paz, **Bolivia,** se encuentra en una casa colonial que data del siglo XV. La colección de joyería y otros objetos preciosos de oro, plata y cobre *(copper)* fueron hechos por los varios grupos indígenas que ocupaban el territorio que ahora es Bolivia. Los objetos de oro son muy valiosos y se guardan en una sección especial. Otros objetos de un gran valor histórico y gran interés son las cerámicas incaicas y pre-incaicas.

Viracocha, *máscara de oro*

Compara con tu mundo *¿Qué tipo de museos hay en tu ciudad o estado? ¿Cuáles te gustan más y por qué?*

8 ¡Para viajar mejor!

Leer
Hablar
Escribir

Lee la información sobre cómo viajar mejor y contesta las preguntas con respuestas completas. Lee las preguntas antes de leer la información.

1. ¿Qué debes hacer en caso de que tengas que ir a eventos especiales?
2. ¿Qué debes llevar para que puedas disfrutar de cada día?
3. ¿Qué debes hacer antes de que salgas?
4. ¿Cómo puedes evitar que tu familia o amigos estén preocupados?

Para que disfrutes tu próximo viaje...

¡Sigue estos consejos!

- Deja tu itinerario con tu familia. Así podrás disfrutar del viaje sin que ellos estén preocupados.
- No olvides ni las gafas de sol ni el paraguas para que puedas disfrutar cualquier tiempo.
- Antes de que salgas, guarda toda la información importante para tu viaje en tu agenda electrónica.
- Lleva poca ropa a menos que tengas que ir a eventos especiales.

9 ¡Consejos, por favor!

Leer
Escribir

Un estudiante ecuatoriano va a pasar tres semanas con tu familia. Lee su correo electrónico y contéstalo usando al menos cuatro conjunciones.

Hola,

Me estoy preparando para el viaje y no sé qué debo llevar. ¿Me puedes dar algunas sugerencias con respecto a ropa y otras cosas prácticas? También, quisiera aprender algo más sobre tu ciudad y estado. ¿Podrías recomendarme algún sitio web? ¡Gracias!

Alberto

Expansión
Escribe un folleto turístico sobre lo que se puede visitar en tu ciudad. Usa conjunciones.

Más práctica Cuaderno *pp. 200–202* Cuaderno para hispanohablantes *pp. 201–203*

¿Comprendiste? Contesta con oraciones completas.

1. ¿Qué harás en caso de que pierdas la cartera?
2. ¿Usarás tus ahorros en caso de que tengas una oportunidad de viajar?
3. ¿Qué recomiendas que haga tu amigo antes de que se gradúe?

Get Help Online
ClassZone.com

GRAMÁTICA en contexto

¡AVANZA! **Goal:** On the Web site represented below, notice how the subjunctive is used. Then practice using the subjunctive to talk about future plans. ***Actividades 10–12***

Contexto 2 *Sitio web*

ESTRATEGIA **Leer**

Make a chart of the subjunctives Draw a table. In **Part 1** write down each use of the subjunctive found on the conference website. Then, put a check mark in the column of **Part 2** that explains why the subjunctive was used.

1. Frases con subjuntivo	2. Razones para usar el subjuntivo		
	Conjunción	Frase adverbial	Duda
antes de que empiecen las sesiones		✓	

AUDIO

Raúl es un estudiante boliviano que se está preparando para ir a una conferencia estudiantil en Lima, Perú. Acaba de descargar e imprimir una página de información de un sitio web, para ver lo que debe llevar y lo que debe saber antes de salir. Va a participar en un programa modelo de la Organización de las Naciones Unidas (ONU) y tiene que leer mucha información.

Conferencia Juvenil Latinoamericana

Conferencia Juvenil Latinoamericana
del 16 al 23 de septiembre
Lima, Perú

Sobre la ONU

Otras conferencias

Contacto

¡Atención!

Delegados del programa modelo de la ONU:

- Deben llegar a la ciudad dos días antes de que empiecen las sesiones.
- Deben esperar en el hotel hasta que lleguen los líderes del proyecto.
- No pueden participar en las actividades sin que tengan asignado un número de registro.
- Deben llevar una computadora portátil para que puedan participar.
- No deben llevar un teléfono celular a las sesiones a menos que sea absolutamente necesario, y sólo con permiso de los líderes del proyecto.
- Deben traer los documentos de identidad en caso de que tengan que entrar en oficinas del gobierno. Deben guardar los objetos valiosos en la caja de seguridad del hotel para que no se pierdan.
- Pueden vestirse informalmente con tal de que no hagan una visita oficial.
- Para más información sobre la primera tarea del proyecto, visiten **www.confelatinatar1uni2p.edu.pe**

10 Comprensión del sitio web

Leer
Escribir

Usa las palabras y expresiones indicadas para crear oraciones sobre las actividades de los delegados, según la lectura.

1. no participar / sin que / tener asignado
2. llegar / antes de que / empezar
3. esperar / hasta que / llegar
4. vestirse / con tal de que / no hacer
5. no llevar / a menos que / ser
6. guardar / para que / no perderse

11 De visita

Hablar
Escribir

Con tu compañero(a), preparen un programa turístico para los estudiantes de intercambio que vienen a su comunidad. Incluyan al menos diez lugares y/o actividades de interés. Luego, presenten sus ideas a la clase. Usen el subjuntivo con conjunciones.

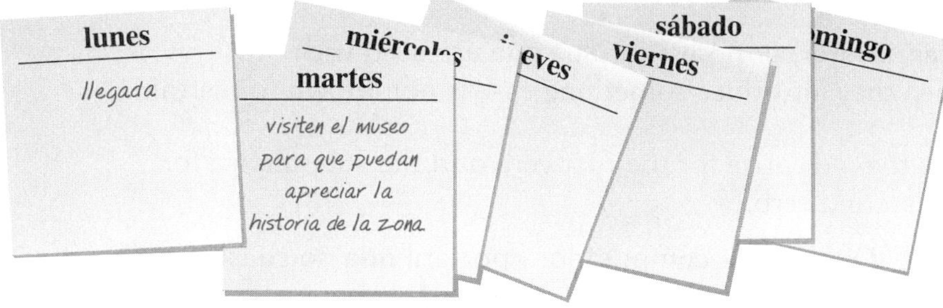

Expansión
Explica cómo cambiarás el itinerario en casos especiales. Usa las expresiones: **con tal que, en caso de que, antes de que...**

12 El fin de semana

Hablar

Con un(a) compañero(a), digan qué planes tienen para el fin de semana.

modelo: tengo que... para que...

1. Voy a... mañana... a menos que...
2. Mis amigos y yo vamos a... con tal de que no...
3. Voy a llevar... en caso de que...
4. No puedo... sin que...
5. Vamos a... para que...
6. Ellos quieren ir a... antes de que...
7. Tú leerás... a fin de que...

A Tengo que comprar más memoria para que pueda usar mi nuevo juego de computadora.

B Yo tengo que comprar un regalo valioso para que mi mamá esté contenta en su cumpleaños.

¿Comprendiste? Completa las oraciones según el sitio web de la conferencia.

1. Los delegados deben esperar en el hotel hasta que...
2. No deben llevar un teléfono celular a menos que...
3. Pueden vestirse informalmente con tal de que...

Presentación de GRAMÁTICA

¡AVANZA! **Goal:** Learn how to use the subjunctive to talk about the unknown. Then practice using the subjunctive to talk about what may or may not be. ***Actividades 13–16***

English Grammar Connection: In English, to talk about people or things that may not exist, you use the **indicative,** but in Spanish you use the **subjunctive.**

I'm looking for **a stamp** that **is** very valuable.	Busco **un sello que sea** muy valioso.

Subjunctive with the Unknown

Animated Grammar ClassZone.com

Verbs like **buscar, querer,** or **necesitar** plus **que** are used with the **subjunctive** when they introduce something that is not known for certain.

Here's how: Use the indicative for the first verb and the **subjunctive** for the second verb.

Quiero una computadora portátil **que** no **cueste** mucho.
I want a laptop computer that does not cost much.

You also need to use the **subjunctive** with expressions that ask about something that may not exist.

¿Hay... que... ? **¿Conoces... que... ?** **¿Tienes... que... ?**

¿**Tienes** un teléfono **que toque** música?
Do you have a phone that plays music?

The **subjunctive** is used in a similar way when these expressions are used with **no** to say that something may not exist or definitely does not exist.

No hay... que... **No conozco... que...** **No tengo... que...**

No conozco a nadie **que publique** poesía.
I don't know anyone who publishes poetry.

To talk about things that definitely do exist, use the **indicative.**

Hay un sitio web que **tiene** la información.
***There is** a Web site that **has** the information.*

Más práctica
Cuaderno *pp. 203–205*
Cuaderno para hispanohablantes *pp. 204–207*

@HomeTutor
Leveled Practice
ClassZone.com

Práctica de GRAMÁTICA

13 Una computadora nueva

Escuchar
Escribir

Escucha el diálogo entre el vendedor y la chica que quiere comprar una computadora nueva. Completa las frases con el verbo apropiado.

La chica quiere una computadora que __1.__ rápida y que __2.__ mucha memoria. El vendedor le dice que no hay ninguna computadora muy rápida que __3.__ barata, pero que sí tiene algunas que __4.__ más lentas y baratas. La chica no quiere ver ninguna computadora que __5.__ más de dos mil dólares. El vendedor no cree que __6.__ ninguna computadora muy buena que __7.__ tan poco dinero, pero dice que tiene modelos que __8.__ bastante eficientes y que cuestan menos de $2.000.

14 No hay nadie

Escribir
Hablar

Completa cada pregunta con el subjuntivo del verbo indicado. Luego, hazle las preguntas a tu compañero(a). Él (o ella) las contestará negativamente.

A ¿Hay alguien en tu clase que sepa utilizar una agenda electrónica?

B No, no hay nadie en mi clase que sepa utilizar una agenda electrónica.

1. ¿Conoces un enlace que (tener) buena información?
2. ¿Hay alguien que (dar una sugerencia) sobre los sitios web?
3. ¿Hay estudiantes que (estar ilusionados) de tener una computadora?
4. ¿Viste a alguien que (temer que) no haya papel en la impresora?
5. ¿Conoces a alguien que (sospechar que) mi computadora es vieja?
6. ¿Hay personas que (no darse cuenta) de la importancia del Internet?

AUDIO

Pronunciación Los sonidos L y LL

La **L** se pronuncia como la ***L*** en inglés. La **LL** tiene varias pronunciaciones regionales: un sonido como la *y* de la palabra *yellow* en inglés, un sonido como la *j* de la palabra *job* en inglés, o un sonido /zh/ como la *s* de la palabra *vision* en inglés.

lavar **la bolsa** **sellos** **llegar**

Trabalenguas

Las tablas de mi balcón mal entablilladas están. Llamen al entablillador que las desentablille y las vuelva a entablillar mejor, que ya se le pagará como buen entablillador.

15 ¿Qué quieren?

Hablar
Escribir

Prepara tu lista de regalos con los artículos que buscas y sus características.

modelo: Mi mamá quiere una bolsa que no sea muy grande.

1. Mi abuelo necesita...
2. Mi papá quiere...
3. Mi hermana busca...
4. Mi hermano desea...
5. Yo espero encontrar...
6. Mi mejor amigo(a) espera recibir...

Expansión
Escribe cinco oraciones con el subjuntivo para describir las características que prefieres que tengan los sitios web.

16 ¿Qué piensas del arte?

Leer
Hablar
Escribir

Comparación cultural

El arte de Tigua

¿Qué importancia tiene el arte indígena?
La pintura de Tigua, un pueblo en el centro de **Ecuador,** representa la vida tradicional de este pueblo de los Andes. Sus imágenes reflejan la historia, los festivales y las leyendas de esta comunidad a fin de que otras personas puedan aprender más de la vida de este pueblo. La comunidad de Tigua-Chimbacucho tiene ahora una galería de pinturas y otras artesanías para que los turistas y coleccionistas puedan apreciar y comprar estas obras de arte.

Día de fiesta en un pueblo quechua
Arte naif, Ecuador

Compara con tu mundo *¿Viste un tipo de arte indígena alguna vez? ¿Dónde?*

Completa las siguientes oraciones con tu opinión.

1. Es importante apoyar a los artistas indígenas y locales para que...
2. Debemos fomentar las expresiones artísticas a fin de que...
3. Los artistas siempre deben expresarse a menos que...

Más práctica Cuaderno *pp. 203–205* Cuaderno para hispanohablantes *pp. 204–207*

¿Comprendiste? Contesta con oraciones completas.

1. ¿Hay alguien en tu clase que tenga un paraguas hoy?
2. ¿Conoces a alguien que envíe cartas por correo?
3. ¿Tienes un(a) amigo(a) que descargue música por Internet?

Get Help Online
ClassZone.com

Todo junto

¡AVANZA! **Goal:** ***Show what you know*** Listen to the conversation between Raúl and other Model UN delegates at the airport. Pay particular attention to how they use the subjunctive. ***Actividades 17–19***

Resumen contextos 1 y 2 Raúl es un estudiante boliviano que va a Lima, Perú, para participar en un programa modelo de la Organización de las Naciones Unidas (ONU) para los países latinoamericanos. Ya se comunicó con algunos participantes en un salón de charlas usando su computadora.

Contexto 3 *Diálogo*

ESTRATEGIA **Escuchar**
List cognates while listening This conversation contains many cognates that make understanding easier. While listening, write down the cognates on a separate sheet. Listen several times so you can find them all.

AUDIO

Ahora Raúl está en el aeropuerto de La Paz, Bolivia, esperando su vuelo a Lima. Allí conoce a otros tres participantes del programa.

Raúl: A ver... ¿qué hora es? Uf, todavía falta una hora y media antes de que pueda abordar el avión... ¿Hola?

Ana: ¡Hola! Veo que tienes información sobre la conferencia en Lima... ¿vas a participar?

Raúl: Sí, sí. ¿Y tú?

Ana: Sí, voy en el mismo vuelo. Me llamo Ana Guerrero. Soy de Cochabamba.

Raúl: Mucho gusto. Yo soy Raúl Méndez, de La Paz.

Ana: Y ellos son Ricardo, de Oruro, y Marilú, de Trinidad. Acabo de conocerlos. Todos vamos a la conferencia.

Ricardo: Hola, Raúl. Soy Ricardo Salcedo. Un placer.

Marilú: Yo soy Marilú Cedeño. Mucho gusto, Raúl.

Raúl: ¿Y ustedes tienen que volar a Lima desde La Paz? ¿No hay otro aeropuerto que quede más cerca de sus ciudades?

Ana: Sí, pero esos vuelos salen muy caros.

Raúl: Bueno, ¿están tan ilusionados con la conferencia como yo?

Marilú: Estoy ilusionadísima... pero, para decir la verdad, ¡estoy un poco nerviosa también! Temo que vaya a ser una experiencia muy intensa.

Ricardo: Uf, parece que sí. ¿Qué les pareció esa tarea que ya nos dieron... ? ¡Y para cumplir antes de que empiece la primera sesión! ¡Qué horror!

Raúl: ¿Una tarea? ¿Para el primer día? ¡No me digan! ¡No me di cuenta!

Ricardo: Hombre, sí... el enlace a la tarea estaba al final de la lista en el sitio web. ¡Y es un trabajo gordo! Tienes que crear un perfil económico, político e histórico de tu ciudad y de tu país.

Raúl: ¡Ay, no! ¿Qué hago? ¡No vi la tarea y no hice nada!

Ana: Bueno, Raúl, tal vez te podamos ayudar un poco, con tal de que nos hagas algún favor en el futuro. ¿Te parece?

Raúl: ¡Lo que tú quieras! ¡Sólo quiero que me ayuden!

Ricardo: Entonces, ¡abre tu computadora portátil y empecemos!

También se dice

Ricardo dice **Es un trabajo gordo** para indicar que tiene mucho trabajo.

- **República Dominicana, Cuba** **Es tremendo trabajo.**
- **Argentina** **Es un trabajo bárbaro.**
- **Perú** **Es una chambaza.**

17 Comprensión del diálogo

Escuchar
Escribir

1. ¿A quiénes conoce Raúl en el aeropuerto?
2. ¿Cuánto falta para que salga el avión?
3. ¿Por qué salen todos del aeropuerto de La Paz?
4. ¿Cómo están los participantes?
5. ¿Para cuándo tienen que hacer la primera tarea?
6. ¿Qué descubre Raúl que no hizo antes de salir?
7. ¿Qué solución le ofrece Ana a Raúl?
8. ¿Qué tiene que usar Ricardo al final?

18 Integración

Leer
Escuchar
Hablar

Lee las especificaciones de tres computadoras portátiles. Escucha el anuncio que pasan por los altoparlantes *(loudspeakers)* de una tienda. Luego decide qué computadora debes comprar.

Fuente 1 Especificaciones

Computadora Portátil PH	$1.255
Procesador M 370 (1.5 GHz), Memoria de 512 MB, Pantalla ancha de 14", Disco Duro de 60GB, DVD (graba y lee CDs y DVDs), Modem 56K y Conexión 10/100Mbps, Peso 2.42kg, Escáner gratis	
Portátil Compactus 3000	**$784**
Procesador de 1.8 GHz, Memoria de 256 MB, Pantalla de 14", Disco Duro de 40GB, DVD Rom y CD-RW (combo), Modem 56K y Conexión 10/100Mbps, Peso 2.43 kg	
Computadora Satelite ABC	**$1.842**
Procesador 3.33 GHz, 1 GB de memoria, Disco Duro de 93.20GB, DVD Super Multi, Pantalla 15.4", Modem 56K Conectada a Internet gratis, Peso 3.4kg	

Fuente 2 Anuncio

Escucha y apunta

- ¿Cuáles son las características de la computadora Letra?
- ¿El precio es atractivo o viste computadoras más baratas?

modelo: La computadora Letra tiene un escáner gratis pero no creo que sea tan buena como la Compactus. No existe ninguna tienda que ofrezca cosas sin sacar beneficio.

19 ¡A escribir!

Escribir

Estás en una conferencia. Escribe un reporte sobre las experiencias que tuviste el primer día. Incluye el vocabulario de la lección y la gramática que aprendiste.

Writing Criteria	Excellent	Good	Needs Work
Content	Your report explains several significant aspects of your chosen topic.	Your report explains some significant aspects of your chosen topic.	Your report explains few aspects of your chosen topic.
Communication	Your report is organized and easy to follow.	Parts of your report are organized and easy to follow.	Your report is disorganized and hard to follow.
Accuracy	You make few mistakes in grammar and vocabulary.	You make some mistakes in grammar and vocabulary.	You make many mistakes in grammar and vocabulary.

Más práctica Cuaderno *pp. 206–207* Cuaderno para hispanohablantes *pp. 208–209*

¿Comprendiste? Termina las frases según el diálogo.

1. Marilú teme que la conferencia...
2. Raúl no sabe que...
3. Ana ofrece ayudar a Raúl para que...

Lectura literaria

¡AVANZA! **Goal:** Read the following excerpt from a story about an imaginary city in Bolivia. Then consider the different ways this city could have responded to errors on their map.

Para leer 

ESTRATEGIA Leer

Take notes on the history While reading about Aguamarina, take notes on a separate sheet to help you understand and remember the events. Write the important years and what happened in each one.

Notas sobre Aguamarina
1953 – El mapa oficial fue publicado con errores.
1954 – ...

Vocabulario para leer

la alcaldía	*oficina del alcalde o jefe de una ciudad*
el presupuesto	*cálculo anticipado de gastos*
descifrar	*descubrir el significado de un mensaje escrito con signos extraños*
adquirir	*conseguir algo*
en blanco	*que no tiene nada escrito*
complejo	*que no es simple, que es difícil de entender*

Nota cultural

Sobre el autor ***Edmundo Paz Soldán (1967–)***
Nació en Cochabamba, Bolivia. Recibió su doctorado en literatura hispanoamericana en la Universidad de California, en Berkeley, y en 1997 ganó el premio «Juan Rulfo». Paz Soldán es el autor de varios libros, entre ellos *Amores imperfectos, Sueños digitales* y la colección de cuentos *Desencuentros.*

Sobre los mapas Los primeros mapas del mundo entero aparecieron en el siglo XVI, después de que Colón llegó al Nuevo Mundo. El mapa creado por Martin Waldseemüller en 1507 es el primero que incluye Latinoamérica, y no era muy exacto si lo comparamos con los mapas modernos.

La ciudad de los mapas

AUDIO

La ciudad de Aguamarina es también conocida como la ciudad de los mapas. Hacia 1953 un error tipográfico hizo que[1] el mapa oficial de la ciudad fuera publicado[2] atribuyendo nombres distintos de los verdaderos a todas sus calles y plazas: la calle Benedicto Romero se llamaba María Dolores y la calle Naucalpán se llamaba Cienfuegos y la Cienfuegos se llamaba Benedicto Romero... La alcaldía no poseía dinero en su presupuesto anual para hacer reimprimir[3] el mapa, de modo que ciudadanos y turistas debieron valerse de él[4] por un año.

Sin embargo, descifrar el mapa, tratar de llegar de un lugar a otro siguiendo nada más que sus instrucciones, se convirtió pronto en el pasatiempo[5] del lugar. Era obvio, la ciudad era pequeña y la gente no necesitaba de mapas para ir de un lugar a otro; el secreto del juego consistía, precisamente, en olvidar esa obviedad[6] y tratar de valerse únicamente del mapa.

....

---

[1] **hizo...** caused [2] **fuera...** to be published [3] to reprint
[4] **valerse...** use it [5] pastime [6] the obvious

Reflexiona

¿Qué caracteriza los mapas de Aguamarina?

Una petición que circuló de mano en mano convenció a la alcaldía de mantener los errores tipográficos de 1953 en el mapa de 1954, o en su defecto cambiar los errores por otros errores. Se eligió la segunda opción.

A pensar
¿Por qué piensas que los ciudadanos hicieron esa petición en vez de corregir el mapa?

....

En los años 60, el error adquirió características de sofisticación al aparecer diversas ediciones clandestinas de mapas que competían y ganaban en originalidad a los que publicaba el municipio. Algunos de estos mapas se publicaban en costosas ediciones limitadas, impresos en seda[7] china o terciopelo[8], numerados y con firma del autor; del mapa Malloy, por ejemplo, en que su creador, un arquitecto casi ciego[9], había eliminado[10] siete calles de la ciudad original y alterado dieciséis nombres de lugares turísticos.

....

[7] silk [8] velvet [9] blind
[10] **había...** had omitted

Una historia de Aguamarina y sus mapas debería[11] necesariamente mencionar estos hitos[12]: en 1971, la publicación de un mapa en blanco; en 1979, la circulación de un mapa de la ciudad de New York como si fuera[13] de Aguamarina; en 1983, el intento fallido[14] de crear un mapa del mismo tamaño de la ciudad; en 1987, el mapa que contaba en clave[15] la leyenda del Minotauro y que motivó la profusión de niños bautizados con los nombres de Ariadna y Teseo; en 1993, el mapa de la ciudad sin alteración alguna, hecho al que se habían desacostumbrado tanto los aguamarinenses[16] que resultó ser el más delirante[17], cruel y complejo de los mapas hechos hasta ahora. ❖

Otras ciudades han tratado[18] de imitar a Aguamarina. No han podido[19].

❖ A pensar
¿Por qué el mapa verdadero resultó ser el más complejo? ¿Piensas que los aguamarinenses querían ese mapa?

---

[11] should [12] milestones [13] **como...** as if it were
[14] **intento...** failed attempt [15] **en...** in code
[16] **hecho...** an action to which the residents of Aguamarina were so unaccustomed
[17] delirious [18] **han...** have tried [19] **No...** have not been able

¿Comprendiste?

1. ¿A qué se deben los primeros errores en el mapa oficial de Aguamarina?
2. ¿Cómo reaccionaron los ciudadanos al ver el mapa defectuoso?
3. ¿Cuál fue la consecuencia de la reacción de los ciudadanos?
4. ¿Cuál era el mapa más difícil de seguir?
5. Aguamarina es una ciudad pequeña. De todos los mapas, ¿cuál es el menos apropiado para esta ciudad?

¿Y tú?

1. ¿Qué tipos de mapas y planos de lugares conoces? En tu opinión, ¿son útiles? ¿Los usas con frecuencia? Da ejemplos.
2. ¿Qué tipo de errores son aceptables en un mapa? ¿Cuáles no? Explica.

Conexiones *Los estudios sociales*

Lenguas indígenas

En Bolivia, Perú y Ecuador, las lenguas indígenas siguen teniendo una gran importancia. Aparte del español, se hablan el quechua (o quichua), el aymara y otras lenguas indígenas. En Bolivia y Perú, el español, el quechua y el aymara son los tres idiomas oficiales del país. En Ecuador, los dos idiomas oficiales son el quechua y el español. También hay poblaciones en Perú, Argentina y Chile que hablan estas lenguas.

Algunas palabras del quechua que se usan también en español e inglés son **cóndor, gaucho, llama** y **quinina.** La palabra **alpaca** viene del aymara.

Proyecto Compara los nombres de las partes del cuerpo en español, quechua y aymara.

español	quechua	aymara
boca	simi	aka
brazo	maqui	ampara
cabeza	uma	ppekke
cuerpo	hanchi	hanchi
diente	kiru	laka chaca
espalda	huassa	iwhani
estómago	wiggsa	pucara
mano	maqui	ampara
ojo	nawi	nalra
pie	chaqui	cayu

1. Busca una palabra en español que tenga la misma traducción en quechua y en aymara.
2. Busca dos palabras en español que se traducen al quechua con la misma palabra. ¿Hay un caso igual en el aymara?

En tu comunidad

¿Sabes qué otros idiomas, además del inglés, se hablan o hablaban en tu ciudad o estado? ¿Con qué países o culturas se asocian estas lenguas?

Lección 1

En resumen

Vocabulario y gramática

Vocabulario

Talk About Personal Items

Personal possessions

la agenda electrónica	*personal organizer*
los ahorros	*savings*
la bolsa	*bag, handbag*
la cartera	*wallet*
distinto(a)	*distinct, different*
el documento (de identidad)	*(identification) document*
las gafas (de sol)	*(sun)glasses*
el monedero	*coin purse*
el paraguas	*umbrella*
precioso(a)	*precious*
sin valor	*worthless*
valioso(a)	*valuable*

Computers, e-mail, online chats

la búsqueda	*search*
la computadora portátil	*portable / laptop computer*
conectarse a Internet	*to connect to the Internet*
la contraseña	*password*
descargar	*to download*
el enlace	*link*
enviar	*to send*
el escáner	*scanner*
imprimir	*to print*
los juegos de computadora	*computer games*
el salón de charlas	*chat room*
el sitio web	*Web site*

Actions

disfrutar de	*to enjoy*
esconder	*to hide*
estar ilusionado(a)	*to be excited, to be thrilled*
evitar	*to avoid*
guardar	*to keep, to put away*

Talk About Requirements

a fin de que...	*in order that*
a menos que...	*unless*
antes de que...	*before*
con tal (de) que...	*as long as*
dar consejos	*to give advice*
dar una sugerencia	*to make a suggestion*
en caso de que...	*in case that*
hasta que...	*until*
para que...	*in order that*
ponerse de acuerdo	*to agree*
sin que...	*without*

Other Phrases

darse cuenta de	*to realize*
sospechar que	*to suspect that*
temer que	*to be afraid that*

Gramática

Nota gramatical: Expressions with **sea** *p. 276*

Subjunctive with Conjunctions

Conjunctions used with Subjunctive		
a fin de que	**con tal (de) que**	**para que**
a menos que	**en caso de que**	**sin que**
antes de que		

No gastes tus ahorros **a menos que sea** necesario.
*Don't spend your savings **unless** it's necessary.*

Without **que,** the verb that follows must be in the **infinitive** form.

Tendrás que comer **antes de salir.**
You'll have to eat before leaving.

Subjunctive with the Unknown

Verbs like **buscar, querer,** or **necesitar** plus **que** are used with the **subjunctive.**

Quiero una computadora portátil **que** no **cueste** mucho.
I want a laptop computer that does not cost that much.

Use the **subjunctive** to ask about something that may not exist, or to say that something does not exist.

¿**Tienes** un teléfono **que toque** música?
Do you have a phone that plays music?

No conozco a nadie **que publique** poesía.
I don't know anyone who publishes poetry.

To talk about things that do exist, use the **indicative.**

Hay un sitio web que **tiene** la información.
***There is** a Web site that **has** the information.*

Lección 1

Repaso de la lección

@HomeTutor
ClassZone.com

Now you can
- talk about personal items
- talk about requirements
- express what does and doesn't exist

Using
- expressions with **sea**
- subjunctive with conjunctions
- subjunctive with the unknown

To review
- vocabulary pp. 272–273

1 Listen and understand

AUDIO

Leonardo va de vacaciones con su familia. Escucha la conversación con su hermana mayor y escribe cinco oraciones sobre lo que van a traer y para qué lo usarán.

To review
- vocabulary pp. 272–273

2 Talk about personal items

Crea oraciones con palabras correspondientes a cada ilustración. Di para qué vas a usar las cosas indicadas. Sigue el modelo.

modelo: Necesito los documentos de identidad para volar dentro del país.

1. 

2. 

3. 

4. 

5. 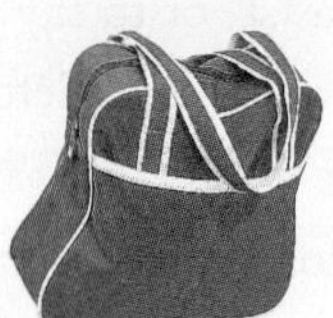

6. 

To review
- subjunctive with conjunctions p. 277
- expressions with **sea** p. 276

3 Talk about requirements

Crea oraciones, según el modelo, para hablar de las computadoras. En los puntos 7 y 8, usa expresiones con **sea.**

modelo: Necesito la contraseña para que...
Necesito la contraseña para que pueda conectarme a Internet.

1. Debemos imprimir la información antes de que...
2. Vas a descargar las gráficas con tal de que...
3. Él se va a conectar a menos que...
4. Yo usaré el escáner en caso de que...
5. Ustedes nos enviarán los enlaces para que...
6. Tú y yo podemos crear un sitio web con tal de que...
7. Ya es de noche, pero tenemos que terminar el blog...
8. Hay que descubrir la contraseña...

To review
- subjunctive with the unknown p. 282

4 Express what does and doesn't exist

Tu amigo dice muchas cosas pero está equivocado. Corrígelo usando la forma negativa y el subjuntivo.

modelo: Hay una tienda que vende carteras buenas.
No hay ninguna tienda que venda carteras buenas.

1. Hay un banco que tiene cuentas de ahorro.
2. Hay una librería que vende libros valiosos.
3. Hay un cibercafé que ofrece servicio de Internet.
4. Hay una computadora portátil que pesa menos de una libra.
5. Hay un juego de computadoras que es muy fácil.

To review
- **Comparación cultural** pp. 278, 284

5 Indigenous artifacts and art

Comparación cultural

1. ¿Qué tipos de objetos se guardan en el Museo de los Metales Preciosos en La Paz?
2. ¿Cuáles son los objetos más valiosos del museo y dónde se guardan?
3. ¿Qué representan las pinturas de Tigua?
4. ¿De qué manera el pueblo de Tigua muestra su arte a los turistas?

Más práctica Cuaderno *pp. 208–219* Cuaderno para hispanohablantes *pp. 210–219*

UNIDAD 5

Los países andinos

Lección 2

Tema:

Nuevos amigos, nuevas oportunidades

¡AVANZA! **In this lesson you will learn to**

- say what would or would not happen
- report what someone said
- talk about the day's activities

using

- **qué** and **cuál**
- conditional tense
- reported speech

¿Recuerdas?

- preterite
- computer vocabulary

Comparación cultural

In this lesson you will learn about

- music in the Andean countries
- archaeological sites in Perú
- geographic variety in the Andean countries

Compara con tu mundo

Estos estudiantes caminan por la Plaza de Armas, el sitio donde se declaró la independencia de Perú por primera vez, en 1820. En la plaza hay una catedral y un monumento dedicado a la independencia. *¿Hay lugares en tu ciudad o estado con significado histórico?*

¿Qué ves?

Mira la foto

¿Cómo son los estudiantes?

¿Cómo se visten?

¿Qué hace la otra gente en la plaza?

¿Qué objetos ves en la plaza?

Online SPANISH CLASSZONE.COM

Featuring...

Cultura INTERACTIVA

Animated Grammar

@HomeTutor

And more...

- Get Help Online
- Interactive Flashcards
- Review Games
- WebQuest
- Conjuguemos.com

Estudiantes en la Plaza de Armas
Trujillo, Perú

Presentación de VOCABULARIO

¡AVANZA! **Goal:** Learn about different ways to relax and socialize. Then practice by talking about things you do at home and with friends. ***Actividades 1–3***

 *¿Recuerdas?* Preterite pp. 37, 42

AUDIO

A A Gladys le gusta mucho estar en **el club** de estudiantes.

B El club de estudiantes es muy **cómodo** y **acogedor.** Aquí puedo hacer muchas cosas como **relajarme** o **dormir una siesta, asistir a las reuniones** del club de **actuación,** o **encontrarme con** mis amigos en nuestros ratos de **ocio** para **charlar, comentar** las noticias, **intercambiar opiniones** o jugar a **las damas** u otros **pasatiempos.** Lo que más me gusta es **el ambiente informal** del lugar y que puedo **pasar un buen rato** lejos del **ruido** de la calle. Además, en la recepción hay un mural donde me puedo informar sobre todas las actividades o hacer la planificación de **un encuentro** cultural. ¡Me gusta mucho estar aquí!

C También hay mucho que hacer en el barrio, cerca del club.

los clubes con música bailable

el vendedor ambulante

los músicos callejeros

Más vocabulario

asistir a un espectáculo *to attend a show*
el billar *billiards*
concluir *to conclude, to finish*
los dados *dice*
formal *formal*
el grupo musical *music group*
la manta *blanket*
la orquesta *orchestra*
relatar *to relate, to tell*
la resolución *resolution*

Expansión de vocabulario p. R11
Ya sabes p. R11

MURAL DEL CLUB

Inscríbase en la recepción. Está después de pasar la entrada, a la derecha. Podrá **disfrutar** de todas las actividades que ofrecemos.

¿Necesita **relajarse**, escapar del **ruido** y los sonidos molestos de la ciudad y poder **dormir una siesta** en paz?

De lunes a sábado,
3–5 p.m.,
clases de relajación y yoga.

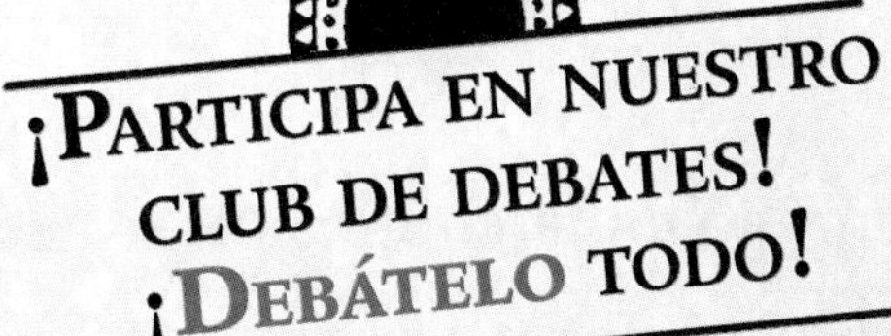

¡PARTICIPA EN NUESTRO CLUB DE DEBATES!
¡DEBÁTELO TODO!

Aquí puedes **discutir** sobre los temas que quieras. ¡Desde **el estreno** de la última película hasta cómo **resolver** los problemas del medio ambiente!

¡Todos los viernes a las 5:30 p.m.!

¡A responder! Escuchar 

Escucha la lista de actividades. Si la actividad es algo que puedes hacer en Internet, levanta la mano derecha. Si es algo que sólo puedes hacer en persona, levanta la mano izquierda.

Práctica de VOCABULARIO

1 ¿Tiene sentido?

Hablar
Escribir

Lee las oraciones y di si las palabras del vocabulario se usan correctamente.

modelo: Mis amigos y yo charlamos sin decir una palabra.
Incorrecto.

1. El grupo musical tocó en el auditorio de la escuela.
2. Julián estaba tan cansado que durmió una siesta.
3. Para jugar al billar se necesitan tres dados.
4. Diana comenta sus problemas con la maestra.
5. La música bailable sólo sirve para relajarse.

2 ¡A pasar un buen rato!

Hablar
Escribir

Di si haces estas actividades en tu tiempo de ocio o no.

modelo: jugar al ajedrez: Nunca juego al ajedrez.

1. bailar
2. jugar a los naipes
3. ver una película
4. jugar a las damas
5. ir a estrenos
6. escuchar música

Expansión
Menciona tres pasatiempos más del vocabulario y explica por qué te gustan o no.

3 ¿Qué pasó en la conferencia?

 ***¿Recuerdas?*** Preterite pp. 37, 42

Hablar
Escribir

Para saber lo que ocurrió ayer en la conferencia, cambia el verbo al pretérito y escoge la palabra correcta de las que están entre paréntesis.

modelo: nosotros / asistir / (a la conferencia / al ajedrez / a la orquesta)
Nosotros asistimos a la conferencia.

1. yo / participar en / (el ocio / el encuentro cultural / el ruido)
2. los invitados / intercambiar / (naipes / opiniones / mantas)
3. nosotros / asistir a / (las damas / el espectáculo / la ficha)
4. Ana / presentar / (una resolución / una siesta / los dados) apropiada
5. ustedes / escuchar / (un grupo musical / un billar / una actuación)
6. el vendedor ambulante / ser / muy (informal / acogedor / cómodo)

Más práctica Cuaderno *pp. 220–222* Cuaderno para hispanohablantes *pp. 220–223*

¿Comprendiste? Contesta con una palabra o frase.

1. ¿Qué juego de mesa te hace pensar mucho?
2. ¿Cómo se llama un conjunto con muchos músicos?
3. Si quieres informarte sobre un tema en especial, ¿adónde vas?

VOCABULARIO en contexto

¡AVANZA! **Goal:** Learn about the first day of the Model UN Conference as you read Gladys' blog. Then discuss the activities already completed as well as those still to come. ***Actividades 4–5***

Contexto 1 *Blog*

ESTRATEGIA **Leer**

Write down the schedule To help you understand Gladys' email, write down her schedule of events at the model United Nations Conference. Include every event she mentions, as well as where the event takes place and whom she meets at the event. Don't worry about not knowing exact hours.

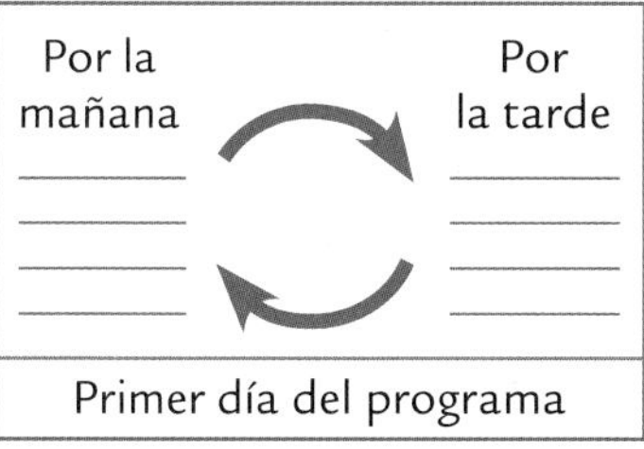

Gladys Belgrano es una joven peruana que está participando en una conferencia de la Organización de las Naciones Unidas (ONU) en Lima. Cada noche, Gladys escribe en su blog para describir qué pasó durante el día.

Blog de Gladys

BLOG DE GLADYS

Sobre el blog

Aquí escribo mis experiencias en la escuela y en otras actividades relacionadas con mi educación. Todas las noches escribo cosas nuevas para que todos sepan qué ocurrió en mi día de actividad.

Enlaces

Archivos

Más fotos

Escribe tus comentarios AQUÍ

CONFERENCIA DE LA ONU EN LIMA

Publicado el 12 de marzo

Participo en una conferencia estudiantil de la ONU. Ya se acabó el primer día del programa. Y ahora estoy relajándome en mi habitación antes de encontrarme con un grupo de gente para salir. ¡Qué día más interesante! Anoche fui a una recepción de bienvenida y conocí, en persona, a los dos estudiantes que conocía del salón de charlas: Raúl y Sofía. Son muy amables, aunque Raúl es un poco desorganizado. Pasé un buen rato charlando con los otros delegados y después... ¡a la cama! Estaba cansadísima.

Hoy asistí a varias reuniones con mi grupo, el de los países andinos. Participamos en unas actividades de grupo y luego intercambiamos opiniones y debatimos varios temas. Mañana participaremos en un encuentro con los delegados del Cono Sur, para resolver un problema económico y presentar nuestras conclusiones. Mucho trabajo, pero súper interesante. 4 comentarios

UN POCO DE DESCANSO

Publicado el 12 de marzo

Dormiré una siesta antes de reunirme con el grupo. Iremos a un salón de baile para estudiantes. También vamos a planear una excursión a Cuzco o a Trujillo. Aquí pueden ver unas fotos con mis compañeros de la conferencia. Mañana publicaré detalles sobre nuestra salida y más información sobre la conferencia. 1 comentario

4 Comprensión del blog

Leer
Hablar

Completa las oraciones sobre la lectura con la información correcta.

1. Mientras escribe, Gladys está...
2. Gladys conoció a...
3. Hoy, Gladys participó en...
4. Mañana el grupo de Gladys va a...
5. Los dos grupos van a...
6. Ahora Gladys quiere...

Nota gramatical

Qué and cuál

Both **qué** and **cuál** can mean *what* in English. **Cuál** can also mean *which.*

¿**Qué** juego vamos a jugar hoy?
***What** game are we going to play today?*

¿**Cuál** de estas tres fichas prefieres?
***Which** of these three game pieces do you prefer?*

Use **qué** if you want someone to *define* or *describe* something. Use **cuál** if you want someone to *select* or to *identify* something.

¿**Qué** tipo de juego es popular en Bolivia?
***What** type of game is popular in Bolivia?*

¿**Cuál** es el nombre de tu juego favorito?
***What** is the name of your favorite game?*

5 Haz la pregunta

Hablar

Léele las siguientes respuestas a un(a) compañero(a) y él (ella) dirá la pregunta usando **qué** o **cuál(es).**

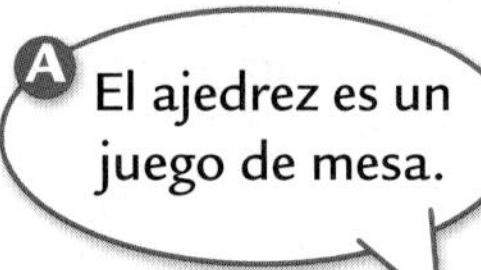

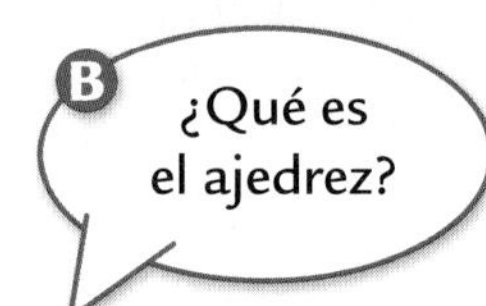

1. Las fichas del ajedrez son: el rey, la reina, la torre, el caballo, el peón y el alfil.
2. Un estreno es la primera vez que se presenta una película o una obra.
3. La música que más me gusta es la música bailable.
4. De estos dos restaurantes, prefiero el restaurante formal.
5. Una charla es una conversación informal.
6. La orquesta del director Jaime Serra se llama Orquesta Serra.
7. Necesito dormir una siesta para relajarme.

¿Comprendiste? Haz una lista de las actividades que Gladys menciona en su blog.

1. ¿Cuántas de estas actividades son para las horas de ocio?
2. ¿Cuántas se relacionan con las sesiones de la conferencia?

Presentación de GRAMÁTICA

¡AVANZA! **Goal:** Learn about the formation and use of the conditional tense. Then talk about things that you would or would not do. ***Actividades 6–9***

 *¿Recuerdas?* Computer vocabulary pp. 272–273

English Grammar Connection: In English, you form the conditional by placing *would* before the main verb. In Spanish, the **conditional** is one word.

I **would bring** a blanket. Yo **llevaría** una manta.

Conditional Tense

To say what someone *would* or *wouldn't* do, use the **conditional** tense.

Here's how: All verbs, whether they end in **-ar, -er,** or **-ir,** have the same endings in the **conditional.** Add the endings directly to the **infinitive** of regular verbs.

Infinitive		conditional endings	
llevar	+	-ía	-íamos
resolver		-ías	-íais
discutir		-ía	-ían

Angélica **discutiría** la situación y **resolvería** el problema con nuestra ayuda.
*Angélica **would discuss** the situation and **she would resolve** the problem with our help.*

Verbs that are irregular in the future tense have the same irregular stem in the **conditional.** You still use the regular conditional endings.

Infinitive	Stem	Infinitive	Stem	Infinitive	Stem
haber	habr-	poner	pondr-	decir	dir-
poder	podr-	salir	saldr-	hacer	har-
querer	querr-	tener	tendr-		
saber	sabr-	venir	vendr-		

Yo **pondría** el escáner aquí. Así lo **tendríamos** al lado de la computadora.
*I **would put** the scanner here. That way **we would have** it next to the computer.*

Más práctica

Cuaderno *pp. 223–225*

Cuaderno para hispanohablantes *pp. 224–226*

Conjuguemos.com

@HomeTutor
Leveled Practice
ClassZone.com

Práctica de GRAMÁTICA

6 De viaje

¿Recuerdas? Computer vocabulary pp. 272–273

Hablar
Escribir

Tu familia va a planear un viaje al Perú. Di qué harías tú para investigar qué lugares de interés deberían visitar.

modelo: conectarse a Internet: Me conectaría a Internet.

1. hacer una búsqueda
2. mirar los enlaces
3. explorar varios sitios web
4. descargar páginas buenas
5. buscar un salón de charlas
6. imprimir información útil
7. poner los detalles más importantes en mi agenda electrónica

7 Decisiones difíciles

Hablar

Entrevista a un(a) compañero(a) para saber qué harían estas personas.

modelo: tu mamá / tiempo libre / dormir una siesta o jugar al ajedrez

A ¿Qué haría tu mamá en su tiempo libre, dormiría una siesta o jugaría al ajedrez?

B Mi mamá jugaría al ajedrez.

1. tus amigos y tú / un rato libre / ir a un restaurante o asistir a un espectáculo
2. tú / después de clases / relajarse o encontrarse con amigos
3. tú y yo / una conferencia / debatir el tema o resolver el problema
4. tu hermana / una fiesta / bailar o charlar con sus amigos y amigas
5. tus amigos y amigas / pasar un buen rato / ir al estreno de una película o escuchar a músicos callejeros

Comparación cultural

La música andina

¿De qué manera la música puede reflejar una cultura?

La música andina se asocia con **Bolivia, Ecuador** y **Perú,** pero se encuentra por todo el mundo. En muchas ciudades grandes de Latinoamérica, EE.UU. y Europa se ven grupos callejeros de músicos andinos. Se podría decir que una de las cosas más características de esta música son sus instrumentos indígenas, como la zampoña y la quena (dos tipos de flauta), el charango (un instrumento de cuerdas hecho del caparazón *[shell]* del armadillo) y muchos otros.

Joven de los Andes tocando la zampoña

Compara con tu mundo *¿Alguna vez viste músicos callejeros en Estados Unidos? ¿Dónde? ¿Qué música tocaban? ¿Qué instrumento(s) musical(es) tocaban?*

8 ¡Tantas posibilidades!

Hablar
Escribir

Forma seis oraciones condicionales mezclando los siguientes elementos y añadiendo otros elementos necesarios.

modelo: Con dos semanas de vacaciones, la profesora tendría tiempo de visitar Ecuador.

con mil dólares con un barco de vela sin ahorros con una computadora sin pasatiempos con dos semanas de vacaciones	yo mi amigo tú la profesora nosotros nuestros(as) amigos(as)	pasar poder saber tener comprar ir	visitar Ecuador de vacaciones por el lago un negocio una casa cómo divertirse

9 ¿Qué harías?

Hablar

Tienes todo el dinero y el tiempo del mundo: ¡puedes hacer lo que quieras! Explícales a tus compañeros(as) seis cosas que harías y por qué las harías.

modelo: Yo viajaría por todo el mundo porque tendría mucho tiempo.

Expansión
Escribe cinco preguntas para saber qué haría o adónde iría un(a) compañero(a).

Más práctica Cuaderno *pp. 223–225* Cuaderno para hispanohablantes *pp. 224–226*

Get Help Online
ClassZone.com

¿Comprendiste? Di qué harían estas personas en un día libre.

1. mi abuelo / relajarse
2. yo / asistir a un espectáculo
3. mi familia y yo / pasar un buen rato
4. mi profesor / poder charlar con muchas personas

GRAMÁTICA en contexto

¡AVANZA! **Goal:** Learn about the different opportunities for entertainment and leisure in Lima. Then discuss which of these activities would interest you. ***Actividades 10–12***

Contexto 2 *Guía del ocio*

ESTRATEGIA Leer

Chart the conditional While reading, make a chart to track the uses of the conditional. In the first column, include the sources of information, including the play review and the two ads. In the second column, write down every use of the conditional in each information source.

Fuente de información	Uso del condicional
Crítica de la obra dramática	

AUDIO

Gladys está asistiendo a una conferencia. Se ofreció para organizar a un grupo de estudiantes para salir por las tardes. Ahora, ella y sus compañeros están mirando una guía del ocio para ver qué posibilidades se presentan.

Espectáculo de
MÚSICA CALLEJERA

Teatro Colina
20:00 hs
del 9 al 30 de septiembre

¡Todos los músicos y grupos musicales callejeros más populares de la ciudad, reunidos para tocar juntos por solamente tres semanas!

«¡Sería una tragedia perderse este espectáculo! Yo lo vería otra vez con muchas ganas.»

—Dámaso Bernardi, *El Diario* de Lima

EL OJO CRÍTICO
por Jorge Echeverría

Juego de mesa

Juego de mesa es una nueva obra dramática. Su estreno fue al principio de esta semana en el Teatro Larco. Como siempre trato de apoyar a obras y artistas nuevos, me gustaría escribir algo bueno sobre esta obra. Pero esto sería pura mentira de mi parte. La actuación no podría ser peor. La obra, que trata sobre un misterio en una casa de campo, no parecería verosímil a un niño de cinco años. (*cont. en la pág. 12*)

Salón de baile estudiantil
AMAZONAS
¡La pachanga empieza aquí!

¿Te gustaría pasar la tarde en un sitio con un ambiente tropical?

¡Ven al salón AMAZONAS para una tarde inolvidable!

- música bailable, los fines de semana desde la 1:00 p.m.
- cinco grupos musicales cada tarde, todos los sábados y domingos
- buffet gratis desde la 1:00 p.m. hasta las 7:00 p.m.!

¡Te quedarías todo el tiempo... pero cerramos a las 7:00 p.m.!

También se dice

En Perú y Ecuador se usa **pachanga** para decir **fiesta.**
- **Argentina** **conga**
- **Colombia** **rumba**
- **Cuba** **guateque**

10 Comprensión de la guía del ocio

Leer
Escribir

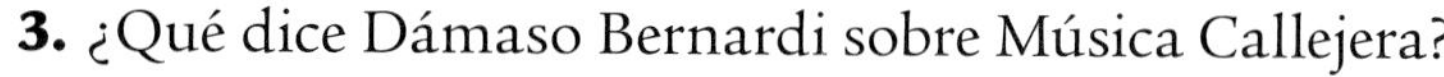

1. ¿Podría decir Jorge Echeverría que *Juego de mesa* es una buena obra?
2. ¿Cómo es la actuación en *Juego de mesa*?
3. ¿Qué dice Dámaso Bernardi sobre Música Callejera?
4. ¿Hasta qué hora te quedarías bailando en Amazonas?
5. ¿Cuántos grupos musicales podrías ver los martes en Amazonas?

11 ¿Qué pasaría?

Hablar
Escribir

Completa cada oración con el condicional de un verbo apropiado.

modelo: Eloíza ____ muchos libros de aventuras.
leería

1. Betina ____ todo el día a los músicos callejeros.
2. Héctor ____ una carta al editor del periódico.
3. Ellos ____ sin parar en el salón de baile.
4. Tú ____ español en Ecuador.
5. Nosotros ____ en avión a Bolivia.

12 En tu lugar...

Leer
Escribir

Tu amigo Iván te escribió este correo electrónico para pedirte consejos. Lee su mensaje y luego contesta, diciéndole qué harías en su lugar.

Hola,

Espero que me puedas dar algunas sugerencias. Tres estudiantes de la conferencia van a quedarse con mi familia este fin de semana. No sé qué les gustaría hacer. ¿Es mejor que nos quedemos en casa jugando a las damas y charlando o debo llevarlos a conocer Lima? Sospecho que nadie tiene mucho dinero pero quiero que todos pasen un buen rato. Por favor, escríbeme hoy con algunas ideas.

Iván

Expansión
Si sales con los amigos de Iván, di qué ropa llevarías, cómo irías y qué harías antes y después de la salida.

¿Comprendiste? Contesta con oraciones completas según la guía del ocio.

1. ¿Iría la gente a ver *Juego de mesa*?
2. ¿Adónde iría la gente a quién le gusta la música?

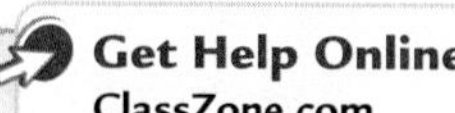

Presentación de GRAMÁTICA

¡AVANZA! **Goal:** Learn how to report information that someone else has told you. Then practice by talking about what other people have said. ***Actividades 13–16***

English Grammar Connection: In English, to report what someone *said*, you can use the simple past, the past progressive, or the conditional tense. In Spanish, a variety of tenses can be used for reported speech as well.

Simple past tense:	Nico **said that** he **went** to the movies.
Past progressive tense:	Nico **said that** he **was going** to the movies.
Conditional tense:	Nico **said that** he **would go** to the movies.

Reported Speech

Animated Grammar ClassZone.com

Use **reported speech** to relay information about what someone said, without using a direct quote.

Here's how:

The second verb in a sentence with **reported speech** can use the preterite, the imperfect, or the conditional.

To report what people said they did, use the preterite.

Nico dijo, «Fui al teatro». *Nico said, "I went to the theater."*	Nico **dijo que fue** al teatro. *Nico **said that he went** to the theater.*

To report what people said they were planning to do, use the imperfect.

Nico dijo, «Voy al teatro». *Nico said, "I'm going to the theater."*	Nico **dijo que iba** al teatro. *Nico **said that he was going** to the theater.*

To report what people said they would do in the future, use the conditional.

Nico dijo, «Iré al teatro». *Nico said, "I will go to the theater."*	Nico **dijo que iría** al teatro. *Nico **said that he would go** to the theater.*

Remember that if you use **decir** to express what someone told *another* person to do, you use the **subjunctive** for the second verb.

Nico **dice** que **vayas** al teatro.
*Nico says that **you should go** to the theater.*

Más práctica

Cuaderno *pp. 226–228*

Cuaderno para hispanohablantes *pp. 227–230*

@HomeTutor Leveled Practice ClassZone.com

Práctica de GRAMÁTICA

13 El ocio

Escuchar
Escribir

Alejandra estuvo con sus amigos. Escucha lo que dice y contesta las preguntas con respuestas completas.

1. ¿Con quiénes dijo Alejandra que se encontró ayer y dónde?
2. ¿Adónde dijo Alejandra que fueron y qué le interesó más?
3. ¿Qué dijo Alejandra de la comida en casa de Javier y Marta?
4. ¿Qué le pasó a Marta durante todo el día?
5. ¿Qué dijo Alejandra que hicieron después de la comida?

14 Una entrevista

Escribir

Para saber lo que dijo el crítico de espectáculos, escribe las oraciones en el condicional. Sigue el modelo.

modelo: Dijo que los actores (dar) una conferencia de prensa.
Dijo que los actores darían una conferencia de prensa.

1. Explicó que el estreno (ser) en enero.
2. Dijo que los otros críticos (debatir) sobre la película.
3. Comentó que (grabar) un CD con la música de la película.
4. Dijo que la historia (concluir) con la segunda parte de la película.
5. Dijo que (haber) una recepción para celebrar con los actores.
6. Anunció que la orquesta (tocar) en la plaza.
7. Dijo que su familia (asistir) otra vez al espectáculo.

Expansión
Escribe cinco posibles cosas más que el crítico dijo que pasarían.

AUDIO

Pronunciación La letra p

La **p** en español tiene un sonido más suave que la **p** en inglés y se pronuncia sin la explosión de aire de la **p** en inglés. La posición de la letra **p** en una palabra no afecta su sonido.

portátil **publicar**
carpintero **imprimir**

Refrán

Pocos pelos pero bien peinados.

15 ¡Tarde!

Hablar

Algunas personas llegaron tarde a un espectáculo. Tu compañero(a) te pregunta qué van a hacer las personas y tú le contestas lo que dijeron según los comentarios siguientes.

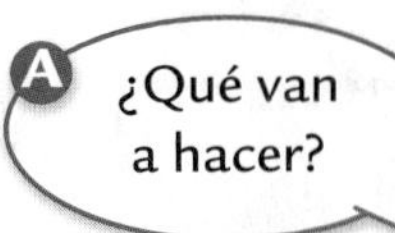

modelo: «Volvamos mañana.»

1. «Preguntemos cómo empezó el espectáculo.»
2. «Tomaré un refresco para calmar los nervios.»
3. «Escucharé la orquesta desde afuera.»
4. «Leeré las opiniones en el periódico.»
5. «Esperemos a los actores para saludarlos.»

Expansión
Repórtale tres comentarios más a tu compañero(a).

16 ¿Qué dijo?

Leer
Hablar
Escribir

Comparación cultural

Maravillas de Perú

¿Qué nos dicen las ruinas antiguas sobre una cultura? Varias civilizaciones dominaron la historia de **Perú.** En Trujillo se pueden ver dos pirámides de la cultura moche (100–700 a.C.), y en Chiclayo, se encuentra la tumba moche del Señor de Sipán. Los científicos dijeron que era un descubrimiento muy importante porque el sitio todavía estaba intacto. Machu Picchu, la famosa ciudad inca montañosa, ha inspirado a millones de personas. Entre ellas está el poeta Pablo Neruda, que dijo en un poema que Machu Picchu era la «alta ciudad de piedras escalares... la madre de piedra, espuma *(mist)* de cóndores.»

Machu Picchu

Compara con tu mundo *¿Hay sitios históricos cerca de tu ciudad? ¿Dónde? ¿Qué importancia tienen?*

Contesta las siguientes preguntas con respuestas completas.

1. ¿Qué dijeron los científicos cuando descubrieron la tumba del Señor de Sipán?
2. ¿Qué dijo Pablo Neruda de la ciudad de Machu Picchu?
3. ¿Qué crees que quiso decir Pablo Neruda cuando utilizó la frase «espuma de cóndores» para definir a Machu Picchu?

Más práctica Cuaderno *pp. 226–228* Cuaderno para hispanohablantes *pp. 227–230*

¿Comprendiste? ¿Qué harían las personas siguientes en el caso de una emergencia?

1. la maestra / llamar al bombero
2. nosotros / salir tranquilamente
3. todos / reunirse afuera
4. los bomberos / llegar pronto

Get Help Online
ClassZone.com

Todo junto

¡AVANZA! **Goal:** ***Show what you know*** Notice how Gladys and her friends use the conditional to discuss possible activities in Peru. Then talk about these activities and which ones would interest you. ***Actividades 17–19***

Resumen contextos 1 y 2 Gladys es una estudiante peruana que está participando en un programa estudiantil en Lima. Acaba de conocer a varios estudiantes de Bolivia.

Contexto 3 *Diálogo*

ESTRATEGIA **Escuchar**
List all the possibilities As you read, make a list of possible places to go in Peru. Write the place, how to get there (by train, plane, etc.), what to see or do there, and who (Raúl, Gladys, Ana, Marilú, and/or Ricardo) wants to go.

AUDIO

Gladys y sus compañeros hacen planes para hacer una excursión para explorar otra parte del país, pues tienen unos días festivos la semana que viene.

Gladys: Bueno, la señora Suárez me dijo que podía acompañarnos si hacemos una excursión. Mañana tenemos que avisarle adónde queremos ir así que deberíamos discutirlo hoy.

Ricardo: A mí me gustaría ver Cuzco. ¡Sería una aventura inolvidable! La combinación de las montañas, las ruinas de los incas, la arquitectura colonial... sería increíble. Además, sería posible hacer una excursión en tren de Cuzco a Machu Picchu.

Gladys: Sí, y también hay muchos pueblitos que venden artesanías.

Raúl: Deberíamos ir allí entonces.

Ana: Ay, pero yo estoy muy ilusionada con la idea de ir a Trujillo. Me fascina la cultura moche. Y hay otros pueblos y ciudades cercanos con ruinas, como Lambayeque y Chiclaya.

Gladys: Y también la playa Huanchaco. Un amigo me dijo que el surfing es muy popular allí.

Raúl: ¿Ruinas y surfing a la vez? ¡Genial! Entonces, estamos decididos, ¿no?

Marilú: No quiero complicar las cosas, pero a mí me gustaría hacer una excursión por el río Amazonas. Podríamos tomar una excursión desde Iquitos. Pasaríamos por el río en un barco muy cómodo donde también comeríamos y dormiríamos. Y los guías nos llevarían a explorar la selva amazónica.

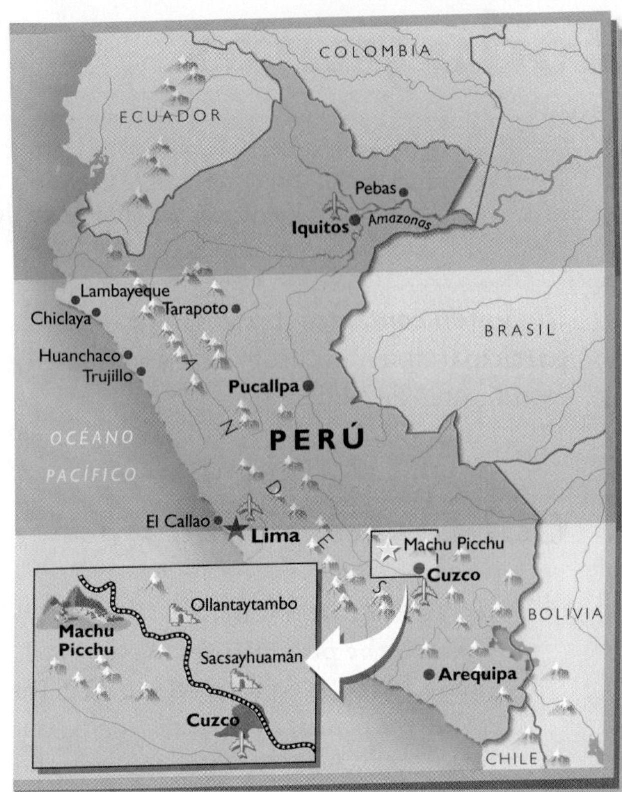

Ricardo: Ay, sí... veríamos la selva tropical, los pájaros, los delfines de agua dulce, los monos... y ¡las pirañas!

Raúl: ¡Pirañas! ¡Fenomenal! Entonces, vamos al Amazonas, ¿verdad?

Gladys: Oye, Raúl, ¡tranquilo, hombre! ¡Quieres hacerlo todo! Bueno, debatamos la cuestión para resolverla pronto. ¡No nos queda mucho tiempo!

17 Comprensión del diálogo

Escuchar Hablar Escribir

Contesta las preguntas.

1. ¿Quién dijo que acompañaría a los delegados en la excursión?
2. ¿Cuáles son los tres destinos principales considerados para la excursión?
3. ¿Qué podrían hacer los chicos en la ciudad de Cuzco?
4. ¿Qué podrían hacer en la región alrededor de Cuzco?
5. ¿Qué dijo Ana que podrían ver en Trujillo?
6. ¿Cuáles serían otros atractivos de la excursión a Trujillo?
7. ¿Cómo visitarían el río Amazonas y qué harían allí?
8. ¿Qué dijo Gladys que deberían hacer para resolver la cuestión?

Expansión
Escoge una excursión que hayas hecho o que te gustaría hacer. ¿Qué lugar es? ¿Qué harías? ¿Qué verías?

18 Integración

Leer
Escuchar
Hablar

Lee las noticias locales de un periódico. Hay un artículo sobre un debate en la comunidad. Escucha la información que pasan por la radio. Explica lo que dijo el alcalde. Di qué harías tú.

Fuente 1 Artículo político

NOTICIAS LOCALES

¿El desarrollo o la protección?

EL PASADO MARTES hubo una conferencia para debatir el desarrollo económico de nuestra comunidad. El alcalde y representantes de varios comités se encontraron para discutir proyectos y planear nuestro futuro. Un tema fue el desarrollo de los parques alrededor del lago. El alcalde quiere que los parques atraigan más turismo y propuso varios proyectos, como la construcción de dos hoteles. Los dos representantes del comité para la belleza de la comunidad no estuvieron de acuerdo y dijeron que sería mucho más importante proteger la ecología de los parques. Discutieron por mucho tiempo pero no llegaron a ninguna resolución.

Fuente 2 Radio Comunidad

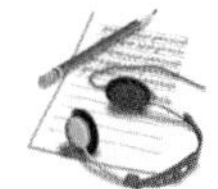

Escucha y apunta

- ¿Qué anunció el alcalde?
- ¿Cómo reaccionaron los comités?
- ¿Qué prometieron los representantes del comité para la belleza de la comunidad?

modelo: El alcalde dijo que iban a construir hoteles porque esto atraería a más turistas. Los comités de representantes dijeron que organizarían otra reunión. Yo haría lo siguiente...

19 Mi profesión favorita

Escribir

Habla con un familiar sobre su profesión. Escribe un ensayo de tres a cinco párrafos sobre sus experiencias. Escribe qué harías tú en su lugar. Mientras escribes, enfócate en el uso de los tiempos pasados y condicional.

Writing Criteria	Excellent	Good	Needs Work
Content	Your essay includes many details about the profession.	Your essay includes some details about the profession.	Your essay includes few details about the profession.
Communication	Your essay is organized and easy to follow.	Parts of your essay are organized and easy to follow.	Your essay is disorganized and hard to follow.
Accuracy	You make few mistakes in grammar and vocabulary.	You make some mistakes in grammar and vocabulary.	You make many mistakes in grammar and vocabulary.

Más práctica Cuaderno *pp. 229–230* Cuaderno para hispanohablantes *pp. 231–232*

¿Comprendiste? ¿Qué dijo que querría hacer? Usa el condicional para completar las oraciones.

1. Ricardo dijo que...
2. Ana dijo que...
3. Sofía dijo que...
4. Raúl dijo que...

Get Help Online
ClassZone.com

Lectura literaria

¡AVANZA! **Goal:** Read about the role chess played in the death of the Inca ruler Atahualpa and then discuss other popular games like checkers, backgammon, and Parcheesi.

Para leer 

ESTRATEGIA Leer

Note causes and effects While reading, use words and arrows to show causes and effects (on a different sheet). Start with the Spaniards discovering something important, and end with Atahualpa being sentenced to death. To reflect the actions, use a verb in each cause and each effect; an effect of a certain action becomes the cause of the next action. Add as many causes and effects as you need for this story.

CAUSA #1: Los españoles descubrieron que Atahualpa y Huáscar estaban luchando.

→ EFECTO #1: ____________________ = CAUSA #2

→ EFECTO #2: ____________________ = CAUSA #3

→ EFECTO #3: Atahualpa fue condenado a muerte.

Vocabulario para leer

la pieza	*una ficha de un juego de mesa*
los lances	*movimientos destacados o estratégicos durante un juego*
las jugadas	*movimientos que se hacen al participar en un juego*
la torre	*una de las fichas del ajedrez*
la partida	*el juego completo, del principio al fin*
el (jaque) mate	*jugada definitiva para ganar un juego de ajedrez*

Nota cultural

Sobre el autor ***Ricardo Palma (1833–1919)***
Nació en Lima, Perú. Aunque estudió leyes, siempre se interesó por la literatura y las tradiciones de su país. Su libro *Tradiciones peruanas* describe momentos históricos y culturales de Perú, que fueron tomados de la tradición oral.

Sobre el imperio inca Atahualpa y su hermano mayor Huáscar fueron los últimos emperadores del imperio inca. Atahualpa gobernó en el norte del imperio y Huáscar en la parte sur. Cuando llegaron los españoles, descubrieron que los dos emperadores estaban luchando por la división del imperio. Francisco Pizarro usó esa rivalidad y capturó a Atahualpa en la ciudad de Cajamarca.

Los incas ajedrecistas

El ajedrez llegó a España de la mano de los moros, quienes disfrutaban mucho de este juego. Para principios del siglo XV, el ajedrez ya era un juego muy popular en España, sobre todo entre los capitanes del ejército. Cuando los conquistadores españoles llegaron al Nuevo Mundo, uno de los elementos culturales que incorporaron fue el ajedrez.

Se sabe, por tradición, que los capitanes Hernando de Soto, Juan de Rada, Francisco de Chaves, Blas de Atienza y el tesorero[1] Riquelme se congregaban todas las tardes, en Cajamarca, en el departamento[2] que sirvió de prisión al Inca Atahualpa desde el día 15 de noviembre de 1532, en que se efectuó la captura del monarca, hasta la antevíspera[3] de su injustificable sacrificio, realizado el 29 de agosto de 1533.

....

[1] treasurer [2] room
[3] two days before

Reflexiona

¿A quién habían capturado los capitanes españoles?

Atahualpa y Francisco Pizarro acuerdan la cantidad por el rescate del rey inca, *Theodore de Bry*

Honda preocupación abrumaría[4] el espíritu del Inca en los dos o tres primeros meses de su cautiverio, pues aunque todas las tardes tomaba asiento junto a Hernando de Soto, su amigo y amparador[5], no daba señales de haberse dado cuenta de la manera como actuaban las piezas ni de los lances y accidentes del juego. Pero una tarde, en las jugadas finales de una partida empeñada[6] entre Soto y Riquelme, hizo ademán[7] Hernando de movilizar el caballo, y el Inca, tocándole ligeramente en el brazo, le dijo en voz baja:

—No, capitán, no... ¡El castillo!

La sorpresa fue general. Hernando, después de breves segundos de meditación, puso en juego la torre, como le aconsejara Atahualpa, y pocas jugadas después sufría Riquelme inevitable *mate*.

[4] must have overwhelmed [5] protector
[6] heated [7] **hizo...** he started to move

A pensar
¿Por qué fue tan sorprendente el consejo que Atahualpa le dio a Hernando de Soto?

Después de aquella tarde, y cediéndole[8] siempre las piezas blancas en muestra de respetuosa cortesía, el capitán don Hernando de Soto invitaba al Inca a jugar una sola partida, y al cabo de[9] un par de meses el discípulo era ya digno del maestro. Jugaban de igual a igual. ❖

❖ A pensar
¿Qué indica la frase «el discípulo era ya digno del maestro»?

....

La tradición popular asegura que el Inca no habría sido condenado[10] a muerte si hubiera permanecido[11] ignorante en el ajedrez. Dice el pueblo que Atahualpa pagó con la vida el *mate* que por su consejo sufriera[12] Riquelme en memorable tarde. En el famoso consejo[13] de veinticuatro jueces, consejo convocado[14] por Pizarro, se impuso a Atahualpa la pena de muerte[15] por trece votos contra once. Riquelme fue uno de los trece que suscribieron[16] la sentencia.

---

[8] assigning him [9] **al...** at the end of
[10] **no...** wouldn't have been condemned [11] **hubiera...** had remained
[12] suffered [13] council [14] called [15] **pena...** death penalty [16] signed

PARA Y PIENSA

¿Comprendiste?

1. ¿Cómo llegó el ajedrez al Nuevo Mundo?
2. ¿Qué hacían los capitanes españoles cada tarde? ¿Dónde lo hacían? ¿Quién más estaba presente?
3. ¿Cómo aprendió el Inca Atahualpa a jugar al ajedrez?
4. ¿Cómo trató Soto a Atahualpa después del *mate* a Riquelme?
5. Según la tradición popular, ¿qué conexión puede haber entre el ajedrez y la muerte de Atahualpa?

¿Y tú?

¿Qué juegos de mesa te gustan? ¿Cuándo los juegas?

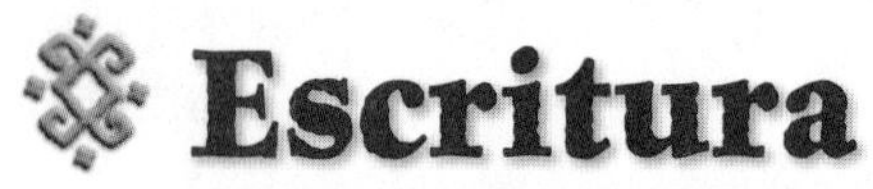

Escritura

Descripción de un viaje

Vas a escribir sobre un viaje que te gustaría hacer a Bolivia, Perú o Ecuador. Antes de empezar a escribir haz la actividad para organizar tus ideas.

1 Prepárate para escribir

ESTRATEGIA **Limita el tema de una composición** Antes de escribir, es necesario enfocarse en el tema y limitarlo. Primero, divide la información que tienes en categorías. Luego, selecciona lo más importante.

Vas a hacer un viaje de una semana a Bolivia, Perú o Ecuador. Tienes poco tiempo y debes organizar el viaje con cuidado. Primero, haz una lista de:

- todos los sitios que te gustaría visitar en cada país
- los tipos de alojamiento que quieres
- las actividades que quieres hacer
- los medios de transporte que vas a usar cuando estás allí

Luego, escoge **un solo país** y piensa en lo que puedes hacer en una semana. Tendrás que eliminar varias cosas de tu lista porque no habrá tiempo para todas. Completa la siguiente tabla con no más de dos actividades por día.

lunes	martes	miércoles	jueves	viernes	sábado	domingo
Viaje de ida						Viaje de regreso

2 Escribe

ESTRATEGIA **Escribe un borrador *(draft)* siguiendo una organización de cinco párrafos**

Párrafo 1 Introducción Di adónde irías y por qué escogiste ese país.

Párrafos 2 a 4 Información Describe las categorías que elegiste. Incluye y explica las actividades de la tabla. Usa el condicional.

Párrafo 5 Conclusión Resume las ventajas del viaje.

3 Revisa tu composición

Intercambia el borrador con un(a) compañero(a) y corrígelo.

- ¿Están claras las actividades de tu compañero(a)? ¿Hay información para cada categoría?
- ¿Son correctas las formas del condicional ?
- ¿Hay una introducción y una conclusión interesantes?

Me interesa mucho la historia de los indígenas. Por eso me ~~gustara~~ gustaría ir a Perú. El primer día iría a Machu Picchu en un autobús. El segundo día pasearía por Lima, la capital. Allí ~~habría~~ hay tiendas y universidades importantes. Me dijeron que Perú es tan lindo que volvería todos los años.

Lección 2

En resumen

Vocabulario y gramática

Vocabulario

Talk About the Day's Activities

asistir a un espectáculo	*to attend a show*	el estreno	*debut, premiere*
dormir una siesta	*to take a nap*	la ficha	*game piece*
encontrarse con	*to meet up with*	el grupo musical	*music group*
pasar un buen rato	*to have a good time*	el juego de mesa	*board game*
relajarse	*to relax*	la manta	*blanket*
el ajedrez	*chess*	la música bailable	*dance music*
el billar	*billiards*	la orquesta	*orchestra*
los dados	*dice*	los naipes	*cards*
las damas	*checkers*	el pasatiempo	*pastime*
		el ocio	*leisure*

Report What Someone Said

asistir a una reunión	*to attend a meeting*
charlar	*to chat*
comentar	*to comment on, to talk about*
concluir	*to conclude, to finish*
debatir	*to debate*
el encuentro	*encounter*
intercambiar opiniones	*to exchange opinions*
relatar	*to relate, to tell*

Other Words and Actions

acogedor(a)	*cozy, welcoming*	el (la) músico(a) callejero(a)	*street musician*
la actuación	*acting*	la resolución	*resolution*
el ambiente	*atmosphere*	resolver	*to solve*
discutir	*to discuss, to argue*	el ruido	*noise*
formal	*formal*	el (la) vendedor(a) ambulante	*street vendor*
informal	*informal, casual*		

Gramática

Nota gramatical: Qué and **cuál** *p. 302*

Conditional Tense

Add the **conditional** endings directly to the **infinitive** of regular verbs.

Infinitive		Conditional endings	
llevar		-ía	-íamos
resolver	+	-ías	-íais
discutir		-ía	-ían

Infinitive	Stem	Infinitive	Stem
haber	**habr-**	**poner**	**pondr-**
poder	**podr-**	**salir**	**saldr-**
querer	**querr-**	**tener**	**tendr-**
saber	**sabr-**	**venir**	**vendr-**
decir	**dir-**	**hacer**	**har-**

Yo **pondría** el escáner aquí. Así lo **tendríamos** al lado de la computadora.

Reported Speech

The second verb in a sentence with **reported speech** can use the preterite, the imperfect, or the conditional.

Nico **dijo que fue** al teatro.
*Nico **said that he went** to the theater.*

Nico **dijo que iba** al teatro.
*Nico **said that he was going** to the theater.*

Nico **dijo que iría** al teatro.
*Nico **said that he would go** to the theater.*

Remember that if you use **decir** to express what someone told *another* person to do, you use the **subjunctive** for the second verb.

Nico **dice** que **vayas** al teatro.
*Nico says that **you should go** to the theater.*

Lección 2

Repaso de la lección

¡LLEGADA!

@HomeTutor
ClassZone.com

Now you can
- say what would or would not happen
- report what someone said
- talk about the day's activities

Using
- conditional tense
- reported speech

To review
- vocabulary p. 298–299

1 Listen and understand

AUDIO

Vas a escuchar información sobre un concurso de radio organizado por una emisora en La Paz, Bolivia. Mientras escuchas escribe el nombre de los tres candidatos y lo que dijeron que harían.

To review
- vocabulary p. 298–299

2 Talk about the day's activities

Di qué hicieron las personas indicadas, en varias partes de la ciudad, según los dibujos. Sigue el modelo.

modelo: Sr. Blanco y Sra. Rojas
El señor Blanco y la señora Rojas asistieron a una reunión.

1. Sra. Mendoza

2. Pedro y Ramón

3. María Rosa y Lorena

4. Hernán

5. Ariel y Sara

6. Carlos y Luisa

To review
• conditional tense p. 303

3 Say what would or would not happen

¿Qué harían las personas en las situaciones indicadas? Forma oraciones con verbos en el condicional.

modelo: Beto y Leticia / un club
Beto y Leticia jugarían a las damas en un club.

1. César y Beatriz / un restaurante elegante
2. yo / una reunión de estudiantes
3. tú / un espectáculo
4. nosotros / una discoteca
5. ustedes / un café

To review
• reported speech p. 308

4 Report what someone said

Unos amigos te llamaron de sus teléfonos celulares y te dejaron mensajes en tu contestadora automática. ¿Qué dijeron que iban a hacer?

modelo: «Hola, soy Felipe. Voy a ir a un estreno en el teatro.»
Felipe dijo que iba a ir a un estreno en el teatro.

1. «Soy Silvio. ¡Escucha! Mañana vamos a jugar al billar a las doce.»
2. «¡Hola! Habla Marisa. Esta tarde voy a comprar los CDs de música bailable que te gustan.»
3. «Te habla Ricardo. Estaré trabajando de vendedor ambulante.»
4. «Oye, habla Pedro. Mañana te comento lo que discutí con Pablo.»

To review
• **Comparación cultural** pp. 304, 310

5 Music and archaeological sites in the Andes

Comparación cultural

1. ¿Cuáles son los instrumentos que se asocian con la música andina?
2. ¿En qué países se toca esta música?
3. ¿Con qué cultura se asocia Machu Picchu?
4. ¿En qué condición estaba Machu Picchu cuando fue descubierto?

Más práctica Cuaderno *pp. 231–242* Cuaderno para hispanohablantes *pp. 233–242*

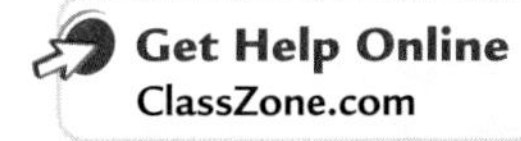

Comparación cultural

Variedad geográfica

Lectura y escritura

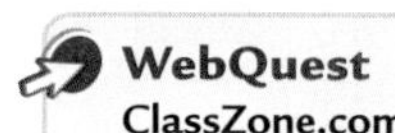

1. **Leer** Lee las descripciones que dan Dolores y Antonio sobre la geografía de sus países.

2. **Escribir** Usa las descripciones que hicieron Dolores y Antonio, y escribe una composición sobre la geografía de la región donde tú vives.

ESTRATEGIA Escribir

Gather and organize cultural information
Gather cultural information using the Internet or the library. Organize it using a chart showing region name, location, and comments/details.

Nombre de la región	Lugar
Características geográficas	

Paso 1 Usa la información de tu tabla para ayudarte a escribir. Escribe tu introducción en el primer párrafo.

Paso 2 Escribe un párrafo sobre cada característica que quieres explicar.

Paso 3 Escribe un párrafo como una conclusión con tus comentarios. Luego revisa la gramática y la ortografía.

Compara con tu mundo

Compara la geografía de tu región con las regiones donde viven Dolores y Antonio. ¿Hay variedad de geografía? ¿Hay animales diferentes o parecidos? ¿Cómo es la arquitectura?

Cuaderno *pp. 243–245* Cuaderno para hispanohablantes *pp. 243–245*

Perú

Dolores

Hola, soy Dolores. Soy de Lima y quiero que conozcas mi país. ¡Perú es un país con zonas geográficas muy distintas! La cordillera de los Andes pasa por el centro, por eso nunca estás lejos de las montañas. Las ruinas de la famosa ciudad inca de Machu Picchu están en los picos del sur de los Andes. La montaña más alta se llama Huascarán y tiene 6.768 metros de altura. Y también tenemos parte del famoso Amazonas, ¡uno de los ríos más grandes del mundo!

Una ciudad muy importante es Cuzco, por su larga historia. Esta ciudad fue la capital del imperio inca. Todavía hay muchos edificios coloniales en su centro histórico. Otra ciudad con mucha arquitectura colonial es Arequipa, que tiene un ambiente muy tradicional y moderno a la vez. A Arequipa también se la conoce como «la ciudad de los volcanes.»

Antonio

¡Hola! ¡Bienvenidos a Ecuador! Soy Antonio y vivo en Quito. Vamos a charlar sobre mi país...

La parte oeste de Ecuador está a una gran altitud. El pico más alto de los Andes, en Ecuador, es Chimborazo, que tiene 6.310 metros de altura. Muchos alpinistas y turistas vienen al país para escalar las montañas y admirar su belleza. ¡Muchos de los picos son volcanes!

Pero la "joya natural" de Ecuador son las islas Galápagos. Estas islas están a más de 900 km. de nuestra costa. Son montañosas y rocosas, con muchos volcanes. En 1835, el explorador Charles Darwin las visitó y se dio cuenta de que las islas tenían muchas especies de animales únicas: muchos tipos de reptiles, animales acuáticos y aves, como este piquero de patas azules. Hoy, las islas son controladas por el gobierno para proteger sus especies únicas. Las islas recibieron su nombre por los galápagos, unas tortugas gigantes que viven allí.

Ecuador

EL DESAFÍO

VIDEO DVD

El desafío de hoy tiene dos partes. Primero, es necesario que los equipos busquen en Internet una receta para hacer guacamole. Luego, deben ir a un restaurante famoso donde hacen el mejor guacamole de Cuernavaca y preparar guacamole para el chef del restaurante.

Antes del video

1. ¿Dónde crees que está María? Describe esta foto. ¿Qué crees que está pasando?

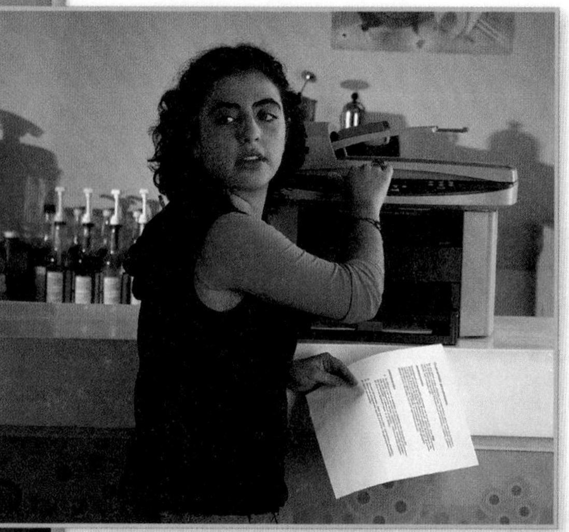

2. Mira esta foto y describe lo que está pasando. ¿Qué crees que está haciendo Marco?

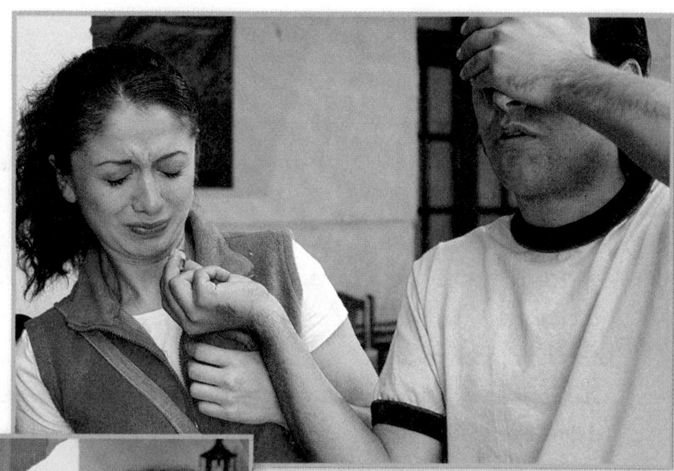

3. ¿Qué crees que pasó aquí? En tu opinión, ¿qué equipo crees que va a ganar este desafío?

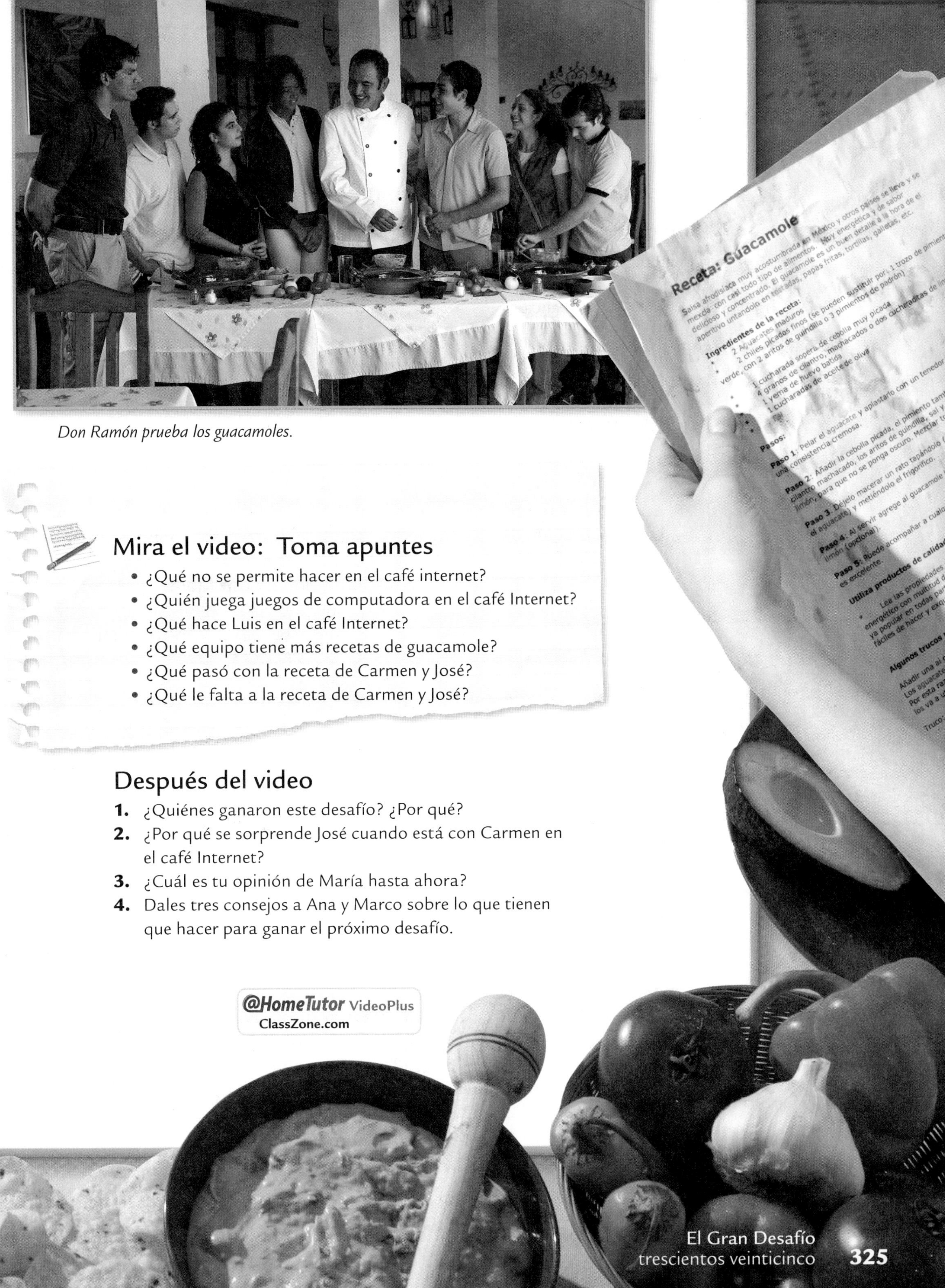

Don Ramón prueba los guacamoles.

Mira el video: Toma apuntes

- ¿Qué no se permite hacer en el café internet?
- ¿Quién juega juegos de computadora en el café Internet?
- ¿Qué hace Luis en el café Internet?
- ¿Qué equipo tiene más recetas de guacamole?
- ¿Qué pasó con la receta de Carmen y José?
- ¿Qué le falta a la receta de Carmen y José?

Después del video

1. ¿Quiénes ganaron este desafío? ¿Por qué?
2. ¿Por qué se sorprende José cuando está con Carmen en el café Internet?
3. ¿Cuál es tu opinión de María hasta ahora?
4. Dales tres consejos a Ana y Marco sobre lo que tienen que hacer para ganar el próximo desafío.

@HomeTutor VideoPlus
ClassZone.com

UNIDADES 1-5

Repaso inclusivo

Options for Review

1 Escucha, comprende y transmite

Escuchar Hablar

Escucha este mensaje telefónico de tu tío y escoge la respuesta apropiada.

modelo: ¿Dónde está tu tío?
a. Guayaquil
b. Cuenca
c. Quito
Dijo que estaba en Quito.

1. ¿Cuándo va a estar libre?
   a. el viernes y el sábado
   b. el sábado y el domingo
   c. el domingo y el lunes
2. ¿Adónde le gustaría ir?
   a. a un restaurante
   b. a una reunión
   c. a una fiesta
3. ¿Qué tiene que comprar?
   a. música callejera
   b. regalos para la familia
   c. un libro sobre edificios coloniales
4. ¿Qué dijo del espectáculo?
   a. que le gusta escuchar a músicos nuevos
   b. que los organizadores de la conferencia lo recomiendan
   c. que debe ser un sitio acogedor

2 Explica lo que hacías

Escribir

Escribe un ensayo sobre lo que hacías con tu familia cuando eras niño(a). ¿Qué reflejaban esas actividades sobre tu vida y personalidad? Escribe por lo menos tres párrafos usando el pretérito y el imperfecto. Incluye palabras que te describan.

3 Organiza un congreso

Hablar

Con un(a) compañero(a), presenten la posibilidad de un congreso internacional en su comunidad. Para organizar sus ideas, consideren cuál sería el tema o enfoque del congreso, a quiénes invitarían, qué incluirían en la agenda y qué harían con los delegados en su tiempo libre. Preparen una presentación para compartir sus ideas con la clase. Utilicen el condicional.

4 Mejora tu comunidad

Hablar

Tú y un(a) compañero(a) tienen que decidir qué hace falta *(is missing)* en su comunidad. Tienen patrocinadores para un proyecto especial. ¿Qué proyecto presentarían y por qué? Para expresar sus ideas, usen oraciones como las del modelo. Luego, decidan qué van a proponer y preparen los detalles que van a presentar a los patrocinadores. No olviden usar el subjuntivo cuando sea necesario.

modelo: **Problema** No hay ningún lugar acogedor donde los jóvenes puedan reunirse para charlar y tomar un refresco.
Solución Queremos tener un lugar donde los jóvenes puedan reunirse, que sea acogedor, que sirva refrescos, que tenga cómo conectarse a Internet...

5 Entrevista, informa y analiza

Hablar
Escribir

Tú y tus compañeros(as) son inversionistas *(investors)* y quieren investigar qué productos o servicios hacen falta en su comunidad. Primero, cada persona del grupo debe entrevistar a varias personas de la comunidad y preguntarles qué hace falta. Luego, el grupo se reúne para informar y analizar los resultados de las encuestas. Después de decidir qué productos o servicios quieren ofrecer, organicen su propuesta para presentarla en clase. Recuerden que los verbos en el futuro son importantes para promocionar un producto.

6 Diseña un lugar para comer

Hablar

Con unos(as) compañeros(as), diseñen un restaurante nuevo para su comunidad. Entre otros detalles, incluyan información sobre el lugar, la comida y el servicio. Presenten sus ideas a la clase con mandatos para persuadirlos de que es el mejor restaurante de la comunidad.

7 Escribe una solicitud a un concurso

Escribir

Decidiste participar en un concurso para recibir a un(a) estudiante de intercambio *(exchange)* durante un año. Escribe una solicitud *(application)* de al menos tres párrafos en la que describas por qué tu familia sería ideal, qué podría hacer el (la) estudiante en tu escuela y comunidad, y a qué lugares de interés lo (la) llevarías.

UNIDAD 6

España

¿Dónde vivimos?

Lección 1

Tema: ***La vida en la ciudad***

Lección 2

Tema: ***Fuera de la ciudad***

«¡Hola!

Somos José Luis y Amparo. Somos españoles.»

Almanaque cultural

Geografía: Península más grande de Europa. Tres mares: Océano Atlántico, mar Mediterráneo y mar Cantábrico con montañas, campos y playas.

Comidas: pulpo a la gallega, cazuela de mariscos, paella, tortilla española

Gente famosa: David Bisbal (cantante), Penélope Cruz (actriz), Pedro Almódovar (director), Pablo Picasso (pintor), Federico García Lorca (poeta)

Lenguas: castellano, catalán, gallego y vascuence.

Tortilla española

Festival de la tapa malagueña, Málaga

La deliciosa comida española España es conocida por sus sabrosas comidas. Los pescados y los mariscos son ingredientes principales en muchos de sus platos, como la cazuela y la paella. Una tradición española es la de comer tapas, que son pequeños platos de diferentes comidas. *¿Cuál es la comida típica de tu región?*

Arquitectura moderna Ciudades como Madrid y Barcelona muestran un fuerte contraste de arquitectura. Allí hay edificios antiguos de estilo gótico pero también hay enormes construcciones modernas, llenas de luces. En estas ciudades cosmopolitas se establecen empresas de todo el mundo. *¿Cuál es el edificio más alto de tu ciudad o región?*

Torre Agbar, Barcelona

El brasilero Robinho jugando para el equipo de fútbol Real Madrid

Una pasión deportiva El fútbol es el deporte favorito de los españoles. España tiene equipos muy importantes, como el Barza y el Real Madrid. Muchos jugadores de Europa y Latinoamérica pasan a jugar para equipos españoles. Este deporte, también conocido como balompié, es la pasión del público español. *¿Cuál es el equipo de fútbol de tu ciudad, región o estado?*

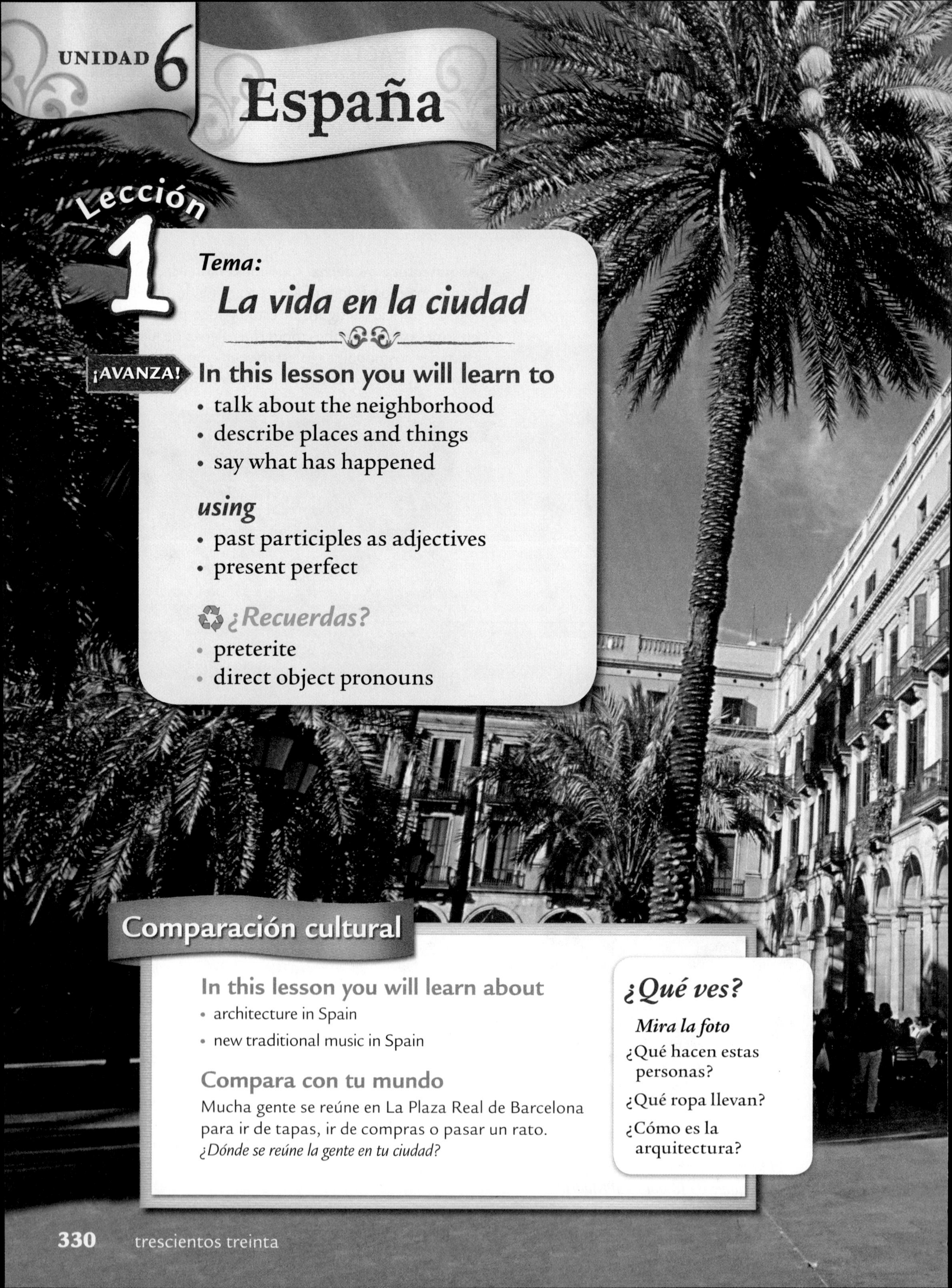

UNIDAD 6

España

Lección 1

Tema:

La vida en la ciudad

¡AVANZA! **In this lesson you will learn to**

- talk about the neighborhood
- describe places and things
- say what has happened

using

- past participles as adjectives
- present perfect

¿Recuerdas?

- preterite
- direct object pronouns

Comparación cultural

In this lesson you will learn about

- architecture in Spain
- new traditional music in Spain

Compara con tu mundo

Mucha gente se reúne en La Plaza Real de Barcelona para ir de tapas, ir de compras o pasar un rato. *¿Dónde se reúne la gente en tu ciudad?*

¿Qué ves?

Mira la foto

¿Qué hacen estas personas?

¿Qué ropa llevan?

¿Cómo es la arquitectura?

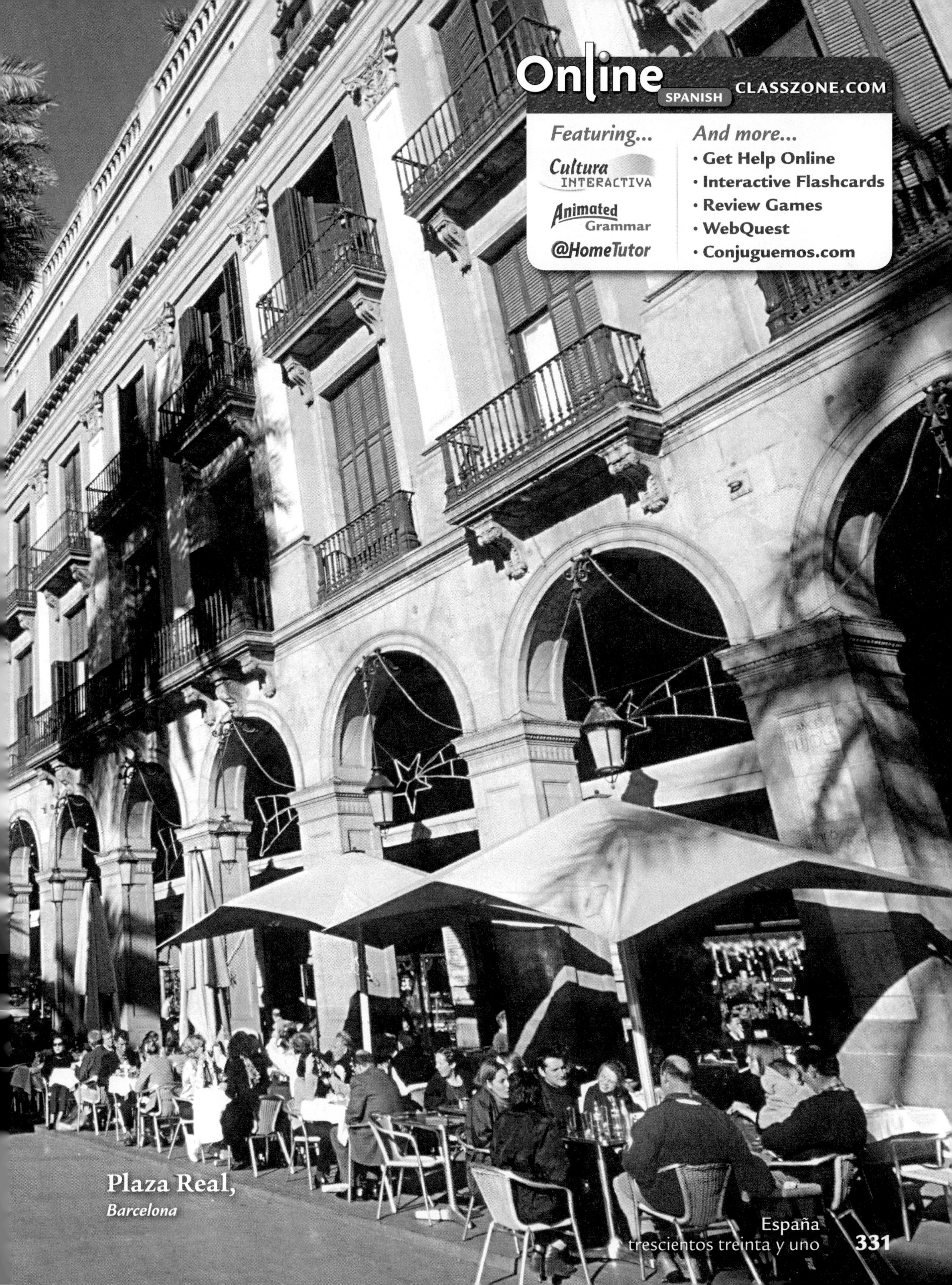

Plaza Real,
Barcelona

Presentación de VOCABULARIO

¡AVANZA! **Goal:** Learn new words to talk about people and places. Then practice what you learned by describing a neighborhood. ***Actividades 1–2***

 *¿Recuerdas?* Preterite pp. 37, 42

AUDIO

A Hola, me llamo Amparo. Mi familia y yo vivimos aquí. Nuestro **piso** es grande y tiene **una terraza** estupenda. Yo **aprovecho** su posición estratégica para ver quién **toca el timbre** y **enterarme de** todo lo que pasa en **la manzana.**

B Nosotros cuidamos nuestro piso: tratamos de no **ensuciar, romper** o **desordenar** nada. Y si algo está **roto,** lo **arreglamos** rápido.

Más vocabulario

(sacar) el billete *(to buy) a ticket*
dejar *to leave (behind)*
el fregadero *kitchen sink*
(abrir/cerrar) el grifo *(to turn on/turn off) faucet*
el kiosco *kiosk*
el lío *mess*
la mesita *nightstand, end table*
(subir a/bajar de) el metro *(to get on/to get off) the subway*
el microondas *microwave*
ordenar *to organize*
quitar *to take away*
el refrigerador *refrigerator*
el sello *stamp*

Expansión de vocabulario p. R12
Ya sabes p. R12

C El barrio es muy bueno y práctico; todas las tiendas están cerca. Para **hacer los mandados,** sólo tengo que caminar un minuto. **La verdulería, la lechería** y **la ferretería** están una al lado de la otra y tienen **ofertas** muy buenas. **El correo** también está muy cerca. También voy a...

la carnicería

la frutería

el cajero automático

la bombonería

la estación de metro

la fuente

el buzón

la pastelería

la florería

D Aquí puedo hacer muchas cosas: **ir de tapas** con mis amigos o ir a mirar **los escaparates** de las tiendas. A veces voy a **dar una vuelta** por el parque y me siento en **un banco.** ¡Me encantan mi piso y mi barrio!

¡A responder! Escuchar

Vas a escuchar una lista de palabras. Si es una cosa que tienes en la cocina de tu casa, levanta la mano derecha. Si es un lugar en tu barrio o pueblo, levanta la mano izquierda.

@HomeTutor
Interactive Flashcards
ClassZone.com

Práctica de VOCABULARIO

1 ¿Dónde se compra?

Hablar
Escribir

Explica dónde se compran los siguientes artículos.

verdulería	ferretería	lechería
frutería	florería	carnicería
bombonería		

modelo: rosas: Las rosas se compran en una florería.

1. manzanas, uvas, naranjas
2. herramientas para la construcción
3. chuletas de cerdo, pollo, bistec
4. lechuga, tomates, espinacas
5. queso, helado, yogur
6. bombones, caramelos

Expansión
Di dos cosas más que se compran en cada tienda. Si es necesario, usa tu diccionario.

2 Búscalo en el barrio

 ***¿Recuerdas?*** Preterite pp. 37, 42

Hablar
Escribir

Usa el pretérito para explicar lo que hizo cada persona.

modelo: Mónica / sacar
Mónica sacó dinero del cajero automático.

1. Pepe y Lola / entrar

2. Arturo / subir

3. tú / poner

4. nosotros / ir

5. yo / hacer

6. ellos / dar

Más práctica Cuaderno *pp. 246–248* Cuaderno para hispanohablantes *pp. 246–249*

¿Comprendiste? Contesta con oraciones completas.

1. ¿Qué haces cuando llegas a una casa y quieres que te abran la puerta?
2. ¿En qué parte del baño te lavas las manos?
3. Cuando estás en el parque y quieres descansar, ¿en dónde te sientas?

Get Help Online
ClassZone.com

VOCABULARIO en contexto

¡AVANZA! **Goal:** Read and listen to the following comic strip, paying special attention to the words used to talk about the apartment and the neighborhood. ***Actividades 3–4***

Contexto 1 *Historieta*

ESTRATEGIA Leer

Analyze the conversations On a separate sheet, draw six boxes, each box matching a panel of the comic strip below. Use the sample questions to help you analyze and understand the dialogue in each box.

CUADRO UNO
• ¿Qué personajes hay? • ¿Hay alguna emoción? • ¿Qué problema hay? • ¿Qué soluciones hay?

AUDIO

Amparo Prado escribe una historieta *(comic strip)* para el periódico de su escuela. Ella vive en Madrid y describe escenas de la vida diaria de su piso y su barrio.

Planeta Barrio

¿Cómo que tu madre viene? ¡Necesito ordenar el piso!
¿No te lo dije? Ella me avisó hace un mes... llega a la una.

Tendremos que limpiar todo, ¡el microondas, el refrigerador y los lavabos!
Tú y Amparo podéis hacerlo muy rápido.

¿Cómo nosotras? ¡¿Y tú?!
Bueno, cariño, yo puedo ir a la verdulería y a la carnicería...
¡Y preparar la comida! ¡Yo tengo que ordenar este piso!

Papá, también ve a la pastelería que está al otro lado de la ciudad...
¡Vale! Tendré que tomar el metro...

Hola, Amparo. ¡Déjame pasar!
Doña Rosario, ¡espere...!
¿Así que tu abuela llega hoy y tu madre acaba de enterarse?

Hola, Silvana. ¡Ay!, ¿pero cómo ensuciaste tanto la cocina?
¡Otro día en Planeta Barrio!

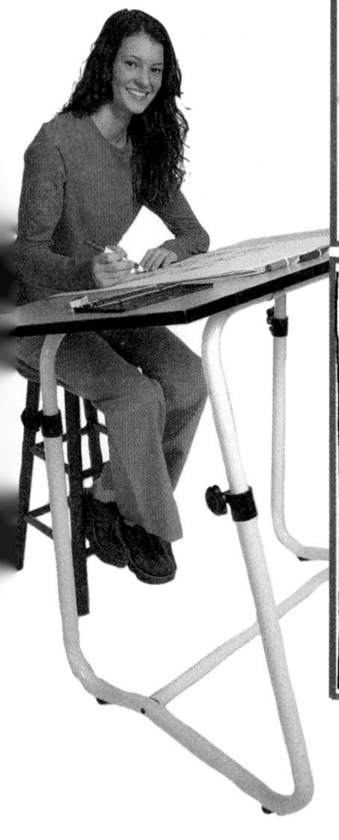

También se dice

La palabra **vale** es muy común en España. Se utiliza en el lenguaje oral para expresar aprobación, como la palabra **¡bueno!**

- **Argentina** listo
- **Perú** sale
- **México** órale
- **Colombia** chévere

3 Comprensión de la historieta

Leer Hablar Escribir

Contesta las siguientes preguntas sobre la lectura.

1. ¿La mamá de Amparo se entera de que tiene que hacer qué inmediatamente?
2. ¿Qué cosas tienen que limpiar Amparo y su madre?
3. ¿Adónde va a ir Rodrigo?
4. ¿Qué tiene que hacer Rodrigo para ir a la pastelería?
5. ¿Dónde estuvo doña Rosario esa mañana?

4 Los mandados

Escribir

Organiza la lista de compras de Rodrigo para agrupar lo que necesita de los siguientes lugares: verdulería, carnicería, frutería, pastelería, heladería, panadería y lechería. ¡Ojo! Rodrigo debe ir también a otros lugares.

lechuga	cebolla	pan
tomates	periódico	pastel
chuletas de cerdo	naranjas	queso
herramientas	fresas	rosas y plantas

Expansión
Rodrigo tiene que ir a la ferretería, al kiosco y a la florería. ¿Qué cosas de su lista incluyes en cada categoría?

Comparación cultural

Un banco sin fin

¿Cómo contribuye el talento artístico de un arquitecto a mejorar los lugares públicos? El Parc Güell en Barcelona, **España,** fue diseñado por el famoso arquitecto catalán Antoni Gaudí. Es una maravilla de fantasía porque los edificios, bancos, murallas y otras superficies están decorados con mosaicos de colores brillantes. Gaudí también diseñó muchos otros edificios en Cataluña.

Parc Güell, Barcelona

Compara con tu mundo *¿Qué edificios u otras construcciones originales y famosas hay en tu ciudad o región? Descríbelos.*

¿Comprendiste? Indica si las siguientes palabras son parte de un piso o un objeto.

Get Help Online ClassZone.com

1. la terraza
2. la bañera
3. el balcón
4. la entrada
5. el lavabo
6. la mesita
7. la ducha
8. el horno

Presentación de GRAMÁTICA

¡AVANZA! **Goal:** Learn about the formation and use of past participles as adjectives. Then practice using past participles for description. ***Actividades 5–8***

English Grammar Connection: In English, as in Spanish, the **past participle** of many verbs can be used as an adjective. In English, it usually ends in *-ed* and is frequently used with the verb *to be* to describe people, places, and things.

The article is **published.** El artículo está **publicado.**

Past Participles as Adjectives

Animated Grammar
ClassZone.com

Past participles are frequently used with the verb **estar** to describe the result of an action.

Here's how: To form the **past participle,** drop the infinitive ending and add **-ado** to **-ar** verbs or **-ido** to **-er** and **-ir** verbs.

arreglar → **arreglado** **esconder** → **escondido** **pedir** → **pedido**

When the past participle is used as an adjective, be sure the ending agrees in number and gender with the noun it describes.

agrees
El **horno** está **arreglado.**
*The oven is **fixed.***

agrees
Las **tapas** están **pedidas.**
*The appetizers are **ordered.***

Irregular Past Participles

Infinitive	Past Participle	Infinitive	Past Participle
abrir	abierto	**ir**	ido
decir	dicho	**morir**	muerto
descubrir	descubierto	**poner**	puesto
escribir	escrito	**resolver**	resuelto
freír	frito	**romper**	roto
hacer	hecho	**ver**	visto
imprimir	impreso	**volver**	vuelto

La ducha no funciona. Está **rota.**
*The shower is not working. It's **broken.***

Todas las mesas están **puestas.**
*All the tables are **set.***

Más práctica
Cuaderno *pp. 249–251*
Cuaderno para hispanohablantes *pp. 250–252*

@HomeTutor
Leveled Practice
ClassZone.com

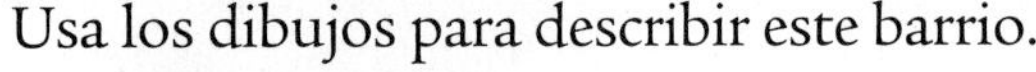

Práctica de GRAMÁTICA

5 En el barrio

Hablar
Escribir

Usa los dibujos para describir este barrio.

modelo: desordenar todo el día
La tienda está desordenada todo el día.

1. cerrar por la noche

2. abrir toda la mañana

3. romper hoy

4. siempre ordenar

5. bien iluminar

6. siempre abrir

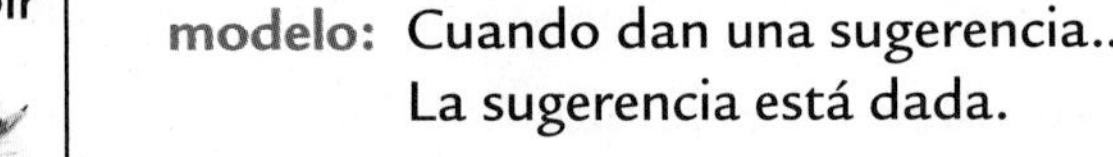

6 Las descripciones

Hablar
Escribir

Describe el resultado de cada acción usando un participio pasado.

modelo: Cuando dan una sugerencia...
La sugerencia está dada.

1. Cuando pierdo mis gafas de sol...
2. Cuando resolvemos un problema...
3. Cuando concluyen una reunión...
4. Cuando nos relajamos...
5. Cuando tú guardas tus documentos...
6. Cuando conecto mi computadora a Internet...
7. Cuando cierran una ventana...
8. Cuando yo hago una buena oferta...

7 Los quehaceres

Hablar

Escucha las sugerencias de tu compañero(a). Usa los participios pasados para explicar que los quehaceres ya están hechos.

modelo: ordenar la habitación

A: Espero que ordenes tu habitación esta tarde.

B: Mi habitación ya está ordenada.

1. arreglar la ducha
2. quitar los platos de la mesa
3. hacer los mandados
4. mandar una carta por correo
5. escribir un correo electrónico
6. poner el reloj en la mesita
7. hacer las tareas de la escuela
8. lavar la bañera
9. reciclar las latas
10. ordenar el garaje
11. ordenar el escaparate
12. no dejar los platos en el fregadero

Expansión
Inventa cinco sugerencias de tu maestro(a) y explica que ya están hechas.

8 Pintar con palabras

Escribir

Escribe una descripción de una habitación de tu casa o apartamento. Incluye por lo menos cinco participios pasados como adjetivos.

modelo: La puerta y las ventanas están abiertas. La cama está hecha un lío, pero el resto de la habitación está ordenado...

Expansión
Léele la descripción a un(a) compañero(a) para que éste(a) dibuje lo que escucha.

AUDIO

Pronunciación La letra h

La **h** nunca tiene sonido en español; es muda. Cuando va seguida por una vocal, el sonido que se pronuncia es la vocal después de la **h.**

hambre **héroe** **prohibir** **hogar** **huésped**

Me han dicho que has dicho un dicho que han dicho que he dicho yo. Pero el que te lo ha dicho mintió.

Más práctica Cuaderno *pp. 249–251* Cuaderno para hispanohablantes *pp. 250–252*

PARA Y PIENSA

¿Comprendiste? Completa cada descripción con el verbo **estar** y el participio pasado del verbo indicado.

1. el grifo / cerrar
2. el timbre / romper
3. la lechería / abrir
4. los pisos / vender

GRAMÁTICA en contexto

¡AVANZA! **Goal:** Notice how past participles are used as adjectives in the following interview. Then practice using past participles to describe people, places and things. ***Actividades 9–11***

¿Recuerdas? Direct object pronouns p. R27

Contexto 2 *Entrevista*

ESTRATEGIA **Leer**

Analyze the characters Based on this reading, analyze what you know so far about Amparo's parents, grandmother, and neighbors. Draw an 8-pointed star for each person. On each point, write a specific fact about the person.

AUDIO

La revista madrileña *Hoy por hoy* vio la historieta *(comic strip)* «Planeta Barrio» y decidió hacerle una entrevista a Amparo.

La reina de las historietas

HOY por hoy: *Dime, Amparo, ¿le molesta a tu familia que cuentes todos sus secretos en la historieta cada mes?*

Amparo: No, tengo mucha suerte. Mis padres creen que mi trabajo es muy divertido, pero no sé si mi abuela estaría de acuerdo.

Hph: *¿Así que tu abuela no lee la historieta?*

A: ¡Qué va! ¡Claro que no! ¿Te imaginas lo que pensaría al leer todos los comentarios sobre el piso desordenado y sobre mis padres desorganizados?

Hph: *¿Pero no te preocupa que ella pueda leer esta entrevista?*

A: No, porque ella vive en Málaga y casi nunca está enterada de lo que pasa en Madrid. Y aquí sólo viene de visita una vez al año y no lee el periódico escolar.

Hph: *¿Y qué me dices de los vecinos?*

A: Bueno, como ves en la historieta, no importa si la puerta está cerrada o abierta. Los vecinos nunca tocan el timbre... entran al piso a cualquier hora.

Hph: *Gracias por tus comentarios, Amparo. Esperemos que estés preparada para el éxito de esta historieta, porque me parece que está garantizado.*

A: Pues, muchas gracias a vosotros. Tengo mucho material escrito para mis próximas historietas... ¡ya veremos qué pasa en el futuro!

32

9 Comprensión de la entrevista

Leer
Hablar
Escribir

Contesta las siguientes preguntas sobre la entrevista que tuvo Amparo.

1. ¿Qué opinan los padres de Amparo sobre la historieta?
2. ¿Cómo está el piso de Amparo? ¿Cómo son sus padres?
3. ¿Por qué piensa Amparo que su abuela no va a leer la entrevista?
4. Según la entrevistadora, ¿qué está garantizado?
5. ¿En qué condición está el material de las próximas historietas?

10 Mi habitación

 ***¿Recuerdas?*** Direct Object Pronouns p. R27

Hablar
Escribir

Hazle preguntas a un(a) compañero(a) para saber en qué condiciones dejó su casa esta mañana.

modelo: la habitación / ordenar / desordenar

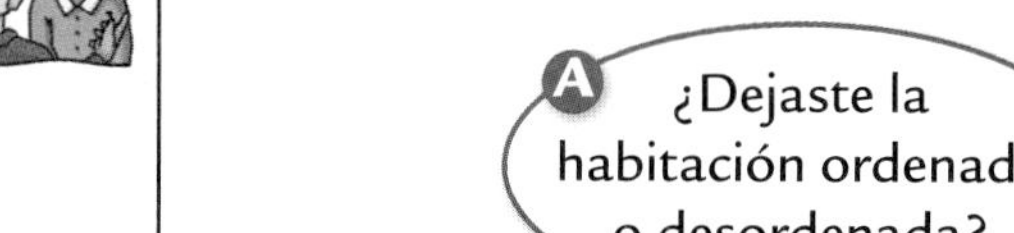

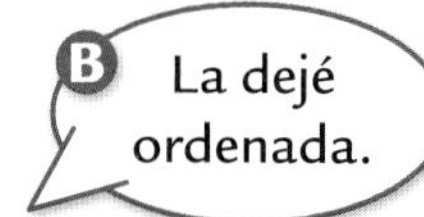

1. la cama / hacer / deshacer
2. las ventanas / abrir / cerrar
3. los zapatos / guardar / tirar
4. el grifo / abierto / cerrado
5. la ropa / colgar / tirar en el suelo
6. el horno / apagar / encender
7. el timbre / romper / arreglar
8. las verduras / preparar / guardar

Expansión
Pregúntale a tu compañero(a) por qué dejó su casa en esas condiciones. Usen los adjetivos en sus preguntas y sus respuestas.

11 ¿Cómo dices que es?

Hablar
Escribir

Con tu compañero(a), asocia los siguientes adjetivos con algo personal o que conozcas.

modelo: Mi casa está separada de las otras casas de la manzana.

separado(a)	divertido(a)	satisfecho(a)	organizado(a)
complicado(a)	abierto(a)	preparado(a)	roto(a)

¿Comprendiste? Utiliza participios pasados para completar las siguientes oraciones basadas en la entrevista con Amparo.

1. Para sus padres, las historietas de Amparo son muy _____ .
2. Como vive en Málaga, su abuela no está _____ de lo que pasa en Madrid.
3. Parece que el éxito de esta historieta está _____ .

Get Help Online
ClassZone.com

Presentación de GRAMÁTICA

¡AVANZA! **Goal:** Learn about the formation and use of the present perfect tense. Then talk about things that have happened in the recent past. ***Actividades 12–15***

English Grammar Connection: The **present perfect** describes an event or action that has taken place. In English, it is formed by combining the verb *has* or *have* and the past participle of the main verb. In Spanish, you use **haber.**

We **have repaired** everything. Nosotros **hemos arreglado** todo.

Present Perfect Tense

Animated Grammar
ClassZone.com

To talk about events that have already happened (or not happened), use the **present perfect** tense.

Here's how: Conjugate the verb **haber** in the present tense and add the past participle of the main verb. In the **present perfect,** the past participle always ends in **-o.**

haber	
he	**hemos**
has	**habéis**
ha	**han**

\+ **past participle**

Ella ya **ha ido** de tapas.
*She **has** already **gone** out to eat.*

Rosa nunca **ha robado** nada.
*Rosa **has** never **stolen** anything.*

When you use **object** or **reflexive pronouns** with the present perfect, you put them *before* the conjugated form of **haber.**

¿Alberto **te ha comprado** el billete?
***Has** Alberto **bought you** the ticket?*

Sí, **me lo ha comprado.**
*Yes, **he has bought it for me.***

There is a written accent over the **i** in the past participle of **-er** and **-ir** verbs with a stem that ends in **a, e,** or **o.**

traer → **traído** **oír** → **oído** **leer** → **leído**

No **he leído** la nueva novela de Pérez Reverte.
***I have** not **read** the new novel by Pérez Reverte.*

Más práctica
Cuaderno *pp. 252–254*
Cuaderno para hispanohablantes *pp. 253–256*

Conjuguemos.com

@HomeTutor
Leveled Practice
ClassZone.com

Práctica de GRAMÁTICA

12 ¿Qué ha hecho Eduardo?

Escuchar
Escribir
Hablar

Escucha la conversación. Escoge el dibujo correcto y di qué ha hecho Eduardo.

modelo: sacar
Ha sacado dinero del cajero automático.

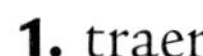

1. traer

2. comprar

3. poder comprar

4. dejar

5. poner

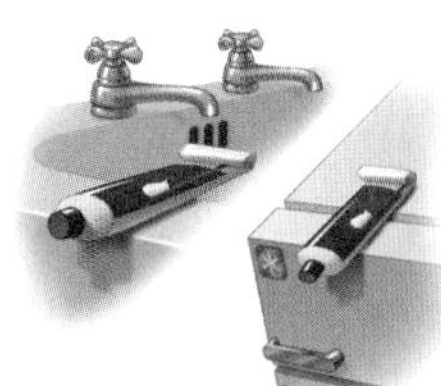

6. poner

13 Anuncios de periódico

Hablar
Leer
Escribir

Lee los anuncios y contesta las preguntas.

Noticias del Barrio

¡Banco González ha abierto un nuevo cajero automático!
Aprovecha este cajero al lado de la Panadería Zamora. La panadería ha extendido su horario hasta las 8 de la noche.

¡Los señores Gil se han jubilado!
Pero la Verdulería Gil no ha cerrado; sólo ha cambiado de nombre. Visita la Verdulería Campos y saluda a Sonia Campos, la nueva dueña.

¡Se ha completado el arreglo de la fuente del Parque Olimpia!
Ha tomado un año y ha costado bastante dinero. ¿Por qué no la visitas?

1. ¿Qué ha hecho la Panadería Zamora?
2. ¿Qué han hecho los señores Gil?
3. ¿Por qué la verdulería se llama Verdulería Campos?
4. ¿Qué ha pasado en el Parque Olimpia?
5. ¿Cuánto tiempo ha tomado la reparación de la fuente?

14 Mi vida hasta ahora

Escribir
Hablar

Prepara una lista de diez cosas interesantes que has hecho en tu vida. Luego, compara tus experiencias con las de tu compañero(a). ¿Qué ha hecho tu compañero(a) que te gustaría hacer también? ¿Qué experiencia de tu compañero(a) no te gusta? Explica por qué.

modelo: **He ido de vacaciones. Mi compañero ha ido a acampar y yo he ido a la playa. Me gustaría acampar y...**

Expansión
Hazle cinco preguntas más a tu compañero(a).
Por ejemplo:
¿Cuándo... ?
¿Por qué... ?
¿Dónde... ?

15 El nuevo rock

Leer
Hablar
Escribir

Comparación cultural

El flamenco: clásico y moderno

El grupo «Ojos de Brujo»

¿Qué importancia tiene la mezcla de dos estilos de música? El flamenco es música que se toca y se canta con el corazón. Expresa los deseos y emociones más íntimas de sus *cantaores,* que es como se les llama a los cantantes de este género. El flamenco es un género musical y un baile tradicional de **España.** Tiene sus raíces en la antigua cultura gitana *(gypsy)* de Andalucía, pero también ha recibido influencias de las culturas árabe y judía. El flamenco ha evolucionado con el tiempo. Varios artistas han incorporado aspectos del flamenco en su música. El guitarrista Paco de Lucía lo ha mezclado con el jazz y la música clásica. La cantante Rosario ha mezclado el flamenco con el rock y el grupo «Ojos de Brujo» lo ha mezclado con hip-hop, rap, funk, reggae y son cubano.

Compara con tu mundo *¿Qué música se escucha en Estadas Unidos que tenga una mezcla con otros estilos? ¿Qué elementos tienen?*

Hay grupos de música norteamericanos que han combinado varios estilos. Escribe un breve ensayo sobre uno de estos grupos: ¿Cuál ha sido el origen del grupo? ¿Qué tipos de música han combinado? ¿En qué éxitos *(hits)* han incorporado los estilos combinados? Usa el presente perfecto.

Más práctica Cuaderno *pp. 252–254* Cuaderno para hispanohablantes *pp. 253–256*

PARA Y PIENSA

¿Comprendiste? ¿Qué han hecho estas personas?

1. tú / dejar tu chaqueta en el tren
2. Mauricio / descubrir un café nuevo
3. mi hermana / venir temprano
4. yo / hablar con mis primos

Get Help Online
ClassZone.com

Todo junto

¡AVANZA! **Goal:** ***Show what you know*** In the following conversation between Amparo and her parents, pay attention to their use of past participles and the present perfect. Then practice by talking about things that have (or haven't) happened. ***Actividades 16–19***

Resumen contextos 1 y 2 Amparo Prado es madrileña y escribe la historieta *(comic strip)* «Planeta Barrio» para el periódico de su escuela. Su historieta llamó la atención de una periodista de la revista madrileña *Hoy por hoy,* quien le hizo una entrevista a Amparo.

Contexto 3 *Diálogo*

ESTRATEGIA **Escuchar**
Use a pyramid to organize possible solutions While listening, use a pyramid to organize the possible solutions identified during the conversation, with the best possible solution at the very top. Then notice how the best solution leads right back to the problem!

AUDIO

La abuela de Amparo, que vive en Málaga, nunca ha leído la historieta que escribe su nieta. La historieta a veces hace chistes de la personalidad de la abuela. Ahora Amparo y sus padres acaban de enterarse de que la abuela llega de visita a Madrid el mismo día que sale una entrevista sobre Amparo y su historieta en una revista madrileña.

Amparo: ¡Papá! ¡Mamá! ¿Han dicho que la abuela viene de visita esta tarde? ¡Pero si estuvo aquí hace sólo un mes!

Padre: Sí, pero en Málaga hace demasiado calor; por eso ha decidido pasar unas semanas aquí.

Amparo: ¡No lo puedo creer! Justo hoy salió la revista con mi entrevista, ¡y está en todos los kioscos de la ciudad! ¡No quiero que ella se entere de la historieta! He escrito algunas cosas que a ella no le van a gustar.

Madre: ¡Qué lío! ¡La situación se ha complicado! Y ahora, ¿qué hacemos?

Amparo: ¡No sé, no sé! Tal vez podemos entretenerla para que no tenga tiempo de comprar revistas...

Padre: Es verdad que tu abuela nunca ha tenido un buen sentido del humor...

Madre: Muy bien, hemos decidido que tenemos que preparar un plan para...

De repente, la puerta, que estaba cerrada, se abre.

Don Ramón: Hola a todos. Soy yo, su vecino favorito. Se ha roto mi televisor y no quería perderme el noticiero... ¿Os importa si uso el microondas para calentar el té un poquitín?

Amparo: Don Ramón, ¡usted me ha dado una idea tremenda!

Don Ramón: ¿Qué has dicho, Amparito?

Amparo: Mi abuela estará una semana de visita en Madrid. ¿Podrían usted y doña Rosario invitarla a ir de tapas o quizás a dar una vuelta por el barrio?

Madre: Creo que has resuelto bien esta situación, Amparo...

Don Ramón: Estaré encantado de daros ese gusto. Y estoy seguro de que doña Rosario no ha planeado nada... Llevaremos a tu abuela por cada lugar de la ciudad.

Amparo: Sí, a pasear por toda la ciudad... ¡menos a los kioscos de revistas!

16 Comprensión del diálogo

Escuchar
Hablar
Escribir

Contesta las preguntas sobre la lectura.

1. ¿Qué ha anunciado el padre de Amparo?
2. ¿Por qué está tan preocupada Amparo?
3. ¿Por qué ha entrado don Ramón en el piso de la familia?
4. ¿Qué pensó Amparo cuando vio a don Ramón?
5. ¿Cómo reaccionó don Ramón cuando Amparo le dijo su idea?

17 Una visita problemática

Hablar
Escribir

Con tus compañeros(as), inventa algún episodio de la visita de la abuela de Amparo. Escriban un diálogo para presentarlo en clase. Usen por lo menos cinco participios como adjetivos y como verbos *(present perfect)*.

Abuela Amparo, los vecinos me han dicho que ha salido un artículo sobre una historieta que escribes todos los meses. ¡Debes estar muy emocionada!

Amparo Ay, abuela, no es nada. La verdad es que no he escrito nada importante.

18 Integración

Leer
Escuchar
Hablar

Lee los anuncios. Luego escucha el mensaje de tu agente con la información sobre los pisos. Después, llama a la agente y pregúntale más sobre los dos pisos que ha recomendado y dile qué has decidido hacer tú.

Fuente 1 Anuncios clasificados

Piso céntrico con 2 habitaciones, cocina, sala y balcón. Barrio tranquilo, edificio antiguo, cerca estación metro Argüelles. Llamar al **2-34-35-25** para más información.

Fabuloso piso de 3 habitaciones, cocina completa, baño y medio, sala y terraza. Estacionamiento incluido. Edificio moderno, mucha luz. Barrio movido, cerca parada de autobús 29, 33, 36. Llamar al **2-42-84-57**.

Piso acogedor en barrio histórico. 1 habitación, baño moderno, cocina simple y salita con muebles. Cerca metro Palacio. Llamar al **2-52-49-39** y dejar nombre y teléfono.

Piso amplio con 2 habitaciones, cocina completa, baño, sala grande y balcón. Cerca centro histórico. Metro Valladolid. Buen precio. Llamar al **2-59-31-90**.

Escucha y apunta

- ¿Qué ha dicho la agente sobre el piso de tres habitaciones?
- ¿Qué detalles ha mencionado sobre los otros pisos?

modelo: Usted ha dicho que el piso de tres habitaciones... Yo he decidido...

19 ¡A escribir!

Escribir

Escribe un ensayo de tres a cinco párrafos sobre las actividades que has hecho y no has hecho todavía este año. Organiza la información. Utiliza el vocabulario sobre las partes de la casa, el barrio y algunas actividades para hacer en la ciudad. Incluye al menos tres ejemplos de participios como adjetivos y cinco en forma de verbos *(present perfect)*.

Writing Criteria	Excellent	Good	Needs Work
Content	Your essay includes many details about your activities.	Your essay includes some details about your activities.	Your essay includes few details about your activities.
Communication	Your essay is organized and easy to follow.	Parts of your essay are organized and easy to follow.	Your essay is disorganized and hard to follow.
Accuracy	You make few mistakes in grammar and vocabulary.	You make some mistakes in grammar and vocabulary.	You make many mistakes in grammar and vocabulary.

Más práctica Cuaderno *pp. 255–256* Cuaderno para hispanohablantes *pp. 257–258*

¿Comprendiste? Escribe oraciones con el participio pasado de los verbos siguientes. Escribe dos oraciones con cada verbo para usar los participios pasados como adjetivos y como verbos.

1. romper **2.** arreglar **3.** hacer **4.** dormir

Get Help Online
ClassZone.com

Lectura literaria

¡AVANZA! **Goal:** Read the following story written by a Spanish author. Then talk about the ways in which nicknames can be both positive and negative.

Para leer 

ESTRATEGIA Leer

Recognize the humor While reading the story, pay special attention to Manolito's sense of humor. To do this, first draw a table with three columns. Use as many rows as you need. In the story, find as many examples of humor as you can and write them in the first column. For each example, explain why it is funny (second column) and how it reflects the culture (third column). Consider how humor can differ across cultures.

Ejemplo	¿Por qué es divertido?	¿Qué elemento cultural hay?

Vocabulario para leer

el tío *amigo, hombre, muchacho*
el camión *vehículo para transportar mercancía por carretera*
el mono *animal parecido al hombre*
fastidiar *hacerle cosas desagradables a alguien*
el colegio *escuela*
el mote *nombre que se da a una persona por una cualidad o condición suya*
meterse con alguien *provocar a alguien*
hacerle gracia a alguien *ser simpático con alguien*

Nota cultural

Sobre la autora ***Elvira Lindo (1962–)***
Nació en Cádiz pero ha vivido en Madrid desde que tenía doce años. Ha escrito guiones *(scripts)* para programas de televisión y también reseñas *(reviews)* de libros para varios periódicos. Se ha destacado por su trabajo en la radio donde ella creó el personaje de Manolito Gafotas. También se ha realizado una película sobre Manolito, dirigida por Miguel Albaladejo.

Sobre los motes Los motes *(nicknames)*, como se llaman en España, o los apodos, como se llaman en Latinoamérica, se basan en características de la apariencia física o de la personalidad de una persona. El uso de apodos es muy común en los países hispanohablantes y generalmente demuestran cariño. Sin embargo, hay que tener cuidado al usarlos para no ofender a nadie. En la selección que estás a punto de leer, el mote de Manolito, «Gafotas», hace referencia a sus gafas grandes, y el de su amigo, «Orejones», se refiere a sus orejas grandes.

Manolito Gafotas

Me llamo Manolito García Moreno, pero si tú entras a mi barrio y le preguntas al primer tío que pase:

—Oiga, por favor, ¿Manolito García Moreno?

El tío, una de dos, o se encoge de hombros[1] o te suelta[2]:

—Oiga, y a mí qué me cuenta[3].

Porque por Manolito García Moreno no me conoce ni el Orejones[4] López, que es mi mejor amigo, aunque algunas veces sea un cochino[5] y un traidor y otras, un cochino traidor, así todo junto y con todas sus letras, pero es mi mejor amigo y mola un pegote[6].

En Carabanchel, que es mi barrio, por si no te lo había dicho[7], todo el mundo me conoce por Manolito Gafotas. Todo el mundo que me conoce, claro. Los que no me conocen no saben ni que llevo gafas desde que tenía cinco años. Ahora, que ellos se lo pierden[8]. ❖

Me pusieron Manolito por el camión de mi padre y al camión le pusieron Manolito por mi padre, que se llama Manolo. A mi padre le pusieron Manolo por su padre, y así hasta el principio de

❖ **A pensar**
¿Por qué crees que las personas conocen a Manolito por el mote y no por su nombre?

---

[1] **se...** shrugs his shoulders [2] **te...** he says to you
[3] **y...** what's it to me [4] big ears [5] pig [6] **mola...** he really rocks
[7] **por...** in case I hadn't told you [8] **ellos...** that's their loss

Lectura literaria *continuación*

los tiempos. O sea, que por si no lo sabe Steven Spielberg, el primer dinosaurio Velociraptor se llamaba Manolo, y así hasta nuestros días. Hasta el último Manolito García, que soy yo, el último mono. Así es como me llama mi madre en algunos momentos cruciales, y no me llama así porque sea una investigadora de los orígenes de la humanidad. Me llama así cuando está a punto de soltarme[9] una galleta o colleja[10]. A mí me fastidia que me llame el último mono, y a ella le fastidia que en el barrio me llamen el Gafotas. Está visto que nos fastidian cosas distintas aunque seamos de la misma familia.

A mí me gusta que me llamen Gafotas. En mi colegio, que es el «Diego Velásquez», todo el mundo que es un poco importante tiene un mote. Antes de tener un mote yo lloraba bastante. Cuando un chulito[11] se metía conmigo en el recreo siempre acababa insultándome y llamándome cuatro-ojos o gafotas. Desde que soy Manolito Gafotas insultarme es una pérdida de tiempo. Bueno, también me pueden llamar Cabezón[12], pero eso de momento no se les ha ocurrido y desde luego[13] yo no pienso dar pistas. Lo mismo le pasaba a mi amigo el Orejones López; desde que tiene su mote ahora ya nadie se mete con sus orejas.

....

A pensar
¿Por qué le gusta a Manolito su mote?

[9] give me [10] **una...** a slap [11] little bully [12] big head
[13] **desde...** of course

Reflexiona

¿Cuál es la historia del nombre «Manolo» según Manolito?

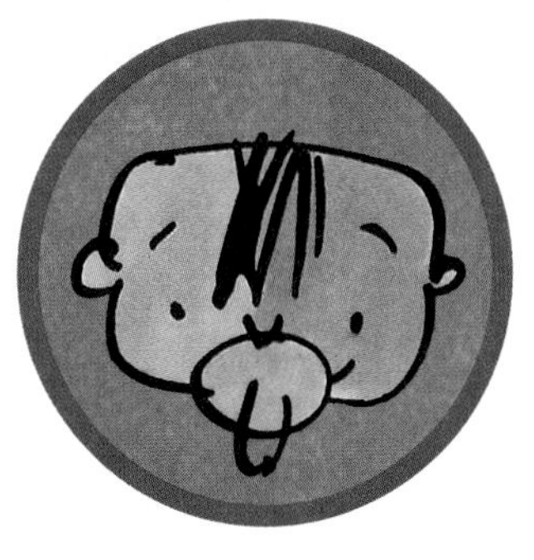

El Imbécil es mi hermanito pequeño, el único que tengo. A mi madre no le gusta que le llame El Imbécil; no hay ningún mote que a ella le haga gracia. Que conste[14] que yo se lo empecé a llamar sin darme cuenta. No fue de esas veces que te pones a pensar con los puños sujetando[15] la cabeza porque te va a estallar[16].

Me salió el primer día que nació. Me llevó mi abuelo al hospital; yo tenía cinco años; me acuerdo porque acababa de estrenar[17] mis primeras gafas y mi vecina la Luisa siempre decía: «Pobrecillo, con cinco años.» ✻

Bueno, pues me acerqué a la cuna[18] y le fui a abrir un ojo con la mano [...] Yo fui a hacerlo con mi mejor intención y el tío se puso a llorar con ese llanto[19] tan falso que tiene. Entonces todos se me echaron encima[20] [...] y pensé por primera vez: «¡Qué imbécil!», y es de esas cosas que ya no se te quitan de la cabeza. Así que nadie me puede decir que le haya puesto el mote aposta[21]; ha sido él, que ha nacido para molestar y se lo merece.

✻ A pensar
¿Por qué la vecina dice «pobrecillo»?

---

[14] **Que...** let me just say [15] **con...** fists pressing [16] explode
[17] **acababa...** I had just worn for the first time [18] cradle [19] cry
[20] **todos...** everybody jumped on me [21] on purpose

¿Comprendiste?

1. ¿Por qué nombre conoce todo el mundo a Manolito?
2. Según Manolito, ¿cuál es la ventaja *(advantage)* de tener un mote?
3. ¿Cómo le puso Manolito el mote a su hermanito?
4. ¿Qué opina la mamá de Manolito de los motes?

¿Y tú?

¿Qué opinas tú de los motes? ¿Tienes un mote? ¿Cómo lo recibiste? ¿Quién(es) lo usa(n)?

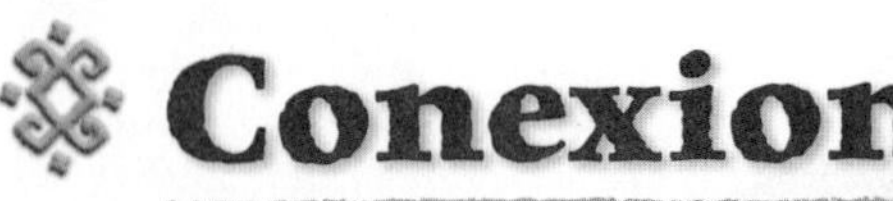

Conexiones *El arte*

Retratos de mujeres

España ha tenido un papel importante en la historia de la pintura. Algunas de las pinturas más antiguas del mundo (16,000–9,000 a.C.) se encuentran en las paredes de las cuevas de Altamira, en el norte del país. También son famosos los pintores religiosos como Francisco de Zurbarán y realistas como Diego Velázquez. El artista más famoso del siglo XVIII

Retrato de una niña, *(1642)*
Velázquez

Retrato de Dora Maar, *(1937)*
Picasso

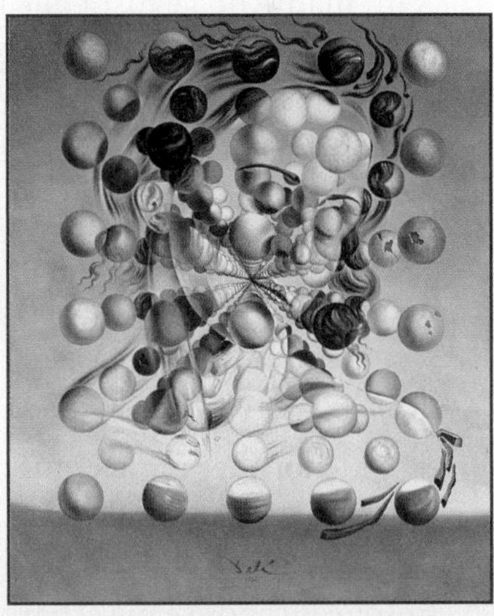

Galatea de las esferas, *(1952)*
Dalí

fue Francisco de Goya, con sus temas sociales y políticos. Además, durante el siglo XX, en España hubo otro gran florecimiento artístico que produjo varios pintores fundamentales del arte moderno. Pablo Picasso fue uno de los padres del cubismo, que representa los objetos desde varias perspectivas con formas geométricas. Los innovadores del surrealismo fueron dos catalanes, Salvador Dalí y Joan Miró. Sus obras tratan de expresar las ideas de la mente subconsciente con imágenes de los sueños *(dreams)*.

Proyecto Mira los tres retratos de mujeres hechos por el pintor realista Velázquez, el pintor cubista Picasso y el pintor surrealista Dalí. Describe cada pintura y compara los colores, las formas y el efecto total de la pintura de cada uno.

En tu comunidad

¿Hay algún lugar en tu comunidad donde puedas ver arte? Piensa en los lugares públicos. ¿Qué ves allí?

Haz una investigación para buscar el retrato de una persona hecho por un(a) artista estadounidense. Compáralo con uno de los retratos de arriba. Utiliza las siguientes preguntas para guiarte: ¿De qué año son los dos retratos? ¿A qué movimientos artísticos pertenecen *(belong)*? ¿En qué se parecen y en qué se diferencian?

En resumen

Vocabulario y gramática

Vocabulario

Talk About the Neighborhood

el banco	*bench*	la frutería	*fruit stand*
la bombonería	*candy store*	la fuente	*fountain*
el buzón	*mailbox*	el kiosco	*kiosk*
el cajero automático	*ATM*	la lechería	*dairy store*
la carnicería	*butcher shop*	la manzana	*(city) block*
el correo	*post office*	la oferta	*offer*
el escaparate	*display window*	la pastelería	*pastry shop*
la estación de metro	*subway station*	la verdulería	*vegetable stand*
la ferretería	*hardware store*	(sacar) el billete	*(to buy) a ticket*
la florería	*flower shop*	(subir a/bajar de) el metro	*(to get on/to get off) the subway*

Say What Has Happened

(abrir/cerrar) el grifo	*(to turn on/to turn off) the faucet*
(tocar) el timbre	*(to ring) the doorbell*
aprovechar	*to take advantage (of something)*
arreglar	*to repair*
dar una vuelta	*to take a walk*
dejar	*to leave (behind)*
enterarse de	*to find out about*
hacer los mandados	*to do errands*
ir de tapas	*to go out to eat*
ordenar	*to organize*
quitar	*to take away*

Describe Places and Things

el balcón	*balcony*	el lío	*mess*
la bañera	*bathtub*	la mesita	*nightstand, end table*
desordenar	*to mess up*	el microondas	*microwave*
la ducha	*shower*	el piso	*apartment*
ensuciar	*to get dirty*	el refrigerador	*refrigerator*
la entrada	*entrance*	romper	*to break*
el fregadero	*kitchen sink*	roto(a)	*broken*
el horno	*oven*	el sello	*stamp*
el lavabo	*bathroom sink*	la terraza	*terrace*

Gramática

Past Participles as Adjectives

To form the **past participle,** drop the infinitive ending and add **-ado** to **-ar** verbs or **-ido** to **-er** and **-ir** verbs.

arreglar → **arreglado** **esconder** → **escondido**

pedir → **pedido**

When the past participle is used as an adjective, the ending agrees in number and gender with the noun it describes.

agrees — El **horno** está **arreglado.**

agrees — Las **tapas** están **pedidas.**

Infinitive	Past Participle	Infinitive	Past Participle
abrir	**abierto**	**ir**	**ido**
decir	**dicho**	**morir**	**muerto**
poner	**puesto**	**escribir**	**escrito**
freír	**frito**	**romper**	**roto**
hacer	**hecho**	**ver**	**visto**
imprimir	**impreso**	**volver**	**vuelto**

Present Perfect Tense

haber	
he	**hemos**
has	**habéis**
ha	**han**

\+ **past participle**

Ella ya **ha ido** de tapas.
*She **has** already **gone** out to eat.*

When you use **object** or **reflexive pronouns** with the present perfect, you put them *before* the conjugated form of **haber.**

¿Alberto **te ha comprado** el billete?
Sí, **me lo ha comprado.**

There is a written accent over the **i** in the past participle of **-er** and **-ir** verbs with a stem that ends in **a, e,** or **o.**

traer → **traído** **oír** → **oído** **leer** → **leído**

Lección 1

Repaso de la lección

@HomeTutor
ClassZone.com

Now you can
- talk about the neighborhood
- describe places and things
- say what has happened

Using
- past participles as adjectives
- present perfect

To review
- vocabulary pp. 332–333

1 Listen and understand

El Sr. Valle es el portero *(doorman)* de un edificio de apartamentos en Madrid. Tiene tres mensajes de diferentes residentes del edificio. Escucha sus mensajes y luego di si las siguientes oraciones son verdaderas o falsas.

1. La Srta. Valdez vive en el apartamento 1C.
2. La Srta. Valdez tiene un problema con el grifo de la cocina.
3. La Srta. Valdez necesita ayuda para mover sus plantas a la terraza.
4. El Sr. Valle ha organizado una fiesta de sorpresa para su esposa.
5. Los invitados van a llegar entre las cinco y las seis de la tarde.
6. El gatito de la Sra. Blanco se ha subido al balcón y no sabe regresar.

To review
- past participles as adjectives p. 337

2 Describe places and things

Son las once de la mañana. Escribe frases con el participio pasado para describir qué pasa en el piso.

modelo: El grifo está abierto.

1. 

2. 

3. 

4. 

5. 

6. 

To review
- present perfect p. 342

3 Talk about your neighborhood

Haz oraciones sobre las actividades en el barrio. ¿Qué han hecho tus vecinos? Utiliza las variantes que aparecen en las columnas.

modelo: Ana / comprar flores / no entrar carnicería
Ana ha comprado flores pero todavía no ha entrado a la carnicería.

Ramona	encontrar a su amigo	no correr
Rafael y Jaime	entrar en la estación de metro	no enviar una carta
Pablito	comer helado	no sacar billetes
Doña Clara	salir de la ferretería	no montar en bicicleta
Don Pepe	alquilar un piso	no sentarse en el banco
Pilar y Gil	ir al parque con su perro	no arreglar el grifo

To review
- present perfect p. 342

4 Talk about what has happened

Lee los mandatos que recibieron las siguientes personas. Luego di qué han hecho y qué no han hecho.

modelo: Paco, limpia la cocina y haz las compras.
Paco ha limpiado la cocina pero no ha hecho las compras.

1. Mónica y Alicia, den una vuelta y vayan al correo.
2. Adela, escribe una carta y envíala.
3. Tú, entra en la bombonería pero no comas.
4. Caminemos hasta el kiosco y compremos el periódico.
5. Señor, abra la farmacia y límpiela.

To review
- **Comparación cultural** pp. 336, 344

5 Architecture and traditional music

Comparación cultural

1. ¿Qué es el Parc Güell?
2. ¿En dónde hay más edificios de Gaudí?
3. ¿Qué culturas han influido en la música flamenca?
4. ¿Qué tipos de música mezcló la cantante Rosario?

Más práctica Cuaderno *pp. 257–268* Cuaderno para hispanohablantes *pp. 259–268*

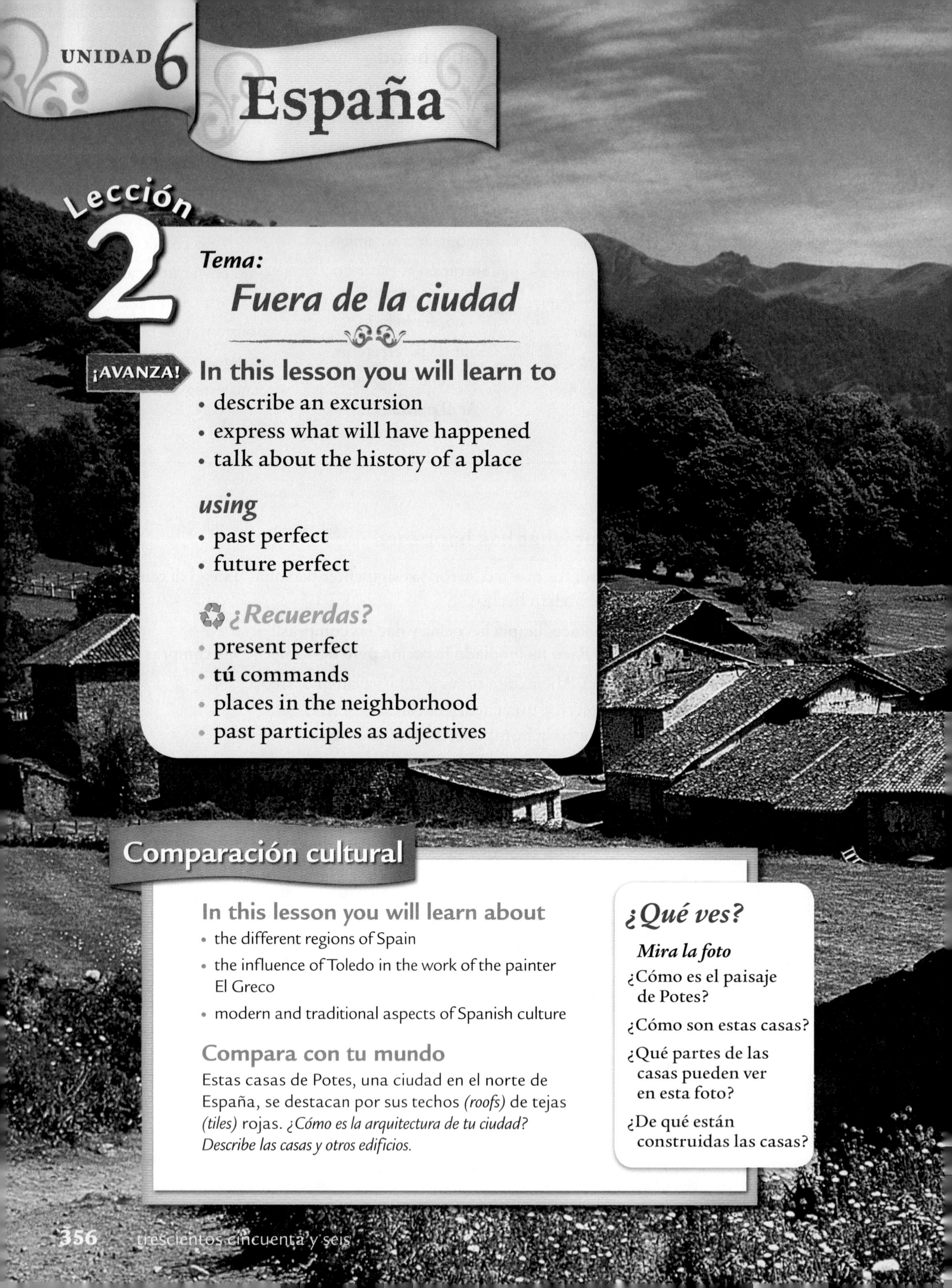

España

Lección 2

Tema:

Fuera de la ciudad

¡AVANZA! **In this lesson you will learn to**

- describe an excursion
- express what will have happened
- talk about the history of a place

using

- past perfect
- future perfect

¿Recuerdas?

- present perfect
- **tú** commands
- places in the neighborhood
- past participles as adjectives

Comparación cultural

In this lesson you will learn about

- the different regions of Spain
- the influence of Toledo in the work of the painter El Greco
- modern and traditional aspects of Spanish culture

Compara con tu mundo

Estas casas de Potes, una ciudad en el norte de España, se destacan por sus techos *(roofs)* de tejas *(tiles)* rojas. *¿Cómo es la arquitectura de tu ciudad? Describe las casas y otros edificios.*

¿Qué ves?

Mira la foto

¿Cómo es el paisaje de Potes?

¿Cómo son estas casas?

¿Qué partes de las casas pueden ver en esta foto?

¿De qué están construidas las casas?

Featuring...

Cultura INTERACTIVA

Animated Grammar

@HomeTutor

And more...

- Get Help Online
- Interactive Flashcards
- Review Games
- WebQuest
- Conjuguemos.com

Casas de techos rojos,
Potes

 Presentación de VOCABULARIO

¡AVANZA! **Goal:** Learn new vocabulary to describe an excursion. Then practice what you learned by talking about real or imagined trips. ***Actividades 1–3***

¿Recuerdas? Present perfect p. 342, **tú** commands p. 97

AUDIO

¡A GRANADA EN TREN!

A Usted puede **hacer una visita guiada** donde podrá **probar las especialidades** de nuestra cocina. **Además,** no tendrá que **pedir direcciones** ni **se perderá.** Podrá caminar tranquilamente por la parte antigua de la ciudad, **pues** nuestros guías le mostrarán la ciudad en **orden cronológico,** y podrá **analizar** cada detalle de la arquitectura.

El interior de La Alhambra

Los famosos **callejones callados** de la ciudad

B Granada es una ciudad excelente para **explorar.** Allí puedes ver el palacio de La Alhambra en el **centro histórico** y descubrir la belleza de sus **callejones callados,** muy diferentes de las calles **ruidosas** de las ciudades grandes.

Más vocabulario

a pesar de que *in spite of, despite*
el asiento numerado *numbered seat*
caerse *to fall down*
el castillo *castle*
consecutivo(a) *consecutive, in a row*
el cuadro *painting*
meterse en problemas *to get into trouble*
el mirador *lookout, outlook*
el plano *city map*
el tapiz *tapestry*
tratarse de *to be about*

Expansión de vocabulario p. R13
Ya sabes p. R13

C

En conclusión, ¡no pierda la oportunidad de disfrutar de las mejores vistas de las murallas, los puentes, el río y las fortalezas de la ciudad! Compre su billete en la taquilla, y mientras espera el tren, puede tomar algo refrescante en la sala de espera. ¡Granada es una experiencia única!

el paisaje

a Madrid
la ruta
A6
LINARES BAEZA
Jodar-Úbeda
Los Propios y Cazorla
Larva
Huesa
Cabra Santo Cristo
Alamedilla G.
Moreda
Iznalloz
GRANADA
Andújar
Espeluy
JAÉN
A2

el vagón
Granada
la vía
el andén

la ventanilla
el pasillo

el conductor

¡A responder! Escuchar

Vas a escuchar diez frases. Si la frase describe una excursión en tren, levanta la mano derecha. Si describe el paisaje que puedes ver, levanta la mano izquierda.

@HomeTutor
Interactive Flashcards
ClassZone.com

Práctica de VOCABULARIO

1 Viajar en tren

Hablar
Escribir

Contesta cada pregunta con una palabra de la lista.

1. ¿Cómo se llama un carro del tren?
2. ¿Dónde puedes sentarte antes de llegar el tren?
3. ¿Dónde compras un billete de tren?
4. Si quieres admirar el paisaje, ¿qué asiento prefieres?
5. ¿Dónde se suben los pasajeros al tren?

la taquilla
el vagón
la ventanilla
el andén
la sala de espera

2 De excursión

 ***¿Recuerdas?*** Present perfect p. 342

Hablar

Tú y tu compañero(a) acaban de encontrarse por casualidad *(chance)* en un café en Granada. Usen el presente perfecto para hacerse preguntas.

modelo: perderse

A: ¿Cuántas veces te has perdido?

B: No me he perdido. Tengo un plano. ¿Y tú? ¿Te has perdido mucho?

1. tomar algo
2. explorar
3. pedir direcciones
4. hacer una visita guiada
5. meterse en problemas
6. probar las especialidades

Expansión
Hazle cinco preguntas más a tu compañero(a) sobre su experiencia en Granada.

3 Saludos de Barcelona

 ***¿Recuerdas?*** **tú** commands p. 97

Escribir

Un amigo te ha escrito desde Barcelona. Escoge la opción correcta para saber sus recomendaciones.

¡Hola! Ven a visitarme. Iremos al __**1.**__ *(centro histórico / asiento numerado), una parte muy* __**2.**__ *(ruidosa / callada) y tranquila, para que aprendas sobre mi ciudad. Consigue un* __**3.**__ *(mirador / plano) y* __**4.**__ *(pide direcciones / prueba las especialidades) para llegar a mi casa. Podemos pasear y* __**5.**__ *(meternos en problemas / tomar algo). Yo no tengo vacaciones, pero* __**6.**__ *(a pesar de / además de) trabajar, puedo dedicar dos días consecutivos a pasear.* __**7.**__ *(En orden cronológico / En conclusión), nos vamos a divertir mucho.*

Pepe

Más práctica Cuaderno *pp. 269–271* Cuaderno para hispanohablantes *pp. 269–272*

¿Comprendiste? Completa con la palabra más apropiada.

1. El _____ pasa por el vagón para revisar los billetes de los pasajeros.
2. La _____ del tren pasa por túneles y sobre _____ que cruzan ríos.

Get Help Online
ClassZone.com

VOCABULARIO en contexto

¡AVANZA! **Goal:** Notice the words that are used to talk about the history and culture of Toledo in the guidebook below. Then practice by comparing Toledo to the city or region where you live. ***Actividades 4–5***

Contexto 1 *Guía del Viajero*

ESTRATEGIA **Leer**
Cluster related words While reading about Toledo, make a mind map to cluster related words. You can create your own categories.

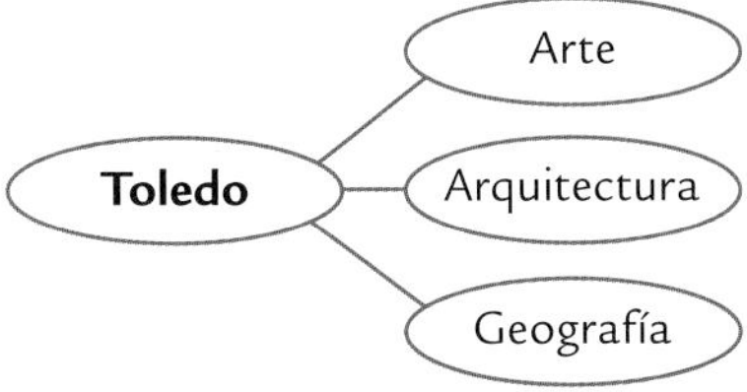

AUDIO

José Luis Barra es de Barcelona, pero está pasando el verano visitando a su primo Francisco en Madrid. Los dos van a pasar un día en Toledo, explorando el centro histórico. La última vez que José Luis visitó Toledo fue hace diez años, así que está leyendo una guía del viajero *(traveler's guide)* para prepararse para la excursión.

Toledo

Toledo tiene de todo. ¡Ven a explorarlo!

Una historia, muchas culturas

Toledo está en la orilla del río Tajo. Turistas de todo el mundo lo visitan para admirar su arte, su arquitectura y su paisaje. Entre 700 y 1600, Toledo fue uno de los centros políticos, religiosos e intelectuales más importantes de la península.

Puedes visitar:

- el Museo de la Santa Cruz, que tiene el último cuadro que pintó El Greco
- el Alcázar, una fortaleza árabe construida sobre las ruinas de una fortaleza romana
- las sinagogas judías de El Tránsito y Santa María la Blanca
- la mezquita árabe del Cristo de la Luz
- la catedral católica gótica

Catedral católica gótica

Museo de la Santa Cruz

Toledo es una ciudad con muchas atracciones. Los visitantes pueden perderse en sus callejones callados o pasear por la ruidosa Calle del Comercio, con sus tiendas y restaurantes. Los que quieren ir fuera del centro, pueden visitar los puentes antiguos de Alcántara y San Martín. Allí tienes una de las vistas más hermosas de la ciudad: las murallas antiguas.

Alcázar

162

4 Comprensión de la guía del viajero

Leer
Hablar
Escribir

Contesta las siguientes preguntas sobre la guía del viajero.

1. ¿Qué río pasa por Toledo?
2. ¿Qué se encuentra en el Museo de la Santa Cruz?
3. ¿Qué es el Alcázar?
4. ¿Cuáles son dos edificios que se asocian con la influencia judía?
5. ¿Cuál es un edificio que se asocia con la influencia cristiana?
6. ¿Cómo es la calle donde se puede ir de compras?

5 Una guía del viajero

Hablar
Escribir

Con tu compañero(a), escribe una breve introducción turística de su región para incluirla en una guía del viajero. Pueden usar la guía sobre Toledo como modelo. Incluyan una descripción general, lugares de interés específicos y actividades que es posible hacer.

Comparación cultural

Las autonomías españolas

Autonomías con idiomas diferentes del castellano (español)

¿En qué se diferencian y se parecen las distintas autonomías de España? **España** está dividida en diecisiete regiones llamadas *comunidades autónomas* o *autonomías.* La división tiene su origen en los antiguos reinos de la península. Algunos de estos reinos habían existido antes de que los moros llegaran al área y todos siempre habían tenido una identidad individual por razones culturales, geográficas y, en muchos casos, lingüísticas. Pero, desde que España se unificó bajo los reyes Fernando e Isabel, el gobierno central trató de disminuir las diferencias regionales. En 1978, la nueva Constitución creó las autonomías, con sus propios cuerpos legislativos ligados *(tied)* al gobierno central. Algunas han mantenido sus idiomas tradicionales: el gallego en Galicia, el euskera en País Vasco, y el catalán y sus dialectos en Cataluña, Valencia y Baleares.

Compara con tu mundo *En tu opinión, ¿tienen los estados de los EE.UU. una identidad individual fuerte? ¿Qué estados tienen una historia política más antigua que los otros?*

¿Comprendiste? Contesta las siguientes preguntas sobre tu región.

1. ¿Hay puentes viejos o antiguos en tu área? ¿De qué están hechos?
2. ¿Hay edificios viejos? ¿Qué funciones tienen?

Presentación de GRAMÁTICA

¡AVANZA! **Goal:** Learn how to form and use the past perfect tense. Then talk about events that had taken place before other events. ***Actividades 6–9***

¿Recuerdas? Places in the neighborhood pp. 332–333, Past participles as adjectives p. 337

English Grammar Connection: The **past perfect** describes actions that had occurred before other actions in the past. In English, it is formed with the verb *had* and the past participle of the main verb. In Spanish, you use **haber.**

We **had** already **eaten** when she called. Ya **habíamos comido** cuando llamó.

Past Perfect Tense

Use the **past perfect** tense to show that an event had already occurred (or not occurred) at a specific moment in the past.

Here's how: Conjugate the verb **haber** in the imperfect tense and add the past participle of the main verb. The past participle always ends in **-o.**

haber		
había	**habíamos**	
habías	**habíais**	+ **past participle**
había	**habían**	

Yo **había visitado** Toledo antes. *I **had visited** Toledo before.*

When used with another verb, the action expressed with the **past perfect** occurred before the other **past action.**

Cuando Felipe **volvió,** sus tíos ya **se habían ido.**
*When Felipe **returned,** his aunt and uncle **had** already **gone.***

The words **ya** and **todavía** are often used with the **past perfect** tense. **Ya** is used in affirmative statements and means *already.*

Irma **ya había salido** cuando Alberto llegó.
*Irma **had already left** when Alberto arrived.*

Todavía is used in negative statements and means *not . . . yet* or *still . . . not.*

Maite **todavía** no **había comprado** el pan cuando la panadería cerró.
*Maite **still hadn't bought** the bread / **hadn't bought** the bread **yet** when the bakery closed.*

Más práctica

Cuaderno *pp. 272–274*
Cuaderno para hispanohablantes *pp. 273–275*

Conjuguemos.com

@HomeTutor Leveled Practice ClassZone.com

Práctica de GRAMÁTICA

6 En tren

Hablar
Escribir

Usa el pasado perfecto para expresar qué había o no había ocurrido cuando Marta subió al tren.

modelo: **el tren / no salir todavía**
El tren no había salido todavía cuando Marta subió.

1. varios pasajeros / ya sentarse
2. algunos pasajeros / no subir todavía
3. vosotros / ya caerse en el andén
4. todos nosotros / ya sacar el billete
5. Marta / no leer sobre la ruta a Toledo todavía
6. Ramón / ya encontrar un asiento de ventanilla
7. el conductor / no revisar los billetes todavía
8. la amiga de Marta / ya perder el tren

Expansión
Pregunta a cinco personas en tu clase qué había ocurrido ya cuando tú llegaste hoy. Luego, escribe lo que aprendiste.

7 En mi barrio

¿Recuerdas? Places in the neighborhood pp. 332–333

Escribir
Hablar

Explica lo que había hecho cada persona en los lugares indicados.

modelo: **Juan fue a la panadería.**
Juan había comprado una barra de pan.

1. Eva y Miguel fueron a la frutería.
2. Tú fuiste a la bombonería.
3. Nosotros fuimos al kiosco.
4. David fue al banco.
5. Yo fui a la farmacia.
6. Ella fue a la lechería.
7. Ellos fueron a la verdulería.
8. Mi hermano fue a la florería.
9. Mis amigos fueron a la pastelería.
10. Él fue a la ferretería.

AUDIO

Pronunciación El sonido rr

La **r** inicial de una palabra y la **rr** tienen el mismo sonido fuerte de /rr/.

reloj **arreglar**
reunirse **socorro**

Trabalenguas

Erre con erre guitarra,
erre con erre barril,
rápido corren los carros,
por la línea del ferrocarril.

8 ¿Había hecho algo?  *¿Recuerdas?* Past participles as adjectives p. 337

Escribir

Expresa el resultado de las siguientes acciones.

modelo: Joaquín había abierto la puerta.
Ahora la puerta está abierta.

1. Renato había cancelado la reservación del viaje en tren.
2. Nosotros habíamos escrito una novela.
3. Los romanos habían construido una muralla.
4. Lisa había analizado los mapas.
5. Tú habías explorado el castillo.
6. El tren había roto las vías.

9 Ayer en la estación

Hablar

Ayer, un(a) compañero(a) y tú leyeron este horario en la estación de tren. Hoy, se hacen preguntas para comparar diferentes destinos *(destinations)* y decir si los trenes estaban a tiempo, atrasados *(delayed)* o cancelados.

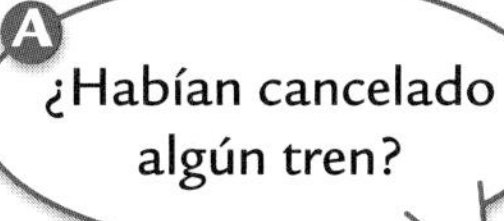

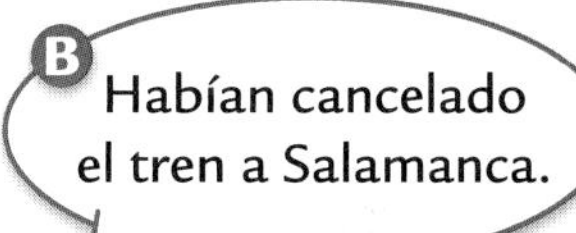

Desde Madrid

Destino	Salida	Llegada	Vía	Condición
ALCALÁ DE HENARES	7:50	9:30	3	A TIEMPO
ARANJUEZ	7:35	8:35	2	ATRASADO HASTA LAS 7:59
ÁVILA	8:47	11:30	3	A TIEMPO
SALAMANCA	10:00	12:24	1	CANCELADO
SEGOVIA	9:55	11:32	2	A TIEMPO
TOLEDO	8:20	10:40	1	ATRASADO

Más práctica Cuaderno *pp. 272–274* Cuaderno para hispanohablantes *pp. 273–275*

¿Comprendiste? Di lo que habían hecho algunos(as) compañeros(as) ayer a las 3:30.

1. hacer la tarea
2. ir de tapas
3. pedir direcciones
4. perderse

GRAMÁTICA en contexto

¡AVANZA! **Goal:** In the following summary of Toledo's history, notice how verbs in the past perfect verb tense help to clarify the chronology of events. Then practice using the past perfect to discuss details of the reading. ***Actividades 10–12***

Contexto 2 *Información histórica*

ESTRATEGIA **Leer**

Make newspaper headlines To help you understand and remember what you read, pick out the five most important events in the history of Toledo and indicate when these events occurred. Put them in chronological order.

Suceso	**Año o siglo**
Los romanos llegaron a Toledo, una ciudad íbera.	

AUDIO

José Luis es un estudiante de Barcelona que está pasando el verano en Madrid. Está leyendo un resumen de la historia de Toledo en una guía del viajero.

Toledo

Los romanos
Cuando los romanos llegaron al río Tajo en 192 a.C., los íberos ya habían construido una colonia importante allí. Los romanos establecieron una fortaleza en el mirador de la ciudad. El Puente de Alcántara, el puente más antiguo de la ciudad, data de la época romana. El imperio romano ya había empezado a desintegrarse cuando los visigodos tomaron Toledo en 418.

TOLEDO

Los visigodos y los moros
Este pueblo había controlado la región por más de cien años cuando llegaron los moros en 711. Éstos construyeron El Alcázar sobre las ruinas de la fortaleza romana. Los moros habían estado allí por casi 350 años cuando Alfonso VI de Castilla tomó control de la ciudad en 1085 y la hizo su capital.

Alfonso X
Durante el gobierno de Alfonso el Sabio, en el siglo XIII, la ciudad ya había crecido mucho. Fue una época de riqueza cultural e intelectual.

Felipe II
En el siglo XVI, Toledo había perdido importancia, por eso Felipe II estableció su corte en Madrid en 1561.

Hoy
En 1986 Toledo fue declarada por la UNESCO Ciudad Patrimonio Mundial.

UNA CALLE ANTIGUA

10 Comprensión de la información histórica

Leer
Hablar
Escribir

Contesta las siguientes preguntas sobre la información histórica.

1. ¿Quiénes fueron los primeros habitantes del área donde más tarde se estableció la ciudad de Toledo?
2. ¿Qué construyeron los romanos al llegar al área?
3. ¿Quiénes conquistaron a los romanos?
4. ¿En qué año llegaron los moros a Toledo?
5. ¿Durante qué época tuvo la ciudad esplendor cultural?
6. ¿Cuándo y por qué disminuyó la importancia política de Toledo?

11 Un paseo por España

Escribir
Hablar

Modifica las siguientes oraciones utilizando el pasado perfecto para decir lo que no habían hecho las personas. Sigue el modelo.

modelo: Yo **comí** manzanas **después** de almorzar.
Yo no **había comido** manzanas **antes** de almorzar.

1. Nosotros paseamos por Las Ramblas después de ver la película.
2. José Luis visitó el Alcázar después de pasar por el puente.
3. Francisco y José Luis decidieron ir a Barcelona después de enero.
4. Paco entró al museo Reina Sofía después de leer el periódico.
5. José Luis comió unas tapas después de visitar los museos.

12 La secuencia histórica

Hablar
Escribir

Con tu compañero(a), prepara una presentación de dos párrafos sobre la historia de Toledo. Utiliza la información histórica de Toledo y organízala, según el gráfico, en orden cronológico. Utiliza el pasado perfecto.

Una historia breve de Toledo

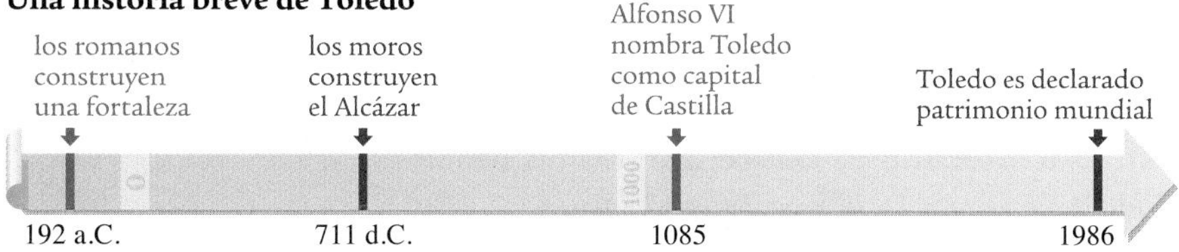

Expansión
Con tu compañero(a) prepara una línea cronológica para reflejar la historia de tu comunidad. Incluyan al menos cinco fechas de eventos y personajes importantes.

PARA Y PIENSA

¿Comprendiste? Contesta las siguientes preguntas sobre tu ciudad o región. Usa el pasado perfecto.

1. Cuando llegaste hoy a la escuela, ¿quiénes de tus compañeros(as) ya habían llegado y quiénes no?
2. Hace cinco años, ¿qué edificios u otros sitios de interés ya se habían construido en tu ciudad y cuáles no?

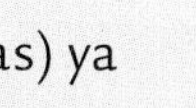

Get Help Online
ClassZone.com

Presentación de GRAMÁTICA

¡AVANZA! **Goal:** Learn about the formation and use of the future perfect tense. Then talk about actions that will have been completed at some point in the future. ***Actividades 13–16***

English Grammar Connection: The **future perfect** describes actions that will have been completed by a certain time in the future. In English, you form it by combining *will have* and the past participle of the main verb. In Spanish, you use the future tense of **haber.**

At 3:00 the train **will have left.** A las 3:00 el tren **habrá salido.**

Future Perfect Tense

Animated Grammar
ClassZone.com

Use the **future perfect** tense to express what will have happened by a certain time in the future.

Here's how: Conjugate the verb **haber** in the future tense and add the past participle of the main verb. In the **future perfect,** the past participle always ends in **-o.**

haber	
habré	**habremos**
habrás	**habréis**
habrá	**habrán**

\+ **past participle**

El lunes, **habremos visto** el famoso cuadro de El Greco.
On Monday, ***we will have seen*** *El Greco's famous painting.*

The **future perfect** is often used with **para** or **dentro de** + a time reference.

Para entonces Elena **habrá explorado** la ciudad.
By *then Elena* ***will have explored*** *the city.*

Dentro de tres meses **habré aprendido** mucho.
Within *three months* ***I will have learned*** *a lot.*

You also use the **future perfect** tense to speculate about something that may have happened in the past.

¿Cómo **se habrá roto** el brazo Miguel?
How ***could*** *Miguel* ***have broken*** *his arm?*

No sé. **Se habrá caído.**
I don't know. ***He must have fallen.***

Más práctica
Cuaderno *pp. 275–277*
Cuaderno para hispanohablantes *pp. 276–279*
Conjuguemos.com
@HomeTutor
Leveled Practice
ClassZone.com

Práctica de GRAMÁTICA

13 ¿Qué habrán hecho?

Escuchar
Hablar

Escucha cada descripción. Luego, decide qué habrán hecho Sofía y Javier durante su excursión.

modelo: Sofía / visitar: Sofía habrá visitado el museo.

1. Sofía y Javier / cruzar
2. Javier / ir
3. Sofía / perderse
4. Sofía / subir
5. Sofía / no hacer
6. Sofía y Javier / tomar

14 Una excursión a Toledo

Leer
Escribir

Lee el folleto sobre la visita guiada que va a hacer Marta en Toledo. Luego escribe lo que habrá ocurrido a las siguientes horas.

modelo: a las 12:00
A las 12:00 Marta ya habrá ido a la Casa-Museo de El Greco.

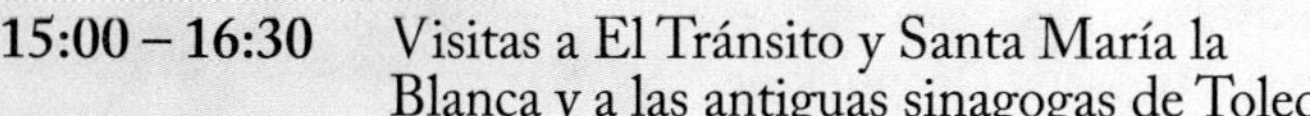

11:15 – 12:15	Casa-Museo de El Greco
12:30 – 13:00	Santo Tomé y el famoso cuadro de El Greco, *El entierro del Conde de Orgaz*
13:00 – 15:00	Tiempo libre para comer y explorar los callejones del centro histórico. El grupo se reunirá a las 15:00 en punto enfrente de la sinagoga de El Tránsito.
15:00 – 16:30	Visitas a El Tránsito y Santa María la Blanca y a las antiguas sinagogas de Toledo.
16:45 – 17:45	Visitar el Museo Sefardí.
18:00 – 20:00	Tiempo libre para tomar algo, ir de tapas, compras o visitar otro lugar de interés. Sugerencias incluyen el monasterio de San Juan de los Reyes, el Museo Visigodo, el Museo de Santa Cruz y el Puente Alcántara.
20:00 en punto:	El autobús sale para Madrid. ¡No te pierdas y no llegues tarde o tendrás que tomar el tren!

sinagoga de El Tránsito

San Juan de los Reyes

Puente Alcántara

1. a las 12:30
2. a las 14:15
3. a las 16:30
4. a las 17:15
5. a las 18:30
6. a las 20:10

15 El año 2050

Hablar
Escribir

Con tus compañeros(as), imaginen cómo habrá cambiado el mundo para el año 2050. Escriban sus ideas sobre cinco de los siguientes temas para presentarlas a la clase.

modelo: los inventos: Para el año 2050, los científicos habrán inventado vehículos solares.

los inventos	gente famosa
los recursos naturales	tu casa
las especies en peligro de extinción	tu familia
la media	tu barrio
las computadoras e Internet	tu ciudad

Expansión
Imagina cinco cosas que no habrán cambiado y comparte tus ideas con tu compañero(a).

16 Descripción de un cuadro

Leer
Escribir

Comparación cultural

El Greco y Toledo

¿Qué influencia tienen las ciudades en la obra de los pintores?
El artista que más se asocia con Toledo, **España,** es El Greco. Él pintó el cuadro más conocido de la ciudad, *Vista de Toledo*. Se encuentran muchos de sus cuadros en esta ciudad antigua, entre ellos, su más famoso, «El entierro del Conde de Orgaz». El Greco, como indica su apodo, era de **Grecia.** Su nombre verdadero era Doménikos Theotokópolous y nació en 1541. En 1577 El Greco ya había llegado a Toledo y allí pintó unas de sus mejores obras. Su estilo se destaca por el uso de colores vivos y sombras *(shadows)* dramáticas y por las caras y manos alargadas *(lengthened)* de sus figuras. Después de mirar este cuadro, todos habremos visto la fuerte relación emocional entre el lugar y el artista.

Vista de Toledo *(1610), El Greco*

Compara con tu mundo *¿Qué colores asocias con tu ciudad? ¿Por qué?*

Mira el cuadro *Vista de Toledo* por El Greco. ¿Cómo es? ¿En qué estación del año crees que se pintó? ¿Qué habrá querido decirnos El Greco con los colores que utilizó? Según la atmósfera del cuadro, ¿cómo crees que eran las calles y el ambiente de la ciudad? Usa palabras del vocabulario para describir tu respuesta.

Más práctica Cuaderno *pp. 275–277* Cuaderno para hispanohablantes *pp. 276–279*

PARA Y PIENSA

¿Comprendiste? ¿Qué habrán hecho estas personas al final del día?

1. yo
2. tú
3. el (la) maestro(a) de español
4. mis amigos(as) y yo

Get Help Online
ClassZone.com

Todo junto

¡AVANZA! **Goal:** ***Show what you know*** In the following conversation between José Luis and his friends, notice how the verb forms he uses show the chronology of different actions. Then practice by talking about a place that you have visited more than once. ***Actividades 17–20***

Resumen contextos 1 y 2 José Luis es un estudiante de Barcelona que está pasando el verano en Madrid con su primo Francisco. Hoy los dos vinieron a Toledo a visitar a su amigo Ignacio.

Contexto 3 *Diálogo*

ESTRATEGIA **Escuchar**
Listen for the contributions
Listen for the contributions made by José Luis, Francisco, and Ignacio to this conversation. Using a table, summarize each person's ideas in your own words.

AUDIO

Ahora, a la una de la tarde, José Luis y Francisco descansan en el piso donde vive Ignacio con sus padres y hablan de cómo pasaron la mañana en Toledo.

José Luis: Toledo es genial, ¿no? Mi familia vino aquí hace diez años. Recuerdo la fecha, porque yo había celebrado mi sexto cumpleaños la semana anterior.

Ignacio: ¡Hace mucho tiempo! Y, ¿qué hicisteis por la mañana?

Francisco: Yo fui a la sinagoga de Santa María la Blanca. Es impresionante... también muy antigua, del siglo XIII. No sabía que se había construido dos siglos antes que la sinagoga de El Tránsito.

José Luis: ¡Quiero verla! Voy a ir allí después de la comida.

Francisco: Pues yo hice una visita guiada del Alcázar. Hay unas vistas fenomenales allí.

José Luis: ¿Sí? ¡También tengo que visitarlo después de la comida!

Ignacio: Y tú, José Luis, ¿qué hiciste? ¡No has dicho ni pío! ¡Me parece que no has visto nada!

José Luis: ¡Me perdí en todos esos callejones pequeños! Y también perdí mi guía del viajero... Me metí en problemas porque anduve en círculos toda la mañana. ¡Pero voy a ver mucho por la tarde!

Francisco: No sé cómo... ya habrá cerrado todo a las cuatro y el último tren a Madrid sale a las siete. Para entonces, no habrás visto ni la mitad de los sitios de interés.

José Luis: Ay, ¿qué puedo hacer? Tal vez podemos pasar la noche aquí.

Ignacio: No sé si mis padres les permitirán quedarse aquí...

José Luis: Ay, ¿qué debo hacer?

Ignacio: Hombre, no sé, pero necesitas un plan... ¡pronto!

También se dice

Francisco utiliza la expresión **ni pío,** para decir que José Luis no ha dicho nada.

- **México** **ni jota**
- **Cuba** **ni esta boca es mía**
- **Perú** **naranjas**

17 Comprensión del diálogo

Escuchar
Hablar
Escribir

Contesta las preguntas sobre la excursión de los chicos a Toledo.

1. ¿Cómo recuerda José Luis la fecha de su primera visita a Toledo?
2. ¿Qué visitó Francisco y qué aprendió del sitio?
3. ¿Cuál de los tres jóvenes vive en Toledo?
4. ¿Cómo pasó José Luis la mañana?
5. ¿Qué problema tienen los chicos y José Luis en particular?

18 ¿Qué hacer?

Hablar
Escribir

Con tu compañero(a), considera las posibles soluciones al problema de los chicos. ¿Deben regresar a Madrid esa tarde? ¿Deben pedir permiso para quedarse? ¿Deben volver a Toledo otro día? Preparen una lista de ventajas y desventajas de cada opción para presentar en clase.

modelo: El último tren habrá partido a las siete. Deberían pedirles permiso a los padres de Francisco para quedarse y aprovechar el día siguiente en Toledo.

Expansión
Después de decidir qué deben hacer los chicos, prepara cinco recomendaciones con el subjuntivo para sus próximos pasos *(steps)*.

19 Integración

Leer
Escuchar
Hablar

Lee este folleto turístico de Barcelona. Luego escucha la visita guiada *(guided tour)*. Explica qué había pasado en la antigüedad en el Palacio Real.

Fuente 1 Folleto turístico

El Palacio Real está en el barrio histórico de Barcelona. En la época de los romanos, el palacio había sido el lugar de reunión más importante de los políticos.

- Todavía se puede ver la muralla de la ciudad, que había sido construida para proteger la ciudad.
- La estructura actual tiene elementos del siglo X. La sala central, por ejemplo, fue construida con un estilo gótico muy hermoso.
- La capilla (*chapel*) de Santa Ágata es otra estructura notable.
- Con los años, muchos visitantes habrán pasado por este palacio para conocer la historia de España.

Fuente 2 Visita guiada

Escucha y apunta

- ¿Qué había ocurrido en el Palacio Real?
- ¿Quiénes habrán visitado el Palacio Real?

modelo: El Palacio Real había sido el centro de reunión de los romanos. Mucha gente habrá visitado el Palacio Real este año.

20 ¡A escribir!

Escribir

Investiga sobre uno de los siguientes lugares cercanos a Madrid: Alcalá de Henares, Segovia, Salamanca o Ávila. Escribe un artículo sobre una excursión a uno de ellos. Incluye una introducción, una descripción general de los sitios de interés más importantes y lo que los visitantes habrán aprendido después de la excursión.

Writing Criteria	Excellent	Good	Needs Work
Content	Your article includes many details about your destination and expectations.	Your article includes some details about your destination and expectations.	Your article includes few details about your destination and expectations.
Communication	Your article is organized and easy to follow.	Parts of your article are organized and easy to follow.	Your article is disorganized and hard to follow.
Accuracy	You make few mistakes in grammar and vocabulary.	You make some mistakes in grammar and vocabulary.	You make many mistakes in grammar and vocabulary.

Más práctica Cuaderno *pp. 278–279* Cuaderno para hispanohablantes *pp. 280–281*

¿Comprendiste? Piensa en un lugar que has visitado varias veces. ¿Qué hiciste la segunda vez que fuiste? ¿Qué habías hecho la primera vez?

Lectura literaria

¡AVANZA! **Goal:** In the following poem by a famous Spanish author, notice how he uses words, like the color green, to create visual images for the reader. Then talk about both the actions and the images that appear in the poem.

Para leer 

ESTRATEGIA Leer

Interpret the images This poem is filled with beautiful and sometimes shocking images, some of which have a deeper meaning. To interpret the images, draw a circle for each image and write García Lorca's words for the image. Inside, draw a smaller circle and write what you think the deeper meaning might be.

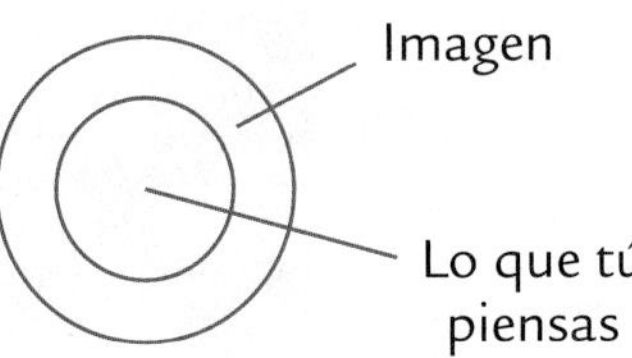

Vocabulario para leer

la sombra	*silueta oscura que proyectan los objetos cuando les da la luz*
soñar	*ver cosas y escenas mientras uno está dormido*
(la) baranda	*estructura que hay en balcones y escaleras para evitar las caídas*
el (la) gitano(a)	*persona que vive viajando, sin lugar fijo para vivir*
la higuera	*árbol que da un fruto dulce, llamado «higo»*
amargo(a)	*sabor, como el café sin azúcar*
herir	*dañar, hacer daño físico o psicológico a alguien*
rezumar	*que deja pasar a través de sus poros o huecos las gotas de líquido*
el rastro	*pistas, huellas que deja algo o alguien al caminar*
el aljibe	*hueco hecho en la tierra para guardar agua*

Nota cultural

Sobre el autor ***Federico García Lorca (1898–1936)*** Federico García Lorca nació en Fuente Vaqueros, en la provincia de Granada, España. Era poeta y dramaturgo, y sus obras dramáticas revolucionaron el mundo del teatro. En poesía se destacó con el *Romancero gitano,* una colección de poemas publicada en 1928 que hablan del amor y de la política española. En «Romance sonámbulo», el poeta describe la llegada de un soldado *(soldier)* herido que regresa de la guerra.

Sobre el romance El romance es una forma poética de origen español en que cada verso *(line)* generalmente tiene ocho sílabas y los versos pares *(even)* tienen la misma rima. Los romances eran muy populares en el siglo XV y la gente podía cantarlos mientras tocaba un instrumento musical. «Romance sonámbulo» es hoy día una canción popular conocida como «Verde».

Romance sonámbulo 

Federico García Lorca

El flautista *(1955), Remedios Varo*

Verde que te quiero verde.
Verde viento. Verdes ramas.
El barco sobre la mar
y el caballo en la montaña.
Con la sombra en la cintura,
ella sueña en su baranda,
verde carne, pelo verde,
con ojos de fría plata.
Verde que te quiero verde.
Bajo la luna gitana
las cosas la están mirando
y ella no puede mirarlas. ❖

Verde que te quiero verde.
Grandes estrellas de escarcha[1]
vienen con el pez de sombra
que abre el camino del alba.
La higuera frota[2] su viento
con la lija[3] de sus ramas,
y el monte, gato garduño[4],
eriza[5] sus pitas[6] agrias.

❖ **A pensar**
¿Sobre quién crees que habla el poema?

[1] frost [2] rubs [3] sandpaper [4] thief
[5] stands on end, raises [6] green plants with spiny leaves

Lectura literaria *continuación*

Pero ¿quién vendrá? ¿Y por dónde?...
Ella sigue en su baranda,
verde carne, pelo verde,
soñando en la mar amarga.

—Compadre, quiero cambiar
mi caballo por su casa,
mi montura[7] por su espejo,
mi cuchillo por su manta.
Compadre, vengo sangrando,
desde los puertos de Cabra[8].
—Si yo pudiera, mocito[9],
este trato se cerraba.
Pero yo ya no soy yo,
ni mi casa es ya mi casa.
—Compadre, quiero morir
decentemente en mi cama.
De acero[10], si puede ser,
con las sábanas de holanda[11].
¿No ves la herida que tengo
desde el pecho a la garganta?

—Trescientas rosas morenas
lleva tu pechera[12] blanca.
Tu sangre rezuma y huele
alrededor de tu faja[13].
Pero yo ya no soy yo,
ni mi casa es ya mi casa.
—Dejadme subir al menos
hasta las altas barandas,
¡dejadme subir!, dejadme
hasta las verdes barandas.
Barandales de la luna
por donde retumba[14] el agua.
Ya suben los dos compadres
hacia las altas barandas.
Dejando un rastro de sangre.

A pensar
¿Qué papel juega la naturaleza en esta descripción?

[7] saddle [8] a town in Spain [9] young man [10] steel
[11] fine cotton [12] shirt front [13] sash [14] rumbles

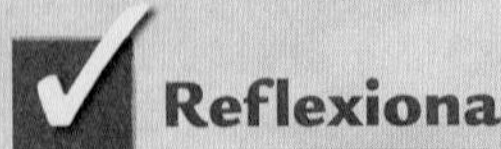

Reflexiona

¿Quién llega y con quién habla? ¿Qué quiere el mocito?

Dejando un rastro de lágrimas.
Temblaban en los tejados [15]
farolillos [16] de hojalata [17].
Mil panderos [18] de cristal
herían la madrugada.

Verde que te quiero verde,
verde viento, verdes ramas.
Los dos compadres subieron.
El largo viento dejaba
en la boca un raro gusto
de hiel [19], de menta y de albahaca [20].
—¡Compadre! ¿Dónde está, dime,
dónde está tu niña amarga?
—Cuántas veces te esperara,
cara fresca, negro pelo,
en esta verde baranda!

Sobre el rostro [21] del aljibe
se mecía [22] la gitana.
Verde carne, pelo verde,
con ojos de fría plata.
Un carámbano [23] de luna
la sostiene sobre el agua.
La noche se puso íntima
como una pequeña plaza.
Guardias civiles [24] borrachos [25]
en la puerta golpeaban.
Verde que te quiero verde.
Verde viento. Verdes ramas.
El barco sobre la mar
Y el caballo en la montaña.

A pensar
Organiza la información de esta estrofa en «acciones» e «imágenes».

A pensar
¿Por qué crees que Lorca escribe: «¿... dónde está tu niña amarga?»

---

[15] roof tiles
[16] lanterns
[17] tin
[18] large tambourines
[19] **gusto...** taste of bile
[20] basil
[21] face
[22] **se...** rocked
[23] icicle
[24] **Guardias...** policemen
[25] drunken

¿Comprendiste?

1. ¿Quiénes son los personajes del poema? ¿Qué hace cada uno?
2. ¿Cómo usa Lorca la naturaleza en el poema?
3. ¿Cuál es la relación entre el mocito, «ella» y el compadre?
4. ¿Qué crees que le pasó al mocito, a «ella» y al compadre?

¿Y tú?

Tradicionalmente, en el mundo hispano el color verde se asocia con la esperanza. ¿Qué aspectos de la esperanza se incluyen en el poema?

Escritura

Una carta al futuro

Vas a escribirte una carta a ti mismo(a) para que abras cuando tengas 30 años. La carta tendrá información sobre ti, tu familia y tus amigos.

1 Prepárate para escribir

ESTRATEGIA **Usa una tabla para hacer predicciones** ¿Qué habrás hecho en el futuro? ¿Qué profesión habrás escogido? ¿Qué habrán hecho tu familia y tus amigos? Organiza tus predicciones en tres grupos: predicciones sobre ti mismo(a), sobre tu familia y sobre tus amigos.

Yo	Mi familia	Mis amigos
¿Qué habré hecho?	¿Qué habrá hecho mi ____ (hermana)?	¿Qué habrán hecho?
¿Qué no habré hecho?	¿Qué no habrá hecho mi ____ ?	¿Qué no habrán hecho?

2 Escribe

ESTRATEGIA **Usa las predicciones para escribir un primer borrador**

Paso 1 Usa las predicciones de la primera columna para escribir el primer párrafo de tu carta. Usa el futuro perfecto para hablar de las acciones que crees que habrás o no habrás hecho.

Cuando tenga treinta años creo que habré hecho muchas cosas. Primero, creo que habré ido a la universidad. Creo que me habré graduado con un título en... Creo que no habré estudiado...

Paso 2 Usa las predicciones de la segunda columna para indicar qué crees que habrán hecho varios miembros de tu familia.

Creo que mi hermana habrá estudiado para ser médica. Creo que mi primo no habrá trabajado todavía...

Paso 3 Usa las predicciones de la tercera columna para indicar qué crees que habrán hecho tus amigos.

Creo que mis amigos me habrán acompañado a la universidad. Creo que ellos se habrán casado...

3 Revisa tu composición

Intercambia el borrador con el de un(a) compañero(a). Lee la carta de tu compañero(a) y subraya todos los verbos.

- Decide si es correcta la conjugación del verbo.
- Haz un círculo alrededor de los verbos con errores.
- Escribe las correcciones.

Creo que mis amigos me habrán acompañado a la universidad. Creo que ellos se habían casado... habrán

Lección 2

En resumen

Vocabulario y gramática

Vocabulario

Describe an Excursion

el andén	*platform*
el asiento numerado	*numbered seat*
callado(a)	*quiet*
el callejón	*alley*
el (la) conductor(a)	*conductor*
el cuadro	*painting*
la entrada	*entrance*
el mirador	*outlook, lookout*
el paisaje	*landscape*
el pasillo	*aisle*
el plano	*city map*
el puente	*bridge*
el río	*river*
ruidoso(a)	*noisy*
la ruta	*route*
la sala de espera	*waiting room*
el tapiz	*tapestry*
la taquilla	*ticket window*
el vagón	*wagon, (railroad) car*
la ventanilla	*train window*
la vía	*track*
la vista	*view*
caerse	*to fall down*
explorar	*to explore*
hacer una visita guiada	*to take a guided tour*
meterse en problemas	*to get into trouble*
pedir direcciones	*to ask for directions*
perder	*to miss*
perderse (ie)	*to get lost*
probar (ue) las especialidades	*to try the specialties*
tomar algo	*to drink something*

Talk About History

analizar	*to analyze*
el castillo	*castle*
el centro histórico	*historical center*
consecutivo(a)	*consecutive, in a row*
en conclusión	*in conclusion*
en orden cronológico	*in chronological order*
la fortaleza	*fortress*
la muralla	*wall*

Other Words and Phrases

a pesar de que	*in spite of, despite*
además	*in addition, additionally*
pues	*so, well*
tratarse de	*to be about*

Gramática

Past Perfect Tense

haber	
había	habíamos
habías	habíais
había	habían

+ past participle

Yo **había visitado** Toledo antes.
I ***had visited*** *Toledo before.*

When used with another verb, the action expressed with the **past perfect** occurred before the other **past action.**

Cuando Felipe **volvió,** sus tíos ya **se habían ido.**

Ya and **todavía** are often used with the **past perfect.**

Irma **ya había salido** cuando Alberto llegó.
Irma ***had already left*** *when Alberto arrived.*

Maite **todavía** no **había comprado** el pan cuando la panadería cerró.
Maite ***still hadn't bought*** *the bread /* ***hadn't bought*** *the bread* ***yet*** *when the bakery closed.*

Future Perfect Tense

haber	
habré	habremos
habrás	habréis
habrá	habrán

+ past participle

El lunes, **habremos visto** el famoso cuadro de El Greco.
On Monday, ***we will have seen*** *El Greco's famous painting.*

The **future perfect** is often used with **para** or **dentro de** + a time reference.

Dentro de tres meses **habré aprendido** mucho.

You also use the **future perfect** tense to speculate about the past.

¿Cómo **se habrá roto** el brazo Miguel?
How ***could*** *Miguel* ***have broken*** *his arm?*

No sé. **Se habrá caído.**
I don't know. ***He must have fallen.***

Lección 2

Repaso de la lección

@HomeTutor
ClassZone.com

Now you can
- describe an excursion
- express what will have happened
- talk about the history of a place

Using
- past perfect
- future perfect

To review
- vocabulary pp. 358–359

1 Listen and understand

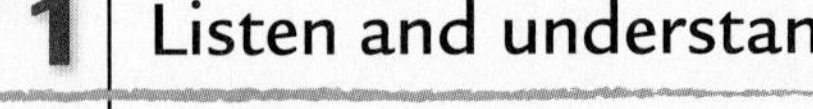

AUDIO

Escucha el siguiente anuncio sobre los beneficios de viajar en tren. Luego, contesta las siguientes preguntas.

1. ¿Qué ya habrá hecho el pasajero del tren cuando llega a la estación?
2. ¿Por qué no será necesario hacer una reservación de hotel?
3. ¿Por qué no será necesario buscar un restaurante para comer?
4. Según el anuncio, ¿cuál es una desventaja *(disadvantage)* de viajar en coche? ¿Y en avión?
5. ¿Qué puedes hacer en tren que no puedes hacer en auto o en avión?
6. ¿Qué harán los conductores del tren?

To review
- past perfect p. 363

2 Describe an excursion

Lee sobre la excursión que hicieron dos amigas. Usa el pasado perfecto para completar las frases.

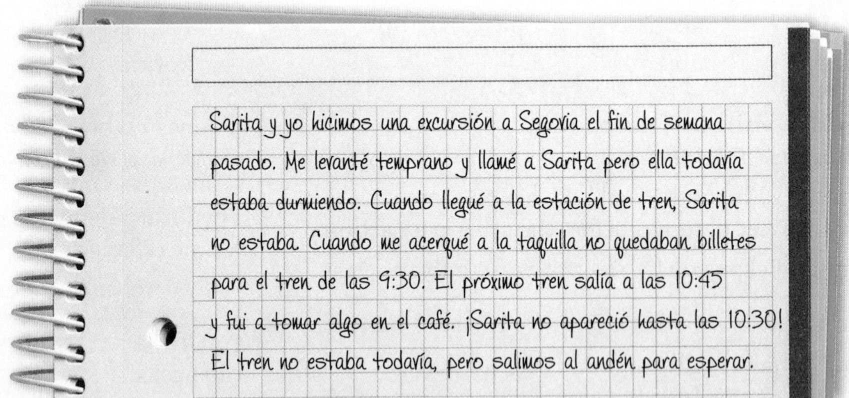

Sarita y yo hicimos una excursión a Segovia el fin de semana pasado. Me levanté temprano y llamé a Sarita pero ella todavía estaba durmiendo. Cuando llegué a la estación de tren, Sarita no estaba. Cuando me acerqué a la taquilla no quedaban billetes para el tren de las 9:30. El próximo tren salía a las 10:45 y fui a tomar algo en el café. ¡Sarita no apareció hasta las 10:30! El tren no estaba todavía, pero salimos al andén para esperar.

1. Yo llamé a Sarita temprano pero ella (no levantarse) todavía.
2. Cuando yo llegué a la estación, Sarita (no llegar) todavía.
3. Todos los billetes para el tren de las 9:30 ya (venderse).
4. Sarita quería un refresco cuando llegó pero yo ya (tomar algo).
5. Por suerte el tren todavía (no salir) cuando Sarita por fin apareció.

To review
- future perfect p. 368

3 Express what will have happened

Haz predicciones sobre qué habrán hecho tu familia y tú y al final de una excursión a Segovia.

1. yo / visitar el centro histórico
2. mi hermano / perderse tres veces
3. mis padres / ver cuadros y tapices interesantes
4. todos nosotros / subir al castillo
5. tú / meterse en problemas

To review
- past perfect p. 363

4 Talk about the history of a place

Mira la línea cronológica y contesta las preguntas sobre la historia de Ávila.

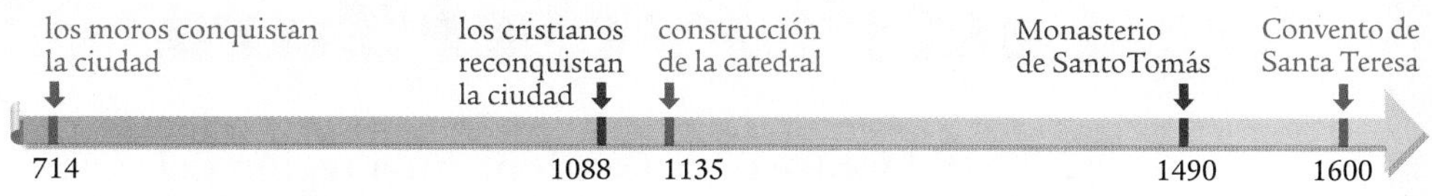

1. ¿Qué culturas habían estado en la zona cuando Ávila fue reconquistada en 1088?
2. ¿Qué construcciones no habían comenzado cuando se empezó a construir la catedral?
3. ¿Qué monumentos importantes ya se habían completado cuando se terminó el Monasterio de Santo Tomás?
4. ¿Se había terminado el convento de Santa Teresa cuando se construyó la catedral?

To review
- **Comparación cultural** pp. 362, 370

5 Regions of Spain and art in Toledo

Comparación cultural

1. ¿Qué pintor se asocia más con la ciudad de Toledo?
2. ¿Qué pinturas famosas pintó allí?
3. ¿Cuántas comunidades autónomas hay en España? ¿Cuál es su origen histórico?
4. ¿Qué lenguas se hablan en las autonomías aparte del español?

Más práctica Cuaderno *pp. 280–291* Cuaderno para hispanohablantes *pp. 282–291*

Comparación cultural

AUDIO

Lo moderno y lo tradicional

Lectura y escritura

WebQuest
ClassZone.com

1. **Leer** Montse es de Cataluña, una región del noreste de España, y Ramón es de Andalucía, en el sur. Lee sus descripciones.

2. **Escribir** Prepara una lista con información sobre tu ciudad y estado. ¿Qué elementos modernos y tradicionales hay? ¿Qué le interesaría saber a una persona que quiere visitar ese lugar? Escribe un ensayo de cinco párrafos.

ESTRATEGIA Escribir

Follow the flow Make a flow chart with shapes and arrows. The circle is the introduction, followed by three interesting aspects (crosses), and the stop sign is the conclusion.

Paso 1 Dibuja una secuencia de figuras y flechas como la que se muestra arriba pero más grande. Escribe notas en cada figura, empezando por la introducción (círculo), que debe incluir una descripción general.

Paso 2 En las cruces escribe tres aspectos interesantes e importantes, tradicionales o modernos. En la figura con forma de señal de PARE escribe una conclusión.

Paso 3 Usando la información del diagrama, escribe el ensayo. Luego revisa la gramática y la ortografía.

Compara con tu mundo

Compara tu ciudad o estado con las regiones donde viven Montse y Ramón. ¿Qué tienen en común? ¿En qué se diferencian? ¿Tu región se parece más a Cataluña o a Andalucía?

Cuaderno *pp. 292–294* Cuaderno para hispanohablantes *pp. 292–294*

Cataluña

Montse

¡Hola! Me llamo Montse Mir y soy de Barcelona, la capital de la región de Cataluña y la segunda ciudad más grande de España.

Barcelona es famosa por Las Ramblas, un paseo largo con cafés, kioscos y tiendas. También hay músicos callejeros, artistas y un ambiente alegre. A mí me gusta mucho el Barrio Gótico, el centro histórico de la ciudad, donde hay muchos edificios antiguos. Los domingos, la gente viene a este barrio para bailar la sardana, nuestro baile tradicional. Las ciudades grandes de Cataluña son importantes por el comercio, la industria y la vida cultural. Pero también tenemos zonas rurales conocidas por la industria de la fruta y por la producción de quesos.

La gente también visita Cataluña para esquiar en los montes Pirineos y disfrutar de las playas de la Costa Brava. ¡Cataluña lo tiene todo!

Ramón

Soy Ramón Jiménez y vivo en Jaén, en la región de Andalucía. Mi región es básicamente rural. Sevilla, la ciudad más grande, tiene la mitad de la población que Barcelona.

En la arquitectura de Andalucía se puede ver claramente la influencia árabe y las típicas casas blancas con techos rojos.

Andalucía tiene geografía muy variada. Tenemos las playas de la Costa del Sol y las montañas de la Sierra Morena y la Sierra Nevada. Aparte del turismo, Andalucía es un centro agrícola y ganadero muy importante, famoso por sus aceitunas, jamones, caballos y toros. Realmente tenemos de todo, desde las cuevas prehistóricas de Ronda hasta los hoteles exclusivos para los famosos que van de vacaciones a Marbella.

Andalucía

EL DESAFÍO

VIDEO DVD

En este desafío, los equipos deben dar una vuelta por un barrio de la ciudad, buscando unas pistas que les dará el profesor. Deben completar una ruta específica y regresar con un objeto de cada lugar. Cada equipo debe regresar con tres objetos.

Antes del video

1. La pista dice: «La vida es dulce.» ¿Adónde crees que tienen que ir?

2. La pista dice: «Una verdura anaranjada con vitaminas buenas para los ojos.» ¿Adónde deben ir?

3. La pista dice: «Mezclar azúcar, huevos y leche, y por ultimo añadir manzanas.» ¿Adónde tienen que ir?

Analizando los resultados del desafío

Mira el video: Toma apuntes

- ¿Qué tienen que leer Carmen y José para enterarse de la noticia de ayer?
- ¿Qué equipo tiene que ir a la verdulería?
- ¿Adónde tienen que ir Luis y María?
- Escribe qué equipo llega primero con los tres objetos.
- Según María, ¿por qué no pueden ganar Marco y Ana?
- ¿Por qué corren todos detrás de Marco al final?

Después del video

1. Lee tus predicciones en la sección de «Antes del video». ¿Tuviste razón?
2. ¿Por qué crees que quiere ser Ana la directora de la ruta?
3. ¿Cuál es el tercer objeto que trajeron Ana y Marco? ¿Dónde lo habrán conseguido? ¿Qué crees que fue su tercera pista?
4. ¿Estás de acuerdo con la decisión del profesor sobre los ganadores? ¿Por qué?

UNIDADES 1-6

Repaso inclusivo

Options for Review

1 Escucha, comprende y contesta

Hablar
Escuchar
Escribir

Escucha esta entrevista de Javier Cabal con Aurelia Blanca, una escritora de la telenovela española *Historias del barrio.* Contesta las preguntas sobre su vida y trabajo.

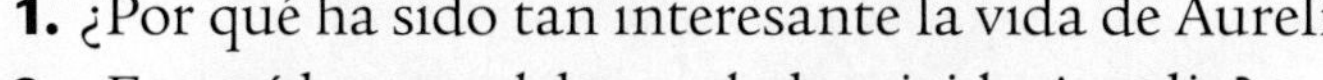

1. ¿Por qué ha sido tan interesante la vida de Aurelia?
2. ¿En qué lugares del mundo ha vivido Aurelia?
3. ¿Dónde había vivido hasta los once años?
4. ¿Qué hizo para aprender nuevas lenguas y hacer nuevos amigos y amigas?
5. ¿En qué se ha inspirado para escribir episodios para la telenovela?
6. ¿Con qué compara Aurelia la vida de su barrio y por qué?

2 Presenta a un(a) famoso(a)

Hablar

Tu compañero(a) es anfitrión(a) *(host)* de un programa de charla en la televisión y te ha invitado a participar. Tú tienes que representar a una persona famosa. Si la persona famosa es ficticia, deben inventar su historia. Preparen preguntas apropiadas para un programa de charla. Usen el pretérito y el imperfecto para contar su historia, y el futuro para decir sus planes.

3 ¡Actúa!

Hablar
Escribir

Con tus compañeros(as), escribe un episodio de *Historias del barrio* o una continuación de la aventura de los tres primos en Toledo. Deben practicar su episodio bastante para poder presentarlo con naturalidad, aunque usen el guión. No olviden incluir mandatos. Deben llevar ropa apropiada con sus papeles el día de la presentación.

4 Presenta tu comunidad

Hablar
Escribir

Prepara una presentación sobre la comunidad, su historia, sus personajes y sus monumentos. Utiliza el presente perfecto y el pasado perfecto apropiadamente.

5 Prepara un folleto

Hablar
Escribir

Con tus compañeros(as), prepara un folleto sobre un fin de semana ideal en su comunidad. Deben incluir información sobre la historia e interés general de la comunidad: dónde quedarse, dónde comer, qué visitar y qué hacer durante el día y la noche. También deben incluir sugerencias para excursiones interesantes a lugares cerca de tu comunidad. Usen el condicional. Finalmente, preséntenle su información y folleto a la clase.

6 Piensa qué habrá pasado

Hablar
Escribir

Con tus compañeros(as), preparen una presentación sobre el futuro de su comunidad: su desarrollo futuro, sus necesidades en el futuro, sus problemas futuros y sus posibles soluciones. ¿Qué habrá ocurrido para entonces? ¿Cómo habrá cambiado su comunidad? ¿Qué debería hacer el departamento de planificación para asegurar el futuro de su comunidad? Piensen en las necesidades comerciales, de vivienda *(housing)*, de entretenimiento, de desarrollo turístico, económico y de transporte. Utilicen expresiones impersonales más el infinitivo y el subjuntivo para dar sus recomendaciones.

7 Mi vida

Escribir

Escribe tu autobiografía. ¿Qué has hecho? ¿Cómo te han formado tus experiencias? ¿Qué no has hecho que todavía esperas hacer? ¿Qué te gustaría hacer? Escribe al menos tres párrafos. Compara tu historia con las de algunos de tus compañeros(as) de clase.

modelo:

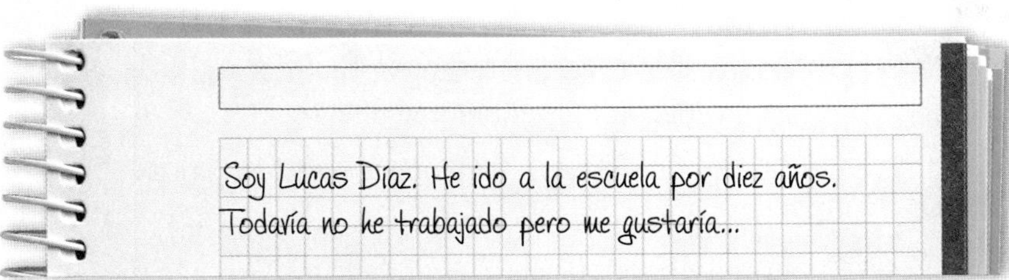

UNIDAD 7

Colombia y Venezuela

Tu pasado y tu futuro

Lección 1

Tema: ***Recuerdos***

Lección 2

Tema: ***Nuevos principios***

«¡Mucho gusto!

Somos Victoria y Esperanza, dos hermanas venezolanas. Y él es Guille, de Colombia.»

Almanaque cultural

Geografía: Cordillera de los Andes, selva amazónica, playas y llanos

Clima: caliente en la costa; frío en la montaña.

Origen del nombre: Colombia: en honor a Cristóbal Colón; Venezuela: diminutivo de Venecia, o «pequeña Venecia»

Comidas: arepas, sancocho, bandeja paisa

Gente famosa: Venezuela: Oscar de León (músico), Gabriela Spanic (actriz), Rómulo Gallegos (escritor). Colombia: Shakira (cantante), Gabriel García Márquez (escritor), Juan Pablo Montoya (automovilista)

Arepas

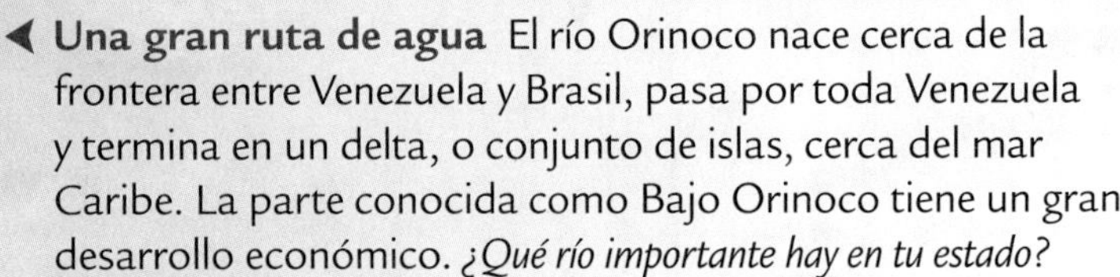

Una gran ruta de agua El río Orinoco nace cerca de la frontera entre Venezuela y Brasil, pasa por toda Venezuela y termina en un delta, o conjunto de islas, cerca del mar Caribe. La parte conocida como Bajo Orinoco tiene un gran desarrollo económico. *¿Qué río importante hay en tu estado?*

Pueblo de Pepeina, a orillas del río Orinoco

Una importante producción de café
Colombia es uno de los principales productores de café. La primera producción comercial de café fue en 1835, en Santander. Ese año se hizo la primera exportación, de aproximadamente 120 libras. Hoy, Colombia le vende café a todo el mundo. *¿Qué se cultiva en tu estado?*

Trabajador juntando granos de café en Colombia

El Día de la Bandera en Caracas, Venezuela

Homenaje a la bandera
En Venezuela se celebra el Día de la Bandera el 12 de marzo. Ese día, la gente participa en desfiles y espectáculos. La bandera tiene los tres colores primarios, rojo, azul y amarillo. También tiene ocho estrellas, que representan las ocho provincias que habían declarado la indepencia de Venezuela en 1811. Los símbolos del escudo *(seal)* representan las ideas de unión, victoria y libertad. *¿Cuántas estrellas tiene la bandera de Estados Unidos? ¿Qué representan las estrellas y qué representan las rayas (stripes)?*

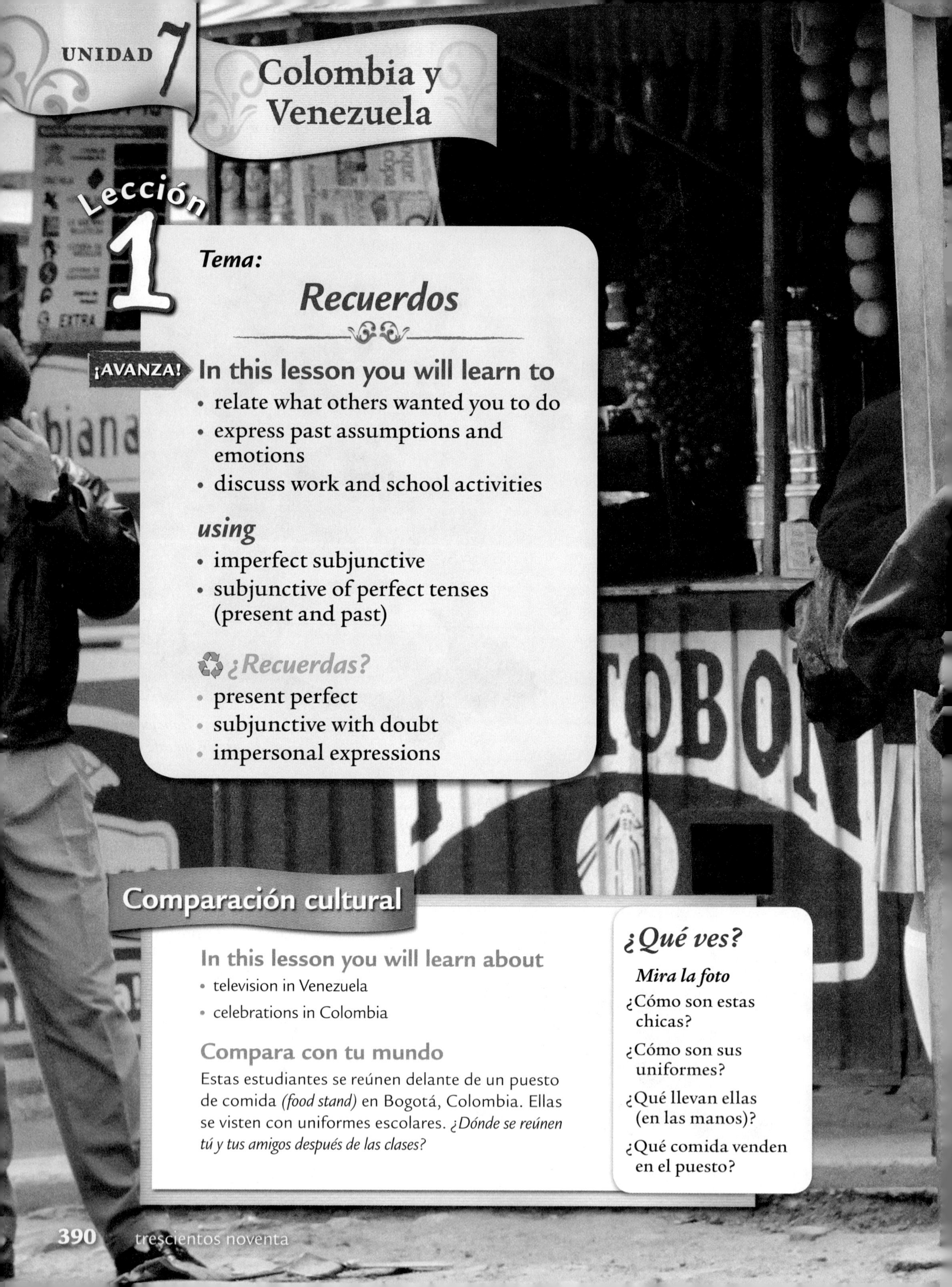

UNIDAD 7

Colombia y Venezuela

Lección 1

Tema:

Recuerdos

¡AVANZA! **In this lesson you will learn to**

- relate what others wanted you to do
- express past assumptions and emotions
- discuss work and school activities

using

- imperfect subjunctive
- subjunctive of perfect tenses (present and past)

¿Recuerdas?

- present perfect
- subjunctive with doubt
- impersonal expressions

Comparación cultural

In this lesson you will learn about

- television in Venezuela
- celebrations in Colombia

Compara con tu mundo

Estas estudiantes se reúnen delante de un puesto de comida *(food stand)* en Bogotá, Colombia. Ellas se visten con uniformes escolares. *¿Dónde se reúnen tú y tus amigos después de las clases?*

¿Qué ves?

Mira la foto

¿Cómo son estas chicas?

¿Cómo son sus uniformes?

¿Qué llevan ellas (en las manos)?

¿Qué comida venden en el puesto?

Featuring...

Cultura INTERACTIVA

Animated Grammar

@HomeTutor

And more...

- Get Help Online
- Interactive Flashcards
- Review Games
- WebQuest
- Conjuguemos.com

Estudiantes colombianas vistiendo uniformes,
Bogotá, Colombia

Presentación de VOCABULARIO

¡AVANZA! **Goal:** Learn new words that relate to work and school activities. Then practice by talking about activities at school or outside of school that interest you. ***Actividades 1–3***

 *¿Recuerdas?* Present perfect p. 342

AUDIO

Hola, me llamo Victoria. Hoy terminé de **redactar el anuario** del año pasado. **¡Salió muy bien!**

Un Mensaje Para Los Graduados

Desde **el comienzo anticipamos** que éste iba a ser un año donde **tomaríamos** muchas **decisiones** importantes para el futuro. Fue un año con muchas **esperanzas** y **estrés**; donde muchos estudiantes **reflexionaron** y **decidieron** si querían seguir estudiando o empezar a **trabajar a tiempo parcial** después de **graduarse**.

la ceremonia de graduación

A todos **nos fue bien** y tenemos muchos **recuerdos** que nunca olvidaremos.

Éstas son las actividades más importantes que hicimos en la escuela, en nuestros **ratos libres** y en **los días feriados**.

¡Éste fue un año inolvidable!

Victoria Lozano

Victoria Lozano

Más vocabulario

la cuenta de ahorros *savings account*
cuidar niños *to baby-sit*
dejar de... *to quit, to give up*
los impuestos *taxes*
llenar una solicitud de empleo *to fill out a job application*
el (la) niñero(a) *babysitter*
repartir periódicos *to deliver newspapers*
la reunión *meeting*
solicitar una beca *to apply for a scholarship*

Expansión de vocabulario p. R14
Ya sabes p. R14

Recuerdos

1) Muchos tomaron parte en el coro de estudiantes.

2) El presidente del club de drama actuó y dirigió dos dramas.

3) El nuevo código de vestimenta es popular.

4) ¡Hay que ponerse en forma y comer una dieta balanceada para no estar estresado!

1.

2.

3.

4.

5.
6.
7.
8.

Empleos

5) La vice-presidenta sirvió de empleada en la cafetería para juntar fondos para su grupo.

6) El estudiante qué trabajó de salvavidas en la piscina de la escuela era miembro del comité estudiantil.

7) La tesorera de la sociedad honoraria trabajó de cajera en un restaurante de comida chatarra.

8) Esperanza fue la diseñadora de la página web del comité de eventos.

¡A responder! Escuchar

Escucha la lista de actividades. Si es algo relacionado con el arte, levanta la mano. Si es algo administrativo, párate.

@HomeTutor

Interactive Flashcards
ClassZone.com

Práctica de VOCABULARIO

1 ¿Qué hacen?

Hablar Escribir

Lee cada descripción y di a cuál de las actividades se refiere.

ponerse en forma
repartir periódicos
redactar el anuario
graduarse
trabajar de cajero(a)
dirigir el club de vela

modelo: Jaime hace mucho ejercicio.
Jaime se pone en forma.

1. Nosotros terminamos el colegio.
2. Octavio trabaja en una tienda. Él toma el dinero cuando la gente compra algo.
3. Tú distribuyes las noticias del día por todo el barrio.
4. Regina organiza los artículos y fotos de los eventos de la escuela.
5. Vilma y Federico organizan las excursiones a la costa, para navegar.

2 ¿Qué has hecho?

¿Recuerdas? Present perfect p. 342

Hablar

Contesta las preguntas de tu compañero(a) sobre las actividades que has o no has hecho.

modelo: reflexionar sobre tus experiencias en el colegio

A ¿Has reflexionado sobre tus experiencias en el colegio?

B Sí, (No, no) he reflexionado sobre mis experiencias en el colegio.

1. solicitar una beca
2. actuar en un drama
3. tomar parte en un club
4. trabajar a tiempo parcial
5. diseñar páginas web
6. cuidar niños

Expansión
Investiga más las respuestas de tu compañero(a). Pregúntale dónde, con quién y por qué ha hecho o no la actividad.

3 Mi primer año

Escribir

Escribe un párrafo sobre tus recuerdos del primer año en el colegio.

Pistas: ¿Qué actividades hiciste? ¿En qué organizaciones y clubes tomaste parte? ¿Qué hiciste para ponerte en forma? ¿Te fue bien?

Más práctica Cuaderno *pp. 295–297* Cuaderno para hispanohablantes *pp. 295–298*

¿Comprendiste? ¿Cuáles de estas actividades normalmente tienen lugar en la escuela?

1. redactar el anuario
2. ser miembro del coro
3. repartir periódicos
4. actuar en un drama
5. cuidar niños
6. trabajar de cajero(a)

Get Help Online
ClassZone.com

VOCABULARIO en contexto

¡AVANZA! **Goal:** Notice the words that Victoria and Esperanza use to talk about school activities in their to-do lists. Then practice the new vocabulary to describe your own activities. ***Actividades 4–5***

Contexto 1 *Horarios*

ESTRATEGIA **Leer**

Use a Venn diagram to compare the twins Victoria and Esperanza are very different, but they are also alike in some ways. Make a Venn diagram to compare their similarities (in the middle) and differences (in the non-overlapping parts of the circles).

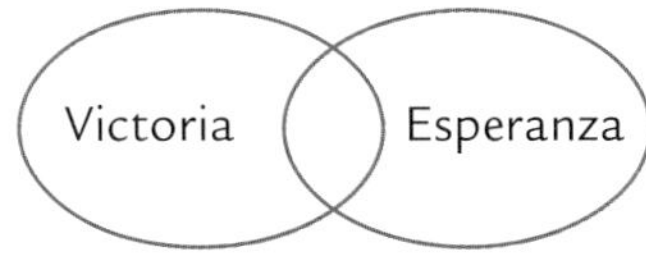

Victoria y Esperanza Lozano son dos estudiantes venezolanas en el penúltimo *(junior)* año de colegio. Aunque son gemelas *(twins)*, son muy diferentes. Cada año, la consejera *(counselor)* académica les pide a todos los estudiantes que hagan un horario de actividades y quehaceres para un día típico. Victoria y Esperanza acaban de hacer sus listas.

Actividades y quehaceres
jueves, 18 de abril

Victoria Lozano

7:00-3:00	Clases.
3:20-3:45	Ir a la reunión con la consejera académica para repasar mi lista e informarme sobre las becas universitarias y cómo solicitarlas.
4:00-4:30	Participar en la práctica de coro.
4:30-5:30	Ir a la reunión del comité estudiantil.
5:30-6:00	Hacer ejercicio en el gimnasio para ponerme en forma y combatir el estrés.
6:00-7:00	Hacer la tarea en casa y tomar decisiones sobre el horario de mañana.
7:30-8:00	Ayudar a mamá a preparar la cena.
8:00-9:00	Cenar con la familia.
9:00-10:00	Llenar la solicitud de empleo para el trabajo a tiempo parcial en el banco.
10:00-10:30	Navegar por Internet para investigar posibles universidades.
10:30-11:00	Decidir qué ropa me pongo mañana.
11:00-11:30	Leer los catálogos de posibles universidades para estar informada.
11:30	Acostarme a dormir.

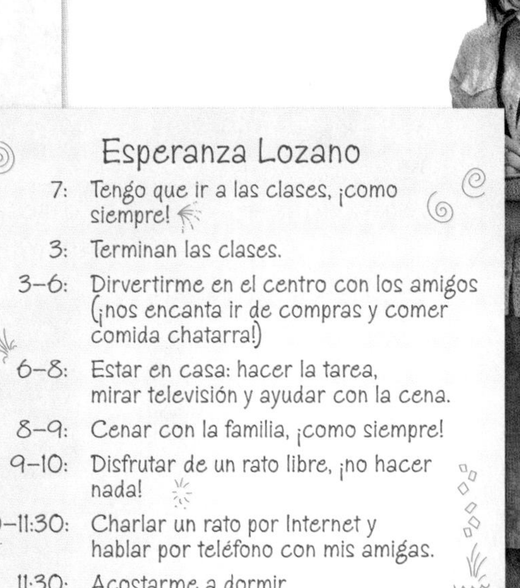

Esperanza Lozano

7:	Tengo que ir a las clases, ¡como siempre!
3:	Terminan las clases.
3–6:	Dirvertirme en el centro con los amigos (¡nos encanta ir de compras y comer comida chatarra!)
6–8:	Estar en casa: hacer la tarea, mirar televisión y ayudar con la cena.
8–9:	Cenar con la familia, ¡como siempre!
9–10:	Disfrutar de un rato libre, ¡no hacer nada!
10–11:30:	Charlar un rato por Internet y hablar por teléfono con mis amigas.
11:30:	Acostarme a dormir.

4 Comprensión de los horarios

Leer
Hablar
Escribir

Contesta las preguntas sobre la lectura.

1. ¿Cuál de las dos hermanas es más organizada? ¿Cómo lo sabes?
2. ¿Cuántas actividades relacionadas con la escuela o con el trabajo menciona Victoria en su lista y cuántas Esperanza? ¿Cuáles son?
3. ¿Qué actividades tienen en común las dos hermanas?
4. ¿Qué hermana piensa mucho en el futuro?
5. ¿Qué hermana piensa más en el presente?

5 El trabajo apropiado

Hablar
Escribir

Según la lectura sobre Victoria y Esperanza, indica quién tiene la personalidad y el carácter apropiados para los siguientes trabajos y explica por qué.

modelo: tesorera del club de computadoras
Victoria sería mejor como tesorera porque es muy organizada y quiere trabajar en un banco.

1. actriz en un drama
2. cajera

3. empleada una tienda de ropa

4. salvavidas

5. diseñadora de páginas web

6. niñera

Expansión
Compara tus ideas con las de un(a) compañero(a). Decidan juntos cuál es el mejor trabajo para cada hermana y expliquen sus razones a la clase.

PARA Y PIENSA

¿Comprendiste? Usa el vocabulario nuevo para contestar estas preguntas.

1. Menciona tres actividades que haces en la escuela durante el día.
2. Menciona tres actividades relacionadas con la escuela o con el trabajo que haces por la tarde o por la noche.

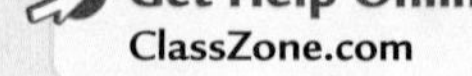

Get Help Online
ClassZone.com

Presentación de GRAMÁTICA

¡AVANZA! **Goal:** Learn how to form the imperfect subjunctive. Then practice by talking about hopes, doubts, emotions, and opinions in the past. ***Actividades 6–9***

¿Recuerdas? Subjunctive with doubt p. 243

English Grammar Connection: In English, you typically use the **conditional** or the **infinitive** after expressions of hope, doubt, emotion, or opinion in the past. In Spanish, you use the **imperfect subjunctive.**

I **hoped** that everything **would turn out** well.	**Esperaba** que todo **saliera** bien.
His mother **wanted** him **to study** more.	Su mamá **quería** que él **estudiara** más.

Imperfect Subjunctive

You already know when to use the present subjunctive. To express the same ideas in the past, use the **imperfect subjunctive.** How do you use it?

Here's how: Expressions of hope, doubt, emotion, or opinion in the past are followed by verbs in the **imperfect subjunctive.**

To form the **imperfect subjunctive,** remove the **-ron** ending of the **ustedes/ellos(as)** preterite form and add the imperfect subjunctive endings.

Infinitive	Preterite
tomar	**tomaron**
saber	**supieron**
pedir	**pidieron**

Endings	
-ra	-´ramos
-ras	-rais
-ra	-ran

The endings are the same for all **-ar, -er,** and **-ir** verbs. Note the accent mark in the **nosotros(as)** form, placed on the vowel immediately before the ending.

El profesor de música **quería** que nosotros **tomáramos** parte en el coro.
The music teacher wanted us to take part in the choir.

Yo **dudaba** que alguien **supiera** la respuesta correcta.
I doubted that anyone would know the correct answer.

Más práctica

Cuaderno *pp. 298–300*
Cuaderno para hispanohablantes *pp. 299–301*

Conjuguemos.com

@HomeTutor Leveled Practice ClassZone.com

Práctica de GRAMÁTICA

6 Mis padres

Hablar
Escribir

Haz frases para decir qué querían los padres que sus hijos hicieran el verano pasado.

modelo: yo / dejar de estar estresado(a)
Mis padres querían que yo dejara de estar estresado.

1. Margarita / pagar los impuestos
2. Marcos y Daniel / salir bien en los exámenes
3. tú / trabajar de salvavidas
4. yo / pedir empleo en la biblioteca
5. Rebeca y Alonso / ser miembros de la sociedad honoraria
6. ustedes / abrir una cuenta de ahorros

7 Los recuerdos

Hablar

Contesta las preguntas de tu compañero(a) sobre las recomendaciones que les diste a tus amigos para una excursión.

modelo: visitar el castillo

A ¿Qué les recomendaste a tus amigos que visitaran?

B Les recomendé que visitaran el castillo.

1. hacer una visita guiada
2. probar las arepas
3. traer de recuerdo un tapiz
4. ver una ceremonia local
5. explorar el centro histórico
6. leer una guía turística

Expansión
Pídele a tu compañero(a) que te explique por qué hizo tres de las recomendaciones a sus amigos.

8 Mentiras  *¿Recuerdas?* Subjunctive with doubt p. 243

Hablar

Inventa frases improbables en el pasado con las ideas siguientes. Tu compañero(a) expresará su duda.

es imposible
no creer
dudar
es improbable
es dudoso
no es verdad

modelo: ser miembro del comité de eventos...

A Yo fui miembro del comité de eventos el año pasado.

B No creo que tú fueras miembro del comité de eventos el año pasado.

1. graduarse en dos años...
2. solicitar una beca...
3. anticipar el futuro...
4. tener un sueldo muy alto...
5. servir de presidente(a)...
6. ser tesorero(a) del club...
7. tener la esperanza de...
8. no tomar ningún día feriado...

9 Recomendaciones de salud

Escribir

Los entrenadores de tu escuela dieron una conferencia sobre la salud de los estudiantes. Lee tus notas y escríbele un correo electrónico a tu compañero(a) que no fue a la conferencia.

modelo: Hola, la conferencia fue interesante. Los entrenadores nos dijeron que era muy importante que...

- ponernos en forma
- aliviar el estrés
- seguir una dieta balanceada
- dejar de comer...
- sólo trabajar a tiempo parcial
- tomar decisiones buenas
- hacer ejercicio todos los días
- dormir ocho horas cada noche

Comparación cultural

La televisión en Venezuela

¿Cómo se relacionan la cultura y los medios de comunicación en los diferentes países? En **Venezuela,** como en Estados Unidos, una manera muy popular de pasar los ratos libres es ver la televisión. Venezuela exporta programas y películas a todo el mundo. Sus telenovelas *(soap operas)* son muy conocidas y se doblan *(are dubbed)* en varios idiomas para poder transmitirlas en otros países. Se puede decir que son las ventanas de Venezuela al mundo. Además de verse en Latinoamérica, las telenovelas venezolanas se ven en Turquía, Mongolia, Egipto, Israel y muchísimos otros países.

Noticiero venezolano en las calles de Caracas

Compara con tu mundo *¿Qué tipos de programas asocias con la televisión estadounidense? En tu opinión, ¿cuáles son los programas estadounidenses más «típicos»? ¿Por qué?*

Más práctica Cuaderno *pp. 298–300* Cuaderno para hispanohablantes *pp. 299–301*

¿Comprendiste? Escribe las oraciones de nuevo con los verbos en el imperfecto.

1. Mis amigos no quieren que yo cuide niños los sábados por la noche.
2. Mis padres esperan que todo salga bien en mi examen.
3. Mi profesor duda que el examen sea demasiado difícil.

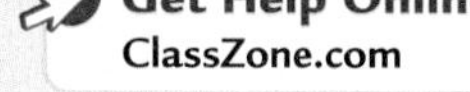

Get Help Online
ClassZone.com

GRAMÁTICA en contexto

¡AVANZA! **Goal:** Notice how Victoria and Tía Esmeralda use the imperfect subjunctive in the letters below. Then practice using the imperfect subjunctive to talk about what friends and family wanted you to do in the past.
Actividades 10–12

Contexto 2 *Cartas*

ESTRATEGIA **Leer**

Use a situational flow chart Create a situational flow chart. On the left, draw two boxes describing Victoria and Esperanza's interests. In the next two boxes, summarize Victoria's letter and the advice she receives.

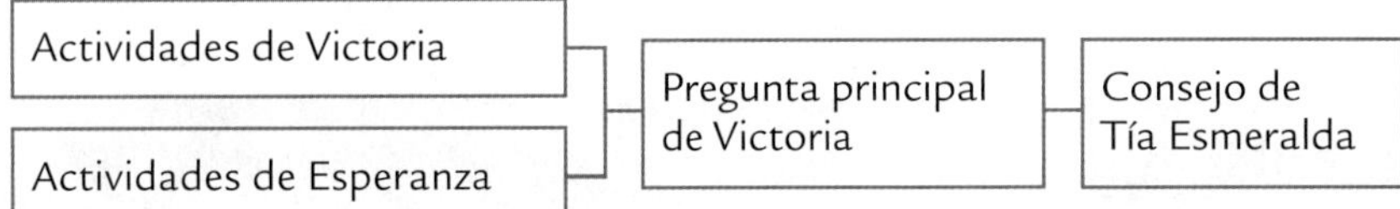

AUDIO

Victoria está preocupada por su hermana y le ha escrito una carta a Tía Esmeralda, una periodista que tiene una columna de consejos en una revista local.

MUJER VENEZOLANA

QUERIDA TÍA ESMERALDA

Querida Tía Esmeralda,

Estoy muy preocupada por mi hermana y no sé qué hacer. Ella no toma parte en actividades fuera de las clases y no hace nada en sus ratos libres. Hablé con ella ayer y le aconsejé que reflexionara un poco sobre su vida y que hiciera algunos planes para el futuro. Temo que ella no pueda asistir a la universidad si no se organiza mejor.

Le recomendé que estudiara más, que participara en más actividades y que empezara a investigar universidades y solicitar becas ahora mismo. Ella me dijo que no le gustaba que yo le dijera cómo vivir su vida y que la dejara en paz. Pero realmente me preocupo por ella. ¿Qué debo hacer?

—Una hermana preocupada

Querida Hermana Preocupada,

Si tu hermana no quiere cambiar, no hay nada que tú puedas hacer. Si ella te pidió que no le dieras más consejos, tú tienes que respetar sus deseos. ¿Por qué no invitas a tu hermana a hacer algo juntas que realmente le gustaría a ella? Eso sería una buena manera de tratar de hacerle ver que las actividades pueden ser divertidas. Pero nada más, ya que te dijo que no le hablaras más del tema, no debes ofrecerle más consejos.

—*Tía Esmeralda*

212

10 Comprensión de las cartas

Leer
Hablar
Escribir

Contesta las siguientes preguntas sobre la lectura.

1. ¿Por qué le escribió Victoria a Tía Esmeralda?
2. ¿Qué le había aconsejado Victoria a su hermana antes de escribir la carta?
3. ¿Qué teme Victoria?
4. ¿Qué le recomendó Victoria a Esperanza?
5. ¿Qué le contestó Esperanza?
6. Menciona dos cosas que Tía Esmeralda le recomendó a Victoria que hiciera.

11 ¡Cuéntame...!

Hablar

Cuéntale a tu compañero(a) sobre una ocasión en que tuviste que hacer algo que no querías hacer.

Pistas: ¿Qué tuviste que hacer? ¿Quién quería que lo hicieras? ¿Por qué no querías hacerlo? ¿Cómo reaccionaste? ¿Cómo terminó?

modelo: Cuando yo tenía seis años, mi hermana quería que yo llevara a su perro para un retrato de la familia, pero no me gustaba el perro...

12 Un problema

Escribir

Escríbele una carta a Tía Esmeralda pidiéndole consejos sobre una situación en que tú querías que alguien (tu mamá, un[a] hermano[a], tus amigos[as], tus maestros[as]) hiciera algo que no quería hacer. Explica claramente lo que tú querías, pedías o decías que esa persona hiciera y cómo reaccionó.

Querida Tía Esmeralda,
Le estoy escribiendo esta carta porque no sé qué hacer. Déjeme explicarle. Le pedí a mi amigo que hiciera...

Expansión
Intercambia tu carta con otra persona. Lee la carta de tu compañero(a) y prepara una respuesta.

PARA Y PIENSA

¿Comprendiste? Di qué querían tu familia, tus amigos y otras personas que tú hicieras la semana pasada.

1. Mis amigos querían que yo...
2. Mis padres querían que yo...
3. Mi maestro(a) quería que yo...
4. Mi hermano(a) quería que yo...

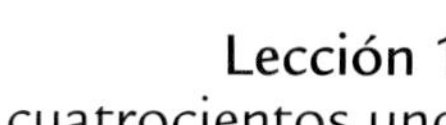

Presentación de GRAMÁTICA

¡AVANZA! **Goal:** Learn the subjunctive forms of the present perfect and past perfect. Then practice by saying how you feel about events that have occurred recently or that had occurred in the past. ***Actividades 13–16***

 *¿Recuerdas?* Impersonal expressions p. 128

English Grammar Connection: In English, you use the present or past perfect to express a reaction to what *has* happened, or *had* happened. In Spanish, you often need to use the **present** or **past perfect subjunctive.**

It's good that Peter **has understood.**	Es bueno que Peter **haya entendido.**
They wished he **had arrived.**	Esperaban que él **hubiera llegado.**

Subjunctive of Perfect Tenses

In Spanish, the **perfect tenses** always use a form of the verb **haber** with the past participle of the main verb. When the subjunctive is required, you must use the subjunctive form of **haber.**

Here's how: Use the **present perfect subjunctive** after a verb in the present tense. You form it with the **present subjunctive** of **haber** plus the **past participle** of the main verb.

haya	**hayamos**		
hayas	**hayáis**	**+**	**past participle**
haya	**hayan**		

Espero que tú **hayas decidido** redactar el anuario este año.
*I hope that **you have decided** to edit the yearbook this year.*

Use the **past perfect subjunctive** after a verb in the past tense. You form it with the **imperfect subjunctive** of **haber** plus the **past participle** of the main verb.

hubiera	**hubiéramos**		
hubieras	**hubierais**	**+**	**past participle**
hubiera	**hubieran**		

Paco **dudaba** que **hubiéramos trabajado** de salvavidas el verano pasado.
*Paco doubted that **we had worked** as lifeguards last summer.*

Más práctica
Cuaderno *pp. 301–303*
Cuaderno para hispanohablantes *pp. 302–305*

Conjuguemos.com

@HomeTutor
Leveled Practice
ClassZone.com

Práctica de GRAMÁTICA

13 Nuestros atletas

 ***¿Recuerdas?*** Impersonal expressions p. 128

Escuchar
Hablar
Escribir

Escucha este informe en la radio sobre los cambios que han hecho los atletas de tu escuela. Expresa tus opiniones sobre lo que has aprendido. Usa las expresiones impersonales que ya sabes.

modelo: increíble / dejar de comer
Es increíble que los atletas hayan dejado de comer comida chatarra.

1. es mejor / no comer
2. es increíble / dejar de tomar
3. es bueno / perder peso
4. es lógico / reducir el estrés
5. es interesante / participar
6. es impresionante / empezar a seguir

14 Descubrimientos

Escribir
Hablar

Escribe tus impresiones sobre la vida de tus familiares. Utiliza las expresiones del banco de palabras.

es asombroso
es sorprendente
es admirable
es impresionante
es extraordinario

modelo: mi tío Joaquín / participar en un partido de fútbol
Era increíble que mi tío Joaquín hubiera participado en un partido de fútbol.

1. mis abuelos / construir su casa
2. mi padre / bailar muy bien tango
3. mis bisabuelos / casarse muy jóvenes
4. mis padres / conocerse en tercer grado
5. mi abuelo Pepe / usar el código de vestimenta
6. mi abuela / cantar en la ópera

AUDIO

Pronunciación La letra r

Si no es la primera letra de la palabra, la letra **r** tiene un sonido suave. Se pronuncia como el sonido de **dd** en **ladder** o de **tt** en **better.**

graduarse	**estrés**
cuidar	**ceremonia**

Trabalenguas

Tres tristes tigres en traje tragan trigo en un trigal.

15 Ojalá hubiera...

Hablar

Tu compañero(a) te dice lo que han decidido estas personas. Di qué hubieras preferido tú que hicieran.

modelo: Jaime: «Voy a cuidar niños; no voy a trabajar en la cafetería.»

A: Jaime ha decidido cuidar niños.

B: Ojalá hubiera decidido trabajar en la cafetería.

1. Mariana: «Voy a llenar una solicitud de empleo; no voy a solicitar una beca.»
2. Juan y Pilar: «Vamos a escribir el comienzo de un cuento; no vamos a escribir un artículo para el periódico estudiantil.»
3. Nosotros: «Vamos a cantar en el coro; no vamos a actuar en el drama.»
4. Gabriel: «Voy a ser vicepresidente del comité estudiantil; no voy a ser secretario del club de español.»
5. Ester y Lila: «No vamos a ir a la fiesta; vamos a ir al cine.»

16 ¿Qué quieren?

Leer
Escribir

Comparación cultural

El carnaval en Barranquilla, *Colombia*

El carnaval

¿Qué importancia tienen las celebraciones típicas de un país? El carnaval es un festival cultural con orígenes religiosos que se celebra durante la semana antes de la Cuaresma *(Lent)*. Hay música, baile, canciones y ropa especial. La ciudad de Barranquilla, en **Colombia,** tiene fama por sus carnavales. Cada año, los barranquilleros toman parte en el carnaval, el cual fue declarado Patrimonio de la Humanidad por la UNESCO en 2003.

Compara con tu mundo *Describe las celebraciones en que toman parte tu familia y tú. ¿Cuándo son? ¿Cuál es su origen?*

Escribe una lista de cinco cosas que querías que hubieran ocurrido durante una celebración.

modelo: Yo quería que mi hermana hubiera cantado canciones divertidas.

Más práctica Cuaderno *pp. 301–303* Cuaderno para hispanohablantes *pp. 302–305*

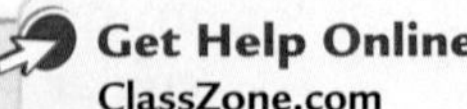

¿Comprendiste? Cambia las oraciones con una expresión impersonal de emoción en el pasado (Era necesario que, Era importante que...).

1. Un compañero ha recibido una beca para la universidad.
2. Los profesores han nombrado a tu amiga para la sociedad honoraria.
3. Los miembros del equipo no se habían puesto en forma.

Todo junto

¡AVANZA! **Goal:** ***Show what you know*** Notice the language that Victoria and Esperanza use to express past assumptions and to relate what they each wanted the other to do. Then practice by expressing your own doubts and assumptions about the past. ***Actividades 17–20***

Resumen contextos 1 y 2 Victoria y Esperanza son hermanas. Victoria es muy organizada y participa en muchas actividades. Victoria le escribió una carta a Tía Esmeralda, la autora de la columna de consejos de la revista, pidiendo recomendaciones sobre su hermana.

Contexto 3 *Diálogo*

ESTRATEGIA **Escuchar**

Use a storyline to track sequence and tones
Listen two times, keeping track of the sequence of events with a storyline. To do this, draw a line that shows events divided by diagonal marks. Listen a third time and add notes about the tones of voice (joking, sarcastic, surprised, angry, etc.).

AUDIO

Esperanza y Victoria discuten por la carta que Victoria mandó a la columna de consejos que tiene Tía Esmeralda en la revista.

Esperanza: Hola, Viki. Veo que sigues con la dieta balanceada. Bueno, que te vaya bien. Para mí, unas empanadas, unas arepas y ya está...

Victoria: Ay, Esperanza. ¡Nunca cambias!

Esperanza: Sí, ya me aconsejaste que comiera mejor y dejara la comida chatarra, pero con tantos consejos que me das... siempre me olvido de todos. Oye, ¿tienes la columna de la Tía Esmeralda?

Victoria: ¿La lees? ¡No sabía que te gustaba! Ejem... todavía la estoy leyendo.

Esperanza: ¡Qué va! La revista está al otro lado de la mesa.

Esperanza toma la revista. Victoria se pone muy nerviosa.

Esperanza: A ver qué pasa con la tía hoy... siempre tomando decisiones, arreglando el mundo...

Victoria: Bueno, no es muy interesante. No le salió bien.

Esperanza sigue leyendo la columna. Victoria parece aun más estresada.

Victoria: Esperanza... ¿Espe? Realmente, no debes...

Esperanza termina de leer la columna y pone la revista en la mesa. Está furiosa.

Esperanza: ¡Victoria! ¡No es posible que hayas escrito esta carta a la revista! ¡No tienes el derecho de hablar de mí con el mundo entero! ¡No puedo creer que me hayas tratado tan mal!

Victoria: Ay, lo siento, ¡pero me preocupo mucho por ti! Quiero que asistas a la universidad después de la graduación y si no te esfuerzas más...

Esperanza: Ya te dije que estoy contenta. ¡Hazme la caridad y déjame en paz! Es increíble que hayas enviado esto a una revista... ¡Qué vergüenza! ¿Cómo puedo salir de la casa? ¿Qué hago?

Victoria: Ay, Espe, ¡lo siento! ¡No llores! Estaba pensando en tu futuro...

Esperanza: «¡Mi futuro!» Pero, ¿qué pasa con «mi presente»?

También se dice

Esperanza utilizó la frase **Hazme la caridad,** que quiere decir **Hazme un favor.**
- Argentina **Hacéme una gauchada.**
- Cuba **Tírame un cabo.**

17 Comprensión del diálogo

Escuchar Hablar Escribir

Contesta las preguntas sobre la lectura.

1. ¿De qué se burló *(made fun of)* Esperanza cuando vio a su hermana en el comedor?
2. ¿Qué le pidió Esperanza a Victoria?
3. ¿De qué se sorprendió Victoria?
4. ¿Cómo reaccionó Esperanza cuando leyó la carta que había escrito Victoria?
5. ¿Cómo se sintió Victoria cuando vio la reacción de su hermana?
6. ¿Qué diferencia hay entre las hermanas?

18 ¡Ojalá no hubiera...!

Hablar

Reflexiona sobre algo que tú hiciste, que te salió mal y que le hizo daño a otra persona. Explica qué hiciste, cómo te salió, cómo afectó a la otra persona y qué hubieras hecho diferente.

modelo: Hice una amiga nueva y pasé menos tiempo con otra amiga... Ojalá hubiera pasado más tiempo con esta otra amiga.

Expansión
Escribe un párrafo sobre lo que hubieras querido y no hubieras querido hacer esta semana.

19 Integración

Leer
Escuchar
Hablar

Lee la biografía de un ex alumno. Luego escucha el discurso durante una reunión de ex alumnos *(class reunion)*. Explica qué has aprendido de la vida de Víctor Espronceda.

Fuente 1 Biografía

VÍCTOR ESPRONCEDA

Víctor Espronceda siempre fue un estudiante popular. Todos querían que participara en los eventos sociales. Le pidieron que organizara eventos de beneficencia en la comunidad. También dirigió el club de teatro y actuó en casi todos los dramas de la escuela. En sus ratos libres trabajaba en una tienda de videos. No es sorprendente que haya seguido la carrera de actor. Sus padres querían que se hubiera graduado de ingeniero pero Víctor se decidió por el arte. Ahora, con más de cinco películas en su currículum, Víctor es uno de nuestros estudiantes más famosos.

Fuente 2 Discurso

Escucha y apunta

- ¿Qué esperaba Víctor Espronceda?
- ¿Hubiera pensado ser un actor famoso?

modelo: Víctor esperaba que todos estuvieran bien y que hubieran visto su película...

20 ¡A escribir!

Escribir

Escríbele una carta a la persona que mencionaste en la actividad número dieciocho. En tu carta, expresa tu arrepentimiento *(regret)* por el daño que le hiciste a esa persona y explica qué no hubieras hecho.

modelo: Querida Alicia,
He decidido escribirte para pedirte perdón. Ojalá...

Writing Criteria	Excellent	Good	Needs Work
Content	Your letter includes many details about your regrets.	Your letter includes some details about your regrets.	Your letter includes few details about your regrets.
Communication	Your letter is organized and easy to follow.	Parts of your letter are organized and easy to follow.	Your letter is disorganized and hard to follow.
Accuracy	You make few mistakes in grammar and vocabulary.	You make some mistakes in grammar and vocabulary.	You make many mistakes in grammar and vocabulary.

Más práctica Cuaderno *pp. 304–305* Cuaderno para hispanohablantes *pp. 306–307*

Get Help Online
ClassZone.com

¿Comprendiste? ¿Recuerdas algunas situaciones en que las acciones de otra persona te afectaron mucho? Completa las oraciones con tus sentimientos.

1. No podía creer que...
2. Me pareció imposible que...
3. No me gustó que...
4. Fue increíble que...

Lectura literaria

¡AVANZA! **Goal:** Read this excerpt of a story about two boys who refuse to let a lack of water prevent them from enjoying their new boat. Then think about other adventures that might be possible with the power of imagination.

Para leer 

ESTRATEGIA Leer

Find the "fantastic" elements Gabriel García Márquez is known for the "fantastic" and "magical" elements in his stories. Make a chart like the one below. In the first column of the chart, write the ordinary elements. In the second column write the fantastic or magical elements.

Elementos comunes	Elementos fantásticos o mágicos

Vocabulario para leer

el muelle *lugar donde están parados los barcos*
el bote de remos *barco pequeño sin motor*
la brújula *instrumento para saber los puntos cardinales*
reacio(a) *que no quiere hacer algo*
dorado(a) *de color amarillo, como el sol*
la bombilla *objeto que produce luz en una lámpara*
la corriente *electricidad*

Nota cultural

Sobre el autor ***Gabriel García Márquez (1928–)***
Nació en Aracataca, Colombia. Su obra más famosa, *Cien años de soledad,* se publicó en 1967. En 1982 García Márquez ganó el premio Nóbel de literatura. Sus novelas y cuentos muestran una mezcla de fantasía y realismo donde muchas veces lo fantástico parece completamente normal.

Sobre el realismo mágico El realismo mágico es una forma de ficción donde los elementos fantásticos aparecen junto a cosas reales. Todos los personajes de la obra aceptan estos elementos como realidad. Se asocia el realismo mágico con Gabriel García Márquez porque, según la mayoría de los críticos, su libro *Cien años de soledad* es considerado como una de las obras más importantes del estilo.

La luz es como el agua

En Navidad los niños volvieron a pedir un bote de remos.

—De acuerdo —dijo el papá—, lo compraremos cuando volvamos a Cartagena.

Totó, de nueve años y Joel, de siete, estaban más decididos de lo que sus padres creían.

—No —dijeron a coro—, nos hace falta ahora y aquí.

—Para empezar —dijo la madre—, aquí no hay más aguas navegables que la que sale de la ducha.

Tanto ella como el esposo tenían razón. En la casa de Cartagena de Indias había un patio con un muelle sobre la bahía[1], y un refugio para dos yates grandes. En cambio[2], aquí en Madrid vivían apretujados[3] en el piso quinto del número 47 del Paseo de la Castellana. Pero al final ni él ni ella pudieron negarse, porque les habían prometido[4] un bote de remos con su sextante[5] y su brújula si se ganaban el laurel[6] del tercer año de primaria, y se lo habían

[1] bay [2] **En...** however [3] squeezed [4] had promised
[5] sextant [6] laurel wreath, a prize for excellence

ganado. Así que el papá compró todo sin decirle nada a su esposa, que era la más reacia a pagar deudas[7] de juego. Era un precioso bote de aluminio con un hilo[8] dorado en la línea de flotación.

—El bote está en el garaje —reveló el papá en el almuerzo—. El problema es que no hay cómo subirlo ni por el ascensor ni por la escalera, y en el garaje no hay más espacio disponible[9].

Sin embargo, la tarde del sábado siguiente los niños invitaron a sus condiscípulos[10] para subir el bote por las escaleras, y lograron llevarlo hasta el cuarto de servicio.

—Felicitaciones —les dijo el papá— ¿Y ahora qué?

—Ahora nada —dijeron los niños—. Lo único que queríamos era tener el bote en el cuarto, y ya está[11].

La noche del miércoles, como todos los miércoles, los padres se fueron al cine. Los niños, dueños y señores[12] de la casa, cerraron

A pensar
¿Por qué crees que los niños quieren un bote?

[7] debts [8] thin line [9] available [10] classmates
[11] **ya...** that's it [12] **dueños...** lords and masters

Reflexiona

¿Dónde vivían los niños antes? ¿Dónde viven ahora? ¿Qué diferencias hay?

puertas y ventanas, y rompieron la bombilla encendida de una lámpara de la sala. Un chorro[13] de luz dorada y fresca como el agua empezó a salir de la bombilla rota, y lo dejaron correr hasta que el nivel llegó a cuatro palmos[14]. Entonces cortaron la corriente, sacaron el bote, y navegaron a placer[15] por entre las islas de la casa. ✣

✣ A pensar
¿Cuánto de realidad y de magia hay en la aventura de los niños?

Esta aventura fabulosa fue el resultado de una ligereza[16] mía cuando participaba en un seminario sobre la poesía de los utensilios domésticos. Totó me preguntó cómo era que la luz se encendía con sólo apretar un botón, y yo no tuve el valor de pensarlo dos veces.

—La luz es como el agua —le contesté—: uno abre el grifo, y sale.

De modo que siguieron navegando los miércoles en la noche, aprendiendo el manejo[17] del sextante y la brújula, hasta que los padres regresaban del cine y los encontraban dormidos como ángeles de tierra firme[18]. Meses después, ansiosos de ir más lejos, pidieron un equipo de pesca submarina. Con todo: máscaras, aletas[19], tanques y escopetas de aire comprimido[20].

....

---

[13] stream [14] palms [15] **a...** as they pleased [16] lighthearted comment
[17] handling [18] **tierra...** dry land [19] fins
[20] **escopetas...** compressed air harpoon guns

¿Comprendiste?

1. ¿En qué época del año ocurre el cuento?
2. ¿Qué gran diferencia geográfica hay entre Cartagena y Madrid?
3. ¿Cómo suben los niños el bote a su apartamento?
4. ¿Cómo solucionan los niños el problema de no tener aguas navegables?
5. ¿Por qué pidieron los niños el equipo de pesca submarina?

¿Y tú?

1. ¿Qué crees que pasará cuando los niños tengan su equipo de pesca submarina?
2. «La luz es como el agua» es un símil, una comparación poética. Inventa otros símiles y explica qué significan.

Conexiones *La música*

El joropo y la cumbia

La fusión de culturas ha resultado en una gran variedad de música y baile en Latinoamérica. Dos ejemplos muy típicos de esta mezcla de influencias son el joropo de Venezuela y la cumbia de Colombia.

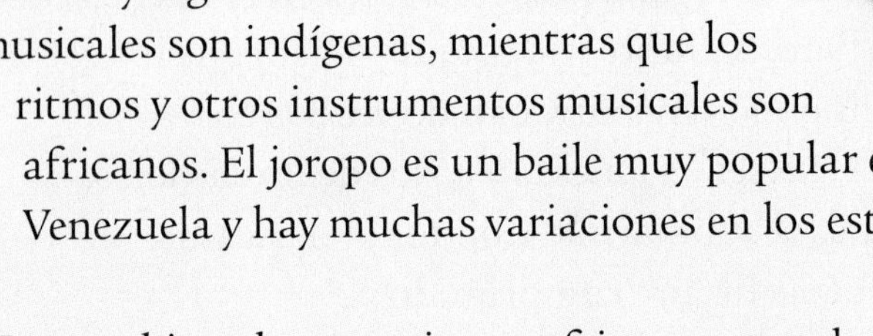

la guitarra

El joropo tiene sus raíces en el flamenco español, particularmente con relación a los movimientos del baile. Pero también muestra una mezcla de otras influencias. Las melodías y algunos de los instrumentos musicales son indígenas, mientras que los ritmos y otros instrumentos musicales son africanos. El joropo es un baile muy popular en Venezuela y hay muchas variaciones en los estilos.

el tambor

La cumbia se basa en ritmos africanos, pero las melodías y los gestos son indígenas. La cumbia ha pasado por muchas etapas *(stages)*. Por ejemplo, durante los años 1950, los mambo-cumbias eran muy populares. Hoy en día, hay músicos que tocan cumbias hip-hop. Pero hay un elemento que nunca cambia; la cumbia es súper bailable y es una de las formas musicales más populares de toda Latinoamérica.

el cuatro

el acordeón

Proyecto Mira las fotos de algunos de los instrumentos que se usan para tocar el joropo y la cumbia y trata de adivinar *(guess)* su lugar de origen: Europa, África o las culturas indígenas de Latinoamérica.

En tu comunidad

¿Hay algún baile tradicional o moderno típico de tu ciudad, estado o región? ¿Cuál es su origen? ¿Cuándo se baila?

Investiga un tipo de música o de baile muy típico de Estados Unidos. ¿Cuándo se originó? ¿Cuáles son sus influencias culturales? ¿Todavía se baila o se toca esta música? ¿Se asocian la música o el baile con algún tipo de celebración?

las maracas

En resumen

Vocabulario y gramática

Vocabulario

Discuss Work and School Activities

School activities and events

el anuario	*yearbook*
la ceremonia	*ceremony*
el código de vestimenta	*dress code*
el comienzo	*beginning, start*
el comité de eventos	*events committee*
el comité estudiantil	*student government*
el coro	*the choir*
el día feriado	*holiday*
la graduación	*graduation*
el rato libre	*free time*
el recuerdo	*memory*
la reunión	*meeting*
la sociedad honoraria	*honor society*
el (la) tesorero(a)	*treasurer*
el (la) vice-presidente(a)	*vice president*

Actions

actuar en un drama	*to act in a play*
graduarse	*to graduate*
irle bien (a alguien)	*to do well (in a class)*
redactar	*to edit*
reflexionar	*to reflect, to look back*
salir bien	*to turn out well*
ser miembro de	*to be a member of*
servir de presidente(a)	*to be / to serve as president*
solicitar una beca	*to apply for a scholarship*
tomar parte en	*to participate, to take part in*

Remember work

la cuenta de ahorros	*savings account*
cuidar niños	*to baby-sit*
el (la) diseñador(a) de páginas web	*Web page designer*
el (la) empleado(a)	*employee*
el empleo	*job*
los impuestos	*taxes*
llenar una solicitud de empleo	*to fill out a job application*
el (la) niñero(a)	*babysitter*
repartir periódicos	*to deliver newspapers*
el sueldo	*salary*
trabajar a tiempo parcial	*to work part-time*
trabajar de cajero(a)	*to work as a cashier*
trabajar de salvavidas	*to work as a lifeguard*

Express Past Assumptions and Emotions

anticipar	*to anticipate*	el estrés	*stress*
la esperanza	*hope*	estresado(a)	*stressed*

Relate What Others Wanted You To Do

la comida chatarra	*junk food*	dirigir	*to lead, to direct*
decidir	*to decide*	ponerse en forma	*to get in shape*
dejar de...	*to quit, to give up...*	tomar decisiones	*to make decisions*
la dieta balanceada	*balanced diet*		

Gramática

Imperfect Subjunctive

Expressions of hope, doubt, emotion, or opinion in the past are followed by verbs in the **imperfect subjunctive.**

To form the **imperfect subjunctive,** remove the **-ron** ending of the **ustedes/ellos(as)** preterite form and add the imperfect subjunctive endings.

Infinitive	Preterite
tomar	**tomaron**
saber	**supieron**
pedir	**pidieron**

drop **-ron** +

Endings	
-ra	**-´ramos**
-ras	**-rais**
-ra	**-ran**

The endings are the same for all **-ar, -er,** and **-ir** verbs.

Subjunctive of Perfect Tenses

Use the **present perfect subjunctive** after a verb in the present tense. You form it as follows:

haya	**hayamos**	
hayas	**hayáis**	**+ past participle**
haya	**hayan**	

Use the **past perfect subjunctive** after a verb in the past tense. You form it as follows:

hubiera	**hubiéramos**	
hubieras	**hubierais**	**+ past participle**
hubiera	**hubieran**	

Lección 1

Repaso de la lección

¡LLEGADA!

@HomeTutor ClassZone.com

Now you can
- relate what others wanted you to do
- express past assumptions and emotions
- discuss work and school activities

Using
- imperfect subjunctive
- subjunctive of perfect tenses

To review
- vocabulary pp. 392–393
- imperfect subjunctive p. 397

1 Listen and understand

Tomás Azuela es el secretario del comité estudiantil. Escucha las notas que tomó en la última reunión. Haz una lista de las actividades que el comité decidió apoyar. Haz otra lista con las actividades que no decidió apoyar y explica por qué.

To review
- imperfect subjunctive p. 397

2 Relate what others wanted you to do

Lee lo que hicieron las siguientes personas. ¿Quién crees que quería que hicieran esas cosas?

modelo: Julio hizo un análisis del libro.
La maestra de literatura quería que Julio hiciera un análisis del libro.

1. María diseñó una página web.
2. Los tíos cuidaron a los niños.
3. Tú repartiste periódicos.
4. Yo trabajé de cajero(a).
5. Nosotros narramos el cuento.

To review
- present perfect subjunctive p. 402

3 Express past assumptions and emotions

Mira los siguientes comentarios y expresa tus dudas. Sigue el modelo.

modelo: Lorenzo ha cuidado a los niños de Antonio Banderas.
Dudo que Lorenzo haya cuidado a los niños de Antonio Banderas.

1. Yo he dejado de comer comida chatarra.
2. Mis amigos se han graduado del colegio a la edad de doce años.
3. Los estudiantes del colegio han pedido un código de vestimenta.
4. Nosotros hemos redactado el anuario en solamente una semana.

To review
- past perfect subjunctive p. 402

4 Remember work and school activities

Haz oraciones completas sobre las actividades del año pasado. Sigue el modelo.

modelo: para graduarte era importante / completar unos cursos
Para graduarte, era importante que hubieras completado unos cursos.

1. para solicitar una beca universitaria era necesario / los estudiantes graduarse del colegio
2. para ponerse en forma era imprescindible / usted seguir una dieta balanceada
3. para evitar el estrés era una buena idea / nosotros hacer ejercicio y ponernos en forma
4. para trabajar en el anuario era lógico / tú escribir y redactar artículos para el periódico estudiantil
5. para trabajar de cajero era mejor / los empleados tener experiencia trabajando en un restaurante

To review
- **Comparación cultural** pp. 399–404

5 Television and celebrations

Comparación cultural

1. ¿Qué tipo de programa de televisión venezolano tiene fama mundial?
2. ¿En qué países se ven?
3. ¿Qué ciudad colombiana tiene una celebración de carnaval famosa?
4. ¿Cuáles son los orígenes de la celebración? ¿Cuánto tiempo dura esa celebración?

Más práctica Cuaderno *pp. 306–317* Cuaderno para hispanohablantes *pp. 308–317*

UNIDAD 7

Colombia y Venezuela

Lección 2

Tema:

Nuevos principios

¡AVANZA! **In this lesson you will learn to**

- talk about career possibilities
- hypothesize
- narrate in the past

using

- **si** clauses
- sequence of tenses

¿Recuerdas?

- impersonal expressions with subjunctive
- conditional
- future
- architectural structures

Comparación cultural

In this lesson you will learn about

- professions and art in Colombia
- universities in Colombia
- schools in Venezuela and Colombia

Compara con tu mundo

Estos estudiantes colombianos celebran su graduación del Instituto de Ciencias de la Salud. *¿Cómo es la ceremonia de graduación en tu colegio?*

¿Qué ves?

Mira la foto

¿Cómo están los estudiantes?

¿Qué tienen en las manos?

¿Qué crees que estudiaron en la universidad?

Online SPANISH CLASSZONE.COM

Featuring...
- Cultura INTERACTIVA
- Animated Grammar
- @HomeTutor

And more...
- Get Help Online
- Interactive Flashcards
- Review Games
- WebQuest
- Conjuguemos.com

Ceremonia de graduación,
Medellín, Colombia

Presentación de VOCABULARIO

¡AVANZA! **Goal:** Learn new words for talking about career possibilities. Then practice by talking about activities at school or outside of school that interest you. ***Actividades 1–3***

 *¿Recuerdas?* Impersonal expressions with subjunctive p. 183, Conditional p. 303

AUDIO

A Hola, soy Guille y tengo un problema. No sé qué hacer después de graduarme. Por eso estoy buscando información en algunos sitios web de **universidades** para ver qué me interesa. Yo sé que es muy importante **seguir una carrera** y **especializarme** en algo que me guste, porque tener **un título** es fundamental para mi futuro como profesional.

HTTP://www.universidad-autónoma-de-viejalinda.ve

UNIVERSIDAD AUTÓNOMA DE VIEJALINDA

En la Universidad Autónoma de Viejalinda tú puedes ser lo que quieras: **ingeniero**, **traductor** o **dueño** de **una empresa**. ¡Si quieres convertirte en un profesional **eficiente**, **cualificado** y **versátil**, nuestra universidad es el lugar ideal!

Enseñamos más de cincuenta carreras y **especialidades**. Nuestras **facultades contratan** a **los profesores más** cualificados y **apasionados** de todo el país.

Usamos **las estrategias** más **flexibles** y **fiables** para enseñar y nuestros alumnos son **educados**, **honestos** y **motivados**. Además, nuestra **escuela técnica** ha podido **establecer** una calidad muy alta en sus especialidades más populares.

NUESTRAS ESPECIALIDADES Y CARRERAS MÁS POPULARES

Contabilidad y Administración de empresas

Relaciones públicas

Idiomas

Ingeniería

Derecho

Economía

B Éstos son algunos de nuestros alumnos más **destacados.**

Mirta Contreras es **una mujer de negocios.**

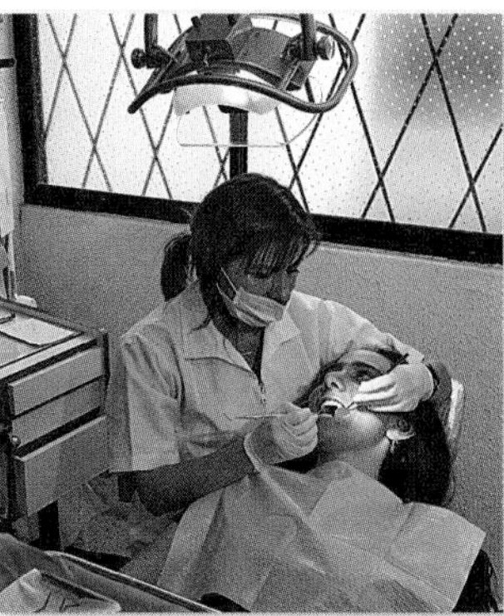

María Perdomo es **dentista.**

Miguel Cabrera es **juez.**

Luisa Rodríguez es **contadora.**

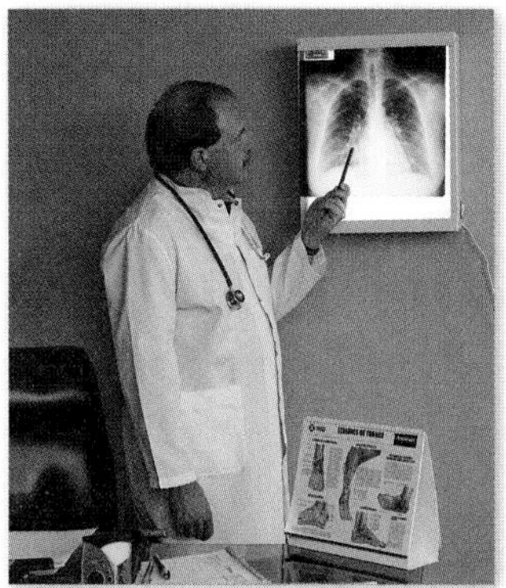

Andrés Ruiz es **médico.**

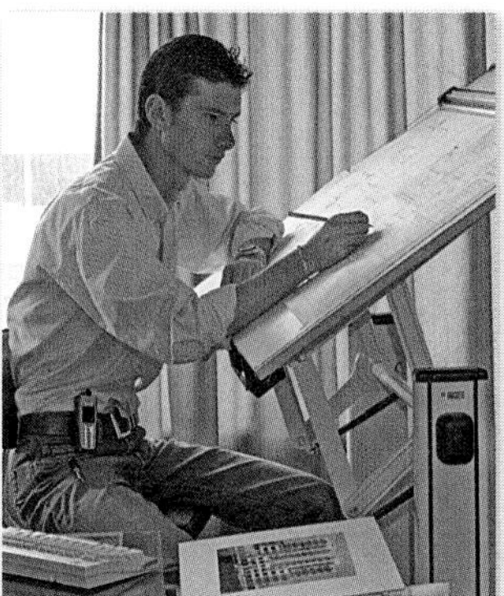

Orlando Sánchez es **arquitecto.**

Más vocabulario

el (la) abogado(a) *lawyer*
el (la) agente de la bolsa *stockbroker*
animado(a) *animated, upbeat*
el curso *course*
el (la) enfermero(a) *nurse*
el (la) gerente *manager*
honrado(a) *honest, honorable*
la iniciativa *initiative*
el (la) peluquero(a) *hairdresser*
el plan financiero *financial plan*
puntual *punctual*

Expansión de vocabulario p. R15
Ya sabes p. R15

¡A responder! Escuchar

Vas a oír el nombre de una profesión y luego una lista de adjetivos. Si el adjetivo describe una cualidad que es importante para la profesión, indícalo con el dedo pulgar hacia arriba, si no, indícalo con el dedo pulgar hacia abajo.

@HomeTutor
Interactive Flashcards
ClassZone.com

Práctica de VOCABULARIO

1 Las profesiones

Hablar
Escribir

Identifica la profesión descrita.

1. diseña edificios y hace planes para su construcción
2. corta el pelo de sus clientes
3. debe estudiar administración de empresas
4. cuida a pacientes en una clínica u hospital
5. traduce documentos de un idioma a otro

gerente
traductor(a)
peluquero(a)
enfermero(a)
arquitecto(a)

2 Las cualidades  ¿Recuerdas? Impersonal expressions with subjunctive p. 183

Hablar
Escribir

Para cada profesión indicada, decide cuál es la cualidad más importante.

modelo: abogado: ¿eficiente u honesto?
Es más importante que un abogado sea honesto.

1. profesor: ¿apasionado o puntual?
2. dentista: ¿cualificado o eficiente?
3. ingeniera: ¿fiable o educada?
4. médico: ¿versátil o animado?
5. agente de bolsa: ¿puntual o flexible?
6. jueza: ¿honrada o motivada?

Expansión
Escoge tres de estas profesiones. Menciona dos cualidades más que una persona debe tener para practicar cada profesión.

3 Una empresa   ¿Recuerdas? Conditional tense p. 303

Hablar
Escribir

Explica quién haría cada trabajo.

modelo: hacer el plan financiero de un negocio
El contador haría el plan financiero de un negocio.

1. contratar a empleados para su empresa
2. enseñar un curso en la universidad
3. llevar la contabilidad de una empresa
4. trabajar muchas horas en la bolsa
5. establecer un hospital para enfermos de cáncer

Más práctica Cuaderno *pp. 318–320* Cuaderno para hispanohablantes *pp. 318–321*

¿Comprendiste? ¿Qué carrera deben seguir estas personas?

1. Jorge estudia derecho.
2. Ángela estudia contabilidad.
3. Rodrigo habla tres idiomas.
4. Carmen quiere ayudar a todos.

VOCABULARIO en contexto

¡AVANZA! **Goal:** In the the following ads, notice what words are used to talk about careers and professions. Then describe your own thoughts about college and a future career using the new vocabulary. ***Actividades 4–6***

 *¿Recuerdas?* Future tense p. 157

Contexto 1 *Anuncios clasificados*

ESTRATEGIA **Leer**
Use an opportunity-analysis chart Use an opportunity-analysis chart to analyze the opportunities that Guille sees in the three ads.

Anuncios	Oportunidades para Guille
Escuela Técnica	
Universidad	
Empresa	

AUDIO

Guille Chávez, un estudiante colombiano, se está preparando para graduarse y buscar un empleo o seguir sus estudios. Le interesa mucho el cine y los idiomas, y tiene habilidad con las computadoras. El consejero académico le pidió que leyera los anuncios del periódico para informarse sobre las posibilidades de trabajo y estudio que hay.

HOMBRES Y MUJERES DE NEGOCIOS

Ingenieros de software (3 años de experiencia, fiables, puntuales)

Contador para crear plan financiero nuevo (7–8 años de experiencia)

Experto en relaciones públicas (3 años de experiencia en la formación de estrategias comunicativas)

Vendedores (la experiencia no es necesaria, los candidatos deben mostrar iniciativa y ser eficientes, versátiles y animados)

Manda C.V. y carta a la casilla N°331-B, periódico El Universal

Escuela Técnica Interamericana

35 años de experiencia formando técnicos profesionales. Carreras en éstas y otras áreas:

- *contabilidad sistémica*
- *análisis y programación de computadoras*
- *cosmetología para peluqueros*
- *urgencias médicas para enfermeros*

¡Formamos personal cualificado para un mercado laboral competitivo! Av. 39 #15-58

(571) 555-3474 • ***www.ETIColombia.r2r.co***

Universidad de San Beltrán Establecida en 1898

Cursos, especialidades y títulos en carreras académicas: idiomas, derecho, ingeniería, negocios, medicina, periodismo, ciencias sociales, ciencias, matemáticas, artes. Profesores cualificados y apasionados, clases pequeñas, atención personal. Nuestro estudiante ideal es motivado, versátil, flexible, con curiosidad intelectual.

¡Educamos a los profesionales del futuro, ahora!

Bogotá • (571)-bel-tran • **www.sanbeltrán.r2r.edu.co**

4 Comprensión de los anuncios clasificados

Leer
Hablar
Escribir

Contesta las siguientes preguntas, según los anuncios.

1. ¿Dónde se estudia la especialidad de peluquería?
2. ¿Qué tipo de estudiantes busca la Universidad de San Beltrán?
3. Si quieres estudiar ciencias sociales, ¿adónde irás?
4. Si quieres estudiar urgencias médicas, ¿dónde estudiarás?
5. ¿A quiénes quiere contratar la empresa? ¿Cómo deben ser los ingenieros de software que busca la empresa?
6. ¿Qué características personales deben tener los vendedores?

5 Conocimientos

Hablar
Escribir

Con tu compañero(a), escriban oraciones para explicar qué cualificaciones, experiencias y características personales ustedes piensan que son importantes para cada profesión. Utilicen el subjuntivo con expresiones impersonales: **es importante..., es necesario..., es imposible...**

modelo: Es importante que un arquitecto sea creativo.

peluquero(a)	conocer las leyes
profesor(a)	saber administración de empresas
contador(a)	asistir a una escuela de belleza
gerente	saber matemáticas
enfermero(a)	conocer anatomía
abogado(a)	saber enseñar

Expansión
Escoge una profesión. Ayuda a tu compañero(a) a prepararse para una entrevista de trabajo relacionada con tu elección. Hazle sugerencias.

6 ¿Qué quisieras ser?

¿Recuerdas? Future tense p. 157

Escribir

Escribe cinco oraciones sobre las profesiones que te interesan y las que no y explica por qué. Utiliza el futuro y las profesiones de la actividad anterior.

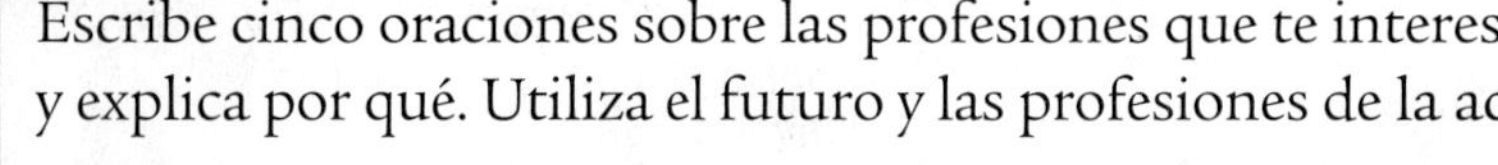

modelo: No seré arquitecto porque me gusta más la ingeniería.

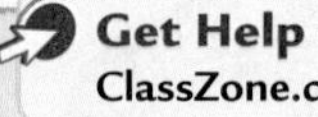

¿Comprendiste? Contesta las preguntas con oraciones completas.

1. ¿Cuáles son las ventajas *(advantages)* y desventajas *(disadvantages)* de ir a una escuela técnica después de graduarse?
2. ¿Cuáles son las ventajas y desventajas de ir a la universidad?
3. ¿Cuál de las opciones te interesa más? ¿Por qué?

 Presentación de GRAMÁTICA

¡AVANZA! **Goal:** Learn how to express a hypothesis. Then practice by talking about what might occur in specific circumstances. ***Actividades 7–10***

¿Recuerdas? Architectural structures pp. 358–359

English Grammar Connection: A clause is a part of a sentence that has a conjugated verb. In a sentence that expresses a hypothesis, both English and Spanish can use the **imperfect subjunctive** in the *if clause* and the **conditional** in the main clause.

If I **were** you, I **would decide** now.
if clause | **main clause**

Si yo **fuera** tú, **decidiría** ahora.
if clause | **main clause**

Si Clauses

A **si** clause is a hypothesis about what will happen or what would happen in particular circumstances. The verb in the **si** clause can be in the **simple present** or the **imperfect subjunctive** form.

Here's how:

To predict the result of a likely event, use the **simple present** in the **si** clause and the **future tense** in the main clause to express the outcome.

Si **dejamos** de comer comida chatarra, **perderemos** peso.
***If we stop** eating junk food, **we will lose** weight.*

To express how things would be if circumstances were different, use the **imperfect subjunctive** in the **si** clause and the **conditional** in the main clause.

Si Ana **cantara** en el coro, no **tendría** tiempo para redactar el anuario.
***If** Ana **were to sing** in the chorus, **she would** not **have** time to edit the yearbook.*

In both cases above, the order of clauses can be reversed.

Perderemos peso **si** **dejamos** de comer comida chatarra.

Ana no **tendría** tiempo para redactar el anuario **si** **cantara** en el coro.

Más práctica

Cuaderno *pp. 321–323*
Cuaderno para hispanohablantes *pp. 322–324*

@HomeTutor
Leveled Practice
ClassZone.com

Práctica de GRAMÁTICA

7 Si yo fuera diferente

Hablar
Escribir

Di lo que pasaría si fueras diferente.

modelo: puntual / no tener problemas en el trabajo
Si yo fuera más puntual no tendría problemas en el trabajo.

1. eficiente / ganar más dinero
2. educado(a) / lograr lo que quiero
3. animado(a) / trabajar en la radio
4. flexible / poder hacer más cosas a la vez
5. cualificado(a) / ser hombre (mujer) de negocios
6. tener iniciativa / contratarme para trabajos de relaciones públicas

Expansión
Elige a un(a) compañero(a) y di qué pasaría si tuviera tres de estas cualidades.

8 ¿Qué hago?  ***¿Recuerdas?*** Architectural structures pp. 358–359

Escuchar
Hablar
Escribir

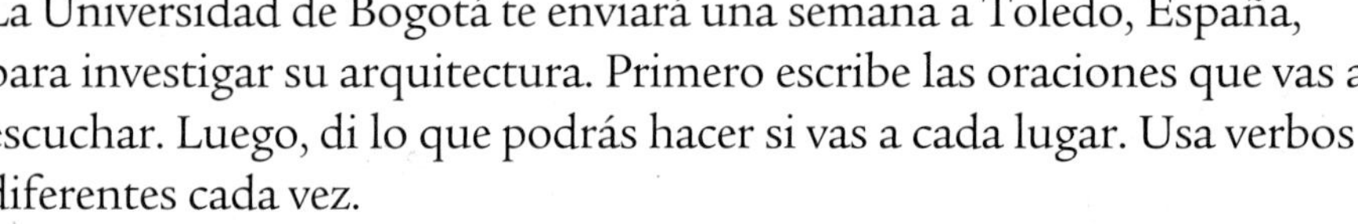

La Universidad de Bogotá te enviará una semana a Toledo, España, para investigar su arquitectura. Primero escribe las oraciones que vas a escuchar. Luego, di lo que podrás hacer si vas a cada lugar. Usa verbos diferentes cada vez.

Pistas: visitar, viajar, entrar, caminar, observar, ver, apreciar

modelo: La Catedral de Toledo tiene la colección de El Greco.
Si voy a la Catedral, podré ver la colección de El Greco.

9 Las profesiones

Hablar

Entrevista a un(a) compañero(a) para saber sus impresiones sobre las profesiones de la lista.

dentista	traductor(a)	juez(a)
ingeniero(a)	peluquero(a)	profesor(a)
abogado(a)	agente de bolsa	médico(a)

modelo: médico(a)

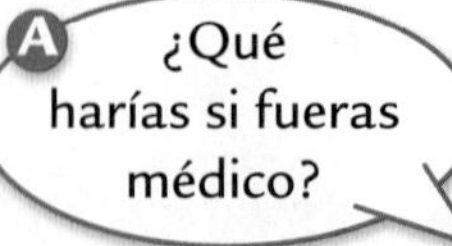

B Si fuera médico, trabajaría en un hospital de niños.

10 ¡A trabajar!

Leer
Hablar
Escribir

Lee el siguiente anuncio y responde a las preguntas.

1. ¿Qué carrera seguirías si asistieras a la Universidad Politécnica de Venezuela?
2. ¿Qué materias *(subjects)* te interesarían más si estudiaras arquitectura?
3. ¿Adónde llamarías si quisieras tener una entrevista? ¿Qué preguntarías?
4. ¿Qué preguntas harías si quisieras estudiar arquitectura?
5. ¿Qué título tendrías si te graduaras?
6. ¿Qué otra carrera escogerías si no te aceptaran en esta universidad?

La Universidad Politécnica de Venezuela

¡te invita a seguir la carrera de arquitectura!

Ofrecemos un nuevo programa de alto nivel. Estudiarás diseño, matemáticas, idiomas y administración de proyectos, y te prepararás para seguir una carrera con muchas oportunidades.

Habla con uno de nuestros consejeros para aprender más sobre esta especialidad.

Llama al (614) POLI-VEN para hacer una cita.

Comparación cultural

Los retratos de Fernando Botero

¿Cómo influye la intuición (intuition) *de un artista en su estilo?* Fernando Botero, el famoso pintor colombiano, se destaca por sus retratos de la gente de su país. Sus obras presentan imágenes de personas de muchas profesiones: militares, políticos, hombres de negocios, peluqueros y jardineros. Las esculturas y figuras de los cuadros de Fernando Botero tienen proporciones exageradas. Botero explica que a él le gustan estas formas de gran volumen por intuición. Aquí, Botero se pinta a sí mismo.

Compara con tu mundo *Mira el cuadro* Autorretrato. *¿Qué características del estilo de Botero puedes ver? ¿Cómo te pintarías tú?*

Autorretrato *(1987), Fernando Botero*

Más práctica Cuaderno *pp. 321–323* Cuaderno para hispanohablantes *pp. 322–324*

¿Comprendiste? Completa las siguientes hipótesis con tus propias ideas.

Get Help Online
ClassZone.com

1. Si ella estudiara derecho...
2. Si mi tío(a) abre una empresa...
3. Si yo fuera profesor(a)...
4. Si él supiera idiomas...
5. Si mi madre cocinara bien...
6. Si tú estudiaras medicina...

GRAMÁTICA en contexto

¡AVANZA! **Goal:** Read Guille's résumé. Then speculate about your own abilities and future plans. ***Actividades 11–13***

Contexto 2 *Hoja de vida*

ESTRATEGIA Leer

Compare yourself with Guille As you read, take notes on what you learn about Guille: his location, his grade in school, what he is interested in, what he does, his qualities, and so on. After you read, use a Venn diagram to compare yourself with Guille.

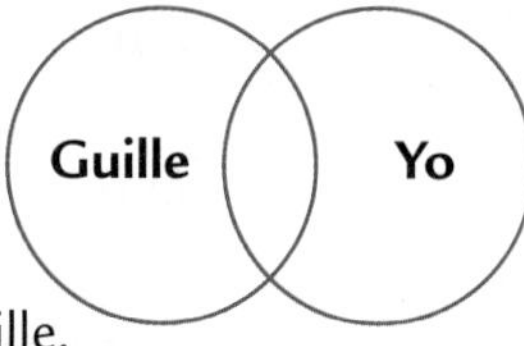

Guille preparó una hoja de vida *(résumé)* con sus intereses e ideas para el futuro.

Guillermo Chávez

Av. 27 #26 Bogotá · (57 1) 5974321 · Guillecha@correo6.rr.co

ESTUDIOS:
Estudiante de último año, Colegio San Bernardino, Bogotá

ACTIVIDADES:
Presidente, Club de Computación; tesorero, Sociedad Honoraria

INTERESES:
Diseño de páginas web, dibujos animados computarizados, idiomas, cine internacional y televisión.

Si pongo esto, ¿pensarán que soy perezoso?

CUALIDADES PROFESIONALES:
Soy una persona puntual, eficiente y fiable. Soy muy motivado: si tengo un proyecto urgente, no descansaré hasta que lo termine. También puedo tomar la iniciativa; por ejemplo, si no tuviera la información necesaria para completar un proyecto, haría preguntas o buscaría más datos para poder terminarlo bien.

METAS PROFESIONALES:
Me gustaría trabajar en el campo de la computación, en un puesto que exija creatividad y talento. Soy muy versátil, así que si el empleo requiere muchas responsabilidades variadas, me gustará mucho. Tengo mucha experiencia con las computadoras, pero nunca he tenido un trabajo con sueldo. Quiero poner en práctica mis conocimientos de diseño y computación para adelantarme profesionalmente y prepararme para el futuro.

Si escribo esto, ¿me considerarán muy egoísta?

11 Comprensión de la hoja de vida

Leer
Hablar
Escribir

Contesta las siguientes preguntas sobre la lectura.

1. Según Guille, ¿cuáles son cinco cualidades profesionales que él tiene?
2. Menciona cuatro actividades o intereses en que participa Guille.
3. ¿Qué tipo de trabajo quiere hacer?
4. ¿Qué haría Guille si no tuviera toda la información necesaria para completar un proyecto?
5. Si Guille incluye «televisión» entre sus intereses, ¿qué teme que piensen las personas que lean su hoja de vida?
6. En relación con las responsabilidades, ¿qué le gustará a Guille?
7. Si consiguiera un trabajo, ¿qué le gustaría poner en práctica?
8. ¿Cómo cree que lo considerarán si dice que tiene talento?

12 Si quisiera ser...

Hablar
Escribir

Indica las clases que Guille debería tomar si quisiera ser director de cine. Sigue el modelo.

física	matemáticas	historia del cine
fotografía	dibujo	geografía

modelo: **Si Guille quisiera ser director de televisión, no tendría que tomar la clase de física.**

13 Mi hoja de vida

Hablar
Escribir

Usa tus ideas y escribe un borrador *(draft)* de tu hoja de vida. Puedes usar la hoja de vida de Guille como modelo.

Pistas: ¿Cómo te llamas?, ¿dónde estudias?, ¿en qué clases eres bueno(a)? ¿Qué trabajos has hecho anteriormente? ¿Qué sabes hacer? ¿Qué quieres lograr en tu futuro?

Expansión
Intercambia tu hoja de vida con la de tu compañero(a). Hablen sobre sus opiniones.

¿Comprendiste? Completa las siguientes oraciones con tus propias ideas y planes para el futuro.

1. Si tuviera más tiempo...
2. Si voy a la universidad...
3. En el futuro estaré muy contento(a) si...

Presentación de GRAMÁTICA

¡AVANZA! **Goal:** Learn the proper sequence of tenses for any sentence with verbs in the indicative and subjunctive. Then talk about what you want or what you wanted others to do. ***Actividades 14–17***

English Grammar Connection: In English, you can use a **past tense** verb and a **present tense** verb in the same sentence. It is also common, in English, to use the **infinitive** instead of the subjunctive. In Spanish, you must match the tense of the indicative and subjunctive verbs.

I **am** glad that you **told** the truth.	**Me alegro** de que **hayas dicho** la verdad.
I **wanted** you **to be** honest.	**Quería** que **fueras** honesto.

Sequence of Tenses

Animated Grammar
ClassZone.com

The **subjunctive** form used depends on the **indicative tense** used in the main clause. How do you know what form of the **subjunctive** to use?

Here's how: You use the **present subjunctive** or **present perfect subjunctive** after the following **indicative tenses.**

simple present	Es bueno que **hayas decidido.**
present progressive	**Está prohibiendo** que **salgas.**
future	**Será** mejor que me **llames.**
present perfect	**He sugerido** que **trabajes** más.

You use the **imperfect subjunctive** or the **past perfect subjunctive** after the following **indicative tenses.**

preterite	**Prohibió** que **saliera.**
imperfect	**Era** bueno que **hubiera decidido.**
***past progressive**	**Estaba prohibiendo** que **salieras.**
conditional	**Preferiría** que **escribieras** más.
past perfect	**Había sugerido** que **salieras.**

*grammar point of the next lesson.

Depending on what you want to express, **ojalá** can be used with any subjunctive form.

Ojalá (que) **sigas** la carrera de derecho.	*I hope you **pursue** a career in law.*
Ojalá (que) **hubieras estudiado** ingeniería.	*I wish you **had studied** engineering.*

Más práctica

Cuaderno *pp. 324–326*
Cuaderno para hispanohablantes *pp. 325–328*

Conjuguemos.com **@HomeTutor**
Leveled Practice
ClassZone.com

Práctica de GRAMÁTICA

14 Todo en orden

Hablar
Escribir

Completa las siguientes oraciones.

modelo: el director de la escuela deseaba / los empleados tener iniciativa
El director de la escuela deseaba que los empleados hubieran tenido iniciativa.

1. era importante / tú pedir una beca
2. el gerente deseaba / mi padre hacer la estrategia de marketing
3. es una lástima / los estudiantes no entender matemáticas
4. la abogada prefiere / su hija estudiar derecho
5. nadie desearía / Jorge estudiar en la facultad de ingeniería
6. me había sorprendido / la administración de empresas ser tan complicada

15 Una entrevista

Hablar

Usa la siguiente información para hacerle preguntas a un(a) compañero(a). Sigue el modelo.

modelo: tus amigos / pedir

A: ¿Qué te piden tus amigos que hagas? ¿Qué te pidieron tus amigos que hicieras la semana pasada? ¿Qué te han pedido tus amigos?

B: Mis amigos me piden que sea honesto con ellos. Mis amigos me pidieron que fuera al cine con ellos. Mis amigos me han pedido que vaya al parque con ellos.

1. el (la) consejero(a) / decir
2. tus padres / rogar
3. tu hermano(a) / esperar
4. el (la) médico(a) / sugerir

Expansión
Pregúntale a tu compañero(a) sobre tres de las situaciones que describió.
Por ejemplo: «Si no fueras honesto(a), ¿qué pasaría?»

AUDIO

Pronunciación La letra t

La **t** tiene un sonido más suave que la **t** en inglés y se pronuncia sin explosión de aire. La posición de la **t** en una palabra no afecta su pronunciación.

título **motivado**

estrategia **contabilidad**

Refrán

Tanto va el cántaro a la fuente, hasta que se rompe.

16 ¿Qué querían?

Escribir

Escribe una lista de cosas que otras personas querían que hicieras en el pasado y lo que quieren ahora.

modelo: **Mis padres querían que asistiera a un programa de español en la universidad. Ahora quieren que vaya a estudiar a España.**

1. tus padres
2. tu maestro(a)
3. el entrenador
4. tu doctor
5. mi hermano
6. mis tías

17 ¿Querían que estudiáramos?

Leer
Hablar
Escribir

Comparación cultural

Universidades

¿Qué influencia tiene la historia en la educación de un país? **Colombia** fue una colonia española importante durante los siglos XVI al XIX, hasta que consiguió la independencia en 1819. Era importante para los colonizadores españoles que el país tuviera escuelas y universidades buenas para educar a sus familias; así no era necesario que sus hijos viajaran a Europa para estudiar. Su primera universidad, la Universidad de Santo Tomás, se estableció en Bucaramanga en 1580, y ha crecido mucho desde su establecimiento. Sus directores quieren que siga ofreciendo una gran variedad de programas académicos.

Universidad de Santo Tomás, Bucaramanga, Colombia

Compara con tu mundo *¿Cuál es la universidad más importante de tu estado o región? ¿Qué otras universidades antiguas de Estados Unidos conoces?*

Contesta las siguientes preguntas sobre la educación en Colombia. Utiliza respuestas completas, concordando *(sequencing)* los tiempos de los verbos correctamente.

1. ¿Por qué querían los españoles que se fundaran universidades en Colombia?
2. ¿Qué quieren los directores de la Universidad de Santo Tomás?

Más práctica Cuaderno *pp. 324–326* Cuaderno para hispanohablantes *pp. 325–328*

¿Comprendiste? Escribe las oraciones de nuevo con los verbos en el pasado.
1. Los maestros se alegran de que los estudiantes sean honestos.
2. Mis padres me han dicho que estudie relaciones públicas.
3. Será muy importante que la empresa contrate a un traductor.

Todo junto

¡AVANZA! **Goal:** ***Show what you know*** Listen to and read the conversation between a Colombian high school student and his guidance counselor as they talk about his future plans. Then describe your own plans and ideas for your future. ***Actividades 18–21***

Resumen contextos 1 y 2 Guille leyó los anuncios de trabajo en el periódico y preparó su hoja de vida para dársela a su consejero escolar.

Contexto 3 *Diálogo*

ESTRATEGIA **Escuchar**

Predict and then check Before listening to the dialogue between Guille and his counselor, list four topics you might expect Guille to talk about based on what you know about him so far.

AUDIO

Guille tiene una reunión con la señora Ramos, la consejera académica, para hablar de su futuro, sus planes y sus ideas de trabajo.

Sra. Ramos: Hola, Guille. ¿Qué tal?

Guille: Hola, señora Ramos. Bien, gracias. Aquí tiene la hoja de vida que preparé.

Sra. Ramos: Muy bien. A ver... ¿así que te gustan el diseño y las computadoras?

Guille: Sí, parece que tengo buena aptitud para todo eso.

Sra. Ramos: Sí, es obvio que tienes mucha experiencia. Entonces, ¿vas a seguir una carrera de tecnología y vas a especializarte en computadoras?

Guille: Creo que sí. No sé...

Sra. Ramos: Parece que no te apasiona la idea. ¿Por qué escogiste esta profesión?

Guille: Porque sé mucho sobre las computadoras y todo el mundo me ha dicho que me prepare para una profesión en que pueda ganar un buen sueldo.

Sra. Ramos: Eso es importante, pero hay otras consideraciones también. Si pudieras trabajar en cualquier campo, sin pensar en el dinero, ¿qué escogerías?

Guille: ¡La televisión y el cine! Si no tuviera que preocuparme por el dinero, escribiría y dirigiría películas para la televisión y el cine internacional.

Sra. Ramos: Entonces, ¿por qué no vas a una universidad que tenga una especialización en cine?

Guille: Es que si no estudio computación, ¡mis padres se morirán de los nervios! Dicen que hay mucha competencia en el campo del cine y que nunca podría ganarme la vida si no tuviera una profesión más segura.

Sra. Ramos: Bueno, Guille, la seguridad es importante, pero la pasión también importa mucho. Eres muy joven para olvidarte de tus sueños.

Guille: Tiene razón, señora Ramos. ¡Pero no sé cómo hablar de eso con mis padres!

También se dice

Guille usa la expresión **se morirán de los nervios** para decir que sus padres se pondrán muy nerviosos.

- **el Caribe** **Les va a dar un soponcio.**
- **América del Sur** **Se van a poner verdes.**

18 Comprensión del diálogo

Escuchar
Hablar
Escribir

Contesta las preguntas sobre el diálogo.

1. ¿Cuáles son las aptitudes que Guille incluyó en su hoja de vida?
2. ¿Por qué eligió la computación como profesión?
3. Si Guille no tuviera que pensar en el dinero, ¿qué profesión preferiría?
4. Si Guille no estudia computación, ¿cómo cree que reaccionarán sus padres? ¿Por qué?
5. ¿Cuál es la opinión de la señora Ramos?

19 Una sorpresa

Hablar
Escribir

Con tus compañeros(as), prepara un diálogo de la conversación que tiene Guille con sus padres para explicarles que quiere seguir una carrera en la televisión y el cine.

modelo:

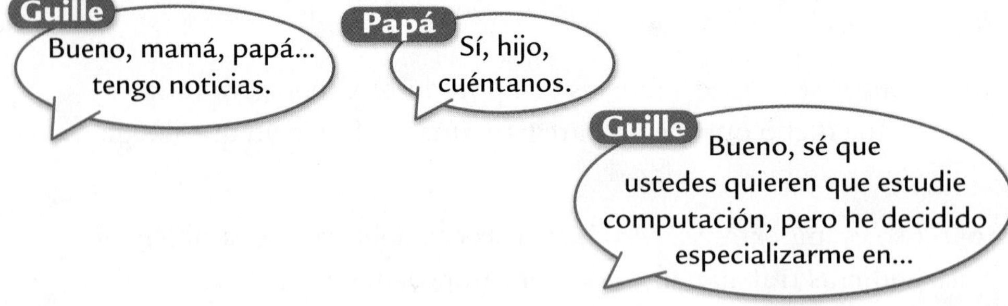

20 Integración

Leer
Escuchar
Hablar

Lee la hoja de vida y la carta de presentación *(cover letter)* de Silvia. Escucha los anuncios que pasan por la radio. Decide qué trabajo le puede interesar a Silvia.

Fuente 1 Hoja de vida

Señor gerente:
Como verá en mi hoja de vida, tengo buena experiencia en el campo de las comunicaciones. Además, soy creativa y eficiente. Me interesaría mucho trabajar en las relaciones públicas de su empresa, si fuera posible.

Si usted tien... y cree que una entrevista p... contratarm...
Atentamen...
Silvia Ro...
Silvia Ro...

Silvia Rodríguez
Calle Simón Bolívar 555
Barranquilla, Colombia
Tel. 50-50-50
srodríguez872@777mail.com

EDUCACIÓN
2002–2005 Universidad de San Carlos, especialidad en comunicación e idiomas.
1999–2002 Academia Internacional de Periodismo, título con honores.

EXPERIENCIA
2003–presente Periodista y fotógrafa para el periódico *El Noticiero de Barranquilla.*
2001–presente Diseñadora de páginas web.
1999–2002 Colaboradora con el anuario de la Academia Internacional.

IDIOMAS: Inglés e italiano

Fuente 2 Anuncios por la radio

Escucha y apunta
- ¿Cuáles son los trabajos anunciados?
- ¿Qué cualificaciones requiere cada trabajo?

modelo: Uno de los trabajos es de administración. Si el candidato hablara inglés sería mejor. Si a Silvia le interesan las relaciones públicas, entonces...

21 ¡A escribir!

Escribir

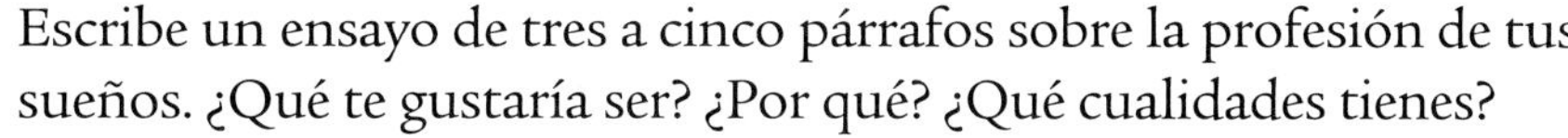

Escribe un ensayo de tres a cinco párrafos sobre la profesión de tus sueños. ¿Qué te gustaría ser? ¿Por qué? ¿Qué cualidades tienes?

Writing Criteria	Excellent	Good	Needs Work
Content	Your essay includes many details about your dream job.	Your essay includes some details about your dream job.	Your essay includes few details about your dream job.
Communication	Your essay is organized and easy to follow.	Parts of your essay are organized and easy to follow.	Your essay is disorganized and hard to follow.
Accuracy	You make few mistakes in grammar and vocabulary.	You make some mistakes in grammar and vocabulary.	You make many mistakes in grammar and vocabulary.

Más práctica Cuaderno *pp. 327–328* Cuaderno para hispanohablantes *pp. 329–330*

PARA Y PIENSA

¿Comprendiste? Di lo que las siguientes personas querían que tú hicieras en el pasado y lo que quieren que tú hagas ahora.

1. Ayer mis padres querían que yo... Ahora quieren que yo...
2. La semana pasada mi mejor amigo(a) me pidió que... Ahora me pide que...

Get Help Online
ClassZone.com

Lectura literaria

¡AVANZA! **Goal:** Read this story about an encounter between a man and a living skeleton. Then consider how literature can help you to stretch your imagination beyond normal, daily-life occurrences.

Para leer 

ESTRATEGIA Leer

Use shapes to help you understand Draw a square or a cube, and in it write any normal, unsurprising things you read in the story. Draw a starburst, and in it write any unusual, surprising things from the story.

Vocabulario para leer

el esqueleto	*skeleton*
la paloma	*pájaro que es símbolo de la paz*
risueño(a)	*que se ríe*
rojizo(a)	*de color rojo*
castañear	*hacer ruido con los dientes por el frío*
los comensales	*personas que están en la mesa para comer*
boquiabierto(a)	*con la boca abierta*
adivinar	*anticipar un evento*
asombrarse	*sorprenderse*
susurrar	*hablar en voz muy baja*
incorporarse	*levantarse*

Nota cultural

Sobre el autor **Evelio Rosero Diago (1958–)**

Evelio Rosero Diago nació en Bogotá e hizo sus estudios universitarios allí. Trabaja como periodista y autor y ha publicado novelas, una novela corta, cuentos y literatura juvenil. En 1992 ganó el Premio Nacional de Literatura.

Nota cultural En la literatura latinoamericana existe una gran tradición de narrar historias en que se mezclan elementos de la realidad cotidiana con elementos mágicos. En este cuento un hombre se encuentra con un esqueleto vivo, al que invita a tomar chocolate. El autor utiliza las situaciones que les pasan al hombre y al esqueleto como un símbolo de la importancia de la tolerancia en la sociedad.

El Esqueleto de Visita

Un día conocí un esqueleto, en el parque. Estaba sentado en un banco de piedra, rodeado[1] de palomas blancas, y sonreía, pensativo. Me pareció muy raro encontrar un esqueleto en pleno[2] parque, dando de comer a las palomas, y tan risueño y tranquilo, como si se acordara de una broma[3], solitario, en mitad de la tarde [...] Me dijo que no tenía nombre. «Ningún esqueleto lo tiene», dijo, y cuando el sol desapareció detrás de las nubes[4] rojizas, se lamentó del frío. Sus dientes castañeaban. Se puso de pie y me propuso[5] que fuéramos a tomar una tacita[6] de chocolate, en cualquier[7] lugar.

....

Al fin encontramos un restaurante que anunciaba: *Chocolate caliente a toda hora.* Al entrar muchos comensales quedaron boquiabiertos. Algunas señoras gritaron; una de las meseras[8] dejó caer una bandeja repleta de tazas[9].

....

[1] surrounded [2] **en...** in the middle of
[3] **como...** as if he were remembering a joke [4] clouds [5] proposed
[6] mug [7] any [8] waitresses [9] **una...** a tray with many mugs

Reflexiona

¿Cuáles son los elementos realistas y cuáles los fantásticos? ¿Qué efecto produce la combinación?

«¿Qué pasa?» pregunté, abochornado[10], aunque ya adivinaba a qué se debía aquel alboroto[11]. «¿Quién es ése?», me respondieron a coro, señalando[12] a mi amigo.

«Perdón —dijo él—. Yo puedo presentarme solo. Soy un esqueleto. Tengan todos muy buenas tardes».

«Oh —se asombró una señora, que llevaba un perrito faldero[13], de pelo amarillo, adornado con un collar de diamantes—. No puede ser. Un esqueleto que habla».

«Pues sí —dijo mi amigo, encogiendo los omóplatos[14]. En realidad todos los esqueletos hablamos».

A pensar
¿Cómo reaccionan las personas en el restaurante a la llegada de un esqueleto? ¿Has visto alguna reacción similar en un lugar público? ¿Por qué?

....

Levantó el dedo índice y pidió a la rubia mesera dos tacitas de chocolate. «Por favor, sea amable». Y sin embargo la mesera nos susurró que tenía órdenes expresas de no atendernos, y que incluso el dueño del restaurante exigía que nos fuéramos inmediatamente.

«Pero si aquí hay chocolate a toda hora», dije.

«Sí —me respondió ella—. Pero no hay chocolate a toda hora para ustedes».

A pensar
¿En qué otras circunstancias crees que ocurre o ha ocurrido este tipo de discriminación?

«Lo suponía —terció[15] mi amigo el esqueleto—. Siempre ocurre lo mismo: desde hace mil años no he logrado que me ofrezcan una sola tacita de chocolate». Y nos incorporamos, para marcharnos[16].

Bueno, lo cierto es que yo me preguntaba cómo haría el esqueleto para beber su tacita de chocolate [...] Pero preferí guardar

---

[10] embarrassed [11] **a...** what the uproar was about [12] pointing
[13] **perrito...** lap dog [14] **encogiendo...** shrugging his shoulder blades
[15] intervened [16] leave

ese misterio: me parecía indiscreto, fuera de tono, preguntar a mi amigo sobre eso. Le dije, por el contrario: «¿Por qué no vamos a mi casa? Lo invito a tomar chocolate».

«Gracias —dijo, con una breve venia [17]—. Una persona como usted no se encuentra fácilmente, ni en trescientos años».

Y así nos pusimos en camino hasta mi casa, que no quedaba lejos.

....

Llegamos a casa cuando anochecía.

Mi mujer abrió la puerta y pegó un alarido [18].

— Tranquila —dije—, es solamente nuestro amigo el esqueleto de visita.

....

Propuse mientras tanto a nuestro amigo que jugáramos un partido de ajedrez. «Oh, sí —dijo—, no hace mucho jugué con Napoleón y lo vencí [19]». Y ya disponíamos [20] las fichas sobre el tablero [21], contentos y sin prisa, en el calor de los cojines [22] de la sala, y con la promesa alentadora [23] de una tacita de chocolate, cuando vi que mi mujer me hacía una angustiosa seña [24] desde la cocina.

....

Ella me explicó enfurruñada [25] que no había chocolate en la alacena [26] [...] Yo ya iba a responder cuando, detrás nuestro, sentimos la fría pero amigable presencia del esqueleto. «No se preocupen por mí —dijo, preocupadísimo [...] Ya es costumbre para mí. Ésta es una época difícil para el mundo. Pero no se preocupen, por favor. Además, debo irme. Acabo de recordar que hoy tengo la oportunidad de viajar a la Argentina, y debo acudir [27]. Ustedes perdonen. Fueron muy formales. Muy gentiles.

---

[17] nod [18] **pegó...** let out a wail [19] I defeated [20] we were arranging [21] board
[22] cushions [23] encouraging [24] gesture [25] sulkingly [26] pantry [27] go

¿Comprendiste?

1. ¿Cómo se conocieron el narrador y el esqueleto?
2. ¿Por qué el esqueleto invitó al narrador a tomar un chocolate?
3. ¿Qué ocurrió en el restaurante?
4. ¿Qué pasó en casa del narrador?
5. ¿Cómo reaccionó el esqueleto al final?

¿Y tú?

1. ¿Consideras el cuento cómico o triste? Explica tu opinión.
2. ¿Has tenido algún encuentro extraño? Explica qué pasó.

Escritura

Reflexiones sobre el año pasado

Vas a escribir un análisis de las actividades que hiciste el año pasado. También vas a hacerte algunas preguntas sobre los actividades para el proximo año.

1 Prepárate para escribir

ESTRATEGIA Haz círculos analíticos Piensa en las actividades que hiciste el año pasado (académicas, después de las clases, con amigos, con la familia, deportes, viajes). Luego dibuja tres círculos grandes. En el primer círculo escribe **Lo que hice el año pasado.** En el segundo escribe **Lo que hice que no volvería a hacer.** En el tercero escribe **Lo que todavía no he hecho que me gustaría hacer.** Agrega la información necesaria en cada círculo.

2 Escribe

ESTRATEGIA Usa los círculos analíticos para escribir un primer borrador

Paso 1 Escribe un párrafo breve con una introducción: dónde vivías el año pasado y a qué escuela ibas.

Paso 2 Usa las actividades del primer círculo para escribir el segundo párrafo.
El año pasado estuve en el club de español de la escuela.

Paso 3 Usa las actividades del segundo círculo para escribir el tercer párrafo.
El año pasado participé en el coro. No volvería a hacerlo porque fue muy difícil.

Paso 4 Usa las actividades del tercer círculo para escribir el cuarto párrafo con lo que te gustaría hacer. Usa cláusulas con **si.**
El año pasado no pude jugar al fútbol. Si tengo más tiempo el próximo año, jugaré.

Paso 5 Escribe una conclusión para resumir lo que harás el año que viene.

3 Revisa tu composición

Intercambia tu borrador con un(a) compañero(a).

Subraya todos los verbos y haz lo siguiente:

- Decide si el tiempo y la conjugación son correctos.
- Indica los verbos que tengan errores con un círculo.
- Escribe las correcciones.

El año pasado no puedo (pude) jugar al fútbol. Si tengo más tiempo el próximo año, jugaba (jugaré).

Lección 2

En resumen

Vocabulario y gramática

Vocabulario

Talk About Career Possibilities

el (la) abogado(a)	*lawyer*	el (la) médico(a)	*doctor*	la especialidad	*major, specialization*
el (la) agente de bolsa	*stockbroker*	la mujer de negocios	*businesswoman*	especializarse en	*to major in*
el (la) arquitecto(a)	*architect*	el (la) peluquero(a)	*hairdresser*	la facultad	*school department*
el (la) contador(a)	*accountant*	el (la) profesor(a)	*teacher*	el idioma	*language*
el (la) dentista	*dentist*	el (la) traductor(a)	*translator*	la ingeniería	*engineering*
el (la) enfermero(a)	*nurse*	la administración de empresas	*business administration*	las relaciones públicas	*public relations*
el (la) gerente	*manager*	la contabilidad	*accounting*	seguir una carrera	*to pursue a career*
el hombre de negocios	*businessman*	el curso	*course*	el título	*degree*
el (la) ingeniero(a)	*engineer*	el derecho	*law*	la universidad	*university*
el (la) juez(a)	*judge*	la escuela técnica	*technical school*		

Starting a business

contratar	*to hire*
el (la) dueño(a)	*owner*
la empresa	*company*
establecer	*to establish*
la estrategia	*strategy*
la iniciativa	*initiative*
el plan financiero	*financial plan*

Skills, interests, and values

animado(a)	*animated, upbeat*	flexible	*flexible*
apasionado(a)	*passionate*	honesto(a)	*honest, sincere*
cualificado(a)	*qualified*	honrado(a)	*honest, honorable*
destacado(a)	*outstanding*	motivado(a)	*motivated*
educado(a)	*educated; polite*	puntual	*punctual*
eficiente	*efficient*	versátil	*versatile*
fiable	*dependable*		

Gramática

Si Clauses

To predict the result of a likely event, use the simple present in the **si** clause and the **future tense** in the main clause to express the outcome.

> **Si** dejamos de comer comida chatarra, **perderemos** peso.
> ***If we stop** eating junk food, **we will lose** weight.*

To express how things would be if circumstances were different, use the **imperfect subjunctive** in the **si** clause and the **conditional** in the main clause.

> **Si** Ana **cantara** en el coro, no **tendría** tiempo para redactar el anuario.
> ***If** Ana **were to sing** in the chorus, **she would** not **have** time to edit the yearbook.*

Sequence of Tenses

Use the present subjunctive or present perfect subjunctive after the following **indicative tenses.**

simple present	Es bueno que hayas decidido.
present progressive	Está prohibiendo que salgas.
future	Será mejor que me llames.
present perfect	He sugerido que trabajes más.

Use the **imperfect subjunctive** or the **past perfect subjunctive** after the following **indicative tenses.**

preterite	Prohibió que saliera.
imperfect	Era bueno que **hubiera decidido.**
***past progressive**	**Estaba prohibiendo** que **salieras.**
conditional	**Preferiría** que **escribieras** más.
past perfect	**Había sugerido** que **salieras.**

*grammar point of the next lesson.

Lección 2

Repaso de la lección

¡LLEGADA!

@HomeTutor ClassZone.com

Now you can
- talk about career possibilities
- hypothesize
- narrate in the past

Using
- **si** clauses
- sequence of tenses

To review
- vocabulary pp. 418–419

1 Listen and understand

AUDIO

Hoy es el primer día de la «Semana de las Carreras» en el colegio. Cada día, personas con empleos diferentes vienen a la escuela para hablar de sus profesiones. Hoy habla la señora Villanueva, que trabaja como traductora. Escucha sus comentarios y contesta las siguientes preguntas.

1. ¿Qué estudió la señora Villanueva en el colegio?
2. ¿Qué le aconsejaron sus amigos y parientes sobre sus estudios?
3. ¿Qué dudaban sus amigos y parientes?
4. ¿Qué estudió ella en la universidad?
5. ¿Qué pensaba hacer después de graduarse?
6. ¿Qué le dijo el hombre que ella conoció?
7. ¿Qué trabajo hace la señora Villanueva ahora?
8. ¿Cuál es la sugerencia que la señora Villanueva les ofrece a los estudiantes?

To review
- **si** clauses p. 423

2 Talk about career possibilities

Di qué profesión tendrá cada persona que estudie las siguientes carreras. Sigue el modelo.

modelo: ingeniería
Si estudias ingeniería, serás ingeniero.

1. contabilidad
2. peluquería
3. administración de empresas
4. ingeniería
5. medicina
6. arquitectura
7. idiomas
8. abogacía

To review
- **si** clauses p. 423

3 Hypothesize

Para cada problema, hay un especialista que puede resolverlo. Sigue el modelo.

modelo: Rafaela / cortarse el pelo muy mal
Si Rafaela se cortara el pelo muy mal, buscaría un peluquero.

1. Laura / recibir un documento en ruso
2. tú / romperse un diente
3. Lalo y Pilar / querer aprender cálculo
4. tú / construir una casa nueva
5. Esteban / tener una fiebre muy alta
6. ustedes / no saber cómo pagar los impuestos

To review
- sequence of tenses p. 428

4 Narrate in the past

El señor Cardona habla con los estudiantes de un colegio sobre sus experiencias académicas y profesionales. Completa sus comentarios con las formas correctas de los verbos indicados.

No era un estudiante bueno. Todos me dijeron que __**1.**__ (estudiar) más y que __**2.**__ (jugar) menos. Pero no me interesaban mis estudios. Después del colegio, fui a una escuela técnica, porque era importante que __**3.**__ (tener) una profesión. Me hice mecánico. Tuve mucha suerte y abrí mi propio negocio. Yo no estaba seguro de que __**4.**__ (poder) encontrar trabajo, pero ¡si había trabajo! Contraté a un asistente, pero teníamos demasiado trabajo; era imposible que nosotros __**5.**__ (trabajar) bastante para completar los proyectos. Por fin mi asistente y yo vimos que era necesario que yo __**6.**__ (contratar) a más gente y que __**7.**__ (establecer) una empresa más grande. Fui a la universidad y estudié administración de empresas. Después hice un plan financiero y esperaba que todo me __**8.**__ (salir) bien.

To review
- **Comparación cultural** pp. 425–430

5 Professions and universities

Comparación cultural

1. ¿Quién es Fernando Botero?
2. ¿Cuáles son algunos de los tipos de personas que retrata?
3. ¿Cuál es la universidad más antigua de Colombia?
4. ¿Por qué hay universidades antiguas en Colombia?

Más práctica Cuaderno *pp. 329–340* Cuaderno para hispanohablantes *pp. 331–340*

Get Help Online
ClassZone.com

Comparación cultural

AUDIO

Educación especializada

Lectura y escritura

WebQuest
ClassZone.com

1. **Leer** Estela es de Colombia y Álvaro es de Venezuela. Los dos van a escuelas muy interesantes. Lee y compara las descripciones de sus escuelas.

2. **Escribir** Después de leer las descripciones que dan Estela y Álvaro, escribe una composición sobre una escuela interesante de tu región.

ESTRATEGIA Escribir

Color-code the information Use different colors for each part of the essay: green for the introduction, blue for interesting details, and red for the conclusion.

Introducción	Detalles interesantes	Conclusión

Paso 1 Haz una lista de escuelas de tu región que se enfoquen en programas especiales. Escoge una. Escribe notas para la introducción usando color verde.

Paso 2 En color azul, escribe notas sobre detalles interesantes (programas, currículum, oportunidades). Luego, en color rojo, escribe notas para una conclusión con tus opiniones.

Paso 3 Usa tus notas de colores como guía para escribir el ensayo.

Compara con tu mundo

Compara tu escuela o la escuela que investigaste con las escuelas especiales a las que van Estela y Álvaro. ¿Qué tienen en común? ¿Cuál es la especialidad de cada una? ¿Cuál de las tres te parece más interesante y por qué?

Cuaderno *pp. 341–343* Cuaderno para hispanohablantes *pp. 341–343*

Álvaro

Hola. Me llamo Álvaro Cedeño y soy de Barquisimeto, Venezuela. Soy alumno del Colegio Aplicación, que ofrece especializaciones en ciencias y humanidades. Es muy moderno: tiene cuatro laboratorios de ciencias y dos de computación.

El colegio tiene una orientación profesional. Los dos años finales de la escuela se llaman la etapa diversificada. En esta etapa la mayoría de los estudiantes ya han decidido qué carrera quieren seguir. Yo estoy tomando muchos cursos de ciencias, porque quiero ser geólogo. En Venezuela la industria del petróleo es muy importante, por eso la geología es una especialización práctica e interesante.

También tenemos muchas oportunidades para participar en clubes deportivos como béisbol, fútbol y voleibol. Si no encuentro trabajo como geólogo, ¡tal vez pueda ser futbolista profesional!

Estela

Hola, me llamo Estela Robles y vivo en Bogotá, Colombia. Estudio en el Colegio José Max León, que está en la ciudad de Cota, a 14 kilómetros de Bogotá. Este colegio ofrece una variedad de cursos y especialidades. Pone mucho énfasis en el respeto por los derechos humanos y en la creación de una conciencia de solidaridad internacional.

A mí me gustan los proyectos que hacemos en la granja del colegio. Allí participamos en actividades relacionadas con la agricultura, el reciclaje y la conservación de los recursos naturales. Como me gusta mucho cuidar los animales domésticos de la granja, pienso que tal vez voy a seguir una carrera como veterinaria después de graduarme.

También estudio el inglés, que es una parte muy importante de nuestro currículum. Los cursos de inglés son intensivos para que aprendamos el idioma rápido. Ojalá que yo pueda aprenderlo bien, ¡es una lengua muy difícil!

EL DESAFÍO

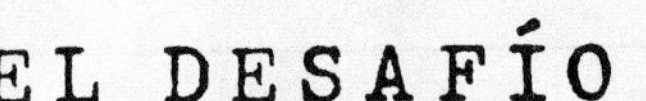

En el desafío de hoy, cada equipo tiene que conseguir un trabajo a tiempo parcial o pensar en una estrategia para conseguir dinero en un tiempo limitado. El equipo que consiga más dinero, gana el desafío.

Antes del video

1. Describe esta foto. ¿Qué crees que está haciendo Carmen?

2. ¿Qué ves en esta foto? ¿Qué crees que está haciendo Marco?

3. ¿Qué tipo de trabajo hacen Luis y María? ¿Qué equipo crees que pueda ganar este desafío?

Llegando a la playa

Mira el video: Toma apuntes

- ¿Dónde cree Luis que esté el profesor Dávila?
- ¿Quién va a llenar una solicitud de empleo?
- Escribe qué equipo decide trabajar en un restaurante.
- ¿Qué tipo de trabajo hace Marco? ¿Lo hace bien? ¿Cómo lo sabes?
- Describe lo que Carmen y Luis quieren vender.
- Describe al turista que observa a los jóvenes.

Después del video

1. Lee tus predicciones en la sección de «Antes del video.» ¿Sabías cuál era el trabajo de cada equipo?
2. En este desafío, Luis y Marco no se llevan muy bien. Evalúa esta situación.
3. ¿Qué piensas de la reacción de María hacia Marco? ¿Por qué dice que es la niñera del grupo?
4. ¿Quién era el turista secreto? ¿Por qué crees que hizo eso?

@HomeTutor VideoPlus
ClassZone.com

UNIDADES 1-7

Repaso inclusivo

Options for Review

1 Escucha, comprende y contesta

Escuchar
Hablar
Escribir

Tía Esmeralda y Carmen escriben columnas de consejos. Una vez por semana hacen un programa en la radio en que comparten algunas de las cartas que han recibido, dan consejos y comparan sus opiniones. Escucha el programa y contesta las preguntas.

1. ¿Dónde trabaja la chica y cuáles son los beneficios de trabajar allí?
2. ¿Qué otra oferta de trabajo ha recibido?
3. ¿Por qué no sabe qué hacer?
4. ¿Qué le recomendó Tía Esmeralda?
5. ¿Qué pensó Carmen?

2 Describe tus experiencias

Escribir
Hablar

Fuiste a acampar el fin de semana pasado a El Sol de México, un lugar para acampar en la playa. Escribe un artículo para el periódico de tu escuela de al menos dos párrafos, con tus experiencias. Utiliza el pasado con verbos regulares e irregulares y el imperfecto.

3 Recomienda

Hablar

Tu compañero(a) y tú tienen que preparar una presentación oral para organizar una teletón en la escuela. La presentación debe incluir una explicación de qué es una teletón y por lo menos ocho recomendaciones para organizar a los voluntarios y las actividades. Utiliza expresiones de mandato afirmativas y negativas y expresiones impersonales con el infinitivo.

4 Haz un diálogo

Hablar
Escribir

Con tus compañeros(as), hagan y actúen un diálogo de cómo será su ciudad en el año 2300. Hablen del medio ambiente, de las tecnologías y de los nuevos inventos que habrá. Utilicen el futuro, las preposiciones **por** y **para** y la forma **ir a + infinitivo.**

5 Crea una empresa

Hablar
Escribir

Un compañero(a) y tú han decidido abrir un negocio cerca de su colegio, después de la graduación. Decidan qué tipo de negocio tendría a estudiantes como clientes. Organicen su plan financiero, sus estrategias y su campaña de relaciones públicas. Presenten sus planes y sus deseos a la clase. Utilicen el subjuntivo con verbos de deseo y el superlativo.

6 Organiza una campaña

Hablar
Escribir

Los clubes siempre buscan más participantes. Con tus compañeros(as), organiza una campaña para que más estudiantes tomen parte en su club. Describan el club, las actividades que organiza, las ventajas que tiene tomar parte en él y sus metas. Usen el subjuntivo después de conjunciones adverbiales y el condicional.

7 Informa

Escribir

Tienes un programa en la televisión sobre las vacaciones. Escribe un guión *(script)* sobre las actividades que hiciste en tus últimas vacaciones. Incluye en el guión una entrevista telefónica sobre las vacaciones de otra persona. Escribe las preguntas y respuestas de la entrevista. Utiliza el presente perfecto, el pasado perfecto y los participios pasados como adjetivos.

UNIDAD 8

El Cono Sur

Hablemos de literatura

Antofagasta
Paraguay
Asunción
Ciudad del Este
Océano Pacífico
Argentina
Santiago
Salto
Uruguay
Rosario
Chile
Buenos Aires
Montevideo
Mar del Plata

Lección 1
Tema: ***Cuentos y poesía***

Lección 2
Tema: ***El drama***

«¿Qué tal?
Somos Mario y Laura. Somos de Argentina.»

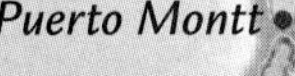

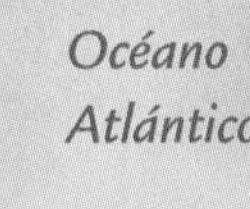

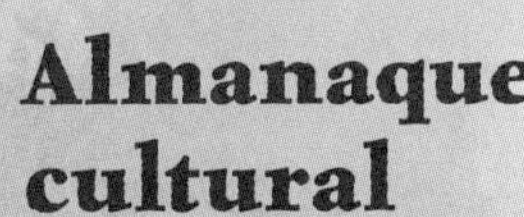

Población: Argentina: 39.537.943, Uruguay: 3.415.920, Paraguay: 6.347.884, Chile: 15.823.957

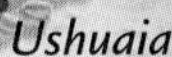

Moneda: peso (Argentina, Uruguay, Chile), guaraní (Paraguay)

Idiomas indígenas: quechua y guaraní

Geografía: desiertos, cordillera, bosque, glaciares y llanuras

Comidas: asado, empanadas, parrillada, locro

Empanadas

Gente famosa: Berta Rojas (guitarrista, Paraguay); Mario Benedetti (escritor, Uruguay); Isabel Allende (escritora, Chile); Raúl Soldi (pintor, Argentina)

Karin Ruby, deportista francesa y campeona de snowboard, en Valle Nevado, cerca de Santiago de Chile

◀ **Deporte en la nieve** Chile recibe turistas de todo el mundo. Allí termina la cordillera de los Andes, que separa Chile de Argentina. Las pistas de esquí son las mejores de Sudamérica. Algunas llegan a los 3000 metros de altura. *¿Dónde hay pistas de esquí en Estados Unidos?*

La Plaza de Mayo Es la plaza principal de Buenos Aires, la capital de Argentina. Allí hay edificios importantes, como la Casa Rosada, que es la casa de gobierno. También está el Banco Nación, la Catedral y el Cabildo, donde se reunían los gobernantes de la época colonial. ▶

Plaza de Mayo, Buenos Aires. Al fondo, la Casa Rosada

Gigantes en tres países Las Cataratas del Iguazú están exactamente entre Argentina, Paraguay y Brasil. Son más de 200 saltos de agua que se originan en el río Iguazú, en medio de un hermoso bosque tropical. *¿Qué espectáculos naturales hay en tu estado?* ▼

Cataratas del Iguazú

UNIDAD 8

El Cono Sur

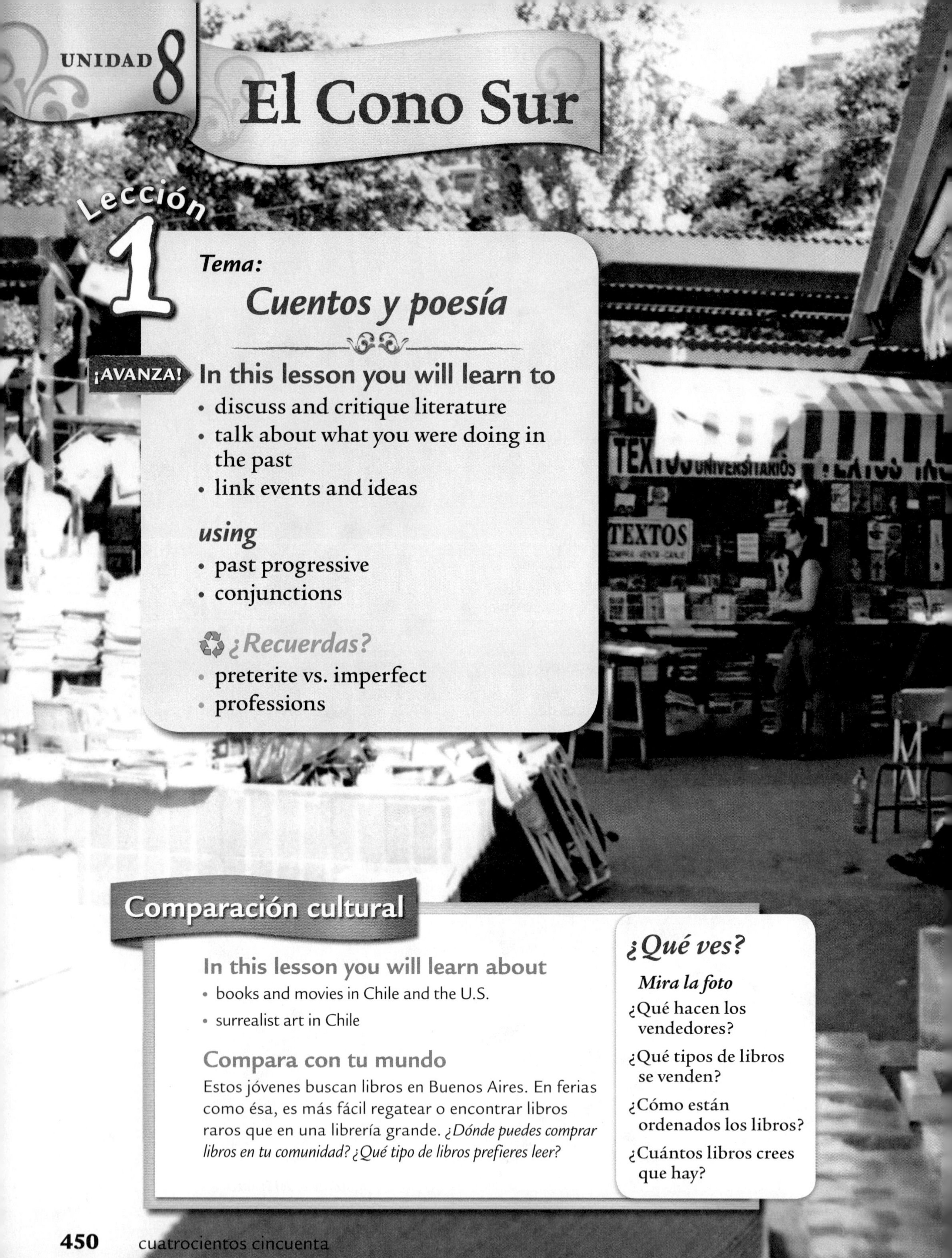

Lección 1

Tema:

Cuentos y poesía

¡AVANZA! **In this lesson you will learn to**

- discuss and critique literature
- talk about what you were doing in the past
- link events and ideas

using

- past progressive
- conjunctions

¿Recuerdas?

- preterite vs. imperfect
- professions

Comparación cultural

In this lesson you will learn about

- books and movies in Chile and the U.S.
- surrealist art in Chile

Compara con tu mundo

Estos jóvenes buscan libros en Buenos Aires. En ferias como ésa, es más fácil regatear o encontrar libros raros que en una librería grande. *¿Dónde puedes comprar libros en tu comunidad? ¿Qué tipo de libros prefieres leer?*

¿Qué ves?

Mira la foto

¿Qué hacen los vendedores?

¿Qué tipos de libros se venden?

¿Cómo están ordenados los libros?

¿Cuántos libros crees que hay?

Online SPANISH CLASSZONE.COM

Featuring...

Cultura INTERACTIVA

Animated Grammar

@HomeTutor

And more...

- Get Help Online
- Interactive Flashcards
- Review Games
- WebQuest
- Conjuguemos.com

Jóvenes en una feria de libros
Buenos Aires, Argentina

Presentación de VOCABULARIO

¡AVANZA! **Goal:** Learn new words that you can use to discuss and critique literature. Then talk about different types of literature. ***Actividades 1–3***

AUDIO

A Eduardo y Laura han organizado un club de lectura en la biblioteca de la escuela. Allí se reúnen a leer y a analizar los distintos **géneros literarios** y **los estilos** de **los autores.**

B ¡Este libro de **poesía** es excelente! Me gustan **la rima** y **el ritmo** de **los versos.**

C **Tan pronto como** leí el primer **capítulo** de esta **novela,** supe que me iba a gustar. Es **una sátira** interesante, **un símil** que **relaciona** la vida de unos animales en un bosque. **En cuanto** termine de leerla, empezaré **unos cuentos románticos** del mismo autor.

D Esta **autobiografía** de José Donoso **narra los sucesos** de su vida. Es interesantísima; se pueden **inferir** detalles de **la realidad** de su tiempo y hacer **un análisis** del carácter del autor.

E **Los temas** de **los ensayos** de Borges son espectaculares por sus diferentes **puntos de vista. El contexto** y **los antecedentes** que utiliza son casi **absurdos,** pero siempre **implican** o **simbolizan** algún problema humano.

F En el club de lectura también se leen **reseñas** de libros interesantes.

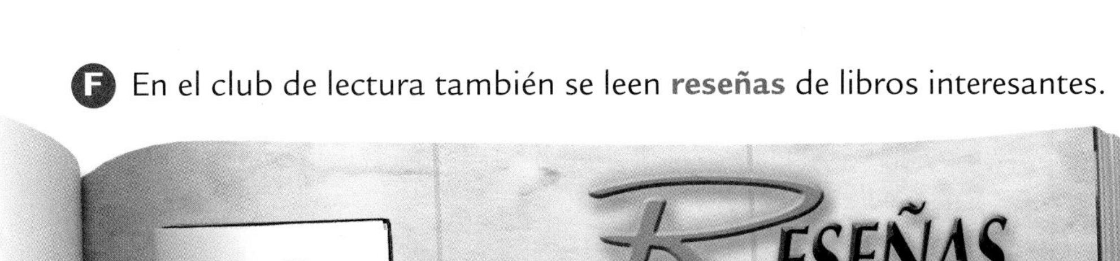

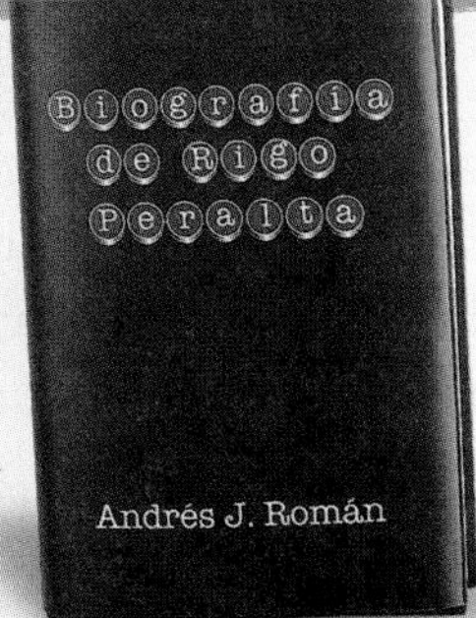

En «La Casa Mar», de Julio Guitea, es impactante **el clímax** que logra el autor en el capítulo veinticinco. Aquí, **la prosa** de Guitea es perfecta cuando narra cómo **los protagonistas** vuelan de una ventana a otra. ¡La novela es excelente y tiene **un desenlace** que puede **significar** muchas cosas!

Esta **biografía** sobre Rigo Peralta debería **titularse** como algún drama de Shakespeare, pues la vida del poeta chileno estuvo llena de momentos muy bellos y muy tristes.

La **obra** de Arminda Herrera es increíble. Y sus poemas están construidos con **estrofas** que parecen **metáforas** musicales.

183

Más vocabulario

el acto *act*
aunque *although*
el cuento policíaco *crime story*
el libro de historietas *comic book*

Expansión de vocabulario p. R16
Ya sabes p. R16

¡A responder! Escuchar

Vas a oír siete frases que describen una obra literaria. Si la frase es más típica para una novela, levanta la mano derecha; si la frase es más típica para una poesía, levanta la mano izquierda.

@HomeTutor
Interactive Flashcards
ClassZone.com

Práctica de VOCABULARIO

1 El club de lectores

Hablar
Escribir

Completa los siguientes comentarios de dos poemas del poeta chileno Pablo Neruda, ganador del premio Nóbel de literatura.

A mí me encantó el poema que __1.__ (se titula / significa) «Oda a los calcetines». ¿Recuerdan el __2.__ (símil / desenlace) en que el poeta compara sus pies con dos pescados de lana *(two fish made of wool)*? Está en la segunda __3.__ (realidad / estrofa). También me gustan mucho las __4.__ (prosas / metáforas) de la tercera estrofa: «bomberos indignos de aquel fuego bordado». Es interesante que Neruda no usa __5.__ (rima / verso) en la poesía, pero si lees la obra en voz alta *(aloud)*, escucharás el magnífico __6.__ (desenlace / ritmo) que tiene.

La «Oda a Federico García Lorca» tiene otro __7.__ (estilo / acto). El __8.__ (capítulo / contexto) es la amistad entre Neruda y Lorca. Por eso podemos __9.__ (implicar / inferir) que Neruda y Lorca eran amigos.

2 Los géneros

Hablar
Escribir

Identifica el género literario según la descripción y escribe oraciones completas para definirlo.

1. un género rico en imágenes, muchas veces escrito en verso
2. una obra de ficción larga, escrita en prosa
3. una obra narrativa corta
4. una obra que narra los sucesos de la vida de alguien
5. un género ilustrado, generalmente escrito para niños

la biografía
la novela
el cuento
la poesía
el libro de historietas

Expansión
Explica qué género prefieres y por qué. Nombra algunos de tus autores preferidos de ese género.

3 Una narración

Escribir

Completa la tabla con información sobre un libro que hayas leído.

Título	Autor(a)	Género	Protagonista(s)	Análisis

Más práctica Cuaderno *pp. 344–346* Cuaderno para hispanohablantes *pp. 344–347*

¿Comprendiste? Escribe el nombre de tu... favorito(a):
1. autor(a) 2. novela 3. poesía 4. género literario

Get Help Online
ClassZone.com

VOCABULARIO en contexto

¡AVANZA! **Goal:** As you read the following short story, identify as many aspects of the literary style that Eduardo uses as you can, and decide whether or not you agree with Laura's comments. Then talk about different types of literature using the new vocabulary. ***Actividades 4–5***

Contexto 1 *Micro cuento*

ESTRATEGIA Leer

List expressions for reacting to literature List expressions that would be useful for reacting to literature. To do this, draw two faces. Next to the smiling one, list positive statements. Next to the frowning one, list negative statements. In both cases, list literary vocabulary.

¡Me encanta el ritmo! ☺
No me gusta ____ . ☹

Eduardo Saravia es un estudiante argentino que participa en un club de escritores jóvenes. Él acaba de escribir un micro cuento y Laura Labarca, una de sus colegas, escribió unos comentarios para ayudarlo con la revisión.

El nuevo espejo

Alejandro era un chico triste. Vivía en una casa triste, en un barrio triste, en una ciudad triste. Una tarde lluviosa y gris, Alejandro salió de la escuela. Mientras sacaba su paraguas, miraba las cosas en el escaparate de una tienda de antigüedades. De repente le llamó la atención un espejo antiguo, en muy mala condición, con unos adornos de árboles y pájaros. Era muy feo, pero a Alejandro le gustó.

«¿Te gusta?» le dijo un hombre viejo que salía de la tienda. «Es muy barato. Te lo venderé por quince pesos.»

Alejandro no pudo resistir y se llevó el espejo a la casa triste y lo colgó en una pared.

Al día siguiente, en cuanto se levantó, fue y se detuvo frente al espejo y se quedó asombrado. Se vio a sí mismo, pero la escena reflejada en el espejo era de un jardín maravilloso bajo un sol brillante.

Un día se acercó y tocó el espejo con la mano, acariciando una de las flores del jardín. «Qué suave es», pensó Alejandro, cerrando los ojos. Cuando los abrió, vio que ya no estaba en su casa triste. Se encontraba en el jardín del espejo, tocando una flor fantástica. Vio un espejo colgado en un muro del jardín. Cuando Alejandro miró su reflejo, vio su casa triste, en su barrio triste, en su ciudad triste, pero él ya no estaba.

¿PUEDES DAR MÁS DETALLES SOBRE EL CONTEXTO Y LOS ANTECEDENTES?

ME GUSTA LA MEZCLA DE LA REALIDAD Y LO ABSURDO.

¡ME ENCANTA EL CLÍMAX! PERO NO SÉ SI ENTIENDO LA METÁFORA. ¿QUÉ SIMBOLIZA EL ESPEJO?

4 Comprensión del micro cuento

Hablar
Escribir

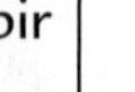

Contesta las siguientes preguntas sobre la lectura.

1. ¿Quién es el protagonista del cuento?
2. ¿La repetición de qué palabra crea un ritmo poético en el primer párrafo?
3. ¿Qué sucesos ocurren en el cuento?
4. ¿Cuál es el clímax del cuento?

5 Mezcla literaria

Hablar
Escribir

Según el cuento «El nuevo espejo», empareja los elementos de cada columna.

1. «él ya no estaba»	**a.** antecedente
2. «un hombre viejo salía de la tienda»	**b.** autor
3. Alejandro	**c.** género
4. Eduardo Saravia	**d.** desenlace
5. cuento	**e.** protagonista
6. la tristeza	**f.** tema

Expansión
Escribe una expansión del cuento donde describes lo que ocurre con el chico en el jardín. Indica qué elementos literarios tiene tu micro cuento.

Comparación cultural

La literatura y el cine

¿Cómo se relacionan las diferentes manifestaciones del arte? Desde que se inventó el cine, libros de varios géneros han servido como fuentes de inspiración para las películas. Por ejemplo, una película americana que se basó en una novela es *De amor y de sombra,* de la autora chilena Isabel Allende. La película es un homenaje *(tribute)* a la libertad y narra una historia de amor durante una época de sucesos políticos dramáticos en **Chile.**

Compara con tu mundo *¿Qué libros conoces que se han convertido en películas? ¿De qué género son los libros? ¿Quiénes son los autores de los libros?*

Escena de la película De amor y de sombra, *(1995)*

PARA Y PIENSA

¿Comprendiste? Piensa en un cuento que hayas leído y contesta las siguientes preguntas.

1. ¿Quién es el (la) protagonista?
2. ¿Cuál es el punto de vista del cuento? (¿Quién lo narra?)
3. ¿Cuál es el tema del cuento?

Get Help Online
ClassZone.com

Presentación de GRAMÁTICA

¡AVANZA! **Goal:** Learn about the past progressive tenses. Then discuss events in the past focusing on the actions that were in progress at a certain time. ***Actividades 6–9***

¿Recuerdas? Preterite vs. imperfect p. 68

English Grammar Connection: In both English and Spanish, you can use the **past progressive** to emphasize that a past action was in progress rather than completed.

Last night, when you arrived, **I was reading.**	Anoche, cuando llegaste, **estaba leyendo.**

Past Progressive

You already know how to form the present progressive to emphasize that a present action is in progress.To say that an action *was* in progress, use the **past progressive.**

Here's how:

The most common form of the **past progressive** is the **imperfect** of **estar** plus the **present participle** of the main verb. In this form, it often expresses an action that was interrupted.

¿Qué **estabas haciendo** cuando te llamé ayer?
*What **were you doing** when I called yesterday?*

Estaba escribiendo un cuento y **escuchando** música.
***I was writing** a short story and **listening** to music.*

To emphasize that an action continued for a period of time and then came to an end, use the **preterite** of **estar** plus the **present participle** of the main verb.

Estuvimos hablando toda la tarde.
***We were talking** all afternoon.*

Use a **preterite** form of the verbs **continuar, seguir,** or **quedarse** with the **present participle** to emphasize the continuation or start of an ongoing action.

Cuando mi hermana se acostó, **me quedé escribiendo** mi autobiografía.
*When my sister went to bed, **I kept on (went back to) writing** my autobiography.*

Más práctica

Cuaderno *pp. 347–349*
Cuaderno para hispanohablantes *pp. 348–350*

Conjuguemos.com

@HomeTutor
Leveled Practice
ClassZone.com

Práctica de GRAMÁTICA

6 Un micro cuento

Hablar
Escribir

Completa el cuento con el pasado progresivo del verbo indicado.

Era una noche romántica. La luna y las estrellas **1.** (iluminar) el cielo de terciopelo *(velvet)* azul. Julieta **2.** (mirar) el jardín desde su balcón. Romeo **3.** (recitar) una poesía. Las flores **4.** (sonreír) de alegría...

De repente, el escritor, que **5.** (escribir) un drama autobiográfico, se dio cuenta de que sus dos hijos **6.** (dormir) en el sofá de su oficina. Habían entrado para desearle las buenas noches y él les había dicho que esperaran un momentito. Eso había sido más de media hora antes. El dramaturgo se sintió avergonzado. Los llevó en brazos a su dormitorio y volvió a su oficina. Romeo **7.** (leer) un libro de historietas mientras lo **8.** (esperar).

Expansión
Escribe el resto del micro cuento y léelo en clase.

7 ¿Quién lo estaba haciendo?

Escuchar
Escribir

Escucha la descripción. Mira las ilustraciones y escribe una oración completa para identificar a las personas y acciones que se mencionan o que no se mencionan en la grabación.

modelo: Una pareja sí estaba jugando al tenis.

1. 

2. 

3. 

4. 

5. 

6. 

8 Biografías de autores  *¿Recuerdas?* Preterite vs. imperfect p. 68

Hablar
Escribir

Haz frases para describir qué estaba haciendo cada autor en un momento importante de su vida.

Jorge Luis Borges

modelo: escribió sus primeros poemas / trabajar en la biblioteca de Buenos Aires
Cuando Borges escribió sus primeros poemas, estaba trabajando en la biblioteca de Buenos Aires.

1. estrenó su obra teatral *La carcajada* / empezar su carrera literaria

Augusto Roa Bastos

2. conoció a García Lorca / viajar por España

Pablo Neruda

3. escribió su autobiografía, *Paula* / reflexionar sobre su vida

Isabel Allende

4. ganó el premio Nóbel de literatura / vivir en Brasil

Gabriela Mistral

Expansión
Di qué estabas haciendo tú en cinco momentos importantes de tu vida.

9 ¿Qué estaban haciendo?

Hablar

Pregúntale a tu compañero(a) qué estaban haciendo estas personas ayer a la hora indicada.

modelo: tu hermano(a) / 3:00 de la tarde

1. tus abuelos / 9:00 de la mañana
2. tu profesor(a) de español / 7:00 de la tarde
3. tú / 10:00 de la noche
4. tu perro / 5:00 de la tarde
5. tus compañeros(as) / 11:00 de la mañana

A: ¿Qué estaba haciendo tu hermano(a) a las tres de la tarde ayer?

B: Mi hermano(a) estaba durmiendo la siesta.

Más práctica Cuaderno *pp. 347–349* Cuaderno para hispanohablantes *pp. 348–350*

¿Comprendiste? Piensa en un evento crítico de tu vida. Recuerda qué estaban haciendo tú y otros miembros de tu familia en ese momento. Luego, escribe cinco oraciones para captar el momento.

Get Help Online
ClassZone.com

GRAMÁTICA en contexto

¡AVANZA! **Goal:** As you read the poem that Laura wrote, notice how she uses the past progressive tense to describe what was happening. Then discuss the poem and use the past progressive tense to describe your own memories of the past. ***Actividades 10–12***

Contexto 2 *Poema*

ESTRATEGIA Leer

Analyze the metaphors Use a chart to analyze the metaphors that Laura uses in her poem. For each metaphor, indicate the meaning. Include any verbs in the metaphors and indicate their tense. See the example below.

Metáfora	Significado	Verbos en la metáfora	Tiempo
un gato grande estaba mirando a los cometas	La luna se movía muy rápido en el cielo y parecía que miraba a los cometas.	estaba mirando	Pasado progresivo

Laura Labarca ha escrito el siguiente poema. Eduardo Saravia lo comentó para ayudarla con la revisión.

Metáforas

Sería mejor si el título fuera más específico

La luna — un gato grande —
estaba mirando a los cometas.
Los cometas — ratoncitos —
dormían entre los planetas.

El gato se cansó y fue
a dormir extendido en su silla.
El sol — un perro amarillo —
entró saludando al día.

¡Me gusta la rima y el ritmo!

Las nubes — pájaros grises —
estaban volando con rapidez.
El sol las vio y trató de comérselas
a todas a la vez.

El perro no pudo y las nubes
estaban llorando. Y por fin el sol se
fue porque el gato ya estaba llegando.

¿Puedes añadir otra estrofa para relacionar el final con el comienzo otra vez?
¿Qué hizo el gato después de llegar?

10 Comprensión del poema

Hablar
Escribir

Contesta las siguientes preguntas sobre la lectura.

1. ¿Con qué compara a la luna la autora? ¿Qué estaba haciendo la luna?
2. ¿Con qué compara a los cometas la autora? ¿Qué estaban haciendo?
3. ¿Con qué compara al sol la autora? ¿Qué hizo el sol mientras la luna estaba durmiendo?
4. ¿Con qué compara a las nubes la autora? ¿Qué estaban haciendo?
5. ¿Qué siguieron haciendo las nubes cuando el perro no se las pudo comer?
6. ¿Qué estaba haciendo el gato cuando el perro se fue, al final?

11 ¿Quién lo estaba haciendo?

Hablar
Escribir

Relaciona cada verbo con el personaje del poema que estaba haciendo tal acción. Escribe oraciones completas. Utiliza el pasado progresivo.

modelo: saludar = El sol estaba saludando al día.

1. mirar
2. volar
3. dormir
4. llorar
5. comer
6. llegar

12 Un juego poético

Escribir
Hablar

Haz una lista de tres sustantivos *(nouns)* y dásela a tu compañero(a). Él o ella debe inventar una metáfora para cada sustantivo de tu lista, relacionando el sustantivo con otra cosa. Tú debes hacer lo mismo con la lista de tu compañero(a). Luego asocia cada sustantivo y metáfora con verbos. Construyan oraciones utilizando el pasado progresivo.

modelo:

sustantivo	metáfora	verbos
parque	una isla verde en un mar de cemento	nadar, caminar, **refugiarse**

Me **estaba refugiando** en el parque, que es una isla verde en un mar de cemento.

Expansión
Con tu compañero(a), escojan las ideas de una de sus tablas y escriban un poema breve. Usen el pasado progresivo más de dos veces.

PARA Y PIENSA

¿Comprendiste? Piensa en un día específico y escribe cinco oraciones para describir tu barrio en ese momento. ¿Qué estaban haciendo las personas? ¿Qué estaba pasando? ¿Qué detalles recuerdas claramente?

Presentación de GRAMÁTICA

¡AVANZA! **Goal:** Learn when to use the subjunctive with certain conjunctions. Then talk about when one event occurred in relation to another event. ***Actividades 13–17***

 *¿Recuerdas?* Professions pp. 418–419

English Grammar Connection: **Conjunctions of time** *(when, until, before, after)* are always followed by the indicative in English. In Spanish, however, the **subjunctive** is sometimes required.

I want to read this **before** they arrive. Quiero leer esto **antes de que** **lleguen.**

Conjunctions

Animated Grammar
ClassZone.com

After some conjunctions the **subjunctive** is always required; after others, the indicative may be used. How do you know what verb form to use?

Here's how: The **subjunctive** is always used after the following **conjunctions.**

a fin de que	**antes de que**	**en caso de que**	**sin que**
a menos que	**con tal (de) que**	**para que**	

Vamos a reunirnos **en caso de que** alguien **tenga** preguntas.
*We are going to meet **in case** anyone **has** questions.*

The following conjunctions can be used with the indicative or the **subjunctive.**

cuando	**en cuanto**	**tan pronto como**
después de que	**hasta que**	

You use the indicative to say that the outcome definitely occurred in the past. You use the **subjunctive** to say that the outcome may occur in the future.

Leí **hasta que** terminé el cuento.
*I read **until I finished** the story.*

Trabajaré **hasta que termine** el poema.
*I will work **until I complete** the poem.*

The conjunction **aunque** is used with the indicative when followed by a known fact, but with the **subjunctive** when it is not known if the information presented is true.

Fact: **Aunque** es tarde, salimos ahora. ***Even though it is*** *late, we are leaving now.*
Uncertain: **Aunque esté** lejos, vamos a pie. ***Even if it may be*** *far, we are going on foot.*

Más práctica
Cuaderno *pp. 350–352*
Cuaderno para hispanohablantes *pp. 351–354*

@HomeTutor
Leveled Practice
ClassZone.com

Práctica de GRAMÁTICA

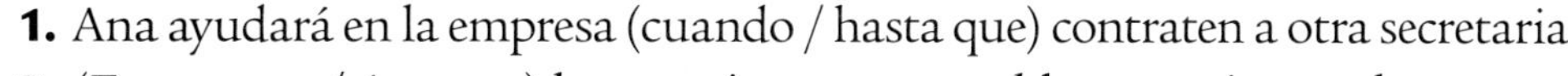

13 Las conjunciones

 ***¿Recuerdas?*** Professions pp. 418–419

Hablar
Escribir

Completa cada frase con la conjunción apropiada.

1. Ana ayudará en la empresa (cuando / hasta que) contraten a otra secretaria.
2. (En cuanto / Aunque) los arquitectos se establezcan, piensan buscar contratos en otros países.
3. (Tan pronto como / Aunque) tenemos un buen plan financiero, nuestra empresa necesita probar otras estrategias.
4. Mi mamá espera que yo encuentre un buen trabajo (aunque / tan pronto como) me gradúe.
5. Dante ya había trabajado varios años en las relaciones públicas (cuando / tan pronto como) abrió su propia agencia de publicidad.

14 La visita de un autor

Hablar
Escribir

Va a haber un evento en la Librería Mundial, cerca de tu casa. Escribe las oraciones y usa las conjunciones apropiadas de la lista.

cuando	aunque
hasta que	tan pronto como
en cuanto	después de que

1. El autor Ariel Dorfman dará su charla ____ la escriba.
2. ____ no he leído sus obras, será interesante escuchar su charla.
3. El año pasado Isabel Allende dio una conferencia; me gustó mucho ____ todavía no había leído nada de ella.
4. ____ ella terminó de hablar, compré su novela y me la firmó.
5. ____ escuche a Dorfman, ¡seguro querré leer todo lo que ha escrito!
6. Espero que estemos en la librería ____ cierre.

Expansión
Escribe un artículo para comentar qué pasó en el evento con Ariel Dorfman. Usa por lo menos cuatro conjunciones.

AUDIO

Pronunciación La y

La **y** funciona como vocal y consonante. Como vocal, en diptongos, se pronuncia como la vocal **i.** Como consonante tiene varias pronunciaciones regionales: un sonido como la *y* de la palabra *yellow* en inglés, un sonido como la *j* de la palabra *job* en inglés, o un sonido /zh/ como la *s* de la palabra *vision* en inglés.

ya **yoga** **ensayo** **ayer**

Trabalenguas

Hoy ya vimos el ayer y ayer imaginamos el hoy;
sin ayer no hay hoy, ni hay hoy sin el ayer.

15 Oraciones en dos tiempos

Hablar
Escribir

Con tu compañero(a), haz oraciones en dos tiempos verbales distintos con la siguiente información. Léanlas a la clase.

modelo: yo escribir / hasta que / terminar mi reseña

A Yo escribiré hasta que termine mi reseña.

B Yo escribí hasta que terminé mi reseña.

1. tú ser famoso(a) / en cuanto / publicar tu sátira
2. nosotros hacer un análisis / cuando / leer el cuento policíaco
3. aunque / Eugenio escribir ensayos / el periódico no querer publicarlos
4. tan pronto como / la profesora explicar / los estudiantes comprender

16 Tan pronto como...

Leer
Escribir

Lee esta carta de tu compañero Eugenio. Contéstale usando las siguientes conjunciones: **hasta que, tan pronto como, cuando, en cuanto** y **aunque.**

Hola, Estoy muy frustrado con la tarea de literatura. ¡No entiendo la poesía! Cuando la leo, me duermo. ¡En cuanto me senté al escritorio esta noche y abrí el libro de poesía, empecé a buscar distracciones! ¿Qué hago? Eugenio

17 ¿Qué te parece?

Leer
Escribir

Comparación cultural

The Onyx of Electra *(1944), Roberto Matta Echaurren*

Los sueños de Roberto Matta

¿Cómo representan los pintores sus sueños? Roberto Matta Echaurren nació en Santiago de **Chile** y fue uno de los miembros del grupo de los surrealistas. La obra de Matta presenta mundos mágicos, fantásticos y de espacios infinitos. La diferencia fundamental de la obra de Matta, en comparación con otros surrealistas, es que el artista chileno utilizaba imágenes de sus sueños.

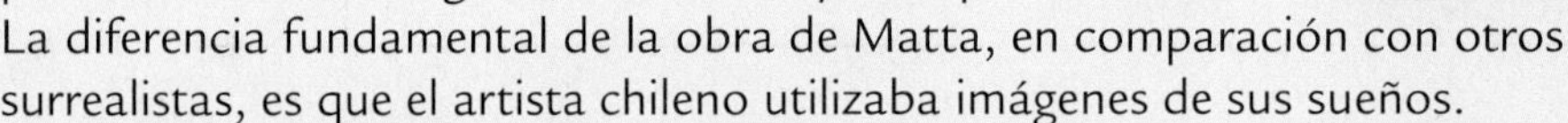

Compara con tu mundo *Describe un sueño que hayas tenido recientemente. Si pintaras ese sueño, di en qué se parecería y en qué no se parecería al cuadro de Roberto Matta.*

Analiza y da tres opiniones sobre el cuadro «The Onyx of Electra». Utiliza el indicativo y el subjuntivo con algunas de las siguientes conjunciones: **aunque, cuando, de manera que, de modo que, así que, hasta que** y **mientras.**

Más práctica Cuaderno *pp. 350–352* Cuaderno para hispanohablantes *pp. 351–354*

¿Comprendiste? Escribe cuatro cosas que no te gustan que tu familia haga mientras estás descansando. Utiliza las conjunciones **cuando, mientras, tan pronto como** y **aunque.**

Get Help Online
ClassZone.com

Todo junto

¡AVANZA! **Goal:** ***Show what you know*** Listen to and read the conversation among a group of young writers from Argentina and Chile. ***Actividades 18–20***

Resumen contextos 1 y 2 Eduardo y Laura son miembros de un club de escritores jóvenes. El grupo se reúne una vez al mes para leer sus obras e intercambiar ideas y comentarios.

Contexto 3 *Diálogo*

ESTRATEGIA **Escuchar**

Expand the lists of expressions Go back to your prior lists of positive and negative expressions for reacting to literature. As you listen to the conversation among the young writers, expand your prior lists by including their comments and expressions. How many expressions do you have in each list by now?

AUDIO

Este mes el grupo de escritores se ha reunido para hablar sobre un nuevo proyecto.

Eduardo: ¡Tengo unas noticias increíbles! El club de cine quiere filmar una de nuestras obras y hacer una película corta.

Mónica: ¡Bárbaro! ¿Qué género literario prefieren?

Eduardo: Quieren un cuento o un capítulo de una biografía o autobiografía.

Laura: Pues, son muy diferentes, ¿no?

Eduardo: Claro. Nos dijeron que escogiéramos nosotros. ¿Qué piensan?

Manuel: Bueno, Eduardo, estabas revisando tu cuento, ¿verdad?

Eduardo: Sí, y Mónica estaba trabajando en una biografía de Isabel Allende.

Manuel: Todavía no he leído el cuento de Eduardo. ¿Cómo es?

Laura: ¡Es buenísimo! El protagonista es un chico muy triste. Un día ve un espejo misterioso y lo compra. Al día siguiente se mira en el espejo y se ve reflejado en un jardín de flores bajo un sol brillante. Al final, él entra por el espejo y cuando mira el reflejo desde el otro lado, ve su casa, pero él ya no está.

Mónica: Es perfecto para una película de fantasía, surrealista, con música misteriosa...

Eduardo: Pero también está buenísima tu biografía, Mónica. Acabo de leer el episodio cuando Isabel Allende estaba trabajando como periodista en Chile y tuvo que salir del país y exiliarse en Venezuela.

Mónica: ¡Qué emocionante! Sería una película de acción; los sucesos y las tragedias personales dentro de un contexto político.

Manuel: ¡Está peludo esto de elegir! Pero tan pronto como decidamos nosotros, los del club de cine pueden empezar el proyecto.

Eduardo: Entonces, sólo hay que evaluar las ventajas y desventajas de cada uno y hacer una adaptación del mejor.

También se dice

La expresión **está peludo** significa **¡Es difícil!** Se dice de diferente formas:

- **Colombia** **¡Es un camello!**
- **Puerto Rico** **¡No es cáscara de coco!**
- **España** **¡Es un rollo!**
- **Cuba** **¡Es un chícharo!**

18 Comprensión del diálogo

Escuchar
Hablar
Escribir

Contesta las preguntas sobre el diálogo.

1. ¿Qué quiere hacer el club de cine?
2. ¿Qué género literario prefieren para el proyecto?
3. ¿Qué estaban haciendo Eduardo y Mónica?
4. ¿Qué estilo tendría una película basada en el cuento de Eduardo?
5. ¿Qué trabajo estaba haciendo Isabel Allende en Chile?
6. Según Manuel, ¿cuándo puede empezar el proyecto la gente del club de cine?

19 Integración

Leer
Escuchar
Hablar

Lee la reseña literaria *(book review)* de una nueva novela que muestran en el escaparate de una librería. Luego escucha una entrevista a su autora. Después, explica lo que aprendiste y di si te interesaría leer la novela.

Fuente 1 Reseña literaria

La nueva novela de Violeta Beltrán narra los sucesos de una familia de inmigrantes españoles en Chile. La protagonista, Camila, cuenta las aventuras de sus parientes en un contexto histórico. La familia estaba aprendiendo a vivir en otro país cuando muchas personas querían que Camila y su familia volvieran a España.Los temas de la obra son los temas típicos de esta autora: el amor y la familia, donde los individuos y los sucesos simbolizan una época histórica.

Fuente 2 Entrevista

Escucha y apunta

- ¿Qué tipo de novela escribió Violeta?
- ¿Qué estaba haciendo la autora cuando pensó en escribir su libro?

modelo: Violeta escribió una novela histórica. Estaba revisando unos papeles de su bisabuela cuando se le ocurrió la idea de escribir. La novela me interesa porque...

20 ¡A escribir!

Escribir

Escribe una reseña de un libro que hayas leído para publicar en el periódico estudiantil. Incluye una introducción a la obra con el título, el (la) autor(a), el género y un resumen breve sobre los aspectos que consideres más importantes. Por ejemplo, los protagonistas, los sucesos y los temas. En tu conclusión debes incluir razones para recomendar o no recomendar la obra.

Writing Criteria	Excellent	Good	Needs Work
Content	Your review includes many details about the book's elements.	Your review includes some details about the book's elements.	Your review includes few details about the book's elements.
Communication	Your review is organized and easy to follow.	Parts of your review are organized and easy to follow.	Your review is disorganized and hard to follow.
Accuracy	Your review has few mistakes in grammar and vocabulary.	Your review has some mistakes in grammar and vocabulary.	Your review has many mistakes in grammar and vocabulary.

Más práctica Cuaderno *pp. 353–354* Cuaderno para hispanohablantes *pp. 355–356*

¿Comprendiste? Cuenta qué estabas haciendo el fin de semana pasado. Utiliza estas conjunciones con el indicativo y el subjuntivo: **aunque, tan pronto como, después (de) que, antes (de) que** y **cuando.**

Lectura literaria

¡AVANZA! **Goal:** Read the following excerpt from a story in which the Chilean poet Pablo Neruda discusses poetic imagery with the postman. Then experiment making your own poetic images to describe elemental aspects of nature such as the rain or sea waves.

Para leer 

ESTRATEGIA Leer

Guess the meaning from the context When you encounter a new expression, think: Do I already know an expression like it in Spanish or English? Also, pay attention to expressions of emotion or intensity. Read the sentence or paragraph as a whole to get a general sense of the meaning. You can create a table like the one below to help you. Don't write down every new expression, only the ones you have trouble with.

Expresión nueva	Expresiones parecidas en inglés o en español	Expresiones de emoción
cartero	carta	tristeza
extrajo	extract	alarmante

Vocabulario para leer

disponerse a *prepararse para*
soltar *dejar libre algo*
la manilla *objeto con que se abre la puerta*
acariciarse *pasarse las manos suavemente por la piel*
someter *obligar, forzar*
suspirar *acción de soltar aire por la boca*

Nota cultural

Sobre el autor ***Antonio Skármeta (1940–)***
Nació en Antofagasta, Chile, y estudió en la Universidad de Chile y en Columbia University. Ha escrito novelas, libros de cuentos y literatura infantil. Su obra más famosa es la novela *Ardiente paciencia (El cartero de Neruda)*, que se adaptó al cine para hacer la película italiana *Il postino (El cartero)*. Skármeta fue embajador chileno en Alemania entre 2000 y 2003. Ahora vive otra vez en Chile, donde se dedica solamente a la literatura.

Sobre Pablo Neruda *Ardiente paciencia* describe las conversaciones entre el famoso poeta chileno Pablo Neruda y su cartero mientras el poeta vive en Italia. En realidad, Neruda nunca vivió en Italia, aunque viajó por Europa y vivió en España por varios años. En 1971 Pablo Neruda ganó el premio Nóbel de literatura.

Ardiente paciencia

(El cartero de Neruda)

Neruda arremetió[1] con su bolsillo[2] y extrajo un billete del rubro[3] «más que regular». El cartero dijo «gracias», no tan acongojado[4] por la suma como por la inminente despedida. Esa misma tristeza pareció inmovilizarlo hasta un grado alarmante. El poeta, que se disponía a entrar, no pudo menos que[5] interesarse por una inercia tan pronunciada. ❖

> ❖ **A pensar**
> ¿Por qué te imaginas que el cartero no quiere irse de la casa del poeta?

—¿Qué te pasa?

—¿Don Pablo?

—Te quedas ahí parado como un poste.

Mario torció[6] el cuello y buscó los ojos del poeta desde abajo:

—¿Clavado[7] como una lanza?

—No, quieto como torre de ajedrez.

—¿Más tranquilo que gato de porcelana?

Neruda soltó la manilla del portón[8], y se acarició la barbilla[9].

—Mario Jiménez, aparte de *Odas elementales,* tengo libros mucho mejores. Es indigno que me sometas a todo tipo de comparaciones y metáforas.

—¿Don Pablo?

—¡Metáforas, hombre!

—¿Qué son esas cosas?

El poeta puso una mano sobre el hombro del muchacho.

—Para aclarártelo[10] más o menos imprecisamente, son modos de decir una cosa comparándola con otra.

—Déme un ejemplo.

Neruda miró su reloj y suspiró.

—Bueno, cuando tú dices que el cielo está llorando.

---

[1] fought, struggled [2] pocket [3] category [4] distressed
[5] **no pudo...** couldn't help but [6] twisted [7] driven in
[8] large door [9] chin [10] explain it to you

Lectura literaria *continuación*

¿Qué es lo que quieres decir?

—¡Qué fácil! Que está lloviendo, pu'[11].

—Bueno, eso es una metáfora.

....

—¡Claro que me gustaría ser poeta!

—¡Hombre! En Chile todos son poetas. Es más original que sigas siendo cartero. Por lo menos caminas mucho y no engordas[12]. En Chile todos los poetas somos guatones[13].

Neruda retomó la manilla de la puerta, y se disponía a entrar, cuando Mario, mirando el vuelo de un pájaro invisible, dijo:

—Es que si fuera poeta podría decir lo que quiero.

—¿Y qué es lo que quieres decir?

—Bueno, ése es justamente el problema. Que como no soy poeta, no puedo decirlo.

....

—Si quieres ser poeta, comienza por pensar caminando. ¿O eres como John Wayne, que no podía caminar y mascar[14] chiclets al mismo tiempo? Ahora te vas a la caleta[15] por la playa y, mientras observas el movimiento del mar, puedes ir inventando metáforas.

—¡Déme un ejemplo!

—Mira este poema: «Aquí en la Isla, el mar, y cuánto mar. Se sale de sí mismo a cada rato. Dice que sí, que no, que no. Dice que sí, en azul, en espuma[16], en galope[17]. Dice que no, que no. No puede estarse quieto[18]. Me llamo mar, repite pegando[19] en una piedra sin lograr convencerla. Entonces con siete lenguas verdes, de siete tigres verdes, de siete perros verdes, de siete mares verdes, la recorre, la besa, la humedece[20], y se golpea el pecho[21] repitiendo su nombre.» —Hizo una pausa satisfecho—. ¿Qué te parece?

A pensar
¿Por qué menciona Neruda su colección de poesía, *Odas elementales*? ¿Qué infieres del intercambio de citas que hacen Neruda y Mario?

A pensar
Lee el poema en voz alta. ¿Qué notas en el sonido de los versos?

[11] informal pronunciation of **pues** [12] gain weight [13] overweight
[14] chew [15] inlet [16] foam [17] gallop [18] still [19] hitting
[20] **la...** surrounds it, kisses it, moistens it [21] **se...** beats its chest

Reflexiona

¿Quiénes se encuentran? ¿Cuál es el interés de uno de los personajes?

—Raro.

—«Raro.» ¡Qué crítico más severo que eres!

—No, don Pablo. Raro no lo es el poema. Raro es como *yo* me sentía cuando usted recitaba el poema.

—Querido Mario, a ver si te desenredas[22] un poco, porque no puedo pasar toda la mañana disfrutando de tu charla.

—¿Cómo se lo explicara? Cuando usted decía el poema, las palabras iban de acá pa'llá.

—¡Como el mar, pues!

—Sí, pues, se movían igual que el mar.

—Eso es el ritmo.

—Y me sentí raro, porque con tanto movimiento me marié[23].

—Te mareaste[24].

—¡Claro! Yo iba como un barco temblando en sus palabras.

Los párpados[25] del poeta se despegaron[26] lentamente.

—«Como un barco temblando en mis palabras.»

—¡Claro!

—¿Sabes lo que has hecho, Mario?

—¿Qué?

—Una metáfora.

—Pero no vale, porque me salió de pura casualidad[27], no más.

—No hay imagen que no sea casual, hijo.

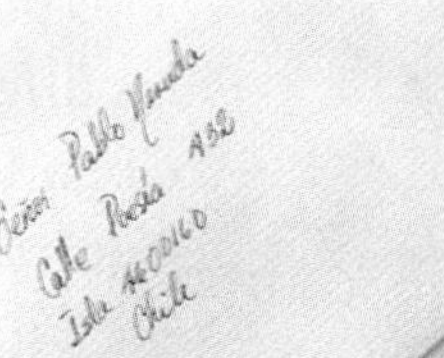

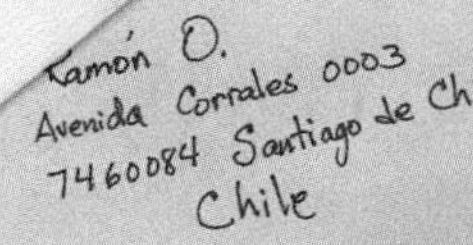

---

[22] **a ver...** sort yourself out [23] mispronunciation of **mareé**
[24] you got dizzy [25] eyelids [26] lifted [27] **de pura...** by sheer chance

¿Comprendiste?

1. ¿Cómo explica el autor lo que es una metáfora?
2. ¿Qué descubrió Mario cuando Neruda recitó su poema sobre el mar? ¿Qué inventó Mario para explicar su reacción al poema? ¿Cómo reaccionó Neruda?
3. ¿Cómo describirías la relación entre Mario y Neruda? Explica tu opinión usando ejemplos de la lectura.
4. ¿Qué crees que Neruda quiso decir en la última línea de la selección?

¿Y tú?

1. ¿Qué tipos de poesía y narrativa te gustan? ¿Qué poetas y novelistas conoces? ¿Cuáles de sus obras recomiendas y por qué?
2. ¿Qué otra metáfora escribirías para representar lo que sintió Mario?

Conexiones *La geografía*

Estaciones opuestas

En los países del hemisferio sur, las estaciones del año son al revés de las estaciones en el hemisferio norte. Cuando escritores del Cono Sur se refieren a la primavera, ¡están hablando de los meses de septiembre, octubre y noviembre!

El ecuador divide a nuestro planeta en el hemisferio norte y el hemisferio sur. En los países que están cerca del ecuador no hay grandes diferencias entre las estaciones; pero cuando el país está lejos del ecuador, como Chile, Argentina, Uruguay y Paraguay, las diferencias entre las estaciones son más evidentes. Las ciudades del sur de Chile y Argentina están cerca de la Antártida. En Ushuaia, Argentina, la ciudad más al sur del mundo, las temperaturas varían entre 64°F en el verano y 5°F en el invierno.

	primavera	verano	otoño	invierno
hemisferio norte	**marzo abril mayo**	**junio julio agosto**	**septiembre octubre noviembre**	**diciembre enero febrero**
hemisferio sur	**septiembre octubre noviembre**	**diciembre enero febrero**	**marzo abril mayo**	**junio julio agosto**

Mira el dibujo del hemisferio sur y la tabla de las estaciones. Luego, contesta las siguientes preguntas.

1. Si quieres estar en un clima frío, ¿en qué dirección viajas en cada hemisferio?
2. ¿En qué lugar son más fríos los inviernos, el norte de Paraguay o el sur de Chile?
3. ¿Qué tiempo haría en julio en el sur de Chile y Argentina? ¿Y en diciembre?

Proyecto Haz una investigación sobre el clima de tu región. ¿Cuánta lluvia recibe durante el año? ¿Cuánta nieve? ¿Cuáles son las temperaturas más altas y más bajas que se han registrado? ¿Cuándo ocurrieron? ¿Cómo ha cambiado el clima de tu región en los últimos cien años?

En tu comunidad

El clima de Estados Unidos varía mucho de un lugar a otro. ¿Cómo es el clima de tu región? ¿Hay cuatro estaciones bien definidas? ¿Cómo es el clima en cada estación del año?

En resumen

Vocabulario y gramática

Vocabulario

Discuss and Critique Literature

absurdo(a)	*absurd*	narrar	*to narrate*
el acto	*act*	la novela	*novel*
el análisis	*analysis*	la obra	*work*
el antecedente	*background event*	la poesía	*poetry*
la autobiografía	*autobiography*	la prosa	*prose*
el (la) autor(a)	*author*	el (la) protagonista	*protagonist, main character*
la biografía	*biography*	el punto de vista	*point of view*
el capítulo	*chapter*	la realidad	*reality*
el clímax	*climax*	relacionar	*to relate*
el contexto	*context*	la reseña	*review*
el cuento	*story, short story*	la rima	*rhyme*
el cuento policíaco	*crime story*	el ritmo	*rhythm*
el desenlace	*ending, outcome*	romántico(a)	*romantic*
el ensayo	*essay*	la sátira	*satire*
el estilo	*style*	significar	*to mean*
la estrofa	*stanza*	simbolizar	*to symbolize*
el género literario	*literary genre*	el símil	*simile*
implicar	*to imply*	el suceso	*event*
inferir	*to infer*	el tema	*theme*
el libro de historietas	*comic book*	titularse	*to be called*
la metáfora	*metaphor*	el verso	*verse*

Link Events and Ideas

aunque	*although*
en cuanto	*as soon as*
tan pronto como	*as soon as*

Gramática

Past Progressive

The most common form of the **past progressive** is the **imperfect** of **estar** plus the **present participle** of the main verb. In this form, it often expresses an action that was interrupted.

¿Qué **estabas haciendo** cuando te llamé ayer?
*What **were you doing** when I called yesterday?*

To emphasize that an action continued for a period of time and then came to an end, use the preterite of **estar** plus the **present participle** of the main verb.

Estuvimos **hablando** toda la tarde.
***We were talking** all afternoon.*

Conjunctions

The **subjunctive** is always used after these **conjunctions.**

a fin de que	**con tal (de) que**	**sin que**
a menos que	**en caso de que**	**para que**
antes de que		

The following conjunctions can be used with the indicative or the **subjunctive.**

cuando	**en cuanto**	**tan pronto como**
después de que	**hasta que**	

- You use the indicative to say that the outcome definitely occurred in the past.
- You use the **subjunctive** to say that the outcome may occur in the future.
- **Aunque** is used with the indicative when followed by a known fact. Use the **subjunctive** when it is not known to be true.

Lección 1

Repaso de la lección

¡LLEGADA!

@HomeTutor
ClassZone.com

Now you can
- discuss and critique literature
- talk about what you were doing in the past
- link events and ideas

Using
- past progressive
- conjunctions

To review
- vocabulary pp. 452–453

1 Listen and understand

AUDIO

Sara Irúñez, una autora paraguaya, está dando una conferencia sobre sus obras. Escucha sus comentarios y luego contesta las siguientes preguntas.

1. ¿Qué le pidieron los organizadores de la conferencia a la señora Irúñez antes de que leyera sus cuentos?
2. ¿Qué estaba haciendo la señora Irúñez cuando empezó a escribir descripciones?
3. ¿Qué le aconsejó el amigo de la señora Irúñez?
4. ¿Qué le pidieron los editores de la revista?
5. ¿Qué otros tipos de literatura ha escrito la señora Irúñez?

To review
- past progressive p. 457
- conjunctions p. 462

2 Discuss and critique literature

Empareja los comentarios de la columna de la izquierda con la terminación correcta de la columna de la derecha. Luego, escribe las oraciones completas.

1. Me gustan los cuentos románticos, con tal de que...
2. Estaba leyendo una novela muy interesante cuando...
3. Voy a escribir unos comentarios sobre el libro para que...
4. Quiero seguir leyendo este poema hasta que...
5. El autor estaba escribiendo su autobiografía en caso de que...
6. La autora del libro de historietas estaba dibujando cuando...

a. identifique el ritmo y los símbolos.
b. se imaginó la escena final.
c. no sean demasiado largos.
d. llegaron unos amigos de visita.
e. algún día se haga famoso.
f. los pueda enviar al autor.

To review
- past progressive p. 457

3 Talk about what you were doing in the past

Escoge una palabra de la lista y di qué estaban haciendo las siguientes personas. Sigue el modelo.

buscar
escribir
leer
ver
pensar

modelo: Ernesto / un poema absurdo / en su cuaderno
Ernesto estaba escribiendo un poema absurdo en su cuaderno.

1. Hernando y Alberto / un drama / en el teatro
2. tú / un ensayo / en la biblioteca
3. nosotros / una biografía / en la base de datos
4. Lorena / en su nuevo cuento

To review
- conjunctions p. 462

4 Link events and ideas

Indica la forma correcta de cada verbo para completar la siguiente reseña de un nuevo libro de poesía.

En su nuevo libro, *La realidad,* el poeta Jorge Marichal ha escrito varios tipos de poemas y experimentado con una variedad de estilos literarios. Marichal nunca descansa; tan pronto como __1.__ (terminar) un libro, empieza a escribir otro. Es interesante que el autor publique con tanta rapidez, con tal de que no __2.__ (afectar) a la calidad de su obra. En caso de que usted no __3.__ (conocer) los poemas de Marichal, sepa que es un poeta que prefiere usar símbolos y metáforas. Aunque la poesía anterior de Marichal __4.__ (tener) un ritmo fijo *(fixed)*, en este libro el poeta varía el ritmo y usa la rima. El resultado es una obra que no se puede mejorar... ¡hasta que este autor __5.__ (publicar) su próxima colección!

To review
- **Comparación cultural** pp. 456, 464

5 Books, movies and surrealist art

Comparación cultural

1. ¿En qué se basó la película *De amor y de sombra*?
2. ¿De qué trata la película?
3. ¿Quién fue Roberto Matta?
4. ¿Qué lo diferenciaba Matta de los otros pintores surrealistas?

Más práctica Cuaderno *pp. 355–366* Cuaderno para hispanohablantes *pp. 357–366*

Get Help Online
ClassZone.com

UNIDAD 8

El Cono Sur

Lección 2

Tema:

El drama

¡AVANZA! **In this lesson you will learn to**

- read and interpret a short play
- talk about unplanned occurrences
- express opinions about a text

using

- **se** for unintentional occurrences
- review: uses of the subjunctive

¿Recuerdas?

- **si** clauses
- literary vocabulary

Comparación cultural

In this lesson you will learn about

- street theater in Uruguay
- theaters in Argentina
- famous writers of Argentina and Chile

Compara con tu mundo

Estos estudiantes tienen que preparar muchas cosas para su obra de teatro, como el escenario *(set)*, disfraces *(costumes)*, luces y música. *¿Te gusta ver o participar en obras de teatro? ¿Qué tipo de obras prefieres?*

¿Qué ves?

Mira la foto

¿Qué hace el actor? ¿Y la actriz?

¿Qué tipo de obra de teatro es?

¿Qué hacen los otros estudiantes?

¿Qué elementos tienen?

Online SPANISH CLASSZONE.COM

Featuring...

Cultura INTERACTIVA

Animated Grammar

@HomeTutor

And more...

- Get Help Online
- Interactive Flashcards
- Review Games
- WebQuest
- Conjuguemos.com

Estudiantes argentinos preparando una obra de teatro

Presentación de VOCABULARIO

¡AVANZA! **Goal:** Learn new words that will help you understand and interpret a short play. Then talk about various aspects of writing and performing a drama. ***Actividades 1–2***

AUDIO

A «Colón agarra viaje a toda costa» es una obra muy interesante; por eso, quiero tomar unas notas antes de representarla. Todos los directores de teatro lo hacen.

Notas del director para la obra de teatro «Colón agarra viaje a toda costa»

¡Importante! Para **dirigir** esta obra hay que investigar los antecedentes históricos que utilizó **el dramaturgo** para describir al personaje principal. **El tema de la obra** es **irónico** y algunos de **los diálogos** son muy cómicos.

Mario es el actor escogido para hacer el papel principal. Es evidente que Cristóbal Colón es un personaje complejo y **singular**, pero hay que **darse cuenta de** que Mario es un actor estupendo. El proceso de creación de esta obra es fascinante porque Colón para muchos fue un **farsante codicioso** y **avaro**. Para otros fue atrevido, **persistente** y con un gran **coraje**.

La dirección de escenografía debe ser excelente, nada que sea poco original. Es obvio que el público tiene que ver los nombres de los barcos.

B Siempre **he soñado con** el éxito, que el público **aplauda** en **el intermedio.** Y cuando termine la obra, **reclamen** que el director salga a saludar.

C Es importante que Mario **ensaye** mucho. También tenemos que asegurar que **el vestuario** sea perfecto.

Más vocabulario

el ensayo *rehearsal*
insólito(a) *unusual*
pedir prestado *to borrow*
reclamar *to call, to demand*
el (la) tirado(a) *pauper*

Expansión de vocabulario p. R17
Ya sabes p. R17

¡A responder! Escuchar

Vas a oír siete frases de la presentación de una obra de teatro. Si la frase es verdadera, indícalo con el dedo pulgar hacia arriba. Si la frase es falsa, indícalo con el dedo pulgar hacia abajo.

Práctica de VOCABULARIO

1 El ensayo

Hablar Escribir

Elige una de las palabras entre paréntesis para completar la conversación entre dos estudiantes que van a ser actores en una obra de teatro de su escuela.

Ramón: Hola Beba. ¿Vas a **1.** (ensayar, reclamar) para la obra de teatro?

Beba: Sí. Por si acaso, tengo **2.** (el gesto, el guión) y lo puedo leer si es necesario.

Ramón: También estoy nervioso. ¿Conoces a la **3.** (tirada, dramaturga)?

Beba: Sí, Elena Benegas, también va a **4.** (aplaudir, dirigir) la obra.

Ramón: Te propongo que hagamos un **5.** (intermedio, ensayo) para aprendernos bien la obra.

Beba: Pues me parece bien porque no quiero que piensen que soy una **6.** (avara, farsante).

Ramón: No te preocupes Beba, ya verás que en **7.** (el gesto, el intermedio) todos te van a **8.** (soñar, aplaudir).

Beba: ¡Ojalá! Para ser actriz hay que ser muy **9.** (insólito, persistente).

Ramón: Sí, y hay que tener mucho **10.** (coraje, singular).

2 El teatro

Escribir

Relaciona cada palabra con su concepto. Escribe oraciones completas para definirlas.

modelo: el escenario: El escenario es el lugar del teatro donde se hace la obra.

1. la persona que indica dónde debes sentarte
2. la obra escrita que sirve de guía a los actores
3. abrir las cortinas para que empiece la obra
4. el grupo de objetos, muebles y adornos para la obra
5. guiar a los actores; decirles cómo hacer los diálogos
6. lugar por donde el público se va del teatro

levantar el telón
la escenografía
el (la) acomodador(a)
dirigir
el guión
la salida
el escenario

Más práctica Cuaderno *pp. 367–369* Cuaderno para hispanohablantes *pp. 367–370*

¿Comprendiste? Elige a la persona que se encarga de los elementos siguientes para una obra de teatro.

1. escribir el guión — **a.** el actor o la actriz
2. hacer un papel — **b.** el (la) dramaturgo(a)
3. sentar al público — **c.** el (la) acomodador(a)

VOCABULARIO en contexto

¡AVANZA! **Goal:** Read the descriptions of Christopher Columbus and consider the effect that other people's opinions can or should have on someone's ideas and plans. ***Actividades 3–4***

Contexto 1 *Obra de teatro*

ESTRATEGIA Leer

Chart the opposing views Make a chart like the one to the right. In the first column write all the positive things about Christopher Columbus, and in the second column write all the negative things. What do you think he was really like?

Lo positivo	Lo negativo

Colón agarra viaje a toda costa *(Parte 1)*

AUDIO

La dramaturga argentina Adela Basch escribió esta obra de teatro, donde cuenta cómo ella cree que se le ocurrió a Cristóbal Colón la idea de viajar en busca de nuevas tierras.

Presentador:
Estimado público, hoy vamos a imaginar
la historia de un singular personaje,
de sus búsquedas[1] y de sus viajes.
Para algunos, fue un hombre intrépido
y valeroso...

Presentadora:
Para otros, fue solamente un ambicioso.

Presentador:
Para algunos, fue un gran navegante[2].

Presentadora:
Para otros, fue sólo un farsante.

Presentador:
Para algunos, quiso ir más allá[3]
de los límites del saber.

Presentadora:
Para otros, sólo buscaba honores y poder.

Presentador:
Para algunos, fue un visionario.

Presentadora:
Para otros, trataba de[4] hacerse
millonario.

Presentador:
Para algunos, fue brillante y generoso.

Presentadora:
Para otros, fue avaro y codicioso.

Presentador:
Para algunos, fue todo generosidad
y grandeza.

Presentadora *(Está en babia[5])*:
¿Qué?

Presentador:
Dije: ¡generosidad
y grandeza! ¡Grandeza!
¡Gran-de-za!

Presentadora:
¿Grande ésa? ¿Grande ésa?
¿Grande ésa qué?

Presentador:
¡Grande esa idea que se le
apareció en la cabeza!
¡Salir de viaje!

[1] searches [2] sailor [3] beyond
[4] **trataba...** he was trying to
[5] **Está...** her head is in the clouds

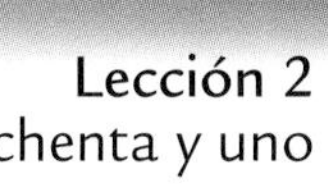

3 Comprensión de la obra de teatro

Hablar
Escribir

Sustituye las siguientas oraciones con expresiones de la lectura que tengan el mismo significado.

modelo: Colón fue un individuo único.
Colón fue **un singular personaje.**

1. Colón fue un impostor.
2. Colón sólo quería ganar dinero.
3. Colón fue un hombre muy inteligente.
4. Colón sólo pensaba en acumular dinero.
5. Colón tenía grandes ideas.

4 ¿Cómo son?

Hablar
Escribir

Haz una lista de tres personas famosas de la historia o la actualidad. Luego, haz una descripción breve de cada persona con un adjetivo desde una perspectiva positiva y otra negativa. Utiliza adjetivos del vocabulario y de la lectura.

modelo: Hernán Cortés
Para algunos fue atrevido. Para otros fue codicioso.

Expansión
Escoge a uno de los personajes de tu lista y usa todos los adjetivos que tú piensas que le corresponden.

Comparación cultural

El carnaval gigante

Comparsa (musical group) *en el carnaval de Montevideo*

¿Qué relación tienen las celebraciones con la historia de un país? El Carnaval en **Uruguay** es una celebración muy larga. Un elemento importante del Carnaval en Montevideo son los tablados: espectáculos musicales callejeros, creados y actuados por murgas (grupos de músicos), dramaturgos, actores y directores. Estas actuaciones informales son un tipo de teatro popular y es típico que sus temas critiquen la sociedad y la política del día. Hay dos requisitos para los tablados de las murgas. Uno es que los cantantes y actores repasen los sucesos más notables del año. El otro es que los músicos usen las formas musicales que más se escucharon durante el año para acompañar la obra.

Compara con tu mundo *¿Hay algún tipo de teatro callejero donde vives? ¿Existen otros tipos de actuaciones callejeras? ¿Cómo son? ¿Dónde y cuándo se presentan?*

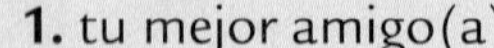

¿Comprendiste? Escribe descripciones para reflejar las opiniones que tú imaginas que las siguientes personas tienen de ti.

1. tu mejor amigo(a)
2. tus vecinos(as)
3. tu abuelo(a)
4. una persona que no te conozca bien

Presentación de GRAMÁTICA

¡AVANZA! **Goal:** Learn how to express accidental or unplanned occurrences using **se** and indirect object pronouns. Then talk about some things that have happened to you unexpectedly. ***Actividades 5–8***

English Grammar Connection: In English, the cause of an unintentional occurrence is the **subject** of the sentence. In Spanish, the occurrence **(verb)** happens *to* someone, so you use an **indirect object pronoun.**

We (accidentally) **broke** the window. **Se nos rompió la ventana.**

Se for Unintentional Occurrences

Unintentional occurrences are expressed in a way that is impersonal, suggesting that no one is responsible for the outcome.

Here's how: The **verb** is expressed with the impersonal pronoun **se** and agrees with the subject. An **indirect object pronoun** indicates the person to whom the action occurred.

Verbs Used to Express Unintentional Occurrences	
acabársele (a uno)	**perdérsele (a uno)**
caérsele (a uno)	**quedársele (a uno)**
ocurrírsele (a uno)	**rompérsele (a uno)**
olvidársele (a uno)	

Se me olvidaron las entradas al teatro.
I forgot the theater tickets.

El tiempo se te acaba.
Your time is running out.

To clarify or emphasize the indirect object pronoun reference, use **a** + **the person** (noun or pronoun).

A Colón se **le** ocurrió buscar una nueva ruta al Oriente.
It occurred to ***Columbus*** *to look for a new route to the East.*

A mí se **me** cayó el vaso, pero **a José** se **le** cayeron los platos.
I *dropped the glass, but* ***José*** *dropped the plates.*

Más práctica
Cuaderno *pp. 370–372*
Cuaderno para hispanohablantes *pp. 371–373*

@HomeTutor
Leveled Practice
ClassZone.com

Práctica de GRAMÁTICA

5 ¡Lo siento!

Hablar

Explícale a tu compañero(a) por qué no has hecho las siguientes cosas.

modelo: llamar / acabársele las baterías del teléfono celular

B Perdona, se me acabaron las baterías del teléfono celular.

1. ir al ensayo / descomponérsele el auto
2. no seguir las direcciones de escenografía / olvidársele los cambios
3. no memorizar tus diálogos / perdérsele el guión
4. quedarse hasta el final / acabársele la paciencia
5. maquillarse / ocurrírsele unas ideas nuevas para el maquillaje

6 Un ensayo difícil

Hablar
Escribir

Completa cada oración con el verbo apropiado.

modelo: Olga tuvo problemas porque... el guión en casa.
Olga tuvo problemas porque se le quedó el guión en casa.

1. Felipe tuvo que inventar el diálogo porque... las líneas.

2. La directora cambió las direcciones de escenografía porque... una idea maravillosa.

3. Armando no pudo levantar el telón porque... el brazo.

4. La señora Olmedo no pudo leer porque... las gafas.

5. El productor canceló la producción porque... el dinero.

6. Andrés no pudo entrar al teatro... las entradas.

7 ¡Excusas!

Escuchar
Escribir

Daniela dio una fiesta el sábado pero varias personas no fueron. El lunes todos le explicaron sus razones. Escucha las explicaciones, elige el dibujo que corresponde, escribe el nombre de la persona y escribe una oración que explique por qué esa persona no fue a la fiesta.

modelo: Rafael
Rafael no fue porque se le descompuso el auto.

1. 

2. 

3. 

4. 

8 La Agenda 24/7

Leer
Escribir

Lee este anuncio. Luego, contesta las preguntas.

1. Qué les pasa a las personas que necesitan la agenda de este anuncio?
2. ¿Por qué necesitan un archivo en la agenda?
3. ¿Por qué necesitan una alarma?
4. La agenda utiliza energía solar. ¿Qué problema soluciona?

Más práctica Cuaderno *pp. 370–372* Cuaderno para hispanohablantes *pp. 371–373*

¿Comprendiste? Menciona cuatro eventos inesperados que te ocurrieron la semana pasada. Utiliza verbos con **se.**

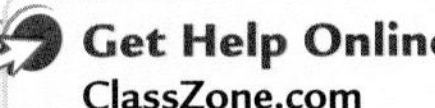

GRAMÁTICA en contexto

¡AVANZA! **Goal:** Read about the ideas that occurred to Columbus to inspire his explorations. Then talk about the effects that unplanned occurrences can have on your life. ***Actividades 9–11***

 *¿Recuerdas?* **Si** clauses p. 423

Contexto 2 *Obra de teatro*

ESTRATEGIA Leer

Write the ideas Find or draw a picture of Christopher Columbus. Around it in speech circles, write (in your own words) at least five of his ideas that you found in the reading.

Colón agarra viaje a toda costa
(Parte 2)

AUDIO

A Colón se le apareció una idea en la cabeza: ¡Salir de viaje! Aquí continúa el drama.

Presentador:
De Colón se sabe poco. Pero existe la certeza[6] de que se le encendió una idea persistente en la cabeza.

Presentadora:
Siempre sintió gran curiosidad por saber qué había más allá.

Presentador:
Ustedes preguntarán: ¿más allá de qué?

Colón:
Me pregunto qué hay más allá de esta orilla, más allá de mi sol y de mi tierra, más allá de mi calle, de mi mesa, de mi silla. Me pregunto si habrá maravillas, ciudades sorprendentes, islas misteriosas, personas diferentes... Me pregunto si habrá lagos[7], montañas, ríos, llanuras[8]. ¡Y siento un irresistible deseo de aventura!

Presentador:
Se sabe muy poco sobre Colón y sobre su vida.

Presentadora:
Pero es seguro que se hacía una pregunta muy atrevida.

Colón:
¿Qué habrá más allá del mar?

Presentador:
También se sabe con certeza que, cada tanto[9], Colón se sentía reclamado...

Presentadora:
¡Por un poderoso y fuerte llamado[10]!

Se escucha golpear[11] a una puerta y no sabemos si está cerrada o está abierta.

[6] certainty [7] lakes [8] plains [9] **cada...** from time to time
[10] **poderoso...** powerful and strong call [11] knocking

9 Comprensión de la obra de teatro

Leer
Hablar
Escribir

Contesta las preguntas sobre la lectura.

1. ¿Cuál fue la idea central que se le ocurrió a Colón?
2. ¿Por qué se le encendió gran curiosidad?
3. ¿Qué se sabe de la vida de Colón?
4. ¿Qué se le presentó al final de esta parte?
5. ¿A quién se refiere el presentador con «ustedes»?
6. ¿Qué preguntas se hacía Colón?
7. ¿Qué se sabía con certeza de Colón?
8. ¿Qué deseo irresistible tenía Colón?

10 ¡Preguntas, preguntas!

¿Recuerdas? **Si** clauses p. 423

Hablar

Pregúntale a tu compañero(a) qué haría en las siguientes situaciones.

modelo: perdérsele las llaves de tu casa

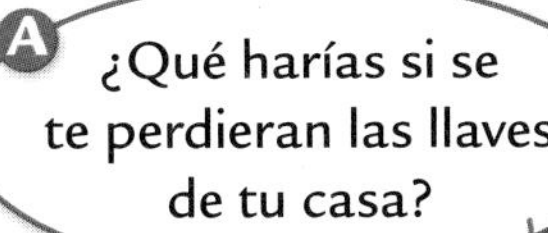

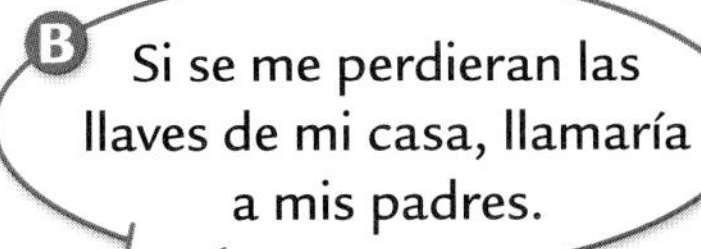

1. caérsele el florero *(vase)* favorito de tu mamá
2. ocurrírsele una idea insólita
3. olvidársele una tarea importante
4. ensuciársele la camisa durante el almuerzo
5. acabársele el tiempo en un examen
6. perdérsele un accesorio
7. rompérsele la ventana de un vecino
8. aparecérsele un(a) viejo(a) amigo(a)

11 La llegada

Hablar
Escribir

Con tu compañero(a), escribe una escena sobre lo que pasó cuando Colón llegó a tierra. Escribe sobre qué pensó, cómo era el lugar y qué hicieron Colón y los otros navegantes. Incluyan las expresiones de abajo.

Pistas: ocurrírsele, aparecérsele, pedir prestado, persistente, coraje, insólito(a)

Expansión
Escriban un párrafo más sobre el regreso de Colón a España.

PARA Y PIENSA

¿Comprendiste? Haz una lista de tres eventos inesperados que te han pasado. Luego, explica cómo cada evento afectó tu vida.

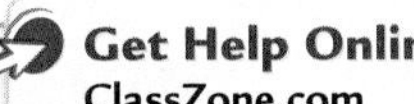

Presentación de GRAMÁTICA

¡AVANZA! **Goal:** Review the various contexts in which to use the subjunctive. Then express opinions, wishes, and doubts about literary texts. ***Actividades 12–15***

¿Recuerdas? Literary vocabulary pp. 452–453

English Grammar Connection: The **subjunctive** is rarely used in English. It is more common to use the **indicative** or the **infinitive** in English.

Subjunctive:	If I **were** you, I wouldn't do it.
Indicative:	I hope that she **goes.**
Infinitive:	I wanted you **to help** me.

REPASO Uses of the Subjunctive

The **subjunctive** expresses ideas whose certainty may not be known.

Here's how: Use the **subjunctive** when there is a change of subject after verbs that express *hope, doubt, influence,* or *emotion.*

Espero que él **se dé** cuenta del error.
Es dudoso que nosotras **podamos** venir.
Recomendó que Ana **escribiera** dramas.
Me alegro de que los actores **sean** tan buenos.

Also use the **subjunctive** to talk about what is **unknown** or **indefinite.**

Buscamos actores que **conozcan** el drama.

Some **conjunctions** are always followed by the **subjunctive.**

Lee el libro **antes de que veas** la película.
Les enseño **para que sepan** todo.

With **conjunctions of time,** use the **subjunctive** if the action may occur in the future.

Me quedaré **hasta que termine** la función.
Vete **tan pronto como** Cristina **llegue.**

Remember that **aunque** is followed by the **subjunctive** when it refers to something whose outcome is not known.

Aunque llueva, jugaremos el partido.

Más práctica

Cuaderno *pp. 372–375*
Cuaderno para hispanohablantes *pp. 374–377*

Conjuguemos.com **@HomeTutor** Leveled Practice ClassZone.com

Práctica de GRAMÁTICA

12 ¿Subjuntivo o indicativo?

 ***¿Recuerdas?*** Literary vocabulary pp. 452–453

Hablar
Escribir

Completa con el subjuntivo, indicativo o infinitivo del verbo indicado.

modelo: Prefiero que las metáforas sean claras en la poesía.

1. Los profesores de literatura creen que es muy importante que nosotros (leer) ejemplos de todos los géneros.
2. Es muy difícil (escribir) el clímax y el desenlace de un cuento.
3. Alejandro busca autores que (soñar) con contar historias singulares.
4. Isabel no duda que ella (tener) talento para la poesía.
5. Ojalá que el autor (publicar) otra colección de cuentos.

Expansión
Haz cinco comentarios sobre lo que esperas, te alegra, o dudas de los escritores.

13 Los editores

Hablar

Tú eres un(a) autor(a) con una obra nueva para publicar. Tu compañero(a) es un(a) editor(a) que te da sugerencias para que hagas la última revisión.

modelo: aclarar la motivación del protagonista / para que los lectores entender mejor

editor(a) Es importante que aclares la motivación del protagonista.

autor(a) ¿Por qué es importante que aclare la motivación del protagonista?

editor(a) Es importante para que los lectores la entiendan mejor.

1. simplificar el argumento / sin que perder el impacto
2. explicar lo que ya pasó / antes de que presentar algo nuevo
3. no terminar la historia / hasta que todo quedar claro
4. eliminar el diálogo / a menos que ser imprescindible

AUDIO

Pronunciación La z

En Latinoamérica se pronuncia la **z** como /s/. Recuerda que el sonido /s/ también se produce por las combinaciones **ce** y **ci**. En España, la **z** y la combinación **ce** o **ci** se pronuncian como la *th* de la palabra *thin* en inglés.

zorro	**z**oológico
ra**z**onar	almor**z**ar

Refrán

Zapatero, a tus zapatos.

14 Una recomendación

Escribir

Tú y tu amigo(a) siempre se hacen sugerencias de lecturas. En un correo electrónico explícale una obra que has leído recientemente y haz algunas sugerencias específicas para que tu amigo(a) disfrute la obra al máximo. Usa por lo menos cinco ejemplos del subjuntivo.

modelo:

```
Hola,
Acabo de leer la última novela del paraguayo Augusto
Roa Bastos y creo que te gustará. Aunque...
```

15 Se me ocurre que...

Leer
Escribir

Comparación cultural

Teatro Colón, Buenos Aires, Argentina

Los teatros: monumentales obras de arte

¿Cómo puede un edificio convertirse en una obra de arte? Hay varios teatros antiguos importantes en los países del Cono Sur. Uno de los teatros más famosos de Latinoamérica es el Teatro Colón de Buenos Aires, **Argentina.** Este edificio tiene un estilo italiano con adornos franceses. Su construcción duró veinte años y se completó en 1908. En 1966 el famoso pintor argentino Raúl Soldi realizó la decoración de la Cúpula del Teatro. Su técnica es hacer la pintura al óleo sobre tela y luego pasarla al muro. Soldi donó la obra a la ciudad de Buenos Aires.

Compara con tu mundo *Nombra un teatro de tu región y menciona los espectáculos que presenta. Di algún detalle que te guste del teatro.*

Escribe la forma correcta del verbo en el siguiente párrafo.

Es importante que tú __**1.**__ (explicar) cómo se pinta una cúpula, para que yo __**2.**__ (poder) entender que __**3.**__ (ser) muy complicado. __**4.**__ (Haber) dos formas de __**5.**__ (pintar): tú lo __**6.**__ (poder) pintar directamente en el muro o lo __**7.**__ (poder) hacer primero en una tela. A mí __**8.**__ (occurírsele) que la forma más fácil de hacerlo es la primera.

Más práctica Cuaderno *pp. 372–375* Cuaderno para hispanohablantes *pp. 374–377*

¿Comprendiste? Haz una lista de tres libros que te hayan gustado mucho. Escribe una frase usando el subjuntivo para expresar una opinión, una emoción o una duda sobre cada libro.

Get Help Online
ClassZone.com

Todo junto

¡AVANZA! **Goal:** ***Show what you know*** Read and listen to the continuation of the drama about Columbus. Then relate what you can say to encourage someone to undertake a difficult task. ***Actividades 16–19***

Resumen contextos 1 y 2 Este drama presentado aquí en cuatro partes cuenta cómo Cristóbal Colón tuvo la idea de viajar a nuevas tierras.

Contexto 3 *Obra de teatro*

ESTRATEGIA Escuchar
List the reasons for and against going
While listening, use a chart to write down reasons Columbus receives for going and reasons he raises for not going.

Razones para ir	Razones para no ir

Colón agarra viaje a toda costa

(Parte 3)

AUDIO

En esta tercera parte del drama Cristóbal Colón recibe un mensaje donde alguien le dice que se vaya de viaje a descubrir nuevos horizontes.

Colón está en su casa, seguramente pensando en lo que pasa. Golpean a la puerta, que dentro de un instante va a estar abierta.

Colón:
¿Quién es?

Presentador:
¡Cartero!

Le entrega una botella con un mensaje. Colón lo lee, interesadísimo.

Colón:

¿Te vas a pasar la vida preguntando y preguntando? ¿Por qué no tratás de hacer algo? El mundo no termina a la vuelta de la esquina[12], pero eso solamente lo ve el que camina. ¡Vamos! Detrás del horizonte siempre hay algo más. Hay rutas desconocidas con mil posibilidades, hay montañas, ríos, selvas y ciudades.

Colón interrumpe por un momento la lectura del mensaje. Tiene unas ganas bárbaras de salir de viaje. Pero no sabe bien qué hacer.

Sí, sí, pero ¿qué hago? Yo no tengo barcos, ni botes, ni veleros[13] y, sobre todo, no tengo dinero. Soy un seco, un tirado y no voy a cruzar el mar a nado[14]. ¿Qué hago, qué hago, qué hago?

Sigue leyendo el mensaje. Tal vez encuentre alguna palabra que le dé coraje[15].

[12] **a...** around the corner
[13] ships
[14] **a...** swimming
[15] courage

También se dice

Colón dice **Soy un seco** para explicar que no tiene dinero.

- **Puerto Rico** **No tengo un chavo.**
- **Cuba** **Estoy sin un kilo.**
- **Colombia** **No tengo ni cinco.**
- **República Dominicana** **No tengo ni un chele.**
- **España** **No tengo un duro.**

16 Comprensión de la obra de teatro

Escuchar
Hablar
Escribir

Contesta las preguntas sobre la escena.

1. ¿Qué se le había ocurrido a Colón al principio del drama?
2. ¿Quién llamó a la puerta y qué le dio a Colón?
3. Según el mensaje, ¿qué hay detrás del horizonte?
4. Según el mensaje, ¿qué ve el que camina?
5. ¿Qué le dice la carta a Colón que haga?
6. ¿Qué necesita Colón para salir de viaje?
7. Al final, ¿por qué Colón sigue leyendo el mensaje?
8. ¿Cómo Colón no quiere cruzar el mar?

17 ¡Un proyecto singular!

Hablar
Escribir

Con tu compañero(a), escribe una lista de características que es probable que tenga una persona interesada en tener una aventura similar a la de Colón. Puede ser la misma aventura de Colón u otra diferente. Puedes escoger aventuras que pasan en el futuro o eventos del presente como la exploración de otros planetas o del fondo *(bottom)* del mar. Luego, escriban una lista de razones lógicas para apoyar el proyecto. Discute las dos listas con tu compañero(a) y luego, preséntenlas en clase.

18 Integración

Leer
Escuchar
Hablar

Lee las reseñas *(reviews)* a una obra de teatro que salieron en una revista de espectáculos. Luego, escucha la opinión de otro crítico en la televisión. Explica si la obra tiene elementos interesantes o no, y por qué.

Fuente 1 Críticas

El mundo es un pañuelo

Campos: Lo que más me gustó de la obra *El mundo es un pañuelo* fue el intermedio. Cuando bajó el telón, me fui a tomar un refresco. Sin duda el escenario y el vestuario son muy buenos. Pero el guión es aburrido y, aunque los actores estaban haciendo todo lo posible, la obra resultó ser un desastre. Recomiendo que no pierdan su tiempo ni su dinero. Se me ocurrió que quizás sea mejor ir a un partido de fútbol.

Ríos: A mí me encantó la nueva obra dramática de Martín Caso. *El mundo es un pañuelo* es lo mejor que ha escrito. El director Alfredo Durán hizo un trabajo genial. La escenografía es fabulosa y el vestuario excelente. El éxito de la obra se debe al guión. Caso entiende lo absurdo de la vida y lo trata con amor y humor. No se pierdan una noche de risa; vayan a ver *El mundo es un pañuelo.*

Fuente 2 Reporte televisivo

Escucha y apunta
- ¿Qué elementos importantes destaca el crítico de la televisión?
- ¿Qué espera el crítico de la televisión?

modelo: El crítico de la televisión destaca los actores y la escenografía. Desea que la próxima obra sea mejor. Para mí hay otros elementos interesantes. En su crítica, Raúl dijo...

19 ¡A escribir!

Escribir

Has decidido mandarle una carta a varias personas, donde describes un proyecto y solicitas dinero y equipo. Describe el tipo de viaje. En el segundo párrafo, explica lo que necesitas y los beneficios de hacer ese viaje.

Writing Criteria	Excellent	Good	Needs Work
Content	Your letter includes many reasons for supporting your trip.	Your letter includes some reasons for supporting your trip.	Your letter includes few reasons for supporting your trip.
Communication	Your letter is organized and easy to follow.	Parts of your letter are organized and easy to follow.	Your letter is disorganized and hard to follow.
Accuracy	Your letter has few mistakes in grammar and vocabulary.	Your letter has some mistakes in grammar and vocabulary.	Your letter has many mistakes in grammar and vocabulary.

Más práctica Cuaderno *pp. 376–377* Cuaderno para hispanohablantes *pp. 378–379*

¿Comprendiste? Un(a) compañero(a) ha decidido pasar un año estudiando español en Argentina pero está un poco preocupado(a). Dale sugerencias para que se sienta mejor.

1. (No sabe si tiene dinero suficiente.) Si se te acaba el dinero...
2. (Teme que no le guste la familia argentina.) No temas que...
3. (No cree que hable suficiente español.) No dudes que...

Lectura literaria

¡AVANZA! **Goal:** Read the final scene of the play about Columbus. Then talk about the challenges and rewards of a venture like Columbus' and its modern-day equivalents.

Para leer 

ESTRATEGIA Leer

Analyze the action Break down this section of the play into parts (see below). Summarize the action in each part.

Parte 1	Parte 2	Parte 3	Parte 4
Colón lee el mensaje en la botella.			
El mensaje dice que debe ir a ver a los reyes.			

Vocabulario para leer

la carabela *barco que utilizó Colón para navegar hasta América*
el desaliento *cansancio, falta de ganas*
la hazaña *acción heroica*
los rumbos *rutas, caminos*
conceder *dar*
el grito *hablar en voz muy alta*
estar harto(a) *estar cansado(a) de algo*

Nota cultural

Sobre la autora **Adela Basch (1946–)**
Nació en Buenos Aires. Su primer trabajo fue traductora de libros del inglés al español. En 1979 escribió su primera obra de teatro, *Abran cancha, que aquí viene don Quijote de la Mancha.* En sus obras, siempre incluye juegos de palabras muy graciosos. En 2002 fundó Ediciones Abran Cancha, una editorial alternativa que promueve el encuentro entre adultos y jóvenes para hablar de temas literarios.

Sobre Colón En español se llama Cristóbal Colón. En inglés se llama Christopher Columbus, pero su nombre original es Cristoforo Colombo. Nació en 1451 en Génova, Italia. El drama que empezaste a leer y que termina en esta sección cuenta su primer viaje a América de una manera divertida.

Colón agarra viaje a toda costa (Parte 4)

Carabelas de Cristóbal Colón, *Daniel Zuloaga*

En esta cuarta y última parte de la obra, Colón, después de leer un mensaje que le mandaron en una botella, decide ir a ver a los reyes[16] de Castilla y Aragón en busca de apoyo financiero para sus planes de viaje...

Colón escucha que alguien llama a su puerta.

Colón:
¿Quién es?

Presentador:
¡Botellerooooo! Perdón, cartero.

Colón sale a la puerta que, por supuesto, está abierta y encuentra una botella con un mensaje. Lo lee en voz alta.

Colón:
Vamos, Colón, el mar te espera. Sea como sea[17], tenés que conseguir tres carabelas. No dejes que el desaliento te inunde el corazón[18]. Andá[19] a ver a los reyes de Castilla y Aragón.

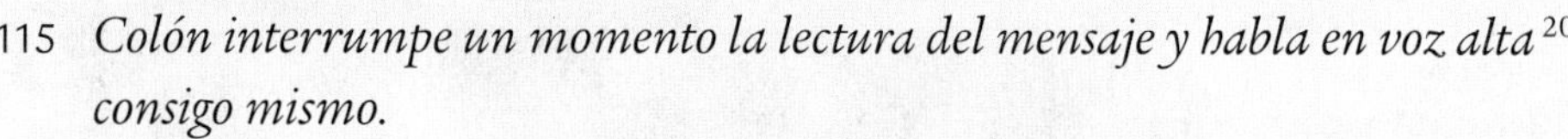

Colón interrumpe un momento la lectura del mensaje y habla en voz alta[20] consigo mismo.

Pero si ya fui como veinte veces y no pasa nada. Siempre me dicen: vuelva otro día, vuelva otro día.

Sigue leyendo el mensaje.

¿Y quién te dijo que hoy no es otro día?

Colón se va. ❖

Presentadora:
¡Atención! ¡Atención!

Presentador:
Vamos a informar a la población.

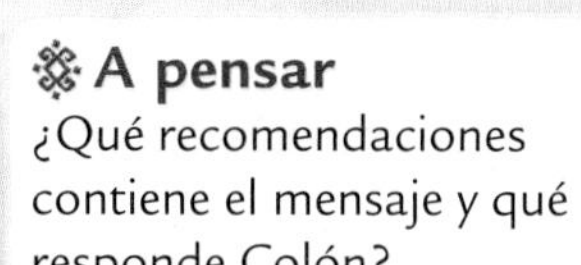

❖ **A pensar**
¿Qué recomendaciones contiene el mensaje y qué responde Colón?

[16] king and queen [17] **Sea...** Any way you can
[18] **te...** flood your heart [19] Go [20] **en...** aloud

Presentadora:
¡Los reyes de Castilla y Aragón han logrado unificar España y se creen capaces de cualquier hazaña! ¡Los reyes de Castilla y Aragón empiezan a soñar con la expansión!

Presentadora:
¡Y ahora tal vez les interese el proyecto de Colón!

Presentador:
¡A la reina de Castilla los bellos ojos le brillan[21] cuando piensa en la otra orilla!

El presentador y la presentadora se van. Y nos encontramos ante la reina de Castilla y el rey de Aragón en sus tronos. Colón entra, hace una reverencia y permanece de pie.

Colón:
¡Salud, altezas[22]! Espero que ahora estén dispuestos a financiar mi empresa. Les ofrezco una aventura insólita y valiente: navegar hacia el oeste para llegar a Oriente. ¡Internarse en el misterio del mar abierto, buscar otros rumbos y otros puertos!

Reina:
Cristóbal Colón, me has convencido. Empezá a prepararte. Tu pedido ha sido concedido.

Presentador:
Las carabelas y sus navegantes van por un camino que nadie tomó antes.

A pensar
¿Cuál es el «camino» a que se refiere el presentador?

Presentadora:
Van a enfrentar lo que nadie ha visto y nadie ha oído. ¡Van al encuentro de lo desconocido!

[21] shine [22] your highness (pl.)

Reflexiona
¿Qué ha logrado Colón hasta este momento?

Colón y su tripulación[23] ya llevan muchos días navegando sin ninguna indicación de las tierras que buscan. Desesperados, los hombres empiezan a quejarse...

Cristóbal Colón muestra la isla Guanahaní a sus marineros

Colón:
¿Qué son esos gritos? ¿Qué pasa?

Luis y Pedro:
¡Que-re-mos vol-ver a ca-sa!

Colón:
Tengan un poco de paciencia. Ya falta poco.

Luis:
¡Qué paciencia ni qué ocho cuartos![24] Ya estamos hartos.

Colón:
¡Qué mar, qué cielo, qué día! ¡Qué mar... avilla! ¡Creo que estamos cerca de la orilla!

Pedro:
¡Tieee... ! ¡Tieeee... ! ¡Tieeeeeeee... !

¡TIERRA! ¡TIERRA! ¡TIERRA!

Presentador:
Estimado público, agradecemos mucho su valiente compañía en esa difícil y osada[25] travesía[26].

Presentadora:
¡Aquí ponemos fin a la navegación y en este momento termina la función!

---

[23] crew [24] **¡Qué...** What do you mean, patience! [25] daring [26] crossing

¿Comprendiste?

1. ¿Cuáles son las mayores dificultades de Colón en hacer su viaje?
2. ¿Quiénes, por fin, financian la expedición y por qué?
3. ¿Por qué crees que la tripulación quiere regresar a casa?
4. ¿Qué significa cuando Pedro dice «Tierra»?

¿Y tú?

1. ¿Adónde te gustaría viajar?
2. ¿Se te ocurrió ir a buscar lugares desconocidos? ¿Cuáles serían?
3. ¿Qué recomendaciones le darías a Colón si fueras el rey o la reina de España?

Escritura

Mi autobiografía

Vas a escribir una autobiografía breve de cinco párrafos. Además de la información personal, como el lugar donde naciste, lugares donde viviste y escuelas a las que fuiste, incluirás experiencias personales.

1 Prepárate para escribir

ESTRATEGIA Haz una lista Escribe los tres sucesos más importantes de tu vida (pueden ser sucesos emocionantes, cómicos, tristes o experiencias interesantes).

2 Escribe

ESTRATEGIA Analiza causa y efecto Usa el siguiente diagrama para analizar cada uno de los tres sucesos que escogiste y ver qué efectos han tenido en tu vida.

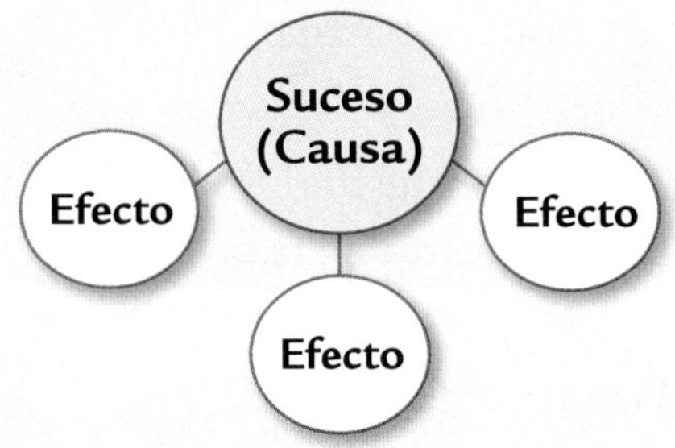

Paso 1 Escribe una introducción breve con tus datos: lugar y año de nacimiento, escuelas, actividades favoritas.

Pasos 2 a 4 Escribe tres párrafos para describir los tres sucesos más importantes de tu vida y cómo te han afectado. Usa la lista de causa y efecto del diagrama.

Cuando tenía diez años, mi familia se mudó a Florida. Fue un suceso muy importante porque allí aprendí muchos deportes acuáticos.

Paso 5 Escribe un párrafo con lo que haces actualmente y lo que esperas en el futuro. Piensa en los tiempos verbales que has aprendido hasta ahora y úsalos.

3 Revisa tu composición

Intercambia tu autobiografía con un(a) compañero(a). Lee la autobiografía de tu compañero(a) y subraya todos los verbos. Para cada verbo, haz lo siguiente:

- Decide si son correctos el tiempo y la conjugación del verbo. Presta atención particular al uso del pretérito y el imperfecto en los párrafos 1 a 4, y al uso del subjuntivo, el condicional y el futuro en el párrafo 5.
- Indica los verbos que tengan errores con un círculo.
- Escribe las correcciones.

> Cuando nací, mi familia (vivió) [vivía] en Missouri.
>
> Una vez, decidieron pasar el día nadando en el río. A mí no me gustaba nadar, por eso les (dijo) [dije] que (fuera) [iba] a quedarme en casa porque me dolía la cabeza. Yo quería tocar la guitarra. Como no quería que ellos se (enteraron) [enteraran] de mis planes, (esperaré) [esperé] hasta que ellos (salieran) [salieron].

Lección 2

En resumen

Vocabulario y gramática

Vocabulario

Read and Interpret a Short Play

el accesorio	*accessory*
el (la) acomodador(a)	*usher*
aplaudir	*to clap*
el diálogo	*dialog*
la dirección de escenografía	*stage direction*
dirigir	*to direct*
el (la) dramaturgo(a)	*playwright*
ensayar	*to rehearse*
el ensayo	*rehearsal*
el escenario	*stage*
la escenografía	*scenery*
el gesto	*gesture*
el guión	*script*
el intermedio	*intermission*
la obra de teatro	*play*
la salida	*exit*
(levantar / bajar) el telón	*(to raise / to lower) the curtain*
el vestuario	*wardrobe*

Other Words and Phrases

avaro(a)	*miserly*
codicioso(a)	*greedy*
el coraje	*courage*
el (la) farsante	*fraud*
insólito(a)	*unusual*
pedir (i) prestado	*to borrow*
persistente	*persistent*
reclamar	*to call, to demand*
singular	*unique*
soñar (ue) con	*to dream of, about*
el (la) tirado(a)	*pauper*

Gramática

Se for Unintentional Occurrences

The **verb** of an unintentional occurrence is expressed with the impersonal pronoun **se** and agrees with the subject. An **indirect object pronoun** indicates the person to whom the action occurred.

Verbs Used to Express Unintentional Occurrences	
acabársele (a uno)	**perdérsele (a uno)**
caérsele (a uno)	**quedársele (a uno)**
ocurrírsele (a uno)	**rompérsele (a uno)**
olvidársele (a uno)	

Se me olvidaron las entradas al teatro.
I forgot the theater tickets.

REPASO Uses of the Subjunctive

The **subjunctive** expresses ideas whose certainty may not be known.

Hope:	**Espero** que él **se dé** cuenta del error.
Doubt:	**Es dudoso** que nosotras **podamos** venir.
Influence:	**Recomendó** que Ana **escribiera** dramas.
Emotion:	**Me alegro de** que los actores **sean** tan buenos.
Unknown:	**Buscamos** actores que **conozcan** el drama.
Conjunctions:	Les enseño **para que sepan** todo. Vete **tan pronto como** Cristina **llegue.** **Aunque llueva,** jugaremos el partido.

Lección 2

Repaso de la lección

¡LLEGADA!

@HomeTutor ClassZone.com

Now you can
- read and interpret a short play
- talk about unplanned occurrences
- express opinions about a text

Using
- **se** for unintentional occurrences
- review: uses of the subjunctive

To review
- vocabulary pp. 478–479

1 Listen and understand

AUDIO

Carmela Castelo hace comentarios de teatro para una emisora de radio de Buenos Aires. Hoy está hablando de su reacción a una nueva obra de teatro. Escucha sus comentarios y luego contesta las siguientes preguntas.

1. Según Carmela Castelo, ¿es buena *El avaro codicioso*?
2. ¿Qué les recomienda Carmela Castelo que hagan a sus radioyentes?
3. ¿Por qué estaba bien que el dramaturgo no estuviera en el teatro?
4. ¿Qué se le ocurrió a Carmela Castelo durante el primer acto?
5. ¿Cuáles son dos aspectos de la producción que le gustaron a Carmela Castelo?
6. ¿Por qué no pudieron bajar el telón el director y los actores?

To review
- review: uses of the subjunctive p. 488

2 Read and interpret a short play

Escoge la palabra apropiada para completar cada oración. Luego cambia el verbo al subjuntivo.

1. Siempre quiero que (los intermedios / los ensayos) (ser) largos. Me gusta tomarme un refresco tranquilamente entre los actos.
2. ¡La ropa es fenomenal! (El maquillaje / El vestuario) es un aspecto importante para que la producción (tener) éxito.
3. Esta obra teatral tiene un (escenario / guión) muy bueno. El clímax es muy misterioso. No creo que la obra (fracasar).
4. Los actores necesitan (entrar / ensayar) más. Es probable que (olvidárseles) las líneas.
5. No me gusta que el público (dirigir / aplaudir) durante una escena.
6. (Los acomodadores / Las direcciones de escenografía) son muy interesantes. Es raro que no (haber) más público en el teatro.

To review
- **se** for unintentional occurrences p. 483

3 Talk about unplanned occurrences

Mira los dibujos para describir qué les pasa a las personas indicadas. Usa **se** y sigue el modelo.

modelo: el técnico / el equipo de sonido
Al técnico se le descompuso el equipo de sonido.

1. 

yo / las líneas

2. 
nosotros / el accesorio

3. 
la directora / gran idea

4. 
tú / el violín

To review
- review: uses of the subjunctive p. 488

4 Express opinions about a text

Escoge la forma correcta de cada verbo para completar las oraciones.

1. La actriz no dudaba que (podía / pudiera) hacer bien el papel.
2. La dramaturga buscaba actores que (conocían / conocieran) sus obras.
3. Es increíble que no (hay / haya) más teatros en esta ciudad.
4. No me gusta que el público (habla / hable) mucho durante el drama.
5. Es obvio que el guión (es / sea) bueno.
6. Todo el público se quedó hasta que (cayó / cayera) el telón.

To review
- **Comparación cultural** pp. 482, 490

5 Theaters in the Southern Cone

Comparación cultural

1. ¿En dónde se hacen tablados?
2. ¿Qué son las murgas? ¿Qué son los tablados? ¿Cómo son?
3. ¿Cómo se llama el teatro más importante de Buenos Aires?
4. ¿Qué estilo tiene ese teatro?

Más práctica Cuaderno *pp. 378–389* Cuaderno para hispanohablantes *pp. 380–389*

Comparación cultural

AUDIO

Cuna de autores famosos

Lectura y escritura

1. **Leer** Rafaela es argentina y Aníbal es chileno. A ellos les gusta mucho la literatura. Lee y compara las descripciones de dos de los autores más notables de sus países, ganadores del Premio Cervantes.

2. **Escribir** Después de leer sobre los autores favoritos de Rafaela y de Aníbal, elige un(a) escritor(a) importante de tu país. Busca información en Internet o en la biblioteca. Luego usa una tabla para organizar la información.

Nombre	Obras	Temas	Género	Premios
Carl Sandburg, Illinois, 1878	*Poemas de Chicago y Abraham Lincoln*	historia	poesía, cuentos	Premio Pulitzer

Paso 1 En Internet o en la biblioteca, busca información sobre un autor importante de tu país.

Paso 2 Organiza la información en una tabla de cinco columnas como la de arriba, incluyendo el nombre del autor, el lugar y el año en que nació, sus obras más importantes, los temas que trataba, los género(s) y sus premios.

Paso 3 Usa la información para escribir un ensayo de tres a cinco párrafos. Incluye una introducción, detalles y tus conclusiones o reflexiones. Luego revisa la gramática y la ortografía.

Compara con tu mundo

Compara el (la) escritor(a) de tu ensayo con los autores mencionados por Rafaela y Aníbal. ¿Tienen estilos parecidos? ¿Qué temas tratan? ¿Cuál es la diferencia más notable entre ellos?

Cuaderno *pp. 390–392* Cuaderno para hispanohablantes *pp. 390–392*

See these pages come alive!

Rafaela

Hola, soy Rafaela Buchman y vivo en Buenos Aires, Argentina. Me encanta la literatura y quiero contarles que tres autores argentinos han ganado el premio Cervantes: Jorge Luis Borges, Ernesto Sábato y Adolfo Bioy Casares. A mí me encanta la obra de Borges, porque es un autor fascinante. Nació en Buenos Aires, vivió en Europa por un tiempo, y luego regresó a Buenos Aires, donde trabajó en la Biblioteca Nacional por muchos años. Escribía en español y en inglés, y sabía mucho latín. Sus cuentos son una mezcla de fantasía y realidad, con imágenes de laberintos, espejos y sueños. Ganó el premio Cervantes en 1979. Cuando aceptó el premio, dijo que «el escritor tiene que sentir, luego soñar, y luego dejar que le lleguen las fabulas».

Argentina

Aníbal

¿Qué tal? Me llamo Aníbal Duarte y soy de Santiago de Chile. Me encanta escribir y pienso estudiar literatura en la Universidad de Santiago. Mi autor favorito es Gonzalo Rojas. Este escritor nació en Lebu, trabajó en el periódico El Tarapacá y luego creó la revista Letras. Estudió derecho en la Universidad de Santiago, dio clases en el Colegio Alemán de Valparaíso y participó en la creación de la universidad de esa ciudad. Fue consejero cultural en China y encargado de negocios en Cuba. Ganó muchísimos premios, entre ellos el Premio Cervantes en el año 2004.

Chile

VIDEO
DVD

EL DESAFÍO

En este último desafío, los equipos deben hacer una pequeña obra de teatro, escrita por ellos mismos. Pueden elegir el tema que quieran. Y pueden usar el vestuario, el maquillaje y los accesorios que prefieran. Pero, tienen que trabajar todos juntos, aunque la puntuación es por equipo.

Antes del video

1. Describe esta foto. ¿Dónde está el profesor? ¿Por qué crees que está allí?

2. ¿Qué está haciendo Marco? ¿Qué crees que necesita?

3. Describe esta foto. ¿Cómo es el escenario? ¿Qué crees que va a pasar allí?

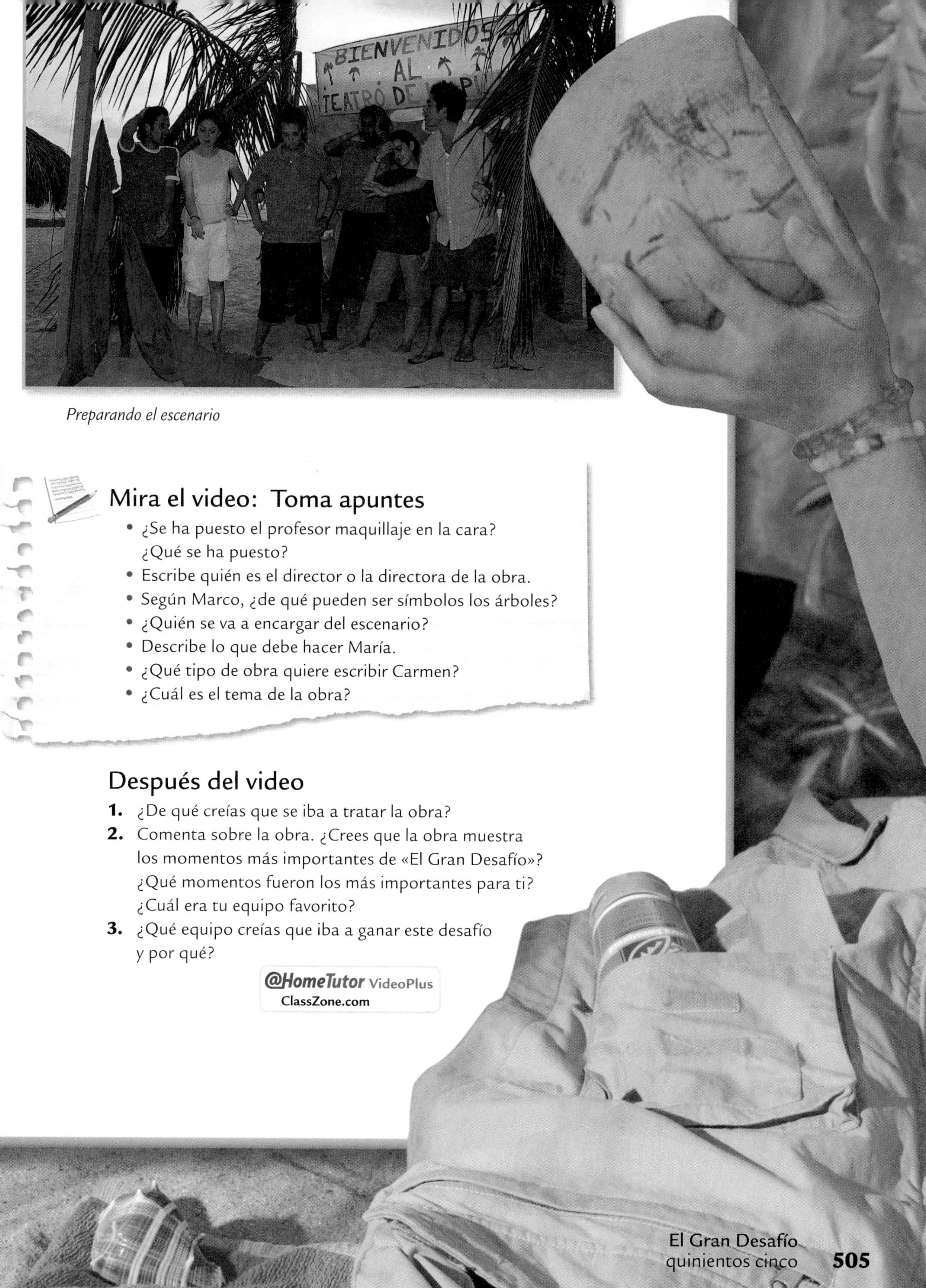

Preparando el escenario

Mira el video: Toma apuntes

- ¿Se ha puesto el profesor maquillaje en la cara? ¿Qué se ha puesto?
- Escribe quién es el director o la directora de la obra.
- Según Marco, ¿de qué pueden ser símbolos los árboles?
- ¿Quién se va a encargar del escenario?
- Describe lo que debe hacer María.
- ¿Qué tipo de obra quiere escribir Carmen?
- ¿Cuál es el tema de la obra?

Después del video

1. ¿De qué creías que se iba a tratar la obra?
2. Comenta sobre la obra. ¿Crees que la obra muestra los momentos más importantes de «El Gran Desafío»? ¿Qué momentos fueron los más importantes para ti? ¿Cuál era tu equipo favorito?
3. ¿Qué equipo creías que iba a ganar este desafío y por qué?

@HomeTutor VideoPlus
ClassZone.com

UNIDADES 1-8

Repaso inclusivo

Options for Review

1 Escucha y comprende

Escuchar
Hablar
Escribir

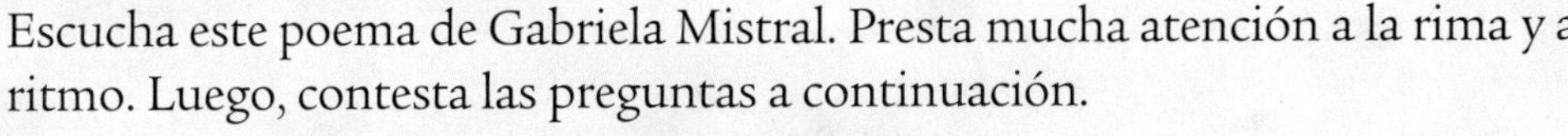

Escucha este poema de Gabriela Mistral. Presta mucha atención a la rima y al ritmo. Luego, contesta las preguntas a continuación.

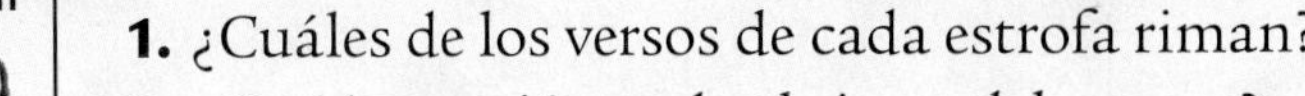

1. ¿Cuáles de los versos de cada estrofa riman?

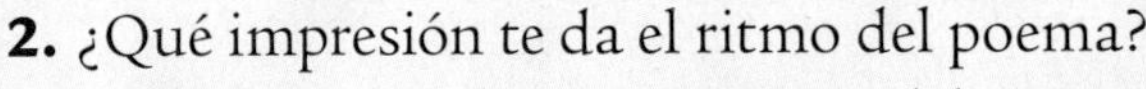

2. ¿Qué impresión te da el ritmo del poema?

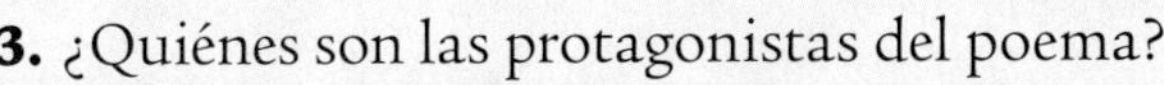

3. ¿Quiénes son las protagonistas del poema?

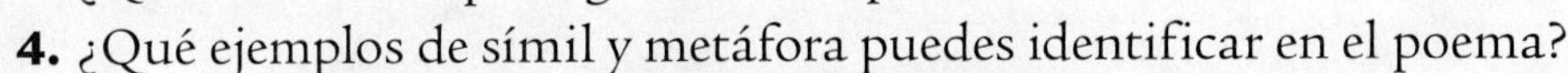

4. ¿Qué ejemplos de símil y metáfora puedes identificar en el poema?
5. ¿Con qué compara la poetisa a las dos niñas del poema?
6. ¿Qué serán las dos chicas al final del poema?

2 Escribe un guión

Escribir
Hablar

Con un(a) o dos compañeros(as), escribe un guión breve para una obra de teatro cómica. Incluye los elementos que debe tener el guión de un drama (nombre de los personajes, escena, narrador, etc.). Escribe sólo el primer acto. Usa expresiones como **se le ocurrió.** Luego presenten el guión a la clase.

3 Planea tus vacaciones

Escribir

Escoge tres lugares adonde te gustaría ir de vacaciones. El primer lugar debe ser una ciudad grande, el segundo un lugar lejos de la ciudad y el tercero un campamento. Escribe un ensayo en que explicas por qué elegiste esos lugares y qué harías en cada uno. Usa el condicional.

4 Escribe un diálogo

Hablar
Escribir

Con tus compañeros forma un grupo de cuatro personas. Cada uno representará a un héroe de la vida diaria (por ejemplo bombero[a], policía, médico[a] o trabajador[a]). Escriban un diálogo donde cada uno empiece con la frase **Si yo fuera** y luego expliquen lo que harían. Los otros miembros del grupo deben decirle cosas como **es importante que...** o **yo quisiera que tú...**

5 Escribe una carta

Escribir

Escríbeles una carta a unos patrocinadores para que donen dinero para un proyecto de acción social que tú organizas. Cuéntales lo que has hecho ya y lo que has planeado. Luego explícales qué harás en el futuro para lograr tus objetivos.

6 Investiga y reporta

Leer
Escribir
Hablar

En Internet, busca un sitio en español sobre los problemas del medio ambiente en Latinoamérica. Imprime la página. Subraya los verbos en el pretérito y haz un círculo alrededor de los verbos en el imperfecto. Luego escribe una lista de mandatos para resolver los problemas que se mencionan en esa página. Léele los mandatos a la clase.

7 Opina

Hablar

Tu compañero(a) y tú son consejeros(as) de una empresa que hace aviones. Ustedes les dan sus opiniones sobre cómo habrán cambiado los aviones en 150 años. Pueden hacer comentarios positivos o negativos. Usen el futuro perfecto para su descripción.

¿?Entre dos

Pair Activities

Folletos

Estudiante A

Tu compañero(a) y tú quieren hacer un folleto para los parques Irsu y Rifi. Tú sabes algunas actividades que pueden hacer en los parques y tu compañero(a) sabe qué otras actividades pueden hacer. Túrnense para preguntar y contestar en qué parque pueden hacer qué actividad.

Estudiante A: ¿Dónde podemos...?

Estudiante B: Podemos... en el parque... ¿Dónde podemos...?

En Rifi puedes...	En Irsu puedes...

Rifi · Irsu · Rifi · Irsu

¿Cuáles de estas actividades hicieron ustedes el año pasado?

Folletos

Estudiante B

Tu compañero(a) y tú quieren hacer un folleto para los parques Irsu y Rifi. Tú sabes algunas actividades que pueden hacer en los parques y tu compañero(a) sabe qué otras actividades pueden hacer. Túrnense para preguntar y contestar en qué parque pueden hacer qué actividad.

Estudiante A: ¿Dónde podemos...?

Estudiante B: **Podemos... en el parque... ¿Dónde podemos...?**

En Rifi puedes...	En Irsu puedes...

Irsu · Rifi · Irsu · Rifi

¿Cuáles de estas actividades hicieron ustedes el año pasado?

Entre dos • Lección 2

El verano pasado

Estudiante A

Ésta es una foto que sacó Elisa, la hermana de Ana. Túrnense tu compañero(a) y tú para preguntar quién hizo las actividades de las fotos el verano pasado y luego contestar con el nombre de la persona.

Estudiante A: ¿Quién...?

Estudiante B: ... ¿Quién...?

¿Quiénes son los más activos?
¿Quiénes son los más tranquilos?

los hermanos menores de Oscar

el nieto menor de Enrique

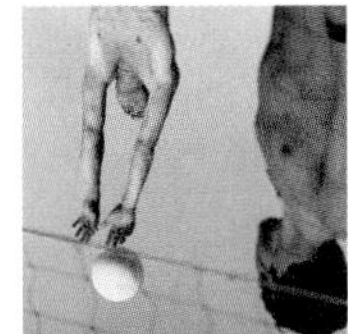

la nuera de Enrique y la tía de Luis

El verano pasado

Estudiante B

Ésta es una foto que sacó Elisa, la hermana de Ana. Túrnense tu compañero(a) y tú para preguntar quién hizo las actividades de las fotos el verano pasado y luego contestar con el nombre de la persona.

Estudiante A: ¿Quién...?

Estudiante B: ... ¿Quién...?

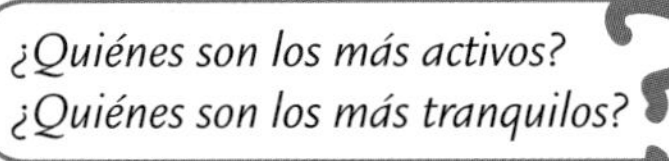

¿Quiénes son los más activos?
¿Quiénes son los más tranquilos?

el cuñado de Elisa

el hermano menor de Luis y el suegro de Ana

el sobrino mayor de Elisa

Entre dos • Lección 1

Proyecto de acción social

Estudiante A

Tu compañero(a) y tú van a elegir a dos estudiantes para organizar la campaña de publicidad para un comedor para gente sin hogar. Túrnense para preguntar y decir qué información falta de los candidatos de las fotos.

Estudiante A: ¿Qué hizo...?

Estudiante B: ... ¿Qué más hizo...?

Con base en esa información, elijan un(a) presidente y un(a) vice presidente.

Estudiante A: ¿A quién eligirías...?

Estudiante B: ... Y tú, ¿a quién...?

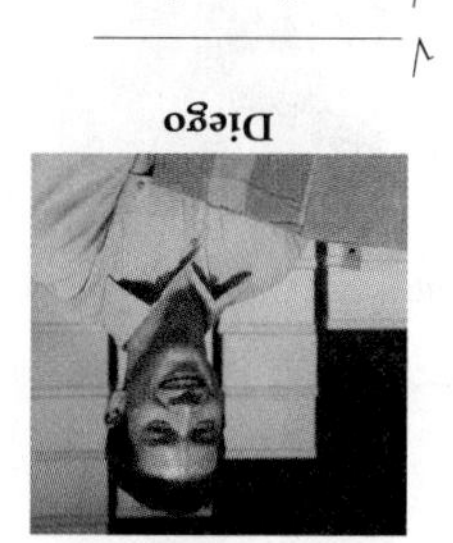

Diego

√ ____________

√ cumplir con los objetivos de reciclaje

Jasmín

√ ____________

√ colaborar en el diseño de anuncios de prensa y radio con mucha creatividad

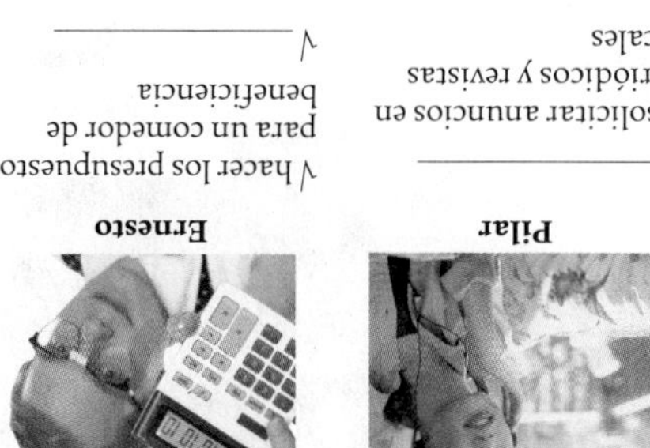

Pilar

√ ____________

√ solicitar anuncios en periódicos y revistas locales

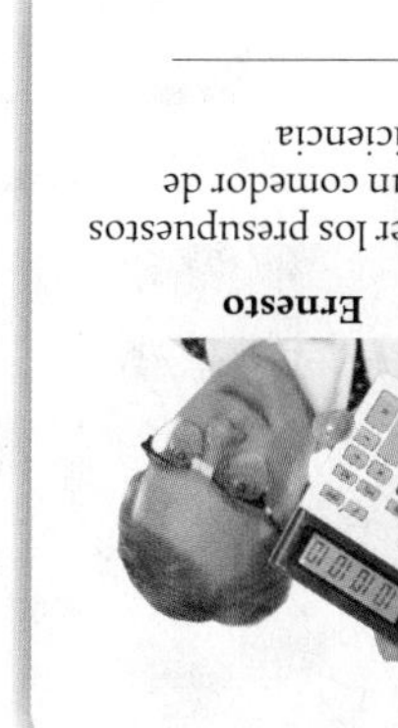

Ernesto

√ hacer los presupuestos para un comedor de beneficiencia

√ ____________

Presidente: ____________

Vice presidente: ____________

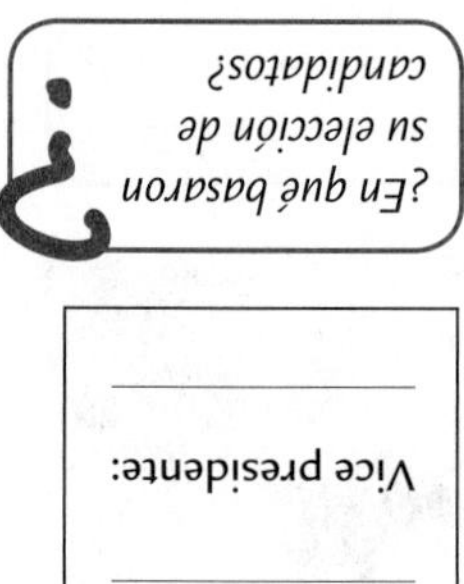

¿En qué basaron su elección de candidatos?

Proyecto de acción social

Estudiante B

Tu compañero(a) y tú van a elegir a dos estudiantes para organizar la campaña de publicidad para un comedor para gente sin hogar. Túrnense para preguntar y decir qué información falta de los candidatos de las fotos.

Estudiante A: ¿Qué hizo...?

Estudiante B: ... ¿Qué más hizo...?

Con base en esa información, elijan un(a) presidente y un(a) vice presidente.

Estudiante A: ¿A quién eligirías...?

Estudiante B: ... Y tú, ¿a quién...?

Diego

√ delegar tareas para cumplir con sus objetivos

√ ____________

Jasmín

√ escribir artículos para proyectos de acción social

√ ____________

Pilar

√ recaudar fondos para su club de teatro

√ ____________

Ernesto

√ ____________

√ organizar los horarios de los voluntarios

Presidente: ____________

Vice presidente: ____________

¿En qué basaron su elección de candidatos?

Entre dos • Lección 2

¡A investigar!

Estudiante A

Con tu compañero(a), túrnense para preguntar y decir qué hicieron las personas de las fotos. Luego reaccionen usando expresiones impersonales con el verbo en infinitivo.

Estudiante A: ¿Qué hizo/hicieron...?

Estudiante B: ...

Estudiante A: Es importante...

	qué hicieron	tu reacción
los editores		
el fotógrafo		
el patrocinador		

la telespectadora

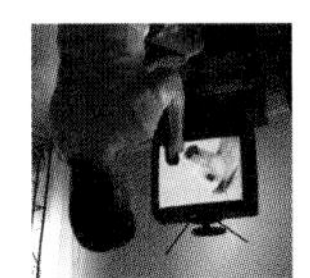

donar para apoyar los programas educativos

el fotógrafo

los editores

la candidata

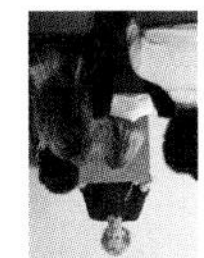

otorgar una entrevista

el patrocinador

el público

comprar los periódicos, sólo leer los titulares

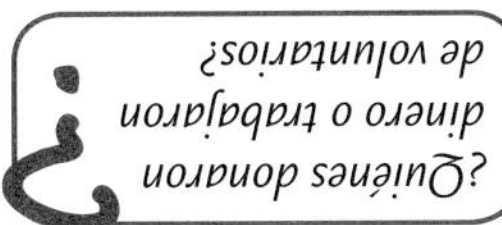

¡A investigar!

Estudiante B

Con tu compañero(a), túrnense para preguntar y decir qué hicieron las personas de las fotos. Luego reaccionen usando expresiones impersonales con el verbo en infinitivo.

Estudiante A: ¿Qué hizo/hicieron...?

Estudiante B: ...

Estudiante A: Es importante...

	qué hicieron	tu reacción
la candidata		
la telespectadora		
el público		

la telespectadora

el fotógrafo

sacar fotos para las reseñas de restaurantes

los editores

elegir las mejores fotos para su reseña

la candidata

el patrocinador

organizar el teletón

el público

¿Quiénes donaron dinero o trabajaron de voluntarios?

Proyectos para el planeta

Estudiante A

Tu compañero(a) y tú trabajan para una agencia de publicidad que quiere patrocinar un proyecto nuevo. Túrnense para preguntar qué proyecto cumple con las preferencias de su agencia, y elige el mejor.

Estudiante A: ¿Qué proyecto...?

Estudiante B: ... ¿Qué proyecto...?

Agencia TeleMerca		
¿Qué proyecto...	Soluciones	Renovación
nvestigará el medio ambiente		
trabajará para disminuir el efecto invernadero		
planificará para eliminar inundaciones		
combatirá la deforestación		

Agencia Míralotodo

Proyecto Terramundo

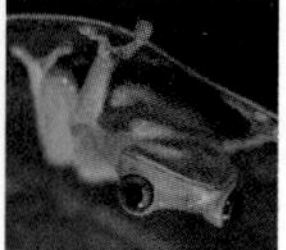
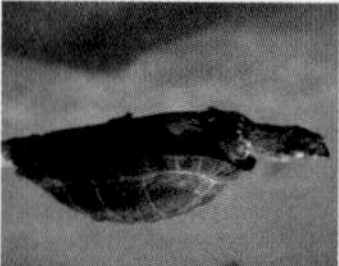

Proyecto Transformación

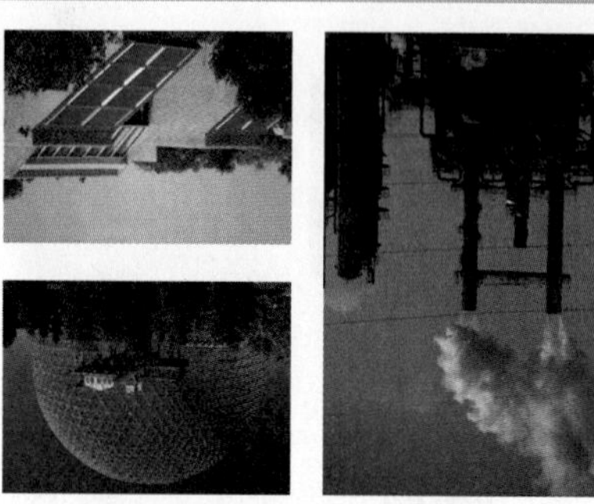

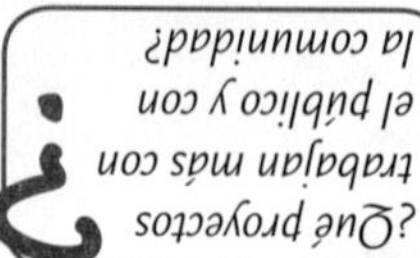

¿Qué proyectos trabajan más con el público y con la comunidad?

Proyectos para el planeta

Estudiante B

Tu compañero(a) y tú trabajan para una agencia de publicidad que quiere patrocinar un proyecto nuevo. Túrnense para preguntar qué proyecto cumple con las preferencias de su agencia, y elige el mejor.

Estudiante A: ¿Qué proyecto...?

Estudiante B: ... ¿Qué proyecto...?

Agencia Míralotodo		
¿Qué proyecto...	Terramundo	Transformación
protegerá especies en peligro de extinción		
informará sobre el medio ambiente		
desarrollará innovaciones con los recursos		
colaborará para reutilizar basura		

Agencia Telemerca

Proyecto Soluciones

Proyecto Renovación

¿Qué proyectos trabajan más con el público y con la comunidad?

Entre dos • Lección 2

Novedades en breve

Estudiante A

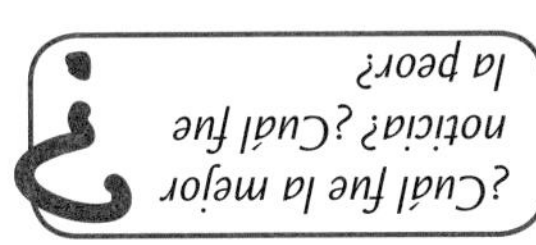

Tu compañero(a) y tú tienen las noticias en breve de dos periódicos digitales sobre novedades en las ciencias. Se desconectan del Internet y no pueden leer el artículo entero. Túrnense para comparar y reaccionar a las noticias según el modelo.

Estudiante A: **¡Qué raro! Según el artículo, penalizaron a... por...**

Estudiante B: **Bueno, parece que... contamina...**

Estudiante A: **Es lógico (raro / una lástima / bueno / necesario / peligroso) que...**

Noticias del rincón científico

Penalizan al científico Robles-Pérez por inventar SolAire, purificador de aire...

Acampa Ocampo comercializa Tiendas EcoAluminio y prospera, critican algunos...

La Recicleta es un fracaso, advierte la organización Ciudadanos Responsables...

Joven de 14 años gana el premio "Científico Modelo" por su Esmógrafo...

¿Cuál fue la mejor noticia? ¿Cuál fue la peor?

Novedades en breve

Estudiante B

Tu compañero(a) y tú tienen las noticias en breve de dos periódicos digitales sobre novedades en las ciencias. Se desconectan del Internet y no pueden leer el artículo entero. Túrnense para comparar y reaccionar a las noticias según el modelo.

Estudiante A: **¡Qué raro! Según el artículo, penalizaron a... por...**

Estudiante B: **Bueno, parece que... contamina...**

Estudiante A: **Es lógico (raro / una lástima / bueno / necesario / peligroso) que...**

Novedades del planeta

Descubren que el SolAire no mejora el aire sino que lo contamina...

La compañía LucEs Oro invierte tres millones de dólares en la Recicleta...

Satisface el Esmógrafo al público: es útil y despierta la conciencia social sobre el smog...

¿Solución para la gente sin hogar? Donan miles de tiendas de campaña de aluminio reciclado...

¿Cuál fue la mejor noticia? ¿Cuál fue la peor?

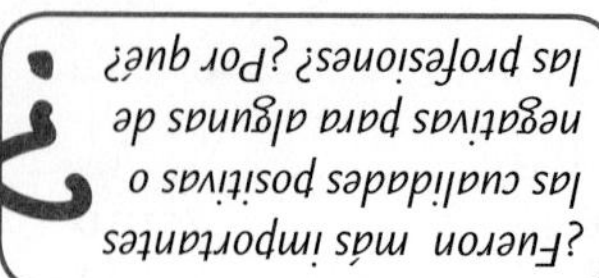

Entre dos • Lección 1

Las cualidades

Estudiante A

Tu compañero(a) y tú trabajan para una agencia de empleo. Para cada puesto, tienen dos candidatos con experiencia similar pero con distintas cualidades. Túrnense para juntar la información y decidir qué candidato es el mejor para cada puesto.

Estudiante A: ¿Cómo es...?

Estudiante B: Es... ¿Cómo es...?

Estudiante B: Sugiero que ... porque...

Estudiante A: Estoy de acuerdo. (No estoy de acuerdo. Prefiero que... porque...)

Puesto	Candidato	Cualidades	Candidato	Cualidades
Trabajador social	**Karin**		**Pedro**	trabajador simpático un poco desorganizado
Detective	**Óscar**	atrevido comprensivo un poco presumido	**Agustín**	
Programador	**Juana**		**Manuel**	simpático brillante un poco perezoso
Piloto	**Carmen**	sobresaliente organizada muy competitiva	**Paula**	

¿Fueron más importantes las cualidades positivas o negativas para algunas de las profesiones? ¿Por qué?

Las cualidades

Estudiante B

Tu compañero(a) y tú trabajan para una agencia de empleo. Para cada puesto, tienen dos candidatos con experiencia similar pero con distintas cualidades. Túrnense para juntar la información y decidir qué candidato es el mejor para cada puesto.

Estudiante A: ¿Cómo es...?

Estudiante B: Es... ¿Cómo es...?

Estudiante B: Sugiero que ... porque...

Estudiante A: Estoy de acuerdo. (No estoy de acuerdo. Prefiero que... porque...)

Puesto	Candidato	Cualidades	Candidato	Cualidades
Trabajador social	**Karin**	paciente modesta un poco tímida	**Pedro**	
Detective	**Óscar**		**Agustín**	considerado dedicado un poco orgulloso
Programador	**Juana**	sincera razonable un poco inconsiderada	**Manuel**	
Piloto	**Carmen**		**Paula**	ingeniosa práctica un poco tímida

¿Fueron más importantes las cualidades positivas o negativas para algunas de las profesiones? ¿Por qué?

Entre dos • Lección 2

¿Qué profesión tiene?

Estudiante A

Tu compañero(a) y tú quieren adivinar las profesiones de las personas del cuadro. Antes de preguntarse qué hace cada persona, identifiquen la profesión de las personas en las fotos y piensen en algunas pistas. Luego, túrnense para preguntar y decir qué hacen las personas y adivinar *(guess)* su profesión.

Estudiante A: ¿Qué hace...?

Estudiante B: Trabaja con... (Apaga... / Protege...)

Estudiante A: ¿Es...?

	¿Qué hace / lleva / usa?	Profesión
Álvaro		
Graciela		
Felipe		
Beni		

Mario

Patricia

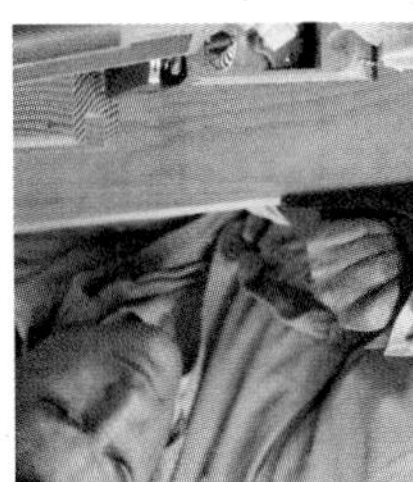
Álex

Luis

¿Quiénes tienen profesiones artísticas? ¿Quiénes tienen que mantenerse en forma?

¿Qué profesión tiene?

Estudiante B

Tu compañero(a) y tú quieren adivinar las profesiones de las personas del cuadro. Antes de preguntarse qué hace cada persona, identifiquen la profesión de las personas en las fotos y piensen en algunas pistas. Luego, túrnense para preguntar y decir qué hacen las personas y adivinar *(guess)* su profesión.

Estudiante A: ¿Qué hace...?

Estudiante B: Trabaja con... (Apaga... / Protege...)

Estudiante A: ¿Es...?

	¿Qué hace / lleva / usa?	Profesión
Mario		
Patricia		
Álex		
Luis		

Álvaro

Graciela

Felipe

Beni

¿Quiénes tienen profesiones artísticas? ¿Quiénes tienen que mantenerse en forma?

Entre dos • Lección 1

Nos falta...

Estudiante A

Cuando llegan a Perú, tu compañero(a) y tú no tienen todas las cosas que necesitan y piensan comprarlas por Internet. Tu compañero(a) busca en sitios de computación y cámaras mientras tú buscas en sitios de ropa y accesorios. Túrnense para preguntar si los sitios web tienen lo que buscan.

Estudiante A: ¿Tienen... que...?

Estudiante B: Sí, (No, no) tienen... ¿Tienen... que...

— cartera / (yo) poder usar para guardar el pasaporte — bolsa / servir para llevar una computadora portátil — paraguas / resistir vientos fuertes — gafas de sol / transformar la energía solar en electricidad

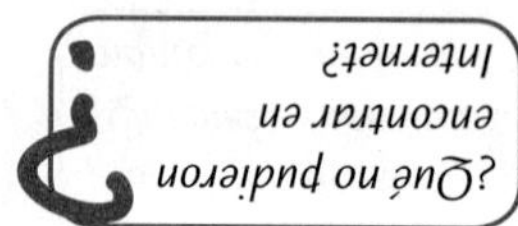

Lo que encuentras en sitios de computación y cámaras

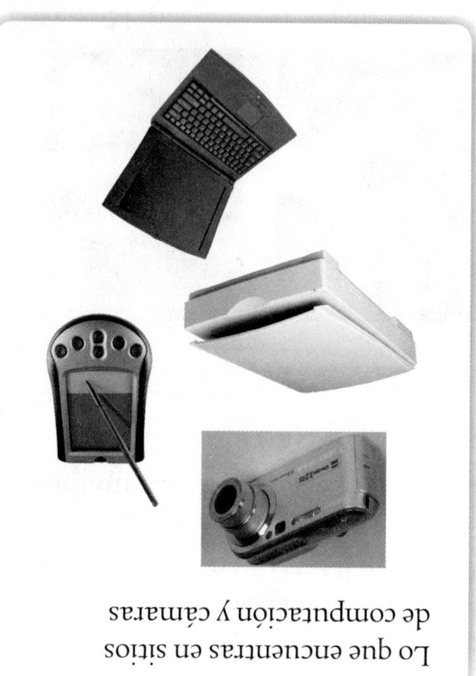

Nos falta...

Estudiante B

Cuando llegan a Perú, tu compañero(a) y tú no tienen todas las cosas que necesitan y piensan comprarlas por Internet. Tu compañero(a) busca en sitios de computación y cámaras mientras tú buscas en sitios de ropa y accesorios. Túrnense para preguntar si los sitios web tienen lo que buscan.

Estudiante A: ¿Tienen... que...?

Estudiante B: Sí, (No, no) tienen... ¿Tienen... que...

— computadora portátil / tener una pantalla ancha — agenda electrónica / no llamar la atención *(attract attention)* — cámara digital / ser más pequeña que un teléfono celular — escáner / (yo) poder esconder en la cómoda

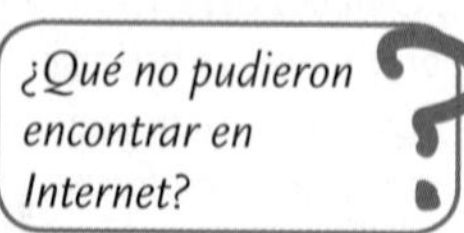

Lo que encuentras en sitios de ropa y accesorios

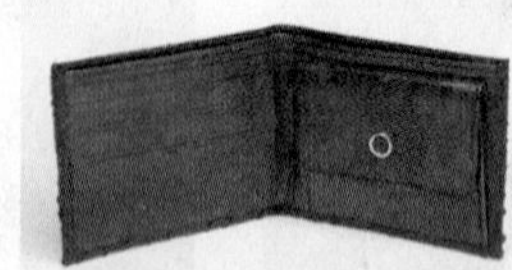

Entre dos • Lección 2

Si pudiéramos...

Estudiante A

Tu compañero y tú están hablando de cómo vivirían o qué harían si tuvieran la oportunidad. Túrnense para preguntar y decir cómo viviría o qué haría cada uno según el modelo.

Estudiante A: ¿Qué harías si tuvieras la oportunidad?

Estudiante B: **Pues, jugaría más a... con... Y tú, ¿qué harías...? (Y tú, ¿qué más harías?)**

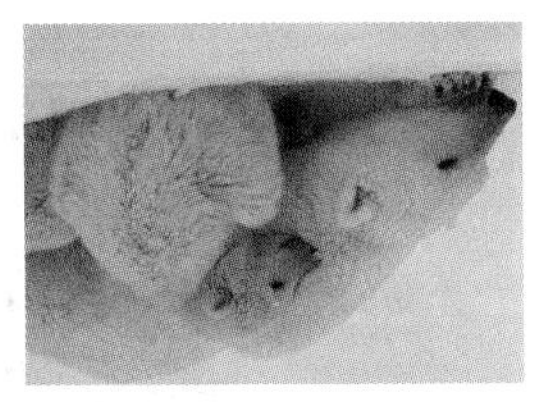

¿Quién trabajaría más para ayudar a la comunidad o el planeta?

Si pudiéramos...

Estudiante B

Tu compañero y tú están hablando de cómo vivirían o qué harían si tuvieran la oportunidad. Túrnense para preguntar y decir cómo viviría o qué haría cada uno según el modelo.

Estudiante A: ¿Qué harías si tuvieras la oportunidad?

Estudiante B: **Pues, jugaría más a... con... Y tú, ¿qué harías...? (Y tú, ¿qué más harías?)**

¿Quién trabajaría más para ayudar a la comunidad o el planeta?

Entre dos • Lección 1

¿Qué has hecho?

Estudiante A

Tu compañero(a) se mudó a un barrio nuevo hace dos semanas. Tú quieres saber si conoce bien el vecindario. Pregúntale qué ha hecho según las pistas del cuadro y decide si lo conoce bien o no.

Estudiante A: ¿Has...?

Estudiante B: Sí, ya (No, todavía no) he...

no: 30 min. sí

no: al final sí

Luego, mira las fotos y contesta las preguntas de tu compañero(a) sobre los preparativos para una fiesta que vas a dar en tu casa hoy.

Estudiante A: ¿Has...?

Estudiante B: **Sí, ya (No, todavía no) he... (Voy a...)**

¿Has...?	sí	no
dar una vuelta por la plaza		
probar los pasteles de la pastelería		
pasar por correos		
ver los periódicos en el kiosco		
Conclusión: Sí (No) lo conoce bien, pero (y) tiene que...		

¿Qué criterios usaron para llegar a su conclusión? ¿Por qué?

¿Qué has hecho?

Estudiante B

Hace dos semanas que te mudaste a un barrio nuevo. Contesta las preguntas de tu compañero(a) con base en las fotos.

Estudiante A: ¿Has...?

Estudiante B: **Sí, ya (No, todavía no) he...**

sí no

no sí

Tu compañero(a) está preparándose para hacer una fiesta hoy. Hazle preguntas según el cuadro para saber como podrás ayudar.

Estudiante A: ¿Has...?

Estudiante B: **Sí, ya (No, todavía no) he... (Voy a...)**

¿Has...?	sí	no
comprar la comida		
limpiar el baño		
sacar la basura		
preparar el pastel		
Conclusión: Podré ayudar a...		

¿Qué criterios usaron para llegar a su conclusión? ¿Por qué?

Entre dos • Lección 2

En vías paralelas

Estudiante A

Tu compañero(a) y tú quieren poner las fotos de sus viajes en orden cronológico. Túrnense para preguntar y decir qué hicieron antes, después, primero, etc.

Estudiante A: ¿Qué hiciste antes de tomar el tren?

Estudiante B: Antes, yo... ¿Y qué hiciste después de...?

FOTOS DE TU COMPAÑERO(A)

Fotos de tu compañero(a)

¿? ¿? ¿?

Tus fotos

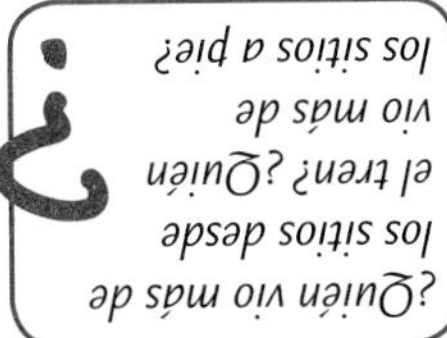

¿Quién vio más de los sitios desde el tren? ¿Quién vio más de los sitios a pie?

En vías paralelas

Estudiante B

Tu compañero(a) y tú quieren poner las fotos de sus viajes en orden cronológico. Túrnense para preguntar y decir qué hicieron antes, despues, primero, etc.

Estudiante A: ¿Qué hiciste antes de tomar el tren?

Estudiante B: Antes, yo... ¿Y qué hiciste después de...?

FOTOS DE TU COMPAÑERO(A)

Fotos de tu compañero(a)

¿? ¿?

Tus fotos

¿Quién vio más de los sitios desde el tren? ¿Quién vio más de los sitios a pie?

Entre dos • Lección 1

Anuario para los graduados

Estudiante A

Tu compañero(a) y tú están redactando el anuario. Tienen dos fotos para cada persona: una de su niñez y una de este año. Túrnense para preguntar y decir qué hacía y cómo era cada persona de niño(a), y qué hizo este año. Luego reaccionen usando expresiones impersonales como **Es increíble (lógico/asombroso/sorprendente) que...**

Estudiante A: ¿Qué hacía... de niño(a)? ¿Cómo era?

Estudiante B: ... ¿Qué hizo... este año?

Estudiante A: Es increíble que...

¿Cuáles de los graduados cambiaron más? ¿Cuáles menos?

CARLA

actuar en cinco dramas y dirigir un drama

FELIPE

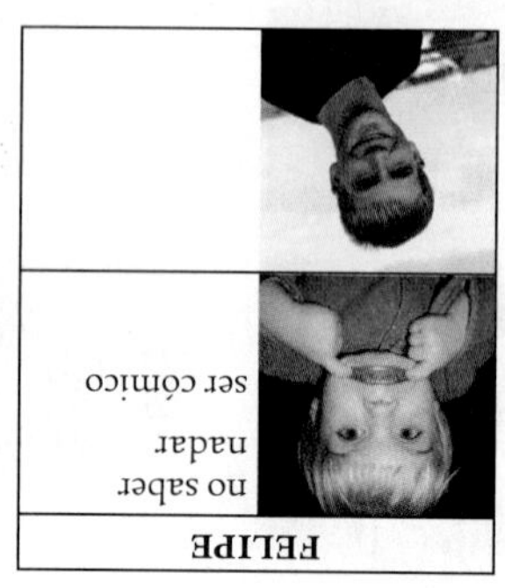

no saber nadar

ser cómico

REBECA

ser la estrella del equipo de fútbol

RUBÉN

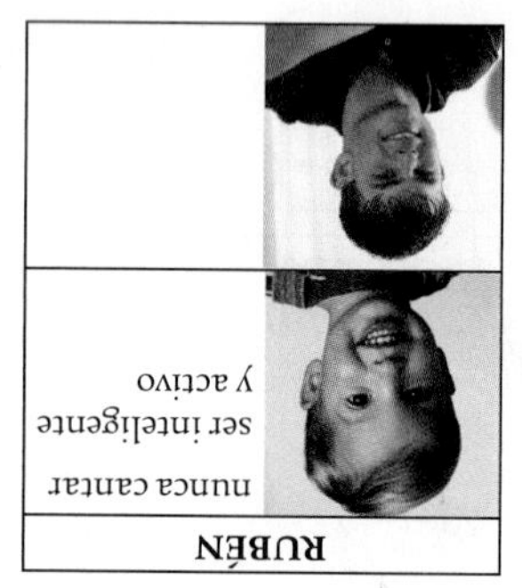

nunca cantar

ser inteligente y activo

Anuario para los graduados

Estudiante B

Tu compañero(a) y tú están redactando el anuario. Tienen dos fotos para cada persona: una de su niñez y una de este año. Túrnense para preguntar y decir qué hacía y cómo era cada persona de niño(a), y qué hizo este año. Luego reaccionen usando expresiones impersonales como **Es increíble (lógico/asombroso/sorprendente) que...**

Estudiante A: ¿Qué hacía... de niño(a)? ¿Cómo era?

Estudiante B: ... ¿Qué hizo... este año?

Estudiante A: Es increíble que...

¿Cuáles de los graduados cambiaron más? ¿Cuáles menos?

CARLA

jugar en el campo

ser tímida y simpática

FELIPE

entrenarse para salvavidas

REBECA

practicar muchos deportes

ser atlética

RUBÉN

tomar parte en el coro de estudiantes

Entre dos • Lección 2

Las carreras

Estudiante A

Tu compañero(a) y tú son consejeros en la universidad. Túrnense para

- preguntar y decir qué cualidades e intereses tienen los estudiantes
- sugerir la mejor carrera para cada estudiante, usando una frase con **Si es..., podrá...**
- explicar por qué no recomendaron la otra carrera, usando una frase con **Si fuera..., podría...**

Estudiante A: ¿Cómo es...?

Estudiante B: **Es... Le interesa(n)...**

Estudiante A: Si es... y si le interesa(n)..., podrá ser...

Estudiante B: **Estoy de acuerdo. Si fuera (más/menos)..., podría ser...**

	Juanita	Rosa	Victoria	Rodrigo	Luis	Elena
Cualidades			extrovertida, independiente	ambicioso, no intelectual		atrevida, buena escritora
Intereses			cosmetología, artes	matemáticas		derecho, noticias
Posibles carreras	profesora / agente de la bolsa	trabajadora social / médica			ingeniero / arquitecto	abogada / periodista

Entre dos Unidad 7

Las carreras

Estudiante B

Tu compañero(a) y tú son consejeros en la universidad. Túrnense para

- preguntar y decir qué cualidades e intereses tienen los estudiantes
- sugerir la mejor carrera para cada estudiante, usando una frase con **Si es..., podrá...**
- explicar por qué no recomendaron la otra carrera, usando una frase con **Si fuera..., podría...**

Estudiante A: ¿Cómo es...?

Estudiante B: **Es... Le interesa(n)...**

Estudiante A: Si es... y si le interesa(n)..., podrá ser...

Estudiante B: **Estoy de acuerdo. Si fuera (más/menos)..., podría ser...**

	Juanita	Rosa	Victoria	Rodrigo	Luis	Elena
Cualidades	intelectual, no ambiciosa	impaciente, estudiosa			artístico , no muy práctico	
Intereses	matemáticas	anatomía, biología			geometría, edificios	
Posibles carreras			peluquera / dueña de una peluquería	profesor / agente de la bolsa		abogada / periodista

¿Hay alguien que podría seguir las dos carreras? ¿Quién(es)?

Entre dos • Lección 1

El club de lectura

Estudiante A

Tú compañero(a) y tú están hablando de la reunión del club de lectura. Túrnense para preguntar y decir qué estaban haciendo todos al final de la reunión. Sigan el modelo.

Estudiante A: ¿Quién estaba buscando cuentos con ilustraciones...?

Estudiante B: Fue... ¿Quién estaba...?

Víctor / cuento

Elena / ensayo

Ramón / estrofa

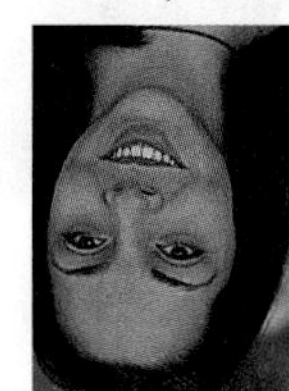
Luisa / cuento policíaco

Alfredo / símil (metáfora)

¿quién?	buscar cuentos con ilustraciones
¿quién?	leer una obra de la vida de Cervantes
¿quién?	criticar el fin de un cuento
¿quién?	preparar una reseña de una obra de 23 capítulos
¿quién?	disfrutar de la rima y ritmo de sus versos favoritos

¿Quiénes deberían colaborar en proyectos literarios? ¿Por qué?

El club de lectura

Estudiante B

Tú compañero(a) y tú están hablando de la reunión del club de lectura. Túrnense para preguntar y decir qué estaban haciendo todos al final de la reunión. Sigan el modelo.

Estudiante A: ¿Quién estaba...?

Estudiante B: ... ¿Quién estaba...?

Ana / biografía

Carlos / libro de historietas

María / poesía

Pablo / novela

Marisol / desenlace

¿quién?	narrar los sucesos de un crimen misterioso
¿quién?	recitar parte de un poema
¿quién?	comparar los estilos de dos autores en un análisis literario
¿quién?	hablar de comparaciones de nubes *(clouds)* a animales
¿quién?	describir el contexto de una narrativa corta

¿Quiénes deberían colaborar en proyectos literarios? ¿Por qué?

Entre dos • Lección 2

¿Qué dicen las reseñas?

Estudiante A

Tu compañero(a) y tú están leyendo reseñas sobre una obra de teatro antes de ir a verla. Túrnense para hacerse preguntas y reaccionar según las pistas del cuadro. Contesten según la información de las fotos.

Estudiante A: ¿Cuál es...?

Estudiante B: Es... ¿Quiénes son...?

Estudiante A: Son... ¿Quién...?

Estudiante B: ...

Estudiante A: Espero que... (Es importante/ raro/ bueno/ una lástima que...)

Tú preguntas...	Tú reacción
cuál / ser / obra de teatro / y / quién / ser / dramaturgo	
quién / dirigir / obra de teatro	
quiénes / ensayar / mucho	
a quiénes / olvidárseles / guión	

¿Piensan ver esta obra de teatro o preferirían investigar otras? Expliquen su respuesta.

Jaime y Lupe

los miembros de la Sociedad de Bellas Artes

el dueño del periódico

Mariana y Agustín

¿Qué dicen las reseñas?

Estudiante B

Tu compañero(a) y tú están leyendo reseñas sobre una obra de teatro antes de ir a verla. Túrnense para hacerse preguntas y reaccionar según las pistas del cuadro. Contesten según la información de las fotos.

Estudiante A: ¿Cuál es...?

Estudiante B: Es... ¿Quiénes son...?

Estudiante A: Son... ¿Quién...?

Estudiante B: ...

Estudiante A: Espero que... (Es importante/ raro/ bueno/ una lástima que...)

Tú preguntas...	Tú reacción
quiénes / ser / actores principales	
quiénes / hacer el papel de / farsantes codiciosos y avaros	
quiénes / ser / patrocinadores	
alguien / reclamar / que / no venderle / más entradas / quién	

¿Piensan ver esta obra de teatro o preferirían investigar otras? Expliquen su respuesta.

Shakespeare

César y Alejandro

Rodrigo

Martín, Alfredo y Sonia

Entre dos
Unidad 8

Recursos

Unidad 1
Lección 1

Expansión de vocabulario

Vamos a acampar

Ya sabes

Sports

el básquetbol	basketball
el béisbol	baseball
el ciclismo	bicycle racing
el fútbol americano	football
la natación	swimming
el tenis	tennis
el voleibol	volleyball

Travel

el boleto	ticket
confirmar el vuelo	to confirm a flight
el equipaje	luggage
hacer la maleta	to pack a suitcase
la identificación	identification
el itinerario	itinerary
la maleta	suitcase
el pasaporte	passport
pasar por la aduana	to go through customs
pasar por seguridad	to go through security
el reclamo de equipaje	baggage claim
la tarjeta de embarque	boarding pass
viajar	to travel

Prepositions of location

al lado (de)	next to
cerca (de)	near
debajo (de)	under
delante (de)	in front (of)
dentro (de)	inside (of)
detrás (de)	behind
encima (de)	on (top of)
frente a	across from
lejos (de)	far (from)

Expansión de vocabulario

Outdoor activities

la linterna	flashlight
la sudadera (con capucha)	(hooded) sweatshirt
los pantalones deportivos	sweatpants
los guantes	gloves
la bufanda	scarf

Travel

alquilar un auto	to rent a car
cambiar dinero	to exchange money
hacer un recado / una diligencia	to run an errand
la estación de servicio	service station
echar gasolina	to get gasoline
llenar el tanque	to fill the tank
la grúa	tow truck
la multa	parking ticket, fine

Nature

el lago	lake
la laguna	pond
el arroyo	creek
la bahía	bay
la península	peninsula
el bosque húmedo / tropical	rain forest

Animals

el oso	bear
el ciervo	deer
la ardilla	squirrel
la hormiga	ant
el mosquito	mosquito
la mosca	fly
la abeja	bee

Unidad 1 Lección 2

Expansión de vocabulario

Vamos a la playa

Ya sabes

Beach activities

bucear	to scuba-dive
el mar	sea
nadar	to swim
la playa	beach
tomar el sol	to sunbathe
el traje de baño	bathing suit

Family

la abuela	grandmother
el abuelo	grandfather
la hermana	sister
el hermano	brother
la hija	daughter
el hijo	son
la madre	mother
el padre	father
el (la) primo(a)	cousin
la tía	aunt
el tío	uncle

Family vacations

el alojamiento	lodging
estar de vacaciones	to be on vacation
la habitación	hotel room
la habitación individual	single room
la habitación doble	double room
hacer / tener una reservación	to make / to have a reservation
el hotel	hotel
ir de vacaciones	to go on vacation
ver las atracciones	to go sightseeing
visitar un museo	to visit a museum

Expansión de vocabulario

Beach activities

la silla para recostarse	beach chair
la arena	sand
las piedras	pebbles
el delfín	dolphin
el tiburón	shark
la ballena	whale
la foca	seal
el (la) salvavidas	lifeguard

Snack foods and drinks

el batido	milkshake
el helado en barquillo	ice-cream cone
las papitas	chips
las galletas saladas	crackers
las galletitas	cookies
el chicle	chewing gum
los dulces	candy
la limonada	lemonade

Family relationships

divorciado(a)	divorced
la mamá	mom
el papá	dad
el (la) medio(a) hermano(a)	half brother / half sister
el (la) hermanastro(a)	stepbrother / stepsister
el (la) hijo(a) único(a)	only child
adoptivo(a)	adopted
los (las) gemelos(as)	twins

Pets

la mascota	pet
el conejo	rabbit
la rana	frog
el hámster	hamster

¡Todos para uno y uno para todos!

Ya sabes

Money

el dinero	money
el dinero en efectivo	cash
el dólar	dollar
el euro	euro
la tarjeta de crédito	credit card

Media

Internet	Internet
el radio	radio
la televisión	television
el televisor	television set

Expressions of frequency

de vez en cuando	once in a while
muchas veces	often, many times
mucho	a lot
nunca	never
siempre	always
todos los días	every day

Expansión de vocabulario

Money

el trabajo a tiempo parcial	part-time job
las monedas	coins
los billetes	bills, notes
los centavos	cents
el cheque de pago de sueldo	paycheck
el estipendio (semanal)	(weekly) allowance

Media

el editorial	publishing company
la empresa de mercadeo	marketing company

Advertisements

contestar un anuncio	to answer an ad
el cartel	poster
la encuesta	survey
el eslogan	slogan

Volunteer activities

hacer una pasantía	to be an intern
la guardería de niños	day-care center
la caridad	charity
la caminata con fondos para caridad	charity walk
la carrera con fondos para caridad	charity race
el (la) tutor(a)	tutor
dar tutoría	to tutor
el centro para la comunidad	community center
el asilo para animales	animal shelter
limpiar las jaulas	to clean cages
la silla de ruedas	wheelchair
entrenar los perros guías	to train guide dogs
leerles a los ciegos	to read to the blind
el lenguaje de señas	sign language

Organizing

el requisito	requirement

Unidad 2 Lección 2

Expansión de vocabulario

¿Cómo nos organizamos?

Ya sabes

Community

ayudar	to help
celebrar	to celebrate
compartir	to share

Expressing opinions

Creo que sí.	I think so.
Creo que no.	I don't think so.
En mi opinión...	In my opinion . . .
Es buena idea / mala idea.	It's a good idea / bad idea.
Me parece que...	It seems to me . . .
necesitar	to need
pensar (ie)	to think
preferir (ie)	to prefer
querer (ie)	to want

Expansión de vocabulario

Television

el (la) presentador(a)	host
el reality show	reality show
el programa de concursos	game show
el programa de variedad	variety show
el talk show	talk show
la telenovela	soap opera
el programa matutino	morning show
el programa nocturno	late-night show
la canción tema	theme song

Editorial work

redactar	to compose
la redacción	essay
el borrador	rough draft

Telethon

sonar (ue)	to ring
Se desconectó la llamada.	My call was cut off.
La línea está ocupada.	The line is busy.
Los teléfonos no dejan de sonar.	The phones are ringing off the hook.
colgar (ue) el teléfono	to hang up the phone
La llamada no quiere entrar.	I can't get through.
el número gratis	toll-free number

Unidad 3 Lección 1

Expansión de vocabulario

¿Cómo será el futuro?

Ya sabes

Social action

comenzar (ie)	to begin
fracasar	to fail
pedir (i)	to ask for
poder (ue)	to be able, can
servir (i)	to serve
tener éxito	to be successful

Social responsibilities

limpio(a)	clean
limpiar	to clean
el problema	problem
sucio(a)	dirty
vivir	to live

Expansión de vocabulario

Outer space

el continente	continent
la luna	moon
el espacio	space
la nave espacial	spaceship
el extraterreste	alien

Environment

el (la) guardabosques	forest ranger
los incendios forestales	forest fires
el humo	smoke
el huracán	hurricane
el cartón	cardboard
el vidrio	glass
el mundo	world
la vida	life
la energía	energy

Endangered species

la ballena	whale
la tortuga	turtle
la foca	seal
el manatí	manatee
el jaguar	jaguar
el panda	panda
el águila	eagle

Social responsibilities

el seguro (de salud, de auto, de vida)	insurance (health, car, life)

Unidad 3 Lección 2

Expansión de vocabulario

Por un futuro mejor

Ya sabes

Social awareness

aprender	to learn
enseñar	to teach
importar	to be important
interesar	to interest
recomendar (ie)	to recommend

Impersonal expressions

Es bueno...	It's good . . .
Es importante...	It's important . . .
Es necesario...	It's necessary . . .

Expansión de vocabulario

Inventions

el telecomando, el control remoto	remote control
el robot	robot
automático(a)	automatic
poderoso(a)	powerful
el poder	power
el televisor de pantalla plasma	plasma-screen TV
el vehículo híbrido	hybrid vehicle
los consumidores	consumers

Social awareness

el partido (republicano, demócrata, independiente)	(Republican, Democratic, Independent) party
el (la) presidente	president
el (la) vicepresidente	vice president
el alcalde, la alcaldesa	mayor
el (la) gobernador(a)	governor
el (la) senador(a)	senator
el (la) representante	representative
el (la) juez	judge
las leyes	laws
la constitución	constitution

Unidad 4 Lección 1

Expansión de vocabulario

¿Quién te inspira?

Ya sabes

Personality characteristics

artístico(a)	artistic
atlético(a)	athletic
cómico(a)	funny
desorganizado(a)	disorganized
estudioso(a)	studious
heroico(a)	heroic
inteligente	intelligent
organizado(a)	organized
perezoso(a)	lazy
serio(a)	serious
simpático(a)	nice
trabajador(a)	hard-working
valiente	brave

Role models

el héroe	hero
la heroína	heroine

Professions

el (la) agente de viajes	travel agent
el (la) auxiliar de vuelo	flight attendant
el (la) camarógrafo(a)	cameraman / camerawoman
el (la) deportista	sportsman / woman
el (la) director(a)	director
el (la) director(a) de la escuela	school principal
el (la) guionista	screenwriter
el (la) maestro(a)	teacher

Expansión de vocabulario

Personality characteristics

listo(a)	clever, smart
callado(a)	quiet
extrovertido(a)	outgoing
tonto(a)	silly
travieso(a)	mischievous
talentoso(a)	talented
creativo(a)	creative
ambicioso(a)	ambitious
motivado(a)	motivated
apasionado(a)	passionate
animado(a)	animated, upbeat
optimista	optimistic
pesimista	pessimistic

Features

canoso(a)	gray-haired
calvo(a)	bald
el pelo oscuro	dark hair
el pelo ondulado	wavy hair
el pelo rizado	curly hair
el pelo lacio	straight hair
los frenillos	braces
los rayitos	highlights
la cola de caballo	ponytail
llevar el pelo suelto	to wear your hair down
el flequillo	bangs
las trenzas	braids

Unidad 4 Lección 2

Expansión de vocabulario

¿Quiénes son los héroes?

Ya sabes

Everyday people

el (la) amigo(a)	friend
la chica	girl
el chico	boy
el (la) estudiante	student
el hombre	man
la mujer	woman
la persona	person

Emotions

cansado(a)	tired
contento(a)	content
deprimido(a)	depressed
emocionado(a)	excited
enojado(a)	angry
nervioso(a)	nervous
ocupado(a)	busy
tranquilo(a)	calm
triste	sad

Expansión de vocabulario

Goals

el aprecio	recognition
jubilarse	to retire
ganarse la lotería	to win the lottery
encontrar la cura para...	to find the cure for . . .
el cáncer, el SIDA, la enfermedad del corazón	cancer, AIDS, heart disease
obtener un postgrado	to get a graduate degree
disfrutar de...	to enjoy . . .
viajar por el mundo	to travel the world

Professions

el (la) banquero(a)	banker
el (la) recepcionista	receptionist
el (la) intérprete	interpreter
el (la) comediante	comedian
el (la) autor(a)	author
el (la) decorador(a) de interiores	interior designer
el (la) diseñador(a) de modas	fashion designer
el (la) diseñador(a) gráfico(a)	graphic designer
el (la) cirujano(a)	surgeon
el (la) trabajador(a) de limpieza	custodian
el (la) agente (de deportes, de talento)	(sports, talent) agent
el (la) agente de relaciones públicas	public relations agent
el (la) agente de servicio al cliente	customer service agent
el (la) planificador(a) (de eventos, de bodas)	(event, wedding) planner
el bailarín, la bailarina	dancer
el (la) anunciador(a)	announcer
el (la) consejero(a)	guidance counselor
el jefe, la jefa	boss

Unidad 5 Lección 1

Expansión de vocabulario

Comuniquémonos entre naciones

Ya sabes

Clothing

el abrigo	coat
la blusa	blouse
las botas	boots
los calcetines	socks
la camisa	shirt
la camiseta	T-shirt
el chaleco	vest
la chaqueta	jacket
el cinturón	belt
la falda	skirt
la gorra	cap
los jeans	jeans
los pantalones	pants
los pantalones cortos	shorts
la pulsera	bracelet
la ropa	clothing
las sandalias	sandals
el sombrero	hat
el suéter	sweater
el traje	suit
el vestido	dress
los zapatos	shoes

Technology

la dirección electrónica	e-mail address
escribir correos electrónicos	to write e-mails
estar en línea	to be online
hacer clic en	to click on
el icono	icon
el mensajero instantáneo	instant messaging
el ratón	mouse
el software	software
el teclado	keyboard

Expansión de vocabulario

Personal possessions

el reproductor de mp3 (eme pe tres)	mp3 player
el llavero	key chain
la licencia de conducir	driver's license
el permiso de conducir	driver's permit
los audífonos	headphones
el casillero	locker
los lentes de contacto	contact lenses
el álbum de fotos	photo album
regalar	to give (as a gift)
el tesoro	treasure
brillante	shiny
opaco(a)	dull

Technology

cortar y pegar	to cut and paste
borrar	to delete
el archivo adjunto	attachment
la sonrisa, la carita feliz (emoticono)	smiley face (emoticon)
escribir a máquina	to type
charlar en línea	to chat online
la cadena de e-mail	e-mail chain (forward)
arroba	@ (at)
punto com	.com (dot com)
el blog	blog
comenzar (ie) / terminar la sesión	to log on / to log off
la memoria	memory
funcionar	to work, function
arreglar	to fix
programar	to program
el virus	virus
el idioma	language

Unidad 5 Lección 2

Expansión de vocabulario

Nuevos amigos, nuevas oportunidades

Ya sabes

After-school activities

andar en patineta	to skateboard
caminar	to walk
el centro comercial	shopping center, mall
escuchar música	to listen to music
jugar al fútbol	to play soccer
leer un libro	to read a book
levantar pesas	to lift weights
mirar la televisión	to watch television
montar en bicicleta	to ride a bike
pasar un rato con los amigos	to spend time with friends
practicar deportes	to practice / play sports
el tiempo libre	free time
tocar la guitarra	to play the guitar

Entertainment

el cine	movie theater; the movies
el concierto	concert
la fiesta	party
la gala	gala; formal party
el partido	. . . game
de básquetbol	basketball . . .
de béisbol	baseball . . .
de fútbol	soccer . . .
la película...	. . . film
de aventuras	action
de ciencia ficción	science fiction
de fantasía	fantasy
de terror	horror

Expansión de vocabulario

Leisure activities

hacer un crucigrama	to do a crossword puzzle
hacer un rompecabezas	to do a puzzle
practicar yoga	to practice yoga
pintar	to paint
coser	to sew

Work

la presentación	presentation
aplazar las responsabilidades	to procrastinate
la sala de conferencias	boardroom
el podio	podium
hacer una lluvia de ideas	to brainstorm
mientras	while

Atmosphere

incómodo(a)	uncomfortable
tenso(a)	tense

Instruments

el piano	piano
la flauta	flute
el saxofón	saxophone
el tambor	drum
la trompeta	trumpet
el violín	violin

Music

el rap	rap
alternativa	alternative
la música electrónica	electronic music, techno
el ritmo	rhythm
la letra	lyrics

Unidad 6 Lección 1

Expansión de vocabulario

La vida en la ciudad

Ya sabes

Parts of a home

el apartamento	apartment
el armario	closet; armoire
la casa	house
la cocina	kitchen
el comedor	dining room
el cuarto	room; bedroom
la escalera	stairs
el jardín	garden
el patio	patio
el piso	floor (of a building)
la planta baja	ground floor
la sala	living room

Furniture

la alfombra	rug
la cama	bed
las cortinas	curtains
el espejo	mirror
la lámpara	lamp
los muebles	furniture
el sofá	sofa, couch

Chores

barrer el suelo	to sweep the floor
cortar el césped	to cut the grass
darle de comer al perro	to feed the dog
hacer la cama	to make the bed
lavar los platos	to wash the dishes
limpiar la cocina	to clean the kitchen
pasar la aspiradora	to vacuum
planchar la ropa	to iron
poner la mesa	to set the table
los quehaceres	chores
sacar la basura	to take out the trash

Expansión de vocabulario

Apartment building

el ascensor	elevator
la escalera mecánica	escalator
el parqueo subterráneo	underground parking
el (la) conserje	building custodian
la calefacción	heating
el aire acondicionado	air conditioning
el (la) proprietario(a)	landlord

Parts of a home

el traspatio	backyard
la cerca	fence
el garaje	garage
el patio español	back porch
el sótano	basement

Furniture and other items

la almohada	pillow
la mecedora	rocking chair
la bombilla	light bulb
el despertador	alarm clock
la videograbadora	VCR
el congelador	freezer
el triturador de basura	garbage disposal

In the neighborhood

el centro de restaurantes de comida rápida	food court
la heladería	ice-cream shop
el salón de belleza	beauty salon
la peluquería	hair salon, barbershop
la juguetería	toy store
la tienda de discos	music store
el campo de golf	golf course
el municipio	town hall, city hall
la discoteca	discotheque
el centro recreativo	recreation center

Unidad 6 Lección 2

Expansión de vocabulario

Fuera de la ciudad

Ya sabes

City life

la acera	sidewalk
la avenida	avenue
el barrio	neighborhood
la catedral	cathedral
la ciudad	city
la cuadra	city block
el edificio	building
la estación de tren	train station
la oficina de turismo	tourist office
la parada de autobús	bus stop
la plaza	plaza; square
el rascacielos	skyscraper
tomar un taxi	to take a taxi

Rural life

acampar	to camp
el (la) agricultor(a)	farmer
la agricultura	agriculture
dar una caminata	to hike
hacer una excursión	to go on a day trip
la montaña	mountain
montar a caballo	to ride a horse
pasear	to go for a walk
pescar	to fish

Life in the past

antiguo(a)	ancient
la civilización	civilization
la estatua	statue
la herramienta	tool
el monumento	monument
la pirámide	pyramid
la religión	religion
las ruinas	ruins
el templo	temple
la tumba	tomb

Expansión de vocabulario

In the country

la granja	farm
el granero	barn
las llanuras	plains, fields
el pasto	grass
la oveja	sheep
la vaca	cow
el toro	bull

On the train

la cortina	curtain
el asiento reservado	reserved seat
facturar las maletas	to check baggage
el asiento reclinable	reclining seat
la bandeja	tray

In the city

la bandera	flag
el garaje público	public parking garage
el parquímetro	parking meter
la calle sin salida	dead end
el desvío	detour
la calle de una vía	one-way street
el semáfaro	stoplight
el cruce	crosswalk
el transvía	trolley
el peatón	pedestrian
la zona peatonal	pedestrian-only zone
la arquitectura	architecture
el diseño	design
la estructura	structure
... está en remodelación	. . . is being remodeled
el asfalto	asphalt
el concreto	concrete
el ladrillo	brick
el acero	steel

Unidad 7 Lección 1

Expansión de vocabulario

Recuerdos

Ya sabes

School activities

estudiar	to study
el examen	exam
hacer la tarea	to do homework
sacar una buena / mala nota	to get a good / bad grade
tomar apuntes	to take notes

Health and fitness

doler (ue)	to hurt, to ache
fuerte	strong
hacer ejercicio	to exercise
herido(a)	hurt
mantenerse (ie) en forma	to stay in shape
la salud	health
saludable	healthy; healthful
sano(a)	healthy
seguir (i) una dieta balanceada	to follow a balanced diet

Expansión de vocabulario

School activities

recordar (ue)	to remember
olvidar	to forget
la detención	detention
el recreo	recess
la asamblea	assembly
un día libre por la nieve	snow day
¿Me puede dar una nota de permiso?	Can I have a hall pass / permission slip?

Sports

los deportes de pista y campo	track and field
correr a campo traviesa	to run cross-country
el (la) porrista	cheerleader
la gimnasia	gymnastics
hacer snowboard	to snowboard
saltar	to jump
hacer trucos	to do tricks
el hockey	hockey

Balanced diet

las grasas	fats
los carbohídratos	carbohydrates
las proteínas	protein

Part-time jobs

el (la) dependiente	salesclerk
el (la) tutor(a)	tutor
el (la) lavaplatos	dishwasher
el (la) árbitro(a)	referee
el (la) interno(a)	intern
el (la) ayudante	assistant
el (la) camarero(a) de hotel	housekeeper
el (la) cadi	caddie

Unidad 7 Lección 2

Expansión de vocabulario

Nuevos principios

Ya sabes

School subjects

el arte	art
las ciencias	science
el español	Spanish
la historia	history
el inglés	English
las matemáticas	math

Businesses

el almacén	department store
la farmacia	pharmacy
la heladería	ice-cream shop
la joyería	jewelry store
la librería	bookstore
la panadería	bakery
la pastelería	pastry shop
la zapatería	shoe store

Skills

bailar	to dance
cantar	to sing
cocinar	to cook
correr	to run
dibujar	to draw
editar	to edit
escribir	to write

In business

la hoja de vida	résumé
la carta de presentación	cover letter
el préstamo	loan
el contrato	contract
las ganancias	profits
despedir (i)	to fire
el mercadeo	marketing

Expansión de vocabulario

Career possibilities

la medicina	medicine
la filosofía	philosophy
la comunicación	communication
la biología	biology
la física	physics
la literatura	literature
el periodismo	journalism
la psicología	psychology
la computación	computer science
la educación (primaria, secundaria)	(elementary, secondary) education
las artes y letras	liberal arts
la matrícula	tuition
la ayuda financiera	financial aid

Professions

el (la) ingeniero(a) (civil, mecánico, químico)	(civil, mechanical, chemical) engineer
el (la) psicólogo(a)	psychologist
el (la) nutricionista	nutritionist
el (la) granjero(a)	farmer
el (la) estilista de modas	fashion stylist
el (la) asistente dental	dental hygenist
el (la) optometrista	optometrist
el (la) terapeuta (físico[a])	(physical) therapist

beneficios	benefits
días personales	personal days
jubilación privada	pension plan
seguro médico	medical insurance
sueldo	salary

Cuentos y poesía

Ya sabes

Literary terms

el argumento	plot
contar (ue)	to tell (a story)
la leyenda	legend
el mensaje	lesson; message
la narración	narration
el personaje	character

Time and frequency

el año pasado	last year
anteayer	the day before yesterday
antes de	before
a veces	sometimes
después (de)	afterward; after
durante	during
entonces	then; so
frecuentemente	frequently
generalmente	in general; generally
hoy	today
luego	later; then
mañana	tomorrow
más tarde	later on
el mes pasado	last month
normalmente	usually; normally
por fin	finally
primero	first
la semana pasada	last week

Expansión de vocabulario

Books and reading

el club de lectura	book club
la tarjeta de la biblioteca	library card
el (la) antagonista	antagonist
el (la) crítico(a)	critic
el reconocimiento	recognition, acknowledgment

Discuss and critique literature

surreal	surreal
clásico(a)	classic
moderno(a)	modern
horrible	horrible
repetitivo(a)	repetitive
intenso(a)	intense
complejo(a)	complex
sencillo(a)	simple
chistoso(a)	funny
cautivador(a)	captivating
trágico(a)	tragic
irónico(a)	ironic
poco original	not very original, unoriginal
deslumbrante	dazzling
obvio(a)	obvious, predictable
el suspenso	suspense
el sueño	dream

Unidad 8 Lección 2

Expansión de vocabulario

El drama

Ya sabes

Evaluative terms

aburrido(a)	boring
agrio(a)	sour
barato(a)	inexpensive
bueno(a)	good
caliente	hot (temperature)
delicioso(a)	delicious
divertido(a)	fun
dulce	sweet
fino(a)	fine
fresco(a)	fresh
interesante	interesting
malo(a)	bad
picante	spicy
sabroso(a)	tasty
salado(a)	salty
único(a)	unique

Theater

el actor	actor
la actriz	actress
la comedia	comedy
el (la) director(a)	director
el drama	drama
la escena	scene
el guión	screenplay
hacer un papel	to play a role

Useful words

demasiado	too; too much
desde	from
entre	between
hasta	to
si	if
sobre	about
tal vez	perhaps, maybe
todavía	still; yet

Expansión de vocabulario

Personal opinion phrases

Admiro la manera en que...	I admire the way . . .
Supongo que...	I am assuming that . . .
Perdí el interés cuando...	I lost interest when . . .
Me simpatiza el papel de...	I like the role of . . .
lo fascinante	the fascinating thing
Es evidente que...	It's evident that . . .
tomar en cuenta que	to take into account that
lo interesante	the interesting thing
por ejemplo	for example
darse cuenta de	to realize

Theater

ponerse de pie para aplaudir	to give a standing ovation
el reparto	cast
el director de reparto	casting director
los ejercicios de calentamiento	warm-ups
el auditorio	auditorium
el disfraz	costume
la máscara	mask
la peluca	wig
la base	foundation
el rubor	blush
el pintalabios, el lápiz	lipstick
el rímel	mascara
la sombra de ojos	eye shadow

Para y piensa

Self-Check Answers

Lección preliminar

p. 5

A Lucía le gusta estar en casa, navegar por Internet, estar en línea y escribir.

A Lucía no le gusta acampar, hacer la tarea o hacer cola.

p. 9

1. Nosotros somos estudiantes.
2. Yo salgo para México.
3. Ella está emocionada.
4. Ellos van a pescar.

p. 11

1. Yo vengo.
2. Juan entiende.
3. Ustedes compiten.
4. Tú cuentas.
5. Yo tengo.
6. Ellas dicen.

p. 15

1. No conozco Miami.
2. Soy estudiante.
3. Beto está enojado.

p. 19

1. Yo me ducho.
2. Paco se levanta.
3. Nosotros nos acostamos.
4. Tú te vistes.

p. 24

1. Soy menor que Rosa.
2. Soy más alto(a) que Rosa.
3. Tengo tantos amigos como Rosa.

Unidad 1

p. 34

Answers will vary. Possible answers include:

1. la estufa de gas, la olla, el saco de dormir, la tienda de campaña
2. hacer caminatas, hacer una excursión, escalar montañas

p. 36

1. navegar por rápidos- sí
2. tomar transporte público- no
3. escalar montañas- sí
4. meterse en la tienda de campaña- no

p. 39

1. Yo utilicé la estufa de gas.
2. Los vendedores ofrecieron un descuento.
3. Nosotros seguimos el sendero.
4. Yo pagué la tarifa más barata.

p. 41

1. organizó
2. viajaron
3. usé

p. 44

1. ¿Tuvieron descuentos en las tarifas?
2. ¿Pusieron el equipo en la camioneta?
3. ¿Durmieron bien en el saco de dormir?

p. 47

1. Tuviste que enfocarte en el equipo necesario.
2. ¡Fue como un problema de lógica!
3. El padre le prestó la camioneta.

p. 51

Answers will vary. Sample responses include:

1. El autor usa el título "Hermandad" porque siente una relación con la naturaleza.
2. Al principio, el autor tiene la actitud de que comparado con la grandeza del cielo de la noche, él es muy pequeño. Al final, después de recibir "un mensaje" de las estrellas, se siente parte de este universo enorme.
3. El autor cambia el orden de los elementos en el título y en la última línea de cada estrofa para describir los papeles de los elementos en los procesos naturales y para ilustrar que cada elemento de la naturaleza tiene una relación con y depende de los otros.
4. La conclusión del poema "Viento, agua, piedra" describe que los elementos de la naturaleza tienen una calidad transitoria.

p. 60

1. hacer surf- sí
2. pararse en la orilla- no
3. merendar- no
4. ver el amanecer- sí

p. 62

1. Sergio, Olga y Rosita se marearon.
2. Llevaron los chalecos salvavidas durante el viaje entero.
3. Sandra conoció a Santiago, un surfista.

p. 65

Answers will vary. Sample responses include:

1. Mi familia pasaba las vacaciones en la playa.
2. Nosotros nos reuníamos con mis abuelos, navegábamos en velero y jugábamos al voleibol playero. Nos quedábamos en un hotel con vista del mar.

p. 67

1. se refrescaban
2. se recostaba
3. observaba
4. pensaba

p. 70

Answers will vary. Students must use preterite verbs in their answers to numbers 1 and 3. In their answer to number 2, the first verb must be in the preterite and the following verbs must be in the imperfect. Sample responses include:

1. Yo fui a Cancún.
2. Cuando llegué, hacía sol y calor.
3. Yo me recosté en la playa, nadé en el mar y recogí caracoles en la orilla.

p. 73

1. fui
2. era, hizo
3. miraba, pensaba

p. 77

Answers will vary. Sample responses include:

1. Tita y su familia vivían en el rancho de Mamá Elena.
2. Todas las mujeres de la familia participaban en la preparación del chorizo.
3. Planchar, bordar y coser ropa eran actividades diarias de las mujeres.
4. Pedro Muzquiz era el señor que quería venir a hablar con Mamá Elena para pedir la mano de Tita.
5. La relación entre Mamá Elena y sus hijas era una de represión. Sus hijas sentían que no tenían mucha independencia y que tenían que estar en casa y cuidar de ella.

Unidad 2

p. 94

Answers will vary. Sample responses include:

1. Los voluntarios organizan campañas para solicitar dinero para ayudar a la gente pobre o sin hogar, ayudan en los hospitales y los hogares de ancianos y limpian los parques y las calles.
2. Anuncios en la prensa, en las emisoras de radio o en los canales de televisión son medios de comunicación útiles para las campañas.
3. En mi comunidad, puedo recoger y reciclar periódicos, revistas, papel, latas, botellas y bolsas de plástico.

p. 96

1. Profesor, ¿podría no darnos ninguna tarea esta noche?
2. Mamá y Papá, ¿podrían comprarme un carro?
3. ¿Podrías ayudarme en la planificación de un proyecto?

p. 99

Answers will vary. Sample responses include:

Ven a los eventos sociales de la escuela.
Sé simpático(a) a otros estudiantes.
Habla con los estudiantes en tus clases para hacer amigos.
No seas tímido(a).
¡No comas la comida de la cafetería!
No llegues tarde a las clases.

p. 101

Answers will vary. Sample responses include:

Colabora con un grupo escolar y organiza un evento para estudiantes.
Ayuda a recoger basura en la escuela.
Sé voluntario(a) para solicitar dinero para actividades y excursiones.
No olvides que es importante ser parte de la comunidad escolar.
¡No vengas a las reuniones si no quieres trabajar!
¡No seas perezoso(a); da tu tiempo para mejorar la escuela!

p. 104

1. Pongan los platos en las mesas.
2. Encienda la estufa.
3. Preparen la comida.

p. 107

Answers will vary. Sample response:

Para estudiar para un examen, organiza todas las cosas que necesitas, como libros y apuntes. Lee los apuntes y escribe preguntas importantes sobre lo que no sabes muy bien. No tengas prisa. Busca la información en el libro y repásala otra vez. No olvides pedirle ayuda a un compañero de clase si la necesitas.

p. 111

Answers will vary. Sample responses include:

1. Barbarita fue a ver a Tita porque se asustó mucho.
2. Tita le dio una taza de tilo para calmarla.
3. Barbarita estaba repasando el preámbulo a la constitución y abriendo la puerta de la nevera para sacar un refresco cuando apareció San Guiven.
4. San Guiven traía un pavo debajo del brazo y le pidió a Barbarita empezarle una colecta y hacerle un santuario.
5. Barbarita aceptó la misión y piensa hacer más latas para la colecta con la ayuda de Tita.

p. 120

Answers will vary. Sample response:

Para mí, las partes más importantes de un periódico son los artículos de opinión, las reseñas de libros y películas y la columna de consejos.

p. 122

1. titular- sí
2. cita- sí
3. gráfica- sí
4. columna de consejos- no
5. carta al editor- sí
6. foto- sí

p. 125

1. Sí, descríbela./ No, no la describas.
2. Sí, publícalas./ No, no las publiques.
3. Organízalos mañana./ No los organices hoy.
4. Sí, envíamelas./ No, no me las envíes.

p. 127

1. díganos
2. dénnoslo
3. no los olvides
4. no lo traduzca

p. 130

Answers will vary. Possible responses include:

1. Fue bueno apoyar la teletón.
2. Es importante escribir una carta al editor.
3. Es necesario incluir subtitulación para sordos en los programas.

p. 133

Answers will vary. Possible responses include:

1. Es buena idea traer unas cámaras de video.
2. ¡Vean la generosidad de todos!

p. 137

Answers will vary. Sample responses include:

1. Son muchas las personas que felicitan al papá la mañana de su cumpleaños.
2. Cuando todos desfilan por la recámara para presentar sus respetos al Papá, la narradora y sus papás están bajo las sábanas y todavía no se han vestido. Todos los demás ya están vestidos.
3. Papá no quiere despertarse. Mamá tiene vergüenza porque dice que se ve horrible. La narradora se siente atrapada; que no puede levantarse hasta que todos hayan felicitado a Papá.
4. El papel de la abuela en la celebración es supervisar los buenos deseos de todo el mundo.
5. La narradora describe a la abuela como enojona y dice que la regaña por estar en el mismo cuarto de sus padres. La relación entre la mamá y la abuela parece difícil. Se queja de ella, pero Papá no le hace caso. Sin embargo, es obvio que la abuela lo quiere mucho a su hijo y a su familia.

Unidad 3

p. 154

Answers will vary. Sample responses include:

1. Las sustancias químicas en el aire y el daño a la capa de ozono causan el smog y la contaminación.
2. Podemos usar recursos naturales, como el sol y el viento para reemplazar los recursos no renovables. También, podemos desarollar innovaciones para proteger la capa de ozono y disminuir los riesgos de la contaminación.

p. 156

los temblores- no las inundaciones- sí
el smog- no los derrumbes- sí

p. 159

1. Mis abuelos descansarán en la playa.
2. Yo iré al museo con mi hermana.
3. Nosotros volveremos a la seis.
4. Mi madre querrá cenar a las siete.

p. 161

Answers will vary. Possible answers include:

Viviremos en una ciudad protegida contra el medio ambiente.

Las ciudades estarán dentro de un globo de vidrio.

La contaminación será tan fuerte que no podremos salir al aire libre.

La capa de ozono no nos protegerá del sol.

No tendremos recursos no renovables.

No habrá árboles ni flores, ni plantas.

Los autos volarán y usarán la energía solar; no necesitarán gasolina.

p. 164

1. El desarollo excesivo no es bueno para el medio ambiente.
2. En nuestro viaje, pasamos por zonas de mucha erosión.
3. Quiero ir a Honduras por el buen tiempo y para ver Copán.

p. 167

Answers will vary. Possible responses include:

1. A Nicolás le interesa un proyecto relacionado con la energía solar porque sabe que no tendremos suficiente petróleo para los vehículos en el futuro. Él piensa que necesitaremos más innovaciones tecnológicas para solucionar el problema y quiere hacer lo que pueda para mejorar la situación.
2. Usan la energía solar para secar los granos de café.

p. 171

Answers will vary. Sample responses include:

1. Las edades que menciona el autor son la niñez, la juventud y la vejez.
2. Según el autor, los niños pueden comer caramelos, jugar y cazar estrellas y mariposas. La juventud es un tiempo lleno de imaginación, sueños y descubrimiento. La vejez es un tiempo de contemplar las experiencias y de tener la sabiduría que sólo pertenece a los ancianos.
3. Según el autor, la felicidad de una persona depende de su actitud.
4. La conclusión del ensayo significa que todas las partes de la vida son especiales; cada edad tiene sus propios encantos.

p. 180

Answers will vary. Sample response:

Para prosperar, una persona o un negocio debe invertir su tiempo y su dinero en una manera responsable. Tiene que respetar la ley y también los valores de la sociedad.

p. 182

Answers will vary. Sample response:

Un producto nuevo debe ser novedoso. Debe satisfacer las necesidades específicas del público.

p. 185

Answers will vary. Sample responses include:

1. Es mejor que una compania tenga una conciencia social a que sólo quiera satisfacer a los inversionistas.
2. Es importante que protejamos nuestros recursos naturales.
3. Es raro que no todas las personas cuiden el medio ambiente.

p. 187

1. Es preferible que los inventos solucionen un problema y despierten la conciencia social.
2. Es necesario que cada participante llene una solicitud y mande una foto.

p. 190

Answers will vary. Sample answers include:

1. Es increíble que haya un canal que conecta a los océanos Atlántico y Pacífico.
2. Es difícil que vayas a la playa para nadar en el invierno.
3. Es mejor que usted. invierta dinero en las compañías que cuidan el medio ambiente.
4. Es imprescindible que los doctores nos adviertan de los peligros de no comer comidas nutritivas.

p. 193

Answers will vary. Sample responses include:

1. MejorAire es un invento novedoso porque puede ayudar mucho a los atletas que tienen problemas respiratorios. Es importante que los atletas sepan si la calidad del aire es buena y que no les va a causar problemas antes de seguir adelante.
2. Liliana no debe aceptar la oferta. Liliana necesita proteger su idea. También, es imprescindible que busque la ayuda de otros antes de tomar una decisión tan importante.
3. Es muy importante que Liliana saque una patente. Es mejor que proteja su idea antes de vender los derechos a una compañía.
4. Es necesario que Liliana consulte con un abogado.

p. 197

Answers will vary. Sample responses include:

1. El diálogo tiene lugar en la selva.
2. El hombre quiere buena vista así que el zopilote le dará la suya. Quiere ser fuerte, y el jaguar le dará fuerza. Quiere caminar sin cansarse, y el venado le ofrece sus piernas. Quiere adivinar la llegada de las lluvias, y por eso el ruiseñor le dice que le avisará con su canto. Desea ser astuto y y el zorro le enseñará a serlo. El hombre quiere trepar a los árboles, por eso la ardilla le dará sus uñas. El hombre quiere conocer las plantas medicinales y la serpiente las marcará en el campo para él.
3. La chachalaca gritó «Pobres animales» al final porque quiere que los animales sepan que uno no puede darle la felicidad a otra persona. Los animales le dieron al hombre cosas que ellos necesitan para sobrevivir, pero él siempre estará triste.
4. Él quiere encontrar la felicidad y piensa que esas cosas lo ayudarán a ser feliz.
5. Sí, estoy de acuerdo. Pienso que la felicidad viene de adentro.

Unidad 4

p. 214

Answers will vary. Possible answers include:

1. comprensivo, considerado, dedicado, paciente, sincero, sobresaliente, ingenioso, razonable
2. comprensiva, generosa, orgullosa, paciente, sincera, razonable
3. atrevida, dedicada, paciente, sobresaliente, ingeniosa

p. 216

1. guapo, atrevido, orgulloso
2. paciente, tímida, popular
3. capaz, inteligente, presumida, impaciente, desagradable
4. comprensivo, considerado, enérgico

p. 219

1. Tú quieres que yo conserve agua.
2. Mis hermanos esperan que su entrenador les dé una oportunidad.
3. Nosotros deseamos que ustedes reciclen los periódicos.
4. Yo no quiero que tú gastes todo tu dinero.

p. 221

1. Manuel espera que la situación no sea tan grave como parece.
2. Manuel quiere que todos miren el monitor.
3. Es importante que Manuel piense en una solución.
4. Es necesario que Ramona examine el sistema de aire acondicionado para ver cómo funciona.

p. 224

1. sea
2. estudie
3. saques

p. 227

Answers will vary. Sample answers include:

1. Mis padres dejan que yo sólo use la computadora después de hacer la tarea.
2. Mi profesor prohíbe que los estudiantes hablen cuando él presenta una lección.
3. Yo espero que mis amigos puedan venir a la fiesta el viernes.
4. Mi amigo(a) aconseja que estudiemos mucho para el examen de biología.

p. 231

Answers will vary. Sample responses include:

1. América deduce que su tía Paulina tiene una relación muy linda con sus hijos porque vienen a visitarla todos los domingos.
2. Él es esposo de Paulina y tío de América.
3. América se pone triste cuando piensa en su hija porque ellas no tienen una buena relación. Ella se siente responsable por los errores de su hija.
4. En la casa de Ester, América vio fotos de los hijos de Paulina con caras sonrientes en las tarjetas de Navidad.
5. Ella piensa que una madre debe escuchar y orientar a sus hijos, y más importante, darles la libertad de cometer errores. Dice que puede guiarles sólo si se lo piden.

p. 240

1. La valentía es importante en las profesiones de bombero y policía.
2. Las profesiones de artista, músico, periodista y político pueden traer la fama.
3. En las profesiones de cartero, veterinario y escritor no se arriesga la vida.

p. 242

El padre de Enrique es sincero y vive con honor y valentía. Va al trabajo todos los días, cuida de su familia y siempre está listo para hacer cualquier sacrificio por su familia.

p. 245

Answers will vary. Sample answers include:

1. Es improbable que todos los estudiantes de mi escuela tengan que escribir un artículo para el periódico escolar.
2. Dudo que mi maestro de español toque la guitarra con tres músicos caribeños.
3. Es imposible que mis vecinos sean superhéroes que protegen a los ciudadanos.

p. 247

1. sepa
2. vaya
3. estén

p. 250

Answers will vary. Sample answers include:

1. Me enoja que él no quiera ser detective; no es un chico razonable.
2. Mis tíos sienten que no puedan vernos con más frecuencia.
3. ¡Yo me alegro de que nosotros vayamos a mi restaurante favorito para celebrar mi cumpleaños!

p. 253

Answers will vary. Sample answers include:

1. Dudo que él duerma ahora.
2. No estoy seguro de que ella venga temprano.
3. Me alegro de que tengas éxito.
4. No me sorprende que ellos vuelvan hoy.

p. 257

Answers will vary. Sample responses include:

1. Miguel y Juanita nacieron en Nueva York, Estados Unidos. Sus padres nacieron en la República Dominicana.
2. La manera de saludarse y la costumbre de pedir la ñapa en el mercado representan dos diferencias culturales.
3. Tía Lola les aconseja a Miguel y Juanita que pidan su ñapa cuando vayan al mercado.
4. Según Miguel, lo que le hace a una persona ser un verdadero americano, además de haber nacido en Estados Unidos y hablar en inglés, es actuar como un americano. Él da los ejemplos de tener los Yanquis como su equipo de béisbol preferido y de gustarle los *hot dogs* más que el arroz con habichuelas.
5. Él quiere demostrar que aunque parece dominicano, es americano. Saluda al agente como los americanos; le da un apretón de manos.

Unidad 5

p. 274

Answers will vary. Possible answers include:
1. chat.yahoo.com, AOL
2. itunes, Kazaa, Napster
3. Google, Yahoo, Lycos
4. Amazon.com, ebgames.com

p. 276

1. paraguas- sí
2. escáner- no
3. computadora portátil- sí
4. agenda electrónica- sí
5. monedero- sí
6. mochila- no

p. 279

Answers will vary. Sample responses include:
1. En caso de que pierda la cartera, yo me aseguraré de que llevo identificación conmigo, y que tengo fotocopias de lo que hay adentro.
2. En caso de que tenga una oportunidad de viajar, yo (no) usaré mis ahorros.
3. Antes de que se gradúe, yo recomiendo que mi amigo participe en un club estudiantil.

p. 281

1. Los delegados deben esperar en el hotel hasta que lleguen los líderes del proyecto.
2. No deben llevar un teléfono celular a menos que sea absolutamente necesario.
3. Pueden vestirse informalmente con tal de que no hagan una visita oficial.

p. 284

1. No, no hay nadie en mi clase que tenga un paraguas hoy./ Sí, hay alguien que tiene un paraguas hoy.
2. No, no conozco a nadie que envíe cartas por correo./ Sí, conozco a alguien que envía cartas por correo.
3. No, no tengo un amigo que descargue música por Internet./ Sí, tengo un amigo que descarga música por Internet.

p. 287

1. Marilú teme que la conferencia vaya a ser una experiencia muy intensa.
2. Raúl no sabe que hay una tarea que tiene que cumplir antes de que empiece la primera sesión de la conferencia.
3. Ana ofrece ayudar a Raúl para que pueda hacer la tarea antes de que él empiece la conferencia.

p. 291

Answers will vary. Sample responses include:
1. Los primeros errores en el mapa oficial de Aguamarina se deben a un error tipográfico.
2. Al ver el mapa defectuoso, los ciudadanos trataron de descifrarlo y ir de un lugar a otro siguiendo nada más que sus instrucciones.
3. La consecuencia de la redacción de los ciudadanos fue tratar de valerse únicamente del mapa. Esto se convirtió en el pasatiempo del lugar.
4. El mapa más difícil de seguir era el mapa del 1993, que no tenía ninguna alteración.
5. El mapa menos apropiado para Aguamarina es el mapa de 1979.

p. 300

Answers will vary. Sample responses include:
1. El ajedrez me hace pensar mucho.
2. una orquesta
3. Si quiero informarme sobre un tema en especial, voy a la biblioteca o busco información en Internet.

p. 302

participar en una conferencia estudiantil de la ONU, relajarse, encontrarse con un grupo de gente, ir a una recepción de bienvenida, hablar en el salón de charlas, charlar con otros delegados, asistir a varias reuniones, participar en unas actividades de grupo, intercambiar opiniones, debatir varios temas, participar en un encuentro, dormir una siesta, reunirse con el grupo, ir a un salón de baile, planear una excursión
1. Ocho de las actividades son para las horas de ocio.
2. Siete de las actividades se relacionan con las sesiones de la conferencia.

p. 305

1. Mi abuelo se relajaría.
2. Yo asistiría a un espectáculo.
3. Mi familia y yo pasaríamos un buen rato.
4. Mi profesor podría charlar con muchas personas.

p. 307

1. La gente no iría a ver *Juego de mesa.*
2. La gente a quien le gusta la música iría al Teatro Colina para ver el espectáculo de Música Callejera y al salón Amazonas para bailar y escuchar música.

p. 310

1. La maestra dijo que llamaría al bombero.
2. Nosotros dijimos que saldríamos tranquilamente.
3. Todos dijeron que se reunirían afuera.
4. Los bomberos dijeron que llegarían pronto.

p. 313

1. Ricardo dijo que le gustaría ver Cuzco.
2. Ana dijo que estaría muy ilusionada con la idea de ir a Trujillo porque le fascina la cultura moche.
3. Marilú dijo que le gustaría hacer una excursión por el río Amazonas en barco.
4. Raúl dijo primero que deberían ir a Cuzco. Luego, dijo que le gustaría ir a Trujillo para hacer surfing y ver las ruinas. Al final, dijo que querría ir al Amazonas para ver las pirañas.

p. 317

1. El ajedrez llegó al Nuevo Mundo con los conquistadores españoles.
2. Cada tarde los capitanes españoles se congregaban en Cajamarca para jugar al ajedrez en el departamento que sirvió de prisión al Inca Atahualpa durante su cautiverio.
3. El Inca Atahualpa aprendió de Hernando de Soto a jugar al ajedrez. Tomaba asiento junto a él todas las tardes.
4. Le cedía las piezas blancas para mostrar su respeto, y le invitaba a jugar una sola partida.
5. El Inca no habría sido condenado a la muerte si hubiera permanecido ignorante en el ajedrez. Se dice que Atahualpa pagó con la vida el *mate* que sufrió Riquelme por su consejo a Soto. En el consejo de los jueces el voto de Riquelme hizo la diferencia entre recibir o no recibir la pena de muerte.

Unidad 6

p. 334

1. Cuando llego a una casa y quiero que me abran la puerta, toco el timbre.
2. Me lavo las manos en el lavabo.
3. Cuando estoy en el parque y quiero descansar, me siento en un banco.

p. 336

1. piso	5. objeto
2. objeto	6. objeto
3. piso	7. objeto
4. piso	8. objeto

p. 339

1. El grifo está cerrado.
2. El timbre está roto.
3. La lechería está abierta.
4. Los pisos están vendidos.

p. 341

1. divertidas
2. enterada
3. garantizado

p. 344

1. Tú has dejado tu chaqueta en el tren.
2. Mauricio ha descubierto un café nuevo.
3. Mi hermana ha venido temprano.
4. Yo he hablado con mis primos.

p. 347

Answers will vary. Sample answers include:

1. No puedo cocinar porque la puerta del horno está rota. *(adjetivo)*
   Nuestro perrito ha roto muchas cosas en la casa. *(verbo)*
2. El técnico vino y ahora el horno está arreglado. *(adjetivo)*
   Mi mamá ha arreglado el piso porque mis abuelos nos visitan hoy. *(verbo)*
3. Por fin, mi proyecto para la clase de ciencias está hecho. *(adjetivo)*
   ¿Han hecho el anuncio en la estación de radio? *(verbo)*
4. El bebé está dormido. *(adjetivo)*
   La chica ha dormido mucho porque está enferma. *(verbo)*

p. 351

1. Todo el mundo lo conoce por «Manolito Gafotas».
2. Según Manolito, la ventaja de tener un mote es que ahora ya nadie se mete con él por sus gafas. Él dice que insultarlo es una pérdida de tiempo desde que tiene su mote.
3. Manolito le puso el mote «El Imbécil» a su hermanito el día en que nació. Cuando fue al hospital para verlo, se acercó a la cuna y le fue a abrir un ojo con la mano. Su hermano se puso a llorar con su llanto falso y Manolito pensó «¡Qué imbécil!». Le puso ese mote porque piensa que su hermano ha nacido para molestar y se lo merece.
4. A la mamá de Manolito no le gustan los motes. Manolito dice que no hay ningún mote que le haga gracia a ella.

p. 360

1. conductor
2. vía, los puentes

p. 362

Answers will vary. Sample responses include:

1. Sí, hay varios puentes viejos en mi área. Están hechos de metal y piedra.
2. Sí, hay muchos edificios viejos en mi área. Son iglesias, tiendas, bibliotecas, y escuelas.

p. 365

Answers will vary. Sample responses include:

1. Elizabeth ya había hecho la tarea cuando su mamá llegó a casa.
2. Miguel y Ángela todavía no habían ido de tapas.
3. Roberto ya había pedido direcciones a la ventanilla cuando se dio cuenta de que habían cancelado el tren.
4. David se había perdido en el centro de la ciudad.

p. 367

Answers will vary. Sample responses include:

1. Cuando llegué hoy a la escuela, Esteban y Alicia ya habían llegado. Juan, Emilia y Susana todavía no habían llegado.
2. Hace cinco años, mi escuela, las iglesias, y el museo histórico ya se habían construido. La biblioteca nueva y el centro comercial todavía no se habían construido.

p. 370

Answers will vary. Sample responses include:

1. Yo habré ido a la escuela y hecho toda la tarea.
2. Tú habrás jugado un partido de fútbol muy importante.
3. El maestro de español habrá mirado los exámenes.
4. Mis amigos y yo habremos pasado un rato en el centro.

p. 373

Answers will vary. Sample response:

Yo he visitado el Museo de Ciencias varias veces. La segunda vez que fui, vi una película de IMAX sobre los animales en África. Yo ya había visto todas las exhibiciones la primera vez que fui, pero no había tenido tiempo de ver esa película.

p. 377

Answers will vary. Sample responses include:

1. Los personajes del poema son el mocito, «ella» y el compadre. «Ella», sueña en su baranda. El compadre y el mocito suben hacia las altas barandas.
2. Lorca utiliza palabras como «escarcha» y «sombra» para destacar el dolor y amargura que sentía el mocito al volver de la guerra.
3. El mocito regresa de la guerra y busca a su novia. El compadre es el padre de la novia.
4. El mocito va a morir por la herida que tiene desde el pecho hasta la garganta. Su novia ya murió. El compadre seguirá montando a caballo porque ya no tiene casa.

Unidad 7

p. 394

1. sí 3. no 5. no
2. sí 4. sí 6. no

p. 396

Answers will vary. Sample answers include:

1. voy a mis clases, almuerzo con mis amigos, voy a reuniones con el consejero académico
2. soy miembro del coro, reparto periódicos, trabajo de niñera

p. 399

1. Mis amigos no querían que yo cuidara a niños los sábados por la noche.
2. Mis padres esperaban que todo saliera bien en mi examen.
3. Mi profesor dudaba que el examen fuera demasiado difícil.

p. 401

Answers will vary. Sample responses include.

1. Mis amigos querían que yo fuera a una fiesta con ellos.
2. Mis padres querían que yo me quedara en casa con ellos.
3. Mi maestro(a) quería que yo estudiara para el examen.
4. Mi hermano(a) quería que yo limpiara su cuarto.

p. 404

Answers will vary. Sample responses include:

1. Era bueno que un compañero hubiera recibido una beca para la universidad.
2. Era impresionante que los profesores hubieran nombrado a tu amiga para la sociedad honoraria.
3. Era raro que los miembros del equipo no se hubieran puesto en forma.

p. 407

Answers will vary. Sample responses include:

1. No podía creer que él no me hubiera dicho la verdad.
2. Me pareció imposible que mis amigos hubieran ido al baile sin invitarme.
3. No me gustó que mi madre no me hubiera dejado ir de vacaciones con mis amigos.
4. Fue increíble que mi hermano y su amigo hubieran leído todos los correos electrónicos que había escrito a mis amigas.

p. 411

1. El cuento ocurre en la época de Navidad.
2. En Cartagena hay aguas navegables y en Madrid no.
3. Los niños suben el bote por las escaleras a su apartamento con la ayuda de sus condiscípulos.
4. Los niños cerraron las puertas y ventanas del apartamento y rompieron la bombilla encendida de una lámpara en la sala. Un chorro de luz empezaba a salir de la bombilla rota como agua. Lo dejaron correr hasta que el nivel llegó a cuatro palmos. Cortaron la corriente y navegaron en bote en la casa.
5. Los niños pidieron equipo de pesca submarina para pescar de su bote.

p. 420

1. Jorge debe ser abogado.
2. Ángela debe ser contable.
3. Rodrigo debe ser traductor.
4. Carmen debe ser enfermera/médica/profesora.

p. 422

Answers will vary. Sample responses include:

1. Las ventajas de ir a una escuela técnica son que uno puede estudiar una especialidad y buscar un empleo en menos tiempo. También es más barato que ir a la universidad. La desventaja es que uno no tiene un título cuando termina.
2. La ventaja de ir a la universidad es que uno puede seguir con sus estudios y recibir un título. Las desventajas son que hay que estudiar por mucho tiempo y que las universidades son muy caras.
3. *Students will provide their own answers.*

p. 425

Answers will vary. Sample responses include:

1. Si ella estudiara derecho, podría seguir una carrera de abogada.
2. Si mi tío(a) abre una empresa, yo trabajaré con él/ella.
3. Si yo fuera profesor(a), nunca daría tarea a mis estudiantes.
4. Si él supiera idiomas, trabajaría en otros países.
5. Si mi madre cocinara bien, yo no tendría tanta hambre.
6. Si tú estudiaras medicina, podrías ser enfermero o doctor.

p. 427

Answers will vary. Sample responses include:

1. Si tuviera más tiempo participaría en más actividades en la escuela.
2. Si voy a la universidad me gustaría recibir un título en la administración de empresas.
3. En el futuro estaré muy contento(a) si tengo una carrera que me guste y que me interese.

p. 430

1. Los maestros se alegraban de que los estudiantes fueran honestos.
2. Mis padres me habían dicho que estudiara relaciones públicas.
3. Era muy importante que la empresa contratara a un traductor.

p. 433

Answers will vary. Sample responses include:

1. Ayer mis padres querían que yo sacara la basura. Ahora quieren que yo corte el césped.
2. La semana pasada mi mejor amigo me pidió que le ayudara con su tarea de matemáticas. Ahora me pide que le ayude con su tarea de español.

p. 437

1. El narrador y el esqueleto se conocieron en el parque.
2. El esqueleto le invitó al narrador a tomar un chocolate porque hacía frío.
3. En el restaurante la mesera les dijo que no podría atenderles y el dueño exigía que se fueran del restaurante inmediatamente.
4. En su casa, el narrador propuso que jugaran un partido de ajedrez. El esqueleto aceptó. La esposa del narrador le dijo que no había chocolate en la alacena. El esqueleto les dijo que no se preocuparan y que debía irse.
5. El esqueleto les dijo al narrador y a su esposa que eran muy gentiles.

Unidad 8

p. 454

Answers will vary. Sample answers include:
1. autor- Sandra Cisneros
2. novela- *Como agua para chocolate*
3. poesía- *Viento, Agua, Piedra*
4. género literario- novelas

p. 456

Answers will vary. Sample responses include:
1. El protagonista es un chico que tiene el mote «Manolito Gafotas».
2. El punto de vista del cuento es el de Manolito; él narra el cuento.
3. El tema del cuento es su mote y cómo y por qué se lo pusieron.

p. 459

Answers will vary. Sample answer:
Cuando recibimos la llamada, mi mamá estaba preparando la cena en la cocina. Mi hermana y yo estábamos haciendo nuestra tarea y mi papá estaba mirando las noticias en la sala.

p. 461

Answers will vary. Sample answer:
Era el primer día de la primavera. Mis amigos y yo andábamos. en patineta. Unas chicas estaban caminando y charlando. Un grupo de niños estaba jugando al básquetbol. ¡Todos estábamos divirtiéndonos después de un invierno muy largo!

p. 464

Answers will vary. Sample responses include:
Cuando estoy descansando, no me gusta que nadie entre a mi cuarto.
Mientras yo duermo, no me gusta que mi hermano escuche música.
Tan pronto como empiezo a decansar, no me gusta que nadie haga ningún ruido.
Aunque me gusta hablar con mis amigos por teléfono, cuando estoy descansando, no me gusta que me llamen.

p. 467

Answers will vary. Sample responses include:
indicativo- Aunque era tarde, mis amigos y yo fuimos al cine porque queríamos ver la película.
subjuntivo- Aunque fuera tarde, iremos al cine.
indicativo- Tan pronto como terminé mi tarea, tuve que ir al correo.
subjuntivo- Le dije a mis padres que limpiaría mi cuarto tan pronto como pudiera.
indicativo- Después de que fui al correo, fui a comer con unos amigos.
subjuntivo- Le dije a mi hermano que jugaría béisbol con él después de que limpiara mi cuarto.
subjuntivo- Tuve que llamar a un compañero de clase antes de que empezara mi tarea porque se me olvidaron mis apuntes en la escuela.
indicativo- Cuando fuimos al cine mi amigo me compró unas palomitas.
subjuntivo- Mi amiga me dijo que me compraría unas palomitas cuando fuéramos al cine.

p. 471

Answers will vary. Sample responses include:
1. Una metáfora es un modo de decir una cosa comparándola con otra.
2. Mario descubrió que se sentía raro. Mario inventó una metáfora sin saberlo para explicar su reacción al poema.
3. La relación entre Mario y Neruda es como la de profesor y estudiante.
4. Neruda quiso decir que cualquier persona puede ser poeta si presta atención a las imágenes, porque de ellos viene la poesía.

p. 480

1. b 2. a 3. c

p. 482

Answers will vary. Sample responses include:
1. Para mi mejor amigo, soy cómico(a) y simpático(a).
2. Para mis vecinos, soy responsable y organizado(a).
3. Para mi abuelo(a), soy inteligente, bonito(a) y generoso(a).
4. Para una persona que no me conozca bien, soy tímido(a) y serio(a).

p. 485

Answers will vary. Sample responses include:
Se me olvidó que había una reunión del comité estudiantil.
Se me cayeron todos los libros enfrente de todos en la cafetería.
Se me perdió la cartera en el cine.
Se me rompió el brazo en un partido de fútbol.

p. 487

Answers will vary. Sample responses include:
Se me ensució la camisa de mi amiga y tuve que comprarle una nueva.
Se me olvidaron las entradas al concierto y llegamos tarde porque tuve que ir a casa para recogerlas.
Se me perdieron unos apuntes muy importantes de la clase de ciencias y saqué mala nota en el examen.

p. 490

Answers will vary. Sample answers include:
La casa de Mango Street, Como las García perdieron su acento, Cien años de soledad
Recomiendo que todos lean *La casa de Mango Street* porque los cuentos de Esperanza me inspiraron mucho.
En *Como las García perdieron su acento*, era triste que las chicas tuvieran que dejar su vida en la República Dominicana.
Es dudoso que haya una novela que incluya tantos eventos importantes de la historia de Latinoamérica como *Cien años de soledad.*

p. 493

Answers will vary. Sample responses include:
1. Si se te acaba el dinero es posible que alguien te pueda enviar más por Internet; es muy fácil.
2. No temas que la familia no te vaya a gustar; ¡son unas personas fenomenales!
3. No dudes que no hables suficiente español; ¡tú sabes mucho y yo sé que no vas a tener ningún problema!.

p. 497

Answers will vary. Sample responses include:
1. Colón no puede conseguir el dinero que necesita para su expedición. Ha ido a los reyes varias veces y siempre le dicen que vuelva otro día.
2. Los reyes de Castilla y Aragón financian la expedición porque empiezan a soñar con la expansión y por eso, les interesa el proyecto de Colón.
3. La tripulación quiere regresar a casa porque ya llevan muchos días navegando y no hay ninguna indicación de las tierras que buscan. Se sienten desesperados y por eso empiezan a quejarse.
4. Cuando Pedro dice «Tierra» significa que por fin han llegado a la orilla.

Resumen de gramática

Nouns, Articles, and Pronouns

Nouns

Nouns identify people, animals, places, things, and feelings. All Spanish nouns, even if they refer to objects, are either **masculine** or **feminine.** They are also either **singular** or **plural.** Nouns ending in **-o** are usually masculine; nouns ending in **-a** are usually feminine.

To form the **plural** of a noun, add **-s** if the noun ends in a vowel; add **-es** if it ends in a consonant.

Singular Nouns

Masculine	Feminine
abuelo	abuela
chico	chica
hombre	mujer
papel	pluma
zapato	blusa

Plural Nouns

Masculine	Feminine
abuelo**s**	abuela**s**
chico**s**	chica**s**
hombre**s**	mujer**es**
papel**es**	pluma**s**
zapato**s**	blusa**s**

Articles

Articles identify the class of a noun: masculine or feminine, singular or plural. **Definite articles** are the equivalent of the English word *the.* **Indefinite articles** are the equivalent of *a, an,* or *some.*

Definite Articles

	Masculine	Feminine
Singular	**el** chico	**la** chica
Plural	**los** chicos	**las** chicas

Indefinite Articles

	Masculine	Feminine
Singular	**un** chico	**una** chica
Plural	**unos** chicos	**unas** chicas

Pronouns

Pronouns take the place of nouns. The pronoun used is determined by its function or purpose in a sentence.

Subject Pronouns

yo	nosotros(as)
tú	vosotros(as)
usted	ustedes
él, ella	ellos(as)

Direct Object Pronouns

me	nos
te	os
lo, la	los, las

Indirect Object Pronouns

me	nos
te	os
le	les

Resumen de gramática

Nouns, Articles, and Pronouns (continued)

Pronouns After Prepositions

mí	nosotros(as)
ti	vosotros(as)
usted	ustedes
él, ella	ellos(as)

Reflexive Pronouns

me	nos
te	os
se	se

Adjectives

Adjectives describe nouns. In Spanish, adjectives match the **gender** and **number** of the nouns they describe. To make an adjective plural, add **-s** if it ends in a vowel; add **-es** if it ends in a consonant. The adjective usually comes after the noun in Spanish.

Adjectives

	Masculine	Feminine
Singular	el chico alt**o**	la chica alt**a**
	el chico inteligente	la chica inteligente
	el chico joven	la chica joven
	el chico trabajador	la chica trabajador**a**
Plural	los chicos alto**s**	las chicas alta**s**
	los chicos inteligente**s**	las chicas inteligente**s**
	los chicos jóven**es**	las chicas jóven**es**
	los chicos trabajador**es**	las chicas trabajadora**s**

Sometimes adjectives are shortened when they are placed in front of a masculine singular noun.

Shortened Forms

alguno	**algún** chico
bueno	**buen** chico
malo	**mal** chico
ninguno	**ningún** chico
primero	**primer** chico
tercero	**tercer** chico

Adjectives (continued)

Possessive adjectives indicate who owns something or describe a relationship between people or things. They agree in number with the nouns they describe. **Nuestro(a)** and **vuestro(a)** must also agree in gender with the nouns they describe.

Possessive adjectives also have long forms that follow the noun for emphasis. Expressed without the noun, they act as pronouns.

	Masculine Short Form		Masculine Long Form	
Singular	**mi** amigo	**nuestro** amigo	amigo **mío**	amigo **nuestro**
	tu amigo	**vuestro** amigo	amigo **tuyo**	amigo **vuestro**
	su amigo	**su** amigo	amigo **suyo**	amigo **suyo**
Plural	**mis** amigos	**nuestros** amigos	amigos **míos**	amigos **nuestros**
	tus amigos	**vuestros** amigos	amigos **tuyos**	amigos **vuestros**
	sus amigos	**sus** amigos	amigos **suyos**	amigos **suyos**

	Feminine Short Form		Feminine Long Form	
Singular	**mi** amiga	**nuestra** amiga	amiga **mía**	amiga **nuestra**
	tu amiga	**vuestra** amiga	amiga **tuya**	amiga **vuestra**
	su amiga	**su** amiga	amiga **suya**	amiga **suya**
Plural	**mis** amigas	**nuestras** amigas	amigas **mías**	amigas **nuestras**
	tus amigas	**vuestras** amigas	amigas **tuyas**	amigas **vuestras**
	sus amigas	**sus** amigas	amigas **suyas**	amigas **suyas**

Demonstrative Adjectives and Pronouns

Demonstrative adjectives and pronouns describe the location of a person or a thing in relation to the speaker. Their English equivalents are *this, that, these,* and *those.*

Demonstrative Adjectives

Demonstrative adjectives agree in gender and number with the noun they describe.

Demonstrative Adjectives

	Masculine	Feminine
Singular	**este** chico	**esta** chica
	ese chico	**esa** chica
	aquel chico	**aquella** chica
Plural	**estos** chicos	**estas** chicas
	esos chicos	**esas** chicas
	aquellos chicos	**aquellas** chicas

Demonstrative Adjectives and Pronouns (continued)

Demonstrative Pronouns

Demonstrative pronouns agree in gender and number with the noun they replace.

Demonstrative Pronouns

	Masculine	Feminine
Singular	éste	ésta
	ése	ésa
	aquél	aquélla
Plural	éstos	éstas
	ésos	ésas
	aquéllos	aquéllas

Comparatives and Superlatives

Comparatives

Comparatives are used to compare two people or things.

Comparatives

	más (+)	menos (–)	tan, tanto(s), tanto (=)
with adjectives	**más** serio **que...**	**menos** serio **que...**	**tan** serio **como...**
with nouns	**más** cosas **que...**	**menos** cosas **que...**	**tantas** cosas **como...**
with verbs	Me gusta leer **más que** pasear.	Me gusta pasear **menos que** leer.	Me gusta hablar **tanto como** escuchar.

There are a few irregular comparative words. When talking about the age of people, use **mayor** and **menor.** When talking about qualities, use **mejor** and **peor.**

Age	Quality
mayor	mejor
menor	peor

When comparing numbers, use **de** instead of **que.**
más de cinco...
menos de cinco...

Superlatives

Superlatives are used to set apart one item from a group. They describe which item has the most or least of a quality.

Superlatives

	Masculine	Feminine
Singular	**el más** caro	**la más** cara
	el anillo **más** caro	**la** blusa **más** cara
	el menos caro	**la menos** cara
	el anillo **menos** caro	**la** blusa **menos** cara
Plural	**los más** caros	**las más** caras
	los anillos **más** caros	**las** blusas **más** caras
	los menos caros	**las menos** caras
	los anillos **menos** caros	**las** blusas **menos** caras

The ending **-ísimo(a)** can be added to an adjective to intensify it.

Singular	caldo riqu**ísimo**	sopa riqu**ísima**
Plural	huevos riqu**ísimos**	tortillas riqu**ísimas**

Adverbs

Adverbs tell *when, where, how, how long,* or *how much.* They can be formed by adding **-mente** to the singular feminine form of an adjective.

Adjective		Adverb
alegre	→	alegre**mente**
fácil	→	fácil**mente**
general	→	general**mente**
normal	→	normal**mente**
triste	→	triste**mente**
lento(a)	→	lenta**mente**
activo(a)	→	activa**mente**
rápido(a)	→	rápida**mente**
serio(a)	→	seria**mente**
tranquilo(a)	→	tranquila**mente**

Affirmative and Negative Words

Affirmative or **negative** words are used to talk about indefinite or negative situations.

Affirmative Words	Negative Words
algo	nada
alguien	nadie
algún/alguno(a)	ningún/ninguno(a)
o... o	ni... ni
siempre	nunca
también	tampoco

Verbs: Regular Verbs

Regular verbs ending in **-ar, -er,** or **-ir** always have regular endings.

Simple Indicative Tenses

-ar Verbs

Infinitive	Present Participle	Past Participle
habl**ar**	habl**ando**	habl**ado**

Present	habl**o**	habl**amos**
	habl**as**	habl**áis**
	habl**a**	habl**an**
Preterite	habl**é**	habl**amos**
	habl**aste**	habl**asteis**
	habl**ó**	habl**aron**
Imperfect	habl**aba**	habl**ábamos**
	habl**abas**	habl**abais**
	habl**aba**	habl**aban**
Future	hablar**é**	hablar**emos**
	hablar**ás**	hablar**éis**
	hablar**á**	hablar**án**
Conditional	hablar**ía**	hablar**íamos**
	hablar**ías**	hablar**íais**
	hablar**ía**	hablar**ían**

-er Verbs

Infinitive	Present Participle	Past Participle
vend**er**	vend**iendo**	vend**ido**

Present	vend**o**	vend**emos**
	vend**es**	vend**éis**
	vend**e**	vend**en**
Preterite	vend**í**	vend**imos**
	vend**iste**	vend**isteis**
	vend**ió**	vend**ieron**

-er Verbs

Imperfect	vend**ía**	vend**íamos**
	vend**ías**	vend**íais**
	vend**ía**	vend**ían**
Future	vender**é**	vender**emos**
	vender**ás**	vender**éis**
	vender**á**	vender**án**
Conditional	vender**ía**	vender**íamos**
	vender**ías**	vender**íais**
	vender**ía**	vender**ían**

-ir Verbs

Infinitive	Present Participle	Past Participle
compart**ir**	compart**iendo**	compart**ido**

Present	compart**o**	compart**imos**
	compart**es**	compart**ís**
	compart**e**	compart**en**
Preterite	compart**í**	compart**imos**
	compart**iste**	compart**isteis**
	compart**ió**	compart**ieron**
Imperfect	compart**ía**	compart**íamos**
	compart**ías**	compart**íais**
	compart**ía**	compart**ían**
Future	compartir**é**	compartir**emos**
	compartir**ás**	compartir**éis**
	compartir**á**	compartir**án**
Conditional	compartir**ía**	compartir**íamos**
	compartir**ías**	compartir**íais**
	compartir**ía**	compartir**ían**

Future with ir a + infinitive

Another way to express the future is with the construction **ir a + infinitive**.

voy	vamos
vas	vais
va	van

Ellos **van a venir** mañana.

Verbs: Regular Verbs (continued)

Command Forms

		tú Commands	**usted** Commands	**ustedes** Commands	**nosotros** Commands
-ar Verbs	+	habl**a**	habl**e**	habl**en**	habl**emos**
	–	no habl**es**	no habl**e**	no habl**en**	no habl**emos**
-er Verbs	+	vend**e**	vend**a**	vend**an**	vend**amos**
	–	no vend**as**	no vend**a**	no vend**an**	no vend**amos**
-ir Verbs	+	compart**e**	compart**a**	compart**an**	compart**amos**
	–	no compart**as**	no compart**a**	no compart**an**	no compart**amos**

Subjunctive Forms

Present Subjunctive

-ar Verbs	habl**e**	habl**emos**
	habl**es**	habl**éis**
	habl**e**	habl**en**
-er Verbs	vend**a**	vend**amos**
	vend**as**	vend**áis**
	vend**a**	vend**an**
-ir Verbs	compart**a**	compart**amos**
	compart**as**	compart**áis**
	compart**a**	compart**an**

Imperfect Subjunctive

-ar Verbs	habl**ara**	habl**áramos**
	habl**aras**	habl**arais**
	habl**ara**	habl**aran**
-er Verbs	vend**iera**	vend**iéramos**
	vend**ieras**	vend**ierais**
	vend**iera**	vend**ieran**
-ir Verbs	compart**iera**	compart**iéramos**
	compart**ieras**	compart**ierais**
	compart**iera**	compart**ieran**

Compound Tenses

The **perfect tenses** are formed with a conjugation of the auxiliary verb **haber** and a **past participle.**

Present Perfect	**he** hablado	**ha** hablado	**habéis** hablado
	has hablado	**hemos** hablado	**han** hablado
Present Perfect Subjunctive	**haya** hablado	**haya** hablado	**hayáis** hablado
	hayas hablado	**hayamos** hablado	**hayan** hablado
Past Perfect	**había** hablado	**había** hablado	**habíais** hablado
	habías hablado	**habíamos** hablado	**habían** hablado
Past Perfect Subjunctive	**hubiera** hablado	**hubiera** hablado	**hubierais** hablado
	hubieras hablado	**hubiéramos** hablado	**hubieran** hablado
Future Perfect	**habré** hablado	**habrá** hablado	**habréis** hablado
	habrás hablado	**habremos** hablado	**habrán** hablado

Stem-Changing Verbs

Present Tense

Stem-changing verbs in the present tense change in all forms except **nosotros(as)** and **vosotros(as).**

e → ie

pensar		
	pi**e**nso	pensamos
	pi**e**nsas	pensáis
	pi**e**nsa	pi**e**nsan

Other **e → ie** stem-changing verbs are **cerrar, comenzar, despertarse, empezar, encender, entender, hervir, perder, preferir, querer** and **recomendar.**

o → ue

poder		
	p**ue**do	podemos
	p**ue**des	podéis
	p**ue**de	p**ue**den

Other **o → ue** stem-changing verbs are **acostarse, almorzar, costar, doler, dormir, encontrar, envolver, probar** and **volver.**

e → i

servir		
	s**i**rvo	servimos
	s**i**rves	servís
	s**i**rve	s**i**rven

Other **e → i** stem-changing verbs are **competir, freír, pedir, seguir** and **vestirse.**

u → ue

jugar		
	j**ue**go	jugamos
	j**ue**gas	jugáis
	j**ue**ga	j**ue**gan

Jugar is the only verb with a **u → ue** stem-change.

Stem-Changing Verbs (continued)

Preterite Tense

Stem-changing **-ir** verbs in the present tense also change stems in some forms of the preterite.

e → i

pedir	pedí	pedimos
	pediste	pedisteis
	p**i**dió	p**i**dieron

o → u

dormir	dormí	dormimos
	dormiste	dormisteis
	d**u**rmió	d**u**rmieron

Present Subjunctive

Stem-changing **-ar** and **-er** verbs in the present tense also change stems in the same forms of the subjunctive.

e → ie

pensar	p**ie**nse	pensemos
	p**ie**nses	penséis
	p**ie**nse	p**ie**nsen

o → ue

poder	p**ue**da	podamos
	p**ue**das	podáis
	p**ue**da	p**ue**dan

u → ue

jugar	j**ue**gue	juguemos
	j**ue**gues	juguéis
	j**ue**gue	j**ue**guen

Stem-changing **-ir** verbs in the present tense change stems in *all* forms of the subjunctive.

e → ie, i

preferir	pref**ie**ra	pref**i**ramos
	pref**ie**ras	pref**i**ráis
	pref**ie**ra	pref**ie**ran

o → ue, u

dormir	d**ue**rma	d**u**rmamos
	d**ue**rmas	d**u**rmáis
	d**ue**rma	d**ue**rman

e → i

pedir	p**i**da	p**i**damos
	p**i**das	p**i**dáis
	p**i**da	p**i**dan

Present Participles

Some verbs have stem changes as present participles.

decir	→	d**i**ciendo
dormir	→	d**u**rmiendo
pedir	→	p**i**diendo
poder	→	p**u**diendo
servir	→	s**i**rviendo
venir	→	v**i**niendo
vestir	→	v**i**stiendo

Verbs: Spelling Changes

The following verbs undergo spelling changes in some forms to maintain their pronunciation.

c → qu	Preterite	Subjunctive	Command
buscar			
yo	bus**qu**é	bus**qu**e	
tú	buscaste	bus**qu**es	no bus**qu**es
usted/él/ella	buscó	bus**qu**e	bus**qu**e
nosotros(as)	buscamos	bus**qu**emos	(no) bus**qu**emos
vosotros(as)	buscasteis	bus**qu**éis	
ustedes/ellos(as)	buscaron	bus**qu**en	bus**qu**en

like **buscar**: destacar(se), explicar, implicar, personificar, pescar, practicar, publicar, sacar, secar(se), significar, tocar

g → gu	Preterite	Subjunctive	Command
jugar (ue)			
yo	ju**gu**é	jue**gu**e	
tú	jugaste	jue**gu**es	no jue**gu**es
usted/él/ella	jugó	jue**gu**e	jue**gu**e
nosotros(as)	jugamos	ju**gu**emos	(no) ju**gu**emos
vosotros(as)	jugasteis	ju**gu**éis	
ustedes/ellos(as)	jugaron	jue**gu**en	jue**gu**en

like **jugar**: apagar, arriesgar(se), descargar, encargar(se), investigar, llegar, navegar, otorgar, pagar

z → c	Preterite	Subjunctive	Command
almorzar (ue)			
yo	almor**c**é	almuer**c**e	
tú	almorzaste	almuer**c**es	no almuer**c**es
usted/él/ella	almorzó	almuer**c**e	almuer**c**e
nosotros(as)	almorzamos	almor**c**emos	(no) almor**c**emos
vosotros(as)	almorzasteis	almor**c**éis	
ustedes/ellos(as)	almorzaron	almuer**c**en	almuer**c**en

like **almorzar**: amenazar, analizar, cazar, comenzar, comercializar, cruzar, empezar, especializar(se), idealizar, organizar, penalizar, reemplazar, reutilizar, simbolizar, utilizar

Verbs: Spelling Changes (continued)

i → y	Present	Preterite	Subjunctive*	Command
construir				
yo	construyo	construí	construya	
tú	construyes	construiste	construyas	construye no construyas
usted/él/ella	construye	construyó	construya	construya
nosotros(as)	construimos	construimos	construyamos	(no) construyamos
vosotros(as)	construís	construisteis	construyáis	
ustedes/ellos(as)	construyen	construyeron	construyan	construyan

Present Participle: construyendo
*spelling change also applies in all forms of the **Imperfect Subjunctive**: construyera...
like **construir**: destruir, disminuir, concluir

g → j	Present	Subjunctive	Command
proteger			
yo	protejo	proteja	
tú	proteges	protejas	no protejas
usted/él/ella	protege	proteja	proteja
nosotros(as)	protegemos	protejamos	(no) protejamos
vosotros(as)	protegéis	protejáis	
ustedes/ellos(as)	protegen	protejan	protejan

like **proteger**: recoger

c → j	Preterite	Imperfect Subjunctive
conducir		
yo	conduje	condujera
tú	condujiste	condujeras
usted/él/ella	condujo	condujera
nosotros(as)	condujimos	condujéramos
vosotros(as)	condujisteis	condujerais
ustedes/ellos(as)	condujeron	condujeran

like **conducir**: traducir

Verbs: Irregular Verbs

The following verbs are irregular in some forms. The irregular forms are **boldface.**

abrir

Past Participle	**abierto**

caer(se)

Present	**caigo,** caes, cae, caemos, caéis, caen
Preterite	caí, **caíste, cayó, caímos, caísteis, cayeron**
Present Participle	**cayendo**
Past Participle	**caído**

conocer

Present	**conozco,** conoces, conoce, conocemos, conocéis, conocen

creer

Preterite	creí, **creíste, creyó, creímos, creísteis, creyeron**
Present Participle	**creyendo**
Past Participle	creído

dar

Present	**doy,** das, da, damos, dais, dan
Preterite	**di, diste, dio, dimos, disteis, dieron**
Subjunctive	**dé, des, dé, demos, deis, den**
Commands	da (tú), **no des** (neg. tú), **dé** (usted), **den** (ustedes)

decir

Present	**digo**, dices, dice, decimos, decís, dicen
Preterite	**dije, dijiste, dijo, dijimos, dijisteis, dijeron**
Future	**diré, dirás, dirá, diremos, diréis, dirán**
Conditional	**diría, dirías, diría, diríamos, diríais, dirían**
Commands	**di** (tú), no digas (neg. tú), diga (usted), digan (ustedes)
Past Participle	**dicho**

Verbs: Irregular Verbs (continued)

descubrir

Past Participle	**descubierto**

escribir

Past Participle	**escrito**

estar

Present	**estoy**, **estás, está,** estamos, estáis, **están**
Preterite	**estuve, estuviste, estuvo, estuvimos, estuvisteis, estuvieron**
Subjunctive	**esté, estés, esté,** estemos, estéis, **estén**
Commands	está (tú), **no estés** (neg. tú), **esté** (usted), **estén** (ustedes)

hacer

Present	**hago,** haces, hace, hacemos, hacéis, hacen
Preterite	**hice, hiciste, hizo, hicimos, hicisteis, hicieron**
Future	**haré, harás, hará, haremos, haréis, harán**
Conditional	**haría, harías, haría, haríamos, haríais, harían**
Commands	**haz** (tú), no hagas (neg. tú), haga (usted), hagan (ustedes)
Past Participle	**hecho**

ir

Present	**voy, vas, va, vamos, vais, van**
Preterite	**fui, fuiste, fue, fuimos, fuisteis, fueron**
Imperfect	**iba, ibas, iba, íbamos, ibais, iban**
Subjunctive	**vaya, vayas, vaya, vayamos, vayáis, vayan**
Commands	**ve** (tú), **no vayas** (neg. tú), **vaya** (usted), **vayan** (ustedes)
Present Participle	**yendo**
Past Participle	**ido**

leer

Preterite	leí, **leíste, leyó, leímos, leísteis, leyeron**
Present Participle	**leyendo**
Past Participle	**leído**

morir

Past Participle	**muerto**

poder

Preterite	**pude, pudiste, pudo, pudimos, pudisteis, pudieron**
Future	**podré, podrás, podrá, podremos, podréis, podrán**
Conditional	**podría, podrías, podría, podríamos, podríais, podrían**

poner

Present	**pongo,** pones, pone, ponemos, ponéis, ponen
Preterite	**puse, pusiste, puso, pusimos, pusisteis, pusieron**
Future	**pondré, pondrás, pondrá, pondremos, pondréis, pondrán**
Conditional	**pondría, pondrías, pondría, pondríamos, pondríais, pondrían**
Commands	**pon** (tú), no pongas (neg. tú), ponga (usted), pongan (ustedes)
Past Participle	**puesto**

querer

Preterite	**quise, quisiste, quiso, quisimos, quisisteis, quisieron**
Future	**querré, querrás, querrá, querremos, querréis, querrán**
Conditional	**querría, querrías, querría, querríamos, querríais, querrían**

resolver

Past Participle	**resuelto**

romper

Past Participle	**roto**

saber

Present	**sé,** sabes, sabe, sabemos, sabéis, saben
Preterite	**supe, supiste, supo, supimos, supisteis, supieron**
Future	**sabré, sabrás, sabrá, sabremos, sabréis, sabrán**
Conditional	**sabría, sabrías, sabría, sabríamos, sabríais, sabrían**
Subjunctive	**sepa, sepas, sepa, sepamos, sepáis, sepan**
Commands	sabe (tú), **no sepas** (neg. tú), **sepa** (usted), **sepan** (ustedes)

salir

Present	**salgo,** sales, sale, salimos, salís, salen
Future	**saldré, saldrás, saldrá, saldremos, saldréis, saldrán**
Conditional	**saldría, saldrías, saldría, saldríamos, saldríais, saldrían**
Commands	**sal** (tú), no salgas (neg. tú), salga (usted), salgan (ustedes)

Verbs: Irregular Verbs (continued)

ser

Present	**soy, eres, es, somos, sois, son**
Preterite	**fui, fuiste, fue, fuimos, fuisteis, fueron**
Imperfect	**era, eras, era, éramos, erais, eran**
Subjunctive	**sea, seas, sea, seamos, seáis, sean**
Commands	**sé** (tú), **no seas** (neg. tú), **sea** (usted), **sean** (ustedes)

tener

Present	**tengo, tienes, tiene,** tenemos, tenéis, **tienen**
Preterite	**tuve, tuviste, tuvo, tuvimos, tuvisteis, tuvieron**
Future	**tendré, tendrás, tendrá, tendremos, tendréis, tendrán**
Conditional	**tendría, tendrías, tendría, tendríamos, tendríais, tendrían**
Commands	**ten** (tú), no tengas (neg. tú), tenga (usted), tengan (ustedes)

traer

Present	**traigo,** traes, trae, traemos, traéis, traen
Preterite	**traje, trajiste, trajo, trajimos, trajisteis, trajeron**
Present Participle	**trayendo**
Past Participle	**traído**

venir

Present	**vengo, vienes, viene,** venemos, venís, **vienen**
Preterite	**vine, viniste, vino, vinimos, vinisteis, vinieron**
Future	**vendré, vendrás, vendrá, vendremos, vendréis, vendrán**
Conditional	**vendría, vendrías, vendría, vendríamos, vendríais, vendrían**
Commands	**ven** (tú), no vengas (neg. tú), venga (usted), vengan (ustedes)

ver

Present	**veo,** ves, ve, vemos, veis, ven
Preterite	**vi, viste, vio, vimos, visteis, vieron**
Imperfect	**veía, veías, veía, veíamos, veíais, veían**
Past Participle	**visto**

volver

Past Participle	**vuelto**

Glosario español-inglés

This Spanish-English glossary contains all the active vocabulary words that appear in the text as well as passive vocabulary lists.

a to, at
a fin de que in order that **5.1**
a la vez at the same time
A la(s)... At... o'clock. **I**
a menos que unless **5.1**
a pesar de que in spite of, despite **6.2**
a pie on foot **I**
¿A qué hora es/son...? At what time is/are...? **I**
a veces sometimes **II**
A ver. Let's see.
abandonar to abandon
abierto(a) open
Está abierto(a). It's open. **II**
el (la) abogado(a) lawyer **II, 7.2**
abordar to board **II**
abrazar to hug
el abrigo coat **II**
abril April **I**
abrir to open **I**
abrir el grifo to turn on the faucet **6.1**
en absoluto not at all **1.2**
absurdo(a) absurd **8.1**
lo absurdo the absurd
la abuela grandmother **I**
el abuelo grandfather **I**
los abuelos grandparents **I**
aburrido(a) boring **I**
acabar de... to have just... **I**
acampar to camp **I, II**
el acantilado cliff
acariciar to caress, to stroke
acaso perhaps, maybe
por si acaso just in case
el acceso access **2.2**
el accesorio prop **8.2**, accessory
la acción (*pl.* las acciones) action
el aceite (cooking) oil **II**
la aceituna olive
la acera sidewalk **II**
acercarse to approach
aclarar to clarify, to make clear
acogedor(a) cozy, welcoming **5.2**
el (la) acomodador(a) usher **8.2**
acompañar to accompany; to go or come with
¿Quieres acompañarme a...? Would you like to come with me to...? **I**
aconsejar que to advise that **4.1**
el acontecimiento event, happening
acordarse (ue) de to remember
acostarse (ue) to go to bed **I, II**
Pienso acostarme temprano. I plan to go to bed early.
la actitud attitude
la actividad activity **I**
activo(a) active **II**
el acto act **8.1**
el actor actor **II**
la actriz (*pl.* las actrices) actress **II**
la actuación acting **5.2**; performance
la actuación callejera street performances
actual current, contemporary
la actualidad the present
actuar to act **4.2**
actuar en un drama to act in a play **7.1**
el acuario aquarium **I**
el acuerdo agreement
De acuerdo. Right. Agreed.
estar/no estar de acuerdo con to agree/disagree with **II**
ponerse de acuerdo to agree **5.1**
además in addition, additionally **6.2**
además de besides, in addition to
Adiós. Goodbye. **I**
adivinar to guess
adjunto(a) attached
¿Adónde? (To) Where? **I**
¿Adónde vas? Where are you going? **I**
adquirir (ie) to acquire
la aduana customs
pasar por la aduana to go through customs **II**
adulto(a) adult *(adj.)*
el (la) adulto(a) adult
la advertencia warning **3.2**
advertir (ie, i) to warn **3.2**
el aeropuerto airport **II**
afectar to affect
afeitarse to shave oneself **I, II**
el (la) aficionado(a) fan, sports fan **I**
la agencia agency
la agencia de publicidad ad agency **2.1**
la agencia de viajes travel agency **II**
la agenda electrónica personal organizer **5.1**
el (la) agente agent
el (la) agente de viajes travel agent **II**
el (la) agente de bolsa stockbroker **II, 7.2**
agobiante stifling
agosto August **I**
agotador(a) exhausting **1.1**
agradecer (agradezco) to thank
el (la) agricultor(a) farmer **II**
la agricultura agriculture **II**
agrio(a) sour **II**; bitter
el agua (fem.) water **I**
el agua dulce fresh water **1.1**
las aguas termales hot springs
el aguacate avocado
el (la) ahijado(a) godchild
ahogado(a) stifled, choked
ahora now **I**
ahora mismo right now
ahorrar to save (money, time) **1.1**
los ahorros savings **5.1**
la cuenta de ahorros savings account **7.1**

Glosario español-inglés

el aire air
al aire libre outside, outdoors; open-air **I**
el aire acondicionado air conditioning
el aire puro clean air **II, 3.1**
el ajedrez chess **5.2**
el ajo garlic **II**
al to the **I**
al aire libre outside, outdoors; open-air **I, 1.1**
al extranjero abroad **1.1**
al lado (de) next to **I**
al revés upside down
el ala *(fem.)* wing
alado(a) winged
el albergue juvenil youth hostel **1.1**
el (la) alcalde mayor
la alcaldía mayorship
alcanzar to reach, to attain
alegrarse (de que...) to be happy (that...) **4.2**
alegre happy; upbeat
la alfombra rug **I**
algo something **I, II**
el algodón cotton
alguien someone **I, II**
algún some **II**
Algún día... Some day... **II**
alguno(a) some, any **I, II**
el alimento food
el aljibe cistern
allí there **I**
el almacén (*pl.* los almacenes) department store **II**
almacenar to store
almorzar (ue) to eat lunch **I**
el almuerzo lunch **I**
¿Aló? Hello? (on telephone) **I, II**
el alojamiento lodging **II**
el (la) alpinista mountain climber **II**
alquilar to rent **I**
alto(a) tall **I**
el altoparlante loudspeaker
la altura height
el (la) alumno(a) student
amable nice, friendly; kind
Muy amable. Very kind. **II**
el amanecer sunrise
amargo(a) bitter
amarillo(a) yellow **I**
el ambiente atmosphere **5.2**; setting
ambos(as) both
amenazar to threaten **3.1**
el (la) amigo(a) friend **I**
la amistad friendship **II, 4.2**
el amuleto good-luck charm
añadir to add **II**
el análisis (*pl.* los análisis) analysis **8.1**
analizar to analyze **6.2**
anaranjado(a) orange (color) **I**
ancho(a) wide
los ancianos the elderly **2.1**
andar
andar en patineta to skateboard **I**
el andén (*pl.* los andenes) platform **6.2**
el anillo ring **I, II**
la animación animation **II**
animado(a) animated, upbeat **7.2**
animarse to get interested or excited
el ánimo spirit
el año year **I**
el Año Nuevo New Year
el año pasado last year **I, II**
¿Cuántos años tienes? How old are you? **I**
tener... años to be... years old **I**
anoche last night **I**
la anotación (*pl.* las anotaciones) annotation, entry
anteayer the day before yesterday **I, II**
el antecedente background event **8.1**
antemano: de antemano beforehand **2.1**
antes (de) before **I**
antes (de) que before **5.1**
anticipación: con anticipación in advance **1.1**
anticipar to anticipate **7.1**
antiguo(a) ancient **II**; old
el anuario yearbook **7.1**
anunciar to announce
el anuncio advertisement, ad **II**; announcement **2.1**
el anuncio clasificado classified ad **2.2**
el anuncio de prensa press release
el anuncio personal personal ad **2.2**
apagar to turn off
apagar la luz to turn off the light **II**
apagarse to go out, to burn out
el aparato device
aparecer (aparezco) to appear **4.2**
el apartamento apartment **I**
aparte de besides, apart from
apasionado(a) passionate **7.2**
el apellido last name **II, 1.2**
apenas barely **II**
aplaudir to clap **8.2**
el apodo nickname
apoyar to support **2.1**
el apoyo support
apreciar to appreciate **3.1**
aprender to learn **I**
aprender el español to learn Spanish **I**
apretado(a) tight (clothing)
el apretón (*pl.* los apretones) de manos handshake
aprobar (ue) to pass (a law)
aprovechar to take advantage (of something) **6.1**
los apuntes notes **I**
tomar apuntes to take notes **I**
aquel (aquella) that (over there) **I, II**
aquél (aquélla) that one (over there) **II**
aquellos(as) those (over there) **I, II**
aquéllos(as) those ones (over there) **II**
aquí here **I**
la araña spider **1.1**
el árbol tree **II, 1.1**
el árbol de Navidad Christmas tree
el archivo file
la ardilla squirrel
la arena sand **1.2**
el arete earring **I, II**
el argumento plot **II**
el armario closet; armoire **I**
el aro hoop, ring
el (la) arqueólogo(a) archaeologist
el (la) arquitecto(a) architect **II, 7.2**
la arquitectura architecture
el arrecife (de coral) (coral) reef
arreglar to repair **6.1**
arreglarse to get ready **II**
el arrepentimiento regret
arriesgado(a) risky
arriesgarse to risk **4.2**
la arroba at sign (in e-mail address)
el arroz rice **I**

el arte art **I**
el arte interpretativo performance art
las artes marciales martial arts
las bellas artes fine arts
las artesanías handicrafts **I, II**
el (la) artesano(a) artisan, craftsperson
el artículo article **II, 2.1**
el artículo de opinión editorial **2.2**
los artículos goods, articles **I, II**
los artículos deportivos sporting goods
el (la) artista artist **II, 4.2**
artístico(a) artistic **I**
el asado barbecue
asado(a) roasted
el ascensor elevator **II**
el asco disgust
¡Qué asco! How disgusting! **II**
asegurar to assure
Te lo aseguro. I assure you. **II**
asentir (ie, i) to agree
así this way, like this
así que so, thus
el asiento seat
el asiento numerado numbered seat **6.2**
la asignatura subject (in school)
asistir a to attend **5.2**
asombrarse to be astonished
asombroso(a) surprising
la aspiradora vacuum cleaner **I**
pasar la aspiradora to vacuum **I**
el (la) astronauta astronaut **4.1**
asustarse to get scared
atender (ie) to attend
atento(a) attentive
Muy atento(a). Very attentive. **II**
aterrorizar to terrify, to frighten
el (la) atleta athlete **I**
atlético(a) athletic **I**
las atracciones attractions, sights
ver las atracciones to go sightseeing **II**
atractivo(a) attractive
atraer (atraigo) to attract
atrasar to delay
atrevido(a) daring **4.1**
el aula classroom
aumentar to increase
aún even
aunque although **8.1**
la ausencia absence
auténtico(a) authentic **4.2**
los autitos chocadores bumper cars **I**
la autobiografía autobiography **8.1**
el autobús (*pl.* los autobuses) bus **I**
en autobús by bus **I**
la autoestima self-esteem
el automóvil automobile, car
el (la) autor(a) author **8.1**
el (la) auxiliar de vuelo flight attendant **II**
avanzado(a) advanced **II**
avanzar to advance, to move ahead
avancemos let's advance, let's move ahead
¡Avanza! Advance!, Move ahead!
avaro(a) miserly **8.2**
la avenida avenue **II**
la aventura adventure
avergonzarse to feel embarrassed
el avión (*pl.* los aviones) airplane **I**
en avión by plane **I**
avisar to inform
¡Ay, por favor! Oh, please! **II**
ayer yesterday **I**
la ayuda help
ayudar to help **I**
el ayuno hunger strike; fast
azteca Aztec **II**
el azucar sugar **II**
azul blue **I**

la bahía bay
bailar to dance **I**
el bailarín/la bailarina dancer
el baile dance
bajar to descend **I**
bajar el telón to lower the curtain **8.2**
bajo under, beneath
bajo(a) short (height) **I**
el balcón (*pl.* los balcones) balcony **6.1**
la ballena whale
la balsa raft
la banana banana **I**
bañarse to take a bath **I, II**
el banco bank **II**; bench **6.1**
la bandera flag
la bañera bathtub, tub **6.1**
el baño bathroom **I**
el (la) banquero(a) banker
la baranda railing
barato(a) inexpensive **I, II**
bárbaro: ¡Qué bárbaro! How cool!
el barco boat **I**
en barco by boat **I**
barrer to sweep **I**
el barrio neighborhood **II**
el barro mud
el básquetbol basketball (the sport) **I**
bastante quite
la basura trash, garbage **I**
el basurero garbage container, trash can **II, 3.1**
la batalla battle **II**
el bate (baseball) bat **I**
la batería battery
batido(a) beaten **II**
batir to beat **II**
el bautismo baptism
el (la) bebé baby, infant **1.2**
beber to drink **I**
la bebida beverage, drink **I**
la beca scholarship
el béisbol baseball (the sport) **I**
el (la) beisbolista baseball player
la belleza beauty
bello(a) nice **II**; beautiful
el beneficio benefit
a beneficio de for the benefit of **2.2**
la biblioteca library **I**
el (la) bibliotecario(a) librarian
la bicicleta bicycle **I**
bien well, fine **I**
Bien. ¿Y tú/usted? Fine. And you? (familiar/formal) **I**
irle bien (a alguien) to do well **7.1**
Muy bien. ¿Y tú/usted? Very well. And you? (familiar/formal) **I**
pasarlo bien to have a good time
salir bien to turn out well **7.1**
la bienvenida welcome
bienvenido(a) welcome *(adj.)*
el billar billiards **5.2**
el billete ticket
sacar el billete to buy a ticket **6.1**
la biodiversidad biodiversity **3.1**
la biografía biography **8.1**
la bisabuela great-grandmother **1.2**
el bisabuelo great-grandfather **1.2**
los bisabuelos great-grandparents **1.2**
el bistec beef **I**
la biznieta great-granddaughter **1.2**
el biznieto great-grandson **1.2**
los biznietos great-grandchildren **1.2**
blanco(a) white **I**
en blanco blank
el bloqueador de sol sunscreen **I**
la blusa blouse **I**

la boca mouth **I**
la boda wedding
el boleto ticket **I, II**
el boleto de ida y vuelta roundtrip ticket **II**
bolos: jugar a los bolos to go bowling
la bolsa bag, handbag **5.1**; stock market
la bolsa de plástico plastic bag **2.1**
el (la) bombero(a) firefighter **II, 4.2**
la bombilla light bulb
la bombonería candy store **6.1**
bonito(a) pretty **I**
el boquerón (*pl.* los boquerones) anchovy
bordar to embroider
el borrador eraser **I**; draft
borrar to erase
el bosque forest; woods **II, 1.1**
el bosque lluvioso rain forest
el bosque nuboso cloud forest
el bosquejo story board; sketch
la bota boot **II**
el bote boat
el bote de remos rowboat
la botella bottle
¡Bravo! Bravo! **II**
el brazo arm **I**
brillante brilliant
brillar to shine
la brisa breeze **1.2**
el brócoli broccoli **I**
la broma joke
el bronce bronze
la brújula compass
el (la) buceador(a) scuba diver **II**
bucear to scuba-dive **I**
bueno(a) good **I**
¡Buen provecho! Enjoy! **II**
Buenas noches. Good evening; Good night. **I**
Buenas tardes. Good afternoon. **I**
Bueno, ... Well, ...
¿Bueno? Hello? (on phone) **II**
Buenos días. Good morning. **I**
Es bueno (que...) It's good (that...) **II**
burlarse de to make fun ofbuscar to look for **I**
la búsqueda search **5.1**
el buzón (*pl.* los buzones) mailbox **6.1**

C

el caballero knight
el caballo horse **I**
montar a caballo to ride a horse **I**
la cabeza head **I**
la cabina cabin; booth
el cacao cacao tree
cada each; every
cada tanto from time to time
cada vez más more and more
la cadera hip
caer (caigo) to fall
caerse (me caigo) to fall down **6.2**
el café coffee; café **I**
el cafetal coffee farm
la cafetería cafeteria **I**
el (la) cafetero(a) coffee worker
la caja box
el (la) cajero(a) cashier
el cajero automático ATM **6.1**
el calamar squid
el calcetín (*pl.* los calcetines) sock **I**
la calculadora calculator **I**
el caldo broth **II**
el calendario calendar **II**
calentar (ie) to heat
la calidad quality **I**
cálido(a) warm
caliente hot (temperature) **II**
callado(a) quiet **6.2**
la calle street **I**
el callejón (*pl.* los callejones) alley **6.2**
el calor heat **I**
el calor agobiante stifling heat **1.2**
Hace calor. It is hot. **I**
tener calor to be hot (person) **I**
la cama bed **I**
hacer la cama to make the bed **I**
la cámara camera **I**
la cámara de cine movie camera **II**
la cámara de video video camera **II**
la cámara digital digital camera **I, II**
el (la) camarero(a) (food) server **I**
el (la) camarógrafo(a) cameraman/camerawoman **II**
cambiar to change
cambiar de papel to change roles
el cambio change
caminar to walk **I**
la caminata hike **I**
dar o hacer una caminata to hike, to take a hike **I, II, 1.1**
el camión (*pl.* los camiones) truck
la camioneta SUV, truck **1.1**
la camisa shirt **I**
la camiseta T-shirt **I**
la campaña campaign **2.1**
el campeón (*pl.* los campeones) champion **I**
la campeona champion **I**
el campeonato championship **II**
el Campeonato Mundial Juvenil World Youth Championship
el campo field; the country, countryside **I**
el canal canal; channel
el canal de televisión TV channel **2.1**
la cancha court (sports) **I**
la canoa canoe **1.2**
cansado(a) tired **I**
el (la) cantante singer
cantar to sing **I**
la cantimplora canteen, water bottle **1.1**
el canto chant
la capa de ozono ozone layer **II, 3.1**
el caparazón (*pl.* los caparazones) shell (of an animal)
capaz capable
la capilla chapel
el capítulo chapter **8.1**
captar to capture
la cara face **II**
la carabela caravel
el caracol seashell **1.2**
el cariño affection
la carne meat **I**
la carnicería butcher shop **6.1**
caro(a) expensive **I, II**
¡Qué caro(a)! How expensive! **I**
el (la) carpintero(a) carpenter **II, 4.2**
la carrera race **I**; career **I**
el carrete reel
la carretera highway
el carro car **1.2**

la carroza float
la carta letter
  la carta al editor letter to the editor
  la carta de presentación cover letter
el cartel sign, poster
la cartera wallet **5.1**
el (la) cartero(a) mail carrier; postman/postwoman **II, 4.2**
el cartón cardboard **II**
la casa house **I**
  la casa editorial publishing company
  la casa rodante RV **1.2**
casarse to get married **II**
la cascada waterfall
la cáscara shell (of a nut or seed)
el casco helmet **I**
casi almost **I**
el caso case
  en caso de que in case **5.1**
castaño(a) brown (hair) **I**
el castillo castle **6.2**
la casualidad chance
  por casualidad by chance **6.2**
la catedral cathedral **II**
catorce fourteen **I**
el cautiverio captivity
cazar to hunt **II**
la cebolla onion **II**
celebrar to celebrate **I**
los celos jealousy **II**
  tener celos (de) to be jealous (of) **II**
el celular cellular telephone
la cena dinner **I**
cenar to dine, to have dinner **II**
  la hora de cenar suppertime
las cenizas ashes
el centro center; downtown **I**
  el centro comercial shopping center, mall **I**
  el centro histórico historic center **6.2**
cepillar to brush
  cepillarse los dientes to brush one's teeth **I, II**
el cepillo brush **I, II**
  el cepillo de dientes toothbrush **I, II**
la cerámica ceramics; ceramic **I**
  de cerámica (made of) ceramic **II**
cerca (de) near (to) **I**
el cerdo pork
  la chuleta de cerdo pork chop **II**
el cereal cereal **I**
la ceremonia ceremony **7.1**
cero zero **I**
cerrado(a) closed
  Está cerrado(a). It's closed. **II**
cerrar (ie) to close **I**
  cerrar el grifo to turn off the faucet **6.1**
la certeza certainty
el césped grass, lawn **I**
  cortar el césped to cut the grass **I**
el chaleco vest **II**
  el chaleco salvavidas life jacket **1.2**
el chambelán male attendant
el champú shampoo **I, II**
la chaqueta jacket **I**
charlar to chat **5.2**
¡Chau! Bye!
el cheque check **2.1**
chévere: ¡Qué chévere! How cool!
la chica girl **I**
el chico boy **I**
el chisme gossip
el chiste joke
  hacer chiste de to make fun of
el chorizo sausage
el ciclismo bicycle racing, cycling **II**
el ciclo cycle
  el ciclo de vida life cycle
cien one hundred **I**
la ciencia ficción science fiction
las ciencias science **I**
  las ciencias naturales natural sciences
el (la) científico(a) scientist **II, 4.1**
cierto(a) certain; true
  (No) Es cierto que... It is (not) true that... **II, 4.2**
la cima peak; height
cinco five **I**
cincuenta fifty **I**
el cine movie theater; the movies **I**
  la estrella de cine movie star **II**
el cinturón (*pl.* los cinturones) belt **II**
la cita quotation **2.2**; appointment
  tener una cita to have an appointment **II**
la ciudad city **I, II**
  la ciudad universitaria campus
la ciudadanía citizenship
el (la) ciudadano(a) citizen **3.2**
la civilización (*pl.* las civilizaciones) civilization **II**
claro(a) clear
  Claro. Of course.
  ¡Claro que sí! Of course! **I, II**
la clase class, classroom **I**; kind, type
el (la) cliente client
el clima climate **3.1**; weather
el clímax climax **8.1**
el club club
cobrar to charge (money)
el cobre copper
el coche car **I**; carriage
  el coche tirado por caballo horse-drawn carriage
  en coche by car **I**
el cochinillo suckling pig
cocido(a) cooked **II**
la cocina kitchen **I**; cuisine
cocinar to cook **I**
codicioso(a) greedy **8.2**
el código code
  el código de vestimenta dress code **7.1**
el codo elbow **II**
la cola tail
  hacer cola to get in line **II**
colaborar to collaborate **2.1**
el colegio school, high school
colgar (ue) to hang
el collar necklace **I, II**
el color color
  ¿De qué color es/son...? What color is/are...?
colorido(a) colorful
la columna column **2.2**
  la columna de consejos advice column
el columpio swing, swingset
la comedia comedy **II**
el comedor dining room **I**
  el comedor de beneficencia soup kitchen **2.1**
comentar to comment on, to talk about **5.2**
comenzar (ie) to begin **I**
comer to eat **I**
  comer al aire libre to picnic, to eat outside **I**
comercializar to commercialize, to market **3.2**
cometer to commit
  cometer un error to make a mistake **3.2**
cómico(a) funny **I**
la comida meal; food **I**
  la comida chatarra junk food **7.1**

el comienzo beginning, start **7.1**
el comité committee
el comité de eventos events committee **7.1**
el comité estudiantil student government **7.1**
como since; as, like
como sea however that may be
¿Cómo...? How...?; What? **I**
¿Cómo eres? What are you like? **I**
¿Cómo está usted? How are you? (formal) **I**
¿Cómo estás? How are you? (familiar) **I**
¿Cómo llego a...? How do I get to...? **II**
¿Cómo me queda(n)? How does it (do they) fit me? **II**
¡Cómo no! Of course! **II**
¿Cómo se llama? What's his/her/your (formal) name? **I**
¿Cómo te llamas? What's your name? (familiar) **I**
la cómoda dresser **I**
cómodo(a) comfortable
los compadres godparents
el (la) compañero(a) companion, partner
el (la) compañero(a) de equipo teammate **II**
la compañía company, business
comparar to compare
la comparsa dance troupe
compartir to share **I**
la competencia competition **II**
el (la) competidor(a) competitor
competir (i, i) to compete **II**
complejo(a) complex **3.1**
complicado(a) complicated
el comportamiento behavior
comportarse bien/mal to behave well/badly **4.1**
comprar to buy **I**
comprender to understand **I**
¿Comprendiste? Did you understand?
la comprensión understanding
comprensivo(a) understanding **4.1**
comprometerse to commit oneself
el compromiso commitment **3.2**
la computación computer studies
la computadora computer **I**
la computadora portátil laptop computer **5.1**
común common
en común in common

la comunidad community **II**
con with **I**
con anticipación in advance **1.1**
con cuidado carefully
Con mucho gusto. With pleasure. **II**
Con permiso. Excuse me. **II**
con tal (de) que as long as **5.1**
conceder to grant, to bestow
concentrarse to be concentrated
conciencia: la conciencia social social awareness **3.2**
el concierto concert **I**
concluir to conclude, to finish **5.2**
conclusión : en conclusión in conclusion **6.2**
el concurso contest
conducir (conduzco) to drive **1.2**; to steer
la conducta behavior **4.1**
el (la) conductor(a) conductor **6.2**
conectar to connect **I**
conectar(se) a Internet to connect to the Internet **I, 5.1**
confirmar: confirmar el vuelo to confirm a flight **II**
el conjunto band, musical group; (dance) group
conmigo with me **I, II**
conocer (conozco) to know, to be familiar with; to meet **I**
conocido(a) known
muy conocido(a) well-known
el conocimiento knowledge **II**
el contraste contrast
consecutivo(a) consecutive, in a row **6.2**
conseguir (i, i) to get, to find **1.1**
el (la) consejero(a) counselor, advisor
los consejos advice
dar consejos to give advice **5.1**
conservar to conserve **II**; to keep
la consideración consideration
considerado(a) considerate **4.1**
considerar to consider
construir to build **II**
el (la) consultor(a) consultant
el (la) consultor(a) de informática IT consultant
el consultorio doctor's/dentist's office **II**
el (la) consumidor(a) consumer **II**
la contabilidad accounting **7.2**
el (la) contador(a) accountant **7.2**

la contaminación pollution **II**, **3.1**; contamination
contar (ue) to tell (a story) **II**; to count
contar con to count on; to have, to include
contar con los demás to count on others **2.1**
contento(a) happy **I**
la contestadora answering machine
contestar to answer **I**
el contexto context **8.1**
contigo with you (familiar) **I, II**
contra against
la contraseña password **5.1**
contratar to hire **7.2**
convencer to convince
¡Estoy convencido(a)! I'm convinced! **II**
convertirse en to turn into **4.2**
la cooperación cooperation **2.1**
la copa goblet
la Copa Mundial World Cup **II**
el coraje courage **8.2**
el corazón (*pl.* los corazones) heart **I**
la corbata tie, necktie **II**
el corbatín (*pl.* los corbatines) bow tie **II**
el cordero lamb
la cordillera mountain range
el coro choir **7.1**
la corona tiara
corregir (i, i) (corrijo) to correct
el correo post office **II, 6.1**; mail
el correo electrónico e-mail **I**
correr to run **I**
la corriente electricity
cortar to cut **I**
cortar el césped to cut the grass **I**
la corte entourage, attendants
cortés polite
la cortina curtain **I**
corto(a) short (length) **I**
el cortometraje short documentary **2.2**
la cosa thing **I**
la cosecha harvest
coser to sew
la costa coast
costar (ue) to cost **I**
¿Cuánto cuesta(n)? How much does it (do they) cost? **I**
Cuesta(n)... It (They) cost(s)... **I**
la costumbre custom

cotidiano(a) daily
crear to create
la creatividad creativity **2.1**
crecer (crezco) to grow; to grow up
creer to believe, to think
  Creo que sí/no. I think/don't think so. **II**
  no creer que... to not believe that... **4.2**
la crema de afeitar shaving cream **II**
la cría (*pl.* las crías) brood
criar to raise, to bring up
el crimen (*pl.* los crímenes) crime
la crítica review **II**
criticar to criticize **3.2**
cronológico: en orden cronológico in chronological order **6.2**
el crucero cruise
  hacer un crucero to go on a cruise **1.2**
crudo(a) raw **II**
la cruz (*pl.* las cruces) cross
cruzar to cross **II**
el cuaderno notebook **I**
la cuadra city block **II**
el cuadro painting **6.2**; square
  de cuadros plaid **II**
¿Cuál(es)? Which?; What? **I**
  ¿Cuál es la especialidad de la casa? What is the specialty of the house? **II**
  ¿Cuál es la fecha? What is the date? **I**
  ¿Cuál es tu/su número de teléfono? What is your phone number? (familiar/formal) **I**
la cualidad quality
cualificado(a) qualified **7.2**
cualquier any
cuando when **I**
  cuando sea whenever that may be
¿Cuándo? When? **I**
cuanto
  en cuanto as soon as **8.1**
  en cuanto a as to, as for
cuánto(a) how much **I**
  ¿Cuánto cuesta(n)? How much does it (do they) cost? **I**
cuántos(as) how many **I**
  ¿Cuántos años tienes? How old are you? **I**
  ¿Cuántos(as)...? How many...? **I**
cuarenta forty **I**
el cuarto room; bedroom **I**
cuarto quarter **I**
  ...y cuarto quarter past... (the hour) **I**
cuarto(a) fourth **I**
cuatro four **I**
cuatrocientos(as) four hundred **I**
la cubierta deck (of a boat) **1.2**
el cubo bucket
la cuchara spoon **II**
el cuchillo knife **II**
el cuello neck **II**
la cuenta bill (in a restaurant) **I**
  darse cuenta de to realize **5.1**
  la cuenta de ahorros savings account **7.1**
  tener en cuenta to take into account
el cuento story, short story **8.1**
  un cuento policíaco crime story **8.1**
el cuero leather
  de cuero (made of) leather **II**
el cuerpo body **I**
la cuestión (*pl.* las cuestiones) question, issue **II, 2.2**
el cuestionario questionnaire
la cueva cave
el cuidado care
  con cuidado carefully
cuidar to care for, to take care of
  cuidar niños to baby-sit **7.1**
el cultivo cultivation
la cultura culture
el cumpleaños birthday **I**
  ¡Feliz cumpleaños! Happy birthday! **I**
cumplir con to carry out, to fulfill **2.1**
la cuñada sister-in-law **II, 1.2**
el cuñado brother-in-law **II, 1.2**
la cura cure **II**
curar to cure
curioso(a) curious
cursar to study
el curso course (of study) **7.2**

los dados dice **5.2**
¡Dale! Come on! **II**
la dama female attendant
las damas checkers **5.2**
dañar to damage, to harm **II, 3.1**
el daño damage
la danza dance
  la danza folklórica folk dance
dar (doy) to give **I**
  dar consejos to give advice **5.1**
  dar lo mismo to be all the same
  dar una caminata to hike **I, II**
  dar una sugerencia to make a suggestion **5.1**
  dar una vuelta to take a walk **6.1**
  darle de comer al perro to feed the dog **I**
  darse cuenta de to realize **5.1**
  darse prisa to hurry up
  Me da miedo. It scares me. **II**
  Quisiera darle las gracias a... I would like to thank... **II**
los datos information, data
  la base de datos database
de of, from **I**
  de antemano beforehand **2.1**
  de habla hispana Spanish-speaking
  de la mañana in the morning (with a time) **I**
  de la noche at night (with a time) **I**
  de la tarde in the afternoon (with a time) **I**
  de madera/oro/plata (made of) wood/gold/silver **I**
  de moda in style, fashionable
  De nada. You're welcome. **II**
  de repente suddenly
  de vacaciones on vacation **I**
  ¿De veras?, ¿De verdad? Really?
  de vez en cuando once in a while **I**
debajo (de) underneath, under **I**
el debate debate **2.2**
debatir to debate **5.2**
deber should, ought to **I**
el deber duty **4.2**
decidir to decide **7.1**
décimo(a) tenth **I**
decir (digo) to say **I**
  ¡Te digo la verdad! I'm telling you the truth! **II**
  ¿Diga? Hello? (on phone) **II**
  también se dice... you can also say...
la decisión (*pl.* las decisiones) decision
  tomar decisiones to make decisions **7.1**
la decoración (*pl.* las decoraciones) decoration **I**
decorar to decorate **I**
la dedicación dedication

dedicado(a) dedicated **4.1**
el dedo finger **II**
el dedo del pie toe **II**
el dedo pulgar thumb
la deforestación deforestation **II, 3.1**
dejar to leave (behind) **6.1**
¿Me deja ver? May I see? **I, II**
dejar de... to quit..., to give up... **7.1**
dejar un mensaje to leave a message **I, II**
dejar que to allow that **4.1**
Le dejo... en... I'll give... to you for... (a price) **I, II**
del (de la) of or from the **I**
delante (de) in front (of) **I**
delegar to delegate **2.1**
deletrear to spell
delgado(a) thin
delicioso(a) delicious **II**
los demás others
demasiado too; too much **I, II**
el (la) dentista dentist **II, 7.2**
dentro (de) inside (of) **I, 1.1**
los deportes sports **I**
los deportes acuáticos water sports
los deportes extremos extreme sports
el (la) deportista sportsman, sportswoman **II**
deportivo(a) sports, sporting
deprimido(a) depressed **I**
la derecha: doblar a la derecha to turn right **II**
derecho straight
seguir derecho to go straight **II**
el derecho law (profession) **7.2**
derecho(a) right (side, direction)
el derrumbe landslide **3.1**
desagradable disagreeable **4.1**
el desaliento discouragement
desarrollar to develop **3.1**
el desarrollo development **3.1**
el desastre disaster
desayunar to have breakfast **II**
el desayuno breakfast **I**
descansar to rest **I**
descargar to download **5.1**
descifrar to decipher
descomponer to break (down)
desconocido(a) unknown
lo desconocido the unknown
describir to describe **II, 2.2**
descubrir to discover **II**
el descuento discount **1.1**
desde from **II**; since
la desdicha unhappiness
el desfile parade
desear to wish, to want
el desenlace outcome **8.1**
el deseo desire
desesperado(a) desperate
desesperar to despair
desfilar to parade, to march
el desfile parade
deslizarse to slide
deslumbrante dazzling
el desodorante deodorant **II**
desordenar to mess up **6.1**
desorganizado(a) disorganized **I**
despertarse (ie) to wake up **I, II**
después (de) afterward; after **I**
destacado(a) outstanding **7.2**
destacarse por... to stand out (from others) for..., to be remarkable for... **4.1**
el destino destination
la destrucción destruction **II**
destruir to destroy **3.1**
desvanecerse to vanish
la desventaja disadvantage
el detalle detail
el (la) detective detective **II, 4.1**
detenerse (me detengo) to stop
detrás (de) behind **I**
el día day **I**
Algún día... Some day... **II**
Buenos días. Good morning. **I**
el día feriado holiday **7.1**
los días festivos holidays
¿Qué día es hoy? What day is today? **I**
todos los días every day **I**
el diálogo dialog **8.2**
diario(a) daily
dibujar to draw **I**
el dibujo drawing
los dibujos animados cartoons **2.2**
diciembre December **I**
diecinueve nineteen **I**
dieciocho eighteen **I**
dieciséis sixteen **I**
diecisiete seventeen **I**
el diente tooth **II**
la dieta diet
la dieta balanceada balanced diet **7.1**
seguir una dieta balanceada to follow a balanced diet **II**
diez ten **I**
diferente different
difícil difficult **I**
la dificultad difficulty
el dinero money **I**
el dinero en efectivo cash **II**
el dios god **II**
la diosa goddess **II**
la dirección (*pl.* las direcciones) address **I**; direction
la dirección electrónica e-mail address **I, II**
la dirección de escenografía stage direction **8.2**
pedir direcciones to ask for directions **6.2**
el (la) director(a) principal **I**; director **II**
dirigir (dirijo) to direct, to lead **7.1**; to direct (a play or movie) **8.2**
el disco compacto compact disc **I**
quemar un disco compacto to burn a CD **I**
Disculpe. Excuse me; I'm sorry. **II**
el discurso speech
discutir to discuss; to argue **II, 5.2**
el (la) diseñador(a) designer **II**
el (la) diseñador(a) de páginas web Web page designer **7.1**
el diseño design **2.1**
el disfraz (*pl.* los disfraces) costume
disfrutar (de) to enjoy **5.1**
disminuir to diminish, to decrease **3.1**
disponerse (me dispongo) a... to get ready to...
disponible available
distinguirse to be distinguished
distinto(a) distinct, different **5.1**
distribuir to distribute **2.2**
la diversión fun
divertido(a) fun **I**
¡Qué divertido! How fun! **I**
divertirse (ie, i) to enjoy oneself, to have fun **1.1**
doblar to turn **II**; to fold; to dub
doblar a la derecha/a la izquierda to turn right/left **II**
doce twelve **I**
el (la) doctor(a) doctor **II**
el documental documentary **II**
el documento (de identidad) (identification) document **5.1**
el dólar dollar **I**

doler (ue) to hurt, to ache **I**
el dolor ache
el dolor de estómago stomachache
domingo Sunday **I**
la donación (*pl.* las donaciones) donation
donar to donate **2.2**
donde where
donde sea wherever that may be
¿Dónde? Where? **I**
¿De dónde eres? Where are you from? (familiar) **I**
¿De dónde es usted? Where are you from? (formal) **I**
¿De dónde es? Where is he/she from? **I**
Por favor, ¿dónde queda...? Can you please tell me where ... is? **II**
dorado(a) golden
dormir (ue, u) to sleep **I**
dormir una siesta to take a nap **5.2**
el saco de dormir sleeping bag **1.1**
dormirse (ue, u) to fall asleep **I, II**
dos two **I**
doscientos(as) two hundred **I**
el drama drama **II, 8.2**; play, dramatic work **7.1**
el (la) dramaturgo(a) playwright, dramatist **8.2**
la ducha shower **6.1**
ducharse to take a shower **I, II**
dudar to hesitate
dudar que... to doubt that... **4.2**
dudoso(a) doubtful
Es dudoso que... It's doubtful that... **4.2**
el (la) dueño(a) owner **7.2**
dulce sweet **II**
el agua dulce fresh water **1.1**
durante during **I**
durar to last
el DVD DVD **I**

echar to throw
el (la) ecólogo(a) ecologist
el ecoturismo ecotourism
el ecuador equator
el edificio building **II**
editar to edit **II**
el (la) editor(a) editor **II, 2.2**
la educación education
educado(a) educated; polite **7.2**
el efecto effect
el efecto invernadero greenhouse effect **3.1**
los efectos especiales special effects **II**
eficiente efficient **7.2**
el ejemplo example
el ejercicio exercise
hacer ejercicio to exercise **II**
el ejército army **II**
él he; him **I, II**
el (la) electricista electrician **4.1**
elegir (i, i) (elijo) to choose **2.1**
el elemento element
ella she; her **I, II**
ellos(as) they; them **I, II**
embellecer to beautify
emigrar to emigrate
la emisora (de radio) (radio) station **2.1**
emitir to broadcast **2.2**
emocionado(a) excited **I**
Estoy muy emocionado(a). I'm overcome with emotion. **II**
emocionante exciting
emparejar to match
empatado(a): estar empatado to be tied (a score) **II**
el emperador emperor **II**
empezar (ie) to begin **I**
el (la) empleado(a) employee **7.1**
el empleo job **7.1**
emprender to undertake **3.2**
la empresa company, firm **7.2**
la administración de empresas business administration **7.2**
el (la) empresario(a) businessperson **4.1**
en in **I**; on
en absoluto not at all **1.2**
en autobús by bus **I**
en avión by plane **I**
en barco by boat **I**
en caso de que in case **5.1**
en coche by car **I**
en conclusión in conclusion **6.2**
en cuanto as soon as **8.1**
en línea online **I**
en orden cronológico in chronological order **6.2**
en tren by train **I**
en línea online **I**
estar en línea to be online **I, II**
enamorado(a) in love
estar enamorado(a) de to be in love with **II**
encajar to fit, to be fitting
el encaje lace
encantado(a) magical, enchanted
Encantado(a). Delighted; Pleased to meet you. **I**
encantar to delight **II**
Me encanta... I love...
Sí, me encantaría. Yes, I would love to. **II**
encargarse de to take charge of, to make oneself responsible for **3.2**
encender (ie) to light (a match or fire) **1.1**
encender la luz to turn on the light **II**
encima (de) on top (of) **I**
encontrar (ue) to find **I**
encontrarse (ue) to find oneself; to be located
encontrarse con to meet up with **5.2**
el encuentro encounter **5.2**
la encuesta survey
el (la) enemigo(a) enemy **II**
enero January **I**
la enfermedad sickness, disease
el (la) enfermero(a) nurse **II, 7.2**
enfermo(a) sick **I**
enfocarse (en) to focus (on)
el enfoque focus
enfriar to cool
el enlace link **5.1**
enojado(a) angry **I**
enojarse to get angry **II**
enojono(a) short-tempered
enorme huge, enormous
la ensalada salad **I**
ensayar to rehearse **8.2**
el ensayo essay **8.1**; rehearsal **8.2**
enseñar to teach **I**
ensuciar to get (something) dirty **6.1**
entender (ie) to understand **I**
entenderse bien to understand each other well **II**
entenderse mal to misunderstand each other **II**
enterarse de to find out about **6.1**
entonces then; so **I, II**
la entrada ticket **I**; entrance **6.2**
entrar to enter
entre between **II**
la entrega delivery

el entremés (*pl.* los entremeses) appetizer **II**
entremeterse to meddle
entretener to entertain
el (la) entrenador(a) coach, trainer **II, 4.1**
el entrenamiento training
entrenarse to train **II**
la entrevista interview **II, 2.2**
entrevistar to interview **II, 2.2**
el envase container **2.1**
enviar to send **5.1**
envolver (ue) to wrap **I**
el equilibrio balance
el equipaje luggage **II**
facturar el equipaje to check one's luggage **II**
el equipo team **I**; equipment, gear **1.2**
la erosión erosion **3.1**
el error error, mistake
escalar to climb
escalar montañas to climb mountains **II, 1.1**
la escalera stairs **I**
el escáner scanner **5.1**
la escapada getaway **1.2**
el escaparate display window **6.1**
la escena scene **II**
el escenario stage **8.2**; set, movie set
la escenografía scenery **8.2**
escoger (escojo) to choose
escolar school *(adj.)*, school-related **II**
esconder to hide **5.1**
escribir to write **I**
el (la) escritor(a) writer **II**
el escritorio desk **I**
la escritura writing
escuchar to listen (to) **I**
el escudo coat of arms
la escuela school **I**
la escuela secundaria high school
la escuela técnica technical school **7.2**
la escultura sculpture **II**
ese(a) that... (there) **I, II**
ése(a) that one **II**
el esfuerzo effort
la esmeralda emerald
esos(as) those... (there) **I, II**
ésos(as) those ones **II**
el espacio space, room
la espada sword
los espaguetis spaghetti **II**
el español Spanish **I**
el espanto fright, terror
especial special
la especialidad specialty **II**; major (in college), specialization **7.2**
la especialidad de la casa specialty of the house **II**
especializarse en to major in **7.2**
la especie species
las especies en peligro de extinción endangered species **II, 3.1**
el espectáculo performance, show **5.2**
el espejo mirror **I**
la esperanza hope **7.1**
esperar to wait (for) **I, II**
las espinacas spinach **II**
el espíritu spirit
el esplendor splendor, glory
la esposa wife, spouse **II, 1.2**
el esposo husband, spouse **II, 1.2**
el (la) esposo(a) spouse **1.2**
la espuma mist; foam
esquiar to ski
la esquina corner
en la esquina on the corner **II**
establecer to establish **7.2**
el establecimiento establishment
la estación (*pl.* las estaciones) season **I**; station
la estación de metro subway station **6.1**
la estación de tren train station **II**
el estadio stadium **I**
el estado state
la estancia ranch
el estante shelf
estar to be **I**
¿Está...? Is... there? **I, II**
¿Está bien? OK?
Está abierto(a)/cerrado(a). It's open/closed. **II**
estar de vacaciones to be on vacation **II**
estar en línea to be online **I, II**
estar/no estar de acuerdo con to agree/disagree with **II, 2.2**
No, no está. No, he's/she's not here. **I, II**
la estatua statue **II**
la estatuilla statuette
el este east
este(a) this... (here) **I, II**
éste(a) this one **II**
el estilo style **8.1**
Estimado(a)... Dear...
el estómago stomach **I**
el dolor de estómago stomachache
estos(as) these... (here) **I, II**
éstos(as) these ones **II**
la estrategia strategy **7.2**
estrecho(a) narrow
la estrella star; movie star
la estrella de cine movie star **II**
estremecerse to shudder
estrenar to premiere, to open **II**
el estreno premiere **II, 5.2**
el estrés stress **7.1**
estresado(a) stressed **7.1**
la estrofa stanza **8.1**
el estuco stucco
el (la) estudiante student **I**
el (la) estudiante de intercambio exchange student
estudiar to study **I**
el estudio study
estudioso(a) studious **I**
la estufa stove **1.1**
la estufa de gas gas stove **1.1**
la etapa stage
eterno(a) eternal
el euro euro **I**
evaluar to evaluate **3.2**
evitar to avoid **5.1**
el examen (*pl.* los exámenes) test, exam **I**
la excavación (*pl.* las excavaciones) excavation **II**
¡Excelente! Excellent! **II**
la excursión (*pl.* las excursiones) day trip, excursion; tour
hacer una excursión to go on a day trip **II**
exhibir to exhibit
exigir (exijo) que to demand that **4.1**
exiliarse to to be exiled
el éxito success; hit (song)
tener éxito to be successful **II**
exitoso(a) successful
exótico(a) exotic
experimentar to experience
explicar to explain **II, 2.2**
explorar to explore **6.2**
expresar to express
la extinción (*pl.* las extinciones) extinction
extinguirse to become extinct **3.1**
extranjero: al
extranjero abroad **1.1**

la fachada facade, front of a building
fácil easy **I**
fácilmente easily
facturar el equipaje to check one's luggage **II**
la facultad school, department (in college) **7.2**
la falda skirt **II**
falso(a) false
falta: hacer falta to lack, to be missing
faltar to lack, to be missing
la fama fame **4.2**
la familia family **I**
los familiares family members
famoso(a) famous **II**
la fantasía fantasy
la farmacia pharmacy, drug store **II**
el faro lighthouse
la farsa farce; comical play
el (la) farsante fraud **8.2**
fastidiar to annoy
favorito(a) favorite **I**
febrero February **I**
la fecha date **I**
  ¿Cuál es la fecha? What is the date? **I**
  la fecha de nacimiento birth date **I**
  la fecha límite deadline **2.2**
felicitar to congratulate
¡Felicidades! Congratulations!
feliz happy
  ¡Feliz cumpleaños! Happy birthday! **I**
feo(a) ugly **I**
la feria fair **I**
la ferretería hardware store **6.1**
fiable dependable **7.2**
la ficha game piece **5.2**
fiel faithful **4.1**
fiesta party; holiday
  la fiesta de sorpresa surprise party **I**
  la fiesta nacional national holiday
figurar en to appear in **4.2**
el filete a la parrilla grilled steak **II**
filmar to film **II**
el fin end
  a fin de que in order that **5.1**
  el fin de semana weekend **I, II**
  por fin finally **I, II**
  sin fines lucrativos nonprofit
financiero(a) financial
fino(a) fine, of high quality **II**
el flan custard **II**
flexible flexible **7.2**
flojo(a) loose (clothing)
la flor flower **1.1**
la florería flower shop **6.1**
el florero vase
la fogata campfire **1.1**
el follaje foliage
el folleto brochure
fomentar to support, to foster **3.1**
el fondo back; bottom
  los fondos funds **2.1**
la forma shape, form
  ponerse en forma to get in shape **7.1**
formal formal **5.2**
formar to form
fortalecer (fortalezco) to strengthen
la fortaleza fortress **6.2**
el fósforo match **1.1**
la foto photo, picture **I**
  el foto ensayo photo essay
  tomar o sacar fotos to take pictures **I, II**
el (la) fotógrafo(a) photographer **II, 2.2**
fracasar to fail **II**
el fracaso failure **3.2**
la frecuencia frequency
frecuente frequent
frecuentemente frequently **II**
el fregadero kitchen sink **6.1**
freír (i, i) to fry **II**
el frente front
  en frente de in front of
  frente a across from, facing **II, 1.1**
la fresa strawberry **II**
fresco(a) fresh **II**
  hacer fresco to be cool (weather) **1.2**
los frijoles beans **I**
el frío cold **I**
  Hace frío. It is cold. **I**
  tener frío to be cold (person) **I**
frito(a) fried **II**
la fruta fruit **I**
la frutería fruit stand **6.1**
el fuego fire
  los fuegos artificiales fireworks
la fuente fountain **6.1**; source
fuera (de) outside (of) **1.1**
fuerte strong **I**
la fuerza natural natural force
el (la) fundador(a) founder
fundar to found
el fútbol soccer (the sport) **I**
  el fútbol americano football (the sport) **I**
el futuro future
  En el futuro... In the future... **II**
futuro(a) future

las gafas glasses **5.1**
  las gafas de sol sunglasses **5.1**
la gala gala; formal party **II**
la galleta cookie **I**
el (la) ganadero(a) cattle rancher
el ganado cattle
ganador(a) winning
el (la) ganador(a) winner **I**
ganar to win **I**
  ganarse la vida como... to earn a living as... **II**
el gancho hook
una ganga a bargain **II**
la garganta throat **II**
gastar to spend **2.1**
el (la) gato(a) cat **I**
el gazpacho cold tomato soup **II**
el (la) gemelo(a) twin
generalmente generally, in general **II**
el género literario genre **8.1**
la generosidad generosity
generoso(a) generous **II, 4.1**
genial wonderful, awesome
la gente people **II**
  la gente sin hogar the homeless **2.1**
el (la) gerente manager **7.2**
el gesto gesture **8.2**
el gigante giant
la gimnasia gymnastics
el gimnasio gymnasium **I**
gitano(a) Gypsy
el glaciar glacier
el globo balloon **I**
el gol goal (in sports)
golpear to hit
la goma rubber
la gorra cap **II**
el gorro winter hat **I**
el gozo enjoyment, happiness
el grabado sobre madera wood engraving
el grabador tape recorder **2.2**

Gracias. Thank you. **I**
Gracias por atenderme. Thank you for your service. **II**
Muchas gracias. Thank you very much. **I**
Quisiera darle las gracias a... I would like to thank... **II**
la graduación graduation **7.1**
graduarse to graduate **7.1**
la gráfica graphic **2.2**
la gramática grammar
grande big, large **I**
la grandeza grandeur
el grifo faucet **6.1**
abrir el grifo to turn on the faucet **6.1**
cerrar el grifo to turn off the faucet **6.1**
el grito shout, cry
el grupo group
el guante glove **I**
los guantes de trabajo work gloves **2.1**
guapo(a) good-looking **I**
guardar to keep, to put away **5.1**
la guerra war **II**
el (la) guerrero(a) warrior **II**
la guía guide, guidebook **1.1**
la guía del viajero travel guide
el (la) guía guide *(person)*
el guión (*p* los guiones) screenplay **II**; script **8.2**
el (la) guionista screenwriter **II**
el guisante pea
la guitarra guitar **I**
gustar to like **I**
Me gusta... I like... **I**
Me gustaría... I would like... **I, II**
No me gusta... I don't like... **I**
¿Qué profesión te gustaría tener? What do you want to be? **II**
¿Qué te gusta hacer? What do you like to do? **I**
¿Te gusta...? Do you like...? **I**
¿Te gustaría...? Would you like...? **I**
el gusto pleasure **I**
Con mucho gusto. With pleasure. **II**
El gusto es mío. The pleasure is mine. **I**
Mucho gusto. Nice to meet you. **I**

haber to have
Había una vez... Once upon a time there was/were... ... **II**
ha habido... there have been...
No hay de qué. Don't mention it. **II**
la habitación (*pl.* las habitaciones) hotel room **II**
la habitación doble double room **II**
la habitación individual single room **II**
el (la) habitante inhabitant
hablar to talk, to speak **I**
de habla hispana Spanish-speaking
hablar por teléfono to talk on the phone **I**
¿Puedo hablar con... ? May I speak to...? **I, II**
hacer (hago) to make, to do
Hace calor. It is hot. **I**
Hace frío. It is cold. **I**
Hace muchos siglos... Many centuries ago...
Hace sol. It is sunny. **I**
Hace viento. It is windy. **I**
hacer clic en to click on **I, II**
hacer cola to get in line **II**
hacer ejercicio to exercise **II**
hacer esquí acuático to water-ski **I**
hacer falta to lack, to be missing
hacer fresco to be cool (weather) **1.2**
hacer la cama to make the bed **I**
hacer la maleta to pack a suitcase **II**
hacer la tarea to do homework **I**
hacer los mandados to do errands **6.1**
hacer surf de vela to windsurf **I**
hacer surfing to surf, to go surfing **I**
hacer un papel to play a role **II**
hacer un viaje to take a trip **I, II**
hacer una caminata to hike **1.1**
hacer una excursión to go on an excursion or guided tour **1.1**
hacer una visita guiada to take a guided tour **6.2**
hacerle gracia a alguien to please someone
hecho(a) a mano handmade **II**
Me hace llorar. It makes me cry. **II**
Me hace reír. It makes me laugh. **II**
¿Qué hicieron ustedes? What did you do? (pl., formal) **I**
¿Qué hiciste? What did you do? (sing., familiar) **I**
¿Qué tiempo hace? What is the weather like? **I**
hacerse to become
hacerse mujer to become a woman
hacia toward
hacia abajo down
hacia arriba up
la hamaca hammock
el hambre hunger
tener hambre to be hungry **I**
la hamburguesa hamburger **I**
la harina flour
harto: estar harto(a) to be tired or fed up
hasta to **II**; until
Hasta luego. See you later. **I**
Hasta mañana. See you tomorrow. **I**
hasta que until **5.1**
hay... there is/are... **I**
hay que... one has to..., one must... **I**
la hazaña feat, exploit
la heladería ice cream shop **II**
el helado ice cream **I**
la herencia heritage
la herida wound
herido(a) hurt **I**
herir (ie, i) to wound
la hermana sister **I**
el hermano brother **I**
los hermanos brothers; brother(s) and sister(s) **I**
hermoso(a) handsome; pretty **II**
el héroe hero **II**
heroico(a) heroic **II**
la heroína heroine **II**
la herramienta tool **II**

hervido(a) boiled **II**
hervir (ie, i) to boil **II**
la hierba herb
la hija daughter **I**
el hijo son **I**
los hijos children, son(s) and daughter(s) **I**
la historia history **I**; story
histórico(a) historic; historical **II**
la historieta comic strip
el hogar home
  el hogar de ancianos nursing home **2.1**
  la gente sin hogar the homeless **2.1**
la hoja leaf
  la hoja de vida resume
Hola. Hello., Hi. **I**
el hombre man **I**
  el hombre de negocios businessman **II, 7.2**
el hombro shoulder **II**
el homenaje homage
honesto(a) honest, sincere **7.2**
el honor honor **4.2**
honrado(a) honest, honorable **7.2**
honrar to honor
la hora hour; time **I**
  a la hora que sea – at whatever time that might be
  la hora de cenar – suppertime
  ¿A qué hora es/son...? At what time is/are...? **I**
  ¿Qué hora es? What time is it? **I**
horadar to drill
el horario schedule **I**
el horizonte horizon
el horno oven **6.1**
horrible horrible **I**
el hospital hospital **2.1**
el hostal hostel; inn **II**
el hotel hotel **I, II**
hoy today **I**
  hoy en día nowadays
  Hoy es... Today is . . . **I**
  ¿Qué día es hoy? What day is today? **I**
la huelga labor strike
la huella footprint
el huevo egg **I**
húmedo(a) humid
el huracán (*pl.* los huracanes) hurricane

I

el icono icon **I, II**
la idea idea
  Es buena idea/mala idea. It's a good idea/bad idea. **II**
ideal ideal **I**
idealizar (a alguien) to idealize (someone) **4.1**
la identificación identification, ID **II**
el idioma language **7.2**
  el idioma castellano the Spanish language
la iglesia church
igual equal, the same
Igualmente. Same here; Likewise. **I**
iluminar to illuminate
ilusionado: estar ilusionado(a) to be excited, to be thrilled **5.1**
la imagen (*pl.* las imágenes) image **4.2**
imitar to imitate **4.1**
la impaciencia impatience
impaciente impatient **II, 4.1**
implicar to imply **8.1**
la importancia importance
importante important **I**
  Es importante (que...) It's important (that...) **II**
importar to be important, to matter **II**
imposible impossible
imprescindible: es imprescindible que... it is indispensable that... **3.2**
impresionante impressive, awesome
imprimir to print **5.1**
improbable: es improbable que... It's improbable that... **4.2**
el impuesto tax **7.1**
el incendio fire (accidental)
  el incendio forestal forest fire **II**
incluido(a) included
incluir to include
incontable countless
increíble unbelievable
indígena indigenous, native
inferir (ie, i) to infer **8.1**
la influencia influence
influir to influence
la información information **II**
informal informal, casual **5.2**
informarse to keep informed **3.1**
el informe report

la ingeniería engineering **7.2**
el (la) ingeniero(a) engineer **II, 7.2**
ingenioso(a) clever **4.1**
el inglés English **I**
el ingrediente ingredient **II**
la iniciativa initiative **7.2**
la inmigración immigration
el (la) inmigrante immigrant
la innovación (*pl.* las innovaciones) innovation **3.1**
inolvidable unforgettable **1.1**
el insecto insect
insistir to insist **3.2**
insólito(a) unusual **8.2**
el (la) integrante member
inteligente intelligent **I**
intentar to try
intercambiar opiniones to exchange opinions **5.2**
el intercambio exchange
el interés (*pl.* los intereses) interest
interesante interesting **I**
interesar to interest **II**
el intermedio intermission **8.2**
Internet Internet **I, II**
  conectarse a Internet to connect to the Internet **I**
  navegar por Internet to surf the Web **I**
  por Internet on the Internet
interpretar to perform (a dance)
el (la) intérprete performer
la inundación (*pl.* las inundaciones) flood **3.1**
el invento invention **3.1**
el (la) inversionista investor
invertir (ie, i) to invest **3.2**
la investigación (*pl.* las investigaciones) research **3.1**
investigar to investigate **II, 2.2**
el invierno winter **I**
la invitación (*pl.* las invitaciones) invitation **II**
los invitados guests **I**
invitar to invite **I**
  Te invito. I invite you; I'll treat you. **I**
ir (voy) to go **I**
  ir a... to be going to... **I**
  ir de compras to go shopping **I**
  ir de tapas to go out to eat **6.1**
  ir de vacaciones to go on vacation **II**
  irle bien (a alguien) to do well **7.1**
  Vamos a... Let's... **I**

la irresponsabilidad irresponsibility **3.2**
irse (me voy) to go; to leave **II**
la isla island
el itinerario itinerary **II**
la izquierda: doblar a la izquierda to turn left **II**
izquierdo(a) left (side, direction)

el jabón (*pl.* los jabones) soap **I, II**
el jamón (*pl.* los jamones) (ham **I**
el jarabe syrup
el jardín (*pl.* los jardines) garden **I**
  los jardines botánicos botanical gardens
los jeans jeans **I**
joven (*pl.* jóvenes) young **I**
el (la) joven (*pl.* los jóvenes) young man/woman **II**
las joyas jewelry **I, II**
la joyería jewelry store **II**
jubilarse to retire
el juego game
  el juego de mesa board game **5.2**
  los juegos de computadora computer games **5.1**
  los Juegos Olímpicos Olympic Games **II**
  los Juegos Panamericanos Panamerican Games **II**
jueves Thursday **I**
el (la) juez(a) (*pl.* los jueces, las juezas) judge **7.2**
el (la) jugador(a) player **I**
jugar (ue) to play (sports or games) **I**
  jugar a los bolos to go bowling
  jugar al fútbol to play soccer **I**
  jugar en equipo to play on a team **II**
el jugo juice **I**
  el jugo de naranja orange juice **I**
julio July **I**
junio June **I**
juntar
  juntar fondos to fundraise **2.1**
  juntarse (con) to get together (with) **1.2**
junto a next to **1.1**
junto(a) together
jurar to swear (an oath)
  ¡Te lo juro! I swear to you! **II**

el kayac kayak **1.1**
el kiosco kiosk **6.1**

el lado side
  al lado (de) next to **I**
  por un lado... por otro lado on the one hand... on the other hand **II, 3.2**
el ladrón (*pl.* ladrones) thief
el lago lake
lamentable: Es lamentable que... It's too bad that...
la lámpara lamp **I**
la lana wool
el lápiz (*pl.* los lápices) pencil **I**
largo(a) long
el largometraje feature, full-length movie **2.2**
la lástima shame, pity
  ¡Qué lástima! What a shame! **I, II**
  Es una lástima que... It's a shame that...
lastimarse to hurt oneself
la lata can, metal can **2.1**
  la lata de refresco soda can
  ser una lata to be a nuisance **2.1**
latoso(a) annoying **2.1**
el lavabo bathroom sink **6.1**
lavar to wash **I**
  lavarse to wash oneself **I, II**
  lavarse la cara to wash one's face **I**
  lavarse el pelo to wash one's hair
el lazo lasso
la lección (*pl.* las lecciones) lesson
la leche milk **I**
la lechería dairy store **6.1**
la lechuga lettuce **II**
la lechuza owl
el (la) lector(a) reader
  el lector DVD DVD player **I**
la lectura reading
leer to read **I**
lejos (de) far (from) **I**
el lema motto **2.1**
la leña firewood
lentamente slowly
lento(a) slow **II**
el letrero sign, poster **2.1**
levantar to lift **I**; to raise **8.2**
  levantar el telón to raise the curtain **8.2**
  levantar pesas to lift weights **I**
  levantarse to get up **I, II**
la ley law
  la ley de oro the golden rule
  las leyes laborales labor laws
la leyenda legend **II**
la libertad liberty, freedom
la libra pound (weight)
la librería bookstore **II**
el libro book **I**
  el libro de historietas comic book **8.1**
el liceo high school
el (la) líder leader
la liga league
ligero(a) light (weight)
el limón (*pl.* los limones) lemon **II**
limpiar to clean **I**
limpio(a) clean **I**
el lino linen
el lío mess **6.1**
la lista list
listo(a) ready
la llama flame
  en llamas on fire, burning
la llamada phone call **I**
llamar to call
  llamar a alguien to call someone (by phone) **I, II**
llamarse to be called
  ¿Cómo se llama? What's his/her/your (formal) name? **I**
  ¿Cómo te llamas? What's your name? (familiar) **I**
  Me llamo... My name is... **I**
  Se llama... His/Her name is . . . **I**
el llano prairie, plain
las llanuras plains
la llave key **II**
la llegada arrival **II**
llegar to arrive **I**
  ¿Cómo llego a...? How do I get to...? **II**
llenar to fill (up) **1.1**
  llenar una solicitud de empleo to fill out an application **7.1**
llevar to take, to carry **II**; to wear **I**
llevarse
  bien (mal) to (not) get along **II**
llorar to cry **II**
  Me hace llorar. It makes me cry. **II**

llover (ue) to rain **I**
la lluvia rain
Lo siento. I'm sorry. **I**
la locura craziness
el (la) locutor(a) announcer
lograr to achieve **4.2**
el logro achievement, success **4.2**
luchar to struggle **3.2**
luego later; then **I, II**
  Hasta luego. See you later. **I**
el lugar place **I**
  tener lugar to take place
la luna moon
lunes Monday **I**
la luz (*pl.* las luces) light
  encender la luz to turn on the light **II**

M

la madera wood **I**
  de madera (made of) wood **I, II**
la madrastra stepmother **I**
la madre mother **I**
la madrina godmother **II, 1.2**
la madrugada dawn
el (la) maestro(a) teacher **I**
el maíz corn
mal badly
  Mal. ¿Y tú/usted? Bad. And you? (familiar/formal) **I**
la maleta suitcase **II**
  hacer la maleta to pack a suitcase **II**
malo(a) bad **I**
  Es malo que... It's not good that... **II**
mañana tomorrow **I**
  Hasta mañana. See you tomorrow.
  Mañana es... Tomorrow is ...
la mañana morning **I**
  de la mañana in the morning (with a time) **I**
el mandado errand
  hacer los mandados to do errands **6.1**
mandar to send **I**; to order, to command **I, 4.1**
  mandar tarjetas postales to send postcards **II**
  mandar que to order, command that **4.1**
el mandato command
la manga sleeve
la manifestación (*pl.* las manifestaciones) demonstration
la mano hand **I**
  (estar) hecho(a) a mano (to be) handmade **II**
  ¡Manos a la obra! Let's get to work!
la manta blanket **5.2**
mantener (mantengo) to keep, to maintain **1.2**
  mantener el equilibrio to keep one's balance **1.2**
  mantenerse en forma to stay in shape **II**
la manzana apple **I**; (city) block **6.1**
el mapa map **I**
el maquillaje makeup **II**
maquillarse to put on makeup **I, II**
la máquina machine
el mar sea **I**
la maravilla marvel
marearse to get seasick; to get dizzy **1.2**
la mariposa butterfly **1.1**
los mariscos seafood
marrón (*pl.* marrones) brown **I**
martes Tuesday **I**
marzo March **I**
más more **I**; plus, in addition to
  más de... more than (with numbers) **II**
  Más o menos. ¿Y tú/usted? So-so. And you? (familiar/formal) **I**
  más que... more than... **I, II**
  más... que more... than **I, II**
  más tarde later (on) **I, II**
la máscara mask; masquerade
la mascota pet
las matemáticas math **I**
la materia subject (in school)
el matrimonio marriage; married couple **1.2**
mayo May **I**
la mayonesa mayonnaise **II**
mayor older **I, II**
el (la) mecánico(a) mechanic **4.1**
la medalla medal
  la medalla de oro/plata/bronce gold/silver/bronze medal
el (la) médico(a) doctor **7.2**
el medio medium
  en medio de in the middle of
  por medio de by means of
el medio ambiente environment **II, 3.1**
medio(a) half
  ... y media half past... (the hour) **I**
medioambiental environmental
mejor better **I, II**
la mejora improvement **3.2**
mejorar to improve **II, 3.1**
la memoria memory
menor younger **I, II**
menos less
  ... menos (diez) (ten) to/before... (the hour) **I**
  a menos que unless **5.1**
  menos de... less than... (with numbers) **II**
  menos que... less than... **I, II**
  menos... que less... than **I, II**
el mensaje lesson; message **II**
  dejar un mensaje to leave a message **I, II**
  el mensaje instantáneo instant message
el mensajero instantáneo instant messaging **I, II**
la mente mind
la mentira lie, falsehood
el menú menu **I**
el mercado market **I**
  el mercado al aire libre open-air market **II**
  el mercado laboral labor market
las mercancías merchandise
merendar (ie) to have a snack **1.2**
la merienda afternoon snack **II**
el mes month **I**
  el mes pasado last month **II**
la mesa table **I**
  poner la mesa to set the table **I**
la mesita nightstand, end table **6.1**
la meta goal **4.2**
la metáfora metaphor **8.1**
el metal metal
  de metal (made of) metal **II**
meter
  meter un gol to score a goal **II**
  meterse en to go into **1.1**
  meterse con alguien to provoke someone
  meterse en problemas to get into trouble **6.2**
el metro subway **6.1**; meter
la mezcla mixture
mezclado(a) mixed **II**
mezclar to mix **II**
la mezquita mosque
mi my **I**

mí me **I, II**
el micrófono microphone **II**
el microondas microwave (oven) **6.1**
el miedo fear **I**
  Me da miedo. It scares me. **II**
  ¡Qué miedo! How scary! **I**
  tener miedo to be afraid **I**
la miel honey
el miembro member
  ser miembro de... to be a member of... **7.1**
mientras tanto meanwhile
miércoles Wednesday **I**
la migración (*pl.* las migraciones) migration
mil thousand, one thousand **I**
el milagro miracle
el (la) militar soldier
millón: un millón (de) million, one million **I**
el minuto minute **I**
el mirador outlook, lookout **6.2**
mirar to watch **I**; to look (at)
mismo(a) same
el mito myth
la mochila backpack **I**
la moda style, fashion
  estar de moda to be in style **II**
moderno(a) modern **II**
la modestia modesty
modesto(a) modest **4.1**
moler (ue) to grind
molestar to bother
molesto(a) annoying **2.1**
molido(a) ground (up) **II**
el momento moment
  Un momento. One moment. **I**
la moneda currency
el monedero change purse **5.1**
el monje monk
el mono monkey
la montaña mountain **II**
  la montaña rusa roller coaster **I**
montar to ride **I**; to put up **1.1**
  montar a caballo to ride a horse **I, II**
  montar en bicicleta to ride a bike **I**
el monumento monument **II**
morir (ue, u) to die **II**
el mortero mortar and pestle
la mostaza mustard **II**
mostrar (ue) to show
el mote nickname
motivado(a) motivated **7.2**
la moto acuática personal watercraft **1.2**
la muchacha girl
el muchacho boy
mucho a lot **I**
  Mucho gusto. Nice to meet you. **I**
muchos(as) many **I**
  muchas veces often, many times **I**
mudarse to move, to relocate
los muebles furniture **I**
el muelle dock
la mujer woman **I**
  la mujer de negocios businesswoman **II, 7.2**
el (la) mulo(a) mule
mundial global, world *(adj.)*
el mundo world **II**
la muñeca wrist **II**
la muralla wall **6.2**
el murciélago bat (animal)
el muro wall
musculoso(a) muscular **II**
el museo museum **I**
la música music **I**
  la música bailable dance music **5.2**
  la música folklórica folk music
  la música rock rock music **I**
el (la) músico(a) musician **4.2**
  el (la) músico(a) callejero(a) street musician **5.2**
muy very **I**
  Muy bien. ¿Y tú/usted? Very well. And you? (familiar/formal) **I**

nacer (nazco) to be born
el nacimiento birth
nacional national
nada nothing **I, II**
  De nada. You're welcome. **I, II**
nadar to swim **I**
nadie no one, nobody **I, II**
los naipes cards **5.2**
la naranja orange (fruit) **I**
la nariz (*pl.* las narices) nose **I**
la narración narration **II**
narrar to narrate **8.1**
la natación swimming **I**
la naturaleza nature **II, 1.1**
el (la) navegante navigator
navegar to sail, to go sailing
  navegar por Internet to surf the Web **I**
  navegar por rápidos to go whitewater rafting **1.1**
la Navidad Christmas
la neblina fog
necesario(a) necessary
  Es necesario (que...) It's necessary (that...) **II**
la necesidad need
necesitar to need **I**
el negocio business
  el hombre/la mujer de negocios businessman/businesswoman **II, 7.2**
negro(a) black **I**
nervioso(a) nervous **I**
nevar (ie) to snow **I**
la nevera refrigerator
ni... ni neither... nor **I, II**
la nieta granddaughter, grandchild **1.2**
el nieto grandson, grandchild **1.2**
los nietos grandchildren **1.2**
la nieve snow
ningún none, not any **II**
ninguno(a) none, not any **I, II**
el (la) niñero(a) babysitter **7.1**
la niñez childhood
el (la) niño(a) child **II**
el nivel level
no no **I**
  no sólo... sino también... not only... but also... **II**
  no renovable nonrenewable **3.1**
la noche night; evening **I**
  Buenas noches. Good evening; Good night. **I**
  de la noche at night (with a time) **I**
el nombre name
normalmente normally; usually **I, II**
el norte north
nosotros(as) we; us **I, II**
la nota grade (on a test) **I**
  sacar una buena/mala nota to get a good/bad grade **I**
las noticias news **II, 2.1**
el noticiero news broadcast **2.2**
novecientos(as) nine hundred **I**
novedoso(a) novel, original **3.2**

la novela novel **8.1**
la novela gráfica graphic novel
noveno(a) ninth **I**
noventa ninety **I**
la novia girlfriend; fiancée **II, 1.2**
noviembre November **I**
el novio boyfriend; fiancé **II, 1.2**
la nuera daughter-in-law **1.2**
nuestro(a) our **I**
nueve nine **I**
nuevo(a) new **I**
el número number **I**; shoe size **II**
el número de teléfono phone number **I**
nunca never **I, II**
nutritivo(a) nutritious **I**

o or **I**
o... o either... or **I, II**
el objeto object, item **II**
el oblivio oblivion
la obra work (of art, literature) **8.1**
la obra caritativa charitable work **2.2**
la obra de teatro play, dramatic work **8.2**
el (la) obrero(a) laborer **4.1**
observar to observe **1.1**
el obstáculo obstacle **3.2**
el océano ocean
ocho eight **I**
ochocientos(as) eight hundred **I**
el ocio leisure **5.2**
octavo(a) eighth **I**
octubre October **I**
ocupado(a) busy **I**
ocurrírsele (a alguien) to occur (to someone)
el oeste west
ofender to offend
la oferta merchandise, offering **6.1**; offer
la oficina office **I**
la oficina de turismo tourist office **II**
la oficina del (de la) director(a) principal's office **I**
el oficio occupation **II**
ofrecer (ofrezco) to offer **I, 1.1**
Le puedo ofrecer... I can offer you... (a price) **I**
el oído ear, inner ear (hearing) **II**
Ojalá... I hope..., hopefully...
¡Ojalá! I hope so!
el ojo eye **I**
la ola wave
la olla pot **1.1**
oloroso(a) fragrant
once eleven **I**
la opinión (*pl.* las opiniones) opinion **II**
En mi opinión... In my opinion... **II**
la oración (*pl.* las oraciones) sentence
ordenar to organize **6.1**
la oreja ear, outer ear **I**
organizado(a) organized **I**
organizar to organize **2.1**
el orgullo pride
orgulloso(a) proud **4.1**
estar orgulloso(a) (de) to be proud (of) **II**
originarse to originate
la orilla shore **1.2**
el oro gold
de oro (made of) gold **I**
la orquesta orchestra **5.2**
osado(a) daring
el otoño autumn, fall **I**
otorgar to grant **2.2**
otro(a) other **I**
el (la) oyente listener

la paciencia patience
paciente patient **II, 4.1**
el padrastro stepfather **I**
el padre father **I**
los padres parents **I**
el padrino godfather **II, 1.2**
los padrinos godparents **1.2**
la paella traditional Spanish rice dish **II**
pagar to pay **I**
la página page
la página web Web page **1.2, 7.1**
el país country, nation **I**
el país natal native country
el paisaje landscape **6.2**
el pájaro bird **II, 1.1**
el palacio palace **II**
la paloma dove
el pan bread **I**
la panadería bakery **II**
la pantalla monitor; screen **I, II**
los pantalones pants **I**
los pantalones cortos shorts **I**
la papa potato **I**
las papas fritas French fries **I**
los papás parents
el papel paper **I**; role, part **II**
cambiar de papel to change roles
de papel (made of) paper
el papel de regalo wrapping paper **I**
hacer un papel to play a role **II**
para for; in order to **I**
para que in order that, so that **5.1**
Y para comer/beber... And to eat/drink... **II**
la parada de autobús bus stop
el paraguas umbrella **5.1**
parar to stop
Para y piensa. Stop and think.
pararse to stand (up) **1.2**
parecer to seem
Me parece que... It seems to me... **II**
¿Qué les parece...? What did you think of ...?
parecerse (a alguien) to look like (someone); to be like (someone) **1.2**
parecido(a) alike
la pared wall
la pareja pair
el (la) pariente(a) relative **II, 1.2**
el parque park **I**
el parque de diversiones amusement park **I**
el parque ecológico ecological park, ecoreserve
el parque nacional national park
el párrafo paragraph
la parrilla grill
el filete a la parrilla grilled steak **II**
la parrillada barbecue **I**
hacer una parrillada to barbecue **I**
la parte part
tomar parte en to take part in **7.1**
participar to participate
el partido game (in sports) **I**
el pasado the past
pasado(a) past **I**; last (in time expressions)
el año/mes pasado last year/month **I, II**
la semana pasada last week **I, II**
el (la) pasajero(a) passenger **II**
el pasaporte passport **II**
pasar to happen; to pass, to come in
pasar la aspiradora to vacuum **I**
pasar por la aduana to go through customs **II**
pasar por seguridad to go through security **II**

pasar un buen rato to have a good time **5.2**
pasar un rato con los amigos to spend time with friends **I**
pasarlo bien to have a good time
Pase. Go ahead. **II**
¿Qué pasa? What's happening? **I**
¿Qué te pasa (a ti)? What's the matter (with you)?
el pasatiempo pastime **5.2**, hobby
pasear to go for a walk **I**
el pasillo hallway **I**, aisle **6.2**
el paso step, (dance) step; passage
la pasta de dientes toothpaste **I, II**
el pastel cake **I**
la pastelería pastry shop **II, 6.1**
la patata potato **I**
la patente patent **3.2**
patinar to skate **I**
patinar en línea to in-line skate **I**
los patines en línea in-line skates **I**
el patio patio **I**
el (la) patrocinador(a) sponsor **2.2**
patrocinar to sponsor **2.2**
el pavo turkey
la paz peace
pedir (i, i) to order, to ask for **I**
pedir direcciones to ask for directions **6.2**
pedir prestado to borrow **8.2**
peinarse to comb one's hair **I, II**
el peine comb **I, II**
pelado(a) hairless
pelear to fight **II**
la película... ...movie, film **I**
...de aventuras action... **II**
...de ciencia ficción science fiction... **II**
...de fantasía fantasy... **II**
...de terror horror... **II**
el peligro danger
peligroso(a) dangerous **I**
pelirrojo(a) red-haired **I**
el pelo hair **I**
el pelo castaño/rubio brown/blond hair **I**
la pelota ball **I**
el (la) pelotero(a) baseball player
el (la) peluquero(a) hairdresser **7.2**
la pena trouble, suffering
Es una pena que... It's a shame that...
(no) valer la pena to (not) be worth the trouble
Qué pena que... Too bad that...
penalizar to penalize **3.2**
pensar (ie) to think (of); to plan, to intend **I**
peor worse **I, II**
pequeño(a) little, small **I**
perder (ie) to lose **I**, to miss (a train, an opportunity) **6.2**
perderse (ie) to get lost **6.2**; to miss (out on)
Perdón. Excuse me. **I**
Perdóneme. Forgive me. **II**
perdurar to endure
perezoso(a) lazy **I**
el perímetro perimeter
el periódico newspaper **II, 2.1**
el periódico escolar school newspaper
el periódico estudiantil student newspaper
el (la) periodista reporter **II, 4.2**
el período period, time
permanecer (permanezco) to remain
permanecer de pie to remain standing
el permiso permission
Con permiso. Excuse me. **II**
pero but **I**
el (la) perro(a) dog **I**
persistente persistent **8.2**
persistir to persist **3.2**
la persona person **I**
en persona in person
el personaje character **II**
el personal personnel
personificar to personify **4.1**
pertenecer (pertenezco) to belong
pesado(a) boring; heavy
pesar to weigh
a pesar de que in spite of **6.2**
el pescado fish (as food) **I**
pescar to fish **II**
el petróleo oil, petroleum **II, 3.1**
el pez (*pl.* los peces) fish (the animal) **II, 1.1**
picante hot, spicy **II**
el pie foot **I**
a pie on foot **I**
el dedo del pie toe **II**
la piedra stone
de piedra (made of) stone **II**
la piel skin **I**
la pierna leg **I**
la pieza game piece; piece, composition
la píldora pill
el (la) piloto pilot **II, 4.1**
la pimienta pepper, black pepper **II**
pintar to paint
el (la) pintor(a) painter
la pintura painting **II**
el (la) pionero(a) pioneer
la pirámide pyramid **II**
la piscina swimming pool **I**
el piso floor (of a building) **I**; apartment **6.1**
el primer piso second floor (first above ground) **I**
la pista track (in sports) **II**; clue
el pizarrón (*pl.* pizarrones) chalkboard, board **I**
la pizza pizza **I**
el placer pleasure
el plan financiero financial plan **7.2**
planchar to iron **I**
el planeta planet **3.1**
la planificación planning **2.1**
el plano city map **6.2**
la planta plant
la planta baja first floor, ground floor **I**
el plástico plastic
la plata silver **I**
de plata (made of) silver **I**
el plato plate; dish; course
el plato principal main course **I**
el plato vegetariano vegetarian dish **II**
la playa beach **I**
la plaza plaza, square **II**
la pluma pen **I**
la población (*pl.* las poblaciones) population
la pobreza poverty **2.1**
un poco a little **I**
poco a poco little by little **II**
pocos(as) few
poder (ue) to be able, can **I**
Le puedo ofrecer... I can offer you... **I**
¿Podría ver...? Could I see...? **II**
¿Puedo hablar con... ? May I speak to...? **I, II**

poderoso(a) powerful
el poema poem
la poesía poetry **8.1**
el (la) poeta poet
el (la) policía police officer, policeman/policewoman **II, 4.2**
la política politics **3.2**
el (la) político(a) politician **II, 4.2**
el pollo chicken **I**
el pollo asado roasted chicken **II**
poner (pongo) to put, to place **I**
poner la mesa to set the table **I**
ponerse (me pongo) to put on
ponerse de acuerdo to agree **5.1**
ponerse en forma to get in shape **7.1**
ponerse la ropa to put one's clothes on, to get dressed **I, II**
popular popular **II, 4.1**
la popularidad popularity
por for, by, around
por casualidad by chance **6.2**
por eso for that reason, that's why **II, 4.2**
Por favor. Please. **I**
por fin finally **I, II**
por lo tanto therefore **4.2**
por medio de by means of
¿Por qué? Why? **I**
por un lado... y por otro lado on the one hand... on the other hand **II, 3.2**
por ciento percent
el porcentaje percentage
porque because **I**
portátil portable
el portero doorman
el porvenir future **3.1**
poseer to possess
la posibilidad possibility
posible possible
Es posible que... It's possible that...
el póster poster
el postre dessert **I**
de postre for dessert **I**
practicar to practice **I**
practicar deportes to play or practice sports **I**
practicar surf to surf, to go surfing
práctico(a) practical, down-to-earth **4.2**
el precio price **I**
precioso(a) precious **5.1**
preciso(a) exact, precise
preferible: Es preferible que... It's preferable that... **II**
preferido(a) favorite
preferir (ie, i) to prefer **I**
la pregunta question
el prejuicio prejudice
el premio prize; award **II**
la prensa the press **2.1**
preocupado(a) worried
preocuparse to worry
preparar to prepare **I**
preparar la comida to prepare food, to make a meal **I**
presentar to introduce **I**; to present **II, 2.2**
Te/Le presento a... Let me introduce you to... (familiar/formal) **I**
el (la) presidente(a) president
la presión de grupo peer pressure **II**
prestar to lend **2.1**
presumido(a) presumptuous **4.1**
el presupuesto budget **2.1**
la primavera spring **I**
primero first **II**
el primero de... the first of... (date) **I**
primero(a) first **I**
el (la) primo(a) cousin **I**
la princesa princess **II**
el principio principle **3.2**
la prioridad priority **2.1**
la prisa speed, haste
darse prisa to hurry up
tener prisa to be in a hurry **II**
probar (ue) to taste **II**
probar las especialidades to try the specialties **6.2**
el problema problem **I**
meterse en problemas to get into trouble **6.2**
No hay problema. No problem.
el producto product
la profesión (*pl.* las profesiones) profession **II**
¿Qué profesión te gustaría tener? What do you want to be? **II**
el (la) profesor(a) teacher; professor **II, 7.2**
el programa program
el programa educativo educational program **2.2**
la programación programming
el (la) programador(a) programmer **II, 4.1**
programar to program
progresar to progress **3.2**
prohibir que to prohibit that **4.1**
promocionar to promote
promover (ue) to promote
pronto soon
tan pronto como as soon as **8.1**
la propina tip (in a restaurant) **I**
el propósito purpose, aim **4.2**
la prosa prose **8.1**
prosperar to prosper **3.2**
el (la) protagonista protagonist **8.1**
el protector solar sunscreen
proteger (protejo) to protect **II, 3.1**
proveer to provide
próximo(a) next
el (la) próximo(a) the next **II**
proyectar to project
el proyecto project
el proyecto de acción social social action project **2.1**
publicar to publish **II, 2.2**
la publicidad publicity **2.1**
la publicidad por correo mailing **2.2**
el público audience **2.2**
público(a) public
el transporte público public transportation **1.1**
el pueblo town
el puente bridge **6.2**
la puerta door **I**; gate **II**
el puerto port **1.2**
pues so, well **6.2**; well then
la puesta del sol sunset
el puesto position, job; stand
la pulsera bracelet **II**
el punto dot (in e-mail address)
el punto de vista point of view **II, 8.1**
puntual punctual **7.2**

qué
¿Qué? What? **I**
¡Qué asco! How disgusting! **II**
¡Qué bello(a)! How beautiful! **II**
¡Qué caro(a)! How expensive! **II**
¡Qué divertido! How fun! **I**
¡Qué lástima! What a shame! **I, II**
¡Qué miedo! How scary! **I**
¿Qué día es hoy? What day is today? **I**
¿Qué es esto? What is this? **I**
¿Qué hicieron ustedes? What did you do? (pl., formal) **I**

GLOSARIO español-inglés

¿Qué hiciste tú? What did you do? (sing., familiar) **I**
¿Qué hora es? What time is it? **I**
¿Qué pasa? What's happening? **I**
¿Qué tal? How's it going? **I**
¿Qué te gusta hacer? What do you like to do? **I**
¿Qué tiempo hace? What is the weather like? **I**
quedar
¿Cómo me queda(n)? How does it (do they) fit me? **II**
Por favor, ¿dónde queda...? Can you please tell me where ... is? **II**
quedar apretado(a) to fit tight **II**
quedar bien to fit well **II**
quedar flojo(a) to fit loose **II**
quedar mal to fit badly **II**
quedarse (en) to stay (in) **I, II**
los quehaceres chores **I**
quejarse to complain
quemar to burn
quemar un disco compacto to burn a CD **I**
querer (ie) to want **I**
Quisiera darle las gracias a... I would like to thank... **II**
querido(a) beloved; dear **II**
el queso cheese **I**
quien who
quien sea whoever that may be
¿Quién(es)? Who? **I**
¿Quién es? Who is he/she/it? **I**
quince fifteen **I**
quinientos(as) five hundred **I**
quinto(a) fifth **I**
quitar to take away **6.1**

el radio radio **I**
el (la) radioyente listener (to a radio program)
la raíz (*pl.* las raíces) root
la rama branch
rápidamente rapidly
rápido(a) fast **II**
los rápidos rapids
la raqueta racket (in sports) **I**
raro(a) rare
es raro que... it is strange that... **3.2**
el rascacielos (*pl.* los rascacielos) skyscraper **II**
el rastro trace, trail
el rato time, period
el rato libre free time **7.1**
pasar un buen rato to have a good time **5.2**
el ratón (*pl.* los ratones) mouse **I, II**
la raya stripe
de rayas striped **II**
la razón (*pl.* las razones) reason
tener razón to be right **I**
razonable reasonable **4.1**
reaccionar to react
reacio(a) stubborn
la realidad reality **8.1**
realista realistic **4.2**
realizar to fulfill, to make happen
la recámara bedroom
recaudar fondos to raise funds **2.1**
la recepción (*pl.* las recepciones) reception desk **II, 5.2**
la receta recipe **II**
recibir to receive **I**
el reciclaje recycling **II**
reciclar to recycle **II, 2.1**
reclamar to call, to demand **8.2**
el reclamo de equipaje baggage claim **II**
recoger (recojo) to pick up, to gather **II, 1.2**
recomendar (ie) to recommend **II**
reconocido(a) well-known
recordar (ue) to remember
¿Recuerdas? Do you remember?
recostarse (ue) to lie down **1.2**
el recreo recess
el recuerdo souvenir **I, II**; memory **7.1**
el recurso wile, way
el recurso natural natural resource **II, 3.1**
la red net **II**; network
redactar to edit **7.1**
reemplazar to replace **3.1**
referirse (ie, i) to refer
reflejar to reflect
el reflejo reflection
reflexionar to reflect, to look back **7.1**
el refrán saying
refrescarse to cool down or off **1.2**
el refresco soft drink **I**
el refrigerador refrigerator **6.1**
refugiarse (de) to take refuge (from) **1.2**
regalar to give (a gift)
el regalo present, gift **I**
regañar to scold
regatear to bargain **I, II**
registrar to record, to write down
la regla rule
regresar to return **II**
regular: Regular. ¿Y tú/usted? OK. And you? (familiar/formal) **I**
el reino kingdom
reír (i, i) to laugh
Me hace reír. It makes me laugh. **II**
relacionar to relate **8.1**
las relaciones públicas public relations **7.2**
la relajación relaxation
relajante relaxing
relajarse to relax **5.2**
relatar to relate, to tell **5.2**
el relato tale
la religión (*pl.* las religiones) religion **II**
rellenar to stuff
el reloj watch; clock **I, II**
remar to row, to paddle **1.1**
repartir periódicos to deliver newspapers **7.1**
repasar to review, to reexamine
el repaso review
repetir (i, i) to repeat
el repollo cabbage
el reportaje report
el (la) reportero(a) reporter
representar to represent **4.1**
reprobar (ue) to fail
el requisito requirement
rescatar to rescue
la reseña review **2.2, 8.1**
la reseña literaria book review
la reserva reserve, preserve
la reserva natural nature reserve
la reservación (*pl.* las reservaciones) reservation
hacer/tener una reservación to make/to have a reservation **II**

la resolución (*pl.* las resoluciones) resolution **5.2**
resolver (ue) to solve **5.2**
respetar to respect **3.2**
respirar to breathe **II, 3.1**
responder to reply
la responsabilidad responsibility **II, 3.1**
responsable responsible **II, 3.1**
la respuesta answer
el restaurante restaurant **I**
el resultado result
el resumen summary
  en resumen in summary
resumir to summarize
el reto challenge, dare
el retrato portrait **II**
la reunión (*pl.* las reuniones) meeting **5.2, 7.1**
  la reunión de ex alumnos class reunion
reunirse to get together, to meet **1.2**
reutilizar to reuse **3.1**
revisar to check, to revise
la revista magazine **2.1**
rezumar to ooze
rico(a) tasty, delicious **I**; rich
el riesgo risk **3.1**
la rima rhyme **8.1**
el río river **1.1, 6.2**
la risa laughter
risueño(a) smiling
el ritmo rhythm **8.1**
el robot (*pl.* los robots) robot **II**
rocoso(a) rocky; (made of) rock
la rodilla knee **I**
rojo(a) red **I**
romántico(a) romantic **8.1**
romper to break **6.1**
la ropa clothing **I**
  la ropa elegante formalwear **II**
  ponerse la ropa to put on clothes **II**
el rostro face
roto(a) broken **6.1**
rubio(a) blond **I**
el ruido noise **5.2**
ruidoso(a) noisy **6.2**
las ruinas ruins **II**
el ruiseñor nightingale
el rumbo route
la ruta route **6.2**
la rutina routine **I, II**

sábado Saturday **I**
saber (sé) to know (a fact, how to do something) **I**
el saber learning, knowledge
el sabor flavor **II**
sabroso(a) tasty **II**
sacar to take out
  sacar el billete to buy a ticket **6.1**
  sacar fotos to take pictures
  sacar la basura to take out the trash **I**
  sacar una buena/mala nota to get a good/bad grade **I**
el saco bag, sack
  el saco de dormir sleeping bag **1.1**
el sacrificio sacrifice **4.2**
la sal salt **II**
la sala living room **I**
  la sala de espera waiting room **6.2**
salado(a) salty **II**; salted
el salar salt mine
el salero saltshaker
la salida departure **II**; exit **8.2**
salir (salgo) to leave, to go out **I**
  salir bien to turn out well **7.1**
el salón (*pl.* los salones) de charlas chat room **5.1**
la salud health **I**
saludable healthy; healthful **II**
¡Saludos! Greetings!
  Saludos desde... Greetings from...
el (la) salvavidas lifeguard
la sandalia sandal **II**
el sándwich (*pl.* los sándwiches) sandwich **I**
sano(a) healthy **I**
el (la) santo(a) saint
  el santo patrón / la santa patrona patron saint
la sátira satire **8.1**
satisfacer to satisfy **3.2**
satisfecho(a) satisfied
sazonado(a) seasoned
el secador de pelo hair dryer **I, II**
secar to dry
  secarse to dry oneself **I, II**
  secarse el pelo to dry one's hair **I**
seco(a) dry
el (la) secretario(a) secretary **4.2**
el secreto secret **I**
la sed thirst
  tener sed to be thirsty **I**
la seda silk
seguir (i, i) to follow **1.1**
  seguir adelante to continue on, to carry on **3.2**
  seguir derecho to go straight **II**
  seguir una carrera to pursue a career **7.2**
  seguir una dieta balanceada to follow a balanced diet **II**
según according to
segundo(a) second **I**
seguramente surely
la seguridad security
  pasar por seguridad to go through security
seguro(a) secure, safe; sure
  (no) estar seguro(a) (de) que... to (not) be sure that... **4.2**
seis six **I**
seiscientos(as) six hundred **I**
seleccionar to select
el sello stamp **6.1**
la selva jungle **II, 1.1**
el semáforo stoplight **II**
la semana week **I**
  el fin de semana weekend **I**
  la semana pasada last week **I, II**
  la semana que viene next week
semanal weekly
el sendero path, trail **1.1**
Señor (Sr.) ... Mr. ... **I**
Señora (Sra.) ... Mrs. ... **I**
Señorita (Srta.) ... Miss ... **I**
sentarse (ie) to sit
el sentido del humor sense of humor
sentir (ie, i) to feel; to be sorry **4.2**
  Lo siento. I'm sorry. **I**
  sentir que... to feel or be sorry that... **4.2**
separado(a) separate
septiembre September **I**
séptimo(a) seventh **I**
la sequía drought **3.1**
ser to be **I**
  Es de... He/She is from... **I**
  Es el... de... It's the... of... (day and month) **I**
  Es la.../Son las... It is... o'clock. **I**
  ser de madera/oro/plata to be made of wood/gold/silver **II**
  ser miembro de... to be a member of... **7.1**
  ser originario(a) de to come from
  Soy de... I'm from... **I**

serio(a) serious **I**
ser sobrenatural supernatural being
la serpiente snake **1.1**
la servilleta napkin **II**
servir (i, i) to serve **I**; to be useful
servir de presidente(a) to serve as president **7.1**
sesenta sixty **I**
setecientos seven hundred **I**
setenta seventy **I**
sexto(a) sixth **I**
si if **I**
sí yes **I**
¡Claro que sí! Of course! **I, II**
Sí, me encantaría. Yes, I would love to. **I, II**
siempre always **I**
de siempre usual
la siesta nap **5.2**
dormir una siesta to take a nap **5.2**
siete seven **I**
el siglo century
el significado meaning
significar to mean **8.1**
siguiente following **I**
la silla chair **I**
la silla de ruedas wheelchair
el sillón (*pl.* los sillones) armchair **I**
simbolizar to symbolize **8.1**
el símbolo symbol
el símil simile **8.1**
simpático(a) nice, friendly **I**
simplificar to simplify
sin without **1.1**
sin embargo however, nevertheless **II, 4.2**
sin que without **5.1**
sin valor worthless **5.1**
la sinagoga synagogue
la sinceridad sincerity
sincero(a) sincere **II, 4.1**
singular unique **8.2**
el sitio site
el sitio arqueológico archaelogical site
el sitio Web Web site **I, 5.1**
el smog smog **II, 3.1**
sobre about, concerning **II**; on
el sobrenombre nickname
sobresaliente outstanding **4.1**
la sobrina niece **II, 1.2**
el sobrino nephew **II, 1.2**
la sociedad society **3.2**
la sociedad honoraria honor society **7.1**
el sofá sofa, couch **I**
el software software **II**
la soga rope
el sol sun **I**
el bloqueador de sol sunscreen **I**
Hace sol. It is sunny. **I**
tomar el sol to sunbathe **I**
solamente only
el (la) soldado soldier
solicitar to ask for, to request **2.1**
solicitar una beca to apply for a scholarship **7.1**
la solicitud application
llenar una solicitud de empleo to fill out an application **7.1**
sólo only
no sólo... sino también... not only... but also... **II**
solo(a) alone
soltar (ue) to release
solucionar to solve **3.2**
la sombra shadow
el sombrero hat **I**
la sombrilla beach umbrella; parasol **1.2**
someter to force
soñar (ue) to dream
soñar con to dream about **8.2**
el sonido sound **II**
sonreír (i, i) to smile
la sopa soup **I**
soportar to withstand
sordo(a) deaf
los sordos the deaf
sorprendente surprising **4.2**
sorprender to surprise
sorprenderse de que... to be surprised that... **4.2**
la sorpresa surprise **I**
sospechar que to suspect that **5.1**
su his, her, its, their, your (formal) **I**
subir to go up **I**
subir a la vuelta al mundo/la montaña rusa to ride the Ferris wheel/roller coaster **I**
subrayar to underline
la subtitulación para sordos closed captioning for the hearing-impaired **2.2**
el suceso event **8.1**
sucio(a) dirty **I**
la suegra mother-in-law **II, 1.2**
el suegro father-in-law **II, 1.2**
los suegros in-laws **II, 1.2**
el sueldo salary **7.1**
el suelo floor (of a room) **I**; ground, soil **3.1**
el sueño dream; sleep
tener sueño to be sleepy **II**
la suerte luck
tener suerte to be lucky **I**
el suéter sweater **II**
el sufrimiento suffering **3.2**
sufrir to suffer
la sugerencia suggestion
dar una sugerencia to make a suggestion **5.1**
sugerir (ie, i) que to suggest that **4.1**
sumamente extremely **II**
superar to overcome, to surpass **3.2**
la superficie surface
el supermercado supermarket **II**
el sur south
surfear to surf, to go surfing
el (la) surfista surfer **1.2**
suspirar to sigh
el sustantivo noun
el susto fright, scare
susurrar to whisper

la tabla de surf surfboard **1.2**
tal
con tal (de) que as long as **5.1**
tal vez maybe **I**
talentoso(a) talented
la talla clothing size **II**; carving
el taller workshop
el tamaño size
también also, too **I**
no sólo... sino también... not only... but also... **II**
también se dice... you can also say...
tampoco neither, (not) either **I, II**
tan as
tan pronto como as soon as **8.1**
tan... como as... as **I, II**
tanto as much
tanto como... as much as... **I**
tanto(s)... como as many... as **II**
tanto(a) so much

tantos(as) so many
las tapas: ir de tapas to go out to eat **6.1**
el tapiz (*pl.* los tapices) tapestry **6.2**
la taquilla ticket window **6.2**
tarde late **I**
la tarde afternoon **I**
Buenas tardes. Good afternoon. **I**
de la tarde in the afternoon (with a time) **I**
más tarde later (on) **I, II**
la tarea homework **I**; task
la tarifa fare **1.1**
la tarjeta card
la tarjeta de crédito credit card **II**
la tarjeta de embarque boarding pass **II**
la tarjeta postal postcard **II**
la tarta cake
la tarta de chocolate chocolate cake **II**
el taxi taxi
la taza cup
el té tea **II**
el teatro theater **I**
el teclado keyboard **I, II**
el (la) técnico(a) technician, repairperson **4.2**
los tejidos woven materials
la tela cloth, fabric
la tele TV
el teléfono telephone **I**
¿Cuál es tu/su número de teléfono? What is your phone number? (familiar/formal) **I**
el teléfono celular cellular phone **I, II**
Mi número de teléfono es... My phone number is ... **I**
la telenovela soap opera
el (la) telespectador(a) viewer, TV viewer **2.2**
la teletón (*pl.* las teletones) telethon **2.2**
el (la) televidente viewer, TV viewer
la televisión television **I**
el televisor television set **I**
el telón (*pl.* los telones) curtain (in a theater)
levantar/bajar el telón to raise/lower the curtain **8.2**
el tema theme **8.1**
el temblor earthquake **3.1**
temer que to be afraid that **5.1**
el templo temple **II**
la temporada season
temprano early **I**
el tenedor fork **II**
tener (tengo) to have **I**
¿Cuántos años tienes? How old are you? **I**
tener... años to be... years old **I**
tener calor to be hot (person) **I**
tener celos de... to be jealous of...
tener éxito to be successful **II**
tener frío to be cold (person) **I**
tener ganas de... to feel like... **I**
tener hambre to be hungry **I**
tener lugar to take place
tener miedo to be afraid **I**
tener prisa to be in a hurry **II**
tener que to have to **I**
tener razón to be right **I**
tener sed to be thirsty **I**
tener sueño to be sleepy **II**
tener suerte to be lucky **I**
el tenis tennis **I**
la teología theology
tercero(a) third **I**
el terciopelo velvet
las termas hot springs
terminar to end **I**
la terraza terrace **6.1**
el (la) tesorero(a) treasurer **7.1**
el (la) testigo witness
ti you (sing., familiar) **I, II**
la tía aunt **I**
el tiempo weather; time **I**
¿Qué tiempo hace? What is the weather like? **I**
a tiempo parcial part-time **7.1**
el tiempo libre free time **I, II**
la tienda store **I**
la tienda de campaña tent **1.1**
la tierra land, soil
el timbre doorbell **6.1**
tocar el timbre to ring the doorbell **6.1**
la timidez shyness
tímido(a) shy **II, 4.1**
el tío uncle **I**; guy
los tíos uncles, uncle(s) and aunt(s) **I**
típico(a) typical
el tipo type
el (la) tirado(a) pauper **8.2**
tirar to throw (out); to pull
tirar basura to litter **2.1**
tirarse (de) to jump off
las tiras cómicas comic strips
el titular headline **II, 2.1**
titularse to be called **8.1**
el título (academic) degree **7.2**; title **7.2**
la toalla towel **I, II**
el tobillo ankle **I**
el tocadiscos (*pl.* los tocadiscos) compactos CD player **I**
tocar to play (an instrument) **I**; to touch **I**
todavía still; yet **I**
todo all, everything
todo el mundo everyone
todo junto all together
todos(as) all **I**
todos los días every day **I**
tomar to take **I**
tomar algo to drink something **6.2**
tomar apuntes to take notes **I**
tomar decisiones to make decisions **7.1**
tomar el sol to sunbathe **I**
tomar fotos to take photos **I, II**
tomar parte en to take part in, to participate in **7.1**
tomar un taxi to take a taxi **II**
el tomate tomato **I**
la tormenta storm
el torneo tournament
la tortilla omelet (in Spain) **II**
la tortilla de patatas potato omelet **II**
la tortuga turtle, tortoise
la tortuga gigante giant tortoise
trabajador(a) hard-working **I**
el (la) trabajador(a) worker
el (la) trabajador(a) social social worker **4.1**
trabajar to work **I**
trabajar a tiempo parcial to work part-time **7.1**
trabajar de cajero(a) to work as a cashier **7.1**
trabajar de salvavidas to work as a lifeguard **7.1**
trabajar de voluntario to volunteer **II, 2.1**
el trabajo work; job
traducir (traduzco) to translate **2.2**
el (la) traductor(a) translator **7.2**
traer (traigo) to bring **I**
¿Me puede traer...? Can you bring me...? **II**
el traje suit **II**
el traje de baño bathing suit **II**

GLOSARIO español-inglés

tranquilo(a) calm **I**
la transformación (*pl.* las transformaciones) transformation **3.1**
transformar to transform **II**
el transporte público public transportation **1.1**
trasladarse to move (change residence)
tratar
 tratar de to be about; to try to
 tratar sobre to deal with, to be about
 tratarse de to be about **6.2**
travieso(a) mischievous
trece thirteen **I**
treinta thirty **I**
treinta y uno thirty-one **I**
el tren train **I**
 en tren by train **I**
tres three **I**
trescientos(as) three hundred **I**
la tripulación (*pl.* las tripulaciones) crew
triste sad **I**
la trituradora food processor
triunfar to triumph
el triunfo triumph
el trofeo trophy
el tronco trunk
tu your (sing., familiar) **I**
tú you (sing., familiar) **I**
la tumba tomb **II**
el turismo tourism
 el turismo ecológico ecotourism
 la oficina de turismo tourist office **II**
el (la) turista tourist **II**
turnarse to take turns

U

último(a) last
la uña nail (fingernail or toenail) **II**
único(a) unique **II**; only
la unidad unity **3.2**; unit
unificar to unify
el uniforme uniform **II**
unirse to join
la universidad university **7.2**
uno one **I**
usar to use **I**; to wear **I**
usted you (sing., formal) **I, II**
ustedes you (pl., formal) **I, II**
útil useful
utilizar to use **1.1**
la uva grape **I**
¡Uy! Ugh! **II**

las vacaciones vacation **I**
 (estar) de vacaciones (to be) on vacation **I, II**
 ir de vacaciones to go on vacation **II**
el vacío gap
vacío(a) empty
el vagón (*pl.* los vagones) wagon, railroad car **6.2**
¡Vale! OK!
la valentía bravery **4.2**
valer (valgo) to be worth
valiente brave **II**
valioso(a) valuable **5.1**
el valle valley
el valor value
valorar to value **3.1**
la vanidad vanity
vanidoso(a) vain **4.1**
variar to vary
la variedad variety
varios(as) various
la vasija container
el vaso glass **II**
el (la) vecino(a) neighbor **4.2**
vegetariano(a) vegetarian
el vehículo híbrido hybrid vehicle **II**
veinte twenty **I**
veintiuno twenty-one **I**
la vejez old age
el velero sailboat **1.2**
el venado deer
el (la) vendedor(a) salesclerk, vendor **I**
 el (la) vendedor(a) ambulante street vendor **5.2**
vender to sell **I**
venir (vengo) to come **I**
la venta sale
la ventaja advantage
la ventana window **I**
la ventanilla ticket window **I**; train window **6.2**
ver to see **I**
 A ver. Let's see.
 ¿Me deja ver? May I see? **I, II**
 Nos vemos allí. See you there.
 ver el amanecer to watch the sunrise **1.2**
 ver la puesta del sol to watch the sunset **1.2**
 ver las atracciones to go sightseeing **II**
el verano summer **I**
la verdad truth
 (No) Es verdad que... It is (not) true that... **II, 4.2**
 ¡Te digo la verdad! I'm telling you the truth! **II**
 ¿De verdad? Really?
 ¿Verdad? Really? Right? **I**
verdadero(a) real, true, sincere **4.2**
verde green **I**
la verdulería vegetable stand **6.1**
las verduras vegetables **I**
la vergüenza shame
 darle a uno vergüenza to feel ashamed
versátil versatile **7.2**
el verso verse **8.1**
el vestido dress **I**
vestirse (i, i) to get dressed **I, II**
el vestuario costumes **8.2**; wardrobe
el (la) veterinario(a) veterinarian **II, 4.2**
la vez (*pl.* las veces) time
 a la vez at the same time
 a veces sometimes **II**
 de vez en cuando once in a while **I**
 muchas veces often, many times **I**
 tal vez maybe **I**
la vía track, train track **6.2**
viajar to travel **II**
el viaje trip, journey
 hacer un viaje to take a trip **I**
el (la) vice-presidente(a) vice president **7.1**
la vida life **II**; a living
 el ciclo de vida life cycle
 ganarse la vida como... to earn a living as... **II**
el videojuego video game **I**
el vidrio glass **II**
viejo(a) old **I**
el viento wind
 Hace viento. It is windy. **I**

viernes Friday **I**
el vinagre vinegar **II**
la visita visit
hacer una visita guiada to take a guided tour **6.2**
visitar to visit
visitar un museo to visit a museum **II**
la vista view **6.2**
el vitral stained-glass window
la vivienda housing
vivir to live **I**
vivo(a) bright (colors)
el vocabulario vocabulary
la vocación (*pl.* las vocaciones) vocation
el volante flyer **2.2**
volar (ue) to fly
el volcán (*pl.* los volcanes) volcano **II**
el voleibol volleyball (the sport) **I**
el voleibol playero beach volleyball **1.2**
el (la) voluntario(a) volunteer **II**, **2.1**
trabajar de voluntario to volunteer **II**
volver (ue) to return, to come back **I**
vosotros(as) you (pl., familiar) **I**, **II**
votar to vote **3.1**
la voz (*pl.* las voces) voice
en voz alta out loud
el vuelo flight **II**
confirmar el vuelo to confirm a flight **II**
la vuelta turn
dar una vuelta to take a walk **6.1**
la Vuelta a Francia Tour de France **II**
la vuelta al mundo Ferris wheel **I**
vuestro(a) your (familiar) **I**

y and
... y (diez) (ten) past... (the hour) **I**
... y cuarto quarter past... (the hour) **I**
... y media half past... (the hour) **I**
ya already **I**
el yerno son-in-law **1.2**
yo I **I**
el yogur yogurt **I**

los zahones chaps
zambullirse to dive
la zanahoria carrot **II**
la zapatería shoe store **II**
el zapato shoe **I**
la zona zone, region
el zoológico zoo **I**
el zopilote vulture
el zorro fox

Glosario inglés-español

This English Spanish glossary contains all the active vocabulary words that appear in the text as well as passive vocabulary lists.

to abandon abandonar
about sobre **II**
  to be about tratarse de **6.2**
abroad al extranjero **1.1**
absence la ausencia
absurd absurdo(a) **8.1**
  the absurd lo absurdo
access el acceso **2.2**
to accompany acompañar
according to según
account la cuenta
  savings account la cuenta de ahorros **7.1**
  to take into account tener en cuenta
accountant el (la) contador(a) **7.2**
accounting la contabilidad **7.2**
to ache doler (ue) **I**
to achieve lograr **4.2**
achievement el logro **4.2**
to acquire adquirir (ie)
across from frente a **II**
act el acto **8.1**
to act actuar **4.2**
  to act in a play actuar en un drama **7.1**
acting la actuación **5.2**
action la acción (*pl.* las acciones)
active activo(a) **II**
activity la actividad **I**
actor el actor **II**
actress la actriz (*pl.* las actrices) **II**
ad el anuncio **2.1**
  classified ad el anuncio clasificado **2.2**
  personal ad el anuncio personal **2.2**
to add añadir **II**
  addition: in addition además **6.2**
address la dirección (*pl.* las direcciones) **I**
  e-mail address la dirección electrónica **I, II**
adult el (la) adulto(a)
to advance avanzar
  in advance con anticipación **1.1**
advanced avanzado(a) **II**
advantage la ventaja
  to take advantage (of something) aprovechar **6.1**
adventure la aventura
advertisement el anuncio **II**
advice los consejos
  to give advice dar consejos **5.1**
to advise that aconsejar que **4.1**
advisor el (la) consejero(a)
to affect afectar
affection el cariño
afraid
  to be afraid tener miedo **I**
  to be afraid that temer que **5.1**
after después (de) **I**
afternoon la tarde **I**
  Good afternoon. Buenas tardes. **I**
  in the afternoon de la tarde **I**
afterward después **I**
against contra
agency la agencia
  ad agency la agencia de publicidad **2.1**
agent el (la) agente
ago: Many centuries ago... Hace muchos siglos...
to agree ponerse de acuerdo **5.1**; asentir (ie, i)
  to agree/disagree with estar/no estar de acuerdo con **II, 2.2**
agriculture la agricultura **II**
air el aire
  clean air el aire puro **II, 3.1**
air conditioning el aire acondicionado
airplane el avión (*pl.* aviones) **I**
  by plane en avión **I**
airport el aeropuerto **II**
aisle el pasillo **6.2**
alike parecido(a)
all todos(as) **I**
  all together todo junto
alley el callejón (*pl.* los callejones) **6.2**
to allow that dejar que **4.1**
almost casi **I**
alone solo(a)
already ya **I**
also también **I**
  not only... but also... no sólo... sino también... **II**
although aunque **8.1**
always siempre **I**
analysis el análisis (*pl.* los análisis) **8.1**
to analyze analizar **6.2**
anchovy el boquerón (*pl.* los boquerones)
ancient antiguo(a) **II**
and y
angry enojado(a) **I**
  to get angry enojarse
animated animado(a) **7.2**
animation la animación **II**
ankle el tobillo **I**
annotation la anotación (*pl.* las anotaciones)
announce anunciar
announcement el anuncio **2.1**
announcer el (la) locutor(a)
to annoy fastidiar
annoying molesto(a), latoso(a) **2.1**
answer la respuesta
to answer contestar **I**
answering machine la contestadora
to anticipate anticipar **7.1**
any alguno(a) **I**; cualquier
  not any ningún, ninguno(a) **I, II**
apartment el piso **6.1**, el apartamento **I**

to appear aparecer (aparezco) **4.2**
to appear in figurar en **4.2**
appetizer el entremés (*pl.* los entremeses) **II**
apple la manzana **I**
application la solicitud
to fill out a job application llenar una solicitud de empleo **7.1**
to apply (for) solicitar
to apply for a scholarship solicitar una beca **7.1**
appointment la cita
to have an appointment tener una cita **II**
to appreciate apreciar **3.1**
to approach acercarse
April abril **I**
aquarium el acuario **I**
archaeologist el (la) arqueólogo(a)
architect el (la) arquitecto(a) **II, 7.2**
architecture la arquitectura
to argue discutir **II, 5.2**
arm el brazo **I**
armchair el sillón (*pl.* los sillones) **I**
armoire el armario **I**
army el ejército **II**
around por
arrival la llegada **II**
to arrive llegar **I**
art el arte **I**
fine arts las bellas artes
martial arts las artes marciales
performance art el arte interpretativo
article el artículo **II, 2.1**
artisan el (la) artesano(a)
artist el (la) artista **II, 4.2**
artistic artístico(a) **I**
as como
as long as con tal (de) que **5.1**
as many... as tanto(s)... como **II**
as much as... tanto como... **I, II**
as soon as en cuanto, tan pronto como **8.1**
as for en cuanto a
as... as tan... como **I, II**
ashamed: to feel ashamed darle a uno vergüenza
ashes las cenizas
ask
to ask for pedir (i, i) **I**; solicitar **2.1**
to ask for directions pedir direcciones **6.2**

to assure asegurar
I assure you. Te lo aseguro. **II**
astronaut el (la) astronauta **4.1**
at a
at night de la noche **I**
at the same time a la vez
At what time is/are...? ¿A qué hora es/son...? **I**
At... o'clock. A la(s)... **I**
at sign (in e-mail address) la arroba
athlete el (la) atleta **I**
athletic atlético(a) **I**
ATM el cajero automático **6.1**
atmosphere el ambiente **5.2**
attached adjunto(a)
to attain lograr **4.2**
to attend asistir a **5.2**; atender (ie)
attentive atento(a)
Very attentive. Muy atento(a). **II**
attitude la actitud
to attract atraer (atraigo)
attractions las atracciones
attractive atractivo(a)
audience el público **2.2**
August agosto **I**
aunt la tía **I**
authentic auténtico(a) **4.2**
author el (la) autor(a) **8.1**
autobiography la autobiografía **8.1**
automobile el automóvil
autumn el otoño **I**
available disponible
avenue la avenida **II**
to avoid evitar **5.1**
award el premio **II**
awareness: social awareness la conciencia social **3.2**
Aztec azteca **II**

B

baby el (la) bebé **1.2**
to baby-sit cuidar niños **7.1**
babysitter el (la) niñero(a) **7.1**
background event el antecedente **8.1**
backpack la mochila **I**
bad malo(a) **I**
Too bad that... Qué pena que...
badly mal
bag la bolsa **5.1**, el saco
plastic bag la bolsa de plástico **2.1**
sleeping bag el saco de dormir **1.1**

baggage claim el reclamo de equipaje **II**
bakery la panadería **II**
balance el equilibrio
balcony el balcón (*pl.* los balcones) **6.1**
ball la pelota **I**
balloon el globo **I**
banana la banana **I**
band (musical group) el conjunto
bank el banco **II**
banker el (la) banquero(a)
baptism el bautismo
barbecue la parrillada; el asado **I**
barely apenas **II**
to bargain regatear **I, II**
a bargain una ganga **II**
baseball el béisbol **I**
(baseball) bat el bate **I**
baseball player el (la) pelotero(a), el (la) beisbolista
basketball el básquetbol **I**
bat (animal) el murciélago
bath: to take a bath bañarse **II**
bathing suit el traje de baño **II**
bathroom el baño **I**
bathtub la bañera **6.1**
battery la batería
battle la batalla **II**
bay la bahía
to be ser; estar **I**
to be able poder (ue) **I**
to be about tratar(se) de **6.2**
to be born nacer (nazco)
to be cold tener frío **I**
to be cool (weather) hacer fresco **1.2**
to be excited estar ilusionado(a) **5.1**
to be familiar with conocer (conozco) **I**
to be hot tener calor **I**
to be hungry tener hambre **I**
to be important importar **II**
to be in a hurry tener prisa **II**
to be jealous of... tener celos de...
to be lucky tener suerte **I**
to be on vacation estar de vacaciones **II**
to be online estar en línea **I, II**
to be right tener razón **I**
to be sleepy tener sueño **II**
to be thirsty tener sed **I**
to be useful servir (i, i)

to be... years old tener... años **I**
to be like (someone) parecerse (a alguien) **1.2**
What do you want to be? ¿Qué profesión te gustaría tener? **II**
beach la playa **I**
beach umbrella la sombrilla **1.2**
beans los frijoles **I**
to beat batir **II**
beaten batido(a) **II**
beautiful bello(a) **II**
to beautify embellecer
beauty la belleza
because porque **I**
to become hacerse (me hago)
bed la cama **I**
to go to bed acostarse (ue) **I, II**
to make the bed hacer la cama **I**
bedroom el cuarto **I**; la recámara
beef el bistec **I**
before antes (de) que **5.1**; menos **I**
beforehand de antemano **2.1**
to begin empezar (ie), comenzar (ie) **I**
beginning el comienzo **7.1**
behave: to behave well/badly comportarse bien/mal **4.1**
behavior la conducta **4.1**; el comportamiento
behind detrás (de) **I**
to believe creer
to not believe that... no creer que... **4.2**
to belong pertenecer (pertenezco)
beloved querido(a) **II**
belt el cinturón (*pl.* los cinturones) **II**
bench el banco **6.1**
beneath bajo
benefit el beneficio
for the benefit of a beneficio de **2.2**
besides además de, aparte de
better mejor **I, II**
between entre **II**
beverage la bebida **I**
bicycle la bicicleta **I**
bicycle racing el ciclismo **II**
big grande **I**
bill la cuenta **I**
billiards el billar **5.2**
biodiversity la biodiversidad **3.1**
biography la biografía **8.1**
bird el pájaro **II, 1.1**
birth el nacimiento
birth date la fecha de nacimiento **I**
birthday el cumpleaños **I**
Happy birthday! ¡Feliz cumpleaños! **I**
bitter amargo(a), agrio(a)
black negro(a) **I**
blank en blanco
blanket la manta **5.2**
block (city block) la cuadra **II**; la manzana **6.1**
blond rubio(a) **I**
blouse la blusa **I**
blue azul **I**
board el pizarrón (*pl.* los pizarrones) **I**
to board abordar **II**
boarding pass la tarjeta de embarque **II**
boat el barco **I**; el bote
by boat en barco **I**
body el cuerpo **I**
to boil hervir (ie, i) **II**
boiled hervido(a) **II**
book el libro **I**
bookstore la librería **II**
boot la bota **II**
booth la cabina
boring aburrido(a) **I**; pesado(a)
to borrow pedir prestado **8.2**
both ambos(as)
to bother molestar
bottle la botella
bottom el fondo
bow tie el corbatín (*pl.* los corbatines) **II**
bowling: to go bowling jugar a los bolos
box la caja
boy el chico **I**; el muchacho
boyfriend el novio **II, 1.2**
bracelet la pulsera **II**
branch la rama
brave valiente **II**
bravery la valentía **4.2**
Bravo! ¡Bravo! **II**
bread el pan **I**
to break romper **6.1**
to break down descomponer
breakfast el desayuno **I**
to have breakfast desayunar **II**
to breathe respirar **II, 3.1**
breeze la brisa **1.2**
bridge el puente **6.2**
bright (colors) vivo(a)
brilliant brillante
to bring traer (traigo)
to bring up criar
Can you bring me...? ¿Me puede traer...? **II**
to broadcast emitir **2.2**
broccoli el brócoli **I**
brochure el folleto
broken roto(a) **6.1**
bronze el bronce
brood la cría
broth el caldo **II**
brother el hermano **I**
brother-in-law el cuñado **II, 1.2**
brown marrón (*pl.* marrones) **I**
brown hair el pelo castaño **I**
brush el cepillo **I, II**
to brush cepillar
to brush one's teeth cepillarse los dientes **I, II**
bucket el cubo
budget el presupuesto **2.1**
to build construir **II**
building el edificio **II**
bumper cars los autitos chocadores **I**
to burn quemar
to burn a CD quemar un disco compacto **I**
bus el autobús (*pl.* los autobuses) **I**
bus stop la parada de autobús
by bus en autobús **I**
business el negocio
business administration la administración de empresas **7.2**
businessman el hombre de negocios **II, 7.2**
businessperson el (la) empresario(a) **4.1**
businesswoman la mujer de negocios **II, 7.2**
busy ocupado(a) **I**
but pero **I**
butcher shop la carnicería **6.1**
butterfly la mariposa **1.1**
to buy comprar **I**
to buy a ticket sacar el billete **6.1**
by por
by chance por casualidad **6.2**
by means of por medio de
Bye! ¡Chau!

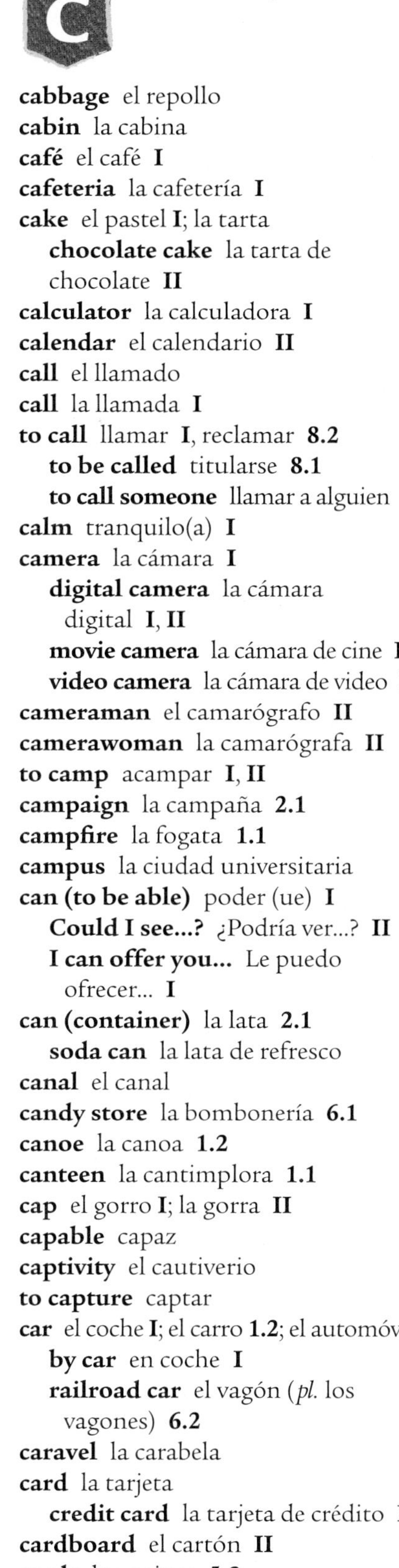

C

cabbage el repollo
cabin la cabina
café el café **I**
cafeteria la cafetería **I**
cake el pastel **I**; la tarta
  chocolate cake la tarta de chocolate **II**
calculator la calculadora **I**
calendar el calendario **II**
call el llamado
call la llamada **I**
to call llamar **I**, reclamar **8.2**
  to be called titularse **8.1**
  to call someone llamar a alguien **II**
calm tranquilo(a) **I**
camera la cámara **I**
  digital camera la cámara digital **I, II**
  movie camera la cámara de cine **II**
  video camera la cámara de video **II**
cameraman el camarógrafo **II**
camerawoman la camarógrafa **II**
to camp acampar **I, II**
campaign la campaña **2.1**
campfire la fogata **1.1**
campus la ciudad universitaria
can (to be able) poder (ue) **I**
  Could I see...? ¿Podría ver...? **II**
  I can offer you... Le puedo ofrecer... **I**
can (container) la lata **2.1**
  soda can la lata de refresco
canal el canal
candy store la bombonería **6.1**
canoe la canoa **1.2**
canteen la cantimplora **1.1**
cap el gorro **I**; la gorra **II**
capable capaz
captivity el cautiverio
to capture captar
car el coche **I**; el carro **1.2**; el automóvil
  by car en coche **I**
  railroad car el vagón (*pl.* los vagones) **6.2**
caravel la carabela
card la tarjeta
  credit card la tarjeta de crédito **II**
cardboard el cartón **II**
cards los naipes **5.2**
care el cuidado
  to take care of cuidar
to care for cuidar
career la carrera
carefully con cuidado
to caress acariciar
carpenter el (la) carpintero(a) **II, 4.2**
carriage el coche
  horse-drawn carriage el coche tirado por caballo
carrot la zanahoria **II**
to carry llevar **II**
  to carry on seguir adelante **3.2**
  to carry out cumplir con **2.1**
cartoons los dibujos animados **2.2**
carving la talla
case el caso
  in case en caso de que **5.1**
  just in case por si acaso
cash el dinero en efectivo **II**
cashier el (la) cajero(a)
castle el castillo **6.2**
casual informal **5.2**
cat el (la) gato(a) **I**
cathedral la catedral **II**
cattle el ganado
  cattle rancher el (la) ganadero(a)
cave la cueva
CD player el tocadiscos (*pl.* los tocadiscos) compactos **I**
to celebrate celebrar **I**
cellular phone el teléfono celular **I, II**; el celular
center el centro **I**
  historic center el centro histórico **6.2**
century el siglo
ceramic la cerámica
  (made of) ceramic de cerámica **II**
ceramics la cerámica **I**
cereal el cereal **I**
ceremony la ceremonia **7.1**
certainty la certeza
chair la silla **I**
chalkboard el pizarrón (*pl.* los pizarrones) **I**
challenge el reto
champion el campeón (*pl.* los campeones), la campeona **I**
championship el campeonato **II**
chance: by chance por casualidad **6.2**
change el cambio
  change purse el monedero **5.1**
to change cambiar
  to change roles cambiar de papel
channel: TV channel el canal de televisión **2.1**
chant el canto
chapel la capilla
chapter el capítulo **8.1**
character el personaje **II**
to charge (money) cobrar
to chat charlar **5.2**
chat room el salón (*pl.* los salones) de charlas **5.1**
check el cheque **2.1**
to check revisar
  to check one's luggage facturar el equipaje **II**
checkers las damas **5.2**
cheese el queso **I**
chess el ajedrez **5.2**
chicken el pollo **I**
  roasted chicken el pollo asado **II**
child el (la) niño(a) **II**
childhood la niñez
children los hijos **I**
choir el coro **7.1**
to choose escoger (escojo)
to choose elegir (i, i) (elijo) **2.1**
chores los quehaceres **I**
Christmas la Navidad
  Christmas tree el árbol de Navidad
church la iglesia
cistern el aljibe
citizen el (la) ciudadano(a) **3.2**
citizenship la ciudadanía
city la ciudad **I, II**
  city block la cuadra **II**; la manzana **6.1**
  city map el plano **6.2**
civilization la civilización (*pl.* las civilizaciones) **II**
to clap aplaudir **8.2**
to clarify aclarar
class la clase **I**
classroom la clase **I**; el aula
clean limpio(a) **I**
to clean limpiar **I**
clear claro(a)
clever ingenioso(a) **4.1**
to click on hacer clic en **I, II**
client el (la) cliente
cliff el acantilado
climate el clima **3.1**
climax el clímax **8.1**
climb escalar
  to climb mountains escalar montañas **II, 1.1**
clock el reloj **I**
to close cerrar (ie) **I**

closed cerrado(a)
closed captioning for the hearing impaired la subtitulación para sordos **2.2**
It's closed. Está cerrado(a). **II**
closet el armario **I**
clothing la ropa **I**
to put on clothes ponerse la ropa **II**
club el club
clue la pista
coach el (la) entrenador(a) **II, 4.1**
coast la costa
coat el abrigo **II**
code: dress code el código de vestimenta **7.1**
coffee el café **I**
coffee farm el cafetal
coffee worker el (la) cafetero(a)
cold el frío **I**
It is cold. Hace frío. **I**
to be cold tener frío **I**
to collaborate colaborar **2.1**
color el color
What color is/are...? ¿De qué color es/son...?
colorful colorido(a)
column la columna **2.2**
advice column la columna de consejos
comb el peine **I, II**
to comb one's hair peinarse **I, II**
to come venir (vengo) **I**
Come on! ¡Dale! **II**
to come back volver (ue) **I**
to come in pasar
to come with acompañar
comedy la comedia **II**
comfortable cómodo(a)
comic book el libro de historietas **8.1**
comic strip la historieta, las tiras cómicas
command el mandato
to command that mandar **4.1**
to comment (on) comentar **5.2**
to commercialize comercializar **3.2**
to commit cometer
to commit oneself comprometerse
commitment el compromiso **3.2**
committee el comité
events committee el comité de eventos **7.1**
common común
community la comunidad **II**
compact disc el disco compacto **I**
companion el (la) compañero(a)
company la empresa **7.2**; la compañía
to compare comparar
compass la brújula
to compete competir (i, i) **II**
competition la competencia **II**
to complain quejarse
complex complejo(a) **3.1**
complicated complicado(a)
computer la computadora **I**
laptop computer la computadora portátil **5.1**
computer studies la computación
concentrated: to be concentrated concentrarse
concert el concierto **I**
to conclude concluir **5.2**
conclusion: in conclusion en conclusión **6.2**
conductor el (la) conductor(a) **6.2**
to confirm confirmar
to confirm a flight confirmar el vuelo **II**
to congratulate felicitar
Congratulations! ¡Felicidades!
to connect conectar **I**
to connect to the Internet conectarse a Internet **I, 5.1**
consecutive consecutivo(a) **6.2**
to conserve conservar **II**
to consider considerar
considerate considerado(a) **4.1**
consideration la consideración
consultant el (la) consultor(a)
consumer el (la) consumidor(a) **II**
container el envase **2.1**; la vasija
contamination la contaminación **II, 3.1**
contest el concurso
context el contexto **8.1**
continue: to continue on seguir adelante **3.2**
contrast el contraste
to convince convencer
I'm convinced! ¡Estoy convencido(a)! **II**
to cook cocinar **I**
cooked cocido(a) **II**
cookie la galleta **I**
cool
How cool! ¡Qué bárbaro!, ¡Qué chévere!
to be cool (weather) hacer fresco **1.2**
to cool enfriar
to cool down or off refrescarse **1.2**
cooperation la cooperación **2.1**
copper el cobre
coral reef el arrecife de coral
corn el maíz
corner la esquina
around the corner a la vuelta de la esquina **8.2**
on the corner en la esquina **II**
to correct corregir (i, i) (corrijo)
to cost costar (ue) **I**
How much does it (do they) cost? ¿Cuánto cuesta(n)? **I**
It (They) cost(s)... Cuesta(n)... **I**
costume el disfraz (*pl.* los disfraces)
costumes (in a play) el vestuario **8.2**
couch el sofá **I**
counselor el (la) consejero(a)
to count contar (ue)
to count on (others) contar con (los demás) **2.1**
countless incontable
country el país **I**; el campo
native country el país natal
courage el coraje **8.2**
course el plato
course (of study) el curso **7.2**
main course el plato principal **I**
court la cancha **I**
cousin el (la) primo(a) **I**
cozy acogedor(a) **5.2**
craftsperson el (la) artesano(a)
craziness la locura
to create crear
creativity la creatividad **2.1**
crew la tripulación (*pl.* las tripulaciones)
crime el crimen (*pl.* los crímenes)
to criticize criticar **3.2**
cross la cruz (*pl.* las cruces)
to cross cruzar **II**
cruise el crucero
to go on a cruise hacer un crucero **1.2**
cry el grito
to cry llorar **II**
It makes me cry. Me hace llorar. **II**
cultivation el cultivo

culture la cultura
cup la taza
cure la cura **II**
to cure curar
curious curioso(a)
currency la moneda
current (contemporary) actual
curtain la cortina **I**
  stage curtain el telón (*pl.* los telones)
  to raise/lower the curtain levantar/bajar el telón **8.2**
custard el flan **II**
custom la costumbre
customs la aduana
  to go through customs pasar por la aduana **II**
to cut cortar **I**
  to cut the grass cortar el césped **I**
cycle el ciclo
  life cycle el ciclo de vida
cycling el ciclismo **II**

daily cotidiano(a); diario(a)
dairy store la lechería **6.1**
damage el daño
to damage dañar **II**
dance el baile; la danza
  folk dance la danza folklórica
to dance bailar **I**
danger el peligro
dangerous peligroso(a) **I**
daring atrevido(a) **4.1**; osado(a)
data los datos
database la base de datos
date la fecha **I**
  birth date la fecha de nacimiento **I**
  What is the date? ¿Cuál es la fecha? **I**
daughter la hija **I**
daughter-in-law la nuera **1.2**
dawn la madrugada
day el día **I**
  day trip la excursión (*pl.* las excursiones)
  every day todos los días **I**
  Some day... Algún día... **II**
  the day before yesterday anteayer **I, II**
  What day is today? ¿Qué día es hoy? **I**
dazzling deslumbrante
deadline la fecha límite **2.2**
deaf sordo(a)
  the deaf los sordos
deal: to deal with, to be about tratar sobre
dear querido(a)
  Dear... Estimado(a)...
debate el debate **2.2**
to debate debatir **5.2**
December diciembre **I**
to decide decidir **7.1**
to decipher descifrar
decision la decisión (*pl.* las decisiones)
  to make decisions tomar decisiones **7.1**
deck (of a boat) la cubierta **1.2**
to decorate decorar **I**
decoration la decoración (*pl.* las decoraciones) **I**
to decrease disminuir **3.1**
dedicated dedicado(a) **4.1**
dedication la dedicación
deer el venado
deforestation la deforestación **II, 3.1**
degree (academic) el título **7.2**
to delay atrasar
to delegate delegar **2.1**
delicious rico(a) **I**; delicioso(a) **II**
to delight encantar **II**
  Delighted. Encantado(a). **I**
to deliver newspapers repartir periódicos **7.1**
delivery la entrega
to demand exigir **4.1**, reclamar **8.2**
  to demand that exigir (exijo) que **4.1**
demonstration la manifestación (*pl.* las manifestaciones)
dentist el (la) dentista **II, 7.2**
deodorant el desodorante **II**
department (in college) la facultad **7.2**
department store el almacén (*pl.* los almacenes) **II**
departure la salida **II**
dependable fiable **7.2**
depressed deprimido(a) **I**
to descend bajar **I**
to describe describir **II, 2.2**
design el diseño **2.1**
designer el (la) diseñador(a) **II**
  Web page designer el (la) diseñador(a) de páginas web **7.1**
desire el deseo
desk el escritorio **I**
to despair desesperar
desperate desesperado(a)
despite a pesar de que **6.2**
dessert el postre **I**
  for dessert de postre **I**
destination el destino
to destroy destruir **3.1**
destruction la destrucción **II**
detail el detalle
detective el (la) detective **II, 4.1**
to develop desarrollar **3.1**
development el desarrollo **3.1**
device el aparato
dialog el diálogo **8.2**
dice los dados **5.2**
to die morir (ue, u) **II**
diet la dieta
  balanced diet la dieta balanceada **7.1**
  to follow a balanced diet seguir una dieta balanceada **II**
different distinto(a) **5.1**; diferente
difficult difícil **I**
difficulty la dificultad
to diminish disminuir **3.1**
to dine cenar **II**
dining room el comedor **I**
dinner la cena **I**
  to have dinner cenar **II**
to direct dirigir (dirijo) **7.1, 8.2**
directions las direcciones
  to ask for directions pedir (i, i) direcciones **6.2**
  stage direction la dirección de escenografía **8.2**
director el (la) director(a) **II**
dirty sucio(a) **I**
  to get (something) dirty ensuciar **6.1**
disadvantage la desventaja
to disagree no estar de acuerdo **2.2**
disagreeable desagradable **4.1**
disaster el desastre
discount el descuento **1.1**
discouragement el desaliento
to discover descubrir **II**
to discuss discutir **5.2**
disgust el asco
  How disgusting! ¡Qué asco! **II**
dish el plato
  vegetarian dish el plato vegetariano **II**
disorganized desorganizado(a) **I**
distinct distinto(a) **5.1**
distinguish: to be distinguished distinguirse
to distribute distribuir **2.2**
to dive zambullirse

dizzy: to get dizzy marearse **1.2**
to do hacer (hago)
  to do errands hacer los mandados **6.1**
  to do well irle bien (a alguien) **7.1**
dock el muelle
doctor el (la) doctor(a) **8.2**; el (la) médico(a) **7.2**
document el documento **5.1**
  identification document el documento de identidad **5.1**
documentary el documental **II**
  short documentary el cortometraje **2.2**
dog el (la) perro(a) **I**
dollar el dólar **I**
to donate donar **2.2**
donation la donación (*pl.* las donaciones)
door la puerta **I**
doorbell el timbre **6.1**
doorman el portero
dot (in e-mail address) el punto
double room la habitación doble **II**
to doubt that... dudar que... **4.2**
doubtful: It's doubtful that... Es dudoso que... **4.2**
dove la paloma
down hacia abajo
to download descargar **5.1**
downtown el centro **I**
draft el borrador
drama el drama **II**
dramatist el (la) dramaturgo(a) **8.2**
to draw dibujar **I**
drawing el dibujo
dream el sueño
to dream soñar (ue)
  to dream about soñar con **8.2**
dress el vestido **I**
dresser la cómoda **I**
to drill horadar
drink la bebida **I**
to drink beber **I**
  to drink something tomar algo **6.2**
to drive conducir (conduzco)
drought la sequía **3.1**
dry seco(a)
to dry secar
  to dry one's hair secarse el pelo **I**
  to dry oneself secarse **I, II**
to dub doblar
during durante
duty el deber **4.2**
DVD el DVD **I**
  DVD player el lector DVD **I**

each cada
ear la oreja **I**
  inner ear (hearing) el oído **II**
early temprano **I**
earn a living as... ganarse la vida como... **II**
earring el arete **I, II**
earth la tierra
earthquake el temblor **3.1**
easily fácilmente
east el este
easy fácil **I**
to eat comer **I**
  to eat lunch almorzar (ue) **I**
  to eat outside comer al aire libre **I**
  to go out to eat ir de tapas **6.1**
ecologist el (la) ecólogo(a)
ecotourism el ecoturismo, el turismo ecológico
to edit editar **II**; redactar **7.1**
editor el (la) editor(a) **II, 2.2**
editorial el artículo de opinión **2.2**
educated educado(a) **7.2**
education la educación
efficient eficiente **7.2**
effort el esfuerzo
egg el huevo **I**
eight ocho **I**
eight hundred ochocientos(as) **I**
eighteen dieciocho **I**
eighth octavo(a) **I**
either tampoco **II**
  either... or o... o **I, II**
  not either tampoco **I**
elbow el codo **II**
the elderly los ancianos **2.1**
electrician el (la) electricista **4.1**
electricity la corriente
element el elemento
elevator el ascensor **II**
eleven once **I**
e-mail el correo electrónico **I**
  e-mail address la dirección electrónica **I, II**
embarrassed: to feel embarrassed avergonzarse
to embroider bordar
emerald la esmeralda
to emigrate emigrar
emperor el emperador **II**
employee el (la) empleado(a) **7.1**
empty vacío(a)
encounter el encuentro **5.2**
end el fin
to end terminar **I**
to endure perdurar
enemy el (la) enemigo(a) **II**
engineer el (la) ingeniero(a) **II, 7.2**
engineering la ingeniería **7.2**
English el inglés **I**
to enjoy disfrutar (de) **5.1**
  Enjoy! Buen provecho! **II**
  to enjoy oneself divertirse (ie, i) **1.1**
enjoyment el gozo
enormous enorme
to enter entrar
entrance la entrada **6.2**
environment el medio ambiente **II, 3.1**
environmental medioambiental
equal igual
equator el ecuador
equipment el equipo **1.2**
to erase borrar
eraser el borrador **I**
erosion la erosión **3.1**
errand el mandado
  to do errands hacer los mandados **6.1**
error el error
essay el ensayo **8.1**
to establish establecer **7.2**
establishment el establecimiento
eternal eterno(a)
euro el euro **I**
to evaluate evaluar **3.2**
even aún
evening la noche **I**
  Good evening. Buenas noches. **I**
event el suceso **8.1**; el acontecimiento
  background event el antecedente **8.1**
every cada
  every day todos los días **I**
everyone todo el mundo
exact preciso(a)
exam el examen (*pl.* los exámenes) **I**
example el ejemplo
excavation la excavación (*pl.* las excavaciones) **II**
Excellent! ¡Excelente! **II**

exchange el intercambio
to exchange opinions intercambiar opiniones **5.2**
excited emocionado(a) **I**
  to be excited estar ilusionado(a) **5.1**
  to get excited animarse
exciting emocionante
excursion la excursión (*pl.* las excursiones)
to excuse
  Excuse me. Perdón **I**; Con permiso. **II**
  Excuse me; I'm sorry. Disculpe. **II**
exercise el ejercicio
to exercise hacer ejercicio **II**
exhausting agotador **1.1**
to exhibit exhibir
exile: to be exiled exiliarse
exit la salida **8.2**
exotic exótico(a)
expensive caro(a) **I, II**
  How expensive! ¡Qué caro(a)! **I**
to experience experimentar
to explain explicar **II, 2.2**
to explore explorar **6.2**
to express expresar
extinct: to become extinct extinguirse **3.1**
extinction la extinción (*pl.* las extinciones)
extremely sumamente **II**
eye el ojo **I**

F

fabric la tela
facade la fachada
face la cara **II**; el rostro
facing frente a **1.1**
to fail fracasar **II**
failure el fracaso **3.2**
fair la feria **I**
faithful fiel **4.1**
fall el otoño **I**
to fall caer (caigo)
  fall asleep dormirse (ue, u) **I, II**
  to fall down caerse (me caigo) **6.2**
false falso(a)
fame la fama **4.2**
family la familia **I**
  family members los familiares
famous famoso(a) **II**
fan (sports) el (la) aficionado(a) **I**
Fantastic! ¡Qué bárbaro!
fantasy la fantasía
far (from) lejos (de) **I**
fare la tarifa **1.1**
farmer el (la) agricultor(a) **II**
fashion la moda
fast rápido(a) **II**
father el padre **I**
father-in-law el suegro **II, 1.2**
faucet el grifo **6.1**
  to turn on the faucet abrir el grifo **6.1**
  to turn off the faucet cerrar el grifo **6.1**
favorite favorito(a) **I**; preferido(a) **I**
fear el miedo **I**
feat la hazaña
feature (movie) el largometraje **2.2**
February febrero **I**
to feed darle(s) de comer **I**
to feel sentir (ie, i)
  to feel like... tener ganas de... **I**
  to feel sorry that... sentir que... **4.2**
Ferris wheel la vuelta al mundo **I**
few pocos(as)
fiancé el novio **II, 1.2**
fiancée la novia **II, 1.2**
field el campo **I**
fifteen quince **I**
fifth quinto(a) **I**
fifty cincuenta **I**
to fight pelear **II**
file el archivo
to fill llenar **1.1**
  to fill out an application llenar una solicitud de empleo **7.1**
to film filmar **II**
film la película
  action... ...de aventuras **II**
  fantasy... ...de fantasía **II**
  horror... ...de terror **II**
  science fiction... ...de ciencia ficción **II**
finally por fin **I, II**
financial financiero(a)
  financial plan el plan financiero **7.2**
to find encontrar (ue) **I**; conseguir (i, i) **1.1**
  to find oneself encontrarse (ue)
  to find out about enterarse de **6.1**
fine fino(a) **II**
finger el dedo **II**
to finish concluir **5.2**
fire el fuego
  (accidental) el incendio
  on fire en llamas
firefighter el (la) bombero(a) **II, 4.2**
firewood la leña
fireworks los fuegos artificiales
first primero **II**
first primero(a) **I**
  the first of... el primero de... **I**
fish (animal) el pez (*pl.* los peces) **II, 1.1**; **(food)** el pescado **I**
to fish pescar **II**
to fit... quedar...
  ...badly ...mal **II**
  ...loose ...flojo(a) **II**
  ...tight ...apretado(a) **II**
  ...well ...bien **II**
  How does it (do they) fit me? ¿Cómo me queda(n)? **II**
fitting: to be fitting encajar
five cinco **I**
five hundred quinientos(as) **I**
flag la bandera
flame la llama
flavor el sabor **II**
flexible flexible **7.2**
flight el vuelo **II**
  to confirm a flight confirmar el vuelo **II**
flight attendant el (la) auxiliar de vuelo **II**
flood la inundación (*pl.* las inundaciones) **3.1**
floor el piso; el suelo **I**
  first or ground floor la planta baja **I**
  second floor (first above ground) el primer piso **I**
flour la harina
flower la flor **1.1**
flower shop la florería **6.1**
to fly volar (ue)
flyer el volante **2.2**
focus el enfoque
to focus (on) enfocarse (en)
fog la neblina
to fold doblar
foliage el follaje
to follow seguir (i, i) **1.1**
  to follow a balanced diet seguir una dieta balanceada **II**

following siguiente **I**
food la comida **I**
  junk food la comida chatarra **7.1**
food processor la trituradora
food server el (la) camarero(a) **I**
foot el pie **I**
  on foot a pie **I**
football el fútbol americano **I**
footprint la huella
for para **I**; por
  for that reason por eso **4.2**
to force someter
forest el bosque **II, 1.1**
  cloud forest el bosque nuboso
  forest fire el incendio forestal **II**
  rain forest el bosque lluvioso
Forgive me. Perdóneme. **II**
fork el tenedor **II**
form la forma
to form formar
formal formal **5.2**
formalwear la ropa elegante **II**
fortress fortaleza **6.2**
forty cuarenta **I**
to found fundar
founder el (la) fundador(a)
fountain la fuente **6.1**
four cuatro **I**
four hundred cuatrocientos(as) **I**
fourteen catorce **I**
fourth cuarto(a) **I**
fox el zorro
fragrant oloroso(a)
fraud el (la) farsante **8.2**
free time el tiempo libre **I, II**
French fries las papas fritas **I**
frequency la frecuencia
frequent frecuente
frequently frecuentemente **II**
fresh fresco(a) **II**
  fresh water el agua dulce **1.1**
Friday el viernes **I**
fried frito(a) **II**
friend el (la) amigo(a) **I**
  to spend time with friends pasar un rato con los amigos **I**
friendly amable
friendship la amistad **II, 4.2**
fright el susto, el espanto
from de **I**; desde **II**
front el frente
  in front of delante de **I**; en frente de
fruit la fruta **I**
  fruit stand la frutería **6.1**
to fry freír (i, i) **II**
to fulfill cumplir con **2.1**; realizar
fun la diversión
fun divertido(a) **I**
  to have fun divertirse (ie) **1.1**
  to make fun of hacer chiste de, burlarse de
  What fun! ¡Qué divertido! **I**
to fundraise juntar fondos **2.1**
funny cómico(a) **I**
furniture los muebles **I**
future futuro(a)
the future el porvenir **3.1**; el futuro
  In the future... En el futuro... **II**

G

gala la gala **II**
game el partido **I**
  board game el juego de mesa **5.2**
  computer games los juegos de computadora **5.1**
  game piece la ficha **5.2**
gap el vacío
garbage la basura **I**
  garbage container el basurero **3.1**
garden el jardín (*pl.* los jardines) **I**
  botanical gardens los jardines botánicos
garlic el ajo **II**
gate la puerta **II**
to gather recoger
gear el equipo
generally generalmente **I, II**
generosity la generosidad
generous generoso(a) **II, 4.1**
genre el género literario **8.1**
gesture el gesto **8.2**
to get conseguir (i, i) **1.1**
  How do I get to...? ¿Cómo llego a...? **II**
  to not get along llevarse mal **II**
  to get along well llevarse bien **II**
  to get angry enojarse **II**
  to get dressed vestirse (i, i) **I, II**
  to get excited animarse
  to get in line hacer cola **II**
  to get in shape ponerse en forma **7.1**
  to get into trouble meterse en problemas **6.2**
  to get lost perderse (ie) **6.2**
  to get off the subway bajar el metro **6.1**
  to get on the subway subir el metro **6.1**
  to get married casarse **II**
  to get ready arreglarse **II**
  to get scared asustarse
  to get together reunirse **1.2**
  to get together (with) juntarse (con) **1.2**
  to get up levantarse **I, II**
getaway la escapada **1.2**
giant el gigante
gift el regalo **I**
girl la chica **I**; la muchacha **I**
girlfriend la novia **II, 1.2**
to give dar (doy) **I**; regalar
  to give advice dar consejos **5.1**
  to give up... dejar de... **7.1**
  I'll give... to you for... Le dejo... en... **II**
glacier el glaciar
glass el vaso **5.2**; el vidrio **II**
glasses las gafas **5.1**
global mundial
glove el guante **I**
  work gloves los guantes de trabajo **2.1**
to go ir (voy) **I**; irse (me voy) **II**
  Go ahead. Pase. **II**
  to be going to... ir a... **I**
  to go bowling jugar a los bolos
  to go for a walk pasear **I**
  to go into meterse en **1.1**
  to go on an excursion hacer una excursión **1.1**
  to go on vacation ir de vacaciones **II**
  to go out salir (salgo) **I**
  to go out to eat ir de tapas **6.1**
  to go shopping ir de compras **I**
  to go sightseeing ver las atracciones **II**
  to go straight seguir derecho **II**
  to go through customs pasar por la aduana **II**
  to go through security pasar por seguridad **II**
  to go to bed acostarse (ue) **I, II**
  to go up subir **I**
  to go whitewater rafting navegar por rápidos **1.1**
  to go with acompañar

goal la meta **4.2**; el gol
goblet la copa
god el dios **II**
godchild el (la) ahijado(a)
goddess la diosa **II**
godfather el padrino **II, 1.2**
godmother la madrina **II, 1.2**
godparents los padrinos **1.2**; los compadres
gold el oro
  (made of) gold de oro **I, II**
golden dorado(a)
good bueno(a) **I**
  Good afternoon. Buenas tardes. **I**
  Good evening. Buenas noches. **I**
  Good morning. Buenos días. **I**
  Good night. Buenas noches. **I**
  It's good (that...) Es bueno (que...) **II**
  It's not good that... Es malo que... **II**
  to have a good time pasar un buen rato **5.2**
Goodbye. Adiós. **I**
good-looking guapo(a) **I**
goods los artículos **I, II**
  sporting goods los artículos deportivos
gossip el chisme
government el gobierno
  student government el comité estudiantil **7.1**
grade la nota **I**
  to get a good/bad grade sacar una buena/mala nota **I**
to graduate graduarse **7.1**
graduation la graduación **7.1**
grammar la gramática
grandchild el (la) nieto(a)
grandchildren los nietos **1.2**
granddaughter la nieta **1.2**
grandeur la grandeza
grandfather el abuelo **I**
grandmother la abuela **I**
grandparents los abuelos **I**
grandson el nieto **1.2**
to grant otorgar **2.2**; conceder
grape la uva **I**
graphic la gráfica **2.2**
  graphic novel la novela gráfica
grass el césped **I**
  to cut the grass cortar el césped **I**
great-grandchild el (la) biznieto(a)
great-grandchildren los biznietos **1.2**
great-granddaughter la biznieta **1.2**
great-grandfather el bisabuelo **1.2**
great-grandmother la bisabuela **1.2**
great-grandparents los bisabuelos **1.2**
great-grandson el biznieto **1.2**
greedy codicioso(a) **8.2**
green verde **I**
greenhouse effect el efecto invernadero **3.1**
Greetings! ¡Saludos!
  Greetings from... Saludos desde...
grill la parrilla
  grilled steak el filete a la parrilla **II**
to grind moler (ue)
ground el suelo **3.1**
ground (up) molido(a) **II**
group el grupo
to grow (up) crecer (crezco)
to guess adivinar
guests los invitados **I**
guide el (la) guía
  guide (book) la guía **1.1**
  travel guide la guía del viajero
guitar la guitarra **I**
guy el tío
gymnasium el gimnasio **I**
gymnastics la gimnasia
Gypsy gitano(a)

hair el pelo **I**
  brown/blond hair el pelo castaño/rubio **I**
hair dryer el secador de pelo **I, II**
hairdresser el (la) peluquero(a) **7.2**
hairless pelado(a)
half medio(a)
  half past... ... y media **I**
hallway el pasillo **I**
ham el jamón **I**
hamburger la hamburguesa **I**
hammock la hamaca
hand la mano **I**
  on the one hand... on the other hand por un lado... por otro lado **II, 3.2**
handbag la bolsa **5.1**
handicrafts las artesanías **I, II**
handmade: (to be) handmade (estar) hecho(a) a mano **II**
handshake el apretón (*pl.* los apretones) de manos
handsome hermoso(a) **II**
to hang colgar (ue)
to happen pasar
  What's happening? ¿Qué pasa? **I**
happy contento(a) **I**; feliz; alegre
  Happy birthday! ¡Feliz cumpleaños! **I**
  to be happy (that...) alegrarse (de que...) **4.2**
hardware store la ferretería **6.1**
hard-working trabajador(a) **I**
to harm dañar **3.1**
harvest la cosecha
hat el sombrero **I**
  winter hat el gorro **I**
to have tener (tengo) **I**; haber
  one has to... hay que... **I**
  there have been... han habido...
  to have a good time pasar un buen rato **5.2**, pasarlo bien
  to have just... acabar de... **I**
  to have to tener que **I**
he él **I**
head la cabeza **I**
headline el titular **II, 2.2**
health la salud **I**
healthful saludable **II**
healthy sano(a) **I**; saludable **II**
heart el corazón (*pl.* los corazones) **I**
heat el calor **I**
  stifling heat el calor agobiante **1.2**
to heat calentar (ie)
heavy pesado(a)
height la cima; la altura
Hello. Hola. **I**
  Hello? ¿Aló?, ¿Bueno?, ¿Diga? **II**
helmet el casco **I**
help la ayuda
to help ayudar **I**
her su **I**; a/de ella **I, II**
herb la hierba
here aquí **I**
  No, he's/she's not here. No, no está. **II**
heritage la herencia
hero el héroe **II**
heroic heroico(a) **II**
heroine la heroína **II**
to hesitate dudar
Hi. Hola. **I**
to hide esconder **5.1**
high school el colegio, la escuela secundaria, el liceo
highway la carretera

hike la caminata **I**
to hike dar o hacer una caminata **I, II, 1.1**
him él **I, II**
hip la cadera
to hire contratar **7.2**
his su **I**
historic(al) histórico(a) **II**
history la historia **I**
hit (song) el éxito
to hit golpear
holiday el día feriado **7.1**
  the holidays los días festivos
homage el homenaje
homeless: the homeless la gente sin hogar **2.1**
homework la tarea **I**
honest honrado(a) **7.2**; honesto(a) **7.2**
honey la miel
honor el honor **4.2**
to honor honrar
honorable honrado(a) **7.2**
hook el gancho
hoop el aro
hope la esperanza **7.1**
  I hope so! ¡Ojalá!
  I hope..., hopefully... Ojalá...
horizon el horizonte
horrible horrible **I**
horse el caballo **I**
  to ride a horse montar a caballo **I**
hospital el hospital **2.1**
hostel el hostal **II**
hot caliente; picante **II**
  It is hot. Hace calor. **I**
  to be hot tener calor **I**
hotel el hotel **I, II**
  hotel room la habitación (*pl.* las habitaciones) **II**
hour la hora **I**
house la casa **I**
housing la vivienda
how
  How? ¿Cómo? **I**
  How are you? ¿Cómo estás? (familiar); ¿Cómo está usted? (formal) **I**
  How beautiful! ¡Qué bello(a)! **II**
  How cool! ¡Qué bárbaro!, ¡Qué chévere!
  How disgusting! ¡Qué asco! **II**
  How do I get to...? ¿Cómo llego a...? **II**
  How does it (do they) fit me? ¿Cómo me queda(n)? **II**
  How expensive! ¡Qué caro(a)! **II**
  How many...? ¿Cuántos(as)...? **I**
  how much cuánto(a) **I**
  How much does it (do they) cost? ¿Cuánto cuesta(n)? **I**
  How old are you? ¿Cuántos años tienes? **I**
  How scary! ¡Qué miedo! **I**
  How's it going? ¿Qué tal? **I**; ¿Qué pasa?
however sin embargo **II, 4.2**
to hug abrazar
huge enorme
humid húmedo(a)
hunger el hambre
  to be hungry tener hambre **I**
to hunt cazar **II**
hurricane el huracán (*pl.* los huracanes)
hurry la prisa
  to be in a hurry tener prisa **II**
to hurry (up) darse prisa
hurt herido(a) **I**
to hurt doler (ue) **I**
  to hurt oneself lastimarse
husband el esposo **II, 1.2**
hybrid vehicle el vehículo híbrido **II**

I yo **I**
  I love... Me encanta...
  I would like... Me gustaría... **II**
  I'm sorry. Lo siento. **I**
ice cream el helado **I**
  ice cream shop la heladería **II**
icon el icono **I, II**
idea la idea
  It's a good idea/bad idea. Es buena idea/mala idea. **II**
ideal ideal **I**
to idealize (someone) idealizar (a alguien) **4.1**
identification document el documento de identidad **5.1**
identification la identificación **II**
if si **I**
to illuminate iluminar
image la imagen (*pl.* las imágenes) **4.2**
to imitate imitar **4.1**
immigrant el (la) inmigrante
immigration la inmigración
impatience la impaciencia
impatient impaciente **II, 4.1**
to imply implicar **8.1**
importance la importancia
important importante **I**
  It's important (that...) Es importante (que...) **II**
impossible imposible
impressive impresionante
improbable: It's improbable that... Es improbable que... **4.2**
to improve mejorar **II, 3.1**
improvement la mejora **3.2**
in en **I**
  in addition además **6.2**
  in advance con anticipación **1.1**
  in case en caso de que **5.1**
  in conclusion en conclusión **6.2**
  in front (of) delante (de) **I**
  in order that a fin de que, para que **5.1**
  in order to para **I**
  in spite of a pesar de que **6.2**
  in the afternoon de la tarde **I**
  in the morning de la mañana **I**
to include incluir
included incluido(a)
to increase aumentar
indigenous indígena
indispensable: It is indispensable that... Es imprescindible que... **3.2**
inexpensive barato(a) **I, II**
infant el (la) bebé **1.2**
to infer inferir (ie, i) **8.1**
influence la influencia
to influence influir
to inform avisar
informal informal **5.2**
information la información **II**; los datos
ingredient el ingrediente **II**
inhabitant el (la) habitante
initiative la iniciativa **7.2**
in-laws los suegros **II, 1.2**
to in-line skate patinar en línea **I**
in-line skates los patines en línea **I**
inn el hostal **II**
innovation la innovación (*pl.* las innovaciones) **3.1**
insect el insecto
inside dentro (de) **I, 1.1**
to insist insistir **3.2**

instant message el mensaje instantáneo
instant messaging el mensajero instantáneo **I, II**
intelligent inteligente **I**
to intend pensar (ie)
interest el interés (*pl.* los intereses)
to interest interesar **II**
  to get interested animarse
interesting interesante **I**
intermission el intermedio **8.2**
Internet Internet **I, II**
  on the Internet por Internet
  to connect to the Internet conectar a Internet **I**
interview la entrevista **II, 2.2**
to interview entrevistar **II, 2.2**
to introduce presentar **I**
  Let me introduce you to... Te/Le presento a... (familiar/formal) **I**
invention el invento **3.1**
to invest invertir (ie, i) **3.2**
to investigate investigar **II, 2.2**
investor el (la) inversionista
invitation la invitación (*pl.* las invitaciones) **II**
to invite invitar **I**
  I invite you. Te invito. **I**
to iron planchar **I**
irresponsibility la irresponsabilidad **3.2**
island la isla
issue la cuestión (*pl.* las cuestiones) **2.2**
itinerary el itinerario **II**
its su **I**

jacket la chaqueta **I**
  life jacket el chaleco salvavidas **1.2**
January enero **I**
jealousy los celos **II**
  to be jealous (of) tener celos (de) **II**
jeans los jeans **I**
jewelry las joyas **I, II**
  jewelry store la joyería **II**
job el empleo **7.1**; el puesto, el trabajo **7.1**
to join unirse
joke la broma, el chiste
journalist el (la) periodista **4.2**
journey el viaje
judge el (la) juez(a) (*pl.* los jueces, las juezas) **7.2**
juice el jugo **I**
  orange juice el jugo de naranja **I**
July julio **I**
to jump off (of) tirarse (de)
June junio **I**
jungle la selva **II, 1.1**
junk food la comida chatarra **7.1**

kayak el kayac **1.1**
to keep guardar **5.1**; conservar
  to keep informed informarse **3.1**
  to keep one's balance mantener el equilibrio **1.2**
key la llave **II**
keyboard el teclado **I, II**
kind amable
  Very kind. Muy amable. **II**
kind (type) la clase
kingdom el reino
kiosk el kiosco **6.1**
kitchen la cocina **I**
knee la rodilla **I**
knife el cuchillo **II**
knight el caballero
to know
  (a fact, how to do something) saber (sé) **I**
  (a person) conocer (conozco) **I**
knowledge el conocimiento **II**; el saber
known conocido(a)
  well-known muy conocido(a)

L

laborer el (la) obrero(a) **4.1**
lake el lago
lamb el cordero
lamp la lámpara **I**
land la tierra
landscape el paisaje **6.2**
landslide el derrumbe **3.1**
language el idioma **7.2**
  the Spanish language el idioma castellano
large grande **I**
last pasado(a); último(a)
  last name el apellido **1.2**
  last night anoche **I**
  last week la semana pasada **I, II**
  last year/month el año/mes pasado **I, II**
to last durar
late tarde **I**
  later (on) más tarde **I, II**
later luego **I, II**
  See you later. Hasta luego. **I**
to laugh reír (i, i)
  It makes me laugh. Me hace reír. **II**
laughter la risa
law el derecho **7.2**; la ley
  labor laws las leyes laborales
lawn el césped **I**
lawyer el (la) abogado(a) **II**; **7.2**
lazy perezoso(a) **I**
to lead dirigir (dirijo) **7.1**
leader el (la) líder
leaf la hoja
to learn aprender **I**
learning el saber
leather el cuero
  (made of) leather de cuero **II**
to leave salir (salgo) **I**; irse (me voy) **7.2**; dejar
  to leave behind dejar **6.1**
  to leave a message dejar un mensaje **II**
left izquierdo(a)
  to turn left doblar a la izquierda **II**
leg la pierna **I**
legend la leyenda **II**
leisure el ocio **5.2**
lemon el limón (*pl.* los limones) **II**
to lend prestar **2.1**
Lent la Cuaresma
less menos
  less than... menos que... **I, II**
  less than... (with numbers) menos de... **II**
  less... than menos... que **I, II**
lesson la lección (*pl.* las lecciones); el mensaje **II**
Let's... Vamos a... **I**
letter la carta
  cover letter la carta de presentación
  letter to the editor la carta al editor
lettuce la lechuga **II**
level el nivel
liberty la libertad

librarian el (la) bibliotecario(a)
library la biblioteca **I**
lie: to lie down recostarse (ue) **1.2**
a lie la mentira
life la vida **II**
  life cycle el ciclo de vida
  life jacket el chaleco salvavidas **1.2**
lifeguard el (la) salvavidas
to lift levantar
  to lift weights levantar pesas **I**
light la luz (*pl.* las luces)
  to turn on the light encender la luz **II**
light bulb la bombilla
light (weight) ligero(a)
to light (a match or fire) encender (ie) **1.1**
lighthouse el faro
like como
to like gustar **I, I**
  Do you like...? ¿Te gusta...? **I**
  I like (don't) like... (No) Me gusta... **I**
  I would like... Me gustaría...; Quisiera... **I**
  I would like to thank... Quisiera darle las gracias a... **II**
  What do you like to do? ¿Qué te gusta hacer? **I**
  Would you like...? ¿Te gustaría...? **I**
line la línea
  to get in line hacer cola **II**
link el enlace **5.1**
list la lista
to listen (to) escuchar **I**
listener el (la) oyente
  (to a radio program) el (la) radioyente
to litter tirar basura **2.1**
little pequeño(a) **I**
little: a little un poco **I**
  little by little poco a poco **II**
to live vivir **I**
living la vida
  living room la sala **I**
  to earn a living as... ganarse la vida como... **II**
locate: to be located encontrarse (ue)
lodging el alojamiento **II**
long largo(a)
  as long as con tal (de) que **5.1**
to look (at) mirar
  to look back reflexionar **7.1**
  to look for buscar **I**
  to look like (someone) parecerse (a alguien) **1.2**
lookout el mirador **6.2**
loose flojo(a)
to lose perder (ie) **I**
lost: to get lost perderse (ie) **6.2**
a lot mucho **I**
loudspeaker el altoparlante
love el amor
  to be in love with estar enamorado(a) de **II**
  Yes, I would love to. Sí, me encantaría. **II**
to lower bajar **8.2**
  to lower the curtain bajar el telón **8.2**
luck la suerte
  to be lucky tener suerte **I**
luggage el equipaje **II**
  to check one's luggage facturar el equipaje **II**
lunch el almuerzo **I**
  to eat lunch almorzar (ue) **I**

M

machine la máquina
magazine la revista **2.1**
mail el correo
mail carrier el (la) cartero(a) **II, 4.2**
mailbox el buzón (*pl.* los buzones) **6.1**
mailing la publicidad por correo **2.2**
to maintain mantener (mantengo) **1.2**
major (in college) la especialidad **7.2**
to major in especializarse en **7.2**
to make hacer (hago)
  (to be) handmade (estar) hecho(a) a mano **II**
  It makes me cry. Me hace llorar. **II**
  It makes me laugh. Me hace reír. **II**
  It scares me. Me da miedo. **II**
  to be made of... ser de... **II**
  to make a mistake cometer un error **3.2**
  to make a suggestion dar una sugerencia **5.1**
  to make decisions tomar decisiones **7.1**
  to make fun of burlarse de
  to make the bed hacer la cama **I**
makeup el maquillaje **II**
  to put on makeup maquillarse **I**
mall el centro comercial **I**
man el hombre **I**
to manage conseguir (i, i) (consigo)
manager el (la) gerente **7.2**
many muchos(as) **I**
map el mapa **I**
  city map el plano **6.2**
March marzo **I**
to march desfilar
market el mercado **I**
  labor market el mercado laboral
  open-air market el mercado al aire libre **II**
marriage el matrimonio
marry: to get married casarse **II**
  married couple el matrimonio **1.2**
marvel la maravilla
mask la máscara
match el fósforo **1.1**
to match emparejar
math las matemáticas **I**
may
  May I see? ¿Me deja ver? **II**
  May I speak to...? ¿Puedo hablar con... ? **II**
May mayo **I**
maybe tal vez **I**; acaso **I**
mayonnaise la mayonesa **II**
mayor el (la) alcalde
mayorship la alcaldía
me mí **I, II**
meal la comida **I**
to mean significar **8.1**
means: by means of por medio de
meanwhile mientras tanto
meat la carne **I**
mechanic el (la) mecánico(a) **4.1**
medal la medalla
  gold/silver/bronze medal la medalla de oro/plata/bronce
to meddle entremeterse
medium el medio
to meet conocer (conozco) **I**; reunirse **1.2**
  to meet up with encontrarse (ue) con **5.2**
  Nice to meet you. Mucho gusto. **I**

meeting la reunión (*pl.* las reuniones) **5.2, 7.1**
member el miembro; el (la) integrante
to be a member of... ser miembro de... **7.1**
memory el recuerdo **7.1**; la memoria
mention: Don't mention it. No hay de qué. **II**
menu el menú **I**
merchandise las mercancías
mess el lío **6.1**
to mess up desordenar **6.1**
message el mensaje **I**
instant message el mensaje instantáneo
to leave a message dejar un mensaje **I, II**
metal el metal
(made of) metal de metal **II**
metaphor la metáfora **8.1**
meter el metro
microphone el micrófono **II**
microwave (oven) el microondas **6.1**
middle: in the middle of en medio de
migration la migración (*pl.* las migraciones)
milk la leche **I**
million un millón (de) **I**
mind la mente
minute el minuto **I**
miracle el milagro
mirror el espejo **I**
mischievous travieso(a)
miserly avaro(a) **8.2**
Miss ... Señorita (Srta.) ... **I**
to miss perder (ie) **6.2**
to be missing hacer falta
to miss (out on) perderse (ie)
mist la espuma
mistake el error
to mix mezclar **II**
mixed mezclado(a) **II**
mixture la mezcla
modern moderno(a) **II**
modest modesto(a) **4.1**
modesty la modestia
moment el momento
One moment. Un momento. **I, II**
Monday el lunes **I**
money el dinero **I**
monitor la pantalla **II**
monk el monje
monkey el mono
month el mes **I**
last month el mes pasado **II**
monument el monumento **II**
moon la luna
more más **I**
more and more cada vez más
more than... más que... **I, II**
more... than más... que **I, II**
more than... (with numbers) más de... **II**
morning la mañana **I**
Good morning. Buenos días. **I**
in the morning de la mañana **I**
mosque la mezquita
mother la madre **I**
mother-in-law la suegra **II, 1.2**
motivated motivado(a) **7.2**
motto el lema **2.1**
mountain la montaña **II**
mountain climber el (la) alpinista **II**
mountain range la cordillera
mouse el ratón (*pl.* los ratones) **I, II**
mouth la boca **I**
to move (relocate) mudarse, trasladarse
movie la película **I**
full-length movie el largometraje **2.2**
movie set el escenario
movie star la estrella de cine **II**
movie theater el cine **I**
the movies el cine **I**
Mr. ... Señor (Sr.) ... **I**
Mrs. ... Señora (Sra.) ... **I**
mud el barro
mule el (la) mulo(a)
muscular musculoso(a) **II**
museum el museo **I**
music la música **I**
dance music la música bailable **5.2**
folk music la música folklórica
rock music la música rock
musician el (la) músico(a) **4.2**
street musician el (la) músico(a) callejero(a) **5.2**
must: one must... hay que... **I**
mustard la mostaza **II**
my mi **I**

N

nail (of finger, toe) la uña **II**
name el nombre
His/Her name is . . . Se llama... **I**
last name el apellido **II, 1.2**
My name is... Me llamo... **I**
What's his/her/your (formal) name? ¿Cómo se llama? **I**
What's your (familiar) name? ¿Cómo te llamas? **I**
nap la siesta **5.2**
to take a nap dormir (ue, u) una siesta **5.2**
napkin la servilleta **II**
to narrate narrar **8.1**
narration la narración **II**
narrow estrecho(a)
national nacional
native indígena
natural resource el recurso natural **II, 3.1**
natural sciences las ciencias naturales
nature la naturaleza **II, 1.1**
navigator el (la) navegante
near (to) cerca (de) **I**
necessary: It's necessary (that...) Es necesario (que...) **II**
neck el cuello **II**
necklace el collar **I, II**
necktie la corbata **II**
need la necesidad
to need necesitar **I**
neighbor el (la) vecino(a) **4.2**
neighborhood el barrio **II**
neither tampoco **I**
neither... nor ni... ni **I, II**
nephew el sobrino **II, 1.2**
nervous nervioso(a) **I**
net la red **II**
network la red
never nunca **I, II**
nevertheless sin embargo **4.2**
new nuevo(a) **I**
New Year el Año Nuevo
news las noticias **II, 2.1**
news broadcast el noticiero **2.2**
newspaper el periódico (*pl.* los periódicos) **II, 2.1**
student newspaper el periódico escolar

next próximo(a)
next to al lado (de) **I**; junto a **1.1**
the next el (la) próximo(a) **II**
nice simpático(a) **I**; amable; bello(a) **II**
Nice to meet you. Mucho gusto. **I**
nickname el mote, el apodo, el sobrenombre
niece la sobrina **II, 1.2**
night la noche **I**
at night de la noche **I**
Good night. Buenas noches. **I**
last night anoche **I**
nightingale el ruiseñor
nightstand la mesita **6.1**
nine nueve **I**
nine hundred novecientos(as) **I**
nineteen diecinueve **I**
ninety noventa **I**
ninth noveno(a) **I**
no no **I**
no one nadie **I, II**
noise el ruido **5.2**
noisy ruidoso(a) **6.2**
none ninguno(a) **I, 5.2**; ningún **II**
nonprofit sin fines lucrativos
nonrenewable no renovable **3.1**
normally normalmente **I, II**
north el norte
nose la nariz (*pl.* las narices) **I**
not
not at all en absoluto **1.2**
not only... but also... no sólo... sino también... **II**
notebook el cuaderno **I**
notes los apuntes **I**
to take notes tomar apuntes **I**
nothing nada **I, II**
noun el sustantivo
novel la novela **8.1**
graphic novel la novela gráfica
novel novedoso(a) **3.2**
November noviembre **I**
now ahora **I**
right now ahora mismo
nowadays hoy en día
nuisance: to be a nuisance ser una lata **2.1**
number el número **I**
phone number el número de teléfono **I**
nurse el (la) enfermero(a) **II, 7.2**
nursing home el hogar de ancianos **2.1**
nutritious nutritivo(a) **I**

O

o'clock: It is... o'clock. Es la.../Son las... **I**
object el objeto **II**
oblivion el oblivio
to observe observar **1.1**
obstacle el obstáculo **3.2**
occupation el oficio **II**
to occur (to someone) ocurrírsele (a alguien)
ocean el océano
October octubre **I**
of de **I**
Of course. Claro.
Of course! ¡Claro que sí!, ¡Cómo no! **I, II**
to offend ofender
offer la oferta
to offer ofrecer (ofrezco) **I, 1.1**
I can offer you... Le puedo ofrecer... **I**
office la oficina **I**
doctor's/dentist's office el consultorio **II**
principal's office la oficina del (de la) director(a) **I**
tourist office la oficina de turismo **II**
often muchas veces **I**
oil el aceite **II**; el petróleo **3.1**
OK regular **I**
OK! ¡Vale!
OK. And you? Regular. ¿Y tú/usted? (familiar/formal) **I**
OK? ¿Está bien?
old viejo(a) **I**; antiguo(a) **II**
How old are you? ¿Cuántos años tienes? **I**
to be... years old tener... años **I**
old age la vejez
older mayor **I, II**
olive la aceituna
Olympic Games los Juegos Olímpicos **II**
omelet la tortilla **II**
on en; sobre
on foot a pie **I**
on the one hand... on the other hand por un lado... y por otro lado **II, 3.2**
on top (of) encima (de) **I**
on vacation de vacaciones **I**
once
once in a while de vez en cuando **I**
Once upon a time there was/were... Había una vez... **II**
one uno **I**
one hundred cien **I**
onion la cebolla **II**
online en línea **I**
to be online estar en línea **II**
only sólo, solamente; único(a)
not only... but also... no sólo... sino también... **II**
to ooze rezumar
open abierto(a)
It's open. Está abierto(a). **II**
to open abrir **I**
open-air al aire libre **I**
opinion la opinión (*pl.* las opiniones) **II**
In my opinion... En mi opinión... **II**
or o **I**
orange (color) anaranjado(a) **I**
orange (fruit) la naranja **I**
orchestra la orquesta **5.2**
order el orden
in chronological order en orden cronológico **6.2**
in order that a fin de que **5.1**
to order pedir (i, i) **I**
to order that mandar que **4.1**
to organize organizar **2.1**, ordenar **6.1**
organized organizado(a) **I**
to originate originarse
other otro(a) **I**
others los (las) demás
ought to deber **I**
our nuestro(a) **I**
outcome el desenlace **8.1**
outdoors al aire libre
outlook el mirador **6.2**
outside al aire libre
outside (of) fuera (de) **1.1**
outstanding sobresaliente **4.1**; destacado(a) **7.2**
oven el horno **6.1**
to overcome superar **3.2**
owl la lechuza
owner el (la) dueño(a) **7.2**
ozone layer la capa de ozono **II, 3.1**

pack: to pack a suitcase hacer la maleta **II**
to paddle remar **1.1**
page la página
  Web page la página web **1.2**, **7.1**
to paint pintar
painter el (la) pintor(a)
painting la pintura **3.2**; el cuadro **6.2**
pair la pareja
palace el palacio **II**
Panamerican Games los Juegos Panamericanos **II**
pants los pantalones **I**
paper el papel **I**
  (made of) paper de papel
  wrapping paper el papel de regalo **I**
parade el desfile
to parade desfilar
paragraph el párrafo
parents los padres **I**
park el parque **I**
  amusement park el parque de diversiones **I**
  ecological park el parque ecológico
  national park el parque nacional
part la parte
  to take part in tomar parte en **7.1**
to participate participar
  to participate in tomar parte en **7.1**
partner el (la) compañero(a)
party fiesta
  surprise party la fiesta de sorpresa **I**
to pass pasar
  to pass (a law) aprobar (ue)
passage el paso
passenger el (la) pasajero(a) **II**
passionate apasionado(a) **7.2**
passport el pasaporte **II**
password la contraseña **5.1**
past pasado(a) **I**
  half past... ... y media **I**
  quarter past... ... y cuarto **I**
the past el pasado
pastime el pasatiempo **5.2**
pastry shop la pastelería **II**, **6.1**
patent la patente **3.2**
path el sendero **1.1**
patience la paciencia
patient paciente **II**, **4.1**
patio el patio **I**
pauper el (la) tirado(a) **8.2**
to pay pagar **I**
pea el guisante
peace la paz
peak la cima
pen la pluma **I**
to penalize penalizar **3.2**
pencil el lápiz (*pl.* los lápices) **I**
people la gente **II**
pepper (black) la pimienta **II**
percent por ciento
percentage el porcentaje
performance el espectáculo **5.2**
  street performance la actuación callejera
perhaps tal vez **I**; acaso **I**
perimeter el perímetro
period el período
permission el permiso
to persist persistir **3.2**
persistent persistente **8.2**
person la persona **I**
  in person en persona
personal
  personal organizer la agenda electrónica **5.1**
  personal watercraft la moto acuática **1.2**
to personify personificar **4.1**
personnel el personal
pet la mascota
pharmacy la farmacia **II**
phone el teléfono **I**
  My phone number is... Mi número de teléfono is... **I**
  phone call la llamada **I**
  What is your phone number? ¿Cuál es tu/su número de teléfono? (familiar/formal) **I**
photo la foto **I**
  photo essay el foto ensayo
  to take photos tomar fotos **I**
photographer el (la) fotógrafo(a) **II**, **2.2**
to pick up recoger (recojo) **II**, **1.2**
to picnic comer al aire libre **I**
picture la foto **I**
piece la pieza
pill la píldora
pilot el (la) piloto **II**, **4.1**
pioneer el (la) pionero(a)
pizza la pizza **I**
place el lugar **I**
to place poner (pongo) **I**
  to take place tener lugar
plaid de cuadros **II**
plains las llanuras
to plan pensar (ie) **I**
planet el planeta **3.1**
planning la planificación **2.1**
plant la planta
plastic el plástico
plate el plato
platform el andén (*pl.* los andenes) **6.2**
play (dramatic work) el drama **7.1**; la obra de teatro **8.2**
to play
  (an instrument) tocar **I**
  (games) jugar **I**
  (sports) jugar (ue), practicar **I**
  to play a role hacer un papel **II**
  to play on a team jugar en equipo **II**
player el (la) jugador(a) **I**
playwright el (la) dramaturgo(a) **8.2**
plaza la plaza **II**
to please
  Please. Por favor. **I**
  to please someone hacerle gracia a alguien
  Pleased to meet you. Encantado(a). **I**
pleasure el gusto **I**; el placer
  The pleasure is mine. El gusto es mío. **I**
  With pleasure. Con mucho gusto. **II**
plot el argumento **II**
plus más
poem el poema
poet el (la) poeta
poetry la poesía **8.1**
point of view el punto de vista **II**, **8.1**
police officer el (la) policía **4.2**
policeman el policía **II**
policewoman la policía **II**
polite educado(a) **7.2**; cortés
politician el (la) político(a) **II**, **4.2**
politics la política **3.2**
pollution la contaminación **II**, **3.1**
pool (billiards) el billar **5.2**
popular popular **II**, **4.1**
popularity la popularidad
population la población (*pl.* las poblaciones)

pork el cerdo
pork chop la chuleta de cerdo **II**
port el puerto **1.2**
portable portátil
portrait el retrato **II**
to possess poseer
possibility la posibilidad
possible posible
It's possible that... Es posible que...
post office el correo **II, 6.1**
postcard la tarjeta postal **II**
to send postcards mandar tarjetas postales **II**
poster el letrero **2.1**, el cartel, el póster
postman el cartero **II**
postwoman la cartera **II**
pot la olla **1.1**
potato la papa **II**; la patata **I**
pound (weight) la libra
poverty la pobreza **2.1**
powerful poderoso(a)
practical práctico(a) **4.2**
to practice practicar **I**
prairie el llano
precious precioso(a) **5.1**
to prefer preferir (ie, i) **I**
preferable: It's preferable that... Es preferible que... **II**
prejudice el prejuicio
premiere el estreno **II, 5.2**
to premiere estrenar **II**
to prepare preparar **I**
present el regalo **I**
the present la actualidad
to present presentar **II, 2.2**
president el (la) presidente(a)
the press la prensa **2.1**
press release el anuncio de prensa
pressure la presión
peer pressure la presión de grupo **II**
presumptuous presumido(a) **4.1**
pretty bonito(a) **I**; hermoso(a) **II**
price el precio **I**
pride el orgullo
princess la princesa **II**
principal el (la) director(a) **I**
principle el principio **3.2**
to print imprimir **5.1**
priority la prioridad **2.1**
prize el premio **II**
problem el problema **I**
No problem. No hay problema.
product el producto
profession la profesión (*pl.* las profesiones) **II**
professor el (la) profesor(a) **II**
program el programa
educational program el programa educativo **2.2**
to program programar
programmer el (la) programador(a) **II, 4.1**
programming la programación
to progress progresar **3.2**
to prohibit that prohibir que **4.1**
project: social action project el proyecto de acción social **2.1**
to project proyectar
to promote promover (ue), promocionar
prop el accesorio **8.2**
prose la prosa **8.1**
to prosper prosperar **3.2**
protagonist el (la) protagonista **8.1**
to protect proteger (protejo) **II, 3.1**
proud orgulloso(a) **4.1**
to be proud (of) estar orgulloso(a) (de) **II**
to provide proveer
to provoke someone meterse con alguien
public público(a)
public relations las relaciones públicas **7.2**
public transportation el transporte público **1.1**
publicity la publicidad **2.1**
to publish publicar **II, 2.2**
publishing company la casa editorial
to pull tirar
punctual puntual **7.2**
purpose el propósito **4.2**
pursue: to pursue a career seguir una carrera **7.2**
to put poner (pongo) **I**
to put away guardar **5.1**
to put on (clothes) ponerse (la ropa) **I, II**
to put on makeup maquillarse **I**
to put up montar **1.1**
pyramid la pirámide **II**

qualified cualificado(a) **7.2**
quality la calidad **I**; la cualidad
quarter cuarto **I**
quarter past... ... y cuarto **I**
question la pregunta; la cuestión (*pl.* las cuestiones) **II, 2.2**
questionnaire el cuestionario
quiet callado(a) **6.2**
to quit... dejar de... **7.1**
quite bastante
quotation la cita **2.2**

race la carrera **I**
racket la raqueta **I**
radio el radio **I**
raft la balsa
railing la baranda
rain la lluvia
to rain llover (ue) **I**
to raise levantar **8.2**; criar
to raise the curtain levantar el telón **8.2**
to raise funds recaudar fondos **2.1**
ranch la estancia
rapidly rápidamente
rapids los rápidos
rare raro(a)
raw crudo(a) **II**
to reach alcanzar
to react reaccionar
to read leer **I**
reader el (la) lector(a)
reading la lectura
ready listo(a)
to get ready arreglarse **II**
to get ready to... disponerse (me dispongo) a...
real verdadero(a) **4.2**
realistic realista **4.2**
reality la realidad **8.1**
to realize darse cuenta de **5.1**
Really? ¿Verdad? **I**; ¿De veras? ¿De verdad?
reason la razón (*pl.* las razones)
for that reason por eso **II, 4.2**

reasonable razonable **4.1**
to receive recibir **I**
reception (desk) la recepción (*pl.* las recepciones) **II**, **5.2**
recess el recreo
recipe la receta **II**
to recommend recomendar (ie) **II**
to record registrar
to recycle reciclar **II**, **2.1**
recycling el reciclaje **II**
red rojo(a) **I**
red-haired pelirrojo(a) **I**
reef el arrecife
to refer referirse (ie, i)
to reflect reflexionar **7.1**; reflejar
reflection el reflejo
refrigerator el refrigerador **6.1**; la nevera
refuge: to take refuge (from) refugiarse (de) **1.2**
region la zona
regret el arrepentimiento
rehearsal el ensayo **8.2**
to rehearse ensayar **8.2**
to relate relatar **5.2**; relacionar **8.1**
relative el (la) pariente(a) **II**; **1.2**
to relax relajarse **5.2**
relaxation la relajación
relaxing relajante
to release soltar (ue)
religion la religión (*pl.* las religiones) **II**
to remain permanecer (permanezco)
to remain standing permanecer de pie
remarkable: to be remarkable for... destacarse por... **4.1**
to remember recordar (ue), acordarse (ue) de
to rent alquilar **I**
to repair arreglar **6.1**
repairperson el (la) técnico(a) **4.2**
to repeat repetir (i, i)
to replace reemplazar **3.1**
to reply responder
report el informe; el reportaje
reporter el (la) periodista **II**; el (la) reportero(a)
to represent representar **4.1**
to request solicitar **2.1**
requirement el requisito
to rescue rescatar

research la investigación (*pl.* las investigaciones) **3.1**
reservation la reservación (*pl.* las reservaciones)
to make/to have a reservation hacer/tener una reservación **II**
reserve la reserva
nature reserve la reserva natural
resolution la resolución (*pl.* las resoluciones) **5.2**
to respect respetar **3.2**
responsibility la responsabilidad **II**, **3.1**
responsible responsable **II**, **3.1**
to make oneself responsible for encargarse de **3.2**
to rest descansar **I**
restaurant el restaurante **I**
to restore restaurar
result el resultado
resume la hoja de vida
to retire jubilarse
to return volver (ue) **I**; regresar **II**
reunion la reunión (*pl.* las reuniones)
class reunion la reunión de ex alumnos
to reuse reutilizar **3.1**
review la reseña **2.2**, **8.1**; la crítica **II**; el repaso
book review la reseña literaria
to review repasar
to revise revisar
rhyme la rima **8.1**
rhythm el ritmo **8.1**
rice el arroz **I**
rich rico(a)
to ride montar **I**; subir a **I**
to ride a bike montar en bicicleta **I**
to ride a horse montar a caballo **I**, **II**
to ride the Ferris wheel/roller coaster subir a la vuelta al mundo/la montaña rusa **I**
right derecho(a)
Right. Agreed. De acuerdo.
Right? ¿Verdad? **I**
to be right tener razón **I**
to turn right doblar a la derecha **II**
ring el anillo **I**, **II**
ring: to ring the doorbell tocar el timbre **6.1**
risk el riesgo **3.1**

to risk arriesgarse **4.2**
risky arriesgado(a)
river el río **1.1**, **6.2**
roasted asado(a)
robot el robot (*pl.* los robots) **II**
rocky rocoso(a)
role el papel **II**
to play a role hacer un papel **II**
roller coaster la montaña rusa **I**
romantic romántico(a) **8.1**
room el cuarto **I**; la habitación (*pl.* las habitaciones) **II**; el espacio
root la raíz (*pl.* las raíces)
route la ruta **6.2**; el rumbo
routine la rutina **I**, **II**
to row remar **1.1**
rowboat el bote de remos
rubber la goma
rug la alfombra **I**
ruins las ruinas **II**
rule la regla
the golden rule la ley de oro
to run correr **I**
to run errands hacer los mandados **6.1**
RV la casa rodante **1.2**

sack el saco, la bolsa **5.1**
sacrifice el sacrificio **4.2**
sad triste **I**
safe seguro(a)
to sail navegar
sailboat el velero **1.2**
saint el (la) santo(a)
salad la ensalada **I**
salary el sueldo **7.1**
sale la venta
salesclerk el (la) vendedor(a) **I**
salt la sal **II**
saltshaker el salero
salty salado(a) **II**
same mismo(a)
Same here. Igualmente. **I**
to be all the same dar lo mismo
sand la arena **1.2**
sandal la sandalia **II**
sandwich el sándwich (*pl.* los sándwiches) **I**
satire la sátira **8.1**
satisfied satisfecho(a)

to satisfy satisfacer **3.2**
Saturday el sábado **I**
sausage el chorizo
to save (money, time) ahorrar **1.1**
savings los ahorros **5.1**
savings account la cuenta de ahorros **7.1**
to say decir (digo) **I**
saying el refrán (*pl.* los refranes)
scanner el escáner **5.1**
to scare
It scares me. Me da miedo. **II**
to get scared asustarse
How scary! ¡Qué miedo! **I**
scene la escena **II**
scenery la escenografía **8.2**
schedule el horario **I**
scholarship la beca
school la escuela **I**; la facultad **7.2**
high school el colegio, la escuela secundaria, el liceo
technical school la escuela técnica **7.2**
school (school-related) escolar **II**
school newspaper el periódico escolar
science las ciencias **I**
science fiction la ciencia ficción
scientist el (la) científico(a) **II, 4.1**
to scold regañar
score: to score a goal meter un gol **II**
screen la pantalla **I, II**
screenplay el guión (*pl.* los guiones) **II**
screenwriter el (la) guionista **II**
script el guión (*pl.* los guiones) **8.2**
scuba diver el (la) buceador(a) **II**
to scuba-dive bucear **I**
sculpture la escultura **II**
sea el mar **I**
seafood los mariscos
search la búsqueda **5.1**
seashell el caracol **1.2**
seasick: to get seasick marearse **1.2**
season la estación (*pl.* las estaciones) **I**; la temporada
seasoned sazonado(a)
seat el asiento
numbered seat el asiento numerado **6.2**
second segundo(a) **I**
secret el secreto **I**
secretary el (la) secretario(a) **4.2**
secure seguro(a)
security la seguridad
to go through security pasar por seguridad
to see ver
Let's see. A ver.
May I see...? ¿Me deja ver...? **I, II**
See you later. Hasta luego. **I**
See you there. Nos vemos allí.
See you tomorrow. Hasta mañana. **I**
to seem parecer (parezco)
It seems to me... Me parece que... **II**
to select seleccionar
self-esteem la autoestima
to sell vender **I**
to send mandar **I**; enviar **5.1**
sentence la oración (*pl.* las oraciones)
separate separado(a)
September septiembre **I**
serious serio(a) **I**
to serve servir (i, i) **I**
to serve as president servir de presidente(a) **7.1**
set: movie set el escenario
to set the table poner la mesa **I**
setting el ambiente
seven siete **I**
seven hundred setecientos **I**
seventeen diecisiete **I**
seventh séptimo(a) **I**
seventy setenta **I**
to sew coser
shadow la sombra
shame la vergüenza
It's a shame that... Es una lástima/una pena que...
What a shame! ¡Qué lástima! **I, II**
shampoo el champú **I, II**
shape la forma
to get in shape ponerse en forma **7.1**
to share compartir **I**
to shave oneself afeitarse **I, II**
shaving cream la crema de afeitar **II**
she ella **I**
shelf el estante
shell la cáscara; el caracol
to shine brillar
ship el barco
shirt la camisa **I**
shoe el zapato **I**
shoe store la zapatería **II**
shop: to go shopping ir de compras **I**
shopping center el centro comercial **I**
shore la orilla **1.2**
short
(height) bajo(a) **I**
(length) corto(a) **I**
shorts los pantalones cortos **I**
short-tempered enojono(a)
should deber **I**
shoulder el hombro **II**
shout el grito
show el espectáculo **5.2**
to show mostrar (ue)
shower la ducha **6.1**
to take a shower ducharse **I, II**
to shudder estremecerse
shy tímido(a) **II, 4.1**
shyness la timidez
sick enfermo(a) **I**
sickness la enfermedad
side el lado
sidewalk la acera **II**
to sigh suspirar
sights las atracciones
to go sightseeing ver las atracciones **II**
sign el letrero **2.1**; el cartel
silver la plata **I**
(made of) silver de plata **I, II**
simile el símil **8.1**
to simplify simplificar
since como; desde
sincere sincero(a) **II, 4.1**; verdadero(a) **4.2**; honesto(a) **7.2**
sincerity la sinceridad
to sing cantar **I**
singer el (la) cantante
single room la habitación individual **II**
sink
bathroom sink el lavabo **6.1**
kitchen sink el fregadero **6.1**
sister la hermana **I**
sister-in-law la cuñada **II, 1.2**
to sit sentarse (ie)
site el sitio
archaelogical site sitio arqueológico
Web site el sitio Web **I**

six seis **I**
six hundred seiscientos(as) **I**
sixteen dieciséis **I**
sixth sexto(a) **I**
sixty sesenta **I**
size el tamaño
clothing size la talla **II**
shoe size el número **II**
to skate patinar **I**
to in-line skate patinar en línea **I**
skateboard la patineta
to skateboard andar en patineta **I**
sketch el bosquejo
to ski esquiar
skin la piel **I**
skirt la falda **II**
skyscraper el rascacielos (*pl.* los rascacielos) **II**
sleep el sueño
to sleep dormir (ue, u) **I**
to be sleepy tener sueño **II**
sleeping bag el saco de dormir **1.1**
sleeve la manga
to slide deslizarse
slow lento(a) **II**
slowly lentamente
small pequeño(a) **I**
to smile sonreír (i, i)
smog el smog **II, 3.1**
snack
afternoon snack la merienda **II**
to have a snack merendar (ie) **1.2**
snake la serpiente **1.1**
snow la nieve
to snow nevar (ie) **I**
so entonces **I, II**; pues **6.2**; así que
so many tantos(as)
so much tanto(a)
so that para que **5.1**
soap el jabón (*pl.* los jabones) **I, II**
soap opera la telenovela
soccer el fútbol **I**
social worker el (la) trabajador(a) social **4.1**
society la sociedad **3.2**
honor society la sociedad honoraria **7.1**
sock el calcetín (*pl.* los calcetines) **I**
sofa el sofá **I**
soft drink el refresco **I**
software el software **II**
soil el suelo **3.1**; la tierra
soldier el (la) soldado, el (la) militar
to solve solucionar **3.2, 5.2**
some alguno(a) **I, 5.2**; algún **II**
Some day... Algún día... **II**
someone alguien **I, II**
something algo **I, II**
sometimes a veces **II**
son el hijo **I**
son-in-law el yerno **1.2**
soon pronto
as soon as en cuanto, tan pronto como **8.1**
sorry
I'm sorry. Lo siento. **I**
I'm sorry; Excuse me. Disculpe. **II**
to be sorry that... sentir que... **4.2**
So-so. And you? Más o menos. ¿Y tú/usted? (familiar/formal) **I**
sound el sonido **II**
soup la sopa **I**
soup kitchen el comedor de beneficencia **2.1**
sour agrio(a) **II**
source la fuente
south el sur
souvenir el recuerdo **I, II**
space el espacio
spaghetti los espaguetis **II**
Spanish el español **I**
Spanish-speaking de habla hispana
to speak hablar **I**
May I speak to...? ¿Puedo hablar con...? **I, II**
Spanish-speaking de habla hispana
special especial
special effects los efectos especiales **II**
specialization la especialidad **7.2**
specialty la especialidad **II**
specialty of the house la especialidad de la casa **II**
species la especie
endangered species las especies en peligro de extinción **II, 3.1**
speech el discurso
speed la prisa
to spell deletrear
to spend gastar **2.1**
spicy picante **II**
spider la araña **1.1**
spinach las espinacas **II**
spirit el espíritu; el ánimo
spite: in spite of a pesar de que **6.2**
splendor el esplendor
sponsor el (la) patrocinador(a) **2.2**
to sponsor patrocinar **2.2**
spoon la cuchara **II**
sporting deportivo(a)
sports los deportes **I**
extreme sports los deportes extremos
water sports los deportes acuáticos
sportsman/woman el (la) deportista **II**
spouse el (la) esposo(a) **1.2**
spring la primavera **I**
square la plaza **4.2**; el cuadro
squid el calamar
squirrel la ardilla
stadium el estadio **I**
stage el escenario **8.2**; la etapa
stage direction la dirección de escenografía **8.2**
stairs la escalera **I**
stamp el sello **6.1**
to stand (up) pararse **1.2**
to stand out (from others) for... destacarse por... **4.1**
stanza la estrofa **8.1**
star la estrella
movie star la estrella de cine **II**
start el comienzo **7.1**
state el estado
station la estación (*pl.* las estaciones)
(radio) station la emisora (de radio) **2.1**
subway station la estación de metro **6.1**
train station la estación de tren **II**
statue la estatua **II**
statuette la estatuilla
to stay quedarse **II**
to stay in shape mantenerse en forma **II**
to stay in... quedarse en... **I**
steak: grilled steak el filete a la parrilla **II**
to steer conducir (conduzco)
step el paso
stepfather el padrastro **I**
stepmother la madrastra **I**
stifling agobiante
still todavía **I**
stock market la bolsa
stockbroker el (la) agente de bolsa **II, 7.2**
stomach el estómago **I**
stomachache el dolor de estómago

Glosario inglés-español

stone la piedra
  (made of) stone de piedra **II**
to stop parar; detenerse (me detengo); dejar de
stoplight el semáforo **II**
store la tienda **I**
to store almacenar
storm la tormenta
story el cuento **8.1**, la historia
  crime story el cuento policíaco **8.1**
  short story el cuento **8.1**
  story board el bosquejo
stove la estufa **1.1**
  gas stove la estufa de gas **1.1**
straight: to go straight seguir derecho **II**
strange: It is strange that... Es raro que... **3.2**
strategy la estrategia **7.2**
strawberry la fresa **II**
street la calle **I**
  street vendor el (la) vendedor(a) ambulante **5.2**
  street performance la actuación callejera
to strengthen fortalecer (fortalezco)
stress el estrés **7.1**
stressed estresado(a) **7.1**
strike
  hunger strike el ayuno
  labor strike la huelga
stripe la raya
  striped de rayas **II**
strong fuerte **I**
to struggle luchar **3.2**
stubborn reacio(a)
stucco el estuco
student el (la) estudiante **I**; el (la) alumno(a)
  exchange student el (la) estudiante de intercambio
  student newspaper el periódico estudiantil
studious estudioso(a) **I**
study el estudio
to study estudiar **I**; cursar
to stuff rellenar
style el estilo **8.1**; la moda
  to be in style estar de moda **II**
subject (in school) la materia, la asignatura
subway el metro **6.1**
  to get on the subway subir el metro **6.1**
  to get off the subway bajar el metro **6.1**
success el logro **4.2**; el éxito
successful exitoso(a)
  to be successful tener éxito **II**
suddenly de repente
to suffer sufrir
suffering el sufrimiento **3.2**
sugar el azucar **II**
to suggest that sugerir (ie, i) que **4.1**
suggestion la sugerencia
  to make a suggestion dar una sugerencia **5.1**
suit el traje **II**
suitcase la maleta **II**
  to pack a suitcase hacer la maleta **II**
to summarize resumir
summary el resumen
  in summary en resumen
summer el verano **I**
sun el sol **I**
  It is sunny. Hace sol. **I**
to sunbathe tomar el sol **I**
Sunday el domingo **I**
sunglasses las gafas de sol **5.1**
sunrise el amanecer
sunscreen el bloqueador de sol **I**
sunset la puesta del sol
supermarket el supermercado **II**
suppertime la hora de cenar
support el apoyo
to support apoyar **2.1**; fomentar **3.1**
sure seguro(a)
  to not be sure that... no estar seguro(a) (de) que... **4.2**
surely seguramente
to surf hacer surfing **I**, practicar surf, surfear
  to surf the Web navegar por Internet **I**
surface la superficie
surfboard la tabla de surf **1.2**
surfer el (la) surfista **1.2**
to surpass superar **3.2**
surprise la sorpresa **I**
to surprise sorprender
  to be surprised that... sorprenderse de que... **4.2**
surprising sorprendente **4.2**; asombroso(a)
survey la encuesta
to suspect that sospechar que **5.1**
SUV la camioneta **1.1**
to swear jurar
  I swear to you! ¡Te lo juro! **II**
sweater el suéter **II**
to sweep barrer **I**
sweet dulce **II**
to swim nadar **I**
swimming la natación **I**
swimming pool la piscina **I**
swing el columpio
sword la espada
to symbolize simbolizar **8.1**
synagogue la sinagoga
syrup el jarabe

table la mesa **I**
  to set the table poner la mesa **I**
tail la cola
to take tomar **I**; llevar **II**
  to take a bath bañarse **I, II**
  to take a guided tour hacer una visita guiada **6.2**
  to take a nap dormir (ue, u) una siesta **5.2**
  to take a shower ducharse **I, II**
  to take a taxi tomar un taxi **II**
  to take a trip hacer un viaje **I, II**
  to take a walk dar una vuelta **6.1**
  to take advantage (of something) aprovechar **6.1**
  to take away quitar **6.1**
  to take care of cuidar
  to take charge of encargarse de **3.2**
  to take notes tomar apuntes **I**
  to take out the trash sacar la basura **I**
  to take part in tomar parte en **7.1**
  to take photos tomar fotos **I, II**
  to take place tener lugar
  to take refuge (from) refugiarse (de) **1.2**

talented talentoso(a)
to talk hablar **I**
to talk about comentar **5.2**
to talk on the phone hablar por teléfono **I**
tall alto(a) **I**
tape recorder el grabador **2.2**
tapestry el tapiz (*pl.* los tapices) **6.2**
task la tarea
to taste probar (ue) **II**
tasty rico(a) **I**; sabroso(a) **II**
tax el impuesto **7.1**
taxi el taxi
tea el té **II**
to teach enseñar **I**
teacher el (la) maestro(a) **I**; el (la) profesor(a) **II, 7.2**
team el equipo **I**
teammate el (la) compañero(a) de equipo **II**
technician el (la) técnico(a) **4.2**
telephone el teléfono **I**
cellular phone el teléfono celular **I, II**
telethon la teletón (*pl.* las teletones) **2.2**
television la televisión **I**
television set el televisor **I**
to tell contar (ue) **II**; relatar **5.2**
I'm telling you the truth! ¡Te digo la verdad! **II**
temple el templo **II**
ten diez **I**
tennis el tenis **I**
tent la tienda de campaña **1.1**
tenth décimo(a) **I**
terrace la terraza **6.1**
to terrify aterrorizar
test el examen (*pl.* los exámenes) **I**
to thank agradecer (agradezco)
I would like to thank... Quisiera darle las gracias a... **II**
Thank you. Gracias. **I**
Thank you for your service. Gracias por atenderme. **II**
that
that one (over there) aquél(aquélla) **II**
that one (there) ése(a) **II**
that... (over there) aquel(aquella) **I, II**
that... (there) ese(a) **I, II**
theater el teatro **I**
their su **I**
them ellos(as) **I, II**
theme el tema **8.1**
then luego; entonces **I, II**
theology la teología
there allí **I**
Is... there? ¿Está...? **II**
there is/are... hay... **I**
therefore por lo tanto **4.2**; por eso
these
these ones (here) éstos(as) **II**
these... (here) estos(as) **I, II**
they ellos(as) **I**
thief el ladrón (*pl.* ladrones)
thin delgado(a)
thing la cosa **I**
to think pensar (ie) **I**; creer
I think/don't think so. Creo que sí /no. **II**
What did you think of ...? ¿Qué les parece...?
third tercero(a) **I**
thirst la sed
to be thirsty tener sed **I**
thirteen trece **I**
thirty treinta **I**
thirty-one treinta y uno **I**
this
this one (here) éste(a) **II**
this... (here) este(a) **I, II**
those
those ones (over there) aquéllos(as) **II**
those ones (there) ésos(as) **II**
those... (over there) aquellos(as) **I, II**
those... (there) esos(as) **I, II**
thousand mil **I**
to threaten amenazar **3.1**
three tres **I**
three hundred trescientos(as) **I**
throat la garganta **II**
to throw (out) tirar, echar
thumb el dedo pulgar
Thursday el jueves **I**
thus así que
ticket la entrada **4.2**; el boleto **I, II**; el billete **6.1**
roundtrip ticket el boleto de ida y vuelta **II**
to buy a ticket sacar el billete **6.1**
tie la corbata **II**
tie: to be tied (in sports) estar empatado **II**
tight (clothing) apretado(a)
time la hora **I**; la vez (*pl.* las veces); el rato **5.2**; el tiempo
at the same time a la vez
At what time is/are...? ¿A qué hora es/son...? **I**
free time el tiempo libre **I, II**; el rato libre **7.1**
from time to time cada tanto
part-time a tiempo parcial **7.1**
to have a good time pasar un buen rato **5.2**
What time is it? ¿Qué hora es? **I**
tired cansado(a) **I**
to be tired or fed up estar harto(a)
title el título
to a **I**; menos **I**; hasta **II**
today hoy **I**
Today is . . . Hoy es... **I**
What day is today? ¿Qué día es hoy? **I**
toe el dedo del pie **II**
together junto(a)
all together todo junto
to get together reunirse
Toltecs los toltecas **II**
tomato el tomate **I**
tomb la tumba **II**
tomorrow mañana **I**
See you tomorrow. Hasta mañana. **I**
Tomorrow is ... Mañana es... **I**
too también **I**; demasiado **II**
too much demasiado **I, II**
tool la herramienta **II**
tooth el diente **II**
toothbrush el cepillo de dientes **I, II**
toothpaste la pasta de dientes **I, II**
tortoise la tortuga
to touch tocar
Tour de France la Vuelta a Francia **II**
tourism el turismo
tourist el (la) turista **II**
tourist office la oficina de turismo **II**
tournament el torneo
toward hacia
towel la toalla **I, II**
town el pueblo
trace el rastro
track
(in sports) la pista **II**
(for trains) la vía **6.2**
train el tren **I**
by train en tren **I**

to train entrenarse **II**
trainer el (la) entrenador(a) **4.1**
training el entrenamiento
to transform transformar **II**
transformation la transformación (*pl.* las transformaciones) **3.1**
to translate traducir (traduzco) **2.2**
translator el (la) traductor(a) **7.2**
transportation el transporte
public transportation el transporte público **1.1**
trash la basura **I**
trash can el basurero **II, 3.1**
to travel viajar **II**
travel agency la agencia de viajes **II**
travel agent el (la) agente de viajes **II**
treasurer el (la) tesorero(a) **7.1**
tree el árbol **II, 1.1**
trip el viaje
to go on a day trip hacer una excursión **II**
to take a trip hacer un viaje **I**
triumph el triunfo
to triumph triunfar
trophy el trofeo
trouble
get into trouble meterse en problemas **6.2**
to (not) be worth the trouble (no) valer la pena
truck la camioneta **1.1**; el camión (*pl.* los camiones)
true verdadero(a) **4.2**; cierto(a)
It is (not) true that... (No) Es cierto/verdad que... **II, 4.2**
trunk el tronco
truth la verdad
I'm telling you the truth! ¡Te digo la verdad! **II**
to try intentar
to try the specialties probar las especialidades **6.2**
to try to tratar de
T-shirt la camiseta **I**
Tuesday el martes **I**
turkey el pavo
to turn doblar **II**
to take turns turnarse
to turn into convertirse en **4.2**
to turn off the faucet cerrar el grifo **6.1**
to turn off the light apagar la luz **II**
to turn on the faucet abrir el grifo **6.1**
to turn on the light encender (ie) la luz **II**
to turn out well salir bien **7.1**
to turn right/left doblar a la derecha/a la izquierda **II**
turtle la tortuga
TV la tele
twelve doce **I**
twenty veinte **I**
twenty-one veintiuno **I**
twin el (la) gemelo(a)
two dos **I**
two hundred doscientos(as) **I**
type el tipo; la clase
typical típico(a)

Ugh! ¡Uy! **II**
ugly feo(a) **I**
umbrella el paraguas **5.1**
unbelievable increíble
uncle el tío **I**
under debajo (de) **I**; bajo **I**
to underline subrayar
underneath debajo (de) **I**
to understand entender (ie), comprender **I**
Did you understand? ¿Comprendiste?
to misunderstand each other entenderse mal **II**
to understand each other (well) entenderse (bien) **II**
understanding comprensivo(a) **4.1**
understanding la comprensión
to undertake emprender **3.2**
unforgettable inolvidable **1.1**
unhappiness la desdicha
uniform el uniforme **II**
to unify unificar
unique único(a) **II**; singular **8.2**
unit la unidad
unity la unidad **3.2**; unit
university la universidad **7.2**
unknown desconocido(a)
the unknown lo desconocido
unless a menos que **5.1**
unlikely: It's unlikely that... Es improbable que **4.2**
until hasta que **5.1**, hasta
unusual insólito(a) **8.2**
up hacia arriba
upside down al revés
us nosotros(as) **I, II**
to use usar **I**; utilizar **1.1**
useful útil
usher el (la) acomodador(a) **8.2**
usual de siempre
usually normalmente **II**

vacation las vacaciones **I**
(to be) on vacation (estar) de vacaciones **I, II**
to go on vacation ir de vacaciones **II**
vacuum cleaner la aspiradora **I**
to vacuum pasar la aspiradora **I**
vain vanidoso(a) **4.1**
valley el valle
valuable valioso(a) **5.1**
value el valor
to value valorar **3.1**
to vanish desvanecerse
vanity la vanidad
variety la variedad
various varios(as)
to vary variar
vase el florero
vegetables las verduras **I**
vegetable stand la verdulería **6.1**
vegetarian vegetariano(a)
velvet el terciopelo
vendor: street vendor el (la) vendedor(a) ambulante **5.2**
versatile versátil **7.2**
verse el verso **8.1**
very muy **I**
Very well. And you? Muy bien. ¿Y tú/usted? (familiar/formal) **I**
vest el chaleco **II**
veterinarian el (la) veterinario(a) **II, 4.2**
vice president el (la) vice-presidente(a) **7.1**
video game el videojuego **I**
view la vista **6.2**
viewer: TV viewer el (la) telespectador(a) **2.2**; el (la) televidente

vinegar el vinagre **II**
to visit visitar
to visit a museum visitar un museo **II**
vocabulary el vocabulario
vocation la vocación (*pl.* las vocaciones)
voice la voz (*pl.* las voces)
volcano el volcán (*pl.* los volcanes) **II**
volleyball el voleibol **I**
beach volleyball el voleibol playero **1.2**
volunteer el (la) voluntario(a) **II, 2.1**
to volunteer trabajar de voluntario **II, 2.1**
to vote votar **3.1**
vulture el zopilote

to wait (for) esperar **I, II**
waiting room la sala de espera **6.2**
to wake up despertarse (ie) **I, II**
to walk caminar **I**
to go for a walk pasear **I**, dar una vuelta **6.1**
wall la muralla **6.2**; el muro, la pared
wallet la cartera **5.1**
to want querer (ie) **I**; desear
war la guerra **II**
wardrobe el vestuario **8.2**
warm cálido(a)
to warn advertir (ie, i) **3.2**
warning la advertencia **3.2**
warrior el (la) guerrero(a) **II**
to wash lavar **I**
to wash one's face/hair lavarse la cara/el pelo **I**
to wash oneself lavarse **I, II**
watch el reloj **I, II**
to watch mirar **I**
to watch television mirar la televisión **I**
water el agua (fem.) **I**
fresh water el agua dulce **1.1**
waterfall la cascada
to water-ski hacer esquí acuático **I**
wave la ola
we nosotros(as) **I**
to wear llevar **I**; usar
weather el tiempo **I**; el clima
What is the weather like? ¿Qué tiempo hace? **I**
Web page la página web **1.2**
Web site el sitio web **I, 5.1**
wedding la boda
Wednesday el miércoles **I**
week la semana **I**
last week la semana pasada **I, II**
next week la semana que viene
weekend el fin de semana **I, II**
weekly semanal
to weigh pesar
welcome la bienvenida
welcome bienvenido(a)
You're welcome. De nada. **I, II**
well bien **I**; pues **6.2**
to do well irle bien (a alguien) **7.1**
to turn out well salir bien **7.1**
Very well. And you? Muy bien. ¿Y tú/usted? (familiar/formal) **I**
Well, ... Bueno, ...
well-known reconocido(a)
west el oeste
whale la ballena
what qué
What? ¿Qué? ¿Cuál? **I**; ¿Cómo?
What a shame! ¡Qué lástima! **I, II**
What are you like? ¿Cómo eres? **I**
What color is/are...? ¿De qué color es/son...?
What day is today? ¿Qué día es hoy? **I**
What do you like to do? ¿Qué te gusta hacer? **I**
What fun! ¡Qué divertido!, **I**
What is the date? ¿Cuál es la fecha? **I**
What is the weather like? ¿Qué tiempo hace? **I**
What luck! ¡Qué casualidad!
What time is it? ¿Qué hora es? **I**
What's happening? ¿Qué pasa? **I**
What's his/her/your (formal) name? ¿Cómo se llama? **I**
What's your (familiar) name? ¿Cómo te llamas? **I**
wheelchair la silla de ruedas
when cuando **I**
When? ¿Cuándo? **I**
where donde
Where? ¿Dónde? **I**
(To) Where? ¿Adónde? **I**
Can you please tell me where ... is? Por favor, ¿dónde queda...? **II**
Where are you from? ¿De dónde eres/es usted (familiar/formal)? **I**
Where are you going? ¿Adónde vas? **I**
Where is he/she from? ¿De dónde es? **I**
Which? ¿Cuál(es)? **I**
a while un rato
once in a while de vez en cuando **I**
to whisper susurrar
white blanco(a) **I**
Who? ¿Quién(es)? **I**
Who is he/she/it? ¿Quién es? **I**
Why? ¿Por qué? **I**
That's why. Por eso. **II**
wide ancho(a)
wife la esposa **II, 1.2**
to win ganar **I**
wind el viento
It is windy. Hace viento. **I**
window la ventana **I**
display window el escaparate **6.1**
stained-glass window el vitral
ticket window la ventanilla **I**; la taquilla **6.2**
train window la ventanilla **6.2**
to windsurf hacer surf de vela **I**
wing el ala (fem.)
winged alado(a)
winner el (la) ganador(a) **I**
winning ganador(a)
winter el invierno **I**
to wish desear
with con **I**
with me conmigo **I, II**
With pleasure. Con mucho gusto. **II**
with you (familiar) contigo **I, II**
without sin **1.1**; sin que **5.1**
to withstand soportar
witness el (la) testigo
woman la mujer **I**
wonderful genial
wood la madera **I**
(made of) wood de madera **I, II**
woods el bosque **1.1**
wool la lana

work el trabajo; la obra **8.1**
to work trabajar **I**
charitable work la obra caritativa **2.2**
Let's get to work! ¡Manos a la obra!
to work as a cashier trabajar de cajero(a) **7.1**
to work as a lifeguard trabajar de salvavidas **7.1**
to work part-time trabajar a tiempo parcial **7.1**
worker el (la) trabajador(a)
social worker el (la) trabajador(a) social **4.1**
workshop el taller
world el mundo **II**
World Cup la Copa Mundial **II**
worried preocupado(a)
to worry preocuparse
worse peor **I, II**
worth: to be worth valer (valgo)
worthless sin valor **5.1**
wound la herida
to wound herir (ie, i)
to wrap envolver (ue) **I**
wrapping paper el papel de regalo **I**
wrist la muñeca **II**
wristwatch el reloj **II**
to write escribir **I**
writer el (la) escritor(a) **II**
writing la escritura

year el año **I**
last year el año pasado **I**
New Year el Año Nuevo
to be... years old tener... años **I**
yearbook el anuario **7.1**
yellow amarillo(a) **I**
yes sí **I**
Yes, I would love to. Sí, me encantaría. **I, II**
yesterday ayer **I**
the day before yesterday anteayer **I, II**
yet todavía **I**
yogurt el yogur **I**
you
(*pl.*, **familiar)** vosotros(as) **I, II**
(*pl.*, **formal)** ustedes **I, II**
(*sing.*, **familiar)** tú **I**; ti **II**
(*sing.*, **formal)** usted **I, II**
young joven (*pl.* jóvenes) **I**
young man/woman el (la) joven (*pl.* los jóvenes) **II**
younger menor **I, II**
your
(formal) su **I**
(*pl.*, **familiar)** vuestro(a) **I**
(*sing.*, **familiar)** tu **I**
youth hostel el albergue juvenil **1.1**

zero cero **I**
zone la zona
zoo el zoológico **I**

Índice

A

B

ÍNDICE

C

D

E

O

P

ÍNDICE

Q

R

S

V

Y

Z

Créditos

Acknowledgements

Unidad 1

"Hermandad" and "Viento, agua, piedra" by Octavio Paz. © Octavio Paz, 1959. Reprinted by permission.

From *Como agua para chocolate* by Laura Esquivel. Copyright © 1989 by Laura Esquivel. Used by permission of Doubleday, a division of Random House, Inc.

Unidad 2

From *En la Ocho y la Doce* by Roberto G. Fernández. Copyright © 2001 by Roberto G. Fernández. Reprinted by permission of Houghton Mifflin Harcourt Publishing Company. All rights reserved.

From *Caramelo* by Sandra Cisneros. Copyright © by 2002 Sandra Cisneros. Translation copyright © 2002 by Lilana Valenzuela. Published by Vintage Español and originally in hardcover by Alfred A. Knopf, Inc., divisions of Random House. Reprinted by permission of Susan Bergholz Literary Services, New York. All rights reserved.

Unidad 3

"La Mejor Edad" by Carlos Balaguer. © Carlos Balaguer. Reprinted by permission of the author.

Unidad 4

From *El sueño de América* by Esmeralda Santiago. Copyright © 1996 por Esmeralda Santiago. Reprinted by permission of HarperCollins Publishers.

From *Cuando Tía Lola vino de visita a quedarse* by Julia Álvarez. Copyright © 2001 by Julia Álvarez. Translation copyright © 2004 by Liliana Valenzuela. Published by Dell Yearling, an imprint of Random House Books for Children. Reprinted by permission of Susan Bergholz Literary Services, New York and Stuart Bernstein Representation for Artists, New York. All rights reserved.

Unidad 5

Excerpts from "La ciudad de los mapas," from *Desencuentros* by Edmundo Paz Soldán. © 2004, Edmundo Paz Soldán. Reprinted by permission of Santillana USA Publishing Company, Inc.

Unidad 6

Excerpt from *Manolito Gafotas* by Elvira Lindo. © 1994, Elvira Lindo. 1994, Santillana, S. A. Reprinted by permission of RDC Agencia Literaria, Madrid, Spain.

Romance sonámbulo by Federico García Lorca © Herederos de Federico García Lorca. From *Obras Completas* (Galaxia Gutenberg, 1996 edition). All rights reserved. For information regarding rights and permissions, please contact lorca@artslaw.co.uk or William Peter Kosmas, Esq., 8 Franklin Square, London W14 9UU.

Unidad 7

Gabriel García Márquez, "La luz es como el agua" from the work *Doce Cuentos Peregrinos* by Gabriel García Márquez. © Gabriel García Márquez, 1981. Reprinted by permission of Agencia Literaria Carmen Balcells, S.A.

Excerpt from "El esqueleto de visita" by Evelio Rosero Diago. © Evelio Rosero Diago. Reprinted by permission of the author.

Unidad 8

Excerpt from *El cartero de Neruda (Ardiente paciencia)* by Antonio Skármeta. © 1986, Antonio Skármeta. Reprinted by permission of Plaza & Janés Editores, S. A.

Excerpt from *Colón agarra viaje a toda costa* by Adela Basch. © 1992, Adela Basch. Reprinted by permission of Santillana Argentina, S. A.

Photography

Cover *center* David Noton Photography; *bottom right* Scott Markewitz/Taxi/Getty Images; **Title Page** David Noton Photography; **Back Cover** top left Steve Dunwell/The Image Bank/Getty Images; *top center* Joseph Rodriguez/Gallery Stock Limited; *top right* Panoramic Images/Getty Images; *bottom left* Doug Armand/Getty Images; *bottom center* David Noton Photography; *bottom right* P. Pet/zefa/Corbis; **iv** *top right* Allan Penn/Holt McDougal/Houghton Mifflin Harcourt; *bottom left* David H. Wells/Odyssey Productions, Inc.; *bottom right* Albert Gea/Reuters/Landov; **v** *bottom* Stewart Cohen/Getty Images; **vi** *bottom right* Pete Olsen/Holt McDougal/Houghton Mifflin Harcourt; **vii** *top left* Pixel Images, Inc./Holt McDougal/Houghton Mifflin Harcourt; *top right* Greg Johnson/Danita Delimont; **viii** *bottom right* Pete Olsen/Holt McDougal/Houghton Mifflin Harcourt; **ix** *top left* Jeff Greenberg/Alamy; *top right* Ken Karp/Holt McDougal/Houghton Mifflin Harcourt; **x** *bottom right* Pete Olsen/Holt McDougal/Houghton Mifflin Harcourt; **xi** *top left* Sonda Dawes/The Image Works, Inc.; *top right* Basco/gtphoto; **xii** *bottom right* Pete Olsen/Holt McDougal/Houghton Mifflin Harcourt; **xiii** *top left* Clive Brunskill/Getty Images; *top right* Paulo Cunha/Agencia EFE; **xiv** *bottom right* Pete Olsen/Holt McDougal/Houghton Mifflin Harcourt; **xv** *top left* Patricio Realpe, Stringer/AP Images; *top right* Robert Frerck/Odyssey Productions, Inc.; **xvi** *bottom right* Pete Olsen/Holt McDougal/Houghton Mifflin Harcourt; **xvii** *top left* Tips Images; *top right* Robert Frerck/Odyssey Productions, Inc.; **xviii** *bottom right* Pete Olsen/Holt McDougal/Houghton Mifflin Harcourt; **xix** *top left* Timothy Ross/The Image Works, Inc.; *top right* Leon Duquel/Duque Munera Tia; **xx** *bottom right* Pete Olsen/Holt McDougal/Houghton Mifflin Harcourt; **xxi** *top left* Cy Hire/Tom Stack & Asscociates; *top right* Allan Penn/Holt McDougal/Houghton Mifflin Harcourt; **xxviii** *both* Pete Olsen/Holt McDougal/Houghton Mifflin Harcourt; **xxix** *all* Pete Olsen/Holt McDougal/Houghton Mifflin Harcourt; **xxx** Jorge Albán/Holt McDougal/Houghton Mifflin Harcourt; **xxxi** *all* Allan Penn/Holt McDougal/Houghton Mifflin Harcourt; **xxxii** Time Life Pictures/Getty Images; **xxxiii** *top right* Jay Penni/Holt McDougal/Houghton Mifflin Harcourt; *bottom left* Jorge Albán/Holt McDougal/Houghton Mifflin Harcourt; **xxxiv** Allan Penn/Holt McDougal/Houghton Mifflin Harcourt; **xxxv** *both* Michael Goss/Holt McDougal/Houghton Mifflin Harcourt; **xxxvi** *top left* H. Sitton/Zefa/Corbis; *top right* Fadigati, Foodstock - StockFood Munich/StockFood America; *bottom* Steve Vidler/SuperStock; **xxxvii** *top left* Max Montecinos/Reuters Pictures; *top right* Martha Granger/EDGE Productions/Holt McDougal/Houghton Mifflin Harcourt; *center right* Gary Cook/Alamy; *bottom right* Danny Lehman/Corbis; **C2** *banner* Colored engraving, 1599. The Granger Collection, New York; *left* Michael & Patricia Fogden/Minden Pictures; *bottom right* Engraving, 19th century. The Granger Collection, New York; **C3** *top left* Steve Kaufman/Peter Arnold, Inc.; *top right* Mayan corn god, Oaxaca. Earthenware, circa 500 CE. Private collection. Photograph © Bridgeman Art Library; *bottom* Muisca tunjo votive , depicting the Ceremony of El Dorado. Copper and gold alloy, pre-Colombian. Galeria Cano, Bogotá, Colombia. Photograph © Bridgeman Art Library; **C4** *banner* Texas Department of Transportation; *center left* John E. Kelly/FoodPix; *top left* Lois Ellen Frank/Corbis; *bottom center* Leigh Beisch/Foodpix/Jupiter Images; *center right* Judd Pilossof/FoodPix; **C5** *top* Anders Ryman/Corbis; *top inset* Finley - StockFood Munich/StockFood America; *center right* Thomas Eckerle/NewsCom/PictureArts; *center left* Linny Morris Cunningham/NewsCom/Picture Arts; **C6** *banner* Allan Penn/Holt McDougal/Houghton Mifflin Harcourt; *bottom right* Zaheeruddin Abdullah/AP Images; *left* Victor Fraile/Reuters/Landov; **C7** *top left* Albert Gea/Reuters/Landov; *top right* Desmond Boylan/Reuters/Corbis; *top right inset* PhotoSpin; *bottom right* Victor Fraile/Reuters/Landov; **C8** *banner* Kelly-Mooney Photography/Corbis; *banner, inset* Joseph McCullar/ShutterStock; *center left* Alan Copson City Pictures/Alamy; *bottom* AFP/Getty Images; **C9** *top left* Zuma Press/NewsCom; *center right* AFP/Getty Images; *bottom left* Roberto Candía/AP Images; **C10** *banner* SuperStock/age fotostock; *top left* Reuters/Corbis; *bottom* Doug Bryant/DDBStock; **C11** *top* Reuters/Corbis; *center* Enrique Marcarian/Reuters/Corbis; **C12** *banner* Ric Ergenbright/Corbis; *left* Jay Penni/Holt McDougal/Houghton Mifflin Harcourt; *bottom* David H. Wells/Odyssey Productions, Inc.; **C13** *top right* Eduardo Abad/Agencia EFE; *top left* David Sanger Photography/Alamy; *bottom left* Danny Lehman/Corbis; **C14** *banner, center left* Allan Penn/Holt McDougal/Houghton Mifflin Harcourt; *bottom right* Robert Frerck/Odyssey Productions, Inc.; **C15** *top left* Reuters/Corbis; *center right, bottom left* Allan Penn/Holt McDougal/Houghton Mifflin Harcourt; *bottom right* Robert Frerck/Odyssey Productions, Inc.; **C16** *banner* Digital Stock; *top left* H. Sitton/Zefa/Corbis; *bottom* Galen Rowell/Odyssey Productions, Inc.; **C17** *top* Nevada Wier/Corbis; *center right* Hubert Stadler/Corbis; *center left* Richard Cummins/Corbis; **C18** *banner* PhotoDisc; *banner inset* Allan Penn/Holt McDougal/Houghton Mifflin Harcourt; *center left* Ryan Soderlin/Salina Journal/AP Images; *bottom right* Jacqueline Larma/AP Images; **C19** *left* Virtual Media Production; *top right* Russell Gordon/Odyssey Productions, Inc.; *bottom right* Helen Montoya/Zuma Press; **C20** *banner* AFP/Getty Images; *banner, inset* Rob Crandall/Stock Connection/IPN; *center left* Oscar Navarrete/Agencia EFE; *bottom right* David Dudenhoefer/Odyssey Productions, Inc.; **C21** *top right* AFP/Getty Images; *left* Michele Burgess/Index Stock Imagery; *bottom right* Charles & Josette Lenars/Corbis; **C22** *banner* Danny Lehman/Corbis; *top left* Anders Ryman/Corbis; *bottom* Marco Cristofori/age fotostock; **C23** *top left* Time Life Pictures/Getty Images; *top right* Robert Frerck/Odyssey Productions, Inc.; *bottom left* Gary Cook/Alamy; **C24** *banner* Marcelo Del Pozo/Reuters/Landov; *left* Miguel Rajmil/Agencia EFE; *bottom right* Emilio Morenatti/Agencia EFE; *bottom* *right inset* Image Club Graphics; **C25** *top left* Chico Sánchez/Agencia EFE; *top right* Image Club Graphics; *center right* © Ana Martinez/Reuters/Corbis; *center inset, bottom right* Image Club Graphics; *bottom left* Jeffrey Arguedas/Agencia EFE; **0** *bottom right* Digital Vision/Getty Images; *bottom left* Arthur Tilley/Taxi/Getty Images; **1–2** Stuart Cohen/Getty Images; **2** *both* Allan Penn/Holt McDougal/Houghton Mifflin Harcourt; **3** *all* Allan Penn/Holt McDougal/Houghton Mifflin Harcourt; **4** *modelo* Yellow Dog Productions/Getty Images; *1* DK Stock/Getty Images; *2* PhotoValley/Alamy; *3* Peter Titmuss/Alamy; *4* Soundsnaps/ShutterStock; *5* Myrleen Ferguson Cate/PhotoEdit; *6* Royalty-Free/Corbis; **6** *top left* Mitchell Zachs/AP Images; *top right* Stockbyte; *bottom left* PhotoDisc; *bottom right* Susan Walsh/AP Images; **7** *top left* Victor Straffon/NewsCom/Mexsport; *top right* Royalty-Free/Corbis; *bottom right* Ciro Cesar/NewsCom/La Opinion; *bottom left* PhotoDisc; **12** *top right, background* Allan Penn/Holt McDougal/Houghton Mifflin Harcourt; *center right* HIRB/Index Stock Imagery; *center left, bottom left, bottom right* Jorge Albán/Holt McDougal/Houghton Mifflin Harcourt; **13** *both* Allan Penn/Holt McDougal/Houghton Mifflin Harcourt; **15** "Dalí Paints Gala in Front of a Mirror" (1972-1973), Salvador Dalí. Museo Dalí, Figueras, Spain. © 2007 Salvador Dalí, Gala-Salvador Dalí Foundation/Artists Rights Society (ARS), New York/Erich Lessing/Art Resource, NY; **16** *top left* Erik Lam/ShutterStock; *all others* Allan Penn/Holt McDougal/Houghton Mifflin Harcourt; **17** *all* Allan Penn/Holt McDougal/Houghton Mifflin Harcourt; **20** *top* Burke/Triolo Productions/Getty Images; *center* Wayne Johnson/ShutterStock; *bottom* Robert Fried/Alamy; *background* Jay Penni/Holt McDougal/Houghton Mifflin Harcourt; **21** *top* Vidura Luis Barrios/Alamy; *center* Krzysztof Dydynski/Lonely Planet Images; *bottom* Paul Cowan/ShutterStock; **24** *modelo left* PhotoObjects/Jupiterimages Corporation; *modelo right* ShutterStock; *1 left* PhotoDisc; *1 right* Royalty-Free/Corbis; *2 left* Jay Penni/Holt McDougal/Houghton Mifflin Harcourt; *2 right* Jorge Albán/Holt McDougal/Houghton Mifflin Harcourt; *3 left* SuperStock; *3 right* Comstock; *4 left* Comstock/SuperStock; *4 right* Image 100/Alamy; *5 left, 5 right* Comstock; *6 left* Rubberball; *6 right* PhotoDisc; *7 left* Jorge Albán/Holt McDougal/Houghton Mifflin Harcourt; *7 right* PhotoDisc; *8 left* Ingvald Kaldhussater/ShutterStock; *8 right* PhotoObjects/Jupiterimages Corporation; **26** *top left* Tracy Frankel/The Image Bank/Getty Images; *top right* José Luis Pelaez, Inc./Corbis; *bottom left* Thinkstock/Alamy; *bottom right* Image100/SuperStock; **28** *Javier* Jay Penni/Holt McDougal/Houghton Mifflin Harcourt; *Sandra* Pixel Images, Inc./Holt McDougal/Houghton Mifflin Harcourt; *bottom right* Angelo Caggiano Photography, Inc./StockFood America; **29** *top left* Martin Parr/Magnum Photos; *center right* Ron Brazil/NewsCom/Zuma Press; *bottom* Panoramic Images/Getty Images; **30–31** Pixel Images, Inc./Holt McDougal/Houghton Mifflin Harcourt; **32** *top* David Young-Wolff/PhotoEdit; *center right* Paul A. Souders/Corbis; *center, center left* David Young-Wolff/PhotoEdit; *bottom left, bottom right* Rubberball Productions/ImageState; *canteen* Brand X Pictures; **33** *parrot* PhotoDisc/Getty Images; *kayak* Carlos S. Pereyra/age fotostock; *rafting* Royalty-Free/Corbis; *fishing* Len Holsborg/Photonica/Getty Images; *left* Lee Foster/Lonely Planet Images; *middle row, top inset* PhotoSpin; *beach* Kent Knudson/Index Stock Imagery; *bus* Jeff Greenberg/PhotoEdit; **35** *car* SuperStock; *all others* Jay Penni/Holt McDougal/Houghton Mifflin Harcourt; **38** "Volcan Iztaccihuatl", Dr. Atl (Gerardo Murillo). Oil on Canvas. Private Collection. Bridgeman Art Library; **39** *modelo* Creatas/age fotostock; *1* Titus Lacoste/Getty Images; *2* Ryan McVay/Getty Images; *3* BananaStock/age fotostock; *4* ThinkStock/age fotostock; *5* Yellow Dog Productions/Getty Images; *6* Rubberball/Alamy; 7 Michael Newman/PhotoEdit; *8* Stuart Cohen/The Image Works, Inc.; *9* Lori Adamski Peek/Getty Images; **40** Jay Penni/Holt McDougal/Houghton Mifflin Harcourt; **44** Jonathan Blair/Corbis; **45** Jay Penni/Holt McDougal/Houghton Mifflin Harcourt; **48** Steve Northup/Time Life Pictures/Getty Images; **49** "Big Dipper. No. 1" (1997), El Hortelano. Oil on canvas, 75 cm. x 75 cm. VEGAP/Art Resource, NY; **50** "Tornado" (1941), Mario Carreno. Oil on canvas, 31" x 41". Digital Image © The Museum of Modern Art/Licensed by SCALA/Art Resource, NY; **52** *top right* Paul B. Southerland/The Daily Oklahoman/AP Images; *map insets* Corbis; **53** *3* Stockdisc/Alamy; **56–57** Greg Johnson/Danita Delimont; **58** Martin Barraud/Getty Images; **59** *canoeing* Frank Pedrick/The Image Works, Inc.; *volleyball* Kayte M. Deioma/PhotoEdit; *surfer* Rick Doyle/Corbis; *top* Neil Rabinowitz/Corbis; *bottom* SuperStock; **60** *right* J. Silver/SuperStock; *left* Richard Hamilton Smith/Royalty-Free/Corbis; *bottom left* Royalty-Free/Corbis; *center, bottom* Chris Mellor/Lonely Planet Images; *center, top* Rudi Von Briel/PhotoEdit; *background* George Hunter/SuperStock; **61** *bottom left* Pixel Images, Inc./Holt McDougal/Houghton Mifflin Harcourt; **64** Peter Guttman/Corbis; **65** *modelo* Mike Surowiak/Getty Images; *1* Jeff Greenberg/The Image Works, Inc.; *2* David Sanger Photography/Alamy; *3* BananaStock/PictureQuest; *4* Javier Pierini/Getty Images; *5* Cro Magnon/Alamy; *6* age fotostock/SuperStock; *7* AbleStock/Index Stock Imagery; *8* Stockdisc/PunchStock; *9* David R. Frazier Photolibrary, Inc./Alamy; **70** Scala/Art Resource, NY; **73** *inset* Christoph Wilhelm/Getty Images; **74** James Leynse/Royalty-Free/Corbis; **75** Arau/CineVista/AviaCSA/The Kobal Collection; **76** Mirimax/Photofest; **77** Celio Pedrosa/Holt McDougal/Houghton Mifflin Harcourt; **82–83** Steve Bly/Alamy; **83** *bottom* Robert Fried/Alamy; **84** *background* Allan Penn/Holt McDougal/Houghton Mifflin Harcourt; *all others* Pete Olsen/Holt McDougal/Houghton Mifflin Harcourt; **85** *background* Allan Penn/Holt McDougal/Houghton Mifflin Harcourt; *top left* Pete Olsen/Holt McDougal/Houghton Mifflin Harcourt; **88** *bottom right* Renee Comet Photography, Inc./StockFood America; *Roberto* Ken Karp/Holt McDougal/Houghton Mifflin Harcourt; *Irma* Allan Penn; **89** *right* Macduff Everton; *top left* Mary Altaffer/AP Images; *bottom* Tim Boyle/Getty Images; **90–91** Jeff Greenberg/Alamy; **92** *right* M. Thomsen/Zefa/Corbis; *left* age fotostock/SuperStock; *bottom* Steve Skjold/Alamy; **93** *left* Jay Penni/Holt McDougal/Houghton Mifflin Harcourt; *right* Allan Penn/Holt McDougal/

Houghton Mifflin Harcourt; **95** Allan Penn/Holt McDougal/Houghton Mifflin Harcourt; **98** Courtesy of El Museo del Barrio; **104** "The Market" (c. 1940s), Pablo O'Higgins. Color lithograph, 12 x 13 in. Collection of the Art Museum of the Americas, Organization of American States; **105** Allan Penn/Holt McDougal/Houghton Mifflin Harcourt; **106** *all* Allan Penn/Holt McDougal/Houghton Mifflin Harcourt; **107** SW Productions/PhotoDisc Green/Getty Images; **112** *right* Najilah Feanny/Corbis; *left* Joe Reidle/Getty Images; **116–117** Ken Karp/Holt McDougal/Houghton Mifflin Harcourt; **118** *left* Ken Karp/Holt McDougal/Houghton Mifflin Harcourt; *right* Jay Penni/Holt McDougal/Houghton Mifflin Harcourt; **119** *top* Ed Bock/Corbis; *bottom* J.F. Rault/Corbis Sygma; **121** Ken Karp/Holt McDougal/Houghton Mifflin Harcourt; **124** *bottom* Kevin Winter/TimePix/Getty Images News and Sport; *top center* Holt McDougal/Houghton Mifflin Harcourt; **126** *top* David Young-Wolff/PhotoEdit; *bottom* Myrleen Ferguson Cate/PhotoEdit; *center* Don Smetzer/PhotoEdit; **130** Jill LeVasseur/Holt McDougal/Houghton Mifflin Harcourt; **131** Ken Karp/Holt McDougal/Houghton Mifflin Harcourt; **134** Eric Gay/AP Images; **142** *bottom right* Jeff Greenberg/age fotostock; **143** *bottom* Jeff Greenberg/age fotostock; **144** *background* Allan Penn/Holt McDougal/Houghton Mifflin Harcourt; *all others* Pete Olsen/Holt McDougal/Houghton Mifflin Harcourt; **145–146** *background* Allan Penn/Holt McDougal/Houghton Mifflin Harcourt; **145** *top left* Pete Olsen/Holt McDougal/Houghton Mifflin Harcourt; **147** Nick Ut/AP Images; **148** *bottom right* Lew Robertson/FoodPix; *bottom left* Jay Penni/Holt McDougal/Houghton Mifflin Harcourt; **149** *bottom* Alfredo Maíquez/Lonely Planet Images; *top left* Robert Frerck/Odyssey Productions, Inc.; *center right* Daniel LeClair/Reuters/Landov; *center inset* Funerary urn with feline lid, Ixil, Quiché, Guatemala. Early postclassic period (900-1200). Polychrome earthenware. Museo Popol Vuh, Guatemala. Photograph by Bridgeman Art Library; **150–151** Michael J. Doolittle/Peter Arnold, Inc.; **152** *background* Guy Jarvis/School Division/Houghton Mifflin Harcourt; *top* BananaStock/SuperStock; *center* Blackout Concepts/Alamy; *bottom right* Chris Gotshall/Sea World Orlando/AP Images; *bottom center* PhotoDisc; *bottom left* Joseph Sohm/Visions of America/Corbis; **153** *background* PhotoDisc; *top left* Dennis MacDonald/age fotostock; *top right* Mireille Vaultier/Alamy; *bottom left* Peter Arnold Inc./Alamy; *bottom right* Walter Astrada/La Nación/AP Images; **155** *top left* Sonda Dawes/The Image Works, Inc.; *bottom right* Frans Lemmens/Getty Images; *bottom left* Jay Penni/Holt McDougal/Houghton Mifflin Harcourt; **156** INSADCO Photography/Alamy; **158** *top* Jay Penni/Holt McDougal/Houghton Mifflin Harcourt; *modelo* Flip Chalfant/Getty Images; *1* Ellis Neel/AP Images; *2* Geri Engberg/The Image Works, Inc.; *3* age fotostock/SuperStock; *4* Jeff Greenberg/age fotostock; *5* Jeff Greenberg/PhotoEdit; *6* Patricio Crooker/fotosbolivia/The Image Works, Inc.; **160** *bottom left* Jay Penni/Holt McDougal/Houghton Mifflin Harcourt; **164** © Luiz Claudio Marigo/naturepl.com; **165** *top center* Jay Penni/Holt McDougal/Houghton Mifflin Harcourt; *inset* Miguel Ángel Molina/Agencia EFE; **167** PhotoDisc/GettyImages; **168** Courtesy of Carlos Balaguer; **169** "Feria" (2006), Graciela Genoves. Oil on canvas. © Zurbaran Galeria/SuperStock; **170** "Valencian Sketch no. 1" Joaquín Sorrolla y Bastida. Museo Sorolla, Madrid, Spain. Scala/Art Resource, New York; **171** Jenny Tylden-Wright/Getty Images; **172** *top left* Michael & Patricia Fogden/Corbis; *top right* Werner Forman/Art Resource, New York; *center right* Guy Jarvis/School Division/Houghton Mifflin Harcourt; *bottom left* Brand X Pictures/Alamy; **174** *1* Ronnie Kaufman/Corbis; *2* Jeff Greenberg/The Image Works, Inc.; *3* David Seri/age fotostock; *4* Joe Sohm/Alamy; *5* Dave G. Houser/Post-Houserstock/Corbis; *6* Amy Wrynn/Holt McDougal/Houghton Mifflin Harcourt; **176–177** Basco/gtphoto; **178–179** *all* Jay Penni/Holt McDougal/Houghton Mifflin Harcourt; **181** *bottom left* Jay Penni/Holt McDougal/Houghton Mifflin Harcourt; **182** Jay Penni/Holt McDougal/Houghton Mifflin Harcourt; **184** Danny Lehman/Corbis; **185** *modelo* Guy Jarvis/School Division/Houghton Mifflin Harcourt; *1* age fotostock/SuperStock; *2* David Young-Wolff/Alamy; *3* Bill Frisch/Brand X Pictures/age fotostock; *4* Kuzma/ShutterStock; *5* Dennis MacDonald/age fotostock; *6* Bob Daemmrich/The Image Works, Inc.; **186** *left* Marcio José Sánchez/AP Images; *bottom right* Jay Penni/Holt McDougal/Houghton Mifflin Harcourt; **189** Blend Images/Alamy; **190** "View of San Antonio de Oriente" (1957), José Antonio Velásquez; Honduran (b.1906, d.1983) oil on canvas, 26 x 37". Collection of the Art Museum of the Americas, Organization of American States; **191** Jay Penni/Holt McDougal/Houghton Mifflin Harcourt; **193** Michael Newman/PhotoEdit; **194** age fotostock/SuperStock; **195** *both* Justin Kerr; **196** Justin Kerr; **197** Justin Kerr; **201** *right* PhotoObjects/Jupiterimages Corporation; *left* Royalty-Free/Corbis; **202–203** Keith Pritchard/Boating Images Photo Library/Alamy; **203** *bottom right* Brandon Cole /Marine Library/Alamy; **204** *background* Allan Penn/Holt McDougal/Houghton Mifflin Harcourt; *all others* Pete Olsen/Holt McDougal/Houghton Mifflin Harcourt; **205** *background* Allan Penn/Holt McDougal/Houghton Mifflin Harcourt; *top left* Pete Olsen/Holt McDougal/Houghton Mifflin Harcourt; **207** Organics Image Library/Alamy; **208** *Enrique* Allan Penn/Holt McDougal/Houghton Mifflin Harcourt; *Inez* Jay Penni/Holt McDougal/Houghton Mifflin Harcourt; *bottom right* Foodcollection/StockFood America; **209** *top left* Nicholas Pitt/Alamy; *right* Copyright © 2008 by David Dudenhoefer and Odyssey Productions, Inc.; *bottom left* David Dudenhoefer/Odyssey Productions, Inc.; *bottom left inset* Phil Schermeister/Corbis; **210–211** Clive Brunskill/Getty Images; **212** *top* Jay Penni/Holt McDougal/Houghton Mifflin Harcourt; **213** *top left* Topham/The Image Works, Inc.; *top center* Bob Daemmrich/The Image Works, Inc.; *bottom left* Digital Vision Inc./SuperStock; *bottom center* PhotoDisc; *bottom right* Michael Rosenfeld/Getty Images; *top right* Arnie Rosner/Index Stock Imagery; **214** Ralph Notaro/Getty Images; **215** *bottom left* PhotoDisc; *all others* Jay Penni/Holt McDougal/Houghton Mifflin Harcourt;

216 Nicolas Osorio/eStock Photo/Alamy; **219** AP Images; **224** Andres Leighton/AP Images; **225** *both* Jay Penni/Holt McDougal/Houghton Mifflin Harcourt; **226** Jay Penni/Holt McDougal/Houghton Mifflin Harcourt; **228** Paco Torrente/Agencia EFE; **229** "Plazoleta Rodolfo Walsh" (2000), Graciela Genoves. Oil on canvas. © Zurbaran Galleria/Superstock; **231** Rob & Sas/Corbis; **232** *all* Bettmann/Corbis; **236–237** Tony Arruza/Corbis; **238** *left* Paulo Cunha/Agencia EFE; *right* Jorge Albán/Holt McDougal/Houghton Mifflin Harcourt; *background* Allan Penn/Holt McDougal/Houghton Mifflin Harcourt; **239** *top* Eric Fougere/Corbis Sygma; *background* Allan Penn/Holt McDougal/Houghton Mifflin Harcourt; *secretary* Rubberball; *carpenter* Rubberball; *musician* PhotoDisc; *police Officer* Rubberball; *bottom right* PhotoDisc/Getty Images; *bottom center* Jorge Albán/Holt McDougal/Houghton Mifflin Harcourt; *bottom left* SSC/SuperStock; **241** Allan Penn/Holt McDougal/Houghton Mifflin Harcourt; **245** "Marpacífico" ("Hibiscus") (1943), Amelia Pelaez. Oil on canvas. 45 1/2" x 35". Gift of IBM. Collection of the Art Museum of the Americas, Organization of American States; **246** *top right* Ariel Skelley/Corbis; *center* Lew Robertson/Corbis; *bottom right* John Henley/Corbis; **250** "Mi Futuro y mi Tierra" (2003), Oscar Ortiz. Colored pencil on paper, 63.5 cm x 48.2 cm. The Bridgeman Art Library; **251** Allan Penn/Holt McDougal/Houghton Mifflin Harcourt; **252** *Silvia* Dynamic Graphics Group/Creatas/Alamy; *Enrique* Allan Penn/Holt McDougal/Houghton Mifflin Harcourt; *postman* Henry Ditlz/Corbis; *Rebeca* Allan Penn/Holt McDougal/Houghton Mifflin Harcourt; **253** Stock4B/Getty Images; *background* Guy Jarvis/School Division/Houghton Mifflin Harcourt; **254** Associated Press; **255** *top* Angelo Cavalli/age fotostock; **256** *top* Giraud Philippe/Corbis; **257** *both* Guy Jarvis/School Division/Houghton Mifflin Harcourt; **262–263** Jorge Albán/Holt McDougal/Houghton Mifflin Harcourt; **263** *bottom right* Jorge Albán/Holt McDougal/Houghton Mifflin Harcourt; **264** *background* Allan Penn/Holt McDougal/Houghton Mifflin Harcourt; *all others* Pete Olsen/Holt McDougal/Houghton Mifflin Harcourt; **265** *background* Allan Penn/Holt McDougal/Houghton Mifflin Harcourt; *top left* Pete Olsen/Holt McDougal/Houghton Mifflin Harcourt; **266** Mark J. Terrill/AP Images; **268** *bottom left* Allan Penn/Holt McDougal/Houghton Mifflin Harcourt; *bottom right* Laura Jihansen/StockFood America; **269** *center right* Walter Wust/Agencia EFE; *bottom* Hubert Stadler/Corbis; *top left* Andrés Stapff/Reuters Pictures; **270–271** Patricio Realpe, Stringer/AP Images; **272** Allan Penn/Holt McDougal/Houghton Mifflin Harcourt; **273** *top* Allan Penn/Holt McDougal/Houghton Mifflin Harcourt; **275** Allan Penn/Holt McDougal/Houghton Mifflin Harcourt; **278** Ancient Art & Architecture - All rights reserved/Danita Delimont; **279** Martha Granger/EDGE Productions/Holt McDougal/Houghton Mifflin Harcourt; **280** *bottom right* Allan Penn/Holt McDougal/Houghton Mifflin Harcourt; *center left* Robert Frerck/Odyssey Productions, Inc.; **284** *center* Mireille Vautier/The Art Archive; *computer* Ingvald Kaldhussater/ShutterStock; *book* Artville; *purse* Stockbyte; *PDA, umbrella, wallet* PhotoObjects/Jupiterimages Corporation; **285** *center* Allan Penn/Holt McDougal/Houghton Mifflin Harcourt; **287** *top left* Ingvald Kaldhussater/ShutterStock; **288** 2003 Dave Feiling Photography; **289–290** Digital Vision/Getty Images; **289** *top, 2nd from top* Digital Vision/Getty Images; *3rd from top* PhotoDisc/Getty Images; *4th from top* Digital Vision/Getty Images; *bottom* Artville; **290** Artville; **291** Digital Vision/Getty Images; **294** *1, 2, 4, 5, 6* PhotoObjects/Jupiterimages Corporation; *3* Ingvald Kaldhussater/ShutterStock; **296–297** Robert Frerck/Odyssey Productions, Inc.; **298** *center* Allan Penn/Holt McDougal/Houghton Mifflin Harcourt; *bottom left* Jeff Greenberg/age fotostock; *bottom center* Pablo Corral Vega/Corbis; *bottom right* Martha Granger/EDGE Productions/Holt McDougal/Houghton Mifflin Harcourt; **299** *background* Jay Penni/Holt McDougal/Houghton Mifflin Harcourt; **301** *top* Allan Penn/Holt McDougal/Houghton Mifflin Harcourt; *bottom* Inga Spence/Index Stock Imagery; **304** 2006 by Robert Frerck/ Odyssey Productions, Inc.; **306** *center* Martha Granger/EDGE Productions/Holt McDougal/Houghton Mifflin Harcourt; *bottom* Jeff Greenberg/age fotostock; **310** Wes Walker/Lonely Planet Images; **311** *right* Allan Penn/Holt McDougal/Houghton Mifflin Harcourt; **314** Courtesy, Museo Ricardo Palma en Miraflores, Lima, Peru; **315** *top left* Mireille Vautier/Museo Pedro de Osma, Lima/The Art Archive; *bottom right* PhotoObjects/Jupiterimages Corporation; **316** Bildarchiv Preussischer Kulturbesitz/Art Resource, New York; **317** Bettmann/Corbis; **322–323** E. Hummel /Zefa/Corbis; **323** James Gritz/PhotoDisc/Getty Images; **324** *background* Allan Penn/Holt McDougal/Houghton Mifflin Harcourt; *bottom left* Pete Olsen/Holt McDougal/Houghton Mifflin Harcourt; **325** *background* Allan Penn/Holt McDougal/Houghton Mifflin Harcourt; *mouse* Tan Kian Khoon/ShutterStock; *all others* Pete Olsen/Holt McDougal/Houghton Mifflin Harcourt; **328** *bottom left* Jay Penni/Holt McDougal/Houghton Mifflin Harcourt; *bottom right* Holt McDougal/Houghton Mifflin Harcourt; **329** *top left* Jesús Domínguez/Agencia EFE; *top left inset* Paco Torrente/Agencia EFE; *right* Andreu Dalmau/Agencia EFE; *bottom left* Emilio Naranjo/Agencia EFE; **330–331** Tips Images; **332** *top left* Jay Penni/Holt McDougal/Houghton Mifflin Harcourt; *top center* Robert Harding World Imagery/Getty Images; *bottom left* Arcaid/Alamy; *bottom right* Elizabeth Whiting & Associates/Alamy; **333** *top left* Oliver Strewe/Lonely Planet Images; *top center* San Rostro/age fotostock; *top right* HIRB/Index Stock Imagery; *center left* Alberto Paredes/age fotostock; *center* David Young-Wolff/Alamy; *center right* Terry Williams/Getty Images; *bottom left* age fotostock/SuperStock; *bottom center* Steve Hamblin/Alamy; *bottom right* Steve Vidler/SuperStock; **335** *bottom left* Jay Penni/Holt McDougal/Houghton Mifflin Harcourt; **336** Steve Vidler/SuperStock; **340** *inset* Jay Penni/Holt McDougal/Houghton Mifflin Harcourt; **344** *top* Alberto Bocos Gil/AFP/Getty Images; *bottom* Alberto Bocos Gil/AFP/Getty Images; **345** Jay Penni/Holt McDougal/Houghton Mifflin Harcourt; **348** Bernardo Pérez/NewsCom/El País Photos; **349–351** Illustration by Emilio Urberuaga. Courtesy of Alfaguara Press/GrupoSantillana; **352** *left,* "Portrait of a Little Girl" (ca. 1638–44), Diego Rodríguez de Silva y Velázquez(Spanish, 1599–

1660). Oil on canvas, 51.5 cm x 41 cm. Courtesy of The Hispanic Society of America, New York, (A108); *center,* "Portrait of Dora Maar" (1937), Pablo Picasso. Oil on canvas. Musée Picasso, Paris. © 2007 Estate of Pablo Picasso/Artists Rights Society (ARS), New York/Photograph by Peter Willi/SuperStock; *right,* "Galatea of the Spheres" (1952), Salvador Dalí. Oil on canvas. Gala-Salvador Dalí Foundation, Figueres, Spain. © 2007 Salvador Dalí, Gala-Salvador Dalí Foundation/Artists Rights Society (ARS), New York./Bridgeman Art Library; **356–357** Michael Busselle/Getty Images; **358** *top, background* Barry Mason/Alamy; *tour* David Young-Wolff/Alamy; *center, bottom* Robert Frerck/Odyssey Productions, Inc.; **359** *top* Robert Frerck/Odyssey Productions, Inc.; *center* Doug Scott/age fotostock; *bottom left* Jack Fields/Corbis; *bottom right* Alan Oliver/Alamy; **361** *top right* age fotostock/SuperStock; *center left* age fotostock/SuperStock; *bottom* Jorge Albán/Holt McDougal/Houghton Mifflin Harcourt; *bottom right* Jay Penni/Holt McDougal/Houghton Mifflin Harcourt; **366** *background* Jay Penni/Holt McDougal/Houghton Mifflin Harcourt; *center left* Francesc Muntada/Corbis; *bottom* Jorge Albán/Holt McDougal/Houghton Mifflin Harcourt; *bottom right* Jay Penni/Holt McDougal/Houghton Mifflin Harcourt; **369** *top* age fotostock/SuperStock; *center* Francesc Muntada/Corbis; *bottom* Javier Larrea/age fotostock; **370** "View of Toledo" (c.1597-99), El Greco (Domenico Theotocopuli). Oil on canvas. Metropolitan Museum of Art, New York. Photograph by Francis G. Mayer/Corbis; **371** *center right* Jay Penni/Holt McDougal/Houghton Mifflin Harcourt; **373** Robert Frerck/Odyssey Productions; **374** The Granger Collection, New York; **375** *background* Linehan & Jones/MicroArt; *top* "El Flautista" ("The Flutist") (1955), Remedios Varo. Oil on masonite, 75 x 93 cm. The Art Archive/Museum of Modern Art Mexico/Dagli Orti; **376** *background* Linehan & Jones/MicroArt; *right* Tia Magallon/Getty Images; **382–383** Bill Bachmann/Danita Delimont; **383** *bottom right* Simon Harris/eStock Photo; **384** *background* Allan Penn/Holt McDougal/Houghton Mifflin Harcourt; *all others* Pete Olsen/Holt McDougal/Houghton Mifflin Harcourt; **385** *background* Allan Penn/Holt McDougal/Houghton Mifflin Harcourt; *all others* Pete Olsen/Holt McDougal/Houghton Mifflin Harcourt; **388** *bottom left* Jay Penni/Holt McDougal/Houghton Mifflin Harcourt; *bottom right* Scott Dalton; **389** *top left* Sergi Reboredo/Peter Arnold, Inc.; *center right* Sean Sprague/Peter Arnold, Inc.; *center inset* Royalty-Free/Corbis; *bottom* Leslie Mazoch/AP Images; **390–391** Timothy Ross/The Image Works, Inc.; **392** *background* Guy Jarvis/Holt McDougal/Houghton Mifflin Harcourt; *top left* Jay Penni/Holt McDougal/Houghton Mifflin Harcourt; *center* Leon Duquel/Duque Munera Tia; **393** *background* Guy Jarvis/Holt McDougal/Houghton Mifflin Harcourt; *1* Martin Siepmann/imagebroker/Alamy; *2* ArenaPal/Topham/The Image Works, Inc.; *3, 4* HIRB/Index Stock Imagery; *5* Bob Daemmrich/The Image Works, Inc.; *6* Jim Smith/Alamy; *7* Tony Freeman/PhotoEdit; *8* ImageState/Alamy; **395** *both* Jay Penni/Holt McDougal/Houghton Mifflin Harcourt; **396** *modelo* Tony Freeman/PhotoEdit; *1* ArenaPal/Topham/The Image Works, Inc.; *2* SuperStock/Alamy; *3* Blend Images/Alamy; *4* Volvox/Index Stock Imagery; *5* David Young-Wolff/PhotoEdit; *6* Sean Sprague/The Image Works, Inc.; **399** Rob Crandall/The Image Works, Inc.; **400** *inset* José Luis Peláez, Inc./Corbis; *background* Jay Penni/Holt McDougal/Houghton Mifflin Harcourt; **404** Jose Miguel Gomez/Reuters/Corbis; **405** *right* Jay Penni/Holt McDougal/Houghton Mifflin Harcourt; **407** Big Cheese Photo/age fotostock; **408** R. Grazioli/Corbis Sygma; **412** *top left* PhotoDisc; *top right* Shadows & Light Limited/PAL-Topham/The Image Works, Inc.; *center right* Bob Daemmrich/The Image Works, Inc.; *center left, bottom right* Artville; **416–417** Leon Duquel/Duque Munera Tia; **418** *top left* Jay Penni/Holt McDougal/Houghton Mifflin Harcourt; *bottom left* Sergio Pitamitz/SuperStock; **419** *bottom left* Tomás del Amo/Index Stock Imagery; *top right* Comstock Images/Alamy; *all others* Jorge Albán/Holt McDougal/Houghton Mifflin Harcourt; **421** *bottom right* Jay Penni/Holt McDougal/Houghton Mifflin Harcourt; **425** "Self Portrait" (1987), Fernando Botero (b.1932) Oil on canvas. Private Collection/James Goodman Gallery, New York/The Bridgeman Art Library; **430** Scott Dalton; **431** *top right* Jay Penni/Holt McDougal/Houghton Mifflin Harcourt; **435** *bottom* Jay Penni/Holt McDougal/Houghton Mifflin Harcourt; **442–443** Chad Ehlers/Alamy; **443** *bottom right* Robert Fried/Alamy; **444** *background* Allan Penn/Holt McDougal/Houghton Mifflin Harcourt; **445** *background* Allan Penn/Holt McDougal/Houghton Mifflin Harcourt; *all others* Pete Olsen/Holt McDougal/Houghton Mifflin Harcourt; **448** *bottom right* Fadigati, Foodstock - StockFood Munich/StockFood America; *bottom left* Allan Penn/Holt McDougal/Houghton Mifflin Harcourt; **449** *top left* Max Montecinos/Reuters Pictures; *center right* Kevin Maloney/Aurora/IPN; *bottom* Francois Gohier/Photo Researchers, Inc.; **450–451** Cy Hire/Tom Stack & Asscociates; **452** *all* Allan Penn/Holt McDougal/Houghton Mifflin Harcourt; **453** *background* Jay Penni/Holt McDougal/Houghton Mifflin Harcourt; *all others* Guy Jarvis/Holt McDougal/Houghton Mifflin Harcourt; **456** *center right* Miramax/The Kobal Collection/Portela, Graciela; *center right inset* Thurston Hopkins/Getty Images; **459** *modelo* Horacio Villalobos/Corbis; *1* Sophie Bassouls/Corbis; *2* Luis Lemus/Corbis; *3* Ed Kashi/Corbis; *4* Bettmann/Corbis; **460** *bottom right* Allan Penn/Holt McDougal/Houghton Mifflin Harcourt; *bottom left* Guy Jarvis/School Division/Houghton Mifflin Harcourt; **464** *center right* "The Onyx of Electra" (1944), Roberto Matta-Echaurren. Oil on Canvas,"50 1/8 x 6". The Museum of Modern Art, New York, NY. Anonymous Fund. (963.1979) Photo credit: Digital Image © The Museum of Modern Art/Licensed by Scala/Art Resource, NY; **465** Allan Penn/Holt McDougal/Houghton Mifflin Harcourt; **467** Eric Robert/Corbis Sygma; **468** Sophie Bassouls/Corbis; **469** *background* Corbis Sygma; **470** Corbis Sygma; **471** *stamp* Guy Jarvis/School Division/Houghton Mifflin Harcourt; *envelopes* Elizabeth Tustian/Holt McDougal/Houghton Mifflin; **476–477** Allan Penn/

Holt McDougal/Houghton Mifflin Harcourt; **478** *center* Holt McDougal/Houghton Mifflin Harcourt; **479** *top left* Adrian Weinbrecht/Getty Images; *right* Allan Penn/Holt McDougal/Houghton Mifflin Harcourt; *center left* Royalty-Free/Corbis; **481** Allan Penn/Holt McDougal/Houghton Mifflin Harcourt; **482** Andrés Stapff/Reuters/Corbis; **486** *top* Allan Penn/Holt McDougal/Houghton Mifflin Harcourt; *bottom right* Allan Penn/Holt McDougal/Houghton Mifflin Harcourt; **490** Westend 61/Alamy; **491** Allan Penn/Holt McDougal/Houghton Mifflin Harcourt; **494** Courtesy of Adela Basch; **495** *top right* Museo Naval Madrid/Dagli Orti/The Art Archive; *bottom right* PhotoDisc/Getty Images; **496** Allan Penn/Holt McDougal/Houghton Mifflin Harcourt; **497** Monastery of the Rabida, Palos, Spain/Dagli Orti/The Art Archive; **502–503** Daniel García/AFP/Getty Images; **503** *bottom right* Manuel H. de León/AP Images; **504** *background* Allan Penn/Holt McDougal/Houghton Mifflin Harcourt; *all others* Pete Olsen/Holt McDougal/Houghton Mifflin Harcourt; **505** *background* Allan Penn/Holt McDougal/Houghton Mifflin Harcourt; *all others* Pete Olsen/Holt McDougal/Houghton Mifflin Harcourt; **510** *climbing* Gary Russ/Holt McDougal Photo; *butterfly* Digital Vision; *trail, campfire* Holt McDougal Photo; *bus* Sam Dudgeon/Holt McDougal Photo; *tent, bike* Getty Images/PhotoDisc; *raft* Corbis; **511** *family* Corbis; *jet boat, seashells, relaxing* Getty Images/PhotoDisc; *sunset, canoe* Image Ideas; *volleyball* Stockbyte; **512** *deliveryman* Jupiter Images; *grass* Getty Images/Stockbyte; *headphones* Getty Images/Digital Vision; *calculator* Ingram Publishing; **513** *reading* Sam Dudgeon/Holt McDougal Photo; *tv* Dennis Fagan/Holt McDougal Photo; *photographer, newspaper, stock reports* Corbis; *journalists, meeting* Holt McDougal Photo; *reporter, speech* Getty Images/PhotoDisc; **514** *frog, turtle, recycling, smoke stacks, windmills, cars, testing soil* Comstock; *wetlands* Jupiter Images; *amazon* Getty Images/PhotoDisc; *house solar panels, kids with jar* Getty Images/Digital Vision; *polar bear* Corel; *truck, flood* Corbis; **516** *Augustin* ImageState; *all others* Getty Images/PhotoDisc; **517** *Mario, Luis* Don Couch/Holt McDougal Photo; *Patricia, Graciela Corbis; Alex, Felipe* Getty Images/PhotoDisc; *Alfaro* George Alban/Holt McDougal Photo; *Obed* Victoria Smith/Holt McDougal Photo; **518** *camera, wallet* Holt McDougal Photo; *scanner, pda, laptop, sunglassess, messenger bag* Getty Images/PhotoDisc; *umbrella* Don Couch/Holt McDougal Photo; **519**, *soccer game, shaking hands* Getty Images/PhotoDisc; *band, gameboard* Sam Dudgeon/Holt McDougal Photo; *polar bears* Jupiter Images; *orchestra* Goodshoot; *hammock* Peter Van Steen/Holt McDougal Photo; *garbage* Don Couch/Holt McDougal Photo; **520** *making cookies, bathroom, garbage, groceries* Corbis; *bedroom* Getty Images/PhotoDisc; *green beans* Brand X Pictures; *fountain* Don Couch/Holt McDougal Photo; *atm* Cindy Bland Verheyden/Holt McDougal Photo; *pastries, post office* Victoria Smith/Holt McDougal Photo; *train* Flat Earth; *kiosk* Sam Dudgeon/Holt McDougal Photo; **521** *cobblestone, tower* John Langford/Holt McDougal Photo; *Plaza de Armas* Ricardo Alcaraz/Holt McDougal Photo; *red train* Holt McDougal Photo; *orange train, bridges, castle, street* Don Couch/Holt McDougal Photo; **522** *plant, Carla* Getty Images/Digital Vision; *making face, overalls, Felipe, Ruben* Corbis; *watermelon, Rebeca* Getty Images/PhotoDisc; **523** *Juanita, Rosa* Getty Images/Stockdisc; *Victoria* Que Net; *Rodrigo* Corbis; *Luis* Comstock; *Elena* Holt McDougal Photo; **524** *Victor* Corbis; *Elena* BananaStock/Jupiter Images; *Ramon* BananaStock/Alamy; *Luisa, Ana, Pablo, Marisol* Holt McDougal Photo; *Alfredo, Carlos, Maria* Marty Granger/Holt McDougal Photo; **525** *mimes, clapping* Getty Images/PhotoDisc; *cell phone, Shakespearean couple, director, actor with script* Corbis; *actor in blue coat, actor in vest* Victoria Smith/Holt McDougal Photo.

All other photography © Jorge Albán/Holt McDougal/Houghton Mifflin Harcourt Publishing Company.

Every effort has been made to contact the copyright holder of the images used herein. Mistakes or omissions brought to our attention will be fixed in later editions.

Illustration

5 Eric Larsen; **8** Rob Saunders; **19** James Yamasaki; **22** James Yamasaki; **28–29** Mike Reagan; **36** Eric Larsen; **52** Steve McEntee; **61** Charlene Potts; **62** Charlene Potts; **66** Charlene Potts; **67** Charlene Potts; **69** Eric Larsen; **71** Charlene Potts; **88–89** Mike Reagan; **100** Anna Veltfort; **101** Eric Larsen; **103** Anna Veltfort; **109–110** *top* Susan Gal; **115** Eric Larsen; **129** *all* Eric Larsen; **135** *top* Enríque Sanchez; **137** *top* Enríque Sanchez; **148** Mike Reagan; **161** Vilma Ortiz-Dillon; **163** Eric Larsen; **187** Eric Larsen; **208** Mike Reagan; **223** Eric Larsen; **249** Eric Larsen; **261** James Yamasaki; **268–269** Mike Reagan; **281** Steve McEntee; **283** Eric Larsen; **292** Steve McEntee; **294** *modelo* Steve McEntee; **305** Eric Larsen; **309** *bottom right* Eric Larsen; **312** Steve McEntee; **320** Vilma Ortiz-Dillon; **328** Mike Reagan; **334** Vilma Ortiz-Dillon; **335** Lauren Scheuer; **338** Vilma Ortiz-Dillon; **339** Eric Larsen; **343** Steve McEntee; **354** James Yamasaki; **362** Steve McEntee; **364** Eric Larsen; **367** Steve McEntee; **381** Steve McEntee; **388–389** Mike Reagan; **403** Eric Larsen; **409–410** Raul Colón/Morgan Gaynin, Inc.; **425** *top* Steve McEntee; **429** Eric Larsen; **435** *top* Joe Cepeda; **436** *top* Joe Cepeda; **448–449** Mike Reagan; **458** James Yamasaki; **461** Steve McEntee; **463** Eric Larsen; **472** Steve McEntee; **478** Polo Barrera; **484** Rob Saunders; **485** James Yamasaki; **489** Eric Larsen; **501** Rob Saunders.

All other illusrations by Robin Storesund or Chris Wilson/Holt McDougal/Houghton Mifflin Harcourt.